SULTZ & YOUNG'S

Health Care USA

Understanding Its Organization and Delivery

TENTH EDITION

James A. Johnson
Central Michigan University

Kimberly S. Davey
Samford University

Richard G. Greenhill
Texas Tech University Health Sciences Center

JONES & BARTLETT
LEARNING

World Headquarters
Jones & Bartlett Learning
25 Mall Road
Burlington, MA 01803
978-443-5000
info@jblearning.com
www.jblearning.com

Jones & Bartlett Learning books and products are available through most bookstores and online booksellers. To contact Jones & Bartlett Learning directly, call 800-832-0034, fax 978-443-8000, or visit our website, www.jblearning.com.

21177-1

Production Credits

Vice President, Product Management: Marisa R. Urbano
Vice President, Product Operations: Christine Emerton
Director, Content Management: Donna Gridley
Manager, Content Strategy: Carolyn Pershouse
Director of Product Management: Matthew Kane
Product Manager: Sophie Fleck Teague
Content Strategist: Tess Sackmann
Project Coordinator: Paula-Yuan Gregory
Director, Project Management and Content Services: Karen Scott
Project Manager: Kristen Rogers
Project Specialist: Belinda Thresher
Digital Project Specialist: Rachel DiMaggio
Director of Marketing: Andrea DeFronzo
Senior Marketing Manager: Susanne Walker
Content Services Manager: Colleen Lamy
Vice President, Manufacturing and Inventory Control: Therese Connell
Composition: Exela Technologies
Project Management: Exela Technologies
Cover Design: Kristin E. Parker
Text Design: Kristin E. Parker
Media Development Editor: Faith Brosnan
Rights & Permissions Manager: John Rusk
Rights Specialist: Maria Leon Maimone
Cover Image (Title Page, Chapter Opener): © STILLFX/iStock /Getty Images Plus/Getty Images.
Printing and Binding: LSC Communications

Library of Congress Cataloging-in-Publication Data

Names: Johnson, James A., 1954- author. | Davey, Kimberly S., author. | Greenhill, Richard G., author. | Young, Kristina M. Sultz & Young's health care USA.
Title: Sultz & Young's health care USA : understanding its organization and delivery / James A. Johnson, Kimberly S. Davey, Richard G. Greenhill. Other titles: Sultz and Young's health care USA
Description: Tenth edition. | Burlington, MA : Jones & Bartlett Learning, [2022] | Preceded by Health care USA / Kristina M. Young, Philip J. Kroth. Ninth edition.. [2018]. | Includes bibliographical references and index.
Identifiers: LCCN 2021038922 | ISBN 9781284211603 (paperback)
Subjects: MESH: Delivery of Health Care | Health Policy | United States | BISAC: BUSINESS & ECONOMICS / Accounting / Financial
Classification: LCC RA418 | NLM W 84 AA1 | DDC 362.1–dc23
LC record available at https://lccn.loc.gov/2021038922

6048

Printed in the United States of America
26 25 24 23 22   10 9 8 7 6 5 4 3 2 1

Brief Contents

Contents

Contents

Foreword

As coauthors of the ninth edition of *Sultz & Young's Health Care USA: Understanding Its Organization and Delivery,* we are privileged to provide this Foreword for the tenth edition. We introduce the new edition, noting this text's remarkable number of course adoptions that have continued over a period spanning 24 years of an ever-changing and evolving healthcare delivery system in the United States. With great pride, we note that repeated course adoptions for over 2 decades attest to the text's continued relevance, both among instructors and students.

As we retire from our roles as coauthors, we enthusiastically welcome the new coauthors, Drs. James Johnson, Kim Davey, and Richard Greenhill, whose vast experience and acumen will ensure both the preservation and advancement of the legacy of *Sultz & Young's Health Care USA: Understanding Its Organization and Delivery.* Each of the coauthors brings an impressive history of authorship and academic and professional accomplishments across an array of the many fields of endeavor encompassed by the U.S. healthcare system. Their backgrounds include in-depth experience with many dimensions of health services planning, administration, quality assessment, and extensive in-class and online teaching experience. This latter attribute is highly relevant to maintaining the text's acclaimed instructor and student friendliness, both in terms of text content and its accompanying instructor and student resources. Evidenced by their scholarly research and authorship, the coauthors

are well positioned to provide objective and insightful content on the plethora of topics and policy issues that characterize today's U.S. healthcare delivery system.

We applaud the coauthors for incorporating a health systems thinking perspective throughout the text. Health systems thinking will continue to be of paramount importance to the education of future professionals as service coordination, quality, and cost considerations remain focal points in healthcare administration and policy. In addition, emphasis on health systems thinking is timely and relevant as the Council on Education for Public Health Accreditation cites health systems thinking as a core competency and a key component of public health course syllabi.

Other features of the tenth edition merit note, including discussions of increasingly important topics within the healthcare delivery system. One example is interprofessional education. Interprofessional education recognizes the need for integrated educational experiences among professional students to facilitate collaborative and coordinated services to patients and communities across a spectrum ranging from personal health care to community public health. Another example is elaboration of the impact of health policy with examples and illustrations, including a new chapter, *Public Policy and the Role of Government in Health Care.* A third example is joining health systems research and health policy with the increasing importance and impact of data analytics. Finally, we note that the co-authors draw upon their extensive international experience with references to comparative health systems and inclusion of an appendix on the Canadian health system.

These comparisons will be valuable to students' critical thinking in considering policy directions, evaluations, and decisions about U.S. healthcare delivery. Particularly in light of the COVID-19 pandemic, the co-authors incorporate important perspectives on global health and the range of crises that can influence health systems. These perspectives lend a rich, broad, and highly relevant perspective to the healthcare delivery system in the United States.

The tenth edition will be published more than a decade after passage of the Patient Protection and Affordable Care Act of 2010 (the ACA). Since 2010, the ACA has withstood more than 60 attempts at Congressional repeal and two Supreme Court challenges, coupled with 2016–2020 presidential promises to overturn it. In 2021, the ACA remains in full force and effect with a new federal administration enacting orders to facilitate ongoing citizen enrollment. Despite challenges, the ACA succeeded in securing health insurance coverage for over 20 million previously uninsured Americans, many of whom were in the lowest income categories. It also enacted numerous cost reduction, business integrity, and quality-improvement innovation experiments. Results of the effectiveness of those improvement and innovation experiments continue with ongoing evaluations to assess outcomes.

Numerous ongoing and future challenges confronting U.S. health care include:

- Reining in the current COVID-19 pandemic
- Discerning and devising proactive preparation for future global health threats
- Addressing underfunded and undervalued public health services and infrastructure
- Addressing escalating healthcare costs

- Deploying an integrated healthcare workforce through interprofessional education
- Addressing changing demographics: the burdens of an increasing aged, chronically ill population
- Addressing health disparities and social determinants of health and as critical components of the delivery system
- Confronting health policy issues in a socially and politically polarized nation

The current federal administration has pledged to address proactively these daunting challenges. History teaches us to be cautious about expectations. Notwithstanding, the tenth edition is a remarkable accomplishment following on the heels of the past four years of the federal administration's health policy uncertainty.

The new coauthors meld a dynamic combination of academic, research, teaching, international perspectives, and administrative experiences that enliven the text's content and maintain its current relevance. We greatly admire the coauthors' commitment to compile the tenth edition amid the current morass of U.S. healthcare and policy issues.

The *About the Authors* section outlines the coauthors' credentials. We applaud their dedication to make the tenth edition a valuable asset to the education of future healthcare and public health professionals.

Kristina M. Young, MS
Clinical Assistant Professor, Emerita
School of Public Health and Health Professions
State University of New York at Buffalo

Philip J. Kroth, MD, MSc
Professor and Chair, Department of
Biomedical Informatics
Professor, Department of Internal Medicine
Western Michigan University, Homer Stryker,
MD School of Medicine

Preface

As the continuation of a very long and prestigious history, the tenth edition of *Health Care USA: Understanding Its Organization and Delivery* provides the most current information, relevant data, and analysis focusing on the health system of the United States. This edition of the book was written by an expert academic team composed of medical social scientist and professor **James A. Johnson**, PhD, MPA, MSc, at Central Michigan University; associate professor **Kimberly S. Davey**, PhD, MBA, MA, at Samford University; and assistant professor **Richard G. Greenhill**, DHA, MS, MBA, FACHE, at Texas Tech University. Furthermore, to facilitate a comparative perspective, it also includes a chapter on Canadian health care written by two health professionals in Canada, Oluwatosin Omolade Dotun-Olujinmi, DHA, and Felix Asekomhe, MD.

The core topics of this book, organized as 15 chapters, include an overview of the healthcare system; historical and benchmark developments; public policy and the role of government; financing health care; the healthcare workforce; hospitals and integrated delivery systems; ambulatory primary care; long-term care and specialized services; behavioral health services; public and population health; health information technology, and quality; health services and systems research; crisis response and preparedness; rural health care; and health care in the future.

In order to facilitate learning, the authors have included cases based on actual events, discussion questions, interviews with leaders, key terms and an extensive glossary, as well as chapter references and websites. Collectively, this range of resources within the book provides for an invigorating learning opportunity. Furthermore, an instructors manual and course support documents were developed by Naomi Deshore, DHA, RN, and are available with the book.

About the Authors

James A. Johnson, PhD, MPA, MSc, is a medical social scientist who specializes in organizational and health systems development. He is a full professor in the School of Health Sciences and Doctor of Health Administration (DHA) Program at Central Michigan University (CMU), where he teaches courses in comparative health systems, organizational behavior, and health systems thinking. Prior to joining the faculty at CMU, Professor Johnson was Chairman of the Department of Health Administration and Policy at Medical University of South Carolina. He is a very active scholar and health science writer with over 100 journal articles and 20 books published. One book read worldwide is *Comparative Health Systems: Global Perspectives*, where he and co-researchers analyzed the health systems of 20 different countries. He is also the co-author of the recently published *Health Systems Thinking*. Eighteen of Dr. Johnson's books have been selected for the permanent collection of the National Library of Medicine and two for the library at the World Health Organization (WHO) in Geneva, Switzerland. He is past-editor of the American College of Healthcare Executives (ACHE) *Journal of Healthcare Management*; a Contributing Editor for the *Journal of Health and Human Services Administration*; past senior editor of *Journal of Management Practice*; and global health editor for the *Journal of Human Security and Resilience*. Additionally, Dr. Johnson has served on many boards, including the Scientific Advisory Board of the National Diabetes Trust Foundation; American Public Health Association (APHA) Governing Council; Board of the Association of University Programs in Health Administration (AUPHA); Advisory Board of the Alliance for the Blind and Visually Impaired; Board President of Charleston Low Country AIDS Services; Advisory Board of the Joint Africa Working Group; Advisory Board of the Center for Collaborative Health Leadership; and Board of Advisors for Health Systems of America. He is a regular delegate to the World Health Congress and a member of the Global Health Council. Dr. Johnson completed his PhD at Florida State University.

Kimberly S. Davey, PhD, MBA, MA, is an associate professor of public health and health administration in the School of Public Health at Samford University. She also serves as the director of the undergraduate public health program. Dr. Davey has extensive teaching experience in the areas of health systems, comparative health systems, health policy, leadership, management, marketing, and strategy at both the undergraduate and graduate level. A hallmark of Dr. Davey's teaching is the extensive interdisciplinary and interprofessional nature of her courses and teaching experience. At Samford, she has taught courses across four schools (School of Public Health, Moffett & Sanders School of Nursing, McWhorter School of Pharmacy, and Cumberland School of Law). Dr. Davey has served as co-chair of the Communications Committee for the Health Administration section of the APHA, Chair of the Healthcare

Management, Hospitality Management, and Public Administration track for the Southern Management Association, and Chair of the Communications and Development Committee for the Alabama Health Action Coalition. Dr. Davey is currently serving as a Health Sciences Councilor and member of the Finance Committee for the Council on Undergraduate Research (CUR). She is a reviewer for the APHA, the Association of Schools and Programs of Public Health, Academy of Management, and Southern Management Association. Prior to joining Samford, Dr. Davey served as a faculty member in the Department of Family, Community, and Health Systems at the University of Alabama at Birmingham (UAB) School of Nursing. She completed her PhD in Health Services Administration at UAB, her MBA at Samford University, and her MA in Diplomacy and International Relations at Seton Hall University.

Richard G. Greenhill, DHA, MBA, CPHQ, PMP, FISQua, FACHE, is Assistant Program Director and Assistant Professor at Texas Tech University Health Sciences Center (TTUHSC) in the Dept. Healthcare Management and Leadership - School of Health Professions. His teaching courses include Quality and Risk, Leadership, Health Informatics and Data Analytics, Strategy, Decision Sciences, and Global Health. In addition, he teaches Six Sigma Green Belt and Project Management Certification Prep at the Texas Tech University (TTU) Rawls College of Business in the Professional and STEM MBA Programs.

He brings more than 27 years of experience in prior roles, including executive leadership in healthcare operations, strategy, quality, and project management. He honorably retired from the U.S. Navy after 20 years of service. Dr. Greenhill is deputy editor for the International *Journal for Quality in Health Care*, Communications (IJCOMS) and serves on the Editorial Board of the *Journal of Health Administration Education* (JHAE). He is on the Board of the College for Behavioral Health Leadership (CBHL).

Dr. Greenhill is a seasoned Lean Six Sigma Black Belt (LSSBB) practitioner a Team-STEPPS Master Trainer, Project Management Professional (PMP), Certified Professional in Healthcare Quality (CPHQ), and Fellow of the International Society in Healthcare Quality (FISQua); a Fellow of the American College of Healthcare Executives (FACHE) and founder of the *Improve Healthcare* podcast. He completed his DHA degree at Central Michigan University.

CHAPTER 1

Overview of the U.S. Healthcare System

CHAPTER OVERVIEW

This chapter provides a broad overview of the U.S. health system. Systems theory and thinking are discussed and applied to health care. Key terms and concepts are defined and discussed, such as "health," "health system," and "population health." Additionally, a discussion of the factors and determinants that influence population health and the functioning of the U.S. health system is presented. The chapter also identifies building blocks, or core components, of all health systems. Six Building Blocks were developed by the World Health Organization (WHO) and provide a framework for analyzing health system inputs, processes, and outcomes. Ultimately, the analysis informs health policies aimed at strengthening health systems and improving population health and healthcare delivery. The chapter concludes with a discussion of the major subsystems present in the U.S. health system and stakeholders who have an interest in the system.

The United States has a unique system of healthcare delivery. The United States still has a significant number of people who are without health insurance despite recent healthcare reform efforts. In comparison, other developed countries perceive health care as a right and almost all citizens are entitled to receive at least basic healthcare services. As a result, significant health disparities (or differences) exist and persist in the United States across a number of dimensions such as: race, ethnicity, socioeconomic status, insurance status (e.g., insured versus uninsured), geographic location (e.g., rural versus urban), and supply and distribution of healthcare professionals, among others. The U.S. health "system" is not a system in the true sense, even though it is called a system when reference is made to its various features, components, and services. The system is fragmented because there are numerous private insurance plans and tax-supported public programs. The system has periodically undergone incremental changes, mainly in response to concerns about cost, access, and quality. In spite of these changes, providing at least a basic package of health care at an affordable price to every American remains an unrealized goal.[1]

People outside the United States sometimes wonder why Americans do not have a national healthcare system. The answers lie in the way American culture was shaped by a history that resulted in self-reliance, an aversion to excessive taxes, and a preference for limited government. Also, within the country today, sentiments about health care are paradoxical. Influenced by the American media, Americans have come to believe that the healthcare system may be in need of major reform, but at an individual level, they are mostly satisfied with their own care.[1] The following section provides a discussion of systems theory and insights into what truly constitutes a system.

▶ Systems Theory and Foundations

In *Health Systems Thinking: A Primer*, Johnson, Anderson, and Rossow provide a primer on systems theory and thinking and how it can be applied to healthcare. Ludwig von Bertalanffy articulated and popularized the General Systems Theory in his 1968 book entitled *General System Theory*.[2] In this book, he sought to unify the field of science. His unique contribution, and that of the General Systems Theory, was trying to understand individual parts of a system as well as how these parts interact through recurring patterns to produce a whole. Prior theories had focused on understanding individual parts in great detail, but they had not considered how the individual parts related to the whole system. George Engel, a physician, noted that the human body was made up of subsystems (i.e., cardiovascular, endocrine, and nervous, among other body systems). In response, he developed the "biopsychosocial model" in the 1970s as a way to better understand disease expression. The model is an example of how systems thinking could be applied to health because the model recognized the interaction of biological (i.e., age, gender, genetics, physiologic reactions, tissue health), psychological (i.e., mental health, emotional health, beliefs, and expectations), and sociological (i.e., interpersonal relationships, social support dynamics, and socioeconomics) factors and how these interactions produced different health outcomes for individual patients as well as patient groups or populations.[3] The WHO Health System Framework reflects these factors and will be discussed later in this chapter.

Today, systems theory and thinking has become a popular approach to understanding how all different types of systems work, including the U.S. health system. Contemporary explanations of systems have been articulated; however, these explanations all build on the work of von Bertalanffy and others who contributed to building a unifying theory of systems. Bellinger views a system as "an entity that maintains its existence through the mutual interaction of its parts."[4] Anderson and Johnson define a system as a "group of interacting, interrelated, or interdependent components that form a complex and unified whole."[5] Organizations can be viewed as complex adaptive systems (CASs). These organizations are complex in that they are composed of multiple, diverse, interconnected, and equally important elements. They are also adaptive in that they are capable of changing and learning from experience based on interactions with their dynamic environment. Most organizations, and certainly all health organizations, can be described as CASs that are constantly adjusting to their environment and responding to feedback from within and without their environments. Complexity science sees change as inevitable and, thus, the search for a stable state is futile. CASs continuously adjust because they are open to exchanges and interaction with the environment. We see examples of this in health care with health policy reforms that try to adjust to health realities across the population. We also see examples of policies that have failed to respond to health realities; therefore, health challenges persist. CASs have attributes that are consistent with General Systems Theory and the newly emerging complexity science. These attributes are described in **BOX 1-1**.

BOX 1-1 Attributes of Complex Adaptive Systems

McDaniel RR and Jordan ME. Complexity and Postmodern Theory. In: Johnson JA. *Health Organizations*. Jones and Bartlett Publishers; 2009.

Agents (i.e., People)

CASs consist of a large number of diverse agents that are information processors. There must be adequate diversity within the group of agents to enable the group to develop new solutions to problems and make decisions in unique circumstances. In a CAS, agents have the capacity to exchange information among themselves and with their environment and adjust their own behavior as a function of the information they process. In a health organization, everyone counts; not only does each person contribute his or her talents but the individual must also help others contribute. Managing such a diverse and changing cast of agents are considered most difficult among other tasks in healthcare management.

(continues)

BOX 1-1 Attributes of Complex Adaptive Systems   *(continued)*

Interconnections

The essence of a CAS is captured in the nonlinear relationships among agents. Inputs are not proportional to outputs; small changes can lead to big effects and big changes can lead to small effects. The way in which clinicians interact with each other, coupled with the way they interact with nonclinicians, is often a key determinant of a health organization's ability to succeed. Everyone is busy and everyone has their job to do. The CAS theory teaches us that the successful healthcare manager pays more attention to the relationship system than to the individual agents.

Self-Organization

The CAS theory teaches us that order in a system may well be a result of the properties of the system itself, rather than some intentionality on the part of some external controller. Rather than hierarchical control, CASs are characterized by a decentralized, bottom-up process of co-design. New structures and new forms of behavior spontaneously emerge as agents self-organize themselves into relatively stable patterns of relationships. No matter how hard a nursing home manager tries to control certified nursing attendants, the attendants will organize themselves to do their job in the way that they see fit. Efforts to help them better perceive and perform their job and develop effective organizational analytical skills are likely to pay greater dividends than efforts to get them to simply comply.

Emergence

The behavior of a CAS cannot be obtained by summing the behaviors of the constituent parts but emerges as the result of the pattern of connections among diverse agents. Emergence is a source of novelty and surprise in a CAS. When we treat safety and clinical success as emergent properties of the system, we are more likely to learn from the past behaviors of the system and develop alternative strategies for achieving our goals.

Coevolution

CASs do not simply change; they change the world around. The CAS and its environments co-evolve such that each fundamentally influences the development of the other. The organizations act and others react, often in unexpected and unpredictable ways. When a health organization begins to investigate the purchase of some new information technology, the potential ramifications will almost immediately come to the fore in the decision-making process. When a big payer decides that you should be paid by a system using diagnostic-related groups, you will figure out how to code the illnesses of your clients so that it is profitable for you.

Johnson JA, Anderson DE, Rossow CC. *Health Systems Thinking: A Primer.* Jones & Barlett Learning; 2020.

The attributes of CASs include agents (i.e., people), interconnections, self-organization, emergence, and coevolution, all of which are important attributes of the U.S. health system. However, these attributes do not always function optimally. As discussed earlier in the chapter, the U.S. health system is fragmented because there are numerous private insurance plans and tax-supported public programs. The U.S. health system also lacks a central agent, which results in little integration and coordination. Technological variation exists across the system and there are multiple players that are able to exert influence over the system, resulting in high costs, unequal access, and average health outcomes. Efforts to further integrate across the health system are underway in United States in hopes of creating a cohesive system focused on enhancing the patient experience of care (including quality and satisfaction), improving the health of the population, and reducing the per capita cost of health. These efforts are based with the defining characteristics of complex systems in mind. Johnson, Anderson, and Rossow outline additional defining characteristics of complex systems that should be considered, including[3]:

- *Complex systems tend to be self-stabilizing.* Systems often use feedback loops to facilitate balance between smaller pieces of the subsystem with the larger, more complex system.
- *Complex systems are purposeful.* A complex system is composed of individual parts and smaller subsystems that work together to achieve the goal of the larger, more complex system or whole.
- *Complex systems are capable of using feedback to modify their behavior.* Systems use feedback from inside or outside the system to adapt and innovate.
- *Complex systems can modify their environments.* Systems can influence their environments by modifying their behavior to achieve their purpose or goal due to their interconnectedness.
- *Complex systems are capable of replicating, maintaining, repairing, and organizing themselves.* Systems are able to engage in transformation that allows the system to reengineer or reinvent itself.

The U.S. health system is generating and capturing more data than ever before and making efforts to use the feedback to modify its behavior and environments in ways that help it achieve stability and purpose. **INTERVIEW 1-1** provides an example of how CASs exist in the U.S. health system. The interview discusses the importance of using feedback to transform and adapt business models and operations. The interview also highlights how CASs can be translated and replicated within the healthcare context. Systems thinking is helping healthcare leaders and clinicians create a culture of health that works to improve population health, enhance the patient care experience, and reduce per capita costs, among other system goals/outcomes.

INTERVIEW 1-1　Health Executive and Administrative Fellow Interview

James F. Geiger
President, Lehigh Valley Health Network-Muhlenberg
Bethlehem, PA
Madeline Kemp
Administrative Fellow, Lehigh Valley Health Network
Allentown, PA

Summarize your definition of systems thinking.

Mr. Geiger: My definition of systems thinking is to identify relevant variables associated with the intended or unintended consequences of moving forward on good ideas or business plans. *Systems thinking is a lot more than setting up an exam room, making an appointment, seeing patients, and giving them a prescription. Systems thinking should be second nature on how to look at the whole system and improve the entire process.*

Ms. Kemp: I tend to differentiate systems from strategic planning. While systems thinking may be viewed through the strategic planning and decision-making lens, systems thinking moves beyond traditional silos to consideration for interrelated and interdependent elements, so the system can function better. Systems thinking should involve considering the tangible and intangible benefits of

(continues)

an investment project or significant initiative. We can look at systems thinking from an operational perspective such as the development of our new yet complex $160,000,000 Medical Campus. It is essential to be able to make changes in the business model, adapt to situations, and involve the right people who represent vital processes to minimize delays and generate solutions.

How are systems thinking as a competency beneficial to the practice of healthcare administration? Leaders and managers?

Mr. Geiger: Our Family Health Pavilion—volume, the mix of patients, revenue sources, and types of services—provides a great example of a significant strategic initiative experience. The dynamic nature of the environment created a threefold increase in self-pay patients; changes in reimbursement policies such as Center for Medicare and Medicaid Services (CMS) diagnostic testing; the influence of social services; and higher-volume and higher-risk episodes of care such as increased opiate-related pregnancies and uncertain budget and taxation policies, all eroded our revenue estimates. This strategic business plan was elaborate concerning analysis, committing funds, and doing so in the context of the community. The plan, which involves a complex and lengthy coordination process, is typically 24 months. However, our planning horizon is typically a 20-year outlook. This experience drove our thinking about planning future projects and incorporating more people into the complicated process earlier, rather than later.

Ms. Kemp: The lessons from the Family Health Pavilion are currently being applied to the new Medical Campus project. This experience is teaching me to think through the elements and components of the system to build in more planning processes and people earlier, rather than later, and facilitate change and preparation with scenarios and drills associated with the patient mix and other situations. I want to reiterate: The environmental dynamics requires more forward-thinking, use of scenarios to learn and adapt, more inclusiveness of people earlier due to the complexity of the processes, and overall adaptive leadership. In the future, modeling and forecasting of CMS reimbursement schemes and use of planning scenarios will help teams make better decisions.

In what ways can systems thinking be integrated into strategic planning? Human resource management (HRM), revenue cycle, and quality improvement initiatives?

Mr. Geiger: I will use HRM in the context of our Medical Campus (cancer and musculoskeletal care with eight operating rooms) and Family Health Pavilion experience as the example. First, the HRM process must include more than the posting of vacancies. While the patient experience is second to none, we wanted more problem solvers and quick thinkers to help with putting together the "pieces of the implementation puzzle" as a team. This effort included the finding obvious and the not-so-apparent disconnects in the system associated with implementation processes and flows. These examples represent systems thinking at the front-line level of the organization. Clinical, administrative, and ancillary colleagues are working together, knowing their processes, responsibilities, and interest in the overall system. Getting everyone to the table to problem solve from a systems thinking perspective is a way to employ systems thinking and focus on quality improvement.

Do you believe systems thinking has not readily been adopted by health administrators?

Mr. Geiger: First, as in the case of the Veterans Resource Center, we are incorporating a systems approach—social, cultural, and population health components. Unfortunately, it is more difficult to conduct these projects today because of disincentives (such as lack of payment for the adjunct services that may be provided by such an initiative). Another example is our $3 million Advanced Remote Intensive Care Unit (ICU) Monitoring Unit, where centrally located intensivists monitor 140 critical care units at six facilities. We have saved lives and salary costs associated with centrally located intensivists.

As a result of the second set of eyes, we have prevented litigation, we have produced better-quality care, but there is no revenue associated with providing this service. This situation stifles systems thinking and creativity to be more "holistic." Second, admittedly, in all my undergraduate, graduate, and continuing medical education experience, the topic has never been addressed in my 43 years. I had to learn hard lessons in applying a systems approach to major projects. It is a new paradigm for individuals in my generation.

Ms. Kemp: It is hard to encourage systems thinking because the organization chart reinforces typical approaches to solving problems in isolation. When I worked at the Veterans Affairs Medical Center, I was exposed to interdisciplinary teams called Patient Aligned Care Teams. When it comes to using systems thinking with other groups in the community, unfortunately, the reimbursement structure does not provide healthcare providers who have limited capacity enough incentive to invest seriously. For example, it can be hard to see some major initiatives, such as those aimed at reducing healthcare utilization, translate into quantifiable and tangible benefits, like reduced expenses. Executive leadership would like to test many ideas, as they would likely improve overall care; however, the environment does not permit such investments because health systems already face slim margins.

How can we create a systems thinking culture in health care and prepare future leaders?

Mr. Geiger: Again, the Family Health Pavilion, Medical Campus, and Veterans Resource Center experience helped my team understand the dependencies and interdependencies in achieving goals. It gave the team the opportunity to learn by seeing how we could help and provide a community benefit and thus improve our bottom line. Systems thinking contributed to this. These are also great case studies. I think the use of case studies and more formal application of systems thinking approaches and tools will go a long way to understanding what works and what does not work. Case studies are a great way to learn what works, does not work, and how to be more successful. Also, we must be able to visualize the intangible benefits as part of case studies. Tangible benefits and hard metrics go hand-in-hand with systems and will make it easier to embrace systems thinking more often.

Ms. Kemp: I would like to reiterate and expand on what Jim has stated. To create a culture of health and prepare future leaders, we must embrace the local community needs assessments and provide appropriate incentives to implement complex projects such as those we have discussed. To create a systems thinking culture and prepare future leaders, I think case studies are best for early careerists, as they provide real-life scenarios on how systems thinking can help professionals through complex strategic and operational environments.

Johnson JA, Anderson DE, Rossow CC. *Health Systems Thinking: A Primer.* Jones & Barlett Learning; 2020.

▶ Systems Thinking

Systems thinking has been embraced by healthcare leaders and clinicians in response to the healthcare complexities and challenges they face. The approach reflects fundamentals of the General Systems Theory previously discussed. Systems thinking allows healthcare professionals to assess the interactions and interdependencies among parts of a system and seek out opportunities to generate sustainable solutions, as addressed in Interview 1-1. Johnson, Anderson, and Rossow discuss this emergent approach by highlighting how interactions and patterns between system parts are better understood along with the interrelated nature of system parts to create the whole. This prevents siloed or myopic views and promotes higher levels of understanding. Root causes, bottlenecks, and constraints are also broken down into individual parts or smaller subsystems so that they are better understood. This allows a systematic analysis that often results in innovative and sustainable solutions. Community-based solutions emerge from a careful analysis of trends, inter-actions, and connections at different levels—individual, team, organization, community, state, or national. Solutions can span multiple levels, which can systemically solve problems.[3] Systems theory and thinking are helpful when navigating the rapidly changing contexts of healthcare, as highlighted in Case 1-1. This approach is useful in understanding and addressing fragmentation, lack of coordination, and other system functions that contribute to the United States not having a system that meets the technical definition of a system. There are opportunities for system agents (or stakeholders) to continuously evolve their interconnection to optimize the system so that it emerges in ways that meet population health needs. The following section provides a definition and discussion of a health system.

▶ Health System

WHO defines a health system as "the sum total of all the organizations, institutions, and resources whose primary purpose is to improve health."[6] An agreed-upon definition of health is paramount to the discussion of any health system. Health is too often seen as a concept that applies only to physical well-being or the absence of disease; however, the most widely accepted definition of health is the one first published by WHO in 1948. It defines health as "a state of complete physical, mental, and social well-being and not merely the absence of disease or infirmity."[7] This compre-hensive concept of health is the one used in this book and serves to inform the discussion of the U.S. health system. This definition also recognizes the influence various health determinants have on individual and population health outcomes.

Health determinants are the varied factors that affect the health status of populations or groups of people.[8] Health determinants fall into five broad categories that include policymak-ing, social factors, health services, individual behavior, and biology and genetics, as shown in **FIGURE 1-1**. The determinants interact and are interrelated to produce different health outcomes.

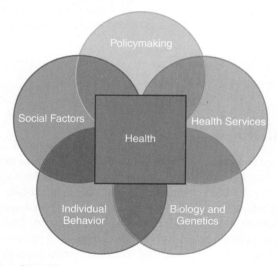

FIGURE 1-1 Determinants of Health

Created by Kim Davey. Based on information from Healthy People 2020. Determinants of health. HealthyPeople.gov. Accessed October 20, 2021. https://www.healthypeople.gov/2020/about/foundation-health-measures/Determinants-of-Health

For example, relationships with peers, family, and friends influence individual health behaviors. Policies and laws regulate certain behaviors (e.g., legal age to purchase alcohol or tobacco products), how certain health services are provided, and many other aspects of the health system.[9]

Population health is the distribution of health outcomes within a population, the determinants that influence distribution, and the policies and interventions that affect the determinants.[10,11] Populations can be defined by geography or grouped according to some common element such as employer, ethnicity, medical condition, or some other grouping element. Population health embraces a comprehensive agenda that addresses the healthy and unhealthy, the acutely ill and the chronically ill, the clinical delivery system, and the public sector. While there are many determinants that affect population health, the ultimate goal for healthcare providers, public health professionals, employers, payers, and policy makers is the same: healthy people comprising healthy populations that create productive workforces and thriving communities.[9] All health systems have common elements or building blocks that are necessary for a functioning health system despite the unique health determinants and population health. The following section provides a discussion of these building blocks.

▶ Health System Building Blocks

The World Health Organization (WHO) utilizes the systems thinking approach through its Health System Framework (see **FIGURE 1-2**), promoting health in ministries and countries all around the world using Health System Building Blocks. WHO identifies six Building Blocks, or core components, of health systems that include service delivery, health workforce, health information, medical technology, health financing, and leadership and governance. These Building Blocks are described in **TABLE 1-1**. A deeper discussion of the Building Blocks is provided in future chapters: service delivery (Chapters 6, 7, 8, 9, 10, and 13), health workforce (Chapter 5),

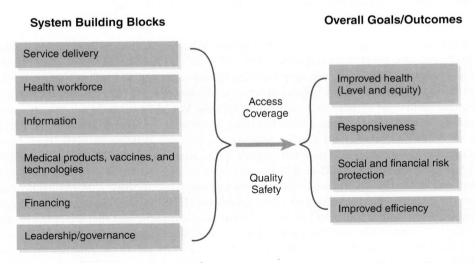

FIGURE 1-2 WHO Health System Framework

TABLE 1-1 Health Systems Building Blocks	
Service Delivery	**Medical Technology**
Good health services are those that deliver effective, safe, quality personal and non-personal health interventions to those who need them, when and where needed, with minimum waste of resources.	A well-functioning health system ensures equitable access to essential medical products, drugs, vaccines, and technologies of assured quality, safety, efficacy, and their scientifically sound and cost-effective use.
Health Workforce	**Health Financing**
A well-performing health workforce is one that works in ways that are responsive, fair, and efficient to achieve the best health outcomes possible, given available resources and circumstances (i.e., there are sufficient staff, fairly distributed; they are competent, responsive, and productive).	A good health financing system raises adequate funds for health, in ways that ensure people can use needed services and are protected from financial catastrophe or impoverishment associated with having to pay for them; it provides incentives for providers and users to be efficient.
Health Information	**Leadership and Governance**
A well-functioning health information system is one that ensures the production, analysis, dissemination, use of reliable and timely information on health determinants, health system performance, and health status improvements.	Leadership and governance involve ensuring that strategic policy frameworks exist and are combined with effective oversight, coalition building, regulation, attention to system design, and accountability.

Johnson JA, Stoskopf C, Shi L. *Comparative Health Systems: A Global Perspective.* 2nd ed. Jones & Barlett Learning; 2018.

health information (Chapter 11), medical technology (Chapter 11), health financing (Chapter 4), and leadership and governance (Chapter 3 and 12). WHO acknowledged a shift toward systems thinking, and the WHO Health System Building Blocks recognize and utilize systems thinking. These Building Blocks not only help us to better understand health systems, but they also provide opportunities for system improvement. WHO, the World Bank, and various governments around the world have a common understanding of these key elements. Some would describe them as critical success factors that are essential to a health system's survival. Furthermore, WHO and other leading international organizations advocate for a "Health in All Policies" (HiAPs) approach, as described in **BOX 1-2**. HiAPs is an approach that serves as a catalyst to compel ministries (or government departments and agencies) to work with the health ministry (or the Department of Health and Human Services [HHS] in the United States) to address the public health implications and potential unintended consequences that affect the health of individuals, communities, and the nation. For example, the Department of Agriculture would engage the Department of Health and Human Services in its policy development process, as would the Department of Transportation.

BOX 1-2 Health in All Policies

Health in All Policies (HiAP) is an approach to public policies across sectors that systematically considers the health implications of decisions, seeks synergies, and avoids harmful health impacts in order to improve population health and health equity. It improves accountability of policymakers for health impacts at all levels of policy-making. It includes an emphasis on the consequences of public policies on health systems, determinants of health and well-being.

One widely accepted way to measure the building blocks, or overall functioning, of a health system is through the lens of the Triple Aim shown in **FIGURE 1-3**. The Institute for Healthcare Improvement (IHI) developed the Triple Aim, a framework for healthcare improvement, in response to increasing healthcare costs, quality concerns, chronic health conditions, and an aging population. The framework consists of simultaneously pursuing three dimensions (thus, the Triple Aim): improving the patient experience of care (including the ability of patients to access high-quality care that patients are satisfied with), the health of the population, and reducing the per capita cost of health. The goal of the framework is to optimize health system performance. The framework recognizes that there are many subsystems, elements, and even individuals that contribute to delivering healthcare in the United States and that accountability is ultimately shared by many stakeholders. The following sections provide a discussion of major subsystems of U.S. healthcare delivery.

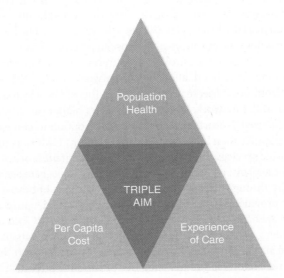

FIGURE 1-3 Institute for Healthcare Improvement Triple Aim for Populations

▶ Major Subsystems of U.S. Healthcare Delivery

The United States does not have a well-integrated and coordinated healthcare delivery system enjoyed by everyone. Instead, there are multiple subsystems developed either through market forces or as a result of policy initiatives to address the needs of certain population segments, as shown in **FIGURE 1-4**. The major subsystems are described in the following sections.[1]

The Managed Care System

Managed care is a system of healthcare delivery that: 1) seeks to achieve efficiencies by integrating the basic functions of healthcare delivery, (2) employs mechanisms to control (manage) utilization of medical services, and (3) determines the price at which the services are purchased and, consequently, how much the providers are paid. It is the most dominant healthcare delivery system in the United States today and is available to most Americans. The primary financiers of the managed care system are employers and the government; however, it is not a private–public partnership. Employers purchase insurance for their own employees, but they do so voluntarily. As a result, many small employers do not provide health insurance to their employees. On the other hand, because employer-based health insurance requires cost sharing, many workers choose not to participate even when the employer pays the bulk of the premium costs. Because of variations in the government programs, beneficiaries are either required to obtain healthcare services through a managed care organization (MCO) or through alternative mechanisms.[1]

There are two main types of MCOs: health maintenance organizations (HMOs) and preferred provider organizations (PPOs). An MCO functions like an insurance company and promises to provide healthcare services contracted under the health plan to the enrollees of the plan. The terms *enrollee* and *member* refer to the individual covered under the plan. The contractual arrangement between the MCO and the enrollee—including the array of covered health services that the enrollee is entitled to—is referred to as the health plan (or *the plan,* for short). The health plan generally uses selected providers from whom the enrollees can choose to receive routine services. HMOs typically require in-network access—that is, the enrollees must receive services from the providers selected by the HMO. PPOs, on the other hand, allow out-of-network access—the enrollees can choose to receive services either from providers that participate in the PPO's selected network or from providers that are not part of the network. The enrollee incurs higher out-of-pocket costs when out-of-network providers are used. Nevertheless, because of the option to choose one's providers, PPO plans have been more popular than HMO plans. Particularly in HMOs, primary care providers or generalists manage routine services and determine the appropriateness of referrals to higher level or specialty services. In these plans, generalists are often referred to as gatekeepers. Some HMOs may deliver services partially through the plan's own hired physicians, but most services are delivered through contracts with providers, such as physicians, hospitals, and diagnostic clinics. Although the employer finances the care by purchasing a plan from an MCO, the MCO is the one responsible for negotiating with providers. HMOs typically use capitation arrangements to pay providers. Under capitation, a negotiated fixed amount per enrollee is paid each month to the provider. This fixed amount is commonly referred to as the per-member per-month rate. Risk is shared between the HMO and the provider who receives the per-member per-month rate, because in exchange for this payment the provider is obligated to deliver whatever contracted services the enrollees might need. PPOs commonly pay the providers a discounted fee that has been negotiated between the PPO and the provider. Providers are willing to discount their services in exchange for being included in the

Managed Care System

Managed care is a system of healthcare delivery that (1) seeks to achieve efficiencies by integrating the basic functions of healthcare delivery. (2) employs mechanisms to control (manage) utilization of medical services, and (3) determines the price at which the services are purchased and consequently how much the providers get paid.

Military and Veterans Systems

The military medical care system is available free of change to active-duty military personnel. it is a well-organized and highly integrated system operated by the U.S. Department of Defense. The VA system provides a broad spectrum of medical, surgical, and rehabilitative care to veterans. It is one of the largest, oldest formally organized healthcare systems in the world.

Vulnerable Population System

In 1965, the U.S. Congress passed two major amendments to the Social Security Act that created the Medicare and Medicaid programs. The government assumed direct responsibility to pay for some of the health care on behalf of two vulnerable population groups—the elderly and the poor. In 1997, the Children Health Insurance Program (CHIP) was enacted to provide health insurance to children living in low income families that did not quality for Medicaid.

Indian Health System

The Indian Health Service (IHS) provides health services to American Indians and Alaska Natives and is an agency with in the Department of Health and Human Services (DHHS) sponsored by the federal government.

Integrated Delivery Systems

An integrated delivery system (IDS) is a network of organizations that provides, or arranges to provide, a coordinated continuum of services to a defined population and is willing to be held clinically and fiscally accountable for the outcomes and health status of that population.

Long-term Care System

The long-term care system is a variety of individualized, well-coordinated services that promote the maximum possible independence for people with functional limitations and that are provided over an extended period of time in accordance with a holistic approach, while maximizing the person's quality of life.

Behavioral Health System

The behavioral care system refers to the individuals, groups, and organizations that provide services that promote mental health, resilience and well-being, treats mental and substance use disorders, and supports individuals that experience and/or are in recovery from these conditions along with their families and communities.

Public Health System

The Centers for Disease Control and Prevention (CDC) defines public health as "the science of protecting and improving the health of families and communities through promotion of healthy lifestyles, research for disease and injury prevention, and detection and control of infectious diseases."

FIGURE 1-4 Major Subsystems of the U.S. Health System

Created by Kim Davey.

PPO's network and being guaranteed a patient population. As insurers, health plans must make actuarial projections of the expected cost of healthcare utilization. They bear the risk that the cost of services delivered could exceed the premiums collected. By underwriting this risk, a plan assumes the role of insurer.[1]

The Military and Veterans Systems

The military medical care system is available free of charge to active-duty military personnel. It is a well-organized and highly integrated system operated by the United States Department of Defense. Comprehensive services cover prevention as well as treatments provided by salaried healthcare personnel. Routine ambulatory care is often available at a dispensary, sick bay, first-aid station, or medical station located close to the military personnel's workplace. Routine hospital services are provided in dispensaries located in military bases, in sick bays aboard ships, and in small base hospitals. Complicated hospital services are provided in regional military hospitals. Dependents of service members, retirees and their dependents, and survivors of deceased members can receive medical care through an insurance program called TRICARE. This program permits the beneficiaries to receive care from military as well as private medical care facilities. Although patients have little choice regarding how services are provided, in general, the military medical care system provides high-quality health care.[1]

War veterans are entitled to receive a wide array of medical and long-term care services through facilities operated by the Veterans Health Administration VA. The VA system provides a broad spectrum of medical, surgical, and rehabilitative care. It is one of the largest, oldest formally organized healthcare systems in the world. The VA, predecessor to the current Department of Veterans Affairs, was established in 1930. In addition to medical care, its mission includes education, training, research, and contingency support and emergency management for the Department of Defense medical care system.[1] The VA system provides care to approximately 9 million veterans at 1,293 healthcare facilities that include 171 medical centers and 1,112 outpatient sites in 2021.[12] The system is divided into 18 Veterans Integrated Service Networks, or VISNs. These regional networks strive improve access and care coordination for veterans in a geographic or local area.[13]

The Vulnerable Population System

In 1965, the United States Congress passed two major amendments to the Social Security Act that created the Medicare and Medicaid programs, and the government assumed direct responsibility to pay for some of the health care on behalf of two vulnerable population groups—the elderly and the poor.[14] Medicaid and Medicare are prime representations of the public sector in the amalgam of private and public approaches for providing access to health care in the United States. Originally created for the elderly, the Medicare program now covers 57 million Americans, including low-income disabled individuals below the age of 65 and people who have end-stage renal disease.[15,16] The Medicaid program finances healthcare services for the poor who qualify based on assets and income below the threshold levels established by each state. The program serves nearly 70.5 million Americans.[17] In 1997, the Children's Health Insurance Program (CHIP) was enacted to provide health insurance to children living in low-income families that did not qualify for Medicaid. Of the 77 million children in the United States, about 45% are enrolled in either Medicaid or CHIP.[18] In the three main public programs, the government finances the insurance, but healthcare services are received mainly through private providers. Medicaid and CHIP enrollees incur few out-of-pocket costs, but Medicare enrollees pay for approximately half of their healthcare costs. This is mainly due to high deductibles, copayments, and certain noncovered services—such as dental, vision, and hearing aids—and gaps in prescription drug coverage (coverage was added to the program in 2005). Poor enrollees can qualify for both Medicaid and Medicare, in which case Medicaid pays for the gaps in Medicare coverage. Most other enrollees purchase private health insurance called Medigap to pay for noncovered Medicare expenses.

Other vulnerable populations—especially uninsured minorities, immigrants, and those living in geographically or economically disadvantaged communities—receive care from safety net providers, including community health centers, physicians' offices, hospital outpatient departments, and emergency rooms, of which community health centers are expressly designed for the underserved.

For over 50 years, federally funded health centers have provided primary and preventive health services to rural and urban underserved populations. The Bureau of Primary Health Care, within the Department of Health and Human Services' Health Resources and Services administration, provides federal support for community-based health centers that include programs for migrant and seasonal farm workers and their families, homeless people, public housing residents, and school-age children. In addition to essential primary care and preventive services, health centers provide enabling services, such as case management, transportation, health education, language translation, and childcare. These services facilitate regular access to care for predominantly minority, low-income, uninsured, and Medicaid patients. The Federally Qualified Health Center (FQHC) program has grown substantially over the years, and in 2019 nearly 1,400 centers operated 13,000 delivery sites providing primary and preventive care to nearly 30 million patients in every state, the District of Columbia, Puerto Rico, the United States Virgin Islands, and the Pacific Basin (or 1 in 11 people). The number of patients seen increased from 9.6 million in 2000 to 29.88 million in 2019.[19] Health centers have contributed to significantly improved health outcomes for the uninsured and Medicaid-recipient populations and have reduced disparities in health care and health status across socioeconomic and racial/ethnic groups.[20,21]

America's safety net, however, is by no means secure, and the availability of safety net providers varies from community to community. Vulnerable populations residing in communities without safety net providers have to forgo care or seek care from hospital emergency rooms, if such services are available in the areas where they live. Safety net providers face enormous pressures due to high demand, particularly in communities that have an increasing number of uninsured and poor people. The inability to shift costs for uncompensated care onto private insurance has become a significant problem because revenues from Medicaid, the primary source of third-party financing for core safety net providers, are inadequate because of funding constraints.[1]

The Indian Health System

The Indian Health Service (IHS) provides health services to Native Americans and Alaska Natives and is an agency within HHS sponsored by the federal government. The IHS provides comprehensive health services to 574 federally recognized tribes in 37 states, or approximately 2.6 million people.[22] The IHS budget appropriation for 2020 was $6 billion, which was up from the system's $5.8 billion budget the previous year. In 2019, IHS expenditures per beneficiary were $4,078. In 2018, there were 40,494 inpatient admissions and 13,752,397 outpatient visits.[23]

Integrated Delivery Systems

An integrated delivery system (IDS) may be defined as a network of organizations that provides, or arranges to provide, a coordinated continuum of services to a defined population and is willing to be held clinically and fiscally accountable for the outcomes and health status of that population. For over a decade now, organizational integration to form IDSs has been the hallmark of the U.S. healthcare industry. Integration in the U.S. healthcare delivery system has occurred in response to cost pressures, development of new alternatives for the delivery of health care, the growing power of MCOs, and the need to provide services more efficiently to populations spread over large geographic areas. An IDS represents various forms of ownership and other strategic linkages among major participants, such as hospitals, physicians, and insurers. The objective is to achieve greater integration of healthcare services along the continuum of care.[1]

The Long-Term Care System

The long-term care system is a variety of individualized, well-coordinated services that promote the maximum possible independence for people with functional limitations and that are provided over an extended period of time in accordance with a holistic approach, while maximizing the person's quality of life. Long-term care needs are not confined only to older Americans, but older Americans are the fastest-growing proportion of the population and are the major consumers of long-term care services. Advances in medical care have made a longer life span possible, with accompanying challenges presented by chronic disease and physical limitations. Long-term care facilities (LTCFs) are institutions such as nursing homes, skilled nursing facilities (SNFs), and assisted living facilities that provide health care to people who are unable to manage independently in the community. This care may represent custodial or chronic care management or short-term rehabilitative services.[24] The site of care delivery categorizes long-term care programs. Institution-based services are those long-term care services provided within an institution such as a nursing home, hospital with inpatient extended care or a rehabilitation facility, or inpatient hospice. Community-based services coordinate, manage, and deliver long-term care services such as adult day-care programs, residential group homes, or care in the recipient's home.

The Behavioral Care System

The behavioral care system refers to the individuals, groups, and organizations that provide services that promote mental health, resilience, and well-being, treat mental and substance use disorders, and support individuals that experience and/or are in recovery from these conditions, along with their families and communities.[25] The Substance Abuse and Mental Health Services Administration (SAMHSA) "is the agency within the DHHS that leads efforts to advance the behavioral health of the nation."[26] Behavioral health conditions are treated by an array of providers representing multiple disciplines working in both public and private settings. The loose coordination of facilities and services has resulted in the mental health delivery system being referred to as a de facto mental health service system, structured with four highly compartmentalized sectors characterized by poor inter-sector communication and isolated funding streams. The behavioral health sector consists of behavioral health professionals, such as psychiatrists, psychologists, psychiatric nurses, psychiatric social workers, and behavioral health clinicians working in outpatient settings. More recently, providers are hiring peer specialists, people with a psychiatric or substance abuse disorder who are trained to help others in accessing care and developing a recovery plan. The human services sector consists of social service agencies, school-based counseling services, residential rehabilitation services, vocational rehabilitation services, criminal justice/prison-based services, and religious professional counselors. The volunteer support network sector consists of self-help groups and family advocacy groups. The primary care sector consists of healthcare professionals, such as internists, family practitioners, pediatricians, and nurse practitioners in private office-based practices, clinics, hospitals, and nursing homes. This sector is often the initial point of contact and may be the only source of mental health services for a large proportion of people with psychiatric or behavioral health disorders. In recent years, there has been a greater recognition of the need for behavioral health professionals and services that are integrated with primary care.

The Public Health System

The Centers for Disease Control and Prevention (CDC) defines public health as "the science of protecting and improving the health of families and communities through promotion of healthy lifestyles, research for disease and injury prevention, and detection and control of infectious diseases."[27] The public health system consists of "all public, private, and voluntary entities that contribute to the delivery of essential public health services within a jurisdiction."[28] Public health is unique in its interdisciplinary approach and methods, its emphasis on preventive strategies, its linkage with government and political decision making, and its dynamic adaptation to new problems placed on the agenda. Above all else, it is a collective effort to identify and address the unacceptable realities that result in preventable and avoidable health and quality of life outcomes. It is the composite of efforts and activities that are carried out by people and organizations committed to these ends.[29] The public health system includes public health agencies at the state and local level, healthcare providers, public safety agencies, human service and charity organizations, education and youth development organizations, recreation and arts-related organizations, economic and philanthropic organizations, and environmental agencies and organizations.

▶ Distinguishing Characteristics of the U.S. Health System

The healthcare system of a nation is influenced by external factors, including the political climate, economic development, technological progress, social and cultural values, the physical environment, and population characteristics, such as demographic and health trends. The combined interaction of these forces influences the course of healthcare delivery in the United States. In the following sections, we summarize the basic characteristics that differentiate the Unites States healthcare delivery system from that of other countries. The main characteristics of the U.S. healthcare system are shown in **FIGURE 1-5** and include[1]:

- No central governing agency and little integration and coordination
- A technology-driven delivery system focusing on acute care
- High costs, unequal access, and average outcomes
- Delivery of health care under imperfect market conditions
- Government as subsidiary to the private sector
- Market justice versus social justice, pervasive throughout health care
- Quest for integration and accountability
- Multiple players and balance of power

FIGURE 1-5 Distinguishing Characteristics of the U.S. Health System
Created by Kim Davey.

No Central Government Agency and Little Integration

The U.S. healthcare system provides a significant contrast to the healthcare systems of other developed countries. The U.S. system is not centrally controlled and has a very complex structure of financing, insurance, delivery, and payment mechanisms. In 2019, the federal government financed the largest share of total health spending (29%) followed by households (28.4%), private businesses (19.1%), state and local governments (16.1%), and private revenues (7.5%).[16] The centrally controlled universal healthcare systems of most developed countries authorize financing and delivery of health care for all residents. The less complex structure of a centrally controlled healthcare system improves efficiency by managing total expenditures through global budgets and by governing the availability and utilization of services through central planning. Because the United States has such a large private system of financing, insurance, and delivery, the majority of insurers and providers are private businesses, independent of the government. Nevertheless, the federal and state governments play an important role in healthcare delivery. They finance healthcare services for publicly insured patients, such as those covered under Medicare and Medicaid. They also determine public sector expenditures and establish reimbursement rates for services delivered to Medicare and Medicaid patients. The government uses various payment mechanisms for providers. Currently, almost all inpatient and home healthcare services delivered to Medicare and Medicaid patients are reimbursed according to a variety of prospective payment methods. Physician reimbursement rates are derived using complex formulas that take into account factors such as time, skill, and intensity of physician work; beginning in 1983, a gradual departure occurred from the previous cost-based reimbursement methods. The government also formulates standards of participation through health policy and regulation and requires providers to comply with the standards and receive federal certification in order to deliver care to Medicare and Medicaid patients. Certification standards are also regarded as minimum standards of quality in most sectors of the healthcare industry.[1]

A Technology-Driven Delivery System Focusing on Acute Care

The United States has been the hotbed of research and innovation in new medical technology. Because of cost implications, almost all nations try to limit the diffusion and utilization of technology through central planning and control. Lack of such controls in the United States promotes innovation, rapid diffusion, and utilization of new technology. Growth in science and technology often creates demand for new services despite shrinking resources to finance sophisticated care. Other factors contribute to increased demand in expensive technological care: patients assume that the latest innovations offer the highest quality, physicians want to try the latest gadgets, and competition among hospitals is often driven by the acquisition of technology. After organizations acquire new equipment and facilities, they are often under pressure to recoup the capital investments. Legal risks for providers and health plans alike may also play a role in discouraging denial of new technology. Although technology has ushered in a new generation of successful interventions, the negative outcomes resulting from its overuse are many. For example, the expense of highly technical interventions increases insurance payments to providers. Insurance premiums rise, and it becomes more difficult for employers to expand coverage. Broad exposure to technology early in medical training affects not only clinical preferences but also future professional behavior and practice patterns. Because medical specialization revolves around technology, an oversupply of specialists in the United States has compounded the rate of technology diffusion.[1]

High Cost, Unequal Access, and Mixed Outcomes

The United States spends twice as much on healthcare as comparable countries.[30] The most recent Organisation for Economic Co-operation and Development (OECD) report based on 2019 data notes that U.S. health spending, with a 17% share of the gross domestic product (GDP), is an outlier when compared with other countries who devote an average of 9.6% to health spending.[31] The high cost of health care has ramifications for the expansion of health insurance to the uninsured, the long-term solvency of publicly financed programs, and other issues of equity and health disparities that remain unaddressed.[1]

Access means the ability of an individual to obtain healthcare services when needed. In the United States, access is restricted to: (1) those who have health insurance through their employers, (2) those covered under a government healthcare program, (3) those who can afford to buy insurance out of their private funds, and (4) those who are able to pay for services privately. Health insurance is the primary means for ensuring access, although some uninsured Americans receive care through the safety net. In 2019, 28.9 million Americans of all ages (10.9% of the population) were uninsured—that is, they were not covered under a private or public health insurance program.[32] For consistent, basic, and routine primary care, the uninsured are unable to see a physician unless they can pay the physician's fees. Those who cannot afford to pay generally wait until health problems develop, at which point they may be able to receive services free of charge in a hospital emergency department. It is well acknowledged that absence of insurance inhibits patients' ability to receive well-directed, coordinated, and continuous health care through access to primary care services and, when needed, referral to specialty services. Experts generally believe that inadequate access to basic and routine primary care services is the main reason that the United States, in spite of being the most economically advanced country, lags behind other developed nations in measures of population health such as infant mortality and overall life expectancy. This belief, however, remains largely unsubstantiated, mainly in view of the fact that the health status of a population is based on many factors, including individual lifestyles and behaviors.[1]

Delivery of Health Care Under Imperfect Market Conditions

In the United States, even though the delivery of services is largely in private hands, health care is only partially governed by free market forces. The delivery and consumption of health care in the United States do not quite meet the basic tests of a free market. Hence, the system is best described as a quasi-market or an imperfect market. There are some key features characterizing free markets. In a free market, multiple patients (buyers) and providers (sellers) act independently. In a free market, patients should be able to choose their provider based on price and quality of services. If it were this simple, patient choice would determine prices by the unencumbered interaction of supply and demand. Theoretically at least, prices are negotiated between payers and providers; however, in many instances, the payer is not the patient but a managed care organization, Medicare, or Medicaid. Because prices are set by agencies external to the market, they are not freely governed by the forces of supply and demand.[1]

Government as Subsidiary to the Private Sector

In most other developed countries, the government plays a central role in the provision of health care. In the United States, the private sector plays the dominant role. This can be explained to some degree by the American tradition of reliance on individual responsibility and a commitment to limiting the power of the national government. As a result, government spending for health care has been largely confined to filling in the gaps left open by the private sector. These gaps include environmental protection, support for research and training, and care of vulnerable populations.[1]

Market Justice Versus Social Justice Pervasive Throughout Health Care

Market justice and social justice are two contrasting theories that govern the production and distribution of healthcare services in the United States. The principle of market justice ascribes the fair distribution of health care to the market forces in a free economy. Medical care and its benefits are distributed on the basis of people's willingness and ability to pay. In contrast, social justice emphasizes the well-being of the community over that of the individual; thus, the inability to obtain medical services because of a lack of financial resources would be considered unjust. A just distribution of benefits must be based on need, not simply one's ability to purchase them in the marketplace. In a partial public and private healthcare system, the two theories often operate side by side; however, market justice principles tend to prevail. Unfortunately, market justice results in the unequal allocation of healthcare services, neglecting critical human concerns that are not confined to the individual but that have broader negative impacts on society.[1]

Quest for Integration and Accountability

The use of primary care as the organizing hub for continuous and coordinated health services was recognized in the United States. It was envisioned that through primary care, other healthcare services would be integrated in a seamless fashion. Although this model gained popularity with the expansion of managed care, its development stalled before it could reach its full potential. The large-scale transition of healthcare delivery to the managed care system in the 1990s was met with widespread criticism, which turned into backlash from consumers, physicians, and legislators. As a result, various compromises were reached. The HMO model that was based on primary care and gatekeeping became less popular than was initially foreseen by its proponents. A compromised PPO model has become dominant in U.S. healthcare delivery; however, current political debates seem to exhibit the need for a model of healthcare delivery that is based on primary care. The PPO model also emphasizes the importance of the patient–provider relationship and how it can best function to improve the health of each individual; however, such a system would fall short of meeting any population-wide objectives without universal access to basic health care. The Affordable Care Act (ACA) was signed into law on March 23, 2010 to increase the affordability of health insurance, to lower the uninsured rate by expanding public and private insurance coverage, and to reduce the costs of health care. It introduced mechanisms like mandates, subsidies, and insurance exchanges. Since the ACA was enacted, the U.S. healthcare system has taken important steps toward providing all Americans with high-quality, affordable health care.[1]

Multiple Players and Balance of Power

The U.S. healthcare system involves multiple players. The key players in the system have been physicians, administrators of health service institutions, insurance companies, large employers, and the government. Big business, labor, MCOs, insurance companies, physicians, and hospitals make up the powerful and politically active special interest groups represented before lawmakers by high-priced lobbyists. Each player has a different economic interest to protect. The problem is that the self-interests of each player are often at odds. For example, providers seek to maximize government reimbursement for services delivered to Medicare and Medicaid patients, but the government wants to contain cost increases. The fragmented self-interests of the various players produce countervailing forces within the system. In an environment that is rife with motivations to protect conflicting self-interests, achieving comprehensive system-wide reforms is next to impossible, and cost containment remains a major challenge. Consequently, the approach to healthcare reform in the United States is characterized as incremental or piecemeal.

▶ Major Stakeholders in U.S. Health System

To understand the healthcare industry, it is important to recognize the number and variety of the stakeholders involved. A stakeholder is an individual, group, organization, or entity that has an interest in an issue, topic, or outcome. The sometimes shared and often conflicting concerns, interests, and influences of these constituent groups cause them to shift alliances periodically to oppose or champion specific reform proposals or other changes in the industry. The major stakeholders in the U.S. health system are shown in **FIGURE 1-6**.

The Public

First and foremost among healthcare stakeholders are the individuals who consume the services. Although all are concerned with the issues of cost and quality, those who are uninsured or underinsured have an overriding uncertainty about access. It remains uncertain as to whether the U.S. public will someday wish to treat health care like other inherent rights, such as education, but the passage of the ACA and recent policy discussions seem to suggest that there is agreement that some basic array of healthcare services should be available to all U.S. citizens.

Employers

Employers constitute an increasingly influential group of stakeholders in health care because they not only pay for a high proportion of the costs but also take proactive roles in determining what those costs should be. Large private employers, coalitions of smaller private employers, and public employers wield significant authority in insurance plan negotiations. In addition, employer organizations representing small and large businesses wield considerable political power in the halls of Congress.

Providers

Healthcare professionals form the core of the industry and have the most to do with the actual process and outcomes of the services provided. Physicians, dentists, nurses, nurse practitioners, physician assistants, pharmacists, podiatrists, chiropractors, and a large array of allied health providers working as individuals or in group practices and staffing healthcare institutions are responsible for the quality and, to a large extent, the cost of the healthcare system. Recognizing the centrality of individual providers to system reform, the ACA and the Medicare Access and CHIP Reauthorization Act (MACRA) are now offering numerous opportunities for the participation of physicians and other healthcare professionals in innovative experimentation with integrated systems of care. The MACRA institutes performance-driven systems of patient care linked to the health outcomes of population groups.[33,34]

FIGURE 1-6 **Major Stakeholders in the U.S. Health System**
Created by Kim Davey.

Hospitals and Other Healthcare Facilities

Much of the provider activity, however, is shaped by the availability and nature of the healthcare institutions in which providers work. Hospitals of different types—general, specialty, teaching, rural, profit or not-for-profit, and independent or multifacility systems—are central to the health-care system. However, they are becoming but one component of more complex integrated delivery system networks that also include nursing homes and other levels of care and various forms of medical practices.

Governments

Since the advent of Medicare and Medicaid in 1965, federal and state governments, already major stakeholders in health care, became the dominant authorities of the system. Governments serve not only as payers but also as regulators and providers through public hospitals, state and local health departments, veterans' affairs medical centers, and other facilities. In addition, of course, governments are the taxing authorities that generate the funds to support the system.

Complementary and Alternative Therapists

Unconventional health therapies—those not usually taught in established medical and other health professional schools—contribute significantly to the amount, frequency, and cost of health care. In spite of the scientific logic and documented effectiveness of traditional, academically based health care, it is estimated that one in three adults use complementary forms of health interventions each year.[35] Complementary medicine consists of using modalities such as nutritional supplements, yoga, acupuncture, or meditation in conjunction with mainstream medical care.[36] Because of their popularity, state Medicaid programs, Medicare, and private health insurance plans provide benefits for some complementary therapies.[37] Alternative medicine uses non-mainstream treatments in place of conventional medicine.[38]

It is estimated that more than $9 billion per year is spent on complementary and alternative forms of health care such as Rolfing, yoga, spiritual healing, relaxation techniques, herbal remedies, energy healing, megavitamin therapy, chiropractic care, and a host of other mind–body healing techniques.[37]

The public's willingness to spend so much time and money on unconventional therapies suggests a substantial level of dissatisfaction with traditional scientific medicine. Thus, as a somewhat paradoxical development, some of the most ancient concepts of alternative health care are gaining broader recognition and acceptance in an era of the most innovative and advanced high-technology medicine. The National Institutes of Health operates the National Center for Complementary and Integrative Health (NCCIH) to fund studies on the efficacy of such therapies.

In recent years, a number of hospitals began offering forms of complementary and alternative medicine. According to an American Hospital Association survey, by 2000, more than 15% of U.S. hospitals had opened complementary or alternative medicine centers.[38] With a market estimated to be worth $34 billion and patients willing to pay cash for treatments, hospitals are willing to rationalize the provision of medically unproven services in response to patient demand.[39]

Health Insurers

The insurance industry has long been a major stakeholder in the healthcare industry. Today, MCO insurance plans are the predominant form of U.S. health insurance. MCOs may be owned by insurance companies, or they may be owned by hospitals, physicians, or consumer cooperatives.

MCOs and the economic pressures they can apply through the negotiation of prepaid fees for healthcare services have produced much of the change occurring in the healthcare system during the past 3 decades. The insurance industry played a major role in the development of the ACA.[40] Under the ACA, the insurance industry contributed annual fees to the federal government to help offset the ACA costs.[41] This fee levy recognizes that the ACA will add millions of new insurance company customers.

The Long-Term Care Industry

The aging of the U.S. population poses a formidable challenge to the country's systems of acute and long-term care. Nursing homes, home-care services, other adult-care facilities, and rehabilitation facilities will become increasingly important components of the nation's healthcare system. The ACA's creation of seamless systems of integrated care that permit patients to move back and forth among ambulatory care offices, acute care hospitals, home care, and nursing homes within a single network of facilities and services will provide a continuum of services required for the complex care of aging patients.

Voluntary Facilities and Agencies

Voluntary not-for-profit facilities and agencies, so called because they are governed by volunteer boards of directors, provide significant amounts of health counseling, health care, and research support and should be considered major stakeholders in the healthcare system. Although the voluntary sector traditionally has not received the recognition it deserves for its contribution to the nation's health care, it is often now viewed as the safety net to replace the services of government or other organizations eliminated by budgetary reductions.

Health Professions Education and Training Institutions

Schools of medicine, public health, nursing, dentistry, pharmacy, optometry, allied health, and other healthcare professions have a significant impact on the nature, quality, and costs of health care. As they prepare each generation of competent healthcare providers, these schools also inculcate the values, attitudes, and ethics that govern the practices and behaviors of those providers as they function in the healthcare system.

Professional Associations

National, state, and regional organizations representing healthcare professionals or institutions have considerable influence over legislative proposals, regulation, quality issues, and other political matters. The lobbying effectiveness of the American Medical Association, for example, is legendary. The national influence of the American Hospital Association and the regional power of its state and local affiliates are also impressive. Other organizations of healthcare professionals, such as the American Public Health Association, America's Health Insurance Plans, the American Nurses Association, and the American Dental Association, play significant roles in health policy decisions. The American insurance industry lobbyists from organizations such as America's Health Insurance Plans had major influences on the provisions of the ACA.

Other Health Industry Organizations

The size and complexity of the healthcare industry encourage the involvement of a great number of commercial entities. Several, such as the insurance industry noted above and the pharmaceutical and medical device industries, have significant influence on the healthcare delivery enterprise.

Research Communities

It is difficult to separate much of healthcare research from the educational institutions that provide for its implementation. Nevertheless, the national research enterprise must be included in any enumeration of stakeholders in the healthcare industry. Government entities, such as the National Institutes of Health and the Agency for Healthcare Research and Quality, and not-for-profit foundations, such as the Robert Wood Johnson Foundation, the Commonwealth Fund, the Henry J. Kaiser Family Foundation, and the Pew Charitable Trusts, exert tremendous influence over healthcare research, policy development, and practice by conducting research, widely disseminating findings, and supporting and encouraging investigations that inform policy decision making.

▶ Continuing Challenges

The United States does not have a well-integrated healthcare delivery system for all citizens. Instead, there are multiple subsystems developed either through market forces or through public initiatives to address the needs of certain population segments. The subsystems include managed care, the military and VA systems, the system for vulnerable populations, and the emerging integrated delivery system. The basic features that characterize the unique healthcare delivery system in the United States include the absence of a central agency to govern the system, little integration and coordination, a technology-driven delivery system focusing on acute care, a costly system that produces unequal access and average outcomes, delivery of health care under imperfect market conditions, government as subsidiary to the private sector, the conflict between market justice and social justice, multiple players and balance of power, and quests for integration and accountability.[1]

As the United States pushes forward with the implementation of legislative initiatives, its experimentation to test strategies to reduce costs, improve quality, and increase access will likely be joined by other emerging concerns. How to improve Americans' health behaviors, how to involve consumers more effectively in healthcare decisions, and how to balance responsibilities and accountability between the government and private sectors remain among the looming challenges of this continuing era of health reform.

▶ Discussion Questions

- Does the U.S. health system meet the definition of a system? Why or why not?
- What is systems theory and thinking?
- What are attributes of complex adaptive systems?
- What is health?

- What is a health system?
- What is population health? Why is a population health approach needed to promote health and wellness?
- What are health determinants? Can you provide an example of each of the determinants?
- What is the WHO Health System Framework?
- What are the WHO Health System Building Blocks? Provide an example of each of the Building Blocks.
- What are the major subsystems of the U.S. healthcare delivery system?
- What are the distinguishing characteristics of the U.S. health system?

CASE 1-1 Systems Thinking for Native American Health Initiative

Written by Nitumigaabow Ryan Champagne

In my experience I have the unique opportunity to lead problem solving teams. As consultants, our customers often contract with our firm, Grand River Community Development, to help solve a problem or overcome a barrier. While their lists usually are tangible and concrete "problems", we look at the organizational systems and culture before attempting to problem solve. Often this includes an organizational assessment. Such assessment allows our teams and the customer to see the "bigger picture" and to focus on systemic or organizational issues versus program and department specific matters. While we employ American Indian consultants from nationwide, we do not utilize consultants who are not versed in systemic solutions. These systems are often complex adaptive systems (CAS) that need a problem solver who understands how relationships, systems, and practices impact organizational culture and productivity. The barrier we often face is getting the customers to understand or embrace the larger need. While I believe they understand and agree, many choose not to explore those type of solutions out of fear of staff resistance, personal resistance, and/or lack of capacity to make such changes.

When thinking about systems thinking one case example comes to mind; it was a rural northern Wisconsin tribe that had a population of about four thousand citizens. They declared a state of emergency due to the high rates of drug usage, dealing, and deaths associated with illegal drugs. The leadership was at a loss on how to combat this crisis. The crisis at hand included the following:

- Twelve deaths related to the sale, consumption, or trafficking of illegal drugs in under four months;
- Elders and community members reported fear of leaving their house after dark due to the illegal drug trafficking and crime associate with such;
- HeadStart reported that 40% of the children were showing signs of developmental delay due to being born chemically addicted or exposed; and
- Current government programming appeared to be ineffective in addressing the crisis.

The first stage was to identify what the crisis entailed. This process included an analysis of the systems. The common themes that emerged included suicide, drugs, unmet behavioral health needs, and crime. The crisis factors allowed for the tribal council to come together to have a unified leadership and shared vision that the status quo was no longer acceptable. The tribal council decided to contract with our firm to gain an outside perspective and lens on the crisis state. The idea was that their staff and citizens where too close to the situation and could not have the systemic view needed to assist with developing real solutions to combat the crisis.

(continues)

CASE 1-1 Systems Thinking for Native American Health Initiative *(continued)*

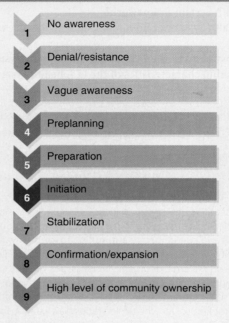

1	No awareness
2	Denial/resistance
3	Vague awareness
4	Preplanning
5	Preparation
6	Initiation
7	Stabilization
8	Confirmation/expansion
9	High level of community ownership

Stages of Community Readiness

Plested, B. A., Jumper-Thurman, P., & Edwards, R. W. (2016). Community readiness manual. The National Center for Community Readiness, Colorado State University, Fort Collins, Colorado.

Grand River conducted a Community Readiness Assessment, to gain an understanding on what the community's current readiness was, which the community scored a (2) and placed them in a domain of Denial/Resistance. This is normal as most individuals whether in a social/environmental crisis state or organizational crisis state have become desensitized to the crisis as the crisis is the status quo or "norm". Post intervention the tool was used again to measure progress and the community scored a (6.75) which raised them between the initiation and stabilization domains.

The next step in the process was having accountability of leadership. This step entailed one-hundred percent of Tribal Council demonstrated support of a drug free community by submitting to a urinalysis and hair screen; enforced "Zero Tolerance Policy" of drug usage or trafficking in government housing; enforced a drug free workplace. At first glance this may not seem like huge accomplishments but in a socialistic form of government where business, government, and citizenship are interconnected this was a feat. The next step entailed a comprehensive organizational assessment, which included a systemic review of all their systems in health and human services. The review extended to collaborative agencies that impacted such systems that included: law enforcement, judicial, housing, education and workforce development, and economic development. The systems assessment established baseline data, identified needs and barriers, and recommended strategies to improve. The assessment served as a detailed roadmap to follow to allow for systemic change.

Preparing for change requires people to change the way they view problems and solutions from a systems thinking perspective. Grand River conducted a Leadership Policy Academy which provided intensive policy training for tribal council. It allowed the leadership to start thinking of their roles as policy makers and systems change, it led to dialogue of strategic planning and visioning. The legislators found value in this new way of thinking that they wanted something for their executive management and management; the Leadership Academy for Tribal Managers was created to meet this need. The tribal managers learned tools to addressing systemic change through: community engagement, implementing change initiatives, leading in a state of crisis, and bridging silos and strategic planning. This was the framework of preparing for systemic change and preparing the human factor.

Grand River along with traditional tribal community leaders started the next stage of community engagement. This stage consisted of conducting a series of: listening sessions; focus groups with elders, cultural advisors, key stakeholders, and consumers; and conducting a community input survey. This stage allowed us to learn of community perceptions, barriers, and problem-solve practical solutions. This stage set the framework of visioning for the community and their vision is what drove the systemic change and community development. Understanding the interconnectedness of these systems and how the community members are the most vital part in solutions was critical in this process, as they are the experts of their community.

Policy development and advocacy stage allowed for: creation of policy and legislation; advocacy with federal, state, and local governments; development of partnerships with local coalitions, state departments, and federal agencies. This stage called on system partners on the local, regional, and macro level to share in the solution process. This process allowed a truly encompassing systemic approach to addressing a crisis in a relatively small community. This set the context for building alliances stage in which Grand River facilitated the process for a formal tribal state partnership and federal partnership. The tribal state partnership addressed social and health disparities; provided funding and technical assistance; and prioritized needs and development of action plan. The tribal federal partnership authorized under the tribal law & order act provided funding, training, and technical assistance development of tribal action plan – priority funding for federal agencies.

The previous steps all were needed to be in place to allow for the final steps of strategic planning, reorganization, and implementation stage. The strategic planning sessions led to key stakeholders and community to recognize the need for reorganization of Health & Human Services. The first step entailed merging fourteen independent siloed programs into three main programs; creation of Human Services Department; and recruitment of a national expert to lead the department. The next phase was to create a Health & Human Services Division which entailed merger of three departments into one division and centralizing core functions and administration; in which increased efficiencies, bridged silos, and reduced costs. Post reorganization a formal strategic plan was adopted that allowed for the following initiatives to occur:

As the chart below demonstrates, these were the major change initiatives that occurred due to a systems thinking perspective; which entailed the ten step Tribal Transformation Process of: (1) Identifying the Crisis; (2) Unified Leadership; (3) Community Readiness; (4) Accountability of Leadership; (5) Organizational Assessment; (6) Policy Institute; (7) Community Engagement; (8) Policy Development & Advocacy; (9) Building Alliances; and (10) Strategic Planning, Reorganization, & Implementation. Within three years Grand River Community Development was able to assist the tribe with twenty-two major self-sustaining initiatives totaling over fifteen million dollars brought-in to the community to start-up such initiatives. The annual profit / cost savings from the initiatives totals more than five million.

Discussion Questions

1. How are the characteristics of complex adaptive systems highlighted in the case?
2. Discuss how systems thinking was used to address the state of emergency that was declared in response to the high rates of drug use, dealing, and death associated with illegal drugs in the tribe.
3. How does the case reflect the Health in All Policies approach?
4. Who were the key stakeholders and what role did they play in the case?

(continues)

CASE 1-1 Systems Thinking for Native American Health Initiative *(continued)*

The System Spectrum and Key Stakeholders

Public Safety	Judicial (Zaagibaa Healing to Wellness Court)	Healthcare (Clinic/Public Health)	Healthcare (Community Based Elder Disability)	Healthcare (Residential)	Human Services (Crisis/Residential)	Human Services (Funding/Case Management)	Workforce Development	Corrections	Cultural
Surveillance Monitoring System	Adult (Alternative to Corrections)	Prescription Drug Monitoring System	Tribal Operated Waivers	Residential Treatment Center	Emergency Shelter	Title IV-E Pass-through Agreement – Child Welfare	YouthBuild	Higher Education in the County Jail	Traditional Healing & Doctoring
Operation Pandora (Interagency Drug Enforcement Approach)	Youth (Early Intervention)	Public Health Awareness Community Campaign	Residential Care Apartment Complex	Permanent Supportive Housing	Peer Supportive Living Homes	Targeted Case Management	Small Business Development in auxiliary health and human services vendors	Clinical Services in the County Jail	Ceremonial Roundhouse
Exclusion & Removal (Banishment)		Patient Centered Medical Home Model				Tribal Wraparound			Family Circles - Grassroots Cultural Intervention
						Comprehensive Community Based Services			

Johnson JA, Anderson DE, Rossow CC. *Health Systems Thinking: A Primer.* Burlington, MA: Jones & Barlett Learning; 2020.

CASE 1-2 Health System Analysis

Written by Kim Davey, PhD, MBA, MA
Samford University, School of Public Health

In this exercise, students are asked to critically analyze the U.S. health system using the WHO Health System Framework. Students will use their analysis to a write case or develop a case presentation. Students will better understand the fundamental and distinguishing characteristics of the U.S. health system through this exercise. If desired, students can select one comparison country to compare and contrast with the U.S. health system. This comparison country will further highlight similarities and differences between health systems. Additionally, a comparative analysis can help students formulate recommendations for addressing health system opportunities and challenges in the United States. Use the sections below to develop a case that analyzes the U.S. health system and a comparison country, if desired.

Section 1: Country Description

This is a great section to use charts and graphs to display and compare information. For each country (i.e., the United States and your comparison country, if desired) provide and compare the following demographic and socioeconomic conditions/information:

- Total population of the country
- Ethnic groups (e.g., British Isles origin, French origin, Asian, African, Arab)
- Religion(s) (e.g., Roman Catholic, Protestant (including Baptist, Lutheran, Methodist, etc.))
- Official language(s) and other languages spoken in the country
- Literacy rate
- Poverty rate
- Employment rate
- Government type (e.g., Constitutional Monarchy, Republic)
- Distribution of the country's population by age, race/ethnicity, location (e.g., urban versus rural), etc.
- Birth rate
- Any additional information that you think is important to understand the health system.

Section 2: History and Evolution of the Healthcare Systems

For each country (i.e., the United States and your comparison country, if desired), provide the following information:

- Describe the history and evolution of the country's healthcare systems.
- Include key dates, pieces of legislation or policies, and establishment of important health programs (e.g., Medicare, Medicaid). What did the legislation do or provide?

Section 3: Health System Analysis Using the WHO Health System Building Blocks Framework

Use the WHO Health System Framework to analyze the U.S. health system. The framework can also be used to compare and contrast the United States and your comparison country, if desired.

Health System Building Blocks

For each country (i.e., the United States and your comparison country, if desired), provide the following information:

(continues)

CASE 1-2 Health System Analysis *(continued)*

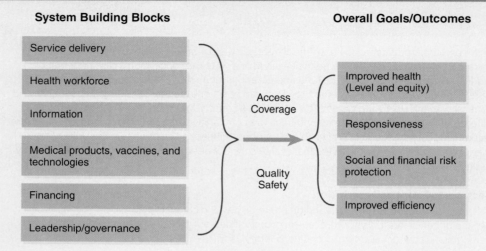

The WHO Health System Framework

Reproduced from the World Health Organization. *Everybody's Business: Strengthening Health Systems to Improve Health Outcomes: WHO's Framework for Action.* World Health Organization; 2007. Accessed June 8, 2021. https://www.who.int/healthsystems/strategy/everybodys_business.pdf

Building Block #1: Health Services

- What are the primary types of healthcare facilities in the country (e.g., primary care clinics, hospitals, community health centers, long-term care, hospice, etc.)? Are they primarily public or private facilities?
- Include any additional information about healthcare facilities or settings where care is provided in the country.

Building Block #2: Healthcare Workforce

- What does the country's healthcare workforce look like? Describe and discuss the distribution of healthcare professionals. For example, what is the number of practicing physicians, nurses, pharmacists, etc.?
- How has the supply of providers changed over time? Are there provider shortages? Surpluses? Are there certain areas with shortages and surpluses?
- What are the specialty areas of healthcare professionals? (e.g., primary versus specialty, etc.) What is the distribution of specialists to generalists/primary care providers in the country?
- What healthcare workforce issues is the country facing? How might these issues influence the health care delivery system in the country now and in the future? (e.g., nurses and physicians in the United States are aging out of the workforce, which has implications for the U.S. healthcare system.)

Building Block #3: Health Information System

- Provide insights into the country's supply and distribution of medical technology.
- What is the status of the country's health information technology infrastructure? Does the country have an underdeveloped or developed healthcare infrastructure?
- Does the country utilize health information technology? Are there any notable ways the country is using or not using technology?

Building Block #4: Essential Medical Products, Vaccines, and Technologies

- What is pharmaceutical spending like in the country? Total expenditures? Per capita?
- How are pharmaceuticals paid for in the country? Are drug prices negotiated in the country?
- Are there any other notables related to pharmaceuticals or the pharmaceutical industry you would like to share?
- Provide insights into the country's supply and distribution of medical products and technology (i.e., number of MRI machines, PET Scanners, Electronic Medical Records, etc.).

Building Block #5: Healthcare Financing

- What do total healthcare expenditures look like in the country? What are the major health expenditure categories in the country?
- What percentage of the country's Gross Domestic Product (GDP) is allocated to health care?
- What is the per capita healthcare expenditure in the country? Again, you are looking for significant trends.
- How is the healthcare system financed in the country? Stated differently, what are the primary sources of funding for the health system (e.g., public programs like Medicare, private options like private health insurance, out-of-pocket)? What is the primary financing source in the country?
- Does the country have universal coverage or a single payer system?
- What types of services are being financed in the country's health system? (e.g., hospital care, preventative care, etc.)
- What services are covered in the country? Who determines what services are provided or covered in the country?
- How are providers (e.g., physicians, nurses, etc.) paid in the country? (e.g., fee-for-service, incentive-based payments, bundled payments, out-of-pocket payments, a mix of payment approaches.)

Building Block #6: Leadership and Governance

- How is the health system organized? What are the major ministries, departments, offices, etc.? What are their roles and functions? For example, the Department of Health and Human Services (DHHS) plays a pivotal role in the U.S. health system. HHS coordinates a number of offices and centers.
- Does the country have health priorities or goals that guide the design of its healthcare system? For example, does market or social justice guide the development of the health system?

Health System Outcomes/Goals

For each country (i.e., the United States and your comparison country, if desired), provide the following information:

Outcome/Goal #1: Improved Health (Population Health)

To understand if health is improving, we have to look at it over time. This is a great section to use charts and graphs to display and compare information.

- What are the leading causes of death? Are these chronic or communicable diseases? A mix?
- Infant mortality rate
- Under 5 mortality rate
- Adult mortality rate
- Life expectancy
- Any additional information that you think is important to understand population health in the country.

(continues)

CASE 1-2 Health System Analysis *(continued)*

Outcome/Goal #2: Responsiveness
- Provide a couple of general examples of health disparities in the country. How are disparities being addressed?

Outcome/Goal #3: Social and Financial Risk (Cost)
- What are the cost projections for the system?
- How are healthcare costs controlled in the country? The term "cost containment" is often used (e.g., cost-containment policies, initiatives).

Outcome/Goal #4: Improved Efficiency (Quality)
- What efforts, if any, has the healthcare system pursued to try and inform consumers/patients/clients about healthcare quality? (e.g., Medicare 5-star rating, hospital compare, physician compare, etc.)
- What quality programs does the country have in place?

Section 5: Health Policies

For each country (i.e., the United States and your comparison country, if desired), provide the following information:
- Identify ONE health policy that was recently passed.
- Why was the policy proposed?
- How does it impact the healthcare system? What building blocks and outcomes does this policy impact? How?
- Who are the stakeholders? What is their "stake" or what is "at stake" related to the problem/issue and policy solution you identify?

Section 6: Strengths and Weakness of the System

For each country (i.e., the United States and your comparison country, if desired), provide the following information:
- What are three to five major strengths of the system?
- What are three to five major weaknesses of the system?
- How should the system move forward based on your analysis?

Reference:

World Health Organization. *Everybody's Business: Strengthening Health Systems to Improve Health Outcomes: WHO's Framework for Action*. World Health Organization; 2007. Accessed June 8, 2021. https://www.who.int/healthsystems/strategy/everybodys_business.pdf.

CHAPTER ACRONYMS

ACA Patient Protection and Affordable Care Act of 2010
CAS Complex Adaptive System
CDC Centers for Disease Control and Prevention
CHIP Children's Health Insurance Program

FQHC Federally Qualified Health Center
HiAPs Health in All Policies
IHS Indian Health Service
HMO Health Maintenance Organization
IDS Integrated Delivery System

IHI The Institute for Healthcare Improvement
LTCF Long-term Care Facility
MACRA Medicare Access and CHIP Reauthorization Act of 2015
MCO Managed Care Organization
NCCIH National Center for Complementary and Ingerative Health

OECD Organisation for Economic Co-operation and Development
PPO Preferred provider organization
SAMHSA Substance Abuse and Mental Health Services Administration
SNF Skilled Nursing Facility
WHO World Health Organization

References

1. Johnson JA, Stoskopf C, Shi L. *Comparative Health Systems: A Global Perspective*. 2nd ed. Jones & Barlett Learning; 2018.

2. von Bertalanffy L. *General System Theory: Foundations, Development, Applications*. George Braziller; 1968.

3. Johnson JA, Anderson DE, Rossow CC. *Health Systems Thinking: A Primer*. Jones & Barlett Learning; 2020.

4. Bellinger G. Systems thinking: an operational perspective of the universe. Published 2004. Accessed June 11, 2021. https://www.systems-thinking.org/systhink/systhink.htm

5. Anderson V, Johnson L. *Systems Thinking Basics: From Concepts to Causal Loops*. Pegasus Communications, Inc.; 1997.

6. World Health Organization. Q&As: health systems. Accessed June 11, 2021. https://www.who.int/topics/health_systems/qa/en/

7. World Health Organization. What is the WHO definition of health? Accessed February 24, 2021. https://www.who.int/about/frequently-asked-questions

8. World Health Organization. Determinants of health. Published February 3, 2017. Accessed February 18, 2021. https://www.who.int/news-room/q-a-detail/determinants-of-health

9. Nash DB, Skoufalos A, Fabius RJ, Oglesby WH. *Population Health: Creating a Culture of Wellness*. 3rd ed. Jones & Barlett Learning; 2021.

10. Kindig D, Stoddart G. What is population health? *Am J Public Health*. 2003;93(3):380-383. doi: 10.2105/AJPH.93.3.380

11. Kindig DA. Understanding population health terminology. *Milbank Q*. 2007;85(1):139-161. doi: 10.1111/j.1468-0009.2007.00479.x

12. U.S. Department of Veterans Affairs. About VHA. Updated July 21, 2021. Accessed June 11, 2021. https://www.va.gov/health/aboutVHA.asp

13. U.S. Department of Veterans Affairs. Veterans Health Administration. Updated July 21, 2021. Accessed July 26, 2021. https://www.va.gov/health/

14. Potter MA, Longest BB Jr. The divergence of federal and state policies on the charitable tax exemption of nonprofit hospitals. *J Health Polit Policy Law*. 1994;19(2):393-419. doi: 10.1215/03616878-19-2-393

15. Centers for Medicare & Medicaid Services. National health expenditure data: historical. Updated December 16, 2020. Accessed June 11, 2021. https://www.cms.gov/Research-Statistics-Data-and-Systems/Statistics-Trends-and-Reports/NationalHealthExpendData/NationalHealthAccountsHistorical

16. Centers for Medicare & Medicaid Services. NHE fact sheet. Updated December 16, 2020. Accessed June 11, 2021. https://www.cms.gov/Research-Statistics-Data-and-Systems/Statistics-Trends-and-Reports/NationalHealthExpendData/NHE-Fact-Sheet

17. Medicaid.gov. September 2020 Medicaid & CHIP enrollment data highlights. Accessed June 11, 2021. https://www.medicaid.gov/medicaid/program-information/medicaid-and-chip-enrollment-data/report-highlights/index.html

18. Centers for Medicare & Medicaid Services. People dually eligible for Medicare and Medicaid. Fact sheet. Accessed June 11, 2021. https://www.cms.gov/Medicare-Medicaid-Coordination/Medicare-and-Medicaid-Coordination/Medicare-Medicaid-Coordination-Office/Downloads/MMCO_Factsheet.pdf

19. Health Resources and Services Administration Bureau of Primary Health Care Health Center Program. Health Center Program: impact and growth. Updated December 2020. Accessed June 11, 2021. https://bphc.hrsa.gov/about/healthcenterprogram/index.html

20. Politzer RM, Schempf AH, Starfield B, Shi L. The future role of health centers in improving national health. *J Public Health Policy*. 2003;24(3):296-306. doi: 10.2307/3343376

21. Shi L, Politzer RM, Regan J, Lewis-Idema D, Falik M. The impact of managed care on vulnerable populations served by community health centers. *J Ambul Care Manage*. 2001;24(1):51-66. doi: 10.1097/00004479-200101000-00007

22. Indian Health Service. About IHS. Accessed June 11, 2021. https://www.ihs.gov/aboutihs/

23. Indian Health Service. IHS profile. Published August 2020. Accessed June 11, 2021. https://www.ihs.gov /newsroom/factsheets/ihsprofile/

24. Centers for Disease Control and Prevention. Nursing homes and assisted living (long-term care facilities [LTCFs]). Updated June 22, 2020. Accessed June 11, 2021. https://www.cdc.gov/longtermcare/

25. Substance Abuse and Mental Health Services Administration. SAMHSA – behavioral health integration. Accessed June 11, 2021. https://www .samhsa.gov/sites/default/files/samhsa-behavioral -health-integration.pdf

26. Substance Abuse and Mental Health Services Administration. About us. Updated June 14, 2021. Accessed July 26, 2021. https://www.samhsa.gov /about-us

27. Centers for Disease Control and Prevention Foundation. What is public health? Accessed June 11, 2021. https://www.cdcfoundation.org/what-public -health

28. Centers for Disease Control and Prevention. The public health system. Updated September 8, 2020. Accessed June 11, 2021. https://www.cdc .gov/publichealthgateway/publichealthservices /originalessentialhealthservices.html#:~:text=Public

29. Turnock BJ. *Public Health: What It Is and How It Works*. 5th ed. Jones & Bartlett Learning; 2012.

30. Squires DAC. U.S. health care from a global perspective: spending, use of services, prices, and health in 13 countries. The Commonwealth Fund. Published October 8, 2015. Accessed June 11, 2016. http://www.commonwealthfund.org/publications /issue-briefs/2015/oct/us-health-care-from-a-global -perspective

31. Organisation for Economic Co-operation and Development. Health expenditure and financing. Accessed June 11, 2021. https://stats.oecd.org/Index .aspx?DataSetCode=SHA

32. Tolbert J, Orgera K, Damico A. Key facts about the uninsured population. Kaiser Family Foundation. Published November 6, 2020. Accessed June 11, 2021. https://www.kff.org/uninsured/issue-brief/key-facts -about-the-uninsured-population/

33. Centers for Medicare & Medicaid Services. Accountable Care Organizations. Updated March 3, 2021. Accessed June 11, 2021. https://www.cms.gov /Medicare/Medicare-Fee-for-Service-Payment/ACO /index.html?redirect=/ACO

34. Centers for Medicare & Medicaid Services. MACRA. Updated November 18, 2019. Accessed June 11, 2021. https://www.cms.gov/Medicare/Quality-Initiatives -Patient-Assessment-Instruments/Value-Based -Programs/MACRA-MIPS-and-APMs/MACRA -MIPS-and-APMs.html

35. National Center for Complementary and Integrative Health. Statistics from the National Health Interview Survey. Accessed June 11, 2021. https://www.nccih .nih.gov/health/statistics-from-the-national-health -interview-survey#2012-nhis

36. National Center for Complementary and Integrative Health. Complementary, alternative, or integrative health: what's in a name? Updated April 2021. Accessed June 11, 2021. https://nccih.nih.gov/health /integrative-health

37. Davis MA, Martin BI, Coulter ID, Weeks WB. US spending on complementary and alternative medicine during 2002–08 plateaued, suggesting role in reformed health care system. *Health Aff*. 2013;32(1):45-52. doi: 10.1377/hlthaff.2011.0321

38. Abelson R, Brown PL. Alternative medicine is finding its niche in nation's hospitals. *New York Times*. Published April 13, 2002. Accessed June 11, 2016. https://www.nytimes.com/2002/04/13/business /alternative-medicine-is-finding-its-niche-in-nation -s-hospitals.html

39. Andrews M. Hospitals are making room for alternative therapies. *Los Angeles Times*. Published January 2, 2012. Accessed June 11, 2016. https://www.latimes .com/health/la-xpm-2012-jan-02-la-he-hospitals -alternative-medicine-20120102-story.html

40. Kaiser Family Foundation. Fact sheet: summary of the Affordable Care Act. Published April 25, 2013. Accessed June 11, 2021. https://files.kff.org /attachment/fact-sheet-summary-of-the-affordable -care-act

41. Kaiser Family Foundation. Summary of the Affordable Care Act. Published April 25, 2013. Accessed June 11, 2016. http://kff.org/health-reform/fact-sheet/summary -of-the-affordable-care-act/

CHAPTER 2

Historical and Benchmark Developments in American Health Care

CHAPTER OVERVIEW

This chapter describes important scientific, political, economic, organizational, and professional influences that transformed health care in the United States from a relatively simple professional service to a huge, complex system. Social scientist James Johnson refers to it as a "complex adaptive system," a term that will be discussed throughout this book.[1] However, as a foundation to the subject matter of this book, a chronological history is presented and benchmark developments are discussed in this chapter. The effects of organized medicine, scientific advances, rising costs, and American values along with assumptions regarding health care are also discussed. The chapter concludes with a brief discussion of the enactment of the Affordable Care Act and its major provisions, as well as an overview of the American Rescue Plan Act of 2021 that was developed in response to the COVID-19 pandemic.

During the colonial period of America's development, health policy was primarily a local activity focused on preventing the spread of epidemic diseases and the enactment of sanitary laws and regulations. Towns and cities appointed inspectors and had the authority to levy fines against property owners who did not follow these rules. In the early 1600s, colonists in Virginia required by law the recording of vital statistics (births, deaths, illnesses, marriages) in log books. When the bubonic plague arrived London in 1665, port cities in the American colonies held British ships offshore in quarantine. Unfortunately, newcomers still brought many infectious diseases, the deadliest being smallpox, which was devastating to the Native American population. During this era, all the major towns along the eastern seaboard, including Boston, Philadelphia, Baltimore, and Charleston, passed quarantine laws. In 1743 a yellow fever epidemic spread in the colonial cities, claiming an estimated 5% of New York City's population. An immigrant physician from Scotland, Cadwallader Colden, recognized a connection between the location of certain homes in the poorest areas with lots of dirty standing water and a higher incidence of disease. He surmised that the cause of yellow fever was poor water supplies, poor diets, and a general condition of filth. His theory translated into a call for clean water and improved sanitation in New York City.

In another port city, Philadelphia, in 1751, under the leadership of Benjamin Franklin, a scientist and politician, and Thomas Bond, a physician, the first hospital in the colony, Pennsylvania Hospital, was built to care for the poor. The founding principles Franklin used in fundraising are still informative today (see **EXHIBIT 2-1**) and guided the hospital through many challenging times,

EXHIBIT 2-1 Five Principles for the Pennsylvania Hospital, 1760

1. Samaritanism: A desire to aid the sick and needy for its own intrinsic value; also called charity.
2. Personal health: A desire to improve the health of oneself and one's family to deal more effectively with disease, disability, and death.
3. Public health: A desire for health as a collective or social responsibility to prevent illness and ensure a healthy populace while reducing the social burden of disease, disability, and death.
4. Economic value: A desire for the hospital to be a source of income and employment and a desire to benefit the community as a whole.
5. Quality of care: A desire to ensure certain levels of quality and recognizing that poor quality and inefficiency impair the other four principles.

Johnson JA, Rossow CC. *Health Organizations: Theory, Behavior, and Development*. 2nd ed. Jones & Bartlett Learning; 2019.

EXERCISE 2-1 Thought Experiment

Mentally transport yourself back to Philadelphia at the time of the founding of the first hospital in the United States. In doing so, describe the environment, social conditions, and population characteristics (you will need to do some internet research to gain the knowledge and understanding you need). Write a three-page description to share with the class. Explain why the founding principles listed in the chapter would have been so important to the success of that hospital and to the city it served.

including the American Revolution, during which the hospital cared for both Continental and British soldiers. One of the signers of the Declaration of Independence, Benjamin Rush, a physician, educator, and social reformer, joined the staff. Use the Thought Experiment in **EXERCISE 2-1** to better process these founding principles.

The Enlightenment philosophy of revolutionary democracy, promulgated in Europe by the ideas of the Genevan philosopher Jean-Jacques Rousseau and the English philosopher and physician John Locke, was an important ideological influence on 18th-century thought about health and the political state. The influence of these philosophers and scientists is especially evident in Thomas Jefferson's declaration that sick populations were the product of sick political systems. He believed despotism produced disease, while democracy liberated health. The American Revolution, also known as the Revolutionary War, led to the formation of a new government, independent from England, based on concepts of liberalism as expressed by Jefferson in the Declaration of Independence in 1776 and democracy as written into the Constitution of 1787 by James Madison. This new democratic republic began a decades-long process of addressing the health needs of its populace that continues today.

▶ Chronology of Health Care

The next section of this chapter offers a chronology of important health care-related events interwoven with developments in public health and medical science since the Revolutionary War period to 2021. This is intended to only be an overview as there are many events, policies, technologies, scientific breakthroughs, and developments at every level of society that are not identified here. The primary resources for this compilation are Johnson and Jones's *The American Medical Association and Organized Medicine*[2]; Johnson's *Introduction to Public Health Management, Organizations, and Policy*[3]; Shi and Johnson's *Public Health Administration: Principles for Population-Based Management*[4]; and the previous edition of *Health Care USA: Understanding its Organization and Delivery* by Young and Kroth.[5] Additional information is sourced from the U.S. Department of Health and Human Services (HHS) website (HHS Historical Highlights | HHS.gov).

1790: The first U.S. census was ordered by George Washington. Taken every 10 years thereafter, this would become a cornerstone for population health and community planning.

1793: The yellow fever epidemic spread in Philadelphia and other major port cities such as Charleston, Baltimore, New York, and New Orleans, where ships arrived from Central and South America.

1796: Edward Jenner, a general practitioner in England, successfully demonstrated smallpox vaccination. While rudimentary inoculations were being done in the port city of Istanbul in the early 1700s, it was not until Jenner's conclusive research that a vaccine proved to be successful. The first smallpox vaccinations in the United States began in Boston in 1800.

1796: The New York State Legislature passed the nation's first comprehensive health law (this was in part a response to the economic impact of the smallpox and yellow fever epidemics). The position of State Commissioner of Health and a New York City Health Office were established.

1798: Congress ordered the creation of the Marine Hospital Service to monitor sailors and protect American ports from incoming diseases. This was the forerunner of the U.S. Public Health Service.

1805: New York City created the nation's first municipal board of health. Propelled by the fear of yellow fever and cholera, Boston, Chicago, New Orleans and many other cities followed in creating boards of health.

1847: The American Medical Association (AMA) was founded. Its stated purpose was and remains "to promote the art and science of medicine and the betterment of public health."[6,7]

1855: Louisiana established the first state board of health, primarily focused on the port city of New Orleans.

1861: The American Civil War began and lasted for 4 years, resulting in approximately 620,000 deaths, mostly due to disease, malnutrition, and dehydration. Public health measures were limited, but some sanitation and quarantine measures were used.

1862: President Lincoln appointed a chemist, Charles M. Wetherill, to serve in the new Department of Agriculture. This was the beginning of the Bureau of Chemistry, forerunner to the U.S. Food and Drug Administration.

1866: New York City passed the Metropolitan Health Bill, the most comprehensive health legislation in the United States at the time.

1869: Massachusetts formed a state board of health, followed by California (1870), Virginia and Minnesota (1872), Maryland (1874), and Alabama (1875).

1871: The first Supervising Surgeon (later called the Surgeon General) was appointed for the Marine Hospital Service, which had been reorganized the prior year.

1872: The American Public Health Association (APHA) was founded.

1879: Congress created a National Board of Health responsible for formulating quarantine regulations between the states.

1880s: State public health laboratories were established in Rhode Island, Michigan, and Massachusetts.

1896: The first national nursing association was founded and in 1911 became the American Nurses Association (ANA).

1898: The American Hospital Association (AHA) was established.

1904: The National Association for the Study and Prevention of Tuberculosis was formed, becoming the first national-level volunteer health organization in the United States.

1904: William Gorgas led a successful campaign of malaria and yellow fever control in the U.S. territory of the Panama Canal.

1906: Upton Sinclair's book *The Jungle* was published to draw attention to unsafe working conditions in Chicago meat packing plants. That same year, Congress passed the Pure Food and Drugs Act.

1906: John D. Rockefeller created a scientific foundation to eradicate hookworm in the American South and later throughout the world. This became one of the many public health accomplishments of what became the Rockefeller Foundation.

1910: The first International Congress on Occupational Diseases was held in Chicago. That same year, New York passed a Workmen's Compensation Act, and most states did the same over the next 10 years. The Carnegie Foundation commissioned an investigation of medical schools, led by Abraham Flexner, that found severely inadequate training and the lack of a science-based approach to medicine. In public health, the first degree specific to the field was awarded at the University of Michigan in 1910.

1912: The Marine Hospital Service became the U.S. Public Health Service, which was authorized to investigate the causes and spread of diseases; study the problems of sewage, sanitation, and water pollution; and publish health information for the general public.

1913: The American Cancer Society was founded.

1916: The polio outbreak in New York spread to cities throughout the United States. The U.S. Surgeon General used what was then a novel approach—warning the public through means such as newspapers, civic organizations, and schools to teach hygiene as a means of prevention.

1918: The H1N1 influenza pandemic began in Kansas and circled the globe, killing at least 30 million people.

1929: Blue Cross was founded based on an insurance plan prototype developed at Baylor University.

1934: The American College of Healthcare Executives (ACHE) was founded.

1935: The Social Security Act was passed to provide a safety net for citizens. This was a central piece of legislation under the leadership of President Franklin D. Roosevelt to address many of the problems caused by the Great Depression. Furthermore, financing was enhanced to allow grants to states for public health education and services. At least a dozen new federal agencies were created between 1933 and 1938 to focus on the nation's health.

1937: The National Cancer Institute (NCI) was established. This was the beginning of what would become a large array of national institutes developed to address specific illnesses through research.

1939: World War II began in Europe, and the United States entered the war in 1941. Health was declared a national priority for the armed forces and the civilian population working for the war effort. General James Stevens Simmons, Director of Preventive Medicine for the U.S. Army, announced: "A civil population that is not healthy cannot be prosperous and will lag behind in the economic competition between nations."[8] Congress began to see health as a national security issue and allocated considerably more resources to communities through the Community Facilities Act.

1946: Due to a major problem with malaria in the southern states, the Center for Controlling Malaria was established in Atlanta, Georgia. After the war, this organization was transformed into the Communicable Disease Center. Now called the Centers for Disease Control and Prevention (CDC), it is the premier epidemiological center for the United States and the world.

1946: Congress passed the Hospital Survey and Construction Act. The legislation sponsored by Senator Lister Hill of Alabama and Senator Harold Burton of Ohio is commonly known as the Hill–Burton Act and sought to answer the national demand for access to medical services by funding construction of hospitals in primarily rural areas.

1952: The polio vaccine was discovered by Jonas Salk at the University of Pittsburgh. This began a nationwide vaccination program and effort to eradicate polio from the United States. Albert Sabin, a researcher at the Medical University of South Carolina in Charleston, developed an oral version of the vaccine that was both safer and easier to administer.

1955: The Indian Health Service (IHS) was established to provide care for American Indians and Alaska Natives.

1956: The Health Amendments Act was authorized to provide funding for traineeships for health professionals from many fields.

1964: The Civil Rights Act was passed, eliminating most legal forms of racial discrimination, including discrimination in the practice of medicine and public health. President Lyndon B. Johnson also pushed for other major social reforms, including a War on Poverty, aid to families and children, and health services for more Americans. Martin Luther King, Jr. famously declared, "Of all forms of inequality, injustice in health care is the most shocking and inhumane."[9]

1965: Medicare and Medicaid legislation was passed to provide health services to the elderly and the poor, along with Aid to Families with Dependent Children (AFDC). The Centers for Medicare and Medicaid Services (CMS) was established.

1970: The Clean Air Act was passed, and a range of federal agencies were created in previous decade to address growing concerns about environmental hazards. These included the Environmental Protection Agency (EPA), the Occupational Safety and Health Administration (OSHA), and the National Institute of Occupational Safety and Health (NIOSH).

1976: The National Consumer Health Information and Health Promotion Act was passed and the Office of Disease Prevention and Health Promotion was created.

1977: The Health Care Financing Administration was created to manage Medicare and Medicaid separately from the Social Security Administration. The United States led the effort for the global eradication of smallpox.

1980: The World Health Assembly declared the eradication of smallpox worldwide.

1980: National health goals were published by the Department of Health, Education, and Welfare (HEW). Goals and objectives have been established under the direction of the Department of Health and Human Services (HHS) in every subsequent decade with the Healthy People 2000, Healthy People 2010, Healthy People 2020, and now Healthy People 2030 initiatives.

1981: Acquired immunodeficiency syndrome (AIDS) was reported in California and New York. An epidemic had begun and would become a global pandemic that changed public health and health care in profound ways. Unfortunately, as so often in the history of disease, many policy decisions were based more on politics and emotional issues than on science. Nevertheless, a concerted effort to fight the epidemic emerged over the coming decades, bringing together public health professionals from federal agencies such as the CDC, FDA, and National Institutes of Health (NIH); state health departments; municipal health agencies; community groups and national associations; universities and private research centers; global organizations like WHO and the United Nations; and foundations both large and small.

1988: The Institute of Medicine (IOM) released a report titled *The Future of Public Health* based on extensive interviews of public health experts and surveys of the health status of every state. It discovered the absence of a shared mission among public health agencies and no commonly accepted definition of their duties. The report called for a plan of action for much needed improvements.[5] A summary statement read:

> An impossible responsibility has been placed on America's public health agencies: to serve as stewards of the basic health needs of entire populations, but at the same time avert impending disasters and provide personal health care to those rejected by the rest of the health system. The wonder is not that American public health has problems, but that so much has been done so well, and with so little.[5]

1996: The Health Insurance Portability and Accountability Act (HIPAA) was enacted. Its purpose is to protect health insurance coverage for workers and their families when they change or lose their jobs. It also established national standards for electronic health care transactions and guidelines for health information privacy and security.

1997: The State Children's Health Insurance Program (SCHIP) was created as the largest expansion of taxpayer-funded health insurance coverage for children in the United States since Medicaid. Like Medicaid, it was designed as a partnership between the federal and state governments.

2001: The 9/11 attacks on the World Trade Center in New York City and the Pentagon prompted investment in disaster preparedness and bioterrorism research.

2003: The President's Emergency Plan for AIDS Relief (PEPFAR) provided funding for HIV/AIDS treatment, prevention, and research, making it the largest global health program focused on a single disease in history.

2006: Massachusetts became the first U.S. state to establish universal health care with enactment of An Act Providing Access to Affordable, Quality, Accountable Health Care. That same year, San Francisco's Board of Supervisors adopted the Health Care Security Ordinance, the first of its kind in the country, in an attempt to provide universal care for all of its residents.

2010: The Patient Protection and Affordable Care Act (hereafter referred to as the Affordable Care Act, or simply the ACA) was enacted in an effort to reform the private health insurance market and to provide better coverage for those with preexisting conditions, college-age citizens, and seniors on Medicare. It included provisions for the establishment of a Center for Medicare and Medicaid Innovation and promoted the use of comparative effectiveness research to inform policy and the management of health systems.

2011: The Department of Health and Human Services released the Healthy People 2020 initiative to establish health goals and objectives for the decade. This is discussed in Chapter 11.

2020: COVID-19 emerged in the United States, spreading rapidly to result in 500,000 American deaths within 1 year. Worldwide, the novel coronavirus became a pandemic affecting every country on Earth. Vaccines were developed in late 2020 and early 2021 to help mitigate morbidity and mortality.

2021: The American Rescue Plan Act was approved to address some of the harsh impact of the COVID-19 pandemic, and President Biden promoted the American Families Plan to further efforts in this regard.

A snapshot of the evolution of the U.S. healthcare system is provided by Shi and Singh in **EXHIBIT 2-2**.

Health care in the 21st century is still emerging, but many of the older themes of American society, such as democracy, federalism, social justice, human rights, and dignity, continue to

EXHIBIT 2-2 Evolution of the U.S. Health Care Delivery System

Development of Science and Technology		
Mid-18th to Late 19th Century	**Late 19th to Late 20th Century**	**Late 20th to 21st Century**

■ Open entry into medical practice
■ Intense competition
■ Weak and unorganized profession
■ Apprenticeship training
■ Undeveloped hospitals
■ Almshouses and pesthouses
■ Dispensaries
■ Mental asylums
■ Private payment for services
■ Low demand for services
■ Private medical schools providing only general education
	■ Scientific basis of medicine
	■ Urbanization
	■ Emergence of the modern hospital
	■ Emergence of organized medicine
	■ Reform of medical training
	■ Licensing
	■ Specialization in medicine
	■ Development of public health
	■ Community mental health
	■ Birth of workers' compensation
	■ Emergence of private insurance
	■ Failure of national health insurance
	■ Medicaid and Medicare
		■ Corporatization
		  • Managed care
		  • Organizational integration
		  • Diluted physician autonomy
		■ Globalization
		  • Global telemedicine
		  • Medical tourism
		  • U.S. health care investment abroad
		  • Migration of professionals
		  • Global health
		■ Era of health care reform
		  • The Affordable Care Act
		  • Prospects for new reforms

Consumer Sovereignty	**Professional Dominance**	**Government and Corporate Dominance**

Beliefs and values/Social, economic, and political constraints provide a link to the nation's founding principles. The impressive advances in science during the past 200 years hold even more promise in the years ahead. The Human Genome Project has been completed at the National Institutes of Health, moving biomedical science from the "germ theory era" to the "genome era." Natural and manmade disasters such as the 9/11 attacks on the World Trade Center in New York City and the Pentagon; mass shootings in schools, churches, and entertainment venues; the devastation of New Orleans by Hurricane Katrina and other climate-related events; the BP oil spill in the Gulf of Mexico; and the COVID-19 pandemic all have resulted in modifications in public policy and health care. Concerns about the delivery of health care, economics, and changing health demographics will continue and modifications in public policy and health care will be needed on an ongoing basis.

▶ Benchmark Developments in U.S. Health Care

In the previous edition of this book, the authors Young and Kroth described several important developments in the history of health care in America. They referred to these as "benchmark" developments to stress their significance.[5] These align historically with various items mentioned in the chronology already provided in this chapter and are worth further elaboration. As described by Young and Kroth, in its earliest history, medical care was dominated by physicians and the hospitals they operated. In the 1800s and early 1900s, participation in U.S. medicine was generally limited to two parties—patients and physicians. Diagnosis, treatment, and fees for services were considered confidential between patients and physicians. Medical practice was relatively simple and usually involved longstanding relationships among physicians, patients, and their families. Physicians set and often adjusted their charges to estimates of patients' ability to pay and collect their own bills. This was an intimate physician–patient relationship that the profession held sacred.

Free from outside scrutiny or interference, individual physicians had complete control over where, when, what, and how they practiced. In 1934, the AMA published this statement: "No third party must be permitted to come between the patient and his physician in any medical matter."[2] The AMA was concerned about such issues as non-physician-controlled voluntary health insurance, compulsory health insurance, and the few prepaid contracts for medical services negotiated by remote lumber or mining companies and a few workers' guilds. For decades, organized medicine repeatedly battled against these and other outside influences that altered "the old relations of perfect freedom between physicians and patients, with separate compensation for each separate service."[2]

As early as the 1800s, some Americans carried insurance against sickness through an employer, fraternal order, guild, trade union, or commercial insurance company. Most of the plans were simply designed to compensate for lost income during sickness or injury by providing a fixed cash payment.[5] Sickness insurance, as it was originally called, was the beginning of social insurance programs that mitigated the risks of income interruption by accident, sickness, or disability. Initially such insurance was provided only to wage earners. Later, it was extended to workers' dependents.

Around 1915, the drive for compulsory health insurance began to build in the United States after most European countries had initiated either compulsory programs or subsidies for voluntary programs. The underlying concern was to protect workers against a loss of income resulting from industrial accidents, which were common at the time. Families with only one wage earner, often already at the edge of poverty, could be devastated by the loss of income caused by sickness or injury, even without the additional costs of medical care.

At the time, life insurance companies sold "industrial" policies that provided lump-sum payments at death, which amounted to $50 or $100 to pay for final medical expenses and funerals. Both Metropolitan Life and the Prudential Insurance Company rose to the top of the insurance industry by successfully marketing industrial policies that required premium payments of 10–25 cents per week.[5]

In 1917, World War I interrupted the campaign for compulsory health insurance in the United States. In 1919, the AMA House of Delegates officially condemned compulsory health insurance with the following resolution:

> The American Medical Association declares its opposition to the institution of any plan embodying the system of compulsory contributory insurance against illness or any other plan of compulsory insurance which provides for medical service to be rendered to contributors or their dependents, provided, controlled, or regulated by any state or the federal government.[2]

Most physician opposition to compulsory health insurance was attributed to an unfounded concern that insurance would decrease, rather than increase, physician incomes and add to their negative experience with accident insurance that paid physicians according to arbitrary fee schedules.[5]

▶ The Great Depression and the Birth of Blue Cross

As the Great Depression shook the nation in 1929, it also threatened the financial security of both physicians and hospitals. Physician incomes and hospital admission rates dropped precipitously as individuals were unable to pay out of pocket for medical care, and hospitals began experimenting with insurance plans. The Baylor University Hospital plan was not the first, but it became the most influential of those insurance experiments. By enrolling 1,250 public school teachers at 50 cents a month for a guaranteed 21 days of hospital care, Baylor created the model for, and is credited with the genesis of, Blue Cross hospital insurance. Baylor started a trend that developed into multihospital plans that included all hospitals in a given area. By 1937, there were 26 plans with more than 600,000 members, and the AHA began approving the plans.[5] Physicians were pleased with the increased availability of hospital care and the cooperative manner in which their bills were paid. The AMA, however, was hostile and called the plans "economically unsound, unethical, and inimical to the public interest."[2]

The AMA contended that urging people "to save for sickness" could solve the problem of financing health care.[2] Organized medicine's consistently antagonistic reaction to the concept of health insurance, whether compulsory or voluntary, is well illustrated by medicine's response to the 1932 report of the Committee on the Costs of Medical Care. The committee's establishment represented a shift from concern about lost wages to concern about medical expenses. Chaired by a former president of the AMA and financed by several philanthropic organizations, a group of prominent Americans from the medical, public health, and social science fields worked for 5 years to address the problem of financing medical care. After an exhaustive study, a moderate majority recommended adoption of group practice and voluntary health insurance as the best way to solve the nation's health care problems. However, even this relatively modest recommendation was rejected by some commission members who in a minority report denounced voluntary health insurance as more objectionable than compulsory insurance. Health insurance, predicted the minority, would lead to "destructive competition among professional groups, inferior medical service, loss of personal relationship of patient and physician, and demoralization of the profession."[5] In 1933, the AMA's House of Delegates again reiterated its longstanding opposition to health insurance of any kind by declaring that the minority report represented "the collective opinion of the medical profession."[2] The dissenting physicians did, however, favor government intervention to alleviate physicians' financial burden, resulting from their obligation to provide free care to low-income populations.

From the early 1900s to the present, there have been many efforts to enact various forms of compulsory health insurance. When the proponents of government-sponsored insurance limited their efforts to older adults and low-income populations, they were finally able to succeed in passing Medicaid and Medicare legislation in 1965. Voluntary insurance against hospital care costs became the predominant health insurance in the United States during those decades. The advocates of government-sponsored health insurance had little success in improving patient access to medical care, but the Blue Cross plans effectively improved hospitals' access to patients.

Following World War II, the federal government boosted the private health insurance industry by excluding health insurance benefits from wage and price controls and by excluding workers' contributions to health insurance from taxable income. The effect was to enable employees to take wage increases in the form of health insurance fringe benefits rather than cash. Also following World War II, the federal government began heavily subsidizing the healthcare industry's expansion through hospital construction and medical research, with physician compensation as an overriding policy objective.

Because insurance companies simply raised their premiums rather than exerting pressure on physicians and hospitals to contain costs, the post-World War II private health insurance system pumped an ever-increasing proportion of the national income into health care. There was little regard for cost growth, with attention focused on avoiding any infringement on physicians' or hospitals' prerogatives to set prices and costs. Medicare and Medicaid followed the same pattern.[5]

▶ Dominant Influence of Government

Although the health insurance industry contributed significantly to the spiraling costs of health care in the decades after World War II, it was only one of several influences. The federal government's coverage of health care for special populations also played a prominent role. Over the years, the U.S. government developed, revised, and otherwise adjusted a host of categorical or disease-specific programs designed to address needs not otherwise met by state or local administrations or the private sector.

In the evolution of the U.S. healthcare delivery system, the policy implications of certain federal initiatives are very important. The government increased its support for biomedical research by establishing the National Institutes of Health in 1930 to support categorical programs that addressed heart disease, cancer, stroke, mental illness, mental disability, maternal and infant care, and many other conditions. In 1935, by granting federal aid to the states for public health and welfare assistance, maternal and child health, and children with disabilities services, the Social Security Act became the most significant social policy ever passed by any Congress. The Social Security Act was the legislative foundation for many significant health and welfare programs, including the Medicare and Medicaid programs.

Programs such as direct aid to schools of medicine, dentistry, pharmacy, nursing, and other professions and their students along with support of health planning, healthcare regulation, and consumer protections were all part of the Kennedy–Johnson presidential policy era called "Creative Federalism."[5] The aggregate annual investment in those programs made the U.S. government the major player and payer in the healthcare field. Between 1964 and 1968, total grant awards to states excluding Social Security and Medicare nearly doubled.[5]

Several programs in addition to Medicare and Medicaid began during the Johnson administration to address mental illness and to support the healthcare professionals' role. The Health Professions Educational Assistance Act of 1963 provided direct federal aid to medical, dental, nursing, pharmacy, and other professional schools, as well as to their students. The Nurse Training Act supported special federal efforts for training professional nursing personnel. During the same period, the Maternal and Child Health and Mental Retardation Planning Amendments initiated comprehensive maternal and child health projects and centers to serve people with intellectual disabilities. The Economic Opportunity Act supported the development of neighborhood health centers to serve low-income populations.

In 1970, in a direction labeled "New Federalism," President Nixon expressed his intent to rescind the federal government's direct administration of several healthcare programs and shift revenues to state and local governments through block grants. Block grants are consolidated grants of federal funds, formerly allocated for specific programs, that a state or local government may use at its discretion. In the meantime, with no effective controls over expenditures, federal and state governments underwrote skyrocketing costs of Medicare and Medicaid. The planners of the Medicare legislation had made several misjudgments according to Young and Kroth.[5] They underestimated the growing number of older adults in the United States, the scope and burgeoning costs of new technology, and the public's rising expectations for use of advanced diagnostic and treatment modalities.

The Medicare and Medicaid programs provided access to many desperately needed healthcare services for older Americans, people with disabilities, and low-income populations. Because rising Medicare reimbursement rates set the standards for most insurance companies, their inflationary effect was momentous. In the mid-1960s, when Medicare and Medicaid were passed, the United States was spending about $42 billion on health care annually, or approximately 8.4% of the gross domestic product (GDP). The costs of U.S. health care are now about $4 trillion and consuming 18% of the GDP. This could rise considerably during the course of the COVID-19 pandemic.

▶ Three Major Healthcare Concerns

The three major healthcare concerns of cost, quality, and access have comprised a generations-long conundrum of the U.S. health delivery system. Virtually all attempts to control one or two of these concerns exacerbated the one or two remaining.[5,6,10] The federal government's improvements in access to care by measures such as post-World War II hospital expansions and Medicare and Medicaid legislation were accompanied by skyrocketing expenditures and quality issues.[11] These measures resulted in the healthcare system's expansions beyond actual need and, while virtually unchecked, funding improved access to competent and appropriate medical care for many; they also resulted in untold numbers of clinical interventions of questionable necessity.

Almost all the federal health legislation since the passage of Medicare and Medicaid and the Balanced Budget Act of 1997 was targeted at reducing costs but with little focus on the reciprocal effects of attenuating access and quality. This concern would later be addressed by the Affordable Care Act in 2010 by promoting and requiring value-based, rather than volume-based reimbursement. This will be discussed more in subsequent chapters.

▶ Efforts at Planning and Quality Control

Two initiatives of the 1960s typified circumstances surrounding federal legislative efforts to address cost, quality, and access concerns. In 1965, the Public Health Service Act was amended to establish the Regional Medical Programs initiative, a nationwide network of medical programs in designated geographic areas to address the leading causes of death: heart disease, cancer, and stroke.[12,13] Through regional medical programs, physicians, nurses, and other health professionals deliberated innovative ways to bring the latest in clinical services to patients. However, representatives of each constituency focused on advocating for funding in their respective disciplines. As a consequence, the regional medical programs added educational and clinical resources but did not materially improve prevention or cost reductions in the treatment of the target conditions. A parallel program, the Comprehensive Health Planning Act, was passed in 1966 to promote comprehensive planning for rational systems of healthcare personnel and facilities in designated regions. The legislation required federal, state, and local partnerships and also required a majority of consumers on every decision-making body.[5]

Almost all the Regional Medical Programs and Comprehensive Health Planning Act programs were dominated by medical and hospital leaders in their regions. Many productive outcomes resulted from the two programs, but conflicts of interest regarding the allocation of research and development funds were common. There was general agreement that the programs were ineffective in achieving their goals.

The Johnson-era programs of 1966–1969, especially Medicare and Medicaid, entrenched the federal government in the business of financing health care. President Johnson's ambitious creative federalism enriched the country's healthcare system and improved the access of many citizens, but it also fueled a persistent inflationary spiral of healthcare costs.

▶ Managed Care Organizations

In 1973, the Health Maintenance Organization Act supported the development of health maintenance organizations (HMOs) through grants for federal demonstration projects. An HMO is an organization responsible for the financing and delivery of comprehensive health services to an enrolled population for a prepaid, fixed fee. HMOs were expected to hold down costs by changing the profit incentive from fee-for-service to promoting health and preventing illness.

The concept was widely accepted, and between 1992 and 1999, HMOs and other types of managed care organizations experienced phenomenal growth, accounting for the majority of all privately insured persons. Subsequently, the fortunes of managed care organizations changed as both healthcare costs and consumer complaints increased. By the 1990s, a consumer and provider backlash resulted in all 50 states enacting protections against managed care access and cost restrictions.[5]

Beginning in 2001, a derivative of managed care organizations, preferred provider organizations (PPOs), gained in popularity. Although PPOs encompass important managed care characteristics, they were organized by physicians and hospitals to meet the needs of private, third-party, and self-insured firms. By 2002, PPOs had captured 52% of covered employees. Today, PPOs remain the most popular form of employer-sponsored health insurance.

▶ Cost Containment and Prospective Hospital Reimbursement

The Reagan administration of the 1980s continued efforts to shrink federally supported programs begun in the 1960s and 1970s. One effort was decentralization of program responsibility to the states through block grants. Block grants consolidate grants of federal funds, formerly allocated for specific programs, so that states may use funding at their discretion and presumably more efficiently than the federal government.

One of the most significant health policy changes of the past decades occurred with the Reagan administration's implementation of the Medicare prospective payment system in hospitals. Based on diagnosis-related groups (DRGs), the system shifted hospital reimbursement from a fee-for-service retrospective mode to a prepaid prospective mode based on patient diagnosis. Designed to encourage efficient use of resources, the DRG system put hospitals at financial risk for charges that exceeded per-case DRG limits. This unprecedented effort to contain healthcare costs was widely adopted as a standard by the health insurance industry.[5]

In an effort to reign in spiraling physician Medicare charges, the administration also created a new payment method, the resource-based relative value scale (RBRVS), to make physician payments equitable across various types of services, specialties, and geographic locations.[5]

▶ Biomedical Advances: Evolution of High-Technology Medicine

Health care in the United States dramatically improved during the 1900s. In the first half of the century, the greatest advances led to the prevention or cure of many infectious diseases. The development of vaccines to prevent a wide range of communicable diseases, from yellow fever to measles, and the discovery of antibiotics saved vast numbers of Americans from early death or disability.

In the second half of the century many technologic advances that characterize today's health care were developed, and the pace of technologic development accelerated rapidly. The following are a few of the seminal medical advances that took place during the 1960s:

- The Sabin and Salk vaccines ended annual epidemics of poliomyelitis.
- The tranquilizers Librium and Valium were introduced and widely prescribed, leading Americans to turn to medicine to cure their emotional as well as physical ills.
- The birth control pill was first prescribed and became the most widely used and effective contraceptive method.
- The heart–lung machine and major improvements in the efficacy and safety of general anesthesia techniques made possible the first successful heart bypass operation in 1964.

In addition, in 1972, computed tomography was invented. Computed tomography (CT), which, unlike x-rays, can distinguish one soft tissue from another, is installed widely in U.S. hospitals and ambulatory centers. This valuable and profitable diagnostic imaging device started an extravagant competition among hospitals to develop lucrative patient services through major capital investments in high-technology equipment. Noting the convenience and profit associated with diagnostic devices such as CT, and a few years later, magnetic resonance imaging (MRI), medical groups purchased the devices and placed them in their own facilities. The profit-driven competition and resulting redundant capacity continued to drive up utilization and costs for hospitals, insurers, and the public. Competition continued unabated with the introduction of even more sophisticated and expensive technology over succeeding years.[5]

New technology, new drugs, and new and creative surgical procedures have made possible a wide variety of life-enhancing and life-extending medical accomplishments. Operations that once were complex and hazardous, requiring hospitalization and intense follow-up care, have become common ambulatory surgical procedures. For example, the use of intraocular lens implants after the removal of cataracts has become one of the most popular surgical procedures. Previously requiring hospitalization, these implants are performed in outpatient settings on approximately 4 million Americans annually. The procedure takes less than 1 hour.

▶ Influence of Interest Groups

Many problems associated with U.S. health care result from a system shared among federal and state governments and the private healthcare industry. The development of fully or partially tax-funded health service proposals initiated waves of lobbying efforts by interest groups for or against the initiatives. Federal and state executives and legislators receive intense pressure from supporters and opponents of healthcare system changes. Lobbying efforts from special interest groups have become increasingly sophisticated and well financed. It is common for former congressional staffers to appear on the payrolls of private interest groups and former lobbyists to assume positions on Capitol Hill. This strong connection between politicians and healthcare lobbyists is evidenced by the record number of dollars spent to defeat the Clinton Health Security Act of 1993 and both "for" and "against" President Obama's healthcare reform plans.

Five major groups have played key roles in debates on tax-funded health services: providers, insurers, consumers, business, and labor. Historically, physicians, the group most directly affected by reforms, developed the most powerful lobbies. Although the physician lobby is still among the best financed and most effective, it is recognized as not representing the values of large numbers of physicians detached from the AMA. In fact, several different medical lobbies exist as a result of political differences among physicians.

The American Medical Association

The American Medical Association (AMA), founded in 1847, is the largest medical lobby, with a membership of 224,503 individuals, yet it represents only 25.6% of physicians and medical students.[2] At the height of its power from the 1940s to the 1970s, the AMA opposed government-provided insurance plans proposed by every president from Truman through Carter.[2] Compromises gained in the final Medicare bill still affect today's program.

In 1989, the AMA changed its relationship with Congress. Initially locked out of White House discussions on the Clinton plan, the AMA was later included and supported, at least publicly, by the Obama plan for expanding healthcare access to all Americans.

Insurance Companies

Even more than physicians, nurses, or hospitals, insurers' political efforts have been viewed as self-serving. The efforts of insurance companies to eliminate high-risk consumers from the insurance pools and their frequent premium rate increases contributed significantly to the focus on cost containment and the plight of the uninsured and underinsured in the debate on health-care reform.

Insurance companies played a strong role in the debates about President Obama's health-care reform effort by appearing to support the general idea while vigorously opposing the idea of a public option, which would severely limit their profits. The amount of dollars spent in lobbying efforts by insurers and others with vested interests in the status quo and in misinforming the public to raise unwarranted fears about the proposed healthcare reform legislation hit a new high in deception and a new low in political machinations.[5]

Consumer Groups

Although provider and insurance groups have been most effective in influencing healthcare legislation, the historically weak consumer movement gained strength. Much of the impetus for healthcare reform on the national scene was linked to pressure on politicians from consumers concerned about rising costs and lack of security in healthcare coverage. Despite widespread disagreement among groups about the extent to which government involvement was needed, all were concerned about the questions of cost, quality, and access in the current healthcare system.

Better educated and more assertive citizens have become more cynical about the motives of leaders in both the political and the health arenas and have become more effective in influencing legislative decisions. A prominent example is the American Association of Retired Persons (AARP). Founded in 1958, the AARP is one of the most influential consumer groups in the healthcare reform movement. Because of its size and research capability, it wields considerable clout among legislators who are very aware that the AARP's 38 million older citizens are among the most determined voters.[14]

Business and Labor

Whenever business groups such as the U.S. Chamber of Commerce are involved in an issue, labor unions will have a strong presence to represent their members' interests. For example, the American Federation of Labor and Congress of Industrial Organizations (AFL-CIO), has had a tremendous influence on national health policy. Closely connected with the AFL-CIO is the Service Employees International Union, which is the largest union representing healthcare workers. During the mid-1940s, labor unions demanded and received healthcare benefits as an alternative to wage increases prohibited by postwar wage and price controls. During the late 1960s, they were able to address the issues of occupational safety and health and achieved passage of the Occupational Safety and Health Act of 1970. Today, occupational safety and health hold prominent places on the national agenda. This has become a high-profile challenge during the COVID-19 era as safety issues permeate healthcare facilities, workplaces, and schools.

Pharmaceutical Industry

In recent years, the highly profitable pharmaceutical industry increased its spending on lobbying tactics and campaign contributions to unprecedented levels. With prescription drug prices and pharmaceutical company profits at record highs, the industry correctly anticipated public and congressional pressure to legislate controls on drug prices and drug coverage for older adults on Medicare.

The pharmaceutical industry played a major role in crafting the 2003 Medicare Part D prescription drug benefit plan. As a result, the final plan prohibited Medicare and the federal government from using its enormous purchasing power to negotiate prices with drug companies.[5]

Public Health Focus on Prevention

Although the groups discussed in the previous section are primarily concerned with the diagnostic and treatment services that constitute most of the U.S. healthcare system, there is an important public health lobby that speaks for health promotion and disease prevention. Often overlooked because of this country's historical emphasis on curative medicine, public health organizations have had to overcome several negative perceptions. Many health providers, politicians, and others associate public health with governmental bureaucracy or link the care of low-income populations with socialism. Nevertheless, the American Public Health Association, founded in 1872, has an aggregate membership of approximately 25,000 and substantial influence on the national scene through its organized advocacy and educational efforts at the federal, state, and local levels. The role of public health will be discussed much more in subsequent chapters of this book. Its prominence has certainly risen in the wake of pandemics such as HIV/AIDS, H1N1, and now COVID-19.[4]

▶ Health Insurance Portability and Accountability Act

The Health Insurance Portability and Accountability Act (HIPAA) was enacted under the Clinton administration in 1996.[12] It had two primary purposes. The first was to help ensure that workers could maintain uninterrupted health insurance coverage if they lost or changed jobs by enabling them to continue coverage through their prior employer's group health plan. Employees using this provision reimburse their former employer directly without company subsidy for their premium costs. The law mandated the renewal of insurance coverage except for specific reasons, such as the nonpayment of premiums. The Act also regulated circumstances in which an insurance plan may limit benefits due to preexisting conditions and offered special enrollment periods for individuals who experience certain changes in family composition, such as divorce or the addition of a dependent.[5,15]

HIPAA's second primary purpose concerned the privacy of personal health information. Prior to HIPAA, no generally accepted set of security standards or general requirements for protecting health information existed in the healthcare industry. At the same time, new technologies were evolving, and the healthcare industry began to shift from paper processes to the use of electronic information systems to pay claims, answer eligibility questions, provide health information, and conduct many other administrative and clinically based functions.[5,15]

Known as the "Administrative Simplification" provisions of the law, they mandated the Department of Health and Human Services (HHS) to establish national standards for regulations protecting the privacy and security of certain health information. To fulfill the mandate,

HHS published national standards known as the "Privacy Rule" and "Security Rule" applicable to virtually all organizations and providers with access to individuals' personal health information. The Security Rule particularly applies to certain health information that is held or transferred in electronic form.[5,15] In 2013 HHS issued final rules under a 2009 law that significantly extended HIPAA's Privacy and Security provisions beyond healthcare organizations and providers to their subcontractors and other business entities that handle electronic patient information.[5,15]

▶ The Balanced Budget Act of 1997

The federal budget negotiations for 1997 reflected pressures to produce a balanced budget and to respond meaningfully to national health issues from consumer and cost-containment perspectives. The resulting Balanced Budget Act (BBA) created sweeping new policy directions for Medicare. The act increased cost sharing among Medicare beneficiaries and extended the prospective payment system introduced with DRGs to hospital outpatient services, home health agencies, skilled nursing facilities, and inpatient rehabilitation facilities.[5] The BBA also opened the Medicare program to private insurers through the Medicare + Choice Program (later renamed Medicare Advantage).

Declines in Medicare spending growth demonstrated the immediate impact of the BBA. After growing at an average annual rate of 11.1% for 15 years, the average annual rate of Medicare spending growth dropped to 1.7%. Finally, the BBA included an initiative, the State Children's Health Insurance Program, which complemented the Medicaid program by targeting uninsured children whose family income was too high to qualify for Medicaid and too low to afford private health insurance.[16] Subsequently renamed the Children's Health Insurance Program (CHIP) and with the goal of enrolling 10 million children, it was the largest expansion of health insurance coverage for children in the United States since Medicaid began. CHIP has been continuously funded since its inception and currently serves more than 10 million children.

▶ Death with Dignity Acts and Other End-of-Life Legislation

November 8, 1994, was a pivotal date in U.S. social legislation when Oregon voters approved the Oregon Death with Dignity Act.[17] The Act legalized physician-assisted suicide by allowing "an adult resident of Oregon, who is terminally ill to voluntarily request a prescription for medication to take his or her life."[17] The person must have "an incurable and irreversible disease that will, within reasonable medical judgment, produce death within six months."[5] The Death with Dignity Act was a response to the growing concern among medical professionals and the public about the extended, painful, and demeaning nature of terminal medical care for patients with certain conditions. An additional consideration was the worry that the extraordinary costs associated with lengthy and futile medical care would exhaust their estates and leave their families with substantial debts.

A survey of Oregon physicians showed that two-thirds of those responding believed that physician-assisted suicide is ethical in appropriate cases.

Physicians must meet multiple requirements before they can write a prescription for a lethal combination of medications. The physician must ensure that the patient is fully informed about

---

EXHIBIT 2-3 Death with Dignity Laws

- California (End of Life Option Act; approved in 2015, in effect from 2016)
- Colorado (End of Life Options Act; 2016)
- District of Columbia (D.C. Death with Dignity Act; 2016/2017)
- Hawaii (Our Care, Our Choice Act; 2018/2019)
- Maine (Death with Dignity Act; 2019)
- New Jersey (Aid in Dying for the Terminally Ill Act; 2019)
- Oregon (Death with Dignity Act; 1994/1997)
- Vermont (Patient Choice and Control at the End of Life Act; 2013)
- Washington (Death with Dignity Act; 2008)

Data from Death with Dignity National Center. In your state. Reviewed July 30, 2021. Accessed July 30, 2021. https://deathwithdignity.org/in-your-state/

---

the diagnosis, the prognosis, the risks, and likely result of the medications and alternatives including comfort care, pain control, and hospice care.

With the burgeoning aged U.S. population and this population group's increasing political strength in numbers, consumer pressure for more states to enact "right-to-die" legislation will be a subject of increasing interest. "Right-to-die" legislation does not only concern older Americans, but any adult with a terminal illness.

As of 2020, eight states and the District of Columbia have enacted death with dignity laws, as shown in **EXHIBIT 2-3**.

▶ The Internet and Health Care

Because data collection and information transfer are critical elements of the healthcare system, the internet has become a major influence in U.S. health care. A Pew Foundation survey report notes that one in three U.S. adults has gone online to diagnose a condition and about half consulted a medical professional about what they found.[18] The internet provides consumers with access to vast resources of health and wellness information, the ability to communicate with others sharing similar health problems, and the ability to gain valuable data about medical institutions and providers that permit well-informed choices about services and procedures. Internet users are becoming more educated and participatory in clinical decision making, challenging physicians and other providers to participate with a more knowledgeable and involved patient population.

Physicians and other healthcare providers also are entering the online world of health communication. Provider-sponsored websites are proliferating at a rapid pace. In addition to information for consumers about providers' training, competencies, and experience, many encourage email or text message exchanges and telehealth portals that provide opportunities to respond to consumers' informational needs as well as diagnostic and therapeutic services.

A wide variety of other web-based entrepreneurial ventures have also begun to take advantage of the huge and growing market of smartphone users with apps that "give consumers access to health information wherever and whenever they need it."[18] Both professionally reliable and questionable entrepreneurs offer consumers opportunities to shop online for pharmaceuticals, insurance plans, medical supplies and equipment, physician services, and other health-related commodities.

▶ The Patient Protection and Affordable Care Act

A centerpiece of President Obama's campaign was to expand health care to universal coverage. Some in the new administration opposed advancing the cause of universal coverage at a time when the President also had to advance his pledges for an economic stimulus package, education reform, and bailouts for banks and the auto industry. Nevertheless, it was believed "that rising medical costs were crippling average families, cutting into corporate profits, and consuming more and more of the federal budget."[19] Decades-long analyses and assessments by the most prestigious academic research and industry experts overwhelmingly noted that the U.S. healthcare system focused on providing excellent care for individuals with acute conditions, but virtually ignored the more basic health service needs of larger populations who could benefit from primary preventive care. The system continued to reward providers for the volume of services delivered with piece-meal reimbursement rather than with financial incentives to maintain or improve health status among populations of service recipients.

Given that a succession of federal administrations beginning in 1945 with President Truman had proposed and failed at enacting some form of universal healthcare coverage, the ACA was an achievement of historic proportion. The groundbreaking nature of the ACA resides in its addressing what were historically intractable systemic problems of cost, quality, and access.

The ACA's intent was to reverse incentives that drive up costs; to enact requirements that increase both accountability for, and transparency of, quality; and to increase access by expanding health insurance coverage to several million Americans.[5] The ACA also adds consumer protections and enhances access to needed services for the nation's most vulnerable populations.[19]

The ACA as originally enacted is more than 900 pages long and written under 10 titles. It is organized under four broad goals:

- Providing new consumer protections
- Improving quality and lowering costs
- Increasing access to affordable care
- Holding insurance companies accountable

Following, as presented in **EXHIBIT 2-4** developed by Young and Kroth,[5] is a brief summary of the law's major provisions excerpted and edited from HHS websites and categorized by the ACA's major goals listed above.

Provisions of the ACA became effective by 2019, yet some have undergone change as the implementation process has proceeded. However, centerpieces of the law such as the new availability of affordable insurance plans and the Medicaid expansion are yielding material results. One among many examples is how states with expanded Medicaid are better able to support the provision of much needed medication-assisted treatment (MAT) for opioid use disorder.[20] After 1 decade since its enactment, it remains too early to speculate on the ACA's success in achieving its overall intended changes in the organization, delivery, efficiency, and effectiveness of a very complex industry. Outcomes will continue to unfold over the coming years. Regulatory and legal changes enacted by the ACA are indeed only two components of the equation. A multitude of other factors such as the nation's economy, the political environment, and provider and consumer

EXHIBIT 2-4 The Affordable Care Act Implementation Provisions

New Consumer Protections

- Establishes a website on which consumers can compare health insurance coverage options and choose their preference.
- Prohibits insurance companies from denying coverage of children based on preexisting conditions.
- Prohibits insurance companies from refusing to sell coverage or renew policies for adults because of preexisting conditions and prohibits insurance companies from charging higher rates because of gender or health status.
- Prohibits insurance companies from denying payments for a subscriber's illness because of technical or other errors discovered in a subscriber's original insurance application.
- Prohibits insurance companies from imposing lifetime dollar limits on essential benefits, such as hospital stays.
- Prohibits insurance companies' use of annual dollar limits on the amount of insurance coverage a patient may receive under new health plans in the individual market and all group plans.
- Provides consumers with a way to appeal coverage determinations or claims to their insurance company and establishes an external review process.
- Provides federal grants to states to establish or expand independent offices to help consumers navigate the private health insurance system.
- Prohibits insurers from dropping or limiting coverage because an individual chooses to participate in a clinical trial; applies to all clinical trials that treat cancer or other life-threatening diseases.

Improving Quality and Lowering Costs

- Provides small business health insurance tax credits to offset costs of employers' contribution to employees' health insurance premiums.
- Provides relief for older Americans' prescription drug costs.
- Requires that all new health plans cover certain preventive services, such as mammograms and colonoscopies, without charging a deductible, copay, or coinsurance.
- Establishes a new $15 billion Prevention and Public Health Fund to invest in proven prevention and public health programs.
- Invests new resources and requires new screening procedures for healthcare providers to boost federal antifraud and waste initiatives in Medicare, Medicaid, and the Children's Health Insurance Program.
- Provides certain free preventive services, such as annual wellness visits and personalized prevention plans for Medicare beneficiaries.
- Establishes a Center for Medicare and Medicaid Innovation to test new ways of delivering care to patients to improve the quality of care and reduce the rate of growth in costs for Medicare, Medicaid, and the Children's Health Insurance Program.
- Establishes a Community Care Transitions Program to help high-risk Medicare beneficiaries avoid unnecessary hospital readmissions by coordinating care and connecting patients to services in their communities.
- Establishes a new Independent Payment Advisory Board to develop and submit proposals to Congress and the President focused on ways to target waste in the system, recommend ways to reduce costs, improve health outcomes for patients, and expand access to high-quality care.

(continues)

EXHIBIT 2-4 The Affordable Care Act Implementation Provisions *(continued)*

- Establishes a hospital Value-Based Purchasing program in traditional Medicare, offering financial incentives to hospitals to improve the quality of care; requires hospitals to publicly report performance for certain diagnoses and patients' perceptions of care.
- Provides incentives for physicians and hospitals to join together to form "Accountable Care Organizations" to better coordinate Medicare beneficiary patient care and improve quality, help prevent disease and illness, and reduce unnecessary hospital admissions.
- Institutes a series of changes to standardize billing and requires health plans to begin adopting and implementing rules for the secure, confidential, electronic exchange of health information.
- Requires any ongoing or new federal health program to collect and report racial, ethnic, and language data to help identify and reduce disparities.
- Provides new funding to state Medicaid programs that choose to cover preventive services for patients at little or no cost to expand the number of Americans receiving preventive care.
- Establishes a national pilot program, Bundled Payments for Care Improvement (BPCI), to encourage hospitals, doctors, and other providers to work together to improve the coordination and quality of patient care by paying a flat rate for a total episode of care rather than billing Medicare for individual services.
- Pays physicians based on value, not volume, through a provision tying physician payments to the quality of care provided.
- Imposes an excise tax on high-cost insurance plans to limit the costs of health insurance plans to a tax-free amount with the intent to generate revenue to help pay for covering the uninsured.

Increasing Access to Affordable Care

- Provides a preexisting condition insurance plan with new coverage options for individuals who have been uninsured for at least 6 months because of a preexisting condition.
- Extends coverage for young adults who will be allowed to stay on their parents' plan until they turn 26 years of age.
- Expands coverage for early retirees through a $5 billion program to provide financial help for employment-based plans to continue providing health insurance coverage to people who retire between the ages of 55 and 65, as well as their spouses and dependents.
- Rebuilds the primary care workforce through new incentives to expand the number of primary care doctors, nurses, and physician assistants through scholarships and loan repayments for primary care doctors and nurses working in underserved areas.
- Provides eligibility for $250 million in new grants to states that have or will implement measures requiring insurance companies to justify premium increases; also may bar insurance companies with excessive or unjustified premium levels from participation in the new health insurance exchanges.
- Provides federal matching funds for states covering some additional low-income individuals and families under Medicaid for whom federal funds were not previously available.
- Provides increased payments to rural healthcare providers to help them attract and retain providers.
- Provides new funding to support the construction of and expansion of services at community health centers, allowing these centers to serve some 20 million new patients across the country.
- Allows states to offer home and community-based services to disabled individuals through Medicaid rather than institutional care in nursing homes through the Community First Choice Option.
- Provides states with two additional years of CHIP funding to continue coverage for children not eligible for Medicaid.
- Makes tax credits available for middle-class individuals with incomes between 100–400% of the federal poverty level who are not eligible for other affordable coverage.

- Enables individuals to purchase health insurance directly in the health insurance marketplace if their employers do not offer health insurance.
- Makes Americans who earn less than 133% of the federal poverty level eligible to enroll in Medicaid; provides states with 100% federal funding for the first 3 years to support this expanded coverage, phasing to 90% federal funding in subsequent years.
- Requires most individuals who can afford it to obtain basic health insurance coverage or pay a fee to help offset the costs of caring for uninsured Americans; if affordable coverage is not available to an individual, they will be eligible for an exemption.
- Creates Health Care Choice Compacts that allow selling health insurance across state lines to increase competition among plans and give consumers more choices.

Holding Insurance Companies Accountable
- Ensures that premium dollars are spent primarily on health care by generally requiring that at least 85% of all premium dollars collected by insurance companies for large employer plans are spent on healthcare services and healthcare quality improvement. For plans sold to individuals and small employers, at least 80% of the premium must be spent on benefits and quality improvement; failing to meet these goals, insurance companies must provide rebates to subscribers.
- Eliminates additional Medicare costs from Medicare managed care plans (Medicare Advantage) and provides bonus payments to Medicare Advantage plans that provide high-quality care.

Data from U.S. Department of Health and Human Services. About the Affordable Care Act. Updated March 23, 2021. Accessed August 29, 2021. https://www.hhs.gov/healthcare/about-the-aca/index.html

reactions and behaviors, to name only a few, will continue to shape the outcomes of this landmark legislation. With the election of President Biden in 2020, there is a strong likelihood of the ACA's core values and goals remaining intact. In fact, Biden was the U.S. Vice President when the legislation was enacted, and furthermore President Biden believes that every American has a right to the peace of mind that comes with knowing they have access to affordable, quality health care. Reliable and affordable access to health insurance does not just benefit families' health; it is a critical source of economic security and well-being for all.[21]

▶ COVID-19

Undoubtedly, the most significant current health event is the COVID-19 pandemic that began globally in 2019 and in the United States in 2020. The result so far in terms of U.S. mortality is over 500,000 deaths as of early 2021. When we consider morbidity and comorbidities, the systemic effects touch every part of our society. The American Rescue Plan will change the course of the pandemic and deliver immediate and direct relief to families and workers impacted by the COVID-19 crisis through no fault of their own. This law is one of the most progressive pieces of legislation in history, as it helps build a bridge to an equitable economic recovery, which in turn helps improve the overall health of the United States.[22]

Much more about this national and global health challenge will be discussed in subsequent chapters and especially highlighted in Chapter 10, Public and Population Health. However, every aspect of the healthcare system has been impacted by this pandemic, and the long-term effects will not be fully realized for years.

▶ Discussion Questions

- Discuss the historical backdrop of health care in the United States. What are at least five milestones?
- Identify 10 pieces of legislation from the chapter and discuss their impact on health care.
- What are the key provisions of the Affordable Care Act? Why are they important in the health improvement of the population?
- Review the chronological developments and choose five to discuss. Why these five?
- What are the five principles of America's first hospital? Where was it located and why? Do these principals have value for today?
- What has been the role of the AMA in influencing health care?
- What other groups in addition to the AMA have been involved in shaping health care? Do an internet search to gain information about the status of these groups today.
- Discuss "death with dignity" laws and provide pros and cons.
- What is HIPAA and why is it important in health care?
- What are DRGs? How did they come about?
- If you could change three things that occurred in the development of U.S. health care, what would they be? How might things have been different as a result?

CASE 2-1 Developing an Agency Training Program

Situation

Evan is the Training Coordinator for a large state public health agency in the Midwest. He is in the process of preparing the agency's new employee orientation program. The objectives of the program are to provide a general overview of the department, services offered, and administrative policies and procedures to efficiently prepare the employees for their job duties. Among the standard topics included in the orientation session will be the requirements of confidentiality surrounding health services to ensure full compliance with the law, as well as other functional responsibilities.

One of the goals of the agency's workforce recruiting program has been to focus on hiring qualified workers for the public health system overall and not just for individual programs and agencies. This recruitment strategy has been successful in attracting professionals from the business field and other areas outside of public health. The pipeline of new recruits will help ensure an adequate supply of professionals for the agency to eliminate the critical public health workforce shortage experienced by many employers within the field.

As many of the agency's new employees will come from positions outside of the field, Evan believes that the orientation program should contain a session or workshop on the 10 greatest achievements in U.S. public health over the last century. He hopes that by including this instruction in the program new employees will develop a base public health competence, enabling them to understand the crucial role public health has played in all aspects of society. The workshop will provide an opportunity for new employees to learn the significance and scope of public health initiatives as well as to broaden their awareness of the needs and challenges within the field.

Background

In 1999, the CDC prepared a list of the notable health achievements that occurred during the 20th century (see **TABLE 2-1**). The choices were based on the opportunity for prevention and the impact on death, illness, and disability in the United States. The list was not ranked by order of importance.

TABLE 2-1   10 Great Health Achievements in the United States (1900–1999)

- Vaccination
- Motor-vehicle safety
- Safer workplaces
- Control of infectious diseases
- Decline in deaths from coronary heart disease and stroke
- Safer and healthier foods
- Healthier mothers and babies
- Family planning
- Fluoridation of drinking water
- Recognition of tobacco use as a health hazard

Next Steps

To develop the workshop, Evan has arranged for several health analysts in the agency to prepare background research on each of the topics on the list. Evan wants the session to be highly informative so the new employees will appreciate these contributions to public health and understand their effect on the health of the U.S population.

Discussion Questions

1. If you were the Training Coordinator, how would you design the workshop to meet the goals of the agency?
2. How will understanding this history help new health professionals to develop a base competence and encourage their career development?
3. What other accomplishments could have been selected for the list? What accomplishments have occurred since 2000?
4. If you were asked to develop a similar training program to focus on major health legislation, what would you include?

CHAPTER ACRONYMS

AARP American Association of Retired Persons

ACA Patient Protection and Affordable Care Act of 2010

ACHE American College of Healthcare Executives

AFDC Aid to Families with Dependent Children

AFL-CIO American Federation of Labor and Congress of Industrial Organizations

AHA American Hospital Association

AIDS Acquired immunodeficiency syndrome

AMA American Medical Association

ANA American Nurses Association

APHA American Public Health Association

BBA Balanced Budget Act

BPCI Bundled Payments for Care Improvement

CDC Centers for Disease Control and Prevention

CHIP Children's Health Insurance Program

CMS Centers for Medicare and Medicaid Services

CT Computed tomography

DRG Diagnosis-related group

EPA Environmental Protection Agency

GDP Gross domestic product

HEW Department of Health, Education, and Welfare

(continues)

CHAPTER ACRONYMS   *(continued)*

HHS Department of Health and Human Services
HIPAA Health Insurance Portability and
Accountability Act
HMO Health maintenance organization
IHS Indian Health Service
IOM Institute of Medicine
MAT Medication-assisted treatment
MRI magnetic resonance imaging
NCI National Cancer Institute

NIH National Institutes of Health
NIOSH National Institute of Occupational Safety
and Health
OSHA Occupational Safety and Health
Administration
PEPFAR President's Emergency Plan for AIDS Releif
PPO Preferred provider organization
RBRVS Resource-based relative value scale
SCHIP State Children's Health Insurance Program

References

1. Johnson JA, Rossow CC. *Health Organizations: Theory, Behavior, and Development.* 2nd ed. Jones & Bartlett Learning; 2019.

2. Johnson JA, Jones WJ. *The American Medical Association and Organized Medicine.* Garland Publishing; 1993.

3. Johnson JA. *Introduction to Public Health Management, Organization, and Policy.* Delmar-Cengage; 2013.

4. Shi L, Johnson JA. *Public Health Administration: Principles for Population-Based Management.* 5th ed. Jones & Bartlett Learning; 2021.

5. Young KM, Kroth PJ. *Health Care USA: Understanding its Organization and Delivery.* 9th ed. Jones & Bartlett Learning; 2019.

6. American Medical Association. About. Accessed July 27, 2021. https://www.ama-assn.org/about

7. American Medical Association. AMA history. Accessed August 15, 2021. https://www.ama-assn.org/about/ama-history/ama-history

8. Simmons JS. *Public Health in the World Today.* Harvard University Press; 1949.

9. Galarneau C. Getting Martin Luther King's words right. Physicians for a National Health Program. Published February 2018. Accessed August 29, 2021. https://pnhp.org/news/getting-martin-luther-kings-words-right/

10. Johnson JA, Stoskopf CE, Shi L. *Comparative Health Systems: A Global Perspective.* 2nd ed. Jones & Bartlett Learning; 2019.

11. Numbers RL. The third party: health insurance in America. In: Vogel MJ, Rosenburg CE, eds. *The Therapeutic Revolution: Essays in the Social History of American Medicine.* University of Pennsylvania Press; 1979.

12. Starr P. Transformation in defeat: the changing objectives of national health insurance, 1915–1980. In: Kindig DA, Sullivan RB, eds. *Understanding Universal Health Programs, Issues and Options.* Health Administration Press; 1992.

13. Stevens R. *In Sickness and in Wealth: American Hospitals in the Twentieth Century.* Basic Books, Inc.; 1989.

14. American Association of Retired Persons. Accessed February 1, 2021. https://www.aarp.org/

15. U.S. Department of Health and Human Services. Accessed January 1, 2021. https://www.hhs.gov/hipaa/

16. HealthCare.gov. The Children's Health Insurance Program (CHIP). Accessed February 5, 2021. https://www.healthcare.gov/medicaid-chip/childrens-health-insurance-program/

17. Death with Dignity National Center. Oregon Death with Dignity Act: a history. Accessed July 27, 2021. https://www.deathwithdignity.org/oregon-death-with-dignity-act-history/

18. Auxier B, Anderson M, Kumar M. 10 tech-related trends that shaped the decade. Pew Research Center. Published December 20, 2019. Accessed August 29, 2021. https://www.pewresearch.org/

19. Kaiser Family Foundation. Summary of coverage provisions in the Patient Protection and Affordable Care Act and the Health Care and Education Reconciliation Act of 2010. Published July 17, 2012. Accessed July 27, 2021. http://kff.org/health-costs/issue-brief/summary-of-coverage-provisions-in-the-patient/

20. Haley S, Johnson JA, Frasier L. *Opioids and Population Health: A Primer.* Jones & Bartlett Learning; 2022.

21. Shi L, Singh DA. *Delivering Health Care in America: A Systems Approach.* 7th ed. Jones & Bartlett Learning; 2019.

22. U.S. Department of the Treasury. Fact sheet: the American Rescue Plan will deliver immediate economic relief to families. Published March 18, 2021. Accessed August 15, 2021. https://home.treasury.gov/news/featured-stories/fact-sheet-the-american-rescue-plan-will-deliver-immediate-economic-relief-to-families

CHAPTER 3

Public Policy and the Role of Government

CHAPTER OVERVIEW

This chapter provides a context for better understanding public policy as it pertains to health care. It briefly traces the philosophical foundation of the American government, especially as it relates to health. The levels of government and the relationships that are promulgated through federalism are discussed. More specifically, the roles of the federal, state, and local governments are addressed, as they are interdependent in the overarching goal of achieving health for the American people.

The context of public policy in the United States was shaped by events that transpired prior to and during the American Revolution of 1776, also known as the Revolutionary War. As discussed in the previous chapter, there was a colonial history that preceded the revolution; however, it was upon the formation of a national government independent from England that public policy became central to the health and well-being of the new country. The Enlightenment philosophy of revolutionary democracy that was promulgated in Europe by the ideas of philosopher Jean-Jacques Rousseau and philosopher and physician John Locke was an important ideological influence on 18th-century thought about health and the political state. Rousseau's *Discourse on Inequality* and *The Social Contract* are cornerstones in political and social thought and make a strong case for democratic government and social empowerment. Locke's *An Essay Concerning Human Understanding* marked the beginning of the modern Western conception of the self, and his *Two Treatises of Government* advocated separation of powers in government. He believed in a social contract between governments and citizens, and that everyone had a natural right to defend their "life, health, liberty, or possessions," which is the basis for the phrase in *The Declaration of Independence* written by Thomas Jefferson as "Life, Liberty, and the pursuit of Happiness." The influence of these philosophers and scientists is especially evident in Jefferson's declaration that sick populations were the product of sick political systems. Furthermore, Jefferson believed despotism produced disease and democracy liberated health. The American Revolution led to the formation of a new government, independent of England, based on concepts of liberalism as expressed in the Declaration of Independence and democracy as written into the Constitution of 1787. Prior to ratification of the Constitution by the States, amendments were added to address fundamental principles of human liberty, which are called the Bill of Rights. This founding document also provided the architecture to be used in creating the structure of government. This organization of government involved the *separation of powers* between three branches: the Executive Branch, composed of the President and Cabinet; the Legislative Branch, made up of two bodies of Congress (the Senate and House of Representatives) to represent the interests of the people and the states through the process of legislation and oversight; and the Judicial Branch, made up of judges and courts, including the United States Supreme Court. Furthermore, the Constitution established two levels of government, the federal and the state. This is often called *federalism* and represents a system of government where two or more levels (i.e., national, state, and local) have certain powers and authority (see **EXHIBIT 3-1**). For example, the United States Constitution ensured that there would be shared power between the federal government and the state governments. As this pertains to health care, for example, the federal branch funds medical research through the National Institutes of Health (NIH) and the state governments license physicians and other health professionals. Typically, each of these levels of government also has a separation of powers between the executive, judicial, and legislative bodies. In a state, the elected executive is the governor, and in a

EXHIBIT 3-1 Overview of the U.S. Political System

As described in Johnson, Stoskopf, and Shi's book *Comparative Health Systems*, the federal government has three branches: **legislative** (the Senate and the House of Representatives), **executive** (the President and the cabinet departments), and **judicial** (federal courts and the U.S. Supreme Court). Each of the states also has its own constitution and its own legislative, executive (Governor and cabinet), and judicial branches.

In general, the states can do anything that is not prohibited by the U.S. Constitution or that is contrary to federal policy. Sometimes, a state might choose to embrace its own laws that do not necessarily align with federal policy; an example of this would be the regulation of recreational and medical marijuana. The major reserved powers of the state include the authority to regulate commerce within the state and exercise law enforcement. This gives states the right to pass and enforce laws that promote health, safety, welfare, and "morality." For example, in health promotion, you might see laws pertaining to the use of tobacco products. Elected politicians representing their constituents make decisions and take actions that are broadly referred to as **public policy**. Policies can take the form of new laws, repeals of existing laws, and interpretations and implementations of laws, executive orders, and court rulings. Throughout the policymaking process, the system of constitutional checks and balances prevails. The president (or governor) often plays an important leadership role in key policy issues. The Constitution grants Congress the power to make laws. The legislative process is often cumbersome as a bill (before it becomes law) goes through both houses of Congress, various committees, and subcommittees. Numerous organizations, called interest groups, which represent the common objectives of their members, try to influence policymakers to protect their members' interests. One example of a powerful interest group is the American Medical Association (AMA). Ultimately, if the president signs the approved bill, it becomes law. The president also has the power to veto (overturn) a bill passed by Congress. Unless a presidential veto is overruled by a two-thirds majority of Congress, it fails to become law. Even after a law has been passed, policymaking continues in the form of interpretation and implementation by the federal agency responsible for implementing the law. For example, the Department of Health and Human Services (DHHS) oversees more than 300 programs related to health and welfare services. It is responsible for 12 different agencies that deal with diverse areas related to public health, such as approval of new drugs and medical devices, health science research, services for children and the elderly, and substance abuse.

city or town, it is typically the mayor. The state legislative body is a legislature or assembly and the local equivalent would be the city or town council, perhaps a county commission. Likewise, there are federal, state, county, and city judges and courts.

▶ Federalism and Policy

A federal system is both a political and philosophical concept that describes how power is given to governments. Federal systems may vary widely in application, but all feature a central government with specific powers over the whole country. In North America, the United States, Canada, and Mexico are structured this way, as are many countries around the world. In general, a federal system allows powers that concern the whole nation to be granted to the federal government. For instance, in most countries with a federal system, only the national government can declare war on another country or make international treaties pertaining to trade or foreign policy matters. State power is more focused on issues that directly affect its residents only; Michigan, for example, cannot dictate what laws Indiana enacts. In Canada, the province of Quebec has French language requirements and Ontario does not. Sometimes the state-level governments must work through problems together. For example, Georgia, Alabama, and Florida have had to work out a water-sharing agreement because rivers and lakes do not always respect state boundary lines and changes in population demographics.

In public policy there are many examples of intergovernmental programs where all levels of the system—federal, state, and local—are involved, such as the control of air pollution or vaccination programs for COVID-19. Sometimes this also requires the involvement of another federal system; for example, the United States working with Canada on the SARS epidemic in 2002 and then in 2009 with Mexico and Canada jointly on the H1N1 influenza pandemic. Intergovernmental initiatives typically also involve the three branches of government since there are issues of law, regulation, funding, authority, and administration. Food and drug regulation is another area that has required the involvement of the executive, judicial, and legislative branches on an ongoing basis, involving government action locally, nationally, and globally to assure the public's health. At the beginning of the 20th century, the Pure Food and Drugs Act of 1906 was passed by Congress to provide federal inspection of meat products and prohibit the manufacture, sale, or transportation of adulterated food products and poisonous medicines. As this domain of public policy grew, it was institutionalized in the Executive Branch with the establishment of the Food and Drug Administration (FDA) in 1930. Subsequent legislation and regulations broadened the scope of this policy area to address ever-changing challenges to an increasingly complex and global society. A recent example is the FDA's involvement with other agencies to address the COVID-19 pandemic. This includes facilitating the development of tests, both diagnostic and serologic; supporting the advance of treatments and vaccines for the disease; and working to ensure that healthcare workers and others have the personal protective equipment and other necessary medical products needed to mitigate it.

While the original organizational architecture of the U.S. federal system as written in 1787 still exists today, there have been amendments to the Constitution and varied interpretations by the courts. Numerous public health and healthcare laws have been enacted by Congress, state legislatures, and local councils and boards. Furthermore, the number and size of public organizations has grown tremendously into a very complex web of departments, agencies, institutes, offices, centers, and collaboratives. Many of these will be described throughout this book, as they are organizations responsible for assuring and promoting health and well-being.

EXHIBIT 3-2 and **3-3** present samples of the range of issues addressed by both federal and state health policy.

There are also many policy issues at the organizational or institutional level. A few examples are provided in **EXHIBIT 3-4**.

EXHIBIT 3-2 Illustrative Health Policy Issues at the U.S. Federal Level

- How should otherwise healthy people be motivated to participate in health insurance programs, thus lowering the average premium?
- What population groups should receive subsidized coverage from tax revenues?
- Because the Constitution does not include the topic of health care as a federal responsibility, how should the federal government participate in supporting health care for all?

- How should the federal government support quality improvement efforts if state boards are not effectively addressing medical error rates?
- The cost of malpractice insurance in some states threatens the supply of providers in some specialties and appears to raise the cost of care, so what is the role of the federal government in avoiding the negative effects of malpractice lawsuits?
- Progress in information technology implementation in health care has lagged behind most other information-intensive service sectors. Are the provisions of the Health Information Technology for Economic and Clinical Health (HITECH) Act sufficient to overcome this problem?
- What services should be covered under Medicare? Medicaid?
- How many health professionals in a subspecialty are sufficient? Armed with the right answer, what should we being doing about any shortages? About any surpluses?

EXHIBIT 3-3 Illustrative Health Policy Issues at State and Local Levels

- What services should be provided and to whom under Medicaid options and waivers?
- How should the professional licensure be conducted so as to encourage quality of care, adequate access, and appropriate competition?
- How should the public university system decide how many professionals to train to ensure adequate access to all sections of the state? To all target groups?
- How aggressive should our state be in implementing and supporting health insurance exchanges?
- What should be the roles of the state insurance regulations and oversight boards in ensuring access to care for the general public and for special populations?
- Should the curative healthcare system, the mental health system, and public health clinics be merged as healthcare access becomes universal?
- What are intended and unintended consequences of sex education policies on health and health services?
- How do we undertake healthcare emergency planning for responses to floods, earthquakes, pandemics, and terrorism? What is the relationship between the state systems (public health and military) and local first responders?

EXHIBIT 3-4 Illustrative Health Policy Issues for Healthcare Institutions

- How much charitable (uncompensated) care should we provide beyond that which is mandated?
- What should be our health information technology strategy?
- Should we undertake joint planning for future services with our local health department?
- How should we go about increasing the proportion of the local population who volunteer as local organ donors?
- Can we rationalize the services provided by local providers, reducing duplication and waste, and still avoid charges of anticompetitive practices?
- What should we be doing to become an effective learning organization?

▶ Public Policy Process

Health policy is an attempt by the government at all levels to address a public issue, problem, or concern. The government, whether it is city, state, or federal, develops public policy in terms of laws, regulations, codes, decisions, and actions. There are three fundamental parts to public policy making: problems, stakeholders, and the policy. A fourth dimension, politics, is also present and results in a policy process that is dynamic and changeable. In this regard, Daniel Dawes has written about the "political determinants of health,"[1] asserting that when a policy issue aligns with a private sector interest or commercial interest and a government value interest, there is greater likelihood of success in advancing an effective agenda.[1] He provides examples of this with Medicare and Medicaid, the Americans with Disabilities Act, the Mental Health Parity and Addiction Equity Act, and the Affordable Care Act. A modified version of his model can be seen in **FIGURE 3-1**, which

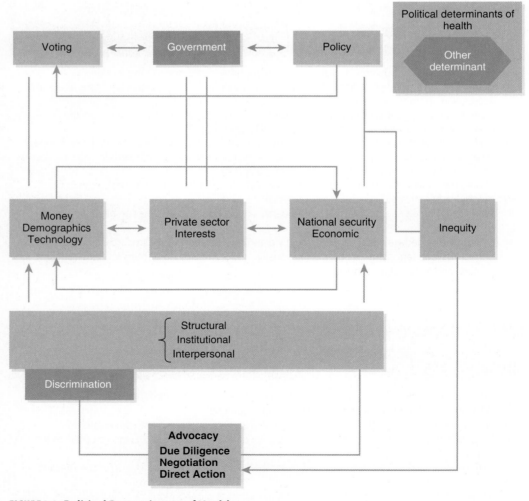

FIGURE 3-1 Political Determinants of Health

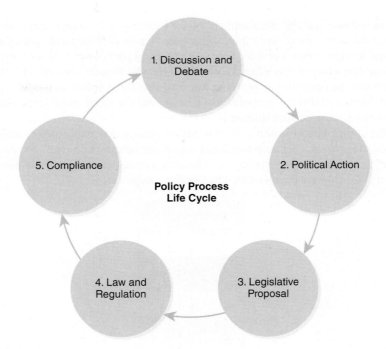

FIGURE 3-2 Policy Life Cycle

uses systems thinking to show various interconnections and interdependencies. He makes the case that this, as with many if not most policy processes, is a "continual strategic process that does not end once a policy is realized but requires constant monitoring by advocates to determine whether a policy or government action is positively or negatively affecting the determinants of health and advancing equity."[1]

In public policy, what is referred to as *the problem* is the issue that needs to be addressed, such as clean water for the City of Flint, Michigan, or the opioid epidemic in West Virginia and throughout the country. The *stakeholders* are the affected individuals or communities along with those who are influential in forming a plan to address the problem in question, such as a city or state. *Policy* is the finalized course of action decided upon by the government, perhaps in the form of a clean water ordinance or a law regulating opioid prescriptions. In some cases, policies are open to interpretation by nongovernmental players, including those in the private sector. This often leads to the infusion of *politics* before the policy is formulated and after it is implemented. As such, most public policies have a life cycle, as shown in **FIGURE 3-2**, and are subject to modification as events and opinions change.

▶ Legislative Policy Process

There are three general categories of public policy: social, economic, and foreign policy. As can be seen in the examples already provided in this chapter, it often spans all three domains. This was especially evident in the evolution of policy for food and medication safety with a series of over 200 laws and the establishment of the FDA and disease control through municipal ordinances, state and federal laws, and the establishment of the Centers for Disease Control and Prevention (CDC). These domains—food, medicines, and disease—cross all three public policy arenas: social, economic, and foreign policy. Food security is now seen as part of national security, and the economics of food continues to shape health behavior. Likewise, disease control, with the emergence of pandemics and the possibility of bioterrorism, spans all three policy arenas with issues such as the economic impact of disease, geopolitics of disease, and the many social justice implications of health disparities associated with disease.

Given the complexity of health care, it is not surprising that public policy making can be a long and arduous process. Each step requires a significant amount of human resources, expertise, time, and debate, and the five-step process can become a struggle of differing opinions, unforeseen complications, and changes in priorities. The five basic steps are:

1. Identify a problem
2. Draft a policy
3. Enact the policy
4. Execute the policy
5. Evaluate the policy

Once the problem has been identified, a policy must be drafted. The U.S government is structured so that, ideally, public opinion has a heavy influence on the formulation of policies. Individuals appeal to their members of Congress to vote for or against a policy. The public also influences and is influenced by media campaigns designed to sway public opinion one way or another. Before a policy is complete, relevant experts weigh in and attempt to create a reasonable, actionable policy that takes into account multiple sides of the issue. Once a policy has been created, the next step is to vote on it. Legislators vote to decide if a policy will become law. In the Senate, the Committee on Labor and Human Resources has jurisdiction over most health bills. The Committee of Finance Subcommittee on Health Care, similar to the Ways and Means Committee in the House of Representatives, has jurisdiction over taxes and revenue for programs such as Medicare, Medicaid, and Maternal and Child Health under the Social Security Act. In **BOX 3-1** you will find a list of characteristics that are common to public policy.

Once a policy is enacted, the government must determine the best ways to implement or execute the new policy. This is usually done through the engagement of one or more of the various agencies tasked with health and public health responsibilities. After a policy has been enacted for some time, it is assessed for its effectiveness. Data are gathered and research is conducted to evaluate the outcome of the policy's implementation. The individuals and communities affected

BOX 3-1 Select Characteristics of Public Policy

- Policy consists of courses of actions rather than mere decisions
- Policy is purposive or goal-oriented
- Policy is what government does, not simply what it intends to do
- Policy is based upon law and is authoritative
- Policy is developed by governments
- Policy is the result of politics

by the policy are usually involved in the process. Community-based participatory research is one tool that is used by the CDC, while comparative effectiveness research is advocated by the Centers for Medicare and Medicaid Services (CMS).

If the outcomes of enacting and implementing a policy are somewhat different from what was expected, adjustments or amendments can be made, or, if the policy proves to be completely ineffective, it can be done away with altogether. Policymaking is not a perfect process, and laws often need to be fine-tuned and modified over many years following enactment. This has been evident with the many changes to Medicare or Medicaid over the past decades as well as the ongoing refinements to the Affordable Care Act.

All health related interest groups have certain interests they seek to promote or defend, **EXHIBIT 3-5** identifies them according to interest group sector or domain.

Unlike governments, health agencies do not have the same authority to enact laws and impose taxes, so they must use a different set of policy instruments to accomplish their goals. There are four broad categories that a range of administrative policy instruments fall into:

- Regulatory development and enforcement
- Health resource allocation
- Information production and dissemination
- Policy advocacy and agenda setting

Regulation: Public organizations receive their regulatory power either through legislation, as described above, or through executive order from the president, governor, or mayor. This authority often involves a directive to establish administrative procedures and an infrastructure for implementation and enforcement. A recent example would be a governor or mayor, in response to COVID-19, ordering a mandate for everyone in their jurisdiction to wear a mask while in public spaces and to limit the number of people in a restaurant.

Allocation: The federal government (and state governments, to some extent) allocates funds to support various health programs. This is typically done through block grants and categorical grants. All block grants are given to the state governments, which are charged with distributing funds appropriately to specific programs, providers, and organizations. The categorical grants give more control over funds to federal agencies than do block grants, which allow the states greater discretion. Block grants are often given in such areas as child and maternal health, mental health, substance abuse, and migrant health. Categorical grants may be targeted at specific programs such as medical research or health professions education.

Information: All major federal agencies have some type of research unit. Many are heavily engaged in research, such as the NIH, the CDC, and the Agency for Healthcare Research

EXHIBIT 3-5   Key Health Care Concerns of Selected Interest Groups

Federal and State Governments
- Cost containment
- Access to care
- Quality of care

Employers
- Cost containment
- Workplace health and safety
- Minimum regulation

Consumers
- Access to care
- Quality of care
- Lower out-of-pocket costs

Insurers
- Administrative simplification
- Elimination of cost shifting

Practitioners
- Income maintenance
- Professional autonomy
- Malpractice reform

Provider Organizations
- Profitability
- Administrative simplification
- Bad debt reduction

Technology Producers
- Tax treatment
- Regulatory environment
- Research funding

and Quality (AHRQ). The activities of these and other federal agencies include basic and social research, surveillance, and policy studies that produce information for dissemination. The agency will often partner with universities and the private sector in both research and dissemination. State governments depend heavily on federally generated data to inform policy and make decisions about how best to structure public health programs and initiatives.

Advocacy: While federal and state agencies do not have any formal legislative authority, as specified in the Constitution's separation of powers doctrine, they do play an important role in the legislative process. This is primarily in the form of providing information and influence to place health issues on the legislative agenda. Sometimes agencies are asked by legislators to design model policies for consideration. They also provide an important counterbalance to information given to legislators by lobbyists and professional associations seeking to shape policy in the directions they prefer.

▶ Ethical Framework for Policy Analysis for Health Programs

All federal and state government programs, whether in health or some other domain, require evaluation. This may be dictated by law or regulation and it is often done at specified intervals over the life of a program or policy. An overarching framework that can help guide the process may involve the following set of considerations, which help assure individual liberties and social justice.[2]

1. *What are the health goals of the proposed policy or program?* Goals should be expressed in terms of health improvement (i.e., the reduction of morbidity or mortality). Even though more specific goals may be formulated—for example, that the participants of a health education program will learn a certain amount of information to protect themselves and their family from COVID-19—the ultimate goal of decreased morbidity and mortality must be in view. Another example would be the reduction of opioid overdose deaths in a given region. The program may also be part of a group of interventions from a variety of agencies and groups that share in reaching the policy goal.

2. *How effective is the program in achieving its stated goals?* The program must be based on the belief that it will achieve its stated goals. For example, health education programs may be effective in transmitting information, but the recipients show little or no behavioral change. This has been seen with measures such as mask wearing or willingness to get a vaccine. It is important that the outcomes of health programs are evaluated to ensure that the desired changes have occurred and that these changes have had an effect on the morbidity and mortality of the target group.

3. *What are the known or potential burdens of the program?* Health programs may involve a number of burdens or harms, but most cluster into three main categories: risks to privacy and confidentiality, particularly in data collection; risks to liberty and self-determination, especially in public health activities designed to contain the spread of disease; and risks to justice, often seen when interventions are targeted only to certain groups with the risk of stigmatization. There may be physical risks as well. For example, mandatory immunization programs may impose health risks to individuals, or spraying to prevent mosquito-borne viruses may endanger individuals who are sensitive to the chemicals being sprayed.

4. *Can burdens be minimized? Are there alternative approaches?* Those who propose health policies and programs are obligated to seek to lessen burdens and harms once they are identified. Contact tracing in sexually transmitted infections programs is routine; however, this practice may pose a threat to confidentiality and privacy. Yet, contact tracing is voluntary; there are no penalties for those who refuse to participate. Therefore, health professionals have an ethical obligation to inform individuals of their right to refuse to disclose the names of their sexual partners or to contact their partners themselves. In addition, if more than one alternative exists, health policy makers are ethically required to choose the alternative that poses the fewest risks to moral concerns such as liberty, privacy, or justice, while not compromising the benefits of the program.

BOX 3-2 Commentary on the Policy Cycle Model of the Policy Process

Although a useful conceptual or analytical tool, the policy cycle model has some limitations as an empirical description of policy-making reality due to its simplification of highly contingent and complex policy processes. The reality of policy making is not as systematic and linear as the model might suggest. Also, the stages are often compressed, skipped, or changed in order entirely. For example, policy formulation can sometimes precede agenda setting, as "solutions seek problems" to which they can be applied.[3] It also does not answer several key questions such as the actual substance of policy, the number and type of relevant actors involved in the process, the exact manner and sequence in which actual policy development processes occur, and whether there exist basic patterns of development in different issue areas, sectors, or jurisdictions. Overall, when using the policy cycle idea, diligent attention has to be paid to the fact that the model is a guideline for the analysis of a far more complex reality.

---

5. *Is the program implemented fairly?* This question determines whether or not there is fair distribution of the benefits and burdens of the proposed program. Social harms can result if stereotypes are created or perpetuated, such as the notion that certain population groups are more vulnerable. This problem may be intensified if other population groups use such stereotyping to come to the erroneous belief that they are at little or no risk because they do not fit the risk profile.

6. *How can the benefits and burdens of a program be fairly balanced?* After the first five steps of the framework have been addressed, a decision must be made as to whether the expected benefits of the proposed policy or program will justify the identified burdens. Inevitably, there will be disagreements over the potential burdens and benefits inherent in the details of a particular program. For instance, taxpayers may focus on the financial burdens of a clean water program that may benefit future generations, while public health professionals only see its benefits. Procedural justice requires that a fair process of decision making is used to resolve such disagreements. This process must seek a balance between communal interests and the liberty rights of individuals, realizing that some infringements on individual liberty are unavoidable. Democratic processes and open hearings can help to ensure that minority positions are presented and considered.

BOX 3-2, with commentary from the International Encyclopedia of the Social and Behavioral Sciences, is intended to further help the reader to understand that the public policy process is not always linear and often involves the balancing of many interests.

▶ Government Responsibilities for Health

The Public Sector

As we proceed in this chapter to gain a better understanding of the scope and scale of the governmental infrastructure, it is important to be aware of the distinctive issues that are at the forefront of public sector organizations. Johnson explains, "while private businesses have some of the constraints, oversights, and pressures of public agencies, the fact is the influence is not as pervasive on a day-to-day basis."[2]

According to Christopher Pollitt, author of *The Essential Public Manager*, the public sector agency faces the issues in **TABLE 3-1** more often or with more magnitude than private businesses might.[4]

TABLE 3-1 Issues and Challenges Facing Public Managers

- Managing in a social–political system
- Working with public pressure and potential protest
- An ever-present sense of accountability
- The need to understand public behavior
- The challenge of rationing resources
- Having to manage influence responsibly
- Assessing multidimensional performance
- Being open and responsive to the media
- Understanding a wider responsibility to a changing society

Federal Responsibilities

The principal entities through which the federal government enacts its responsibilities in promoting and maintaining health include the Department of Health and Human Services (HHS), the Veterans Health System (a component of the Department of Veterans Affairs), and the Department of Defense Military Health System.

The federal government maintains broad policy-making and operational responsibilities to promote and protect the health of U.S. citizens while ensuring the implementation of both preventive and protective public health practices. At the policy level, the federal government plays crucial roles in leading, exercising regulatory powers, and setting health goals, policies, and standards that are models for the nation. It contributes operational and financial resources and supports research, higher education, and advancements in science and technology that contribute to the effectiveness of health delivery at all levels. Federal health responsibilities include[5,6]:

- Ensuring that all levels of government have the capabilities to provide essential public health services (described later in this chapter)
- Taking action when health threats span more than one state, a region, or the entire nation
- Taking action where solutions to public health problems may be beyond the jurisdiction of individual states
- Assisting states when their expertise or resources are not adequate to effectively respond to a public health emergency, such as a natural disaster, bioterrorism, or an emerging disease threat
- Facilitating development of health goals in collaboration with state and local governments and other relevant stakeholders

Federal Agencies Involved in Health

HHS is the primary public health and social service agency of the United States. The Department has a long and rich history that began in 1789 with the passage of an act by Congress for the relief of sick and disabled seamen, thus establishing a network of hospitals for the care of merchant seamen. This became the forerunner of today's U.S. Public Health Service. In 1953 a Cabinet-level Department (Health, Education, and Welfare) was formed and reported directly to the president. Later, in 1980, the education function became its own Department of Education and the health and welfare functions were organized under HHS.[1] The current organizational chart, as shown in Chapter 10, demonstrates the scope and scale of this massive collection of health agencies.

A description of the primary federal health agencies is provided in **TABLE 3-2**.

TABLE 3-2 Federal Health Agencies

Health Resources and Services Administration (HRSA)

HRSA helps provide health resources for medically underserved populations. The main operating units of HRSA are the Bureau of Primary Health Care, Bureau of Health Professions, Maternal and Child Bureau, and the HIV/AIDS Bureau. A nationwide network of community and migrant health centers, augmented by primary care programs for the homeless and the residents of public housing, serve more than 10 million Americans each year. HRSA also works to build the healthcare workforce, and it maintains the National Health Service Corps. The agency provides services to people with AIDS through the Ryan White Care Act programs. It oversees the organ transplantation system and works to decrease infant mortality and improve maternal and child health. HRSA was established in 1982 by bringing together several existing programs. HRSA has nearly 2000 employees, most at its headquarters in Rockville, Maryland.

Indian Health Service (IHS)

IHS is responsible for providing federal health services to American Indians and Alaska Natives. The provision of health services to members of federally recognized tribes grew out of the special government-to-government relationship between the federal government and Indian tribes. This relationship, established in 1787, is based on Article I, Section 8 of the Constitution, and has been given form and substance by numerous treaties, laws, Supreme Court decisions, and Executive Orders. IHS is the principal federal healthcare provider and health advocate for Native Americans, and its goal is to raise their health status to the highest possible level. IHS currently provides health services to approximately 3 million American Indians and Alaska Natives who belong to more than 564 federally recognized tribes in 35 states. IHS was established in 1924; its mission was transferred from the Interior Department in 1955. Agency headquarters are in Rockville, Maryland. IHS has more than 15,000 employees.

Centers for Disease Control and Prevention (CDC)

Working with states and other partners, the CDC provides a system of health surveillance to monitor and prevent disease outbreaks, including bioterrorism events and threats, and it maintains the national health statistics. The CDC also provides for immunization services, supports research on disease and injury prevention, and guards against international disease transmission, with personnel stationed in more than 54 foreign countries. The CDC was established in 1946; its headquarters are in Atlanta, Georgia. The CDC has 11,000 employees.

National Institutes of Health (NIH)

Begun as a one-room Laboratory of Hygiene in 1887, the NIH today is one of the world's foremost medical research centers and the federal focal point for health research. The NIH is the steward of medical and behavioral research for the nation. Its mission is science in pursuit of fundamental knowledge about the nature and behavior of living systems and the application of that knowledge to extend healthy life and reduce the burdens of illness and disability. In realizing its goals, the NIH provides leadership and direction to programs designed to improve the health of the nation by conducting and supporting research in the causes, diagnosis, prevention, and cure of human diseases; in the processes of human growth and development; in the biological effects of environmental contaminants; in the understanding of mental, addictive, and physical disorders; and in the direction of programs for the collection, dissemination, and exchange of information in medicine and health, including the development and support of medical libraries and the training of medical librarians and other health information specialists. Although the majority of NIH resources sponsor external research, there is also a large in-house research program. The NIH includes 27 separate health institutes and centers; its headquarters are in Bethesda, Maryland. The NIH has approximately 19,000 employees.

Food and Drug Administration (FDA)

The FDA ensures that the food we eat is safe and wholesome, that the cosmetics we use will not harm us, and that medicines, medical devices, and radiation-transmitting products, such as microwave ovens, are safe and effective. The FDA also oversees feed and drugs for farm animals and pets. Authorized by Congress to enforce the Federal Food, Drug, and Cosmetic Act and several other public health laws, the agency monitors the manufacture, import, transport, storage, and sale of more than $1 trillion worth of goods annually. The FDA has more than 15,000 employees. Among its staff, the FDA has chemists microbiologists, and other scientists, as well as investigators and inspectors who visit more than 16,000 facilities a year as part of their oversight of the businesses that FDA regulates. Established in 1906, the FDA has its headquarters in Silver Spring, Maryland.

Substance Abuse and Mental Health Services Administration (SAMHSA)

SAMHSA was established by Congress under Public Law 102-321 on October 1, 1992, to strengthen the nation's healthcare capacity to provide prevention, diagnosis, and treatment services for substance abuse and mental illnesses. SAMHSA works in partnership with states, communities, and private organizations to address the needs of people with substance abuse and mental illnesses, as well as community risk factors that contribute to these illnesses. SAMHSA serves as the umbrella under which substance abuse and mental health service centers are housed, including the Center for Mental Health Services (CMHS), the Center for Substance Abuse Prevention (CSAP), and the Center for Substance Abuse Treatment (CSAT). SAMHSA also houses the Office of the Administrator, the Office of Applied Studies, and the Office of Program Services. SAMHSA's headquarters are in Rockville, Maryland; the agency has about 600 employees.

Agency for Toxic Substances and Disease Registry (ATSDR)

Working with states and other federal agencies, ATSDR seeks to prevent exposure to hazardous substances from waste sites. The agency conducts public health assessments, health studies, surveillance activities, and health education training in communities near waste sites on the U.S. Environmental Protection Agency's National Priorities List. ATSDR also has developed toxicity profiles of hazardous chemicals found at these sites. The agency is closely associated administratively with the CDC; its headquarters are also in Atlanta, Georgia. ATSDR has more than 400 employees.

Agency for Health Care Research and Quality (AHRQ)

AHRQ supports cross-cutting research on healthcare systems, healthcare quality and cost issues and effectiveness of medical treatments. Formerly known as the Agency for Health Care Policy and Research, AHRQ was established in 1989, assuming broadened responsibilities of its predecessor agency, the National Center for Health Services Research and Health Care Technology Assessment. The agency has about 300 employees; its headquarters are in Rockville, Maryland.

Turnock BJ. Public Health: What it is and how it Works, 6th Ed. MA: Jones & Bartlett Learning; 2016.

Other Federal Agencies Involved in Public Health

In addition to HHS, there are various federal agencies that work provide health-related public services or have a role in health policy and regulation. These agencies often work in partnership with HHS, but have their own separate missions and responsibilities. These include the Environmental Protection Agency (EPA); the Department of Labor, which houses the Occupational Safety and Health Administration (OSHA); the Department of Agriculture, which performs safety inspections and coordinates the Special Supplemental Nutrition Program for Women, Infants, and Children (WIC); the Department of Homeland Security (DHS); the Department of Veterans Affairs (VA); the Department of Defense (DOD); the Department of Transportation (DOT); and various other agencies and bureaus involved, at least partially. Two of these, the VA and DOD, warrant further discussion.

Veterans Health Administration

First established to provide care for Civil War veterans who were disabled or indigent, the Veterans Health Administration (VHA) system grew to become one of the world's largest healthcare delivery systems. The VHA is a component of the VA and is the country's largest healthcare system and a significant component of America's medical education system. The VA owns and operates 150 hospitals, most of which are affiliated with medical schools, and 819 community-based outpatient clinics throughout the United States. With more than 1,700 sites of care including hospitals, outpatient clinics, rehabilitation centers, and nursing homes, the VHA served nearly 10 million individuals in 2020.

Because the VHA system has a long-term relationship with its patients, it has access to each patient's complete medical record, an advantage over private medicine that, in theory, reduces both costs and medical errors. Likewise, this long-term relationship should be expected to foster more preventive care, higher-quality services, and greater patient satisfaction and cost savings. However, major deficiencies in the VHA health system have come to light regarding egregious delays in veterans' access to services. These have called the system's credibility into question. Administrative and other reforms are underway with the intent to remedy this situation.

Department of Defense Military Health System

The Department of Defense Military Health System operates one of the largest healthcare organizations in the nation and provides both direct healthcare services and support for U.S. active-duty personnel, military retirees, survivors, and their dependents. The system is composed of 15 integrated networks of military hospitals and clinics. Eleven of these facilities are in the United States and four are overseas, including 56 hospitals and 365 clinics that employ more than 58,000 civilians and more than 86,000 military personnel.[5] Components of the system include Army, Air Force, and Navy military treatment facilities and the TRICARE healthcare program. TRICARE is a health insurance program available to those covered under the military health system and offers both managed care and fee-for-service options. TRICARE managed care providers include those at military treatment facilities and a network of civilian providers administered through regional contracts with civilian managed care organizations. The fee-for-service option also covers care provided by civilian providers who have not joined the TRICARE network. TRICARE brings together the healthcare resources of the uniformed services and supplements them with networks of civilian healthcare professionals, institutions, pharmacies, and other suppliers to provide access to high-quality healthcare services.[5]

State and Local Responsibilities

The following sections focus on the central state and local roles in health policy, healthcare delivery, and public health. In reviewing these sections, it is important to note the many relationships, shared resources, and responsibilities between and among the federal, state, and local government sectors. For example, states have significant roles in administering federal grant initiatives, and local health departments carry out important surveillance, data collection, and program implementation activities on behalf of state health agencies.

State Government Roles

State governments have significant influences on healthcare delivery and public health through their departments and agencies, such as health, insurance, education, and social services. States function as regulators of health insurance companies, licensors and regulators of health professionals, regulators of quality of care in state-licensed facilities, and analysts of healthcare costs and quality.[5] Many states also operate mental health institutions, support medical and other health professional schools, and may act as lead organizations to channel federal or other support to local or regional health jurisdictions. Chief among states' obligations is their matching funds requirements for the joint federal/state Medicaid program.[5,6] Also, since the implementation of the ACA, many states have opted to develop and operate health insurance marketplaces either solely or in federal partnerships, creating yet another pivotal role for states in the healthcare system.[5,6] The primary sources of state health agency funding include federal support (53%) and state general funds (24%).[5,6]

The Association of State and Territorial Health Officials (ASTHO) describes characteristics and activities of state health agencies using extensive surveys of 48 states and the District of Columbia.[5,6]

The aggregate state health agency workforce is estimated at 101,000 full-time equivalent employees whose roles encompass a wide range of occupational classifications. The top occupational classifications by average number of full-time equivalent employees in state health agencies include: administrators/managers/administrative staff; public health nurses, nurse practitioners, and environmental health workers; lab workers, social workers, and epidemiologists/statisticians; and physicians, health educators, and nutritionists.

Leadership of state health agencies is carried out by a top state health official, typically in the title of commissioner or state health officer. In 76% of states, this position is appointed by the state governor.[5,6] Almost three-fourths of all top state health officials have medical degrees (MD or DO) and 50% hold a Master of Public Health (MPH) or Master of Public Administration (MPA) degree. In 53% of states, official statutes require the top state official to hold a medical degree (MD or DO).[5,6]

Based upon ASTHO surveys, the following are brief descriptions of six primary categories of state health agency activity. To access more detail on each of the six state categories and other information, readers are encouraged to consult the ASTHO website (https://www.astho.org/).

1. *Administering federal initiatives:* State health agencies have primary responsibilities for the administration and fiscal performance of several federal programs. **TABLE 3-3** lists initiatives for which state health agencies most often report responsibility.
2. *Population-based primary prevention and screening for diseases and medical conditions:* State health agencies engage in a wide array of primary preventive services as listed in **TABLE 3-4**. The most prominent of these relate to tobacco, HIV, sexually transmitted diseases, and now various COVID-19-related services such as screening and vaccination.

TABLE 3-3 State Health Agencies Responsibility for Federal Initiatives

Public Health Emergency Preparedness cooperative agreement (CDC)
Maternal and Child Health—Title V
Vital statistics (National Center for Health Statistics)
Preventive Health and Health Services Block Grant (CDC)
ASPR Hospital Preparedness Program cooperative agreement
National Cancer Prevention and Control Program Grant (CDC)
Immunization funding
Special Supplemental Nutrition Program for Women, Infants, and Children (U.S. Department of Agriculture)
Healthy People initiative
Injury prevention

Data from Association of State and Territorial Health Officials. State health agency activities. Published 2020. Accessed August 9, 2021. https://astho.org/Profile/Volume-Three/Issue-Briefs/Activities/#:~:text=The%20five%20federal%20initiatives%20for,96%25)%2C%20and%20the%20Hospital

TABLE 3-4 Prevention Services Performed by State Health Agencies

Service
Tobacco
HIV
Sexually transmitted disease counseling and partner notification
Nutrition
Physical activity
Injury

Service
Hypertension
Unintended pregnancy
Violence

Data from Association of State and Territorial Health Officials. State health agency activities. Published 2020. Accessed August 9, 2021. https://astho
.org/Profile/Volume-Three/Issue-Briefs/Activities/#:~:text=The%20five%20federal%20initiatives%20for,96%25)%2C%20and%20the%20Hospital

3. *Technical assistance and training:* State health agencies maintain partnerships across local health departments, emergency medical services, healthcare providers, hospitals, laboratories, and other state and community-based organizations. In this role, they provide technical assistance and support on a variety of topics.

4. *Laboratory services:* The most common testing performed by state health agency laboratories is bioterrorism agent testing (96%), foodborne illness testing (96%), and influenza typing (94%). The next most common tests are for newborn screening (73%) and blood lead testing (50%).

5. *Regulation, inspection, and licensing activities:* State health agencies play central roles in enforcing laws and regulations intended to protect health and safety. As **TABLE 3-5** depicts, these activities cover a wide spectrum that affect large segments of the population.

6. *Data collection, epidemiology, and surveillance activities:* State health agencies work with the CDC and other federal agencies to monitor trends and plan appropriate interventions. **TABLE 3-6** lists primary activities that involve data collection and surveillance. Syndromic surveillance systems are of particular importance in anticipating potential health threats and issues. These systems monitor data such as school and employment absenteeism, emergency call systems, volumes of emergency room visits, and other data sources to detect unusual patterns that may signal an evolving health issue.

In addition to the activities noted above, state health agencies, in collaboration with federal agency partners, carry out many more health-related functions. Examples include safeguarding and improving environmental quality, attenuating health disparities, improving health services access, supporting maternal and child health, and advocating for minority and rural health challenges.

Local Government Roles

The National Association of County and City Health Officials (NACCHO) provides detailed descriptions of local health department (LHD) characteristics and activities. These health departments support and deliver a variety of health and health-related services and, as will be discussed in Chapter 10, provide direct patient care services in clinics or health centers, referrals for care, and other services particularly focused on underserved populations. Most LHDs are county-based while others serve cities or towns. LHDs are supported by a variety of revenue sources. Approximately 80% of revenue is contributed from government sources: local funds, state funds, federal direct and pass-through funds, and Medicaid.[7]

TABLE 3-5 Regulation, Inspection, and Licensing Activities Performed by State Health Agencies
Laboratories
Food service establishments
Hospitals
Trauma system
Emergency medical services
Lead inspection
Public swimming pools
Long-term care facilities
Nursing homes
Body piercing and tattooing
Hospice
Campgrounds/RVs
Food processing
Assisted living
Smoke-free ordinances

Reproduced from Association of State and Territorial Health Officials. State health agency activities. Published 2020. Accessed August 9, 2021. https://astho.org/Profile/Volume-Three/Issue-Briefs/Activities/#:~:text=The%20five%20federal%20initiatives%20for,96%25)%2C%20and%20the%20Hospital

LHD activities can be clustered into four main categories: (1) programs and services, (2) emergency preparedness and response, (3) assessment, planning and improvement, and (4) public health policy.

1. *Programs and services:* They engage in a wide variety of activities to promote the positive health status of their communities. Services provided in individual localities depend upon many variables, including state laws and other requirements, community needs and priorities, available funding, and relationships with other health and human services providers and organizations.

TABLE 3-6 Data Collection, Epidemiology, and Surveillance Activities

Reportable diseases

Communicable infectious diseases

Foodborne illnesses

Vital statistics reporting

Morbidity reporting

Perinatal events or risk factors

Behavioral risk factors

Chronic diseases

Syndromic surveillance

Environmental health

Injury

Cancer incidence

Adolescent behavior

Reproduced from Association of State and Territorial Health Officials. State health agency activities. Published 2020. Accessed August 9, 2021. https://astho.org/Profile/Volume-Three/Issue-Briefs/Activities/#:~:text=The%20five%20federal%20initiatives%20for,96%25)%2C%20and%20the%20Hospital

2. *Emergency preparedness and response:* They play important roles in responding to natural and other disasters as well as public health emergencies of many types. Their capacity, coupled with collaborations with an array of other community organizations and healthcare providers, is central in efforts to prevent and control disease outbreaks and environmental hazards. Their advance planning to deal with community public health emergencies is essential for safeguarding the public's health during times of threatening events.

3. *Assessment, planning, and improvement:* Periodic community health assessments, community health improvement planning, and development of strategic plans are mechanisms to help ensure that health departments stay in touch with evolving community needs and plan effective interventions.

4. *Public health policy*: These agencies are often called upon by local governments and communities to assist with the development of policies pertaining to health. One example would be policies for COVID-19 vaccinations and education of the public.

▶ Importance of Systems Thinking in Government

Given the interdependence of federal, state, and local governments along with their myriad agencies and programs, it is best to think in terms of systems thinking, especially the concept of *complex adaptive systems*, as introduced in Chapter 1. A description of the characteristics from Johnson, Anderson, and Rossow's *Health Systems Thinking: A Primer* as they pertain to health care or public health include the following[8]:

1. *Complex systems tend to be self-stabilizing.* A system likely contains many balancing feedback loops, each of which serves to keep some smaller component or subsystem in balance with the larger more complex system. An example would be the various units of the National Institutes of Health remaining on the cutting edge of research within their domain while also serving the larger purpose and mission of medical research.

2. *Complex systems are purposeful.* These systems often seem to function with a mind of their own. An example of this is the work of the Federal Emergency Management Agency (FEMA) in a disaster relief effort. You might have another purposeful agency like the CDC working on the same challenge and very likely state and local government agencies involved.

3. *Complex systems are capable of using feedback to modify their behavior.* All systems do this, providing an essential opportunity for adaptation and innovation. An example would be a health department forming a partnership with an AIDS organization to better provide access to HIV testing.

4. *Complex systems can modify their environments.* Systems can modify their behavior to achieve goals or fulfill a purpose. In doing so, due to the interconnection of everything, they also alter their environments. Concomitant with the change in a systems behavior is the need to identify the links between the system and its environment. An example would be using systems thinking to address water quality issues in a community such as Flint, Michigan.

5. *Complex systems are capable of replicating, maintaining, repairing, and organizing themselves.* This is sometimes referred to as reengineering, reinvention, or organizational transformation. An example of health care would be the incredible growth in scope and scale of the Cleveland Clinics over the last decade or how the Mayo Clinics are now multistate. In the rapidly changing domains of public policy and health care, systems thinking can be perceived as offering valuable insights and guidance for understanding and action. The World Health Organization (WHO) describes systems thinking as "an approach to problem solving that views 'problems' as part of a wider, dynamic system. Systems thinking involves much more than a reaction to present outcomes or events. It demands a deeper understanding of the linkages, relationships, interactions, and behaviors among the elements to characterize the entire system."[8]

Many agencies at every level of government are embracing systems thinking as a means for achieving greater effectiveness. One way this is being done is by including health in all policies, within domains beyond the typical scope of health care or public health. **EXHIBIT 3-6** provides some examples of this.

EXHIBIT 3-6 Public Policy Influences Health

The Sycamore Institute, an independent, nonpartisan public policy research center, has identified various ways public policy can influence health. While not always associated with health, the following public policy areas can have a big health impact.

1. Public policies can create, regulate, and maintain public goods that foster supportive environments for good health.

An example is state roads, highways, sidewalks, and bicycle paths. They are funded by taxes and user fees and are open for use by the public. How these are planned, constructed, connected, and maintained can, for example, impact the accessibility of needed services and the walkability of communities. These factors can create opportunities or barriers to getting care and making the choices that keep people healthy.

2. Public policies can regulate natural resources to prevent harm.

For example, state health departments regulate air and water quality to ensure it is safe. Many people take for granted that the air that they breathe and the water that they drink is safe and healthy. The contaminated water crisis in Flint, Michigan, is an example of a natural resource not being properly regulated to prevent harm.

3. Public policies can set requirements and mandates that protect citizens.

For example, traffic accidents are a leading cause of fatalities and injuries. Mandatory seat belt laws were implemented to address this problem. These laws have increased seat belt usage and decreased the number of motor vehicle-related injuries and fatalities. Laws against alcohol-impaired driving are another example of public policies designed to protect citizens.

4. Public policies can provide direct support in ways that affect the social determinants of health.

One example is the Temporary Assistance for Needy Families (TANF) program, which was created by the U.S. Congress in 1996. The program is jointly funded by the state and federal governments and helps poor families gain self-sufficiency through employment. The program provides temporary cash assistance to help pay for basic needs like food, housing, and transportation while providing opportunities, requirements, and incentives for work training and employment.

5. Public policies can reduce barriers and create opportunities that impact health.

One example of how public policy can create an opportunity to improve health is Tennessee's HOPE Scholarship. The HOPE Scholarship is designed to reduce financial barriers and create the opportunity for some Tennessee students to attend college and attain a higher level of education. Research shows that education and income are generally reliable predictors of health.

6. Public policy can provide incentives and disincentives that influence healthier choices.

For example, many states impose an excise tax on tobacco products. Research has shown that tobacco taxes create a financial disincentive for some individuals to smoke.

Data from the Sycamore Institute. 5 ways public policy impacts health. Published May 4, 2017. Accessed June 5, 2021. https://www.sycamoreinstitutetn .org/5-ways-public-policy-impacts-health/

▶ Discussion Questions

■ Describe the policy life cycle and provide at least one example of how it can pertain to health policy.

■ Discuss federalism and how it impacts health care.

■ Identify several initiatives of the federal government in health care. Give examples.

■ Identify several initiatives of state governments in health care. Give examples.

■ Identify several initiatives of local governments in health care. Give examples.

■ Describe the scope of the Department of Health and Human Services (HHS).

■ What skills are needed to be effective when working in health-related government agencies?

■ What are the administrative policy instruments health agencies can use?

■ What are the five steps in the legislative policy process?

■ Discuss how American history has shaped the U.S. government.

■ How does systems thinking relate to government agencies and policy?

CASE 3-1 The Troubled Launch of HealthCare.gov

In January 2016, the Office of the Inspector General (OIG) of the U.S. Department of Health and Human Services (HHS) issued a "Case Study" entitled "HealthCare.gov: CMS Management of the Federal Marketplace." The launch of HealthCare.gov, on October 1, 2013, had been a public relations disaster.

That negative first impression continued long after the site was salvaged.

The Case Study

The OIG investigation covered 5 years of development and was intended to strengthen the future performance of the Center for Medicare and Medicaid Services (CMS). That case study included **BOXES 3-3** and **3-4**: one on the breakdown and the other on the recovery. The case study was confirmed by other reports as being accurate.

The Various Actors

CMS may have been the focus of the study, but it was neither the only actor nor the only one at fault. Congress, the Supreme Court, the states, the Office of the Secretary of HHS, the White House, and CMS influenced the implementation: "The ingredients are familiar: partisan hurdles thrown up by the GOP, the jumpy political instincts of administration aides, administration insularity, spin that borders on deception, bureaucratic clots, and the bold and sprawling scope of the project."[9]

The Congress

Despite a general consensus that something needed to be done about the uninsured, the process behind the passage of the ACA had been full of twists and turns. Because of the Senate rule requiring 60 senate votes for cloture in the face of a filibuster, every vote was critical; so was the support (or at least acquiescence) of most key health players. As the requests of each player were accepted or compromises reached, the Senate bill grew larger and larger and more and more complex. Then the loss of Senator Kennedy's former seat in the November 2010 election forced quick adoption of the Senate bill by both houses using the reconciliation process.[10] A more thorough vetting of the bill might have smoothed the way for implementation. The totally partisan passage of the bill by the Democrats left the Republican majority in the House dead set against funding its implementation. Consequently, the Office of Consumer Information and Insurance Oversight (OCIIO), which was the implementation

Box 3-3 Key Contributing Factors to Breakdown

PREPARATION AND DEVELOPMENT
March 2010–December 2012

Policy Development Delays: Initial work to create the Federal Marketplace required extensive policy development that delayed HHS and CMS in planning for the technical and operational needs of the HealthCare.gov website.

Poor Transition to CMS: A poor transition of the Federal Marketplace from HHS to CMS early on caused inefficiencies that resulted in communication breakdowns and needlessly complex implementation.

Lack of Clear Leadership: HealthCare.gov lacked clear project leadership to give direction and unity of purpose, responsiveness in execution, and a comprehensive view of progress.

Mismanagement of Key Contract: CMS mismanaged the key website development contract, with frequent changes, problematic technological decisions, and limited oversight of contractor performance.

FINAL COUNTDOWN TO LAUNCH
January 2013–September 2013

Compressed Timeline for Technical Build: CMS continued to change policy and business requirements, which compressed the timeframe for completing the website's technical development.

Resistance to Bad News: CMS leaders and staff failed to recognize the magnitude of problems, became resistant to bad news about the website's development and failed to act on warnings and address problems.

Path Dependency: As problems worsened, CMS staff and contractors became path dependent, continuing to follow the same plan and schedule rather than change course as circumstances warranted.

Corrections Weak and Late: CMS attempted last-minute corrections that were weak and too late to effect change, retaining a fixed deadline for launch, despite poor progress.

Office of the Inspector General. (2016). *HealthCare.gov: CMS management of the federal marketplace: A case study* (Document OEI-06-14-00350), p. iii.

hub at CMS, would have not been funded adequately, if at all. In response, the Secretary downgraded the office to a center (the Center of Consumer Information and Insurance Oversight or CCIIO), so that it was no longer a budget line item. As a result, however, it lost much of its clout within the bureaucracy including control over the contracting process.[11] Later, concern about political pushback led the White House to order a slowdown in the process of writing regulations and contract specifications until after the 2012 elections. This delay negatively impacted the contracting process and in turn led to a crunch before the October 1, 2013 deadline, accompanied by inadequate testing of the website.[11,12] The congressional battle had also left many of the key actors in the White House, HHS, and CMS exhausted and turnover proved high.[12] The OIG case study also reports that some contractors were unwilling to

(continues)

CASE 3-1 The Troubled Launch of HealthCare.gov

(continued)

Box 3-4 Key Contributing Factors to Recovery

LAUNCH, CORRECTION, AND FIRST OPEN ENROLLMENT
October 2013–March 2014

Quick Pivot to New Strategy: CMS and its contractors began correction of website problems immediately following launch, making a quick pivot to change their strategy.

Adoption of Badgeless Culture: CMS and its contractors adopted a badgeless culture that encouraged full collaboration by CMS staff and contractors regardless of employer status and job title, fostering innovation, problem solving, and communication among teams.

Integration of All Functions: CMS integrated all functions into its organizational structure to align with project needs, enhancing CMS and contractor accountability and collaboration.

Planning for Problems: CMS planned for problems, establishing redundant (backup) systems in the event of further breakdowns, and restructuring its key development contract to ensure better performance.

TURNAROUND & SECOND OPEN ENROLLMENT
April 2014–February 2015

Ruthless Prioritization: CMS adopted a policy of ruthless prioritization to reduce planned website functionality, focusing resources on the highest priorities.

Quality over On-Time Delivery: CMS prioritized quality over on-time delivery, employing extensive testing to identify and fix problems and delaying new website functionality if unready for perfect execution.

Simplifying Processes: CMS simplified systems and processes to enable closer monitoring of progress, increased transparency and accountability, and clearer prioritization.

Continuous Learning: CMS adopted continuous learning for policy and technological tasks, balancing project plans with system and team capacity, and changing course as needed to improve operations.

Office of the Inspector General. (2016). *HealthCare.gov: CMS management of the federal marketplace: A case study* (Document OEI-06-14-00350), p. iv.

bid on the Federal Marketplace contracts due to uncertainty about whether the law might be repealed. The 16-day government shutdown on October 1, 2013 also slowed the recovery.

The Supreme Court

The ACA required states to expand their Medicaid programs with extensive federal support. Many states challenged that requirement, as well as the individual mandate, and those cases went to the Supreme Court. The OIG case study reports that some work on the website slowed down because of uncertainties about the Supreme Court's ruling. The Court, on June 28, 2012, upheld the individual mandate but supported the states opposed to Medicaid expansion.

The States

One provision of the bill allowed the states to choose between participating or not in HealthCare.gov. Those decisions had to play out in 50 legislatures and 50 governors' offices. The deadline for the states to submit final plans to CMS was December 14, 2012 and the states' decisions were not reviewed and questions resolved until January 2013. That led to further delays in the specifications for the federal marketplace. Differences in the views of longtime federal employees and newer employees with state insurance backgrounds also led to delays in writing regulations and contract specifications.

Health and Human Services

Established under the Office of the Secretary, the OCIIO had been an innovation-oriented unit in Bethesda, MD with direct hiring authority. It had even successfully developed an ACA browsing site called Plan Finder. Yet some thought that the resources and experiences of CMS with programs such as Medicare Part D were relevant to HealthCare.gov, and that work going on outside Washington would be less associated with the hostility toward Obamacare.

The transition did not go well as the OCIIO changed to CCIIO. Its culture clashed with the very hierarchical culture of CMS, and various functions were parceled out from the new center to CMS's Office of Information Services (OIS), the Office of Acquisition and Grants Management, Office of Financial Management, and Office of Communications. But the small Center staff remained in Bethesda, while those other functions were situated in Baltimore. The OIG case study reported: "[D]ocuments also revealed major differences in understanding between the divisions regarding shared responsibilities and assessments of project progress. In interviews staff in CCIIO and OIS gave very different descriptions of each other's tasks and in some cases could not identify the staff positions or subdivisions responsible for critical project tasks."[13]

Brill (2015) reports interviewing key individuals about who was in charge of the implementation and getting seven different answers. He also asked one official about the existence of a command center and was informed that there were to be four or five command centers—three for CMS, one at HHS, and maybe one at the White House. The OIG report mentions two command centers operated jointly by CMS and its contractors.

According to the OIG case study, when Todd Park, the new White House Chief Technology Officer coming over from the HHS, became concerned, he convinced Secretary Sibelius to hire McKinsey & Co. to assess the CMS process. On March 28, 2013, a McKinsey team report described a process that "for all of its efforts to be polite, depicted a debacle."[11] The McKinsey report referred to the fact that the program design process was not yet completed, and there had been "no end-to-end business process view" across the many government actors. It called for "[f]ast, locked-down decisions" and noted a "lack of any single, empowered decision-making authority." It also hinted at the possibility of delaying the launch. The report was not widely circulated at HHS and was dismissed by White House health policy staff as "second guessing from the sidelines." The Administration was confident CMS was already working on those problems.[11]

The OIG report noted: "In all, CMS received 18 'documented warnings' of concerns regarding the HealthCare.gov build between July 2011 and July 2013, all containing substantial detail about the project's shortcomings and formally submitted to CMS leadership or project managers at CMS" (p. 21).

That case study also noted reluctance within CMS to ask, quoting someone from the center: "You know it has to be bad if I am requesting help" (p. 25).

The White House

Implementation had been a concern at the White House, but it was not always a high priority. It often came behind enrollment and public relations. Economist and staffer David Cutler wrote a letter recommending bringing in an executive familiar with information technology start-ups to head up

(continues)

CASE 3-1 The Troubled Launch of HealthCare.gov
(continued)

the implementation. In late 2011, White House Chief Technology Officer Aneesh Chopra informed HHS and CMS officials about fragmented leadership and recommended the appointment of a project CEO. There was no response. In rollout meetings at the White House during the summer of 2013, President Obama "always ended every meeting by saying something to the effect of 'This is all good, but remember it won't matter, if we don't get the technology right.'"[11] However, the cost-oriented economics staff and the Chief Technology Officers, Chopra at the White House and Todd Park at HHS, were shut out of the process. Senior White House and HHS policy-oriented individuals had no experience with ecommerce start-ups, and CMS leadership thought their experience with large transactional information systems was sufficient to this task. Senior policy staff were more interested in stimulating enrollment and thought good-looking front-end visuals developed directly with experienced contractors meant the project was on track.

As the 2013 elections had approached, the White House political staff slowed down or even stopped the critical work at CMS to write more than 10,000 pages of regulations and system specifications rather than stimulate public criticism.[12]

It is fairly clear that little notice of the problems at CMS reached the President. The OIG report notes a climate of not admitting problems or asking for help at CMS. People were in denial or hoping that the next fix would solve their problems.[13] There was also a certain reluctance to bother the president. Valerie Jarrett, the domestic policy advisor with almost daily access to the president, reportedly responded to an early recommendation about program management with, "The President likes to hear solutions, not problems. If there are problems, bring them to Nancy-Ann (de Parle); she is the one the President put in charge."[11] Nancy-Ann, a CMS director during the Clinton administration, had moved up into a domestic policy role.

Brill notes that while House Republican investigative hearings uncovered many revealing documents about the problems at CMS, the memos of biweekly briefings with the president had only passed along positive reports.

CMS

The downgrading of the managerial hub of HealthCare.gov activity from an office to a center made working there less attractive. The key IT person, Henry Chao, deputy HHS chief technology officer, was assigned to the center, but soon returned to his headquarters job. CCIIO had four directors in four years. John Kingsdale, former CEO of the Massachusetts Connector, already at HHS, turned the lead job down citing insufficient authority.[12]

When the deadline and the delays in writing specifications necessitated a rapid response, the center could only choose from a list of preapproved contracts for an "indefinite-delivery, indefinite-quantity" contract. The chosen one, CGI Federal, had worked for CMS but had little experience with ecommerce. It also had a checkered history of system successes and failures. At one point, there were 55 contractors and subs involved, mostly on extensions of existing contracts, but no assigned integrator nor any shared timeline. There was still, however, the arbitrary commitment to the October 1 launch.

After the McKinsey report, CCIIO hired a consulting firm to do a series of "independent verification and validation reports" concerning contractor progress. It was a technically oriented analysis that identified many risks and problems and questioned whether the system had even been designed with sufficient capacity to handle the launch. That July 17 report, however, apparently was not shared with higher levels of management.

During much of the build period, the health insurance companies were on edge about their interactions with CMS. Karen Ignani, head of Americas Health Insurance Plans, had suggested to CMS officials in Baltimore that the site would not be ready. "Why not let October be a month where people can browse, but not buy? Or perhaps you could delay everything a month? What are your contingency plans?" The response had been that there were no contingency plans and that her problems were all "hypothetical."[11]

As the work fell further and further behind and the July 30 launch of a stripped-down system failed, CMS and the contractors added more people. But it was too little, too late. There were no strategic changes in the application, just more resources. The OIG case study referred to this approach negatively as "path dependent." Then certain functions, such as Spanish language capability, were stripped out to be added back after the launch. The employer mandate and the small business exchange had already been set aside.

The Launch and the Turnaround

On October 1 very few potential enrollees got through to the endpoint of a purchase, and a public uproar ensued. Things improved day by day, but only to slightly less disastrous levels. On top of that, the 16-day federal government shutdown occurred on October 1.

> As a small coterie of grim-faced advisers shuffled into the Oval Office on the evening of Oct. 15, President Obama's chief domestic accomplishment was falling apart ... "We created this problem we didn't need to create. ... And it's of our own doing, and it's our most important initiative."[14]

By October 18, the President had had enough and asked Todd Park and advisor Zionts to take over. He essentially told them that they had no financial, contractual, or procurement constraints and needed to get the job done.[15] They called on contacts in the private sector and within a couple of days a new team of technical experts appeared from around the country.

Here the OIG case study can lead someone astray. It talks about the activities of CMS, the contractors, and an "ad hoc technology team." This team included individuals with experience at Google, Amazon, Facebook, and Twitter, and some who had worked on the Obama election information infrastructure. Some had worked at both. Because one could not volunteer, they were signed on as employees of Quality Software Services, Inc., considered one of the more competent existing contractors, but they took the lead on testing and the integration of functions. They first had to see whether the system could be salvaged. They found no measurement system, so the first day they built a "dashboard" and then got CMS to order in standard monitoring systems. They found the system was slowed because all queries went through the same data base, so they followed industry procedure and established a cache of reusable information, which greatly sped up the system They established a project structure of ignoring blame, no hierarchy of rank or badges, and prioritizing risks and working through them systematically.[15] By January 1, the system was operating tolerably and an improved system was launched for the second enrollment with a new lead contractor, Accenture Federal.

Discussion Questions

1. The two tables in this case show implementation issues in this situation. Which are a function of the task the Obama Administration faced and which are inherent in the way government agencies work?

2. What is your opinion of the prioritization of "Quality over On-Time Delivery"?

3. Thompson (2013) argued that the management of HealthCare.gov should have been handled like a military weapon system program. Does that make sense to you?

4. What might Congress have done to enhance the implementation of the Federally Facilitated Marketplace?

5. What can healthcare provider organizations learn from this story? Does the story fit with your experience?

CHAPTER ACRONYMS

AHRQ Agency for Healthcare Research and Quality

AMA American Medical Association

ASTHO Association of State and Territorial Health Officials

ATSDR Agency for Toxic Substances and Disease Registry

CCIIO Center of Consumer Information and Insurance Oversight

CDC Centers for Disease Control and Prevention

CMHS Center for Mental Health Services

CMS Centers for Medicare and Medicaid Services

CSAP Center for Substance Abuse Prevention

CSAT Center for Substance Abuse Treatment

DHHS Department of Health and Human Services

DHS Department of Homeland Security

DO Doctor of Osteopathic Medicine

DoD Department of Defense

DOT Department of Transportation

EPA Environmental Protection Agency

FDA Food and Drug Administration

FEMA Federal Emergency Management Agency

HHS Department of Health and Human Services

HITECH Health Information Technology for Economic and Clinical Health

HRSA Health Resources and Services Administration

IHS Indian Health Service

LHD Local health department

MD Doctor of Medicine

MPA Master of Public Administration

MPH Master of Public Health

NACCHO National Association of County and City Health Officials

NIH National Institutes of Health

OCIIO Office of Consumer Information and Insurance Oversight

OIG Office of the Inspector General

OIS Office of Information Services

OSHA Occupational Safety and Health Administration

SAMHSA Substance Abuse and Mental Health Services Administration

TANF Temporary Assistance for Needy Families

VA Department of Veterans Affairs

VHA Veterans Health Administration

WHO World Health Organization

WIC Supplemental Nutrition Program for Women, Infants, and Children

References

1. Dawes DE. *The Political Determinants of Health*, Johns Hopkins University Press; 2020.
2. Johnson JA. *Introduction to Public Health Organizations, Management, and Policy*. Delmar-Cengage Learning; 2013.
3. Kingdon JW. *Agendas, Alternatives, and Public Policies*. Little Brown and Company; 1984.
4. Pollitt CC. *The Essential Public Manager*. McGraw Hill; 2003.
5. Johnson JA, Davey KS. *Essentials of Managing Public Health Organizations*. Jones & Bartlett Learning; 2019.
6. Shi L, Johnson JA. *Public Health Administration: Principles for Population-Based Management*. 4th ed. Jones & Bartlett Learning; 2020.
7. Centers for Disease Control and Prevention. United States public health 101. Accessed September 1, 2021. http://www.cdc.gov/stltpublichealth/docs/usph101.pdf
8. Johnson JA, Anderson DE, Rossow CC. *Health Systems Thinking: A Primer*. Jones & Bartlett Learning; 2020.
9. Dickerson J. System malfunction: how politics, partisanship and spin doomed healthcare.gov. *Slate*. 2013. Accessed September 27, 2016. www.slate.com/article/news_and_politics/politics/2013/11/healthcare_gov_doomed_by_partisnship_and_spin_obamacare_s_failed_launch.html
10. McDonough JE. *Inside national health reform*. University of California Press; 2011.
11. Brill S. *America's bitter pill: money, politics, backroom deals, and the fight to fix our broken healthcare system*. Random House; 2015.
12. Emanuel EJ. *Reinventing American health care*. New York, NY: Public Affairs; 2014.
13. Office of the Inspector General of DHSS (OIG). HealthCare.gov: CMS management of the federal

marketplace: A case study (Document OEI-06-14-00350). 2016. Accessed October 19, 2017. https://oig.hhs.gov/oei/reports/oei-06-14-00350.pdf

14. Stolberg SG, Shear MD. Inside the race to rescue a health care site, and Obama. *New York Times*. 2013. Accessed September 27, 2016. https://archive.nytimes.com/www.nytimes.com/indexes/2013/12/01/todayspaper/index.html

15. Schlesinger LA. The spectacular fall and fix of HealthCare.gov. *Harvard Business School Working Knowledge, Cold Call Podcast*. 2016. Accessed October 27, 2016. http://hbswk.hbs.edu/item/the-spectacular-fall-and-fix-of-healthcare-gov?cid=spmailing-13672695-WK%20Newsletter%2010-26-2016

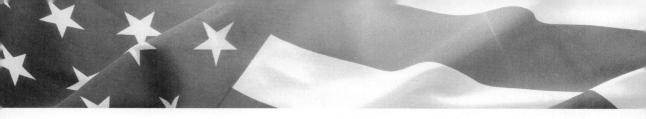

CHAPTER 4

Financing Health Care

CHAPTER OVERVIEW

This chapter reviews the most current data available on National Healthcare Expenditures (NHEs) and sources of payment. It also provides a historical overview of the developments that played major roles in creating the current national healthcare financing infrastructure in the United States. Major factors that affect healthcare costs are discussed as well. Significant trends in healthcare cost and quality are reviewed, along with underlying reasons for changes. The roles of the private sector and government as payers are presented. The chapter concludes with a discussion of legislation that is impacting healthcare financing and reimbursement.

Financing refers to "any mechanism that gives people the ability to pay for health care services."[1] U.S. healthcare financing continues to evolve and is shaped by a variety of influences or factors, including provider, employer, purchaser, consumer, and political factors. These influences produce major tensions that are reflected in ongoing political debates and policy discussions. Financing issues include the role and responsibility of the government as a payer, financial responsibilities of employers as purchasers of health insurance, the impact of payment systems on quality, and other issues. Despite recent health policies, controlling the rising healthcare costs, meeting the needs of aging Americans, reducing health disparities, ensuring health equity, and finding coverage options for uninsured Americans continue to pose fiscal challenges to the U.S. health system.[2]

▶ Overview of National Healthcare Expenditures

National Healthcare Expenditures (NHEs) and trends are reported annually by the National Center for Health Statistics (NCHS), which is part of the Centers for Disease Control and Prevention (CDC); the U.S. Department of Health and Human Services (HHS); and the Centers for Medicare &

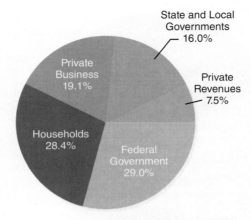

FIGURE 4-1 National Health Expenditures by Funding Source: United States, 2019

Developed by Kim Davey. Based on data from Centers for Medicare & Medicaid Services. NHE fact sheet. Updated December 16, 2020. Accessed February 19, 2021. https://www.cms.gov/Research-Statistics-Data
-and-Systems/Statistics-Trends-and-Reports/NationalHealthExpendData/NHE-Fact-Sheet

Medicaid Services (CMS). Two broad categories of NHEs, historical and projected, are reported. Historical NHEs reflect "annual health spending in the United States by type of good or service delivered (hospital care, physician, and clinical services, retail prescription drugs, etc.), source of funding for those services (private health insurance, Medicare, Medicaid, out-of-pocket spending, etc.) and by sponsor (business, households and governments)."[3] NHE projections "are based on the historical health expenditures and are estimates of spending for health care in the United States over the next decade. Projections are presented by type of good or service delivered (hospital care, physician and clinical services, retail prescriptions, etc.) and by source of funding for those services (private health insurance Medicare, Medicaid, out-of-pocket spending, etc.)."[3] In the United States, NHEs are funded from both public and private sources. In 2019 the federal government financed the largest share of total health spending (29%) followed by households (28.4%), private businesses (19%), state and local governments (16%), and private revenues (7.5%), as shown in **FIGURE 4-1**.[4] The following sections provide an in-depth analysis of how the U.S. health system is financed, starting with an in-depth discussion of NHEs.

In the United States, NHEs grew by 4.6% and totaled more than $3.8 trillion in 2019. This represented 17.7% of the gross domestic product (GDP), or $11,582 per person.[4,5] Looking at total healthcare spending by service category is helpful, as shown in **FIGURE 4-2**. GDP is the broadest quantitative measure of a nation's total economic activity, representing the monetary value of all goods and services produced within a nation's geographic borders over a specified period. Spending is highest for hospital services (31%), followed by spending for physician and clinic services (20%), prescription drugs (10%), nursing care (5%), dental services (4%), home health care (3%), and other health spending that includes nondurable products, residential care, administration, and other state and federal expenditures (27%).[4,5]

NHEs are projected to grow at an average annual growth rate of 5.2% between 2019–2028 and reach $6.2 trillion by 2028. NHEs are projected to grow by 1.1% from 2019–2028, faster than the annual GDP. By 2028, NHEs are projected to represent 19.7% of the GDP, up from 17.7% in 2019. Healthcare spending increases that exceed growth in the overall GDP are not sustainable. This is because the percentage of the GDP used for health care absorbs an increasing share of individuals'

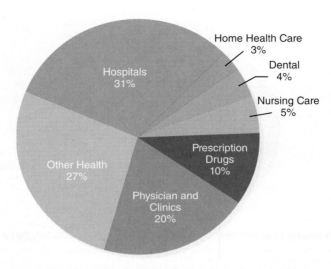

Notes: 'Other health' includes spending on other non-durable products, residential and personal care, administration, and other state and federal expenditures.

FIGURE 4-2   Total Health Spending by Service Category: United States, 2019

Reproduced from Kamal R, McDermott D, Ramirez G, Cox C. How has U.S. Spending on healthcare changed over time? Peterson-KFF Health System Tracker. Published December 23, 2020. Accessed June 9, 2021. https://www.healthsystemtracker.org/chart-collection/u-s-spending-healthcare-changed-time/#item-usspendingovertime_7

incomes and governmental budgets, constraining consumption of other goods and services, with resulting undesirable effects on the national economy.

Healthcare spending has increased across all funding or payer sources. Private health insurance spending grew by 2.9% to $1,195 billion and represented 31% of total NHEs in 2019. Medicare spending grew by 6.7% to $799.4 billion and represented 21% of total NHEs in 2019. Medicaid spending grew by 2.9% to $613.5 billion and represented 16% of total NHEs. From 2018–2028, Medicare is projected to experience the fastest spending grow, with an annual growth rate of 7.6%, since the program was passed in 1965. This growth is fueled by an aging population that is projected to demand more healthcare products and services in the future. Medicare program enrollment is projected to continue to set historic records, which will place pressure on the federal budget. Out-of-pocket spending grew by 3.7% to $1,195.1 billion and represented 31% of total NHEs. Hospital expenditures grew by 6.2% to $1.192 billion, which was significantly faster than the 4.2% growth rate in 2018. Physician and clinical services expenditures grew to $772.1 million, which was also significantly faster than the 4% growth rate in 2018. Prescription drug spending increased by 5.7% to $369.7 billion, which was also significantly faster than the 3.8% growth rate in 2018.[4] Healthcare spending continues to increase across the U.S. health system along with health policies aimed at controlling and reducing costs where possible. Case 4-1 provides an opportunity to craft future health policy to address NHEs in the U.S.

The global COVID-19 pandemic has impacted every aspect of the U.S. healthcare system, including healthcare expenditures. As of 2021, the pandemic has resulted in a historic decline of 0.5% in U.S. healthcare spending. Spending on health services and prescription drugs were both down amid the pandemic. The United States and the world experienced an economic slowdown with reports of lower national GDPs. Despite this downturn, health care still represented a significant and larger portion of the GDP in the United States.[6] Signs in early 2021 indicate that the spending decline may be temporary as better surveillance and control of the virus is achieved. The pandemic will continue to shape and reshape healthcare expenditures in the future as the health system and other sectors of society recover. The following section discusses key drivers of healthcare expenditures in the United States.

▶ Drivers of Healthcare Expenditures

Numerous interrelated factors contribute to healthcare expenditures. As discussed briefly below, key factors include:

- Aging population
- New drugs and medical technology
- Emphasis on specialty medicine
- Large numbers of uninsured and underinsured people
- Volume-based reimbursement incentives
- Labor intensity
- Waste, fraud, and abuse

Aging Population

NHEs are influenced by a variety of factors; an important one is age. Generally, individuals demand more health services and products as they age. Estimates in 2019 placed the population of people 65 years of age and older at 54.2 million, or 16.5% of the population.[7] NHEs by age reveal that personal health spending per person was higher for those over the age of 55, which accounted for 56% of all health spending in the United States.[8] For individuals 55 and over, average personal health spending per person was $6,832.75 in 2016, which was four times higher than average spending per child ($1,791.5) and almost two times higher than average spending for working-age individuals ($4,148).[8] People over the age of 65 are the major consumers of inpatient hospital care. According to the most recent federal data, these individuals account for more than one-third of all hospital stays and nearly one-half of all days of hospital care.[9] In addition, Medicare beneficiaries with chronic conditions account for the majority of all Medicare spending. Thus, a focus on prevention and primary care have taken center stage in the Medicare program and the broader health system. Preventing or stopping the progression of chronic health conditions translates to reduced morbidity and mortality in addition to financial savings for all payer types. Aging has a large effect on federal health spending due to virtually all Americans' eligibility for Medicare at age 65.[10]

Drugs and Medical Technology

New pharmacologic agents, as well as medical and diagnostic technology and services, come at a high price. From 1960 to 2017, retail prescription drug spending in the United States increased from $90 to $1,025 per capita (inflation-adjusted). Out-of-pocket spending on prescription drugs was $144 per capita in 2017, but is projected to increase by over 30% by 2026 for Americans covered by both public and private insurance. From 2014–2018, the price for common generic drugs dropped 37% while the prices for brand-name drugs increased by over 60%. Specialty drugs and few drug patents expiring are driving drug spending and costs. Affordability is an increasing concern for Americans, with one in four Americans reporting difficulty in affording their medications. Older Americans have higher drug spending, which makes prescription drug costs an important cost driver for the Medicare program.[11]

Technologically advanced diagnostic and treatment innovations require expensive equipment, computerization, and highly trained personnel. The large capital investments to finance technological innovations drove economic and professional incentives for their use, unbounded by requirements to justify their cost or the validity of their clinical benefits. The tendency to favor broad, rather than discretionary, use of technology grew with rapidly increasing availability of new technology and its profitability. This is discussed in more detail in Chapter 11.

Focus on Specialty Care

Growth in specialized medicine or care occurred as medical science and technology advanced. Americans' preference for specialty care results in high utilization and rapidly rising costs. Unlike other developed nations, where physician specialists represent half or fewer of physicians, most active physicians in the United States are specialists.[12] This is discussed in more detail in Chapter 5. Since the 1940s, when employers offset post-World War II wage controls with fully paid health insurance benefits, working Americans were insulated from healthcare costs. Americans demanded what they perceived as the "best" care, placing a high value on the use of expensive specialty care. For most, the costs of treatment were irrelevant, and physicians' recommendations were uninhibited by economic considerations for their well-insured patients. Historically, U.S. health insurance models carried no prohibitions against patient self-referrals to specialty care until the 1980s, when managed care placed strong restrictions on patient self-referrals to specialists.

Uninsured and Underinsured Populations

According to United States Census Bureau, among all developed countries of the world, the United States has the highest proportion of population without health insurance coverage. Without health insurance, individuals often do not receive timely preventive, acute, or chronic care. Frequently, this results in their using high-cost emergency care. Un- and underinsured individuals tend to delay seeking care and are more likely than insured individuals to enter care in later stages of disease and require hospitalization.[13] This is discussed in more detail later in the chapter.

Reimbursement Shift from Volume to Value

Both private and government healthcare financing mechanisms continue to be major influences in volume-driven healthcare expenditures. Fee-for-service reimbursement that financially rewards the volume of services delivered continues to provide profit-driven incentives that drive healthcare expenditures. Despite earlier reforms, such as the prospective hospital payment reimbursement system of the 1980s and managed care, the fee-for-service system is still largely in use today. Recent health policies are attempting to move financial incentives toward value-based rather than volume-based approaches. This is discussed in more detail later in the chapter and throughout the textbook.

Labor Intensity

Health care is a labor-intensive industry that employs some of the most highly educated, trained, and compensated individuals in the United States workforce. As such, it is inherently expensive. Employment growth due to technology, the aging population, and other factors are anticipated to continue as significant drivers of healthcare expenditures. This is discussed in more detail in Chapter 5.

Waste, Fraud, and Abuse

The U.S. healthcare system is big business. Just how big? NHEs totaled more than $3.8 trillion in 2019 and are projected to grow at an average annual rate of 5.2% between 2019–2028, reaching $6.2 trillion by 2028, as previously mentioned. The sheer size and complexity of the system means that it is likely to experience waste, fraud, and abuse (see **FIGURE 4-3**). Any of these can cause harm and incur significant costs to individual patients, providers, communities, or the health system at large. The Office of the Inspector General (OIG) defines waste as "the thoughtless or careless expenditure, mismanagement, or abuse of resources to the detriment (or potential detriment) of the United States government. Waste also includes incurring unnecessary costs resulting from inefficient or ineffective practices, systems, or controls."[14] An article published in the *Journal of the American Medical Association* estimated that medical waste accounts for 20–25% of total medical spending. The study identified administrative costs as the largest source of waste, at approximately $226 billion annually. Prices are the second-largest source of waste identified in the article and estimated at $231 to $241 billion annually. The study also identified inefficient, low-value, and uncoordinated care (e.g., lack of preventive care, preventable complications, avoidable admissions, and readmissions) as additional sources of waste that cost the U.S. health system around $205 billion annually. The article found it concerning that the scientific literature did not suggest any recommendations for ways to reduce waste.[15] Future health policies and regulations will be aimed at reducing healthcare waste, fraud, and abuse across the health system (see **FIGURE 4-4**).

The federal government recovered $2.6 billion from healthcare fraud cases in 2019.[16] The persistence of medical fraud has led to a number of laws and regulations, which will be discussed

WASTE	The OIG defines waste as, "the thoughtless or careless expenditure, mismanagement, or abuse of resources to the detriment (or potential detriment) of the U.S. government. Waste also includes incurring unnecessary cost resulting from inefficient or ineffective practices, systems, or controls."
FRAUD	The OIG defines fraud as, "wrongful or criminal deception intended to result in financial or personal gain. Fraud includes false representation of fact, making false statements, or by concealment of information."
ABUSE	The OIG defines abuse as, "excessive or improper use of a thing, or to use something in a manner contrary to the natural or legal rules for its use. Abuse can occur in financial or non-financial settings."

FIGURE 4-3 What Is Healthcare Waste, Fraud, and Abuse?

Developed by Kim Davey. Based on information from the U.S. Agency for International Development Office of Inspector General. What is considered fraud, waste, or abuse? Published April 16, 2018. Accessed February 19, 2021. https://oig.usaid.gov/node/221

in the following sections. The Office of the Inspector General defines fraud as "wrongful or criminal deception intended to result in financial or personal gain. Fraud includes false representation of fact, making false statements, or by concealment of information."[14] Examples of fraud include billing for unnecessary medical services, misrepresenting diagnoses or procedures to increase reimbursements, paying for referrals, billing for no-show patient appointments, upcoding for medical services or procedures, or billing for services that were not provided or documented in a patient's medical record. Committing fraud can result in criminal, civil, and administrative liability and be punished with penalties, fines, and even imprisonment. Additionally, providers can lose their practice licenses, while organizations can be prohibited from participating in federal healthcare programs like Medicare or Medicaid.[17] Abuse is another problem facing the health system.

The Office of the Inspector General defines abuse as "excessive or improper use of a thing, or to use something in a manner contrary to the natural or legal rules for its use. Abuse can occur in financial or non-financial settings."[14] Examples of abuse include billing for unnecessary services, misusing medical codes on claims such as upcoding to increase reimbursement for medical services, or charging excessively for services or supplies. A study found that physicians reported providing unnecessary care including prescription medications, tests, and procedures. Fear of malpractice was cited at the primary reason for over- and unnecessary treatment, followed by pressure from patients. Physicians recommended several strategies for how to reduce overutilization and potential abuse, such as access to a patient's health records from outside providers and organizations, additional training around billing and coding, and more practice guidelines and technology that integrate practice guidelines into the electronic health record

FALSE CLAIMS ACT	The False Claim Act state that it is illegal to submit claims to Medicare or Medicaid that are knowingly false or fraudulent. The Act also prohibits subpar goods or services to be sold to the federal government.
ANTI-KICKBACK STATUTE	Anti-Kickback Statute prohibits paying for patient referrals or providing remuneration (e.g., cash, free rent, expensive meals, medical consultations, medical directorships) for patient referrals.
PHYSICIAN SELF-REFERRAL LAW	The Physician Self-Referral Law prohibits physicians from referring patients to facilities where a physician or a physician's immediate family member has a financial relationship.
EXCLUSION STATUTE	The Exclusion Statute prevents providers (individuals and entities) from participating in federal healthcare programs if they have been convicted of Medicare or Medicaid fraud, patient abuse or neglect, felony convictions for health-related fraud, theft or other financial misconduct, felony convictions for mishandling of controlled substances, defaulting on health education loan or scholarship obligations, receiving kickbacks, submitting false claims, or loss of practice license.

FIGURE 4-4 Key Legislation to Address Healthcare Fraud and Abuse

Developed by Kim Davey. Based on information from the U.S. Department of Health and Human Services Office of Inspector General. Fraud & Abuse Laws. Published April 16, 2018. Accessed February 19, 2021. https://oig.hhs.gov/compliance/physician-education/fraud-abuse-laws/

system.[18] The difference between fraud and abuse center on facts, circumstances, intent, and knowledge, but are closely related concepts. Providers can be subject to civil and criminal penalties for engaging in healthcare abuse. Additionally, providers can lose their practice license while a health organization can be prohibited from participating in a federal healthcare program like Medicare or Medicaid.[17]

Several laws have been passed to address fraud and abuse (see Figure 4-4). Notable laws include the False Claims Act, Anti-Kickback Statute, the Physician Self-Referral Law (or Stark Law), and the Exclusion Statute. The False Claims Act states that it is illegal to submit claims to Medicare or Medicaid that are knowingly false or fraudulent. The Act also prohibits subpar goods or services to be sold to the federal government. The Anti-Kickback Statute prohibits paying for patient referrals or providing remuneration (e.g., cash, free rent, expensive meals, medical consultations, or medical directorships) for patient referrals. The Physician Self-Referral Law prohibits physicians from referring patients to facilities with which the physician or a physician's immediate family member has a financial relationship. The Exclusion Statute prevents providers (individuals and entities) from participating in federal healthcare programs if they have been convicted of Medicare or Medicaid fraud; patient abuse or neglect; felony convictions for health-related fraud, theft, or other financial misconduct; felony convictions for mishandling of controlled substances; defaulting on health education loan or scholarship obligations; receiving kickbacks; submitting false claims; or have lost their practice license.[17]

▶ International Comparison of National Health Expenditures

Although insured Americans view the U.S. healthcare delivery system as superior to that of other developed nations, there are serious questions regarding the value returned for vastly greater expenditures, while citizens of those other nations experience better health outcomes. The Organisation for Economic Co-operation and Development (OECD) is composed of 37 nations committed to democratic principles and economic progress.[19] One of its functions is the compilation of comprehensive comparable statistics on health and health systems across its members.[20] The most recent OECD report, based on 2019 data, notes that U.S. health spending, at 17% of the GDP, is an outlier when compared to other countries, who devote an average of 9.6% to health spending.[21] The United States spends twice as much on health care in comparison with peer or comparable countries, as shown in **FIGURE 4-5**. Spending in the United States has and continues to be driven by payments to hospitals and physicians, as shown in Figure 4-1.[22]

A 2020 Commonwealth Fund report compared the United States to 10 other high-income OECD members. The report included a comparison of healthcare spending, use of services, and prices. The United States had the highest spending, service utilization, and prices. The United States was also the only country in the study group that did not have universal healthcare.[23] Some key findings from the report included:

- The United States spends the most money on health care as a percentage of the GDP, yet it has the lowest life expectancy. OECD members spend 8.8% of their GDP on health care compared with the United States, which spent 16.9% of its GDP on health care in 2019. In 2019, life expectancy in the United States was 78.6 years versus the OECD average of 80.7.[23]

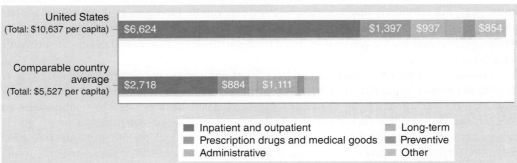

Note: Comparable countries include Austria, Belgium, Canada, France, Germany, Netherlands, Sweden, Switzerland, and the United Kingdom.

FIGURE 4-5 **U.S. Health Spending Compared to Average Peer Country Spending, 2018**

Reproduced from Kurani N, Cox C. What drives health spending in the U.S. compared to other countries. Peterson-KFF Health System Tracker. Published September 25, 2020. Accessed June 11, 2021. https://www.healthsystemtracker.org/brief/what-drives-health-spending-in-the-u-s-compared-to-other-countries/

- The United States also has the highest chronic disease burden at 28%, with more than one-quarter of the U.S. population reporting two or more chronic health conditions. As a result, it has the highest rate of avoidable deaths in the world.[23]
- U.S. per capita private spending for health insurance and other related costs was more than five times the amount spent in Canada, the second-highest-spending country.[23]
- Public per capita spending in the United States was $4,993 and comparable to the OECD average of $3,038. However, Americans have significantly more private and out-of-pocket spending on health care than other OECD members.[23]
- Suicide rates are the highest in the United States, at 13.9 deaths per 100,000. The OECD average is 11.5 deaths per 100,000.[23]
- The United States has the highest rate of obesity, with 40% of the population classified as obese. The average obesity rate for OECD members was 21%. This increases the risks of the developing one or more chronic health conditions such as diabetes, cardiovascular disease, and many other chronic health conditions.[23] These conditions are often expensive to treat and manage over the course of an individual's life.
- The United States has fewer physicians (2.6 per 1,000 people) and fewer annual physician visits (4.0 average visits per capita) when compared with other OECD countries (as of 2019 OECD data).[23]
- The United States uses more expensive technology than other countries, which drives up the cost of care.[23]
- Hospitalization from preventable causes in the United States is among the highest, second only to Germany.[23]
- The United States was the only country whose share of GDP for healthcare spending exceeded the share of GDP expended for social services. The report suggests that the relatively low spending on social services in the United States may be a contributor to poor individual and population health outcomes because health disparities are inadequately addressed.[23]

Financing is an important building block of any health system, as discussed in Chapter 1. Health systems have different funding models, with the U.S. model possibly the most unique and complex in the world. The following sections take a closer look at who is paying for healthcare products and services in the United States and how they are doing so.

▶ Insurance

Basic Insurance Concepts

Insurance is a mechanism for protecting people and organizations from risk.[24] Risk refers "to the possibility of a substantial financial loss from some event."[1] Patients and providers face financial risks, among others, associated with receiving and providing care. Patients may not have sufficient resources to pay for required medical services or catastrophic life events out of pocket without insurance. An insurance company pools and assumes individual risks through the underwriting process. The term insured refers to individuals that have insurance (or are covered by an insurance plan) that provides protection from the risk of significant financial loss. Enrollee and member are interchangeable terms that refer to individuals that are insured by a private health insurance plan. Beneficiary is the term used to refer to individuals that are insured by a public health insurance plan because they are receiving a benefit from the government. Insurance pools individual risks and spreads them over a group so that the financial risk is shared by the group through premiums. Members or beneficiaries also engage in cost sharing, which allows those insured to share some of the risk.

The four main types of cost sharing are premium cost sharing, deductibles, copayments, and coinsurance. A premium refers to the amount members or beneficiaries generally pay for health insurance bi-weekly or monthly. Employer-sponsored health insurance generally requires employees to pay a portion of the insurance premium through wage or payroll deductions, while Medicare beneficiaries pay some premiums out-of-pocket or have a supplemental health insurance plan to help pay for coverage gaps. Insured individuals, covered through both private and public plans, pay for a portion of healthcare costs out-of-pocket through deductibles and copayments. A deductible is the amount the insured must first pay before the insurance plan begins to pay.[1,25] Deductibles vary significantly and plans may have more than one type of deductible (e.g., hospital, outpatient surgery). Copayments and coinsurance are another form of cost-sharing commonly encountered by individuals covered by both private and public plans. The purpose of cost-sharing is to reduce the misuse of insurance benefits.[1] A copayment is a fixed payment amount an insured individual pays for healthcare services after the deductible has been paid or met. For example, a patient could pay $30 for primary care visits and $50 for specialty care provider visits after the patient has met the deductible for their health insurance plan.[26] Coinsurance is a percentage an insured individual pays for healthcare services after the deductible has been paid or met. For example, a patient could pay 20% of $100, or $20, while the health insurance company pays the rest.[27] Insurance plans that utilize coinsurance often have a stop-loss provision. A stop-loss provision is the maximum out-of-pocket payment an insured individual would be required to pay before the plan pays 100% of costs.[1]

Cost sharing is a strategy to control health service utilization and costs. Health insurance leaves insured individuals unaware of the full cost of the service they are receiving and can lead to overutilization or over consumption of health services. Cost sharing makes individuals more sensitive to the costs associated with medical services, which promotes more responsible behavior and utilization.[28] Insurance desensitizes consumers to healthcare costs, which can lead to higher utilization and costs. This is referred to as moral hazard. Moral hazard refers to consumer behavior that leads to higher utilization of healthcare services when the services are covered by insurance.[29] Providers can also create demand for health services and drive up costs through provider-induced demand. Providers, like consumers, are desensitized to service prices and as a result can deliver additional and more expensive services that consumers would not likely use if they had to pay for them out of pocket. Both moral hazard and provider-induced demand contribute to healthcare waste. In response, many countries have implemented supply-side rationing, which focuses on restricting the availability of expensive medical technology and specialty care. Rationing care has been a controversial topic in the United States.[1]

Health insurance plays an important role in the U.S. healthcare system. Several different types of health insurance exist in the United States. There are private forms of health insurance, like employer-sponsored health insurance, and public forms of health insurance like Medicare, Medicaid, and the Children's Health Insurance Program. There are four types of private insurance: group insurance, individual private insurance, self-insurance, and managed care plans. Group insurance refers to when individuals purchase insurance in a group, such as through their employer, which will spread risk among the group members. Individual private health insurance is a type of insurance individuals can purchase directly from an insurer for themselves or their family. This is an option for individuals that are self-employed, for example. Self-insurance or self-funded insurance are health insurance programs that are implemented and controlled by a company itself because the company is large and diversified enough in terms of risk to offer its own insurance rather than paying insurers. Large employers can budget sufficient funds to pay medical claims incurred by their employees, and these plans will often be administered by a private insurer such as Blue Cross Blue Shield. This gives employers control over their health plan.[1] Managed care plans are the type of programs that combine administrative and service costs to achieve better cost control.[1,30] Managed care plays an important role in both public and private insurance plans. The history and evolution of private insurance with a focus on managed care is presented below and then followed by a discussion of public health insurance.

▶ Private Insurance

Evolution of Private Health Insurance

As early as the mid-1800s, a movement by benevolent societies and unions began to insure workers against lost wages resulting from work-related accidents. Later, insurance to cover lost wages resulting from catastrophic illness was added to accident policies.[1,30] It was not until the 1930s that health insurance began paying part or all costs of medical treatment. The basic concept of health insurance is antithetical to the central premise by which "insurance" was historically defined. Whereas insurance originally guarded against the low risk of rare occurrences such as premature death and accidents, the health insurance model that evolved provided coverage for predictable and discretionary uses of the healthcare system as well as unforeseen and unpredictable health events. Known as indemnity insurance because it protected individuals from a portion of financial risk associated with the costs of care, health insurance companies set allowable charges for services, and providers could bill the patient for any excess.[31] Coverage for routine healthcare services added a new dimension to the concept of insurance. Indemnity coverage prevailed until the advent of managed care in the 1970s.

The Rise of Blue Cross and Blue Shield and Commercial Health Insurance

In 1930, a group of Baylor University teachers contracted with Baylor Hospital in Dallas, Texas, to provide coverage for hospital expenses.[1,31] This arrangement created a model for the development of what was to become Blue Cross, a private, not-for-profit insurance empire that grew over the next 4 decades into the dominant form of health insurance in the United States. The Blue Shield plans providing physician payments began shortly after Blue Cross, and by the early 1940s, numerous Blue Shield plans were operating across the country.[24]

The establishment and subsequent growth of the "Blues" signaled a new era in U.S. healthcare delivery and financing. They played a significant role in establishing hospitals as the centers of medical care proliferation and technology and, by reimbursing for expensive services, they put hospital care easily within the reach of middle-class working Americans for the first time. The insulation from costs of care provided by the Blues had a major impact on utilization. By the late 1930s, annual hospital admission rates for Blue Cross enrollees were 50% higher on average than for the nation as a whole.[32] In addition to contributing to increased utilization of hospital services by removing financial barriers, the Blue Cross movement had other lasting impacts on national policy making. Rosemary Stevens noted, "In the United States, the brave new world of medicine was specialized, interventionist, mechanistic and expensive—at least as interpreted, through prepayment, for workers in major organizations."[32] By 1940, the Blue Cross movement was a major financing alternative that suppressed forces that had long lobbied for a form of national health insurance, a concept opposed vehemently by private medicine.[1,32]

Uniform features of all Blue Cross plans included not-for-profit status, supervision by state insurance departments, direct payments through contracts with providers, and the use of community rating. Community-rated insurance allowed all individuals in a defined group to pay single premiums without regard to age, gender, occupation, or health status.[24,31] Community rating helped ensure nondiscrimination against groups with varying risk characteristics to provide coverage at reasonable rates for the community as a whole.

For-profit commercial health insurers entered the market in significant numbers in the decade following the start of Blue Cross and Blue Shield. However, as the commercial insurers entered the marketplace, they used experience-rated insurance and based premiums on groups' historically documented patterns of claims.[1] Unbounded by the requirement for community rating by the not-for-profit Blues, they used experience rating to charge higher premiums to less-healthy individuals and successfully competed for the market of healthier individuals by offering lower premiums. By the early 1950s, commercial insurers had enrolled more subscribers than the Blues.[33] To remain competitive, the Blues were forced to switch to experience-rated insurance to avoid attracting a disproportionate share of high-risk individuals for whom commercial insurance was prohibitively expensive.[32]

▶ Transformation of Health Insurance: Managed Care

The transformation occurred for many reasons. In summary, it resulted from concerns over rising costs and quality issues. Today, health insurance in the United States is synonymous with managed care and managed care organizations (MCOs), also known by the term "health plans." These are the means through which almost all Americans receive health insurance coverage.

Throughout the 1960s and early 1970s, rapidly increasing expenditures accompanied by quality concerns captured the attention of government and private policy makers. Medicare costs were spiraling upward with concerns about quality, and in the private sector, large employers, as the primary private health insurance purchasers, advocated for changes to control costs.[24] These concerns and other factors ultimately resulted in the Nixon administration's proposal for the Health Maintenance Organization (HMO) Act, which was enacted in 1973.[32] Although many employer groups had used principles of managed care in prior decades through contracts with healthcare providers to serve employees on a prepaid basis, provisions of the HMO Act opened participation to the employer-based market, allowing the rapid proliferation of managed care plans.[24] The HMO Act of 1973 provided loans and grants for the planning, development, and implementation of combined insurance and healthcare delivery organizations and required that comprehensive preventive and primary care services be included in the HMO arrangements. The legislation mandated employers with 25 or more employees to offer an HMO option if one was available in their area.[31]

HMOs combined providers and insurers into one organizational entity. Managed care is population-based rather than individually based. The population basis enables the insurer to actuarially determine projected use of services related to age, gender, occupation, and other factors. Population groups' claims histories are used to set premium levels. All forms of managed care entail interdependence between the provision of and payment for healthcare services. It is a system through which care-providing groups or networks and beneficiaries share financial risk with an insurer for medical care and health maintenance. By linking insurance with service delivery and financial risk, managed care intended to reverse the financial incentives in the fee-for-service model, which historically had rewarded providers financially for service volume and focused on illness treatment rather than prevention.

Financial risk sharing between insurers and providers in managed care took two primary forms. The first form is prepayment, or capitation, through which providers are paid a preset amount in advance for services their insured population is projected to need in a given period. Capitation pays providers for services on a per-member per-month basis. Under capitation, providers receive payment whether services are used or not. If providers exceed the predetermined payment level, they may suffer financial penalties. If providers use fewer resources than projected, they may retain the excess as profit. The second form of financial risk sharing is withholds, in which a percentage of the monthly capitated fee is withheld from provider payments to cover potential cost overruns for services such as specialty referrals or hospitalizations. All, part, or none of the withholds may be returned to providers at the end of specified period, depending on financial performance.[31] The key element of all provider prepayment arrangements is cost-conscious, efficient, and effective care. For beneficiaries, managed care transfers financial risk in two forms: copayments and deductibles.

Staff Model

Initially, there were two major types of HMOs. The first was a staff model. It employed groups of physicians to provide most healthcare needs of its members. HMOs often provided some specialty services within the organization and many contracted for services with community specialists. In the staff model, the HMO operated facilities in which its physicians practiced, providing on-site support services such as radiology, laboratory, and pharmacy. The HMO purchased hospital care and other services for its members through fee-for-service or prepaid contracted arrangements. Staff model HMOs were referred to as "closed panel" because they employed the physicians who provided most of their members' care, and those physicians did not provide services outside the HMO membership. Similarly, community-based physicians could not participate in HMO member care without authorization by the HMO.[31]

Individual Practice Associations

The second type of HMO stimulated by the 1973 legislation was the Individual Practice Association (IPA). IPAs are physician organizations composed of community-based, independent physicians in solo or group practices that provide services to HMO members. An IPA HMO did not operate facilities in which members received care, but rather provided its members services through private physician office practices. Like the staff model HMO, the IPA HMO purchased hospital care and specialty services not available through IPA-participating physicians from other providers on a prepaid or fee-for-service basis. Some IPA HMOs allowed physicians to have a nonexclusive relationship that permitted treatment of nonmembers as well as members; however, HMO relationships with an IPA also could be established on an exclusive basis. In this scenario, an HMO took the initiative in recruiting and organizing community physicians into an IPA to serve its members. Because the HMO was the organizing entity in such an arrangement, it was common for the HMO to require exclusivity by the IPA, limiting its services only to that HMO's membership.[31] The staff model and IPA-type organizations illustrate two major types of HMOs, but many hybrid forms of MCOs emerged throughout the 1980s and 1990s in response to cost and quality concerns as well as to purchaser and consumer preferences. The following sections summarize two examples.

Preferred Provider Organizations

Preferred provider organizations (PPOs) are managed care plans that may be owned by various types of organizations such as HMOs, hospitals, physician groups, and physician/hospital joint venture groups.[34] PPOs contract for services from physicians, hospitals, and other healthcare providers to form a network of participating preferred providers who agree to a PPO's cost and utilization control parameters. Employer health benefit plans and health insurance companies may contract with PPOs to purchase healthcare services for their beneficiaries. PPOs exercise purchasing power by negotiating payment rates for services with providers. PPOs derive this power by covering large groups of beneficiaries. Participating providers benefit from a guaranteed flow of business, and physicians are not required to share in financial risk as a condition of participation. By providing predictable admission volume, PPOs help hospitals to project occupancy rates and revenue. Beneficiaries benefit because PPOs do not restrict the use of out-of-network providers. However, using out-of-network providers does incur additional costs, typically in the form of higher copayments.[31] In 2020, PPOs were the most popular managed care plans, encompassing 48% of covered workers among large employers and 45% of covered workers among small employers, as shown in **FIGURE 4-6**.[34]

Point-of-Service Plans

A point-of-service (POS) plan is a hybrid of HMO and PPO plans. It is called "point-of-service" because beneficiaries can select whether to use a provider in a POS-approved network or seek care outside the POS plan network when a particular medical need arises. Although POS plans require beneficiaries to select an in-network primary care provider, POS plans offer the flexibility

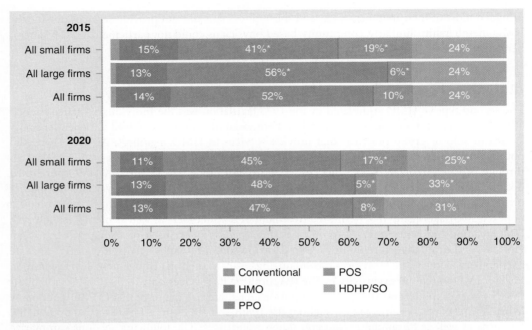

*Enrollment in plan type is statistically different between all small firms and all large firms within year (p < .05).

NOTE: Small firms have 3–199 workers and large firms have 200 or more workers. HMO is health maintenance organization. PPO is preferred provider organization. POS is point-of-service plan. HDHP/SO is high-deductible health plan with a savings option, such as a health reimbursement arrangement (HRA) or health savings account (HSA).

FIGURE 4-6 Distribution of Health Plan Enrollment for Covered Workers, by Plan Type and Firm Size: United States, 2015 and 2020

Reproduced from Kaiser Family Foundation. Employer Health Benefits Survey, 2020. Published October 8, 2020. Accessed June 6, 2021. https://www.kff.org/report-section/ehbs-2020-summary-of-findings/

to choose providers outside of an MCO's approved provider network without requirement of a referral. However, like in PPOs, selecting an out-of-network provider without a primary care referral can incur significant out-of-pocket costs. In 2020, POS plans represented 5% of large firms and 17% of covered employee enrollment in firms with fewer than 200 workers, as shown in Figure 4-6.[34]

Evolution of Managed Care Models

The organizational forms of managed care continued to evolve because of changing market-place conditions, including purchaser preferences, beneficiary demands, and other factors. With the numbers and types of managed care organizations, clear distinctions among them are no longer possible. The emergence of PPOs as the most popular beneficiary choice represented a means to involve insurers and providers in negotiating fees and monitoring utilization while giving beneficiaries more choice. Today, the staff model HMO is almost nonexistent due to many factors, including beneficiary demands for more choice of providers, large capital outlays associated with facility maintenance, and increased competition from IPA models.

Managed Care Backlash

Throughout the 1990s, market factors that enabled large health insurance purchasers to aggressively negotiate provider arrangements contributed to the impact of expenditure-cutting managed care initiatives. The surge in managed care enrollment in the 1990s with decreases in premiums contributed to a decline in the average annual growth of national healthcare expenditures.[35] However, a managed care "backlash" was brewing and began in the late 1990s when organized medicine, other healthcare providers, and consumers protested MCO policies on choice of providers, referrals, and other practices that were viewed as unduly restrictive.[31] A federal commission was established to review the need for guidelines in the managed care industry. In 1998, President Clinton signed legislation that imposed patient protection requirements on private insurance companies providing health coverage to federal workers. Public dissatisfaction with constraints over the right to receive necessary care and the freedom of physicians to refer patients to specialists received wide publicity. Ultimately, the states took the lead in the patients' rights arena and, beginning in 1998, state legislatures enacted more than 900 laws and regulations addressing both consumer and provider protections.[1,36] Over the years, expanded beneficiary choices, patient rights' legislation, rescindments of physician restrictions on referrals, and other factors have served to reverse many of the issues that spawned the backlash.[31] This opened the door to plans that provided more consumer choice; however, consumer choice resulted in higher prices. This resulted in rising healthcare costs and new plans, like high-deductible health plans, that are trying to provide consumer choice but control costs by shifting more of the cost of care to individual plan members.

▶ Employer-Sponsored Health Insurance

Employer-sponsored health insurance is the predominant form of health insurance coverage in the United States and covered 157 million people in 2020. Employers view health insurance as an important employment benefit, with 56% of employers offering employer-sponsored health insurance to their employees. Employees perceive the importance of the benefits, with 72% of employees enrolling in employer-sponsored health insurance. Annual employer-sponsored health insurance premiums were $7,470 for single coverage and $21,342 for family coverage in 2020; both increased by 4%. Employees contribute to employer-sponsored health insurance, and as premiums have increased, so have employee premium contributions. Employees contribute on average 17% ($1,243) for single coverage and 27% ($5,488) for family coverage. PPOs were the dominant employer-sponsored plan type in 2020, with 47% of workers covered. High-deductible health plans with a savings option were the second most popular plan type, representing 31% of employer-sponsored health plans, followed by 13% of employers offering an HMO plan, 8% offering a POS plan, and 1% offering an indemnity plan. Most employer-sponsored health plans, 67%, were self-funded as of 2020, which was up by 6% over the prior year. In addition to premium contributions, deductibles are another way employees engage in cost sharing with their employers. Employee contributions have increased over 25% in the last 5 years and 79% over the last 10 years. The percentage of employees with an annual deductible over $2,000 increased from 19% in 2015 to 26% in 2020.[34]

High-deductible health plans (HDHPs) are emerging form of private health insurance that is growing in popularity among employers and employees. In 2020, HDHPs grew as a form of coverage, with 33% of employees in large firms and 25% in small firms enrolling in these types of health plans. This trend is important because HDHPs substantially increase employees' financial risk for their healthcare costs. HDHPs have lower monthly premiums but higher deductibles when compared to other types of plans. For example, in 2020, an HDHP was a plan that had a deductible of least $1,400 for an individual and $2,800 for a family. Further, a HDHP's total yearly out-of-pocket expenses, including deductibles, copayments, and coinsurance, cannot be more than $6,900 for an individual or $13,800 for a family for in-network services and providers.[37] HDHPs can be combined with either health savings accounts or health reimbursement accounts and are then referred to as consumer-directed health plans (CDHPs). The name recognizes that this type of coverage increases the role consumers play in seeking or shopping for services. The deductible is the amount individuals must pay out of pocket before insurance coverage begins. While in theory, requiring out-of-pocket spending should promote consumers' prudent choices for care, expert observations and preliminary research are raising some concerns. Only a few of the concerns include: a lack of consumer understanding about how plans actually work, especially about provision of no-or low-cost deductibles for preventive services; evidence that consumers are avoiding necessary and appropriate care due to costs; and evidence that out-of-pocket expenses negatively impact consumers' compliance with medically recommended follow-up care, including use of prescription drugs. Some studies suggest that HDHPs' dampening effects on appropriate use of health services in the short term may lead to costly health consequences in the long term.[38,39] As adoption of HDHPs continues to accelerate and HDHPs impact on ever-larger segments of the population, future longitudinal research findings on the effects of these plans will be central to informing policy decisions.

Employers are increasingly focused on the health and wellness of their employees to reduce health insurance costs for the employee and the employer. Health risk assessments are being offered more and more to employees, with 60% of large employers and 42% of small employers offering this health benefit. Biometric screenings are another health benefit increasingly being offered to employees, with 50% of large employers and 33% of small employers offering this benefit. Employers offer incentives for employees to complete these screenings. Incentives can take the form of reduced insurance premiums, gift cards, contributions to health-related savings accounts, or personal time off. Additionally, employers offer health education and programs such as weight management, smoking cessation, or behavioral coaching to employees to help address any risk areas identified through the screenings.[34] The following section discusses the role public insurance plays in the U.S. health system.

▶ Public Insurance

Federal and state governments and, to a lesser extent, local governments, finance healthcare services. Federal funding originally focused on specific population groups (or categories), providing health care for those in government service, their dependents, and particular population groups, such as Native Americans. Public financing supports categorical programs. Categorical programs are designed to provide benefits to a certain category of people who meet the eligibility criteria to become beneficiaries. Today, a combination of public programs, chief among them the federal Medicare program and the joint federal–state Medicaid program, constitutes over 50% of total national care expenditures.[1,3,10] In addition to Medicare and Medicaid, which operate under HHS in the Centers for Medicare & Medicaid Services, HHS has nine other operating divisions with a very broad spectrum of activities covering the entire lifespan of individuals, health professional development, military and veterans' health services, and research.

Medicare

Were it not for the vigorous opposition of the private sector led by the American Medical Association (AMA), the Social Security Act of 1935, the most significant social legislation ever enacted by the U.S. government, would have included a form of national health insurance. It took 30 more years, during which time many presidential and congressional Acts for national health insurance had been proposed and defeated, until Congress enacted Medicare, "Health Insurance for the Aged," as Title XVIII of the Social Security Act Amendments of 1965. When Medicare was enacted, approximately one-half of the elderly did not have any type of health insurance. This insurance usually covered only inpatient hospital costs, and much of healthcare spending was paid for out of pocket.[40] Today, Medicare covers 57 million Americans, including most 65 years and older; younger individuals who receive Social Security Disability Insurance benefits; and individuals with end-stage kidney disease and amyotrophic lateral sclerosis (ALS, or Lou Gehrig's disease) following their eligibility for Social Security Disability Insurance benefits.[4] **FIGURE 4-7** provides characteristics of the Medicare population. As noted earlier in this chapter, in 2019 Medicare expenditures totaled $799.4 billion, and they are projected to grow by 7.6% annually from 2018–2028.[4,5] **FIGURE 4-8** shows average annual growth rates for Medicare and private health insurance spending.

The enactment of Medicare legislation was a historical benchmark, signaling government's entry into the personal healthcare financing arena. The Medicare program was established under the aegis of the Social Security Administration, and hospital payment was contracted to local intermediaries chosen by hospitals. More than 90% of hospitals chose their local Blue Cross association as the intermediary. In response to organized medicine's opposition to government

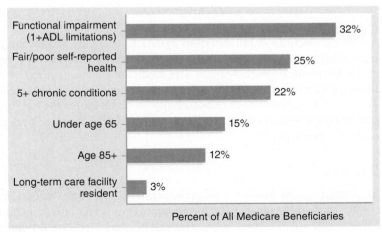

NOTE: ADL is activity of daily living.

FIGURE 4-7 Characteristics of the Medicare Population

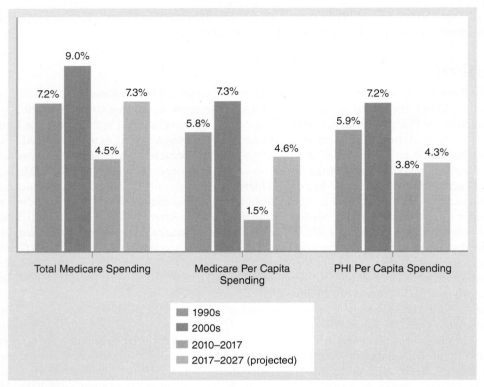

NOTE: PHI is private health insurance.

FIGURE 4-8 Actual and Projected Average Annual Growth Rates in Medicare and Private Health Insurance Spending, 1990-2027

Reproduced from Kaiser Family Foundation. An overview of Medicare. Published February 13, 2019. Accessed June 6, 2021. https://www.kff.org/medicare/issue-brief/an-overview-of-medicare/

certification, the Social Security Administration agreed to accreditation by the private Joint Commission on Accreditation of Hospitals (now the Joint Commission) as meeting the certification requirement for Medicare participation. The Medicare amendment stated that the government should not interfere with medical practice or how services were provided. Ultimately, however, the government's acceptance of responsibility for payment for the care of older adults generated a flood of regulations to address cost and quality control of the services and products for which it was now a major payer.[32]

Medicare Parts

As originally implemented, the Medicare program consisted of two parts, Part A and Part B, which remain fundamentally the same today. In subsequent years, legislative amendments added Parts C and D. Parts A–D are discussed below. **FIGURE 4-9** shows Medicare revenue sources and **FIGURE 4-10** shows Medicare spending by service type. It is important to note that from its inception, Medicare coverage was not comprehensive, and that remains true today. Beneficiaries are required to share costs through deductibles and coinsurance, and many beneficiaries purchase supplemental health insurance policies to assist with costs that Medicare does not cover.

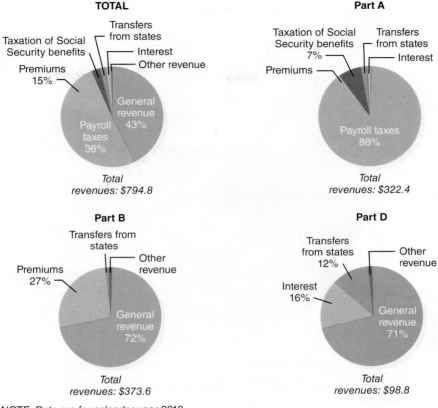

FIGURE 4-9 Sources of Medicare Revenue, 2019

Reproduced from Cubanski J, Neuman T. FAQs on Medicare financing and Trust Fund solvency. Kaiser Family Foundation. Published March 16, 2021. Accessed June 6, 2021. https://www.kff.org/medicare/issue-brief/faqs-on-medicare-financing-and-trust-fund-solvency/

Part A: Hospital Insurance

Part A pays for inpatient hospital care, limited skilled nursing facility care, home health care related to a hospital stay, and hospice care. Part A is mandatory and is financed principally from a 2.9% payroll tax with equal amounts contributed by employees and employers.[1,30] Individuals and couples with incomes over certain thresholds contribute at a higher rate.[30] In general, individuals who have contributed for at least 40 quarter-years of employment (approximately 10 years) are entitled to Part A without paying a premium. However, in 2016, deductibles were $1,288 for a hospital stay of 1 to 60 days, and coinsurance of $161 per day was required for between 21 and 100 days in a skilled nursing facility.[1,30] Medicare does not pay for long-term care in skilled nursing facilities.

Part B: Original Medicare Voluntary Medical Insurance

Part B, supplementary medical insurance, is a voluntary program covering physician services, outpatient hospital services, end-stage renal disease services, outpatient diagnostic tests, medical equipment and supplies, and certain home health services. About 75% of Part B is financed by

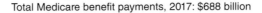

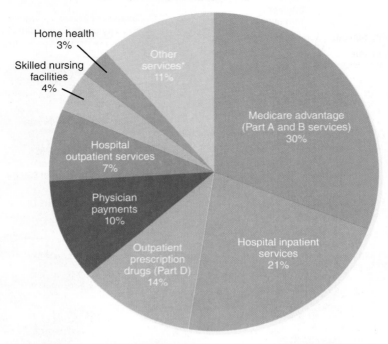

NOTE: *Includes Medicare benefit spending on hospice, durable medical equipment, Part B drugs, outpatient dialysis, outpatient therapy, ambulance, lab community mental health center, rural health clinic, federally qualified health center, and other Part B services.

FIGURE 4-10 **Medicare Benefits Payments by Type of Service, 2017**

Reproduced from Kaiser Family Foundation. An overview of Medicare. Published February 13, 2019. Accessed June 6, 2021. https://www.kff.org/medicare/issue-brief/an-overview-of-medicare/

general federal revenues and 25% by premiums paid by beneficiaries, typically through automatic deductions from monthly Social Security payments. Individuals and couples with incomes over certain thresholds pay higher premiums.[1,30] **FIGURES 4-11** and **4-12** show the Medicare Trust Fund projections and solvency.

Part C: Medicare Advantage

Medicare Part C, "Medicare + Choice," was added by the Balanced Budget Act of 1997. Medicare Part C allowed private health plans to administer Medicare contracts, with beneficiary enrollment on a voluntary basis.[5] The Medicare Prescription Drug, Improvement, and Modernization Act of 2003 (MMA) changed Part C to "Medicare Advantage," revising the administration of Medicare managed care programs to entice additional participation.[1] Part C pays private health plans a capitated monthly payment to provide all Part A and Part B services and Part D services (discussed below) if offered by the plan. Plans can offer additional benefits or alternative cost-sharing arrangements that are at least as generous as the standard Parts A and B benefits under traditional Medicare. In addition to the normal Part B premium, beneficiaries who choose to participate in Part C may pay monthly premiums based on services offered.[1,30]

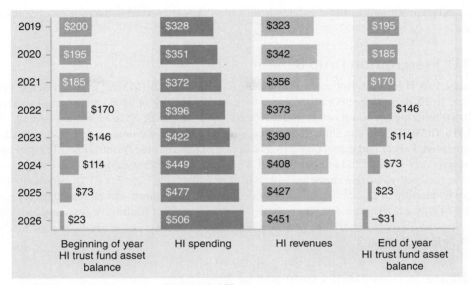

NOTE: HI is Hospital Insurance. Amounts in billions.

SOURCE: KFF analysis of data from the 2020 Annual Report of the Boards of Trustees, Federal Hospital Insurance and Federal Supplementary Medical Trust Funds, April 2020.

FIGURE 4-11 Medicare Trust Fund Solvency

Reproduced from Cubanski J, Neuman T. FAQs on Medicare financing and Trust Fund solvency. Kaiser Family Foundation. Published March 16, 2021. Accessed June 6, 2021. https://www.kff.org/medicare/issue
-brief/faqs-on-medicare-financing-and-trust-fund-solvency/

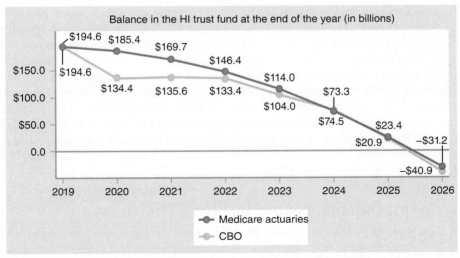

NOTE: HI is Hospital Insurance. Medicare actuaries: Actual data for 2019 and projected data for 2020–2026. CBO: actual data for 2019–2020 and projected data for 2021–2026.

SOURCE: KFF analysis of data from the 2020 Annual Report of the Boards of Trustees, Federal Hospital Insurance and Federal Supplementary Medical Trust Funds, April 2020.

FIGURE 4-12 Hospital Insurance Trust Fund Projections

Reproduced from Cubanski J, Neuman T. FAQs on Medicare financing and Trust Fund solvency. Kaiser Family Foundation. Published March 16, 2021. Accessed June 6, 2021. https://www.kff.org/medicare
/issue-brief/faqs-on-medicare-financing-and-trust-fund-solvency/

Beneficiary enrollment in these private health plans has increased substantially over the past decade.

Part D: Prescription Drug Benefit

Medicare Part D for prescription drug coverage was added by the MMA.[8] Participation is voluntary, and in 2016, participants were required to meet a deductible of $360 and incurred an average estimated monthly premium of $41 and a 25% coinsurance charge up to an annual coverage limit of $3,310. In 2017, CMS enrollment reached approximately 44.5 million individuals. As originally implemented, Part D had a coverage gap that became known as the "donut hole." The gap meant that when costs reached the annual limit of $3,310, beneficiaries would have no coverage until reaching total out-of-pocket spending of $4,850. The Affordable Care Act (ACA) gradually closes the gap by phasing in a combination of drug manufacturer discounts and increased federal subsidies by 2020.[1,30] Prescription drug costs are a significant driver of healthcare costs and specifically Medicare Part D costs. Future health policy is needed to address rising drug costs for Medicare beneficiaries, as well as all Americans.

Medicare Supplement Coverage or Medigap

Medicare is not a comprehensive health insurance plan, and several coverage gaps persist that require beneficiaries to pay out of pocket for healthcare products and services. In response, many beneficiaries opt to purchase additional coverage in the form of Medigap or a Medicare Supplemental Plan (sometimes referred to as MedSup) to help cover these out-of-pocket expenses (e.g., copayments, coinsurance, or deductibles). These plans supplement original Medicare benefits, hence the name Medicare Supplement Coverage. Therefore, an individual must have Medicare Parts A and B to be eligible to purchase a Medigap policy. Medigap coverage is different from a Medicare Advantage (or Part C) plan; however, these coverages are sometimes confused. Medicare Advantage plans are a way to get Medicare benefits, while Medigap supplements the original Medicare benefits and only provides coverage for an individual. Medigap plans have a monthly premium that is paid to a private insurance company in addition to the Medicare Part B premium. Insurance companies must be licensed to sell Medigap policies in a state, which provides some protections for Medicare beneficiaries. The licensing process ensures that Medigap plans comply with federal law and provide real benefits to Medicare beneficiaries. Medigap policies do not generally cover long-term care, vision care, dental care, hearing aids, eyeglasses, or private-duty nursing.[41] **FIGURE 4-13** shows Medicare supplemental coverage rates among Medicare beneficiaries.

Medicare Cost Containment and Quality: A Brief History

Within a few years after implementation, Medicare spending was significantly exceeding projections. Although hospital costs for the growing population of older adults increased more rapidly than expected, the galloping increases over projected Medicare expenses could not be explained by that phenomenon alone. In the decade after Medicare's enactment, several amendments to the Social Security Act made significant changes. In general, amendments during the first 5 years increased the types of covered services and expanded the population of eligible participants. During later periods, amendments addressed concerns about rising costs and quality.

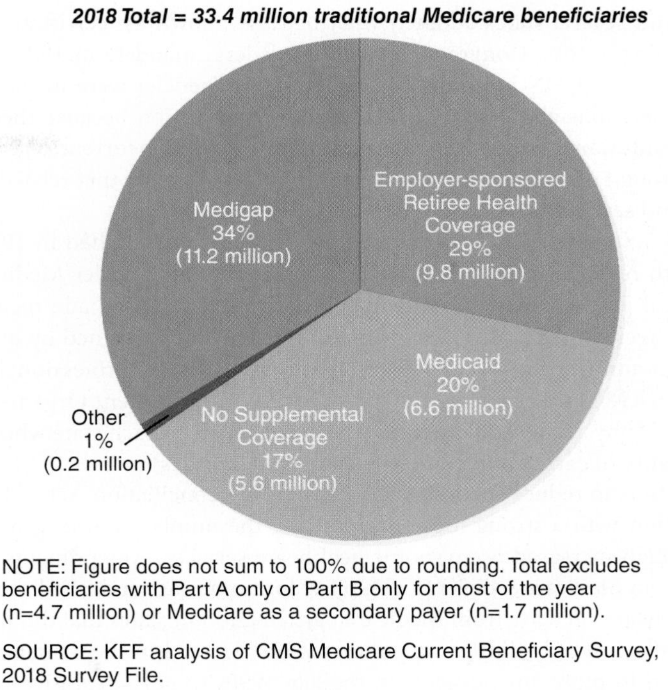
2018 Total = 33.4 million traditional Medicare beneficiaries
Medigap 34% (11.2 million)
Employer-sponsored Retiree Health Coverage 29% (9.8 million)
Medicaid 20% (6.6 million)
No Supplemental Coverage 17% (5.6 million)
Other 1% (0.2 million)
NOTE: Figure does not sum to 100% due to rounding. Total excludes beneficiaries with Part A only or Part B only for most of the year (n=4.7 million) or Medicare as a secondary payer (n=1.7 million).
SOURCE: KFF analysis of CMS Medicare Current Beneficiary Survey, 2018 Survey File.

FIGURE 4-13 Medicare Supplemental Coverage, 2018

Reproduced from Koma W, Cubanski J, Neuman T. A snapshot of sources of coverage among Medicare beneficiaries, 2018. Kaiser Family Foundation. Published March 23, 2021. Accessed June 6, 2021. https://www.kff.org/medicare/issue-brief/a-snapshot-of-sources-of-coverage-among-medicare-beneficiaries-in-2018/

A 1976 study by the U.S. Human Resources Administration reviewed the first 10 years of Medicare hospital expenses and attributed less than 10% of increases to utilization by the older adult population. Almost two-thirds of the increase over projected hospital costs was attributed to huge growth in hospital payroll and non-payroll expenses, including profits.[32]

Medicare's hospital reimbursement mechanism was cost-based and retrospective (or a look back) on a per-day-of-stay basis. This cost-based reimbursement fueled utilization of services and hospital capital expansion, which was augmented by new and expensive medical technology. Paid on a retrospective basis for costs incurred, hospitals had no incentives for efficiency. When Medicare and Medicaid were enacted in 1965, the annual rate of increase in healthcare expenditures was close to the annual increase in GDP. By 1967, healthcare expenditures began rising at double the prior rate. Five years later, federal healthcare expenditures had undergone a sixfold increase over the 1965 level.[32,40]

Medicare Cost Containment and Quality: 1965–1985

In Medicare's first 2 decades, many initiatives attempted to slow spiraling costs and address quality concerns. They were largely unsuccessful. The 1966 Comprehensive Health Planning Act provided federal support to states for conducting local health planning to ensure adequate health facilities and avoid duplication.[42] In 1974, the Health Planning Resources and Development Act replaced the Comprehensive Health Planning Act with local health systems agencies to coordinate and justify health facility and service plans based on quantified population needs.[43] The Act also mandated organizations to obtain approval from a state planning agency before starting any major capital project, and several states adopted what became known as "certificate-of-need (CON)" regulations for this purpose. Congress repealed the federal mandate in 1987, but 36 states still maintain some form of CON program.[43] Health systems agencies were unsuccessful in materially influencing decisions about service or technology expansion because their processes were dominated by institutional and stakeholder vested interests. Concurrent with attempts to slow cost increases through planning, several other initiatives took shape that related to concerns over Medicare costs and service quality.

Professional Standards Review Organizations (PSROs), established in 1972, were the first federal attempt to review the costs and quality of care provided under Medicare. PSROs were composed of local physicians who performed record reviews and made recommendations to local Blue Cross agencies, the Medicare payment intermediary. Plagued by questionable effectiveness and high administrative costs, PSROs were replaced by Professional Review Organizations (PROs) in 1984 and are now known as Quality Improvement Organizations (QIOs).[1,44] QIOs are groups of physicians and other health professionals in each state who are paid by CMS to review the quality of care provided to Medicare beneficiaries.[1]

In another effort to reduce spending, the Omnibus Reconciliation Act of 1980 amended the Medicare legislation with a strong focus on reducing the number and length of Medicare hospitalizations through increased use of home healthcare services. Amendments eliminated many prior restrictions on Medicare recipients' eligibility for home care and lifted the exclusion of for-profit home healthcare agencies from Medicare participation in states that did not require agency licensure. Ironically, not only did the amendments not succeed in their intended purpose, they ultimately resulted in more amendments in the late 1990s to curb explosive home care service expenditures and widespread provider financial abuses.[45]

The rate of Medicare cost growth continued rising despite cost-control efforts of the 1970s and early 1980s for two primary reasons: (1) existing payment methods incentivized the provision of more services, and (2) increases in expensive technology.[46] In addition, Medicare's fee-for-service payment structure was becoming outmoded as employer-sponsored plans, Medicaid, and private insurance companies embraced the managed care principles of prepayment and shared financial risk.

In 1983 Medicare enacted a new case payment system that radically changed hospital reimbursement. The new system shifted hospital reimbursement from a fee-for-service retrospective mode to a prepaid prospective mode, or prospective payment system (PPS). Using diagnosis-related groups (DRGs), the new system provided a patient classification method to relate the type of patients a hospital treated (i.e., age, sex, gender, or diagnoses) to costs.[46] The PPS based hospital payments on established fees-for-services required to treat specific diagnoses rather than on discreet units of services. The DRGs grouped more than 10,000 International Classification of Diseases codes into more than 500 patient categories. Patients within each category are grouped for similar clinical conditions and expected resource use using a Medical Severity-Diagnosis Related Group (MS-DRG).[47] DRGs are a clinically coherent set of patient classes that relate a hospital's case mix to its resource demands and associated costs. The payment an individual hospital receives under this system is calculated using input from a variety of other data known to impact costs, such as hospital teaching status and wage data for its geographic location.[46]

The PPS was intended to provide incentives for the hospital to spend only what was needed to achieve optimal patient outcomes. If outcomes could be achieved at a cost lower than the preset payment, the hospital could retain the balance of unexpended payment. If a hospital spent more to treat a case than allowed, it absorbed the excess costs. The PPS also financially provided for cases classified as "outliers" because of complications.[47] The PPS did not build in allowances to the payment rate for direct medical education expenses for teaching hospitals, hospital outpatient expenses, or capital expenditures. These continued to be reimbursed on a cost basis. By 10 years following implementation by Medicare, forms of the PPS were adopted by 21 state Medicaid programs and about two-thirds of Blue Cross/Shield Plans.[48]

The PPS raised many concerns among healthcare system stakeholders, including fears about premature hospital discharges, hospitals' questionable ability to streamline services to conform to prospective payments, and the home healthcare industry's capacity to accommodate an increased caseload due to earlier discharges. In 1986 Congress established the Prospective Payment Assessment Commission (ProPAC) to monitor the effects of the PPS and evaluate its performance on financial and quality.[32,40,46,49]

"Quicker and sicker" was the slogan popularized by the media during the first years of the PPS to characterize the drive for shorter hospital stays. The media also popularized the term "patient dumping," referring to hospitals transferring patients to other hospitals because they were deemed to be at high risk for expensive and potentially unprofitable services.

Subsequent research on the PPS impact indicated that most concerns were unfounded and that DRGs had a measurable impact on slowing the overall Medicare spending growth rate.[50] Research compared quality indicators before and after PPS implementation, revealing little effect on Medicare patient readmission rates and mortality rates.[49] In a study of almost 17,000 Medicare patients admitted to hospitals for five common serious diagnoses, post-PPS findings saw both a 24% decrease in the average length of stay for these conditions and an overall improvement in mortality rates among the five diagnoses studied.[49]

Concerns about patient dumping were addressed in the 1985 federal budget by the Emergency Medical Treatment and Labor Act (EMTALA), passed into law in 1986. The EMTALA required hospitals to screen everyone who presented in their emergency departments and to treat and stabilize the condition prior to transfer to another hospital. Stiff financial penalties, as well as risk of Medicare decertification by the Joint Commission for inappropriately transferring patients, accompanied the EMTALA provisions.[51]

Concerns about the capacity of the home healthcare industry to meet anticipated increases in demand dissipated quickly. The industry responded by creating new or expanding existing home healthcare services.[51] Hospitals did not experience the predicted negative financial impact, and they actually posted substantial profits. In fact, the federal government partially justified subsequent reductions in prospective payment on the basis that early payments were too high relative to costs. It was even suggested that the large financial surpluses generated by not-for-profit hospitals in the early years of prospective payment fueled hospital costs by making new resources available for investment.[49]

Medicare Cost Containment and Quality: 1986–2006

Historically, physicians set fee-for-service charges, insurers paid their claims, and patients paid any difference between the insured payment and actual bill.[1] Medicare Part B physician reimbursement was established as fee-for-service, based on prevailing fees within geographic areas. Burgeoning Medicare physician annual payment-rate increases averaging 18% between 1975 and 1987 provoked legislative action. In 1984, Congress enacted a temporary price freeze for physician services. Assessments of the price freeze suggested that physicians offset lower fees by increasing the volume of services.[49] Continuing concerns over Medicare's growth in physician payments and overuse of costly specialty care prompted further action.

The 1989 federal budget established a new method of Medicare physician reimbursement effective in 1992, using a resource-based relative value scale (RBRVS) to replace the fee-for-service reimbursement system. The prior payment system, which was based on charges alone, favored the use of more costly diagnostic and surgical procedures over cognitive and primary care services. The RBRVS intended to make physician payments equitable across various types of services, specialties, and geographic locations. To accomplish this, the "resource" components of the scale took into account total physician work, practice expenses, and malpractice expenses. The "value" of physicians' work incorporates elements such as the time required to perform a procedure, physical and mental effort, skill, judgment, and stress. Fee determinations also incorporate geographic differences in price and overall national physician expenditures.[48] Use of the RBRVS scale continues with a committee of the AMA and national medical specialty societies providing input to CMS on annual updates.[52]

Medicare reforms enacted by the PPS, managed care influences, market competition, technology advances, and consumerism continued producing changes in the delivery system. The PPS had demonstrated that "more is not necessarily better," as lengths of stay declined with no apparent negative impact on the quality of patient care. Then, in the early 1990s, the nation witnessed vigorous debates regarding the Clinton administration's proposal for a national health system, the Health Security Act. Although the Act never reached a Congressional vote, months of debate thrust national concerns about escalating Medicare spending, barriers to services, beneficiary costs, and provider choice into the public spotlight. Popular and political sensitivities rose against the backdrop of escalating national predictions about potential insolvency of the Hospital Insurance Trust Fund.[53]

Several trends supported major changes in the Medicare system. First, the Congressional Budget Office projected that Medicare cost growth could not be sustained without cuts in other government programs, major tax increases, or larger budget deficits. Second, as noted earlier in this chapter, Medicare's fee-for-service structure was outmoded, as employer-sponsored plans, Medicaid, and private insurance embraced managed care principles of prepayment. Third, Medicare coverage left significant gaps requiring copays and coinsurance that many beneficiaries were unable to meet. Acknowledging the President's and Congress's discord on a national health reform program, in 1995 Congress focused on slowing Medicare cost growth and achieving broader choices for Medicare beneficiaries through managed care plans as models of cost containment and consumer satisfaction.[54]

The federal budget negotiations for 1997 reflected pressures to produce a balanced budget and to respond meaningfully to national health issues from consumer and cost-containment perspectives. The resulting Balanced Budget Act (BBA) created major new policy directions for Medicare. The BBA proposed to reduce growth in Medicare spending through savings of $115 billion over 5 years, most of which was derived from reductions in payments to providers.[55] As the largest Medicare spender, the BBA targeted hospitals as the source of more than one-third of total anticipated savings. Among several other cost-cutting provisions, it also increased cost-sharing among Medicare beneficiaries.[55] Another major BBA provision extended the PPS to hospital outpatient services, home health agencies, skilled nursing facilities, and inpatient rehabilitation facilities.[1]

Decreased Medicare spending growth between 1998 and 2002 demonstrated the immediate impact of the BBA. After growing at an average annual rate of 11.1% for 15 years, the average annual rate of Medicare spending growth between 1998 and 2000 dropped to 1.7%, resulting in approximately $68 billion in savings.[56] The BBA also opened the Medicare program to private insurers through the Medicare+Choice program. The BBA established federal commissions to carry out monitoring and recommendation functions. These included the Medicare Payment Advisory Commission (MedPAC) and an independent National Bipartisan Commission on the Future of Medicare, whose functions include analyzing numerous dimensions of Medicare's financial condition and benefits design over time and providing advisory reports to Congress.[57,58]

BBA Medicare implementation drew widespread challenges and delays due to opposition from industry stakeholder groups. As a result, just before many of the BBA's provisions took effect, President Clinton signed the Balanced Budget Refinement Act of 1999, providing $17.5 billion to restore cuts to sectors negatively impacted by the BBA and outlining delayed implementation schedules for many of the BBA's original mandates. Due to large MCO withdrawals from the Medicare+Choice program because of reduced Medicare reimbursement and market shifts reducing profitability, in 2000 Congress enacted the Benefits Improvement and Protection Act, which increased participating MCO and provider payments.[56]

In 2001, CMS inaugurated the "Quality Initiative," encompassing every dimension of the healthcare delivery system supported by Medicare payments. The Quality Initiative includes hospitals, nursing homes, home healthcare agencies, physicians, and other facilities.[59] The program collects and analyzes data to monitor conformance with standards of care and performance. Since 2003, the Medicare administration also has continued experimenting with hospital pay-for-performance plans that emphasize the quality of patient outcomes and avoidance of unnecessary costs.[60] Pay-for-performance experiments are reflected in several ACA initiatives to address Medicare costs and quality, discussed in subsequent sections of this chapter.

With the goal of providing public, valid, and user-friendly information about hospital quality, in 2005 Medicare launched the website Hospital Compare in a collaboration with the Hospital Quality Alliance, a public–private partnership organization. Hospital Compare includes common conditions and criteria that assess the consistency of individual hospital performance with evidence-based practice; reporting is required for hospitals to qualify for Medicare payment rate updates.[61] Inaugurated in 2006, data from the Hospital Consumer Assessment of Healthcare Providers and Systems (HCAHPS) surveys was added to Hospital Compare information, providing patient perspectives on their hospital experience.[62]

Medicare Cost Containment and Quality: 2007–Present

In 2007 CMS announced that beginning in 2008, Medicare would no longer pay hospitals for extra costs associated with treatment for what are considered preventable medical errors. This policy change was made through a federal budget mandate that required CMS to identify conditions that: (1) are high cost and/or high volume, (2) result in assignment of a case to a higher payment DRG when the condition is a secondary diagnosis, and (3) could reasonably have been prevented through use of evidence-based treatment guidelines.[63] CMS refers to the conditions covered under this mandate as "hospital-acquired conditions" (HACs) and publishes a list containing 14 categories of such conditions. Examples include catheter-acquired urinary tract infections, foreign objects retained after surgery, surgical site infections, and falls or trauma during hospitalization.[63] Also in 2007, CMS announced that Medicare would no longer pay additional costs for preventable errors known as "never events." The term *never event* was introduced in 2001 by the National Quality Forum (NQF), an independent organization of healthcare experts that advises the federal government on the best evidence-based practices.[3] Never events are egregious, usually preventable errors that result in death or significant disability, such as surgery performed on the wrong body part or use of contaminated drugs or devices in a healthcare setting.[64]

The ACA contained numerous provisions affecting Medicare that reflect the law's overarching population-based approach and the drive to transition from a volume-driven to a value-driven system of care. These provisions are discussed in the following paragraphs. Several of these provisions are discussed in detail in Chapter 6 in the context of hospital care. As available, results from implementation of provisions also are discussed. In reviewing results, remember that for the most part, the provisions have been in effect for only a few years. Given the enormity of the proposed system transformation and the technical and behavioral changes required, it will take many more years of experimentation and research to identify, enact, and embed policies and practices that result in positive balances between costs and quality. Discussed later in this chapter, the Medicare Access and CHIP Reauthorization Act of 2015 (MACRA) will create many more opportunities for experimentation with the links between cost and quality.

Partnership for Patients

Beginning in 2011, CMS dedicated up to $1 billion over 3 years to test care models to reduce hospital-acquired conditions and improve transitions in care. This public–private partnership supported the efforts of physicians, nurses, and other clinicians to make care safer and to better coordinate patients' transitions from hospitals to other settings. More than 6,000 organizations, including more than 3,000 hospitals, joined the Partnership for Patients. CMS estimates that the program has the potential to save 60,000 lives and reduce millions of preventable injuries and complications in patient care, with savings up to $50 billion over 10 years.[65] Following the 2014 release of a positive CMS report on results, leading quality experts raised concerns about the validity of CMS findings.[66,67]

Bundled Payments for Care Improvement

Inaugurated in January 2013, the Bundled Payments for Care Improvement (BPCI) initiative recognized that separate Medicare fee-for-service payments for individual services provided during a Medicare beneficiary's single illness often resulted in fragmented care with minimal coordination across providers and settings and resulted in rewarding service quantity rather than quality. The BPCI links payment for services to an episode of patient care that results in hospitalization. It tests whether, as prior research has shown, bundled payments can align incentives for hospitals, post-acute care providers, physicians, and other healthcare personnel to work closely together across many settings to achieve improved patient outcomes at a lower cost.[68] In 2021, there were 1,707 BPCI participants including, among others, acute care hospitals, physician group practices, home healthcare agencies, and skilled nursing facilities.[69] In April 2016, CMS implemented a mandated "Comprehensive Care for Joint Replacement Model" BPCI for hip and knee replacements, requiring participation by 800 hospitals in 67 geographic areas. In issuing this mandate, CMS noted that more than 400,000 of these procedures are performed annually at a Medicare hospitalization cost of $7 billion, with wide variations in cost and quality.[70]

Comprehensive Primary Care Initiative

Launched in 2012 in select markets, this initiative tested a model to support primary care practices to provide higher-quality, more coordinated, and patient-centered care.[65] It concluded in 2016. In addition to regular fee-for-service payments, CMS paid 497 primary care practices in seven regions throughout the United States a monthly fee to help patients with serious or chronic diseases follow personalized care plans, give patients 24-hour access to care and health information, deliver preventive care, engage patients and their families in care plans, and work together with other doctors, including specialists, to improve care coordination.[65,71] In an evaluation of the Comprehensive Primary Care (CPC) initiative at its midway point in 2014, participating practices reported progress with changes in service delivery, but had not yet shown savings in Medicare expenditures or material improvements in quality of care or patients' experience of care.[71] In April 2016, CMS announced a new program, "Comprehensive Primary Care Plus," commencing in January 2017, which will operate for 5 years. The model incorporates principles of the advanced primary care medical home model and uses a combination of Medicare fee-for-service payments and performance-based financial incentives. Participation is voluntary and medical practices must apply to CMS for inclusion. As of 2021, CMS had recruited 2,737 physician practices and state and commercial health plans utilizing the model.[72]

Federally Qualified Health Center Advanced Primary Care Practice Demonstration

Begun in 2011, this demonstration evaluates the impact of advanced primary care practice on improving care, focusing on prevention, and reducing healthcare costs among Medicare beneficiaries served by Federally Qualified Health Centers (FQHCs). With additional support from CMS in collaboration with the Health Resources and Services Administration (HRSA), the demonstration tested FQHCs' ability to become formally recognized as patient-centered medical homes using teams of physicians and other health professionals to coordinate care for up to 195,000 Medicare patients. Concluded in 2014, the final program evaluation was released in 2016.[73,74]

Accountable Care Organizations

The subject of experimentation in the private sector since 1998, in 2021 there were 838 Accountable Care Organizations (ACOs) of all types operating, with a total of 23.8 million participants across 50 states and the District of Columbia.[75] Today, the ACO concept has been expanded to Medicaid programs and private health insurers. The ACA adopted the ACO model, consisting of groups of providers and suppliers of health care, health-related services, and others involved in caring for Medicare patients to voluntarily work together to coordinate care for the patients they serve under the original Medicare (not the Medicare Advantage) program.[76] ACOs intend to address the costly results of healthcare system fragmentation by ensuring care coordination across multiple providers for the entire spectrum of a patient's needs. The intent under the ACA was to create a variety of ACO organizations with different financial incentive models to track and then identify the models that worked best. ACOs are administered by Medicare and can be structured in several different ways.[76] However, each ACO must be a legally constituted entity within its state and include healthcare providers, suppliers, and Medicare beneficiaries on its governing board. It also must take responsibility for at least 5,000 Medicare beneficiaries for a period of 3 years. To qualify for support under the ACA, ACOs must meet Medicare-established quality measures of care appropriateness, coordination, timeliness, and safety. Medicare recipients participating in ACOs are not restricted from using physicians outside of their ACO.[76,77] Reports on ACOs' quality improvement and financial performance during the early years of this ACA initiative are mixed.[77-79]

Hospital Value-Based Purchasing Program

CMS began implementing value-based purchasing (VBP) pilot projects in 2003; this model has been replicated by private insurers as well, structured to provide incentives to discourage inappropriate, unnecessary, and costly care. Now mandated by the ACA, the VBP program applies to close to 3,000 U.S. hospitals, enabling them to earn incentive payments based on clinical outcomes and patient satisfaction.[80] Quality is measured based on a hospital's Total Performance Score (TPS), which is determined by how well it met a number of specific patient care and outcome objectives. CMS reported that participating hospitals are earning financial incentives for exceeding quality goals.[80]

Hospital Readmissions Reduction Program

The intent of the program is to encourage hospitals to improve the quality and continuity of care through improved communication and care coordination beyond the acute episode that resulted in the initial hospitalization. Discharge planning and education for patients and their caregivers are central to this program and improving care transitions from acute to post-acute care settings. The program's goal is to reduce or prevent avoidable hospital readmissions with 30 days following a patient's initial admission for 6 conditions that include acute myocardial infarction (i.e., heart attack), chronic obstructive pulmonary disease (COPD), heart failure, pneumonia, coronary artery bypass graft (CABG) surgery, and elective primary total hip arthroplasty and/or total knee arthroplasty. In 2009, prior to ACA enactment, 20% of all Medicare fee-for-service payments ($17 billion annually) were for unplanned readmissions.[81] Beginning with discharges on October 1, 2012, the ACA requires CMS to reduce payments to hospitals for the readmission of patients with specified diagnoses within 30 days of discharge from a prior hospitalization.[82] A 2016 analysis compared readmissions rates for targeted conditions before and after implementation of the reduction program. The analysis found reductions in readmissions for targeted and nontargeted conditions alike, suggesting an overall positive impact.[83]

Medicare Access and CHIP Reauthorization Act of 2015

The most significant health policy development of the past decade in terms of cost containment and quality improvement after the ACA is the Medicare Access and CHIP Reauthorization Act of 2015 (MACRA).[84] In addition to repealing a severely flawed Medicare physician reimbursement formula, the "Sustainable Growth Rate," the law has very broad effects on the continued advancement of the population and value-based approaches for public programs and the health system more broadly.[85]

MACRA focuses on quality improvement coupled with value-based payments as the centerpieces of clinical practices. The law establishes a new Quality Payment Program (QPP) that allows physicians to select participation in one of two CMS system options that define the way in which they will be reimbursed for services under Medicare.

The first option is participation in the Merit-based Incentive Payment System (MIPS).[84,86] MIPS eliminates three prior programs that affected physician Medicare payment adjustments and combines them into one program, assigning four weighted performance categories: quality, resource use, clinical practice improvement activities, and meaningful use of certified electronic health record technology.[86] A combined score on performance categories will determine whether physicians receive a Medicare payment increase, no increase, or reduction. The second option is participation in an Alternative Payment Model (APM), such as an ACO, patient-centered medical home (PCMH), or BPCI, in which providers accept some measure of financial risk in return for potentially enhanced reimbursements.[86] Participation in an APM exempts physicians from MIPS payment adjustments and provides an annual lump-sum payment based on 5% of the prior year's estimated aggregate expenditures under the Medicare fee schedule.[86] If physicians do not select a system or are not approved for APM participation, CMS will assign them to a MIPS. Consistent with the ACA's drive toward value-driven performance and departure from volume-driven, fee-for-service reimbursement, APM participation is favored by CMS.[87] This direction was clearly signaled by the 2015 CMS announcement that 30% of traditional Medicare payments would be tied to APMs by the end of 2016 and that 50 % of payments would be tied to these models by the end of 2018. CMS is offering more lucrative potential bonus opportunities and fee increases in APMs as compared with MIPS.[86] Also in this regard, in 2016 CMS announced the availability of $10 million in competitive grants over 3 years to support clinical practices with technical assistance for transition to APMs.[88]

Finally, it is important to recognize that as a new law, the MACRA must undergo a rulemaking process that transitions the law's intent into the implementation details that bring it to life. Rulemaking occurs in dynamic political, economic, and professional environments and can take years. Approximately 1 year after the MACRA's passage, on April 27, 2016, HHS issued the required "Notice of Proposed Rulemaking" to solicit input from stakeholders on implementation of its key provisions. Understandably, the MACRA has evoked strong positions from numerous stakeholders that will surely continue throughout the rulemaking process, with potentially material effects on the law's final impact and the timing of its implementation.[88]

Medicaid

Medicaid became law as Title XIX of the Social Security Act Amendments of 1965.[89,90] Medicaid is administered by CMS and is a joint federal–state program in which federal and state support is shared. The federal government matches state expenditures based on the Federal Medical Assistance Percentage (FMAP), which is adjusted annually based on a state's average personal income compared with the national average. The formula provides higher matching or reimbursements to states with lower per capita incomes compared with the national average.[91] **FIGURE 4-14** shows Medicaid spending and enrollment for the state fiscal year from 1998–2021.

Before Medicaid's implementation, healthcare services for the economically needy were provided through a patchwork of programs sponsored by state and local governments, charitable organizations, and community hospitals. Medicaid is the primary source of medical assistance for millions of low-income and disabled Americans, providing health coverage to many who otherwise would be unable to obtain health insurance.

Medicaid is the third-largest source of healthcare coverage in the United States after private employer-based coverage and Medicare.[92] The Medicaid program covers approximately 1 in 5 Americans.[89] As of September 2020, Medicaid enrollment stood at 70.5 million individuals, including disabled adults and children, the elderly, and 6.7 million children in CHIP.[93] Medicaid represents a major source of national healthcare expenditures, accounting for approximately 16% of total NHEs, or $613.5 billion in 2019.[4] The program also aids 12.2 million Medicare beneficiaries as of 2018, who are referred to as dual eligible (or dual eligibles).[94] A dual eligible is an individual who qualifies to receive both Medicare and Medicaid benefits. Medicaid bears significant responsibility for funding long-term care services because Medicare and private health insurance often furnish only limited coverage for these needs. Medicaid provides coverage for long-term

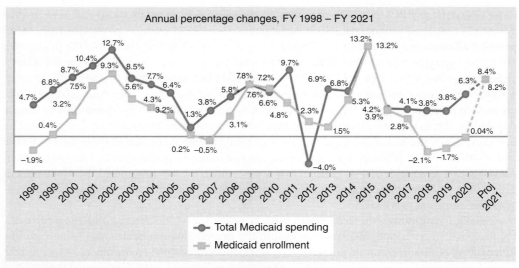

Note: Spending growth percentages refer to state fiscal year (FY).

SOURCE: FY 2020–2021 spending data and FY 2021 enrollment data are derived from the KFF survey of Medicaid officials in 50 states and D.C. conducted by Health management Associates, October 2020. 43 states submitted survey responses by mid-August 2020; state response rates varied across questions. Historic data reflects growth across all 50 states and D.C. and comes from various sources. See Methods of "Medicaid Enrollment & Spending Growth: FY 2020 & 2021" for more information.

FIGURE 4-14 Percentage Change in Medicaid Spending and Enrollment, State Fiscal Year 1998-2021

Reproduced from Rudowitz R, Hinton E, Guth M, Stolyar L. Medicaid enrollment & spending growth: FY 2020 & 2021. Kaiser Family Foundation. Published October 14, 2020. Accessed June 9, 2021. https://www .kff.org/medicaid/issue-brief/medicaid-enrollment-spending-growth-fy-2020-2021/

care services, certain behavioral health services, and Medicare premiums and cost sharing, while Medicare provides coverage for preventive, primary, and acute health care services, and prescription drugs.[94] Medicaid federal guidelines establish a mandated core of basic medical services for state programs, including[95]:

- Inpatient hospital services
- Outpatient hospital
- Early and periodic screening, diagnostic, and treatment services, including immunizations
- Nursing facility
- Home health
- Physician services
- Rural health clinic services
- Federally Qualified Health Center services
- Laboratory and x-ray services
- Family planning services
- Nurse-midwife services
- Certified pediatric and family nurse practitioner services
- Freestanding birth center (when licensed or recognized by the state)
- Transportation to medical care
- Tobacco cessation counseling for pregnant women

The federal government establishes broad program guidelines, but states design, implement, and administer their own Medicaid programs. Because rate-setting formulas, procedures, and policies vary widely among states and the District of Columbia, it is essentially composed of 51 different programs. Medicaid requires states to cover individuals who meet certain minimum categorical and financial eligibility standards. Medicaid beneficiaries include children, pregnant women, adults in families with dependent children, the aged, the blind and/or disabled, and individuals who meet certain minimum income eligibility criteria. Many adults who qualify for Medicaid are working, but earn wages too low to afford private coverage.[89] In general, the program provides three types of coverage[89,90]:

1. Health insurance for low-income families with children
2. Long-term care for older Americans and individuals with disabilities
3. Supplemental coverage for low-income Medicare beneficiaries for services not covered by Medicare, including Medicare part B premiums, deductibles, and coinsurance. These individuals are known as "dual eligibles."

Examples of optional benefits states may cover are prescription drugs, optometry, physical therapy, occupational therapy, chiropractic, dental services, dentures, prosthetics, speech, hearing and language disorder services, respiratory care services, podiatry services, case management, services in an intermediate care facility for individuals with intellectual disability, inpatient psychiatric services for individuals under the age of 21, and hospice, among others.[95] States also have the flexibility to extend coverage to higher income groups under specific circumstances.

Medicaid is funded principally from federal matching dollars to states and state general funds.[89,90] Medicaid is considered a "countercyclical" program in that difficult economic times result in increases in Medicaid eligibility, thereby increasing states' financial burdens as they experience budget stresses. In such instances, Congress may act to increase matching support, as it did during the 2008 Great Recession. Unlike Medicare, which reimburses providers through intermediaries such as Blue Cross, Medicaid directly reimburses service providers. Case 4-2 provides an opportunity to craft future Medicaid health policy to address health insurance and coverage needs in the U.S.

Children's Health Insurance Program

The Balanced Budget Act of 1997 included an initiative, the State Children's Health Insurance Program (SCHIP), which complemented Medicaid by targeting uninsured children whose family income was too high to qualify for Medicaid and too low to afford private health insurance. Subsequently renamed the Children's Health Insurance Program (CHIP), with the goal of enrolling 10 million children, it was the largest expansion of health insurance coverage for children in the United States since Medicaid began. When the program was created, nearly one-fourth of the children in low-income families were uninsured. States have the option to either operate CHIP as a separate program or run it in conjunction with the state's Medicaid program.[1,30] Medicaid and CHIP enrollment was increasing prior to the COVID-19 pandemic, following a decline from 2017 to 2019. The pandemic resulted in an increase in Medicare and CHIP enrollment in every state from February 2020 to November 2020 because of the economy (i.e., widespread job loss) and funds provided to states through the Families First Coronavirus Response Act (FFCRA). Many states saw children shift from CHIP coverage to Medicaid coverage as family income changed. However, every state saw an increase in the number of children enrolled in CHIP or Medicaid from February 2020 to November 2020.[96] Changes in the economy and federal funding contribute to the increase and decrease in the number of enrollees.

Indian Health Service

As discussed in Chapter 1, the Indian Health Service (IHS) provides health services to Native Americans and Alaska Natives and is an agency within HHS sponsored by the federal government. The IHS provides comprehensive health services to 574 federally recognized tribes in 37 states, or approximately 2.6 million people.[97] The IHS budget appropriation for 2020 was $6 billion, which was up from the system's $5.8 billion budget the previous year. In 2019, IHS expenditures per beneficiary were $4,078. In 2018, there were 40,494 inpatients admissions and 13,752,397 outpatient visits.[98]

The Veterans Health Administration

As discussed in Chapter 1, the Veterans Health Administration (VHA) is America's largest integrated healthcare system. The system provides care to approximately 9 million veterans at 1,293 healthcare facilities that include 171 medical centers and 1,112 outpatient sites in 2021.[99] The system is divided into 18 Veterans Integrated Service Networks, or VISNs. These regional networks strive improve access and care coordination for veterans in a geographic or local area. To be eligible to receive care from the VHA, veterans must have served 24 continuous months or the full active-duty period for which they were called (for those who enlisted after September 7, 1980, or entered active duty after October 16, 1981). Veterans may be able to receive VA healthcare benefits if they were discharged due to a disability that was caused or made worse by active duty, were discharged for hardship, or served prior to September 7, 1980. Members of the Reserves or National Guard that have been called to active duty by a federal order and served for the full active period are eligible for VA healthcare benefits.[100] The VHA is the largest provider of graduate medical education in the United States and is a leader in medical and scientific research.[101]

TRICARE and CHAMPVA

TRICARE is a health program sponsored by the Department of Defense (DOD) for uniformed service members and their families, National Guard members and their families, survivors, former spouses, Medal of Honor recipients and their families, and others registered in the Defense Enrollment Eligibility Reporting System (DEERS). There are approximately 9.6 million beneficiaries as of 2020. In terms of annual patient care for 2020, TRICARE provided 109.9 million outpatient visits, 979,900 inpatient admissions, 109,300 births, and 114 million prescriptions.[102] Benefits and plans depend on the beneficiary category previously listed.[103]

The Civilian Health and Medical Program of the Department of Veterans Affairs (CHAMPVA) is a comprehensive health program for eligible beneficiaries provided by the Department of Veterans Affairs to individuals that are not eligible for TRICARE.[104] To be eligible for the program, an individual must be the spouse or child of a veteran who is permanently or totally disabled due to service, a veteran who died from a service-related disability, or a veteran who was permanently or totally disabled from a service-related disability at the time of death. Finally, a surviving spouse or child of a veteran who died in the line of duty (not due to misconduct) is eligible for benefits (although most are eligible for TRICARE, not CHAMPVA).[104] Beneficiaries do not pay premiums; however, there is some cost sharing associated with the plan through coinsurance and deductibles. Beneficiaries pay for 25% of the service costs, up to $3,000 annually, after which point CHAMPVA pays for 100% of the services.[105]

▶ Uninsured Population

The number of uninsured Americans was approximately 28.9 million in 2019, representing 10.9% of the population. The number of uninsured Americans has been steadily increasing since 2016, when the uninsured rate was 10%, then 10.2% in 2017, 10.4% in 2018, and 10.9% in 2019, as shown in **FIGURE 4-15**. Changes in economic conditions and job loss are cited as the primary reasons for the increase in the number of uninsured Americans. Despite recent increases, the uninsured rate remains significantly lower than before the passage of the ACA in 2010, when the uninsured rate was 17.8% (46.5 million Americans).[13]

A profile of uninsured Americans reveals that 73.2% had at least one full-time worker in their family, 85.4% are nonelderly adults, and 77% are U.S. citizens. Further, minorities experience higher uninsured rates. Higher uninsured rates are generally associated with regions and states that did not expand Medicaid coverage through the ACA. The uninsured population persists in the United States due to a lack of employer-sponsored insurance coverage options, cost-prohibitive or lack of affordable employer-sponsored insurance or other private insurance options, and lack of Medicaid expansion in some states. Uninsured nonelderly adults report that they are less likely to receive preventive and chronic health services or to have a health provider or regular source of care. This contributes to 3 in 10 uninsured Americans reporting that they went without needed health care and being three times more likely to delay or go without prescription medications. Additionally, hospitalizations are higher among uninsured people (versus insured individuals) because the uninsured often forgo preventive and chronic care. When hospitalized, the uninsured receive fewer diagnostic and therapeutic services and experience higher mortality rates. The uninsured receive costly medical bills for major medical or emergency services that they must pay for out of pocket. This places a financial strain on individuals and their families, with 75.6% being worried that they will not be able to pay the medical bills.[13] A lack of insurance in the United States results in a lack of access, higher costs, and lower quality.

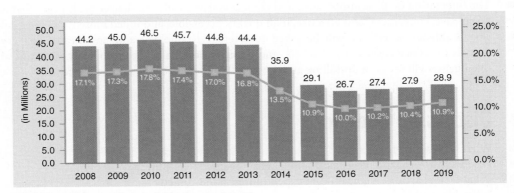

NOTE: Includes nonelderly individuals ages 0 to 64

FIGURE 4-15 **Number of Uninsured and Uninsured Rate Among the Nonelderly Population, 2008-2019**

Reproduced from Tolbert J, Orgera K, Damico A. Key facts about the uninsured population. Kaiser Family Foundation. Published November 6, 2020. Accessed June 9, 2021. https://www.kff.org/uninsured/issue -brief/key-facts-about-the-uninsured-population/

▶ Future of Healthcare Financing

Financing plays an important role in healthcare delivery and continues to undergo transformation to address population health as well as healthcare cost, quality, and access. ACA provisions are reaching millions with affordable health insurance and initiatives such as bundled payments and ACOs linking costs with quality. However, coverage and other gaps remain. MACRA was a historic step toward more equitable provider reimbursements linked with quality of care. Other ongoing initiatives, such as the Hospital Readmissions Reduction Program, are showing promising results. Many other ongoing initiatives will provide health services researchers with valuable information for developing and refining future efforts to control costs and improve quality. The Healthcare Financial Management Association outline financial trends to watch for in the next decade, including[106]:

- Healthcare payers and purchasers will continue to seek a better understanding of the total cost of health care and specifically how cost relates to value.
- Value-based payment and Alternative Payment Models will continue to transition healthcare financing away from the fee-for-service model toward value-based care models.
- Sites of care will continue to expand through the adoption of technology from traditional sites such as clinics and hospitals to homes and workplaces.
- Consumers will drive health care (also referred to as consumer-driven health care) and demand convenience (i.e., hours, care sites, payment, and much more).
- Technology will make it easier to generate, capture, and analyze healthcare data. Health informatics and analytics will be utilized to promote data-driven decision making in all areas of health care.
- Precision medicine will push beyond a "one-size-fits-all" approach to medicine to customize treatments for individual patients. This will help reduce unnecessary care or variations in care because treatments will be designed to be as effective as possible for each specific patient.
- The determinants of health will continue to be a focus and way to influence healthcare costs and outcomes beyond the traditional clinical care system.
- The integration of all administrative and clinical systems will help deliver health care that is responsive, convenient, cost effective, high quality, accessible, and much more.
- The healthcare workforce will be asked to leverage technology and new health delivery models to reduce costs, expand access, and improve population health outcomes. Artificial intelligence will result in upskilling and downskilling in the healthcare workforce.

▶ Discussion Questions

- What is meant by financing?
- Discuss historical and projected National Healthcare Expenditures.
- What factors are driving healthcare expenditures in the United States?
- What are examples of waste, fraud, and abuse?
- What laws have been passed to address fraud and abuse?
- Compare and contrast the U.S. health system with those of other OECD peer countries.

- What is insurance?
- What is risk?
- Can you define basic insurance terminology like insured, enrollee, beneficiary, premium, copayment, coinsurance, deductible, and cost sharing?
- What is moral hazard? How does health insurance create or contribute to moral hazard?
- Discuss how cost sharing applies to health insurance. What is the purpose of cost sharing? Helpful hint: What is the relationship between cost sharing and utilization?
- Can you identify examples of provider-induced demand and supply-side rationing?
- How did private insurance emerge in the United States?
- What are the four types of private insurance?
- How does managed care differ from traditional insurance?
- What are the different managed care models?
- What are some employer-sponsored health insurance trends?
- What is a high-deductible health plan?
- What are examples of public insurance?
- What is Medicare Part A? Discuss the financing of Part A. What services does Part A cover?
- What is Medicare Part B? Discuss the financing of Part B. What services are covered under Part B?
- What is Medicare Part C? What services are covered under Part C?
- What is Medicare Part D? What services are covered under Part D?
- How has the Medicare program evolved since it was passed in 1965?
- Discuss the financing, eligibility, and covered services for the Medicaid program.
- What is the Children's Health Insurance Program?
- What is the Indian Health Service?
- What is the Veterans Health Administration?
- What are TRICARE and CHAMPVA?
- Describe the uninsured population.

CASE 4-1 National Health Policy—What's Next for Healthcare Financing?

Written by Kim Davey, PhD, MBA, MA

You are a staffer working for Senator A. The Senator wishes to make additional health reforms to the Patient Protection and Affordable Care Act, or ACA, to address rising prescription drug costs, insolvency projections for the Medicare program, and other pressing healthcare financing issues. The Senator wants to replace the plan with "something better." The Senator has served for many years on Capitol Hill and is a consummate politician, but is not an expert in health care. The Senator relies on your expertise as a healthcare professional to keep him current on our health system.

- Prepare a memo for the Senator describing the ACA in simple terms and provide recommendations for addressing the Senator's healthcare financing concerns.

Based on cases in Buchbinder SB, Shanks NH, Kite BJ. *Introduction to Health Care Management*. 4th ed. Jones & Bartlett Learning; 2021.

CASE 4-2 Should Our State Expand Medicaid?

As a health policy analyst for the government of one of the states that did not expand Medicaid under the Affordable Care Act (ACA), you have been tasked with exploring whether now is a good time for your state to make a policy change. The Governor has heard about the impact the Medicaid expansion has had in other states. Many of the uninsured in those states have been brought into coverage. Since the federal government is bearing most of the cost of the expansion, this change seems like a no-brainer. In fact, your boss read an article about a candidate for governor in Georgia who asked an audience on the campaign trail to "Raise your hand if you would say no to someone who said, 'Give me a dollar and I'll give you $9 back.'"[1] Further, this is estimated to be costing states between $6 million and $8 million per year. Your boss finds these arguments compelling, needs you to investigate the expansion option further, and has requested input before she makes her decision and a possible recommendation to the legislature. Do some research on the states that have not expanded Medicaid. Pick one to focus on and prepare a proposal for the Governor that addresses the following questions:

1. What does the ACA say about Medicaid expansion in the state and how it needs to work? Who and what will the expansion cover?
2. From the experience of states that have expanded, what are the pros and cons of expansion? What are the relevant political, social, and economic concerns?
3. What is the situation in the state you picked? Why has Medicaid not already expanded?
4. What are the political, social, and economic issues for your state that the Governor needs to consider? Who will be covered? How much will it cost? Is the legislature likely to go along?
5. What is your recommendation to the Governor? Is expansion in your selected state feasible or not?

Reference:

1. Goodnough A. A Georgia candidate's cost saving platform: expand Medicaid. *New York Times.* Published October 21, 2018. Accessed June 9, 2021. https://www.nytimes.com/2018/10/20/health/medicaid-georgia-abrams-midterms.html

Buchbinder SB, Shanks NH, Kite BJ. *Introduction to Health Care Management.* 4th ed. Jones & Bartlett Learning; 2021.

CHAPTER ACRONYMS

ACA Patient Protection and Affordable Care Act of 2010
ACO Accountable Care Organization
AMA American Medical Association
APM Alternative Payment Model
BBA Balanced Budget Act
BPCI Bundled Payments for Care Improvement
CABG Coronary artery bypass graft
CDC Center for Disease Control and Prevention
CDHP Consumer-Directed Health Plan
CHAMPVA Civilian Health and Medical Program of the Department of Veterans Affairs

CHIP Children's Health Insurance Program
CMS Centers for Medicare & Medicaid Services
CON Certificate-of-Need
COPD Chronic obstructive pulmonary disease
CPC Comprehensive Primary Care initiative
DEERS Defense Enrollment Eligibility Reporting System
DOD Department of Defense
EMTALA Emergency Medical Treatment and Labor Act
FFCRA Families First Coronavirus Response Act
FMAP Federal Medical Assistance Percentage

FQHC Federally Qualified Health Centers
GDP Gross Domestic Product
HAC Hospital-Acquired Condition
HCAHPS Hospital Consumer Assessment of Healthcare Providers and Systems
HDHP High-Deductible Health Plan
HHS U.S. Department of Health and Human Services
HMO Health Maintenance Organization
HRA Health reimbursement arrangement
HRSA Health Resources and Services Administration
HSA Health savings account
IHS Indian Health Service
IPA Individual Practice Association
MACRA Medicare Access and CHIP Reauthorization Act of 2015
MCO Managed Care Organization
MedPAC Medicare Payment Advisory Commission
MIPS Merit-based Incentive Payment System
MMA Medicare Prescription Drug, Improvement, and Modernization Act of 2003

MS-DRG Medicare Severity-Diagnosis Related Group
NCHS National Center for Health Statistics
NHE National Healthcare Expenditures
NQF National Quality Forum
OECD Organisation for Economic Co-operation and Development
PCMH Patient-Centered Medical Home
POS Point-of-Service Plan
PPO Preferred provider organizations
PPS Prospective Payment System
ProPAC Prospective Payment Assessment Commission
PRO Professional Review Organization
PSRO Professional Standards Review Organizations
QIO Quality Improvement Organization
QPP Quality Payment Program
RBRVS Resource-Based Relative Value Scale
SCHIP State Children's Health Insurance Program
TPS Total Performance Score
VBP Value-Based Purchasing
VHA Veterans Health Administration

References

1. Shi L, Singh DA. *Essentials of the U.S. Health Care System*. 5th ed. Jones & Barlett Learning; 2019.
2. Kamal R, Cox C, McDermott D, Ramirez G. How has U.S. spending on healthcare changed over time? Peterson-KFF Health System Tracker. Published December 23, 2020. Accessed February 25, 2021. https://www.healthsystemtracker.org/chart-collection/u-s-spending-healthcare-changed-time/#item-usspendingovertime_7
3. Centers for Medicare & Medicaid Services. National health expenditure data. Updated December 17, 2019. Accessed February 19, 2021. https://www.cms.gov/Research-Statistics-Data-and-Systems/Statistics-Trends-and-Reports/NationalHealthExpendData
4. Centers for Medicare & Medicaid Services. NHE fact sheet. Updated December 16, 2020. Accessed February 19, 2021. https://www.cms.gov/Research-Statistics-Data-and-Systems/Statistics-Trends-and-Reports/NationalHealthExpendData/NHE-Fact-Sheet
5. Centers for Medicare & Medicaid Services. National health expenditure data: historical. Updated December 16, 2020. Accessed February 19, 2021. https://www.cms.gov/Research-Statistics-Data-and-Systems/Statistics-Trends-and-Reports/National HealthExpendData/NationalHealthAccountsHistorical
6. Kurani N, Kamal R, Amin K, Ramirez G, Cox C. State of the U.S. health system: 2020 update. Peterson-KFF Health System Tracker. Published December 10, 2020. Accessed February 19, 2021. https://www.healthsystemtracker.org/brief/state-of-the-u-s-health-system-2020-update/
7. U.S. Census Bureau. Quick facts. Published 2020. Accessed February 19, 2021. https://www.census.gov/quickfacts/fact/table/US/PST045219
8. Sawyer B, Claxton G. How do health expenditures vary across the population? Peterson-KFF Health System Tracker. Published January 16, 2019. Accessed February 20, 2021. https://www.healthsystemtracker.org/chart-collection/health-expenditures-vary-across-population/#item-start
9. Centers for Disease Control and Prevention National Center for Health Statistics. Annual Hospital Report portal for the National Hospital Care Survey. Published 2016. Accessed February 20, 2021. https://hehr.nchs.cdc.gov/ahr-beta/#!/js/inpatient
10. Kaiser Family Foundation. An overview of Medicare. Published February 13, 2019. Accessed February 20,

2021. https://www.kff.org/medicare/issue-brief/an-overview-of-medicare/

11. Kamal R, Cox C, McDermott D. What are the recent and forecasted trends in prescription drug spending? Peterson-KFF Health System Tracker. Published February 20, 2019. Accessed February 20, 2021. https://www.healthsystemtracker.org/chart-collection/recent-forecasted-trends-prescription-drug-spending/#item-start

12. American Medical Association. Health workforce mapper. Accessed February 20, 2021. https://www.ama-assn.org/about/research/health-workforce-mapper

13. Tolbert J, Orgera K. Key facts about the uninsured population. Kaiser Family Foundation. Published November 6, 2020. Accessed February 20, 2021. https://www.kff.org/uninsured/issue-brief/key-facts-about-the-uninsured-population/

14. U.S. Agency for International Development Office of Inspector General. What is considered fraud, waste, or abuse? Published April 16, 2018. Accessed February 19, 2021. https://oig.usaid.gov/node/221

15. Shrank WH, Rogstad TL, Parekh N. Waste in the US health care system: estimated costs and potential for savings. *JAMA.* 2019;322(15):1501-1509. doi: 10.1001/jama.2019.13978

16. Livingston S. Feds amassed $2.6 billion from 2019 healthcare fraud cases. *Modern Healthcare.* Published January 9, 2020. Accessed February 20, 2021. https://www.modernhealthcare.com/legal/feds-amassed-26-billion-2019-healthcare-fraud-cases

17. Centers for Medicare & Medicaid Services. *Medicare Fraud & Abuse: Prevent, Detect, Report.* Medicare Learning Network; 2021. Accessed February 19, 2021. https://www.cms.gov/Outreach-and-Education/Medicare-Learning-Network-MLN/MLNProducts/Downloads/Fraud-Abuse-MLN4649244.pdf

18. Lyu H, Xu T, Brotman D, et al. Overtreatment in the United States. *PLoS One.* 2017;12(9):e0181970. doi: 10.1371/journal.pone.0181970

19. Organisation for Economic Co-operation and Development. Where: global reach. Accessed June 11, 2021. https://www.oecd.org/about/members-and-partners/

20. Organisation for Economic Co-operation and Development. Health. Accessed June 11, 2021. https://www.oecd.org/health/

21. Organisation for Economic Co-operation and Development. Health expenditure and financing. Accessed June 11, 2021. https://stats.oecd.org/Index.aspx?DataSetCode=SHA

22. Kurani N, Cox C. What drives health spending in the U.S. compared to other countries. Peterson-KFF Health System Tracker. Published September 25, 2020. Accessed June 11, 2021. https://www.healthsystemtracker.org/brief/what-drives-health-spending-in-the-u-s-compared-to-other-countries/

23. Tikkanen R, Abrams MK. U.S. health care from a global perspective, 2019: higher spending, worse outcomes? The Commonwealth Fund. Published January 30, 2020. Accessed June 11, 2021. https://www.commonwealthfund.org/publications/issue-briefs/2020/jan/us-health-care-global-perspective-2019

24. Morrisey M. *Health Insurance.* 2nd ed. Health Administration Press; 2013.

25. HealthCare.gov. Deductible. Accessed June 11, 2021. https://www.healthcare.gov/glossary/deductible/

26. HealthCare.gov. Copayment. Accessed June 11, 2021. https://www.healthcare.gov/glossary/co-payment/

27. Healthcare.gov. Coinsurance. Accessed June 11, 2021. https://www.healthcare.gov/glossary/co-insurance/

28. RAND Corporation. RAND's Health Insurance Experiment (HIE). Accessed June 11, 2021. https://www.rand.org/health-care/projects/hie.html

29. Feldstein PJ. *Health Policy Issues: An Economic Perspective.* 5th ed. Health Administration Press; 2011.

30. Niles NJ. *Basics of the U.S. Health Care System.* 4th ed. Jones & Barlett Learning; 2021.

31. Kongstvedt PR. *Essentials of Managed Health Care.* 6th ed. Jones & Bartlett Learning; 2013.

32. Stevens R. *In Sickness and in Wealth: American Hospitals in the Twentieth Century.* Basic Books, Inc.; 1989.

33. Thomasson M. Health insurance in the United States. Economic History Association. Accessed June 11, 2021. https://eh.net/encyclopedia/health-insurance-in-the-united-states/

34. Kaiser Family Foundation. 2020 Employer Health Benefits Survey. Published October 8, 2020. Accessed June 11, 2021. https://www.kff.org/report-section/ehbs-2020-summary-of-findings/

35. Smith S, Heffler S, Freeland M. The next decade of health spending: a new outlook. *Health Aff.* 1999;18(4):86-95. doi: 10.1377/hlthaff.18.4.86

36. Morrisey MA, Alexander J, Burns LR, Johnson V. The effects of managed care on physician and clinical integration in hospitals. *Med Care.* 1999;37(4):350-361. doi: 10.1097/00005650-199904000-00005

37. HealthCare.gov. High deductible health plan (HDHP). Accessed June 11, 2021. https://www.healthcare.gov/glossary/high-deductible-health-plan/

38. Agarwal R, Mazurenko O, Menachemi N. High-deductible health plans reduce health care cost and utilization, including use of needed preventive services. *Health Aff.* 2017;36(10). doi: 10.1377/hlthaff.2017.0610

39. RAND Corporation. Analysis of high deductible health plans. Accessed June 11, 2021. https://www.rand.org/pubs/technical_reports/TR562z4/analysis-of-high-deductible-health-plans.html

40. Starr P. *The Social Transformation of American Medicine: The Rise of a Sovereign Profession and the Making of a Vast Industry.* Basic Books, Inc.; 1982.

41. Centers for Medicare & Medicaid Services. What's Medicare Supplement Insurance (Medigap)? Accessed June 11, 2021. https://www.medicare.gov/supplements-other-insurance/whats-medicare-supplement-insurance-medigap

42. Melhado EM. Health planning in the United States and the decline of public-interest policymaking. *Milbank Q.* 2006;84(2):359-440. doi: 10.1111/j.1468-0009.2006.00451.x

43. National Conference of State Legislatures. CON—Certificate of Need state laws. Published December 1, 2019. Accessed June 11, 2021. https://www.ncsl.org/research/health/con-certificate-of-need-state-laws.aspx

44. U.S. Government Accountability Office. Implementation of the PSRO program. Published 1977. Accessed February 21, 2021. https://www.gao.gov/assets/100/98419.pdf

45. Pillemer KA, Levine AS. The Omnibus Reconciliation Act of 1980 and its effects on home health care. *Home Health Care Serv Q.* 1981;2(2):5-39. doi: 10.1300/j027v02n02_02

46. U.S. Department of Health and Human Services Office of the Inspector General. Medicare hospital prospective payment system: how DRG rates are calculated and updated. Published August 2001. Accessed June 11, 2021. https://oig.hhs.gov/oei/reports/oei-09-00-00200.pdf

47. Mistichelli J. Diagnosis-related groups and the prospective payment system: forecasting social implications. Published June 1984. Accessed June 11, 2021. https://repository.library.georgetown.edu/handle/10822/556896

48. McCormack LA, Burge RT. Diffusion of Medicare's RBRVS and related physician payment policies. *Health Care Financ Rev.* 1994;16(2):159-173.

49. Thorpe KE. Health care cost containment: results and lessons from the past 20 years. In: Shortell SM, Reinhardt UE, eds. *Improving Health Policy and Management: Nine Critical Research Issues for the 1990s.* Health Administration Press; 1992:244-246.

50. Russell LB, Manning CL. The effect of prospective payment on Medicare expenditures. *N Engl J Med.* 1989;320(7):439-444. doi: 10.1056/NEJM198902163200706

51. American Academy of Emergency Medicine. EMTALA. Accessed June 11, 2021. https://www.aaem.org/resources/key-issues/emtala

52. American Medical Association. RBRVS overview. Accessed June 11, 2021. https://www.ama-assn.org/about/rvs-update-committee-ruc/rbrvs-overview

53. Davis PA. Medicare: insolvency projections. Congressional Research Service. Updated May 29, 2020. Accessed June 11, 2021. https://www.fas.org/sgp/crs/misc/RS20946.pdf

54. Reischauer RD. Medicare beyond 2002: preparing for the baby boomers. *Brookings Review.* Published June 1, 1997. Accessed June 11, 2021. https://www.brookings.edu/articles/medicare-beyond-2002-preparing-for-the-baby-boomers/

55. Moon M. An examination of key Medicare provisions in the Balanced Budget Act of 1997. The Commonwealth Fund. Published September 1, 1997. Accessed June 11, 2021. https://www.commonwealthfund.org/publications/fund-reports/1997/sep/examination-key-medicare-provisions-balanced-budget-act-1997

56. Medicare Payment Advisory Commission. *Report to the Congress: Medicare Payment Policy.* Medicare Payment Advisory Commission; 2020. Accessed June 11, 2021. http://medpac.gov/docs/default-source/reports/mar20_entirereport_sec.pdf

57. Kahn CN III, Davis K. After the bipartisan commission: what next for Medicare? The Commonwealth Fund. Published October 1, 1999. Accessed June 11, 2021. https://www.commonwealthfund.org/publications/fund-reports/1999/oct/after-bipartisan-commission-what-next-medicare

58. Medicare Payment Advisory Commission. About MedPAC. Accessed June 11, 2021. http://medpac.gov/-about-medpac-

59. Centers for Medicare & Medicaid Services. Quality initiatives - general information. Updated November 17, 2019. Accessed June 11, 2021. https://www.cms.gov/Medicare/Quality-Initiatives-Patient-Assessment-Instruments/QualityInitiativesGenInfo/index.html?redirect=/qualityinitiativesgeninfo/

60. Werner RM, Kolstad JT, Stuart EA, Polsky D. The effect of pay-for-performance in hospitals: lessons for quality improvement. *Health Aff.* 2011;30(4):690-698. doi: 10.1377/hlthaff.2010.1277

61. Centers for Medicare & Medicaid Services. Hospital Compare. Updated October 1, 2020. Accessed June 11, 2021. https://www.cms.gov/medicare/quality-initiatives-patient-assessment-instruments/hospitalqualityinits/hospitalcompare.html

62. Hospital Consumer Assessment of Healthcare Providers and Systems. HCAHPS fact sheet. Published March 1, 2021. Accessed June 11, 2021. https://www.hcahpsonline.org/en/facts/

63. Centers for Medicare & Medicaid Services. Hospital-acquired conditions. Updated February 11, 2020. Accessed June 11, 2021. https://www.cms.gov/Medicare/Medicare-Fee-for-Service-Payment/HospitalAcqCond/Hospital-Acquired_Conditions.html

64. Agency for Healthcare Research and Quality Patient Safety Network. Never events. Published September 7, 2019. Accessed June 11, 2021. https://psnet.ahrq.gov/primer/never-events

65. Centers for Medicare & Medicaid Services. The Affordable Care Act: helping providers help patients.

Accessed June 11, 2021. https://www.cms.gov /Medicare/Medicare-Fee-for-Service-Payment/ACO /Downloads/ACO-Menu-Of-Options.pdf

66. U.S. Department of Health and Human Services. New HHS data shows major strides made in patient safety, leading to improved care and savings. Published May 7, 2014. Accessed June 11, 2021. https://innovation .cms.gov/Files/reports/patient-safety-results.pdf

67. Pronovost P, Jha AK. Did Hospital Engagement Networks actually improve care? *N Engl J Med.* 371:691-693. doi: 10.1056/NEJMp1405800

68. Centers for Medicare & Medicaid Services. Bundled Payments for Care Improvement (BPCI) initiative: general information. Published May 4, 2021. Accessed June 11, 2021. https://innovation.cms.gov /initiatives/bundled-payments/

69. Centers for Medicare & Medicaid Services. BPCI Advanced. Published May 4, 2021. Accessed June 11, 2021. https://innovation.cms.gov/innovation -models/bpci-advanced

70. Centers for Medicare & Medicaid Services. Comprehensive Care for Joint Replacement model. Published May 25, 2021. Accessed June 11, 2021. https://innovation.cms.gov/innovation-models/cjr

71. Dale SB, Ghosh A, Peikes DN, et al. Two-year costs and quality in the Comprehensive Primary Care Initiative. *N Engl J Med.* 2016;374(24):2345-2356. doi: 10.1056/NEJMsa1414953

72. Centers for Medicare & Medicaid Services. Comprehensive Primary Care Plus. Published May 7, 2021. Accessed June 11, 2021. https://innovation.cms.gov /innovation-models/comprehensive-primary-care-plus

73. Centers for Medicare & Medicaid Services. FQHC Advanced Primary Care Practice Demonstration. Published May 4, 2021. Accessed June 11, 2021. https://innovation.cms.gov/innovation-models/fqhcs

74. RAND Corporation. *Evaluation of CMS's Federally Qualified Health Center (FQHC) Advanced Primary Care Practice (APCP) Demonstration: Final Report.* Rand Corporation; 2016. Accessed February 21, 2021. https://downloads.cms.gov/files/cmmi/fqhc -finalevalrpt.pdf

75. Centers for Medicare & Medicaid Services. About the Program. Updated June 22,, 2021. Accessed August 1, 2021. https://www.cms.gov/Medicare/Medicare-Fee -for-Service-Payment/sharedsavingsprogram/about

76. Centers for Medicare & Medicaid Services. Accountable Care Organizations (ACOs): general information. Published June 4, 2021. Accessed June 11, 2021. https:// innovation.cms.gov/innovation-models/aco

77. Gold J. Accountable Care Organizations, explained. *Kaiser Health News.* Published September 14, 2015. Accessed February 21, 2021. https://khn.org/news /aco-accountable-care-organization-faq/

78. Rudin RS, Schneider EC, Volk LA, et al. Simulation suggests that medical group mergers won't

79. undermine the potential utility of health information exchanges. *Health Aff.* 2012;31(3):548-559. doi: 10.1377/hlthaff.2011.0799

79. Bleser WK, Muhlestein D, Saunders RS, McClellan MB. Half a decade in, Medicare Accountable Care Organizations are generating net savings: part 1. *Health Affairs* Blog. Published September 20, 2018. Accessed August 1, 2021. https://www.healthaffairs .org/do/10.1377/hblog20180918.957502/full/

80. Centers for Medicare & Medicaid Services. The Hospital Value-Based Purchasing (VBP) Program. Published February 18, 2021. Accessed June 11, 2021. https://www.cms.gov/Medicare/Quality -Initiatives-Patient-Assessment-Instruments/Value -Based-Programs/HVBP/Hospital-Value-Based -Purchasing

81. U.S. Congressional Budget Office. The long-term outlook for health care spending: sources of growth in projected federal spending on Medicare and Medicaid: an overview. Published November 2007. Accessed June 11, 2021. https://www.cbo.gov/sites/default/files /110th-congress-2007-2008/reports/11-13-lt-health.pdf

82. Centers for Medicare & Medicaid Services. Hospital Readmissions Reduction Program (HRRP). Published August 24, 2020. Accessed June 11, 2021. https://www.cms.gov/Medicare/Medicare-Fee-for -Service-Payment/AcuteInpatientPPS/Readmissions -Reduction-Program

83. Zuckerman RB, Sheingold SH, Orav EJ, Ruhter J, Epstein AM. Readmissions, observation, and the hospital readmissions reduction program. *N Engl J Med.* 2016;374:1543-1551. doi: 10.1056/NEJMsa1513024

84. Centers for Medicare & Medicaid Services. MACRA. Updated November 11, 2019. Accessed June 11, 2021. https://www.cms.gov/Medicare/Quality-Initiatives -Patient-Assessment-Instruments/Value-Based -Programs/MACRA-MIPS-and-APMs/MACRA -MIPS-and-APMs.html

85. Conway PH, Gronniger T, Pham H, et al. MACRA: new opportunities for Medicare providers through innovative payment systems (updated). *Health Affairs* Blog. Published September 28, 2015. Accessed February 25, 2021. https://www.healthaffairs.org /do/10.1377/hblog20150928.050814/full/

86. Centers for Medicare & Medicaid Services. Quality Payment Program. Updated March 23, 2020. Accessed August 1, 2021. https://www.cms.gov/Medicare/Quality -Payment-Program/Quality-Payment-Program

87. Findlay S. Health Policy Brief: Medicare's new physician payment system. *Health Affairs.* Published April 21, 2016. Accessed June 11, 2021. https://www .healthaffairs.org/do/10.1377/hpb20160421.151319 /full/

88. Micklos J, Pierce-Wrobel C, Traylor J. The Center For Medicare And Medicaid Innovation can be a powerful force to accelerate change, but not without key reforms.

Health Affairs Blog. Published February 12, 2020. Accessed June 11, 2021. https://www.healthaffairs.org/do/10.1377/hblog20200204.111760/full/

89. Rudowitz R, Garfield R, Hinton E. 10 things to know about Medicaid: setting the facts straight. Kaiser Family Foundation. Published March 6, 2019. Accessed June 11, 2021. https://www.kff.org/medicaid/issue-brief/10-things-to-know-about-medicaid-setting-the-facts-straight/

90. Centers for Medicare & Medicaid Services. Medicaid facts and figures. Published January 30, 2020. Accessed June 11, 2021. https://www.cms.gov/newsroom/fact-sheets/medicaid-facts-and-figures

91. Mitchell A. Medicaid's Federal Medical Assistance Percentage (FMAP). Congressional Research Service. Published July 29, 2020. Accessed June 11, 2021. https://fas.org/sgp/crs/misc/R43847.pdf

92. Rosso RJ. U.S. health care coverage and spending. Congressional Research Service. Published January 26, 2021. Accessed June 11, 2021. https://fas.org/sgp/crs/misc/IF10830.pdf

93. Medicaid.gov. September 2020 Medicaid & CHIP enrollment data highlights. Accessed February 20, 2021. https://www.medicaid.gov/medicaid/program-information/medicaid-and-chip-enrollment-data/report-highlights/index.html

94. Centers for Medicare & Medicaid Services. People dually eligible for Medicare and Medicaid. Published March 2020. Accessed June 11, 2021. https://www.cms.gov/Medicare-Medicaid-Coordination/Medicare-and-Medicaid-Coordination/Medicare-Medicaid-Coordination-Office/Downloads/MMCO_Factsheet.pdf

95. Medicaid.gov. Mandatory & optional Medicaid benefits. Accessed June 11, 2021. https://www.medicaid.gov/medicaid/benefits/mandatory-optional-medicaid-benefits/index.html

96. Corallo B, Rudowitz R. Analysis of recent national trends in Medicaid and CHIP enrollment. Kaiser Family Foundation. Published April 8, 2021. Accessed June 11, 2021. https://www.kff.org/coronavirus-covid-19/issue-brief/analysis-of-recent-national-trends-in-medicaid-and-chip-enrollment/

97. Indian Health Service. About IHS. Accessed February 19, 2021. https://www.ihs.gov/aboutihs/

98. Indian Health Service. IHS Profile. Accessed June 11, 2021. https://www.ihs.gov/newsroom/factsheets/ihsprofile/

99. U.S. Department of Veterans Affairs. Veterans Health Administration. Accessed August 1, 2021. https://www.va.gov/health/ Updated July 21, 2021.

100. U.S. Department of Veterans Affairs. Eligibility for VA health care. Updated September 17, 2020. Accessed June 11, 2021. https://www.va.gov/health-care/eligibility/

101. U.S. Department of Veterans Affairs. About VHA. Updated April 23, 2021. Accessed June 11, 2021. https://www.va.gov/health/aboutVHA.asp

102. Defense Health Agency. TRICARE facts and figures. Updated August 24, 2020. Accessed June 11, 2021. https://www.tricare.mil/About/Facts

103. Defense Health Agency. TRICARE: eligibility. Updated March 18, 2021. Accessed June 11, 2021. https://www.tricare.mil/Plans/Eligibility

104. U.S. Department of Veterans Affairs. CHAMPVA eligibility. Updated June 10, 2020. Accessed June 11, 2021. https://www.va.gov/COMMUNITYCARE/programs/dependents/champva/champva_eligibility.asp

105. U.S. Department of Veterans Affairs. The Civilian Health and Medical Program of the Department of Veterans Affairs (CHAMPVA). Published November 2016. Accessed June 11, 2021. https://www.va.gov/COMMUNITYCARE/docs/pubfiles/factsheets/FactSheet_01-01.pdf

106. Reese EC. 2020 Vision: what to expect in healthcare finance over the next decade. Healthcare Financial Management Association. Published January 1, 2020. Accessed June 11, 2021. https://www.hfma.org/topics/hfm/2020/january/healthcare-2020s-views-on-healthcares-changing-landscape-from-thought-leaders.html

CHAPTER 5
The Healthcare Workforce

LEARNING OBJECTIVES

After reading this chapter you should be able to:

- Explain how the healthcare workforce influences healthcare delivery.
- Define the key terms such as healthcare professional and specific healthcare professional roles.
- Articulate how interprofessional education and practice influence healthcare delivery.
- Discuss how evidence-based practice and clinical practice guidelines influence healthcare delivery.
- Identify the four primary mechanisms through which health professionals are credentialed and regulated.
- Examine the evolving roles of physicians.
- Explain the evolving roles of nurses.
- Explore the roles of other independent healthcare professionals and allied health professionals.
- Explain the factors that influence the demand for healthcare professionals.
- Discuss healthcare workforce opportunities and challenges.

KEY TERMS

Accreditation
Advanced practice registered nurses (APRNs)
Allied health professionals
Allopathic approach
Behavioral scientists
Certification
Certified nurse-midwives (CNMs)

Chiropractors
Clinical laboratory technologists and technicians
Clinical nurse specialists
Clinical practice guidelines
Credentialing
Dentists
Diversity

Doctor of Medicine (MD)
Doctor of Osteopathic Medicine (DO)
Equity
Evidence-based practice
Generalists
Healthcare professional
Healthcare administrators
Hospitalists

Inclusion	Mid-level practitioners	Physician extenders
International medical graduates (IMGs)	Nuclear medicine technologists	Podiatrists
Interprofessional education	Nurse anesthetists (CRNAs)	Psychologists
Interprofessional practice	Nurse practitioners (NPs)	Radiologic technologists
Job-related burnout	Occupational therapists	Registered nurses (RNs)
Job stress	Optometrists	Registration
Laborists	Osteopathic approach	Rehabilitation counselors
Licensed practical nurse (LPN)	Pharmacists	Social workers
Licensure	Physical therapists	Specialists
Maintenance of Certification (MOC)	Physical therapy assistants or aides	Speech-language pathologists
Medical assistant	Physician assistants (PAs)	Support services
		Therapeutic science practitioners

CHAPTER OVERVIEW

This chapter defines the major healthcare professions with particular emphasis on their educational preparation, credentials, numbers, and roles in the healthcare delivery system. Factors that influence demand for the various healthcare providers are also reviewed. The chapter concludes with a discussion of healthcare workforce policy developments and some expectations for the future.

▶ Background

Health care is one of the nation's largest and most important industries. The U.S. Bureau of Labor Statistics reports that close to 20 million Americans are employed in health care and social assistance as of January 2021.[1] Healthcare professionals work across the healthcare system in a variety of settings or healthcare subsectors. The subsectors provide insights into where health professionals are working, with approximately 7.7 million professionals working in ambulatory healthcare services, or approximately 40%[2]; 5.1 million working in hospitals, or approximately 23%[3]; 3.07 million in nursing and residential care facilities, or approximately 17%[4]; and 3.9 million working in social assistance, or approximately 20% (i.e., individual and family services, community food and housing, emergency and other relief services, vocational rehabilitation, and child daycare services), as shown in **FIGURE 5-1**.[5]

In addition, growth in the healthcare workforce is projected to grow by 15% between 2019 and 2029. This growth will add an estimated 2.4 million new healthcare jobs and outpace the average growth for all other occupations in the United States. The median average wages for healthcare practitioners and technical occupations was almost double that of the median annual wage for all other occupations ($68,190 for healthcare occupations versus $39,810 for all other occupations as of May 2019). An aging population is one of the primary factors cited for the increase in demand for healthcare professionals along with changing delivery and reimbursement models that promote population health and management.[6,7]

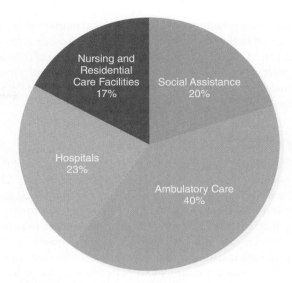

FIGURE 5-1 Subsectors Where Health Professionals Work

Created by Kim Davey. Based on data from the U.S. Department of Labor Bureau of Labor Statistics. Occupational Outlook Handbook. Updated April 9, 2021. Accessed June 11, 2021. https://www.bls.gov/ooh/.

The healthcare workforce plays an important role in influencing healthcare delivery in the United States, particularly related to costs, quality, and access. The healthcare workforce continues to change in size and composition in response to population and overall health trends as well as political, economic, social/demographic, technological, environmental, and legal/regulatory factors. Recent health policy reforms have created incentives that have shifted delivery from acute care facilities to community-based facilities. Although hospitals are still a major employer, recent employment growth has shifted to community-based settings like ambulatory clinics, outpatient surgery centers, home health providers, long-term care facilities, behavioral health clinics, and many other community-based settings. Health policies and reforms work to respond to health trends and shape the healthcare workforce so that it is responsive to health needs.

▶ Healthcare Professionals

The healthcare workforce is composed of more than 200 occupations and different types of healthcare professionals and roles. A healthcare professional is someone who plays a role in delivering health care and includes individuals who provide direct patient care (e.g., physicians, physician assistants, nurses, nurse practitioners, physical therapists, etc.) as well as individuals that indirectly support patients and healthcare delivery (e.g., human resources, finance, marketing, environmental services, information technology, etc., professionals). As the healthcare system continues to change and make use of new technology, new occupations and professional roles will continue to appear and even disappear in some cases as certain sectors expand and others contract. The personnel in those new occupations and professions will be required to possess more specialized knowledge and more sophisticated skills. Specialization to attain higher levels of technical competence also reduces the flexibility of providers to develop more efficient staffing patterns. Specialization among the workforce increases personnel costs, as additional employees are required to perform specific tasks. Smaller service facilities, especially in rural areas, are burdened most by the need for infrequently used specialists. As a result, there is growing acceptance of technology and interdisciplinary education and practice to meet dynamic workforce, delivery, and population health trends. Interprofessional education and practice are efforts to embrace the value of team-based care and growing specialized knowledge and skills among healthcare professionals.[8]

Interdisciplinary Education and Practice

There are a number of healthcare disciplines that participate in the care of the patient: medicine, nursing, pharmacy, physical therapy, occupational therapy, speech therapy, laboratory, and radiology, to name a few. Often these disciplines—in both education and practice—work in parallel, yet very independently and with different goals. All of them have a primary commitment to the patient. The increasing specialization and complexity of health care requires that all disciplines work collaboratively to provide safe, effective, quality care at a decreased cost. Collaboration provides an understanding and appreciation for the roles and contributions of each discipline in the care of the patient and the unique community and population a patient belongs to, as shown in **FIGURE 5-2**. It fosters communication, sharing information about the patient, willingness to listen to another perspective, and the ability to work together to seek understanding.[8]

Interdisciplinary education is a more recent movement and approach to prepare diverse sets of healthcare professionals to work together in practice.[9–11] Interprofessional practice (also referred

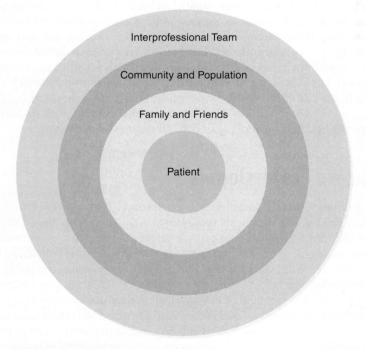

FIGURE 5-2 Interprofessional Collaborative Practice

Developed by Kim Davey. Based on information from the Interprofessional Education Collaborative. *Core Competencies for Interprofessional Collaborative Practice: 2011 Original*. Interprofessional Education Collaborative; May 2011. Accessed June 11, 2021. https://ipec.memberclicks.net/assets/2011-Original.pdf.

to as an interprofessional team) is defined as using a team-based approach to deliver patient care that promotes the health, safety, and outcomes of patients, clients, families, caregivers, and communities.[12] Interprofessional education consists of the foundations of interprofessional practice begin at the beginning of a healthcare student's academic program. Interprofessional education is defined as an educational approach in which two or more disciplines collaborate in the learning process with the goal of enhancing interprofessional interactions, thus enhancing the practice of each discipline.[9] The collaboration enhances communication and decision making, enabling a synergistic influence of grouped knowledge and skills to improve patient safety, outcomes, and satisfaction through evidence-based practice.[10,11] **FIGURE 5-3** provides a checklist of behaviors that foster a collaborative interprofessional team culture. Case 5-1 provides an opportunity to discuss the importance of interdisciplinary education and practice.

Evidence-Based Practice

Evidence-based practice emerged in the 1970s and 1980s in response to data showing wide variation in the applications of medical procedures in different regions of the United States and increased use of questionable, inappropriate, and unnecessary services that added significantly to the increasing costs of health care. Evidence-based practice integrates the best available scientific knowledge (i.e., clinical practice guidelines) with clinical skills and experience while considering the unique needs and preferences of a patient.[13] Clinical practice guidelines are systematically developed protocols used to assist practitioner and patient decisions about appropriate health care by defining the roles of specific diagnostic and treatment modalities in patient diagnosis and management.[14] The protocols contain recommendations that are based on scientific evidence gathered from a rigorous systematic review and synthesis of the published medical literature and are, therefore, described as evidence-based. Evidence-based clinical practice guidelines are considered to be the most objective and least biased clinical practice guidelines that serve as a means to assist in preventing the use of unnecessary treatment modalities and in avoiding negligent events, with patient safety and the delivery of consistent high-quality care as foremost priorities. With government agencies, health systems, third-party payers, and specialty

COLLABORATIVE CULTURE CHECKLIST

Role and Goal Clarification	
Encourages the process of goal, role, task clarification	
Supports division of labor necessary to accomplish group goals	
Communicates in Order to Achieve Team Goals	
Encourages the adoption of an open communication structure where all member input and feedback is heard	
Promotes an appropriate ratio of the group task and members' emotional engagement and group process	

(continues)

COLLABORATIVE CULTURE CHECKLIST (*continued*)

Promotes the use of affirmative dialogue	
Encourages use of effective conflict management strategies	
Employs effective problem-solving and decision-making procedures	
Develops Collaborative Team Norms	
Encourages the establishment of norms that support productivity, innovation, and freedom of expression	
Discourages any group tendency to over legislate individual behavior through the adoption of excessive or unnecessary rules	
Individuals voluntarily conform with norms that promote group effectiveness	
Welcomes diverse perspectives	
Takes Personal Responsibility for the Team's Success	
Members commit to personal and professional development	
Members remain current in their respective fields	
Members actively draw on each other's expertise	
Members promote cohesion and cooperation	
Members take a positive approach to seeking solutions for the team's problems	
Members interact with others outside of the team in ways that promote the team's ability to interface within the larger organizational context	
Members have an understanding of group development and group process	
Employ Energizing Strategies	
Moves toward relationship building	
Engages team members on a personal level	
Makes time for reflection and personal renewal	
Stays appreciative and positive; discovers opportunities in challenges	

FIGURE 5-3 **Checklist of Behaviors That Foster a Collaborative Interprofessional Team Culture**

Weiss D, Tilin FJ, Morgan MJ. *The Interprofessional Health Care Team: Leadership and Development.* Jones & Bartlett Learning; 2018.

societies promoting the use of evidence-based clinical practice guidelines, they have become an integral part of current medical practice. The widespread application of evidence-based clinical practice guidelines is expected to continue to have a significant effect on how physicians and other healthcare professionals practice. Case 5-2 provides an opportunity to consider the importance of interprofessional teams and evidence-based clinical practice.

Credentialing and Regulating Health Professionals

Ensuring a prepared and competent healthcare workforce is essential to promoting high-quality, cost-effective health care to diverse individuals, communities, and populations. Government regulation of the health professions is considered the safeguard to protecting the public from incompetent and unethical practitioners and professionals. How healthcare occupations are regulated and the manner in which regulation is carried out varies from state to state. However, states exercise a significant amount of responsibility in ensuring competent health professionals are practicing in the state. Professional health organizations also play an important role in ensuring a well-trained healthcare workforce through licensing and certification exams and continuing education requirements.

Regulatory restrictions limit healthcare service organizations and agencies in terms of who can perform or practice at certain levels, how they may use personnel, and in limiting their ability to implement innovative ways to provide patient care. Similarly, regulatory restrictions influence educational programs to focus curricula on what has been prescribed by regulatory boards and their related accrediting bodies. Many states have taken steps to revise their credentialing systems to provide greater flexibility and responsiveness to fast-changing healthcare technology.[15] Healthcare professionals, as shown in **FIGURE 5-4**, are regulated through four primary mechanisms:

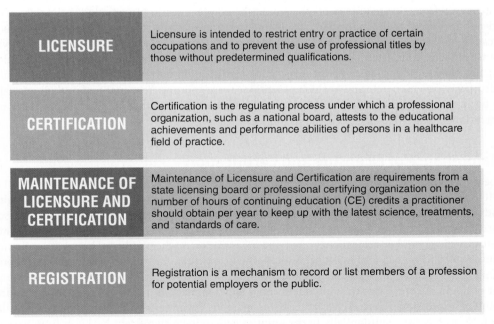

LICENSURE — Licensure is intended to restrict entry or practice of certain occupations and to prevent the use of professional titles by those without predetermined qualifications.

CERTIFICATION — Certification is the regulating process under which a professional organization, such as a national board, attests to the educational achievements and performance abilities of persons in a healthcare field of practice.

MAINTENANCE OF LICENSURE AND CERTIFICATION — Maintenance of Licensure and Certification are requirements from a state licensing board or professional certifying organization on the number of hours of continuing education (CE) credits a practitioner should obtain per year to keep up with the latest science, treatments, and standards of care.

REGISTRATION — Registration is a mechanism to record or list members of a profession for potential employers or the public.

FIGURE 5-4 Four Primary Mechanisms for Regulating Health Professionals

Developed by Kim Davey.

1) state licensure, 2) professional certification, 3) Maintenance of Certification (the newest procedure), and 4) registration.

Licensure

The first mechanism of professional regulation is licensure. Licensure, the most restrictive of the four mechanisms of regulation, is intended to restrict entry or practice of certain occupations and to prevent the use of professional titles by those without predetermined qualifications. Licensure is usually dependent upon passing a national licensing exam. Currently, licensure is provided at the state level where state law defines the legal definition of a discipline and scope of practice. Also, the state regulates the educational and testing requirements that must be met to engage in a particular profession's practice. For example, it is illegal for individuals to perform procedures defined in state statutes as medicine or dentistry or to call themselves physicians or dentists without the appropriate license. Because practicing a medical profession without a state-required license is illegal, licensure is the most powerful mechanism to regulate a profession because of the potential legal penalties, up to and including incarceration. Licensing and state regulation provide the legal basis for preventing an impaired or professionally delinquent individual from practicing.

Certification

The second mechanism of professional regulation is certification. Certification is the regulating process under which a professional organization, such as a national board, attests to the educational achievements and performance abilities of people in a healthcare field of practice. Certification is usually not state-based and is a much less restrictive regulation than licensing. However, states can set practice requirements that could include certification to practice in the state. Certification means that the individual has obtained advanced or specialized training in a particular area of practice consistent with an established body of metrics. For example, this applies to physicians who have completed a residency program and have successfully passed a board certification examination for a particular medical specialty. Certification allows the public, employers, and third-party payers to determine which practitioners are appropriately qualified in their specialty or occupation. Certification generally has no provision for regulating impaired or misbehaving practitioners other than dropping them from certification.

Maintenance of Licensure and Certification

The third mechanism that regulates healthcare occupations is Maintenance of Certification (MOC). Because most occupations in the healthcare field are based on a constantly changing body of knowledge, it is important for all healthcare practitioners to keep up with the latest science, treatments, and standards of care. Traditionally, MOC entailed simple requirements from a state licensing board or professional certifying organization on the number of hours of continuing education (CE) credits a practitioner should obtain per year. CE venues produced educational conferences to meet quality standards and awarded attendees with CE credits based on the number of hours of conference time attendees could apply to meet licensing or certification requirements. The growing financial costs and time to meet the expanding MOC requirements in health professions has risen substantially to the point of generating a significant backlash from various professionals and professional communities.[16]

Registration

The fourth mechanism of regulation is registration. Registration began as a mechanism to facilitate contacts and relationships among members of a profession and potential employers or the public. It is the least rigorous of the regulatory processes, ranging from simple listings or registries of people offering a service, such as private duty nurses, to national registration programs of professional or occupational groups that require educational and testing qualifications. Because most registration programs are voluntary, they do not include parameters for competence or disciplinary actions.[17]

▶ Healthcare Occupations

Space does not allow for a description and discussion of all healthcare occupations, but the following are major occupational categories:

Physicians
Similarities and Differences between MDs and DOs

Physicians play an important role in providing healthcare services by evaluating, diagnosing, and prescribing an intervention or treatment for a patient. There are two types of physicians: the Doctor of Medicine (MD) and the Doctor of Osteopathic Medicine (DO). The differences between these types of physicians center in their treatment philosophies and approaches. MDs use an allopathic approach that views medical treatment as an active intervention to produce a counteracting reaction in an attempt to neutralize the effects of disease.[18] DOs use an osteopathic approach that takes a more holistic approach to health and stresses preventive medicine in their treatment plans by considering how diet, environment, and other factors influence health and treatment.[18] MDs and DOs may use all accepted methods of treatment, including pharmaceutical drugs and surgery. All states require physicians to hold a license to practice medicine. Likewise, physicians must attend an accredited school of medicine that awards a Doctor of Medicine (MD) or a Doctor of Osteopathic Medicine (DO) degree.[7]

Generalists Versus Specialists

Physicians also differ in whether they are a generalist or a specialist. Generally, DOs are generalists while MDs are specialists. Changes in medicine and medical education have led to some shifts and trends for DOs to consider more specialty roles and MDs to consider more generalist roles. Generalists, or primary care providers, are physicians trained in family medicine/general practice, general internal medicine, and general pediatrics in the United States. Primary care providers provide preventive services (e.g., health examinations, immunizations, mammograms, and Pap smears) and treat frequently occurring and less severe problems. Referrals are made to specialists for problems that occur less frequently or require complex diagnostic or therapeutic approaches. Specialists are physicians that focus on particular organ systems or diseases and include areas such as neurology, nephrology, pulmonology, obstetrics and gynecology, cardiology, dermatology, anesthesiology, ophthalmology, pathology, psychiatry, radiology, surgery, specialized internal medicine, pediatrics, and specialty areas. Specialists receive board certification in their specialty areas, which often requires advanced residency training, additional years of practice, and a board or certification exam.[18]

Evolving Physician Roles

Physician roles evolve alongside advances in science and medicine. Hospitalists and laborists are two examples of physician roles that have emerged in recent decades. A hospitalist is a physician who provides care to hospitalized patients. The hospitalist replaces a patient's primary care physician while the patient is hospitalized. A hospitalist monitors the patient from admission to discharge and usually does not have a professional relationship with the patient before or after the hospital admission. This is a new type of physician role that evolved in the 1990s. The hospitalist is usually a generalist.[7]

The laborist is also an emerging specialty role being adopted in hospitals. A laborist is a board-certified physician that provides care to obstetrics and gynecology (OB-GYN) patients in the hospital. The laborist can admit, triage, provide emergency services, manage labor, deliver babies, and generally care for patients who are not assigned to a physician. Laborists, however, can be used by physicians in traditional OB-GYN practices to respond to labor and delivery needs in the hospital during office hours as an OB-GYN physician might otherwise have to close their practice to rush to a delivery or patient in the hospital.[19] Hospitals and physicians are embracing these new physician roles as a way to improve patient safety and outcomes as well as financial performance.

Physician Education

A typical path for training physicians in the United States is completion of education, training, and certification. The pathway to becoming a MD and DO are similar. The "Roadmap to Becoming a Physician" is shown in **FIGURE 5-5** and the sequence is as follows:

1. Receive a 4-year baccalaureate degree with a core in biology, chemistry, math, and many other disciplines and sit for the Medical College Admission Test® (MCAT®).
2. Attend a medical school accredited by the American Association of Medical Colleges (generally 4 years; however, accelerated programs are beginning to emerge that reduce the number of years in medical school).[20]
3. Match with a residency program through the Match® or the National Resident Matching Program® (NRMP®) process. This occurs during the final year of medical school. Medical students select their medical practice area from over 120 options and on Match Day students learn where they will be completing their residency training.
4. Complete residency specialty training accredited by the Accreditation Council for Graduate Medical Education (ACGME) lasting from 3–7 years depending on medical practice or specialty area.
5. Receive certification by one of the American Board of Medical Specialties (ABMS) boards in the medical specialty of the physician's residency by passing a board examination.
6. Complete optional fellowship(s) accredited by the ACGME lasting for 1–4 years each depending on medical practice or specialty area.
7. Complete optional certification(s) by the ABMS boards in the medical subspecialties based on the fellowship(s) completed.

To keep their certification(s) active, most physicians participate in the ABMS Program for Maintenance of Certification. ABMS was established as an independent, not-for-profit organization. ABMS works with member boards to set professional and certification standards that

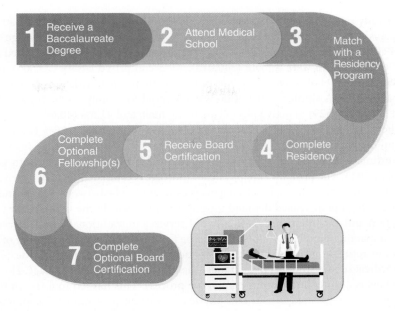

FIGURE 5-5 Roadmap to Becoming a Physician

Developed by Kim Davey. Based on information from the American Association of Medical Colleges. The road to becoming a doctor. Published November 2020. Accessed February 13, 2021. https://www.aamc.org
/system/files/2020-11/aamc-road-to-becoming-doctor-2020.pdf

improve health quality for patients. The MOC program requires periodic professional knowledge self-assessments and/or practice improvement activities in the specialty or subspecialties in which one or more certifications is held. As of 2021, ABMS member boards offer specialty certification in 36 specialties and over 130 subspecialties.[21] The number of subspecialties has continued to increase as the science of medicine has advanced.

Physician Workforce Supply and Distribution

Physicians play a central role in the provisions of health care services. There are 172 Association of American Medical Colleges (AAMC)-accredited medical schools across the United States and Canada that award the MD degree.[22] The Commission on Osteopathic College Accreditation accredits 38 colleges of osteopathic medicine as of the 2020–2021 academic year.[23] Colleges of osteopathic medicine have seen a significant increase in the number of applicants, students, and graduates. Medical school enrollment is important to ensuring a sufficient supply and distribution of physicians in the United States. In 2006, AAMC set a target for a 30% increase in the number of first-year medical students based on 2002 enrollment data (16,448 first-year students in 2002). Although not attained by 2015 as originally planned, the first-year enrollment for 2019 was 21,869 (a 33% increase from 2002).[24,25] In 2020, AAMC consisted of more than 179,000 full-time faculty, 92,000 medical students, 140,000 resident physicians, and 60,000 graduate students and postdoctoral researchers in biomedical sciences.[25] In AAMC's *2019 Medical School Enrollment Survey*, the majority of AAMC-accredited medical schools expressed a concern that the number of residency slots has not kept up with the increasing number of American medical school graduates.[24]

In 2019, there were 938,980 active physicians (including MDs and DOs) practicing in the United States. The largest medical specialty areas were internal medicine (120,171 active physicians), family medicine/general practice (118,198 active physicians), and pediatrics (60,618 active physicians).[26] In 2019, 55.1% (515,443) of active physicians were under the age of 55 while 44.9% (419,693) were 55 or older.[27] In 2019, 63.7% of all active physicians in the United States were male (596,236) and 36.3% were female (340,018). Men comprised 61.3% (73,560) and women comprised 38.7% (46,401) of active physicians practicing in internal medicine, the largest medical specialty area, in 2019. A similar distribution was observed for family medicine/general practice in 2019 with 58.7% (69,329) of active physicians being male and 41.3% (48,693) being female. In pediatrics, the third-largest medical specialty area, women comprised 64.3% (38,928) of active physicians and men comprised 35.7% (21,642).[28]

AAMC estimates a physician shortage of 54,100 to 139,00 physicians in both general and specialty care by 2033. The primary care physician shortage is estimated to be between 21,400 and 55,200 while the shortage of specialty physicians is estimated to be between 33,700 and 86,700 by 2033. Trends driving the increased demand for physician services in the United States include an aging population and expanding access to medical services to traditionally underserved populations. Trends impacting physician supply include the fact that an increasing number of physicians are approaching retirement. Medical schools are actively working to increase the number and diversity of medical school students to help meet the projected physician shortage. However, educating physicians is a time- and resource-intensive process. This has led to a rise in the number of advanced practice registered nurses and physician assistant practitioners as another strategy to meet the demand for general and specialty services. Generally, advanced practice registered nurse and physician assistant programs are 3 years long. The rise in popularity of these programs centers on them being significantly shorter and less expensive.[29] International medical graduates (IMGs) are physicians that receive their medical school education outside the United States or Canada. IMGs help fill residency positions and meet the demand for physician services in the United States. In 2019, IMGs represented 23% of ACGME residents and fellows. IMGs generally practice in primary care roles and often in underserved communities in the United States.

Nevertheless, there are serious shortages in rural and low-income areas that affect the efficiency and quality of medical care. Depending on the region of the country, several of a wide range of medical specialists are in short supply.[30] The South and West are areas projected to have a greater demand for physician services in the future and experience physician shortages.[29] Calculating present and future physician supply needs is a challenging and complex exercise. There is an absence of a national, comprehensive methodology as well as difficulty in assessing physician productivity, or how many patients physicians see or reasonably can see in specified time frames. In addition, wide variations in the number of physicians practicing in various geographic regions remains a pressing problem in the current healthcare delivery system.

Physician Diversity

Diversifying the physician workforce has been a strategic priority for AAMC. In 2018, 56.2% of active physicians were white (516,304), 17.1% were Asian (157,025), 13.7% were of unknown ethnic origin (126,144), 5.8% were Hispanic (53,526), 5% were Black or African American (45,534), 1% were multiple race, non-Hispanic (8,932), .8% were classified as "other" (7,571), and .3% were Native American or Alaska Native (2,570).[31] The number of minority students enrolled in medical schools now constitutes around half of the students accepted to medical school.[32] For the 2018–2019 academic year, 54.6% (10,879) of medical school graduates were white, 21.6% (4,299) were Asian, 8% (1,598) were multiple race/ethnicity, 6.2% (1,238) were Black or African American, 5.3% (1,063) were Hispanic, Latino, or of Spanish origin, and the remainder either

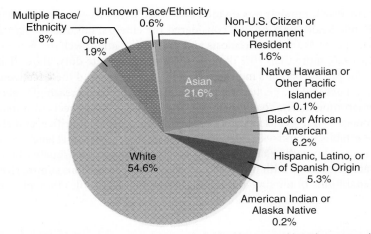

NOTE: Race/ethnicity "alone" indicates that an individual is reported in only one race/ethnicity category. The "Multiple Race/Ethnicity" category includes individuals who selected more than one race/ethnicity response. The "Non-U.S. Citizen or Nonpermanent Resident" category may included individuals with unknown citizenship.

SOURCE: AAMC Data Warehouse: STUDENT and IND as of August 19, 2019

FIGURE 5-6 Physician Diversity, Academic Year 2018–2019

Reproduced from the Association of American Medical Colleges. Figure 13. Percentage of U.S. medical school graduates by race/ethnicity (alone), academic year 2018–2019. In: *Diversity in Medicine: Facts and Figures 2019*. Association of American Medical Colleges; 2020. Accessed February 13, 2021. https://www.aamc.org/data-reports/workforce/interactive-data/figure-13-percentage-us-medical-school-graduates-race/ethnicity-alone-academic-year-2018-2019

were Non-U.S. citizen or permanent residents, unknown Race/Ethnicity, Native Hawaiian or other Pacific Islander, or other.[33] **FIGURE 5-6** captures physician diversity in the United States.

In the last 3 decades, the proportion of female physicians in both active practice and in training has been increasing steadily. In 2013, 46% of trainees in ACGME-accredited residency and fellowship training programs were women.[34] In 2014, 33% of practicing physicians in the United States were women.[35] In 2015, almost 50% of students in AAMC-accredited U.S. medical schools were women.[36] In 2019, women surpassed men to represent the majority, or 50.5%, of medical students.[37] Given these trends, the percentage of female practicing physicians will likely approach that of men in the next 2 decades.

Nurses

Nurses constitute the largest group of healthcare professionals. Nursing was a common employment position for women during the 1800s through association with religious or benevolent groups. A physician, Ann Preston, organized the first training program for nurses in the United States in 1861 at the Woman's Hospital of Philadelphia. Training was open to all women "who wished greater proficiency in their domestic responsibilities."[38]

In the early 1900s, hundreds of new hospitals were built under the aegis of religious orders, ethnic groups, industrialists, and elite groups of civic-minded individuals. Because student nurses were a constantly renewable source of low-cost hospital labor, even some of the smallest hospitals maintained nursing schools.[38] Hospital nursing school programs, therefore, were primarily sources of on-the-job training rather than academic programs. As educational programs evolved, stronger academic components were introduced, eventually leading to baccalaureate degrees instead of hospital diplomas.

Before World War I, nursing was divided into three domains—public health, private duty, and hospital. Public health nursing was considered the elite pursuit and recognized as instrumental in the campaign against tuberculosis and promoting infant welfare. Few nurses worked for hospitals. In 1920, more than 70% of nurses worked in private duty, about half in patients' homes and half for private patients in hospitals. The war emphasized the effectiveness of hospitals, and they soon became the center of nursing education in the increasingly specialized acute care medical environment. The social medicine and public health aspects of nursing were subjugated to the image of nursing as a symbol of patriotism, national sacrifice, and efficiency. The war experience established nurses as dedicated associates in hospital science. Nursing leaders promoted the idea of upgrading the nursing profession through high-quality hospital nursing schools, preferably associated with universities.[39] The following sections summarize the primary educational preparations in nursing and highlight the important roles they play in the healthcare system.

Licensed Practical Nurses

A licensed practical nurse (LPN), or licensed vocational nurse (LVN), works under the direct supervision of a registered nurse (RN) or physician to provide care and administer some medications. One-year LPN/LVN training is offered at approved technical or vocational schools or community or junior colleges. Programs include both classroom study and supervised clinical practice. Like RNs, LPN/LVNs must pass a state licensing examination. Their job responsibilities include observing patients, taking vital signs, keeping records, assisting patients with personal hygiene, and feeding and dressing patients, which are considered activities of daily living (ADLs). According to the U.S. Bureau of Labor Statistics, there were a total of 721,700 LPN/LVNs active in the U.S. workforce who earned an annual median pay of $44,480, or $22.83 per hour, in 2019. The demand for LPN/LVNs is increasing, and overall employment in this occupation is expected to increase by 9% from 2019 to 2029. The U.S. Bureau of Labor Statistics reports that the breakdown the healthcare settings LPN/LVNs work in is as follows: 38% nursing homes and residential care facilities that provide assisted living; 15% state, local, and private hospitals; 13% physician offices; 13% home health care; and 7% government jobs.[40]

Registered Nurses

Registered nurses (RNs) represent the largest healthcare occupation with approximately 3 million members.[41] An RN is a nurse who: 1) holds either a nursing diploma, Associate Degree in Nursing, or bachelor's degree in nursing; 2) has passed the National Council Licensure Examination (NCLEX-RN) administered by the National Council of State Boards of Nursing; and 3) has met all the other licensing requirements mandated by their state's board of nursing. RNs are responsible for recording symptoms of any disease, implementing care plans, coordinating patient care, assisting physicians in the examination and treatment of patients, administering medications and performing medical procedures, supervising other personnel (such as LPNs), and educating patients and families about follow-up care.[7] An RN can be trained in a 2- to 3-year diploma program offered through a hospital, a 2-year associate degree program at a community college or a junior college, or a 4- to 5-year Bachelor of Science degree program at a university or college.[41] Nurses with baccalaureate degrees and preparation are preferred. In August 2020, the American Association of Colleges of Nursing (AACN) found that 41.1% of employers require new nurses to have a bachelor's degree and that 82.4% strongly prefer a bachelor's degree.[42]

Diploma Nurses

Diploma nursing programs are the oldest type of nursing education in the United States; graduates receive a diploma instead of a degree. Today, most diploma nursing programs are affiliated with a college, university, hospital, or health system. The number of nursing programs has decreased to less than 100 operational programs. The majority of these programs are on the East Coast in Pennsylvania and New Jersey.[43]

Associate Degree Nurses

The Associate Degree in Nursing (ADN) is a 2-year program offered by community colleges and some 4-year universities. Many students obtain an ADN and continue their education to receive a Bachelor of Science in Nursing (BSN) degree. There are also 3-year diploma programs for those with an ADN, which are offered by hospitals. The programs tend to be expensive and are being offered less often.

According to the U.S. Bureau of Labor Statistics, there were a total of 3,096,700 RNs active in the U.S. workforce who earned an annual median pay of $73,300, or $35.24 per hour, in 2019. The demand for RNs is increasing, and overall employment in this occupation is expected to increase by 7% from 2019 to 2029. The U.S. Bureau of Labor Statistics reports that the breakdown of the healthcare settings RNs work in is as follows: 60% nursing homes and residential care facilities that provide assisted living, 18% ambulatory healthcare services, 7% nursing and residential care facilities, 5% government jobs, and 3% educational services—state, local, and private.[41] The following are examples the diverse fields RNs work in: addiction, cardiovascular, critical care, genetics, neonatology, nephrology, public health, rehabilitation, and may other areas.

The increasing complexity in health care has forced specialization in nursing as it did in medicine. Nurses with a bachelor's degree can undertake advanced studies in several clinical areas to develop the needed competence for teaching, supervision, or advanced practice. Nurses began to specialize during the 1950s. After World War II, nurses were in short supply, and hospitals began to group the least physiologically stable patients in one nursing unit for intensive care. The more competent nurses cared for the sickest patients. This initiated the critical care nurse specialty and the need for staff nurses continued to grow. By the 1960s, master's degree and doctoral programs were developed for nurses who wished to specialize. Advanced practice nurses took on various advanced practice roles such as nurse practitioners, clinical nurse specialists, nurse anesthetists, or nurse midwives.

Advanced Practice Nurses

Advanced practice registered nurses (APRNs), a type of mid-level provider, or physician extender, are nurses who have education and experience beyond the requirements of an RN. Mid-level providers, or physician extenders, are alternatives to physicians. APRNs generally collaborate with physicians to varying degrees (from close collaborations to independent practice) depending on state laws. APRNs are one category of physician extenders along with physician assistants, physician radiology practitioner assistants, and radiologist assistants. The responsibilities of APRNs exist between those of the RN and physician, which is why they are called mid-level practitioners. APRNs typically obtain a Master of Science in Nursing with a specialty in a field of practice. There are four areas of specialization: clinical nurse specialist, certified RN anesthetist (CRNA), nurse practitioner, and certified nurse-midwife. Many of these certifications allow a nurse to provide direct care, including writing prescriptions.[7] Efforts at healthcare cost containment have increased the demand for cost-effective nurse practitioners. Rural hospitals, with limited reserves of physicians, make substantial use of nurse practitioners and physician assistants. These mid-level practitioners are considered to be a cost-effective means to expand the scope of service in primary care.[44]

Clinical Nurse Specialists A different, but related, type of advanced nursing practice role is the clinical nurse specialist. This specialty role was developed in response to the specific nursing care needs of increasingly complex patients within a hospital setting. Like specialist physicians, clinical nurse specialists are advanced practice specialists with in-depth knowledge and skills that make them valuable adjunct practitioners in specialized clinical settings. The training requirements vary by state but generally include an RN and either a master's or doctoral degree (PhD or DNP) in nursing.[45]

Nurse Anesthetists Nurse anesthetists (referred to as CRNAs) provide anesthesia and related care before, during, and after surgical procedures. They provide pain management and some emergency services. CRNAs administer general anesthesia to put patients to sleep so they feel no pain during surgery. They remain with the patient throughout a procedure to monitor vital signs and adjust the anesthesia as necessary. Nurse anesthetists are RNs now required to have a doctoral degree from an accredited school and must pass the national certification examination. Most nurse anesthetists work with physician anesthesiologists in hospitals, ambulatory surgery centers, and urgent care centers providing comprehensive care to patients requiring anesthesia.

According to the U.S. Bureau of Labor Statistics, there were a total of 44,900 nurse anesthetists active in the U.S. workforce who earned an annual median pay of $115,800, or $55.67 per hour, in 2019. The demand for nurse anesthetists is projected to grow by a significantly higher rate than most other healthcare occupations from 2019 to 2029. A significant increase in the employment of nurse anesthetists the next decade is projected due to the aging population, the increased emphasis on cost reduction in health care, and a growing patient population due to expanding access to healthcare services. The U.S. Bureau of Labor Statistics reports that nurse anesthetists primarily work in hospitals followed by outpatient care centers.[46]

Certified Nurse-Midwives Certified nurse-midwives (CNMs) are RNs who complete a 1- or 2-year master's degree program in nurse midwifery that has been accredited by the American College of Nurse-Midwives Division of Accreditation. Nurse-midwives are primary care providers for women who are pregnant. They must pass the national certification examination to receive the designation of CNM, and they must be recertified every 8 years. They are licensed by the state and also may be required to be certified by the American College of Nurse-Midwives. Currently, almost all midwife-assisted births take place in a hospital or birthing clinic. Although nurse-midwives can perform vaginal deliveries on their own, they all work with obstetricians whom they can call in for complications and unanticipated emergencies or when a patient requires a caesarian section. The average annual salary for certified nurse-midwives is $105,000.[7]

Nurse Practitioners Nurse practitioners (NPs) are RNs with advanced education and clinical experience. Nurse practitioners provide primary and specialty care, and they are allowed to prescribe medicine in most states. Each state specifically defines practice requirements and allowed parameters for this type of APN role. Most nurse practitioners specialize. Neonatal nurse practitioners work with newborns. Pediatric nurse practitioners treat children from infancy through adolescence. School nurse practitioners serve students in elementary and secondary schools, colleges, and universities. Adult and family nurse practitioners are generalists who serve adults and families. Occupational health nurse practitioners work in industries providing on-the-job care. Psychiatric nurse practitioners serve people with psychiatric or emotional problems conditions. Geriatric nurse practitioners care for older adults. Nurse practitioners also work in hospitals and assist surgeons or other interventionists (e.g., cardiologists who perform intra-arterial catheterization and orthopedic surgeons who perform joint replacements) in managing patients in the hospital with pre- and postsurgical regimens. Nurse practitioner services allow physicians to perform a larger number of procedures by freeing them from much of the routine pre- and postprocedure patient management activities.

The current nurse practitioner movement began in the 1960s because of the shortage of physicians. The goal was to have specially prepared nurses augment the supply of physicians by working as primary care providers in pediatrics, adult health, geriatrics, and obstetrics. Nurse practitioners had to overcome resistance from organized medicine and legal difficulties caused by restrictions in most state nurse practice Acts (the statutes defining nursing scope of practice), which prohibited nurses from diagnosing and treating patients. Nurse practitioners sought state-by-state changes in nurse practice Acts, and by 1975 most states had started certifying or accepting the national certification of nurse practitioners, nurse-midwives, and nurse anesthetists.[47]

Two-thirds of the first nurse practitioner programs were brief certificate-granting programs, and one-third were master's programs. The programs primarily trained for practice in pediatrics, midwifery, maternity, family medicine, adult health, or psychiatry. As in most ventures into uncharted territory, several approaches to nurse practitioner preparation were tested. Eventually, a RN with a master's degree became the requirement for national certification and recertification.

According to the U.S. Bureau of Labor Statistics, there were a total of 211,300 nurse practitioners active in the U.S. workforce who earned an annual median pay of $115,800, or $55.67 per hour, in 2019. The demand for nurse practitioners is projected to grow by a significantly higher rate than most other healthcare occupations from 2019 to 2029. A significant increase in the employment of nurse practitioners over the next decade is projected due to the aging population, the increased emphasis on cost reduction in health care, and a growing patient population due to expanding access to healthcare services. The U.S. Bureau of Labor Statistics reports that nurse practitioners primarily work in physician offices followed by hospitals, outpatient care centers, educational services, and offices of other health practitioners.

There are two terminal degrees in nursing—the Doctor of Nursing Practice (DNP) degree and Doctor of Philosophy in Nursing degree. The DNP degree reflects continued specialization and the required preparation needed to practice in the U.S. health system. In contrast, the PhD degree is a research-focused degree. Some advanced practice nurses decide to pursue a PhD; however, the DNP is the professional practice degree for nurses and specifically APRNs.[48]

Physician Assistants

Physician assistants (PAs) are mid-level providers and a type of physician extender who provide a range of diagnostic and therapeutic services to patients. They provide health services under the supervision of a physician, although the degree of supervision required varies among states. PAs are formally trained to provide diagnostic, preventive, and therapeutic healthcare services as delegated by the physician. PAs take medical histories, order and interpret laboratory tests and x-rays, make diagnoses, and prescribe medications as allowed by law. Many PAs are employed in specialties such as internal medicine, pediatrics, family medicine, orthopedics, and emergency medicine. Others specialize in surgery and may provide preoperative and postoperative care and act as first or second assistants during surgery. The emergence of PAs closely parallels that of nurse practitioners. In the 1960s, there was a shortage of healthcare providers. Duke University initiated the first PA program in 1965.[49] Unlike nurse practitioners, who have additional training after completion of an RN, PAs need an undergraduate degree as a requirement for PA school admission. PAs are certified through an examination from the National Commission on Certification of Physician Assistants. Those who pass this exam have the credential Physician Assistant-Certified (PA-C). All physician assistants must be licensed by the state in which they practice.

According to the U.S. Bureau of Labor Statistics, there were a total of 125,260 physician assistants active in the U.S. workforce who earned an annual median pay of $112,260, or $53.97 per hour, in 2019. The demand for physician assistants is projected to grow by 31% from 2019 to 2029, significantly more than most other healthcare occupations. A significant increase in the employment of PAs over the next decade is projected due to the aging population, the increased emphasis on cost reduction in health care, and a growing patient population due to expanding access to healthcare services. The U.S. Bureau of Labor Statistics reports that physician assistants primarily work in physician offices followed by hospitals, outpatient care centers, educational services, and employment services.[50]

Dentists

Dentists prevent, diagnose, and treat tooth, gum, and mouth diseases. They are required to complete 4 years of education at an accredited dental school after completing a bachelor's degree. Dentists are awarded a Doctor of Dental Surgery (DDS), Doctor of Dental Medicine (DDM), or Doctor of Medical Dentistry (DMD) degree. Some states may require a specialty license. To practice in a dental specialty, a dentist must complete a dental residency after dental school in the specialty of choice and then usually must qualify for a special state-based dental license.[51] Dentistry currently includes 12 practice specialties: Dental Anesthesiology, Dental Public Health, Endodontics, Oral and Maxillofacial Pathology, Oral and Maxillofacial Radiology, Oral and Maxillofacial Surgery, Oral Medicine, Orofacial Pain, Orthodontics and Dentofacial Orthopedics, Pediatric Dentistry, Periodontics, and Prosthodontics.[52]

According to the U.S. Bureau of Labor Statistics, there were a total of 151,600 active dentists in the U.S. workforce who earned an annual median pay of $159,200, or $76.54 per hour, in 2019. The demand for dentists is projected to grow by 3% from 2019 to 2029. The U.S. Bureau of Labor Statistics reports that the large majority of dentists are general dentists followed by orthodontists, specialty dentists, oral and maxillofacial surgeons, and prosthodontists. Dentists primarily work in dentist offices followed by government facilities, physician offices, and outpatient care centers.[53]

Pharmacists

Pharmacists are responsible for dispensing prescribed medications. The role of pharmacists is expanding beyond dispensing medication to include advising patients and healthcare providers about the potential side effects of medications, recommending therapeutic alternatives to providers/prescribers, and prescribing medications and monitoring patients after a physician's diagnosis through collaborative practice agreements with physicians. Pharmacists are able to provide certain types of injections like immunizations and manage medication stockpiles during disasters or public health emergencies.[54] Pharmacists must earn a Doctor of Pharmacy (PharmD) degree from one of over 130 colleges of pharmacy accredited by the Accreditation Council for Pharmacy Education.[55] Pharmacy programs grant a PharmD degree after at least 4 years of post-secondary study. The PharmD degree has replaced the Bachelor of Pharmacy degree, which is no longer awarded. To be admitted to a pharmacy program, an applicant must complete at least 2 years of postsecondary study, although most applicants have completed 3 or more years, including courses in mathematics and natural sciences. Many colleges of pharmacy also offer a master's or PhD degree after completion of a PharmD program for pharmacists who want more laboratory or research experience to prepare them for research positions with pharmaceutical companies or to teach at a university. After graduation, a student that completes the PharmD degree may opt to complete 1- to 2- year residences or fellowships that are designed for those who want specialized pharmaceutical training. Pharmacists who want to work in a clinical setting are often required to complete a residency. Each pharmacist is licensed by passing a state examination and completing an internship with a licensed pharmacist. In 1976, the American Pharmaceutical Association created the Board of Pharmacy Specialties. It has since approved ambulatory care pharmacy, cardiology pharmacy, compounded sterile preparations pharmacy, critical care pharmacy, geriatric pharmacy, infectious diseases pharmacy, nuclear pharmacy, nutrition support pharmacy, oncology pharmacy, pharmacotherapy, psychiatric pharmacy, pediatric pharmacy, and solid organ transplantation pharmacy as specialties in which pharmacists may be certified.[56]

According to the U.S. Bureau of Labor Statistics, there were a total of 321,700 pharmacists active in the U.S. workforce who earned an annual median pay of $128,090, or $61.58 per hour, in 2019. The demand for pharmacists is projected to decrease by 3% (10,500 jobs) from 2019 to 2029.[57] Because of the increased use of mail-order pharmacies, the number of jobs in the pharmacy retail segment is expected to decline slightly.[58] However, this trend may change in response to the global COVID-19 pandemic and efforts by the pharmacy profession to expand the role of pharmacists in the U.S. health system. Pharmacists are the most accessible healthcare provider across communities in the United States. The pharmacy profession is looking at how they can potentially expand their role to help provide access to preventative and diagnostic services as well as health education and chronic disease management services. The U.S. Bureau of Labor Statistics reports that pharmacists primarily work in pharmacies and drug stores followed by hospitals (state, local, and private), food and beverage stores, and general merchandise stores.[59]

Podiatrists

Podiatrists treat patients with foot diseases and deformities. Podiatric medicine is concerned with the diagnosis and treatment of diseases and injuries of the lower leg and foot. Podiatrists can prescribe drugs; order radiographs, laboratory tests, and physical therapy; set fractures; and perform surgery. They also fit corrective inserts called orthotics, design plaster casts and strappings to correct deformities, and design custom-made shoes. Podiatrists obtain a Doctor of Podiatric Medicine (DPM) degree from an accredited school in the United States. Students apply to podiatric programs after completing a 4-year degree from an accredited college or university. The 4 years of professional training is similar to that for physicians. Most podiatrists spend 3 or more years completing a residency in a hospital after they graduate.[60] Podiatrists also may take postgraduate training and become board certified in the specialties of primary care in podiatric medicine, diabetic foot wound care and footwear, limb preservation and salvage, or podiatric surgery. All doctors of podiatric medicine are licensed by the state in which they practice.

According to the U.S. Bureau of Labor Statistics, there were a total of 10,500 podiatrists active in the U.S. workforce who earned an annual median pay of $126,240, or $60.69 per hour, in 2019. The demand for podiatrists is projected to experience little to no change from 2019 to 2029.[61] Podiatric care is more dependent on disposable income than other medical services. While Medicare and most private health insurance programs cover acute medical and surgical foot services as well as diagnostic radiographs and leg braces, routine foot care ordinarily is not covered. One notable exception is that Medicare covers diabetic foot care with a podiatrist for those over the age of 65. The U.S. Bureau of Labor Statistics reports that podiatrists primarily work in offices of other health practitioners followed by offices of physicians, government facilities, and hospitals (state, local, and private), while the remaining are self-employed.[62]

Chiropractors

Chiropractors have a holistic approach to treating their patients. They believe the body can heal itself without medication or surgery and treat the whole body without the use of drugs or surgery. Special care is given to the spine because chiropractors believe that misalignment or irritations of spinal nerves interfere with normal body functions. They manipulate the body using their hands or a machine. Chiropractors must be licensed, which requires 2–4 years of undergraduate education, the completion of a 4-year chiropractic college degree, and receipt of passing scores on national and state examinations.

According to the U.S. Bureau of Labor Statistics, there were a total of 51,100 chiropractors active in the U.S. workforce who earned an annual median pay of $70,340, or $33.82 per hour, in 2019. The demand for chiropractors is projected to grow by 4% from 2019 to 2029.[63] This will help meet the increasing demand for chiropractic care as the aging population in the United States becomes more likely to experience musculoskeletal and joint problems and seek chiropractic care.[64] The U.S. Bureau of Labor Statistics reports that chiropractors primarily work in chiropractic offices followed by physician offices.[62]

Optometrists

Optometrists examine patients' eyes to diagnose vision problems and eye disease, prescribe drugs for treatment, and prescribe and fit eyeglasses and contact lenses. Optometrists also test for glaucoma and other eye diseases and diagnose conditions caused by systemic diseases, such as diabetes and high blood pressure, and refer patients to other health practitioners. Optometrists often provide preoperative and postoperative care to cataract patients and patients who have had laser vision correction or other types of eye surgery.[7]

Optometrists must obtain a Doctor of Optometry degree, which requires the completion of a 4-year program at an accredited optometry school. All states require that optometrists be licensed. Applicants for a license must have a Doctor of Optometry degree from an accredited optometry school and must pass both a written national board examination and a national, regional, or state clinical examination. Many states require applications to pass an examination on relevant state laws. Licenses must be renewed every 1–3 years, and continuing education credits are needed for renewal in all states. One-year residency programs are available for optometrists who wish to specialize in family practice optometry, pediatric optometry, geriatric optometry, low-vision rehabilitation, corneal and contact lenses, refractive and ovular surgery, vision therapy and rehabilitation, ocular disease, and community health optometry.[65] An optometrist should not be confused with an ophthalmologist or an optician. An ophthalmologist is a physician who specializes in the treatment of eye diseases and injuries and uses drugs, surgery, or the prescription of corrective lenses to correct vision deficiencies. An optician is a licensed health professional who fits eyeglasses or contact lenses to individual patients as prescribed by ophthalmologists or optometrists.[7]

According to the U.S. Bureau of Labor Statistics, there were a total of 44,400 optometrists active in the U.S. workforce who earned an annual median pay of $115,250, or $55.41 per hour, in 2019. The demand for optometrists is projected to grow by 4% from 2019 to 2029.[66] This is due to the aging population and increased levels of vision insurance coverage.[67] People over 45 years of age visit optometrists and ophthalmologists more frequently because of the onset of vision problems in middle age and the increased likelihood of cataracts, glaucoma, diabetes, and hypertension in old age. The U.S. Bureau of Labor Statistics reports that optometrists primarily work in optometrist offices followed by physician offices and health and personal care stores, while the remaining are self-employed.[68]

Psychologists

Psychologists study the human mind and human behavior. Research psychologists investigate the physical, cognitive, emotional, or social aspects of human behavior. Psychologists in health services fields provide mental health care in hospitals, clinics, schools, or private settings. Psychologists are employed in applied settings, such as business, industry, government, or nonprofit organizations and provide training, conduct research, design organizational systems, and act as advocates for psychology. Psychologists usually specialize and work as clinical psychologists, counseling psychologists, industrial-organizational psychologists, developmental psychologists, social psychologists, and experimental or research psychologists.[7]

A doctoral degree is required for individual practice as a psychologist. Psychologists with a PhD or Doctor of Psychology (PsyD) degree are able to work in universities, healthcare services, elementary and secondary schools, private industries, and government positions as teachers, researchers, clinicians, and counselors. Obtaining either a PhD or PsyD requires 5–7 years of graduate study that culminates in a dissertation based on original research. The PsyD may be based on practical work and examinations rather than a dissertation. In clinical, counseling, and school psychology, the requirement for these degrees includes at least a 1-year internship.[7]

According to the U.S. Bureau of Labor Statistics, there were a total of 192,300 psychologists active in the U.S. workforce who earned an annual median pay of $80,370, or $38.64 per hour, in 2019. Clinical, counseling, and school psychologists represent 89% (171,500) of psychologists in the United States. The demand for psychologists is projected to grow by 3% from 2019 to 2029.[69] This will help meet the demand for mental healthcare providers in the United States. The U.S. Bureau of Labor Statistics reports that psychologists are self-employed followed by employment in elementary and secondary schools, ambulatory healthcare services, government facilities, and hospitals.[70]

▶ Allied Health Professionals

Allied health professionals represent a varied and complex array of healthcare disciplines that support, complement, or supplement the professional functions of physicians, nurses, dentists, or other health professionals in delivering health care to patients. These professionals can provide both direct and indirect patient care. Additionally, they assist in environmental health control, health promotion, and disease prevention. A number of more recent categories of healthcare

01   Technologists and Technicians

Examples: Clinical laboratory technologists and technicians, radiologic technologists, and nuclear medicine technologists.

02   Therapeutic Science Practitioners

Examples: Physical therapists, physical therapy assistance or aids, occupational therapists, and speech-language pathologists.

03   Behavioral Scientists

Examples: Social workers and rehabilitation counselors.

04   Support Services

Examples: Healthcare administrators and medical assistants.

FIGURE 5-7   Allied Health Professional Categories and Examples

Developed by Kim Davey.

specialists were created to implement the new procedures and equipment and the diagnostic, surgical, and therapeutic techniques that proliferated during the last 3 decades. Allied health professionals represent approximately 60% of all healthcare providers.[71]

The range of allied health professionals may be understood best by classifying them according to the functions they serve, as shown in **FIGURE 5-7**, and grouped into the following four categories:

1. Technologists and technicians
2. Therapeutic science practitioners
3. Behavioral scientists
4. Support services

Some allied health disciplines may be included in more than one of these functional classifications.

Technicians and Technologists

There is a rapidly growing number of technicians and technologists, including such major categories as cardiovascular technicians and technologists, clinical laboratory technicians, emergency medical technicians, health information technicians, nuclear medicine technologists, cytotechnologists, histologic technicians and technologists, surgical technologists, occupational safety and health technicians, pharmacy technicians, and many more. Because space does not allow for a discussion of all of these important health vocations, the following descriptions include only some representative disciplines in this allied health category.

Laboratory Technologists and Technicians

Clinical laboratory technologists and technicians have a critically important role in diagnosing disease, monitoring physiologic functions and the effectiveness of interventions, and performing highly technical procedures. Among their roles, clinical laboratory personnel analyze body fluids, tissues, and cells checking for bacteria and other microorganisms; analyze chemical content; test drug levels in blood to monitor the effectiveness of treatment; and match blood for transfusion.[72] Technologists, also known as clinical laboratory scientists or medical technologists, usually have a bachelor's degree in one of the life sciences. Clinical laboratory technicians, also known as medical technicians or medical laboratory technicians, generally require an associate degree or a certificate.[73]

According to the U.S. Bureau of Labor Statistics, there were a total of 337,800 clinical laboratory technologists and technicians active in the U.S. workforce who earned an annual median pay of $53,120, or $25.54 per hour, in 2019. The demand for clinical laboratory technologists and technicians is projected to grow by 7% from 2019 to 2029.[69] This will help meet the demands of an aging population that will have increased needs for the diagnosis of medical conditions and genetic testing. The U.S. Bureau of Labor Statistics reports that clinical laboratory technologists and technicians primarily work in general medical and surgical hospitals followed by medical and diagnostic laboratories, physician offices, junior colleges, colleges, universities, professional schools, and outpatient care centers.[73]

Radiologic and Magnetic Resonance Imaging Technologists

A radiologic technologist works under the supervision of a radiologist, a physician who specializes in the use and interpretation of radiographs and other medical imaging technologies. The radiologic technologist uses radiographs (x-rays), fluoroscopic equipment, and high-tech imaging machines such as ultrasonography, computed tomography, magnetic resonance imaging (MRI), and positron emission tomography (PET). These technologies produce images that allow physicians to study the internal organs, bones, and the metabolic activity of these structures.[74] Formal training programs in radiologic technology range in length from 1 to 4 years and lead to a certificate, associate degree, or bachelor's degree. Two-year associate degrees are the most prevalent. Radiologic technologists must be licensed or certified in most states while few states license MRI technologists. Radiologic technologists tend to specialize after some practice and become MRI technologists.[75]

According to the U.S. Bureau of Labor Statistics, there were a total of 250,700 radiologic and MRI technologists active in the U.S. workforce who earned an annual median pay of $62,280, or $29.94 per hour, in 2019. The demand for clinical laboratory technologists and technicians is projected to grow by 7% from 2019 to 2029. This will help meet the demands of an aging population who will have an increased need for medical imaging to diagnose medical conditions. The U.S. Bureau of Labor Statistics reports that radiologic technologists and MRI technicians primarily work in hospitals followed by physician offices and medical/diagnostic laboratories.[76]

Nuclear Medicine Technology

Nuclear medicine technologists use diagnostic imaging techniques to detect and map radioactive drugs in the human body. They administer radioactive pharmaceuticals to patients and then monitor the characteristics and functions of tissues or organs in which the radiopharmaceuticals localize. Abnormal areas show higher or lower concentrations of radioactivity than do normal ones. Nuclear medicine technologists need an associate or bachelor's degree from an accredited program. Some technologists are prepared in 1-year certificate programs offered by hospitals to those who are already radiologic technologists, medical technologists, or RNs. Nuclear medicine technologists must meet the minimum federal standards on the administration of radioactive drugs and the operation of radiation detection equipment. Certification is common for nuclear medicine technologists, although certification is not required for a license. Certification does meet the requirements for licensure in most states.[77]

According to the U.S. Bureau of Labor Statistics, there were a total of 18,500 nuclear medicine technologists active in the U.S. workforce who earned an annual median pay of $77,950, or $37.48 per hour, in 2019. The demand for nuclear medicine technologists is projected to grow by 5% from 2019 to 2029. This will help meet the demands of an aging population with an increased need for medical imaging to diagnose medical conditions. The U.S. Bureau of Labor Statistics reports that nuclear medicine technologists primarily work in hospitals followed by physician offices, medical/diagnostic laboratories, and outpatient care centers.[77]

Therapeutic Science Practitioners

Therapeutic science practitioners are essential to the treatment and rehabilitation of patients with diseases and injuries of all kinds. Physical therapists, occupational therapists, speech pathology and audiology therapists, radiation therapists, and respiratory therapists are only some of the allied health disciplines in this category.

Physical Therapists

Physical therapists provide services that help restore function, improve mobility, relieve pain, and prevent or limit physical disabilities of patients suffering from injuries or disease. They restore, maintain, and promote overall fitness and health. They review patients' medical histories and measure patients' strength, range of motion, balance, coordination, muscle performance, and motor function. They then develop and implement treatment plans that include exercises to develop flexibility, strength, and endurance. They also may prescribe exercises for patients to do at home. Physical therapists also may use electrical stimulation, hot or cold compresses, and ultrasound to relieve pain and reduce swelling. They teach patients to use assistive and adaptive devices, such as crutches, prostheses, and wheelchairs.[78]

Physical therapists earn a Doctor of Physical Therapy (DPT) degree from an accredited program, which is generally a 3-year program. There are two dominant pathways to earning a DPT. Some students complete a bachelor's degree and then apply to a DPT program, but increasing numbers of colleges and universities are creating a pathway for freshmen to be admitted into 6-year DPT programs that allow students to earn a bachelor's and DPT degree (similar to pharmacy schools where students can complete a 6-year program to earn a PharmD degree and a bachelor's degree). All states require physical therapists to be licensed. Some physical therapists choose to become board-certified in one of eight physical therapy specialty areas, such as orthopedics, sports, or geriatric physical therapy. Board certification in a specialty area requires 2,000 hours of clinical work or completion of a residency program accredited by the American Physical Therapy Association in the specialty area.[78]

According to the U.S. Bureau of Labor Statistics, there were a total of 258,200 physical therapists active in the U.S. workforce who earned an annual median pay of $89,440, or $43.00 per hour, in 2019. The demand for physical therapists is projected to grow by 18% from 2019 to 2029. This will help meet the demands of an aging population with an increased need for physical therapists. The demographic shift will result in a need for more physical therapists to help maintain and restore the mobility of older adults as well as individuals being treated for a number of chronic diseases that can impact mobility, such as diabetes, cardiovascular disease, and obesity. The U.S. Bureau of Labor Statistics reports that physical therapists primarily work in offices followed by hospitals, home health, and nursing or residential care facilities.[78]

Physical Therapy Assistants or Aides

Physical therapy assistants or aides are supervised by physical therapists and assist physical therapists in meeting the needs of an increasing number of patients. Physical therapy assistants observe patients engaged in therapy, help with specific exercises, treat patients via massage and stretching, use devices and equipment like walkers to help patients, and provide patient education based on the treatment plans developed by a physical therapist. Additionally, they assist with office duties such as cleaning, patient transportation, answering the phone, and scheduling patient appointments. Physical therapy assistants or aides earn associate degrees, which takes around 2 years. Upon completion, they take a national certifying examination. All states require either licensure or certification to practice as a physical therapy assistant.[79]

According to the U.S. Bureau of Labor Statistics, there were a total of 149,300 physical therapy assistants or aides active in the U.S. workforce who earned an annual median pay of $48,990, or $23.55 per hour, in 2019. The demand for physical therapy assistants or aides is projected to grow by 29% from 2019 to 2029, significantly faster than other health occupations. This will help meet the demands of an aging population and the rise in chronic diseases that impact health and result in an increased need for physical therapy services. Employment opportunities have grown rapidly in the physical therapy field, and the demand now exceeds the supply. The U.S. Bureau of Labor Statistics reports that physical therapy assistants primarily work in physical therapy offices followed by hospitals, skilled nursing facilities, home health, and physician offices.[79]

Occupational Therapists

Occupational therapists assist patients in recovering from accidents, injuries, or diseases to improve their ability to perform tasks in their daily living and work environments. Occupational therapists work with a wide range of patients, from those with irreversible physical disabilities to those with mental disabilities or disorders. Occupational therapists assist patients in caring for their daily needs such as dressing, cooking, and eating. They also use physical exercises and other activities to increase strength and dexterity, visual acuity, and hand–eye coordination. Occupational therapists instruct in the use of adaptive equipment such as wheelchairs, splints, and aids to improve mobility. They also may design or make special equipment needed by patients at home or at work to perform activities of daily living or work responsibilities. Occupational therapists may collaborate with clients and employers to modify work environments so that clients can maintain employment. They earn a master's degree in occupational therapy, which generally takes 2 to 3 years to complete. A bachelor's degree is required to apply to occupational therapy graduate programs. Doctoral degrees in occupational therapy take 3 or more years to complete. Like pharmacy and physical therapy programs, occupational therapy programs are creating pathways for students to earn a bachelor's and master's degree in 5 years.[80]

According to the U.S. Bureau of Labor Statistics, there were a total of 143,330 occupational therapists active in the U.S. workforce who earned an annual median pay of $84,950, or $40.84 per hour, in 2019. The demand for physical therapy assistants or aides is projected to grow by 16% from 2019 to 2029, faster than other health occupations. This will help meet the demands of an aging population, patients living with chronic diseases, and patients treated for illnesses and disabilities such as Alzheimer's disease, cerebral palsy, autism, and the loss of a limb. The U.S. Bureau of Labor Statistics reports that occupational therapists primarily work in hospitals followed by physical therapy offices, schools, home health, and skilled nursing facilities.[80]

Speech-Language Pathologists

Speech-language pathologists, sometimes called speech therapists, assess, diagnose, and treat patients who have problems with speech, swallowing, and other disorders in hospitals, schools, clinics, and private practice. They help patients improve communication and swallowing disorders due to a variety of causes like stroke, brain injury, hearing loss, developmental delay, Parkinson's disease, autism, and many other conditions. Approximately half of all speech-language pathologists are employed in the education system—from preschools to universities. Speech-language pathologists use written and oral tests and special instruments to diagnose the nature of an impairment and develop an individualized plan of care. They may teach the use of alternative communication methods, including automated devices and sign language. A master's degree and a state license are required to practice.[81]

According to the U.S. Bureau of Labor Statistics, there were a total of 79,120 speech-language pathologists active in the U.S. workforce who earned an annual median pay of $79,120, or $38.04 per hour, in 2019. The demand for speech-language pathologists is projected to grow by 25% from 2019 to 2029, significantly faster than other health occupations. This will help meet the demands of an aging population with increased incidence of conditions such as strokes, brain injuries, and hearing loss, all requiring speech-language therapy intervention. The U.S. Bureau of Labor Statistics reports that speech-language pathologists primarily work in educational settings followed by therapy offices, hospitals, skilled nursing facilities, and private practice.[81]

Behavioral Scientists

Behavioral scientists are crucial in the social, psychological, and community and patient educational activities related to health maintenance, prevention of disease, and accommodation of patients to disability. They include professionals in social work, health education, community mental health, alcoholism and substance abuse services, and other health and human service areas.

Social Work

Social workers diagnose and treat clients, patients, and families in relation to an array of mental, behavioral, and emotional issues. They assist in addressing the personal, economic, and social problems associated with everyday life, illness, injury, and disability. Social workers provide social services in hospitals and other health-related settings. Medical and public health social workers provide patients and families with psychosocial support in cases of acute, chronic, or terminal illness. Mental health and substance abuse social workers assess and treat people with mental illness or those who abuse alcohol, tobacco, or other drugs. A bachelor's degree in social work is required for entry-level positions such as caseworkers or mental health assistants. Clinical social workers require a master's degree and 2 years of supervised experience in a clinical setting. Clinical social workers must pass a clinical exam to be licensed. All states require clinical social workers to be licensed. Doctoral-level programs prepare social workers for advanced clinical practice, research, and academic careers. Generally, states require nonclinical social workers to be licensed or certificatied.[82]

According to the U.S. Bureau of Labor Statistics, there were a total of 713,200 social workers active in the U.S. workforce who earned an annual median pay of $50,470, or $24.26 per hour, in 2019. The demand for social workers is projected to grow by 13% from 2019 to 2029, faster than other health occupations. This will help meet the demands of an aging population and the need for substance abuse treatment providers and mental healthcare providers. The U.S. Bureau of Labor Statistics reports that social workers primarily work as child, family, and school social workers; healthcare social workers; mental health providers and substance abuse socials workers; and other social worker roles. Most social workers work in an office or visit clients in their homes or schools.[82]

Rehabilitation Counselors

A rehabilitation counselor provides personalized counseling, emotional support, and rehabilitation therapy to patients limited by physical, mental, developmental, or emotional disabilities to promote independence. Patients may be recovering from illness or injury, have psychiatric problems, or have intellectual deficits. After an injury or illness is stabilized, the rehabilitation counselor tests the patient's motor ability, skill level, interests, and psychological makeup and develops an appropriate training or retraining plan. The goal is to maximize the patient's ability to function in society. A master's degree in rehabilitation counseling or a related field is required to be licensed or certified as a rehabilitation counselor. Licensing requirements differ from state to state. Usually, counseling services require state licensure, but other services such as vocational training or job placement assistance may not. Licensure usually requires a master's degree and 2,000–4,000 hours of supervised clinical experience. The Commission on Rehabilitation Counselor Certification offers certification, but this is not required for all jobs and in all states.[83]

According to the U.S. Bureau of Labor Statistics, there were a total of 120,200 rehabilitation counselors active in the U.S. workforce who earned an annual median pay of $35,950, or $17.28 per hour, in 2019. The demand for rehabilitation counselors is projected to grow by 10% from 2019 to 2029, faster than other health occupations. This will help meet the demand for substance abuse treatment and mental healthcare providers. The U.S. Bureau of Labor Statistics reports that rehabilitation counselors primarily work in community and vocational rehabilitation services followed by individual and family services, state governments, nursing and residential care facilities, and private practice.[83]

Support Services

Support services are necessary for the highly complex and sophisticated system of health care to function. Service specialists perform administrative, operational, and management duties and often work closely with direct providers of healthcare services. Health information administrators, dental laboratory technologists, electroencephalographic technologists, food service administrators, surgical technologists, and environmental health technologists are just some of the allied health professionals in this category.

Healthcare Administrators

Healthcare administrators, also referred to as medical and health service managers, keep a range of healthcare services and operations running smoothly. Healthcare administrators plan, organize, direct, control, or coordinate medical and health services in hospitals, clinics, nursing care facilities, and group medical practices. Many healthcare administrators are employed in hospital settings, and others work for insurers, clinics, or medical group practices. Bachelor's, master's, and doctoral degree programs in healthcare administration are offered by a variety of colleges and universities. There are also short certificate or diploma programs, usually lasting less than 1 year, in health services administration or in medical office management. However, a bachelor's degree in medical administration currently is considered the minimum entry-level educational degree required for higher-level management positions.[84]

According to the U.S. Bureau of Labor Statistics, there were a total of 422,300 healthcare administrators active in the U.S. workforce who earned an annual median pay of $100,980, or $48.55 per hour, in 2019. The demand for healthcare administrators is projected to grow by 33% from 2019 to 2029, faster than other health occupations. New healthcare administrators are needed to replace those who are retiring and to provide new healthcare services that will emerge and require professionals with business and management skills. The U.S. Bureau of Labor Statistics reports that healthcare administrators primarily work in hospitals followed by physician practices, nursing and residential care facilities, government positions, and outpatient care centers.[84]

Medical Assistants

Medical assistants check patients in for appointments, measure and record vital signs, verify insurance, schedule patient appointments, perform some patient testing, take patient histories, prepare blood samples for laboratory testing, and provide post-visit instructions and general support. Additionally, medical assistants can give patients injections or medications as directed by a physician and permitted by state law. The educational requirements for medical assistants are usually a high school diploma followed by a 1-year training program at a community college, vocational school, technical school, or university. These programs typically lead to a certificate, while some 2-year programs offer an associate degree. Medical assistants are not required to be licensed or certified. However, some employers prefer medical assistants who have been certified by one of several certifying bodies.[85]

According to the U.S. Bureau of Labor Statistics, there were a total of 725,200 medical assistants active in the U.S. workforce who earned an annual median pay of $34,800, or $16.73 per hour, in 2019. The demand for medical assistants is projected to grow by 19% from 2019 to 2029, faster than other health occupations. The demand for medical assistants is driven by the aging population and preventive health services. Physicians and other providers need help with administrative and clinical duties to be able to care for more patients. The U.S. Bureau of Labor Statistics reports that medical assistants primarily work in physician offices followed by hospitals, outpatient care centers, and chiropractor offices.[85]

▶ Factors That Influence Demand for Healthcare Professionals

Without attempting to include all interrelated factors that influence demand for various types of healthcare personnel, it is important to recognize some major determinants of the size and nature of the healthcare employment sector and workforce. Regardless of the potential for legislatively mandated reforms of the healthcare system, the number and skill requirements of each discipline within the healthcare workforce depend on the interdependence of the following factors. **FIGURE 5-8** lists the factors that influence the demand for healthcare professionals.

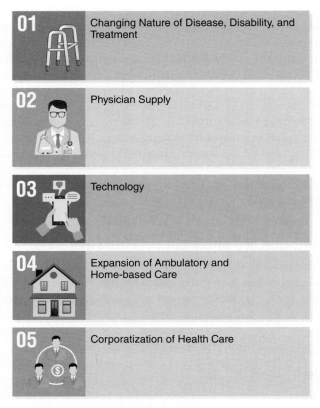

01 Changing Nature of Disease, Disability, and Treatment

02 Physician Supply

03 Technology

04 Expansion of Ambulatory and Home-based Care

05 Corporatization of Health Care

FIGURE 5-8 Factors That Influence the Demand for Healthcare Professionals
Developed by Kim Davey.

Changing Nature of Disease, Disability, and Treatment

The aging of the population and advances in the treatment of acute and life-threatening conditions result in increased survival of people with chronic illness or disabilities. The growing number of patients with deteriorating mental capacities, cardiac conditions, cancer, stroke, head and spinal cord injuries, neonatal deficits, and congenital disorders significantly increases the demand for workers who provide and support prolonged medical treatment, rehabilitation, and nursing home or custodial care.

Physician Supply

Although many categories of healthcare personnel practice independently of physicians, most of the decisions regarding the use of healthcare resources, the acceptance of other therapeutic modalities, and the treatment provided by nonphysicians are still made by physicians. It is therefore important to recognize that the anticipated changes in the numbers and types of physicians will have a direct or indirect impact on the demand for many other types of healthcare personnel.

Technology

Medical and nonmedical technology used in the provision of health care has important implications for the number and skill requirements of the healthcare workforce. Advances in medical imaging, new pharmaceuticals, and health information and communications technologies have the potential to both increase and decrease the demand for various kinds of personnel. Some technologies, such as transluminal coronary angioplasty and positron emission tomography, have led to the elimination of more laborious medical interventions. Others, such as sophisticated remote patient monitoring systems, telehealth, and more robust home care services have facilitated shifts to new service settings, such as ambulatory surgical centers. Also, automation of clinical laboratory testing has reduced the need for laboratory personnel. Advances in artificial intelligence and genomics are revolutionizing and disrupting healthcare delivery. Thus, the mix of skills and the numbers of personnel ebb and flow with the discovery, application, and discontinuation of technologies, treatments, and drugs.

Expansion of Ambulatory and Home-Based Care

Healthcare policies and reforms will continue to shift health service delivery sites from acute care hospitals toward ambulatory, home care, and long-term care settings. With the emphasis on cost containment and value, the home care component of the healthcare industry is expected to expand significantly in the next decade. In addition, there is a growing body of evidence that therapy provided in the home can help patients recover faster, is safer, and reduces hospital readmissions.

Corporatization of Health Care

Solo practice among health professionals is becoming a practice pattern of the past for many reasons. The increase in group practices and hospital employment of physicians, the development of several forms of provider organizations, and new models for physician payment are likely to reduce solo private practice dramatically to only highly specialized and small niches. The assembly of vertically integrated health systems that link hospitals, nursing homes, home care, and other services along with the diversification of health providers into various health-related corporate ventures all reflect the corporatization of health care.

Since the beginning of the Great Recession (2007–2009), employment in health care continued to rise in the fields of ambulatory care, nursing, and residential care. While overall nationwide employment dropped steadily during the Recession, the healthcare industry showed continued growth by adding almost 500,000 jobs. This was also the case during previous economic recessions in 1990 and 2001.[86] Strong growth in the healthcare workforce is likely to continue for the foreseeable future. Between 2014 and 2024, the U.S. Bureau of Labor Statistics predicts a 21.8% increase in healthcare-related jobs compared to an increase of 4.8% projected for all other unrelated jobs.[87]

▶ Emerging Trends in the Healthcare Workforce

The healthcare workforce is rapidly evolving and responding to the complex needs of a diverse range of patients and populations. Diversity, equity, and inclusion (DEI) efforts are underway across the United States. A high-performing and responsive health system reflects its population. Therefore, a workforce that prioritizes DEI is better positioned to serve the diverse health needs of patients, communities, and populations. Job stress and job-related burnout are byproducts of the complex health system and patient needs in the United States. The COVID-19 pandemic highlighted the importance of "caring for the caregivers" to mitigate stress and burnout. Working to mitigate both helps keep the workforce healthy and stable. Failure to keep a stable workforce results in shortages, limited access to certain health professionals and services, increased costs, and many other challenges, undermining population health and well-being. The following sections discuss DEI, job stress, and job-related burnout. There are numerous workforce topics that could be discussed, but the discussion is limited to a few due to page constraints. Case 5-3 provides an opportunity to interview a healthcare professional to better understand professional roles, practice, and emerging trends impacting the healthcare workforce.

Diversity, Equity, and Inclusion

Conversations around diversity, equity, and inclusion (DEI) are rapidly evolving in workplaces across the United States, including those related to health care. DEI programs and positions are emerging to address what has been a slow process to raise awareness about its importance. McKinsey and Company published a series of reports that highlight how the performance gap is widening between organizations that prioritize DEI and those that do not. Financial performance was one dimension in particular that improved over time under diverse executive teams. The report notes that organizations are quickly being categorized as "fast movers," "moderate movers," or "laggards" based on how they are acquiring talent and including DEI in their organizational strategy. The data are clear that DEI efforts must be systematic and a visible strategic priority for organizations.[88] Understanding how diversity, equity, and inclusion are defined can help healthcare organizations design and implement efforts to create diverse, equitable, and inclusive workplaces.

Diversity refers to understanding, accepting, and valuing individual differences such as experience, skills, knowledge, gender, race, culture, age, sexuality, disability, education, religion, class, and many other dimensions. Traditional definitions of diversity have emphasized racial and gender dimensions. For example, research from McKinsey and Company found that companies with high levels of gender, ethnic, and cultural diversity financially outperformed less diverse peer organizations. The results are compelling, finding that greater gender diversity on executive teams was associated with an increased likelihood that the organization would financially outperform a peer organization with less gender diversity. Executive teams composed of 30% or more of female executives were 48% more likely to outperform less gender-diverse organizations. Furthermore, organizations that are more ethnically diverse outperform peer organizations and achieve higher performance than organizations with high levels of gender diversity. This illustrates that diversity compounds, and this compounding can lead to higher and higher levels of performance.[88] There are numerous additional benefits associated with DEI, including higher employee engagement, higher productivity, reduced interpersonal conflict, higher levels of learning, reduced stress and overall higher levels of health, increased resilience and trust, and increased organizational commitment.[89] Today, the definition of diversity is evolving to include age, sexuality, disability, culture, and many other forms of diversity that add value and richness to organizations—and ultimately consumers. Furthermore, the concept of intersectionality is emerging thanks to the work of Professor Kimberlé Crenshaw. Intersectionality is a term coined by Crenshaw to recognize that individuals often possess multiple identities—or "intersecting identities"—that impact how they are viewed, understood, and treated. Organizations often conceptualize diversity based on a single factor such as gender or race. Intersectionality challenges organizations to recognize the multiple and diverse identities of employees. This concept also provides another lens through which to view equity and inclusion in the workplace to reduce bias, discrimination, and feelings of isolation.[90]

Equity refers to organizational policies that support equal opportunities and fairness for everyone in the organization. The organization is focused on ensuring everyone has opportunities for individual growth, development, and advancement. Equity recognizes that differences exist between employees and that these differences are valuable. Therefore, equity-led organizational policies take into consideration individual needs and rebalance organizational structures to address disadvantages faced by different groups of individuals (i.e., minorities, women, and members of the Lesbian, Gay, Bisexual, Transgender, Queer, Intersex, Asexual [LGBTQIA] community, among other examples). Ensuring unbiased talent acquisition (or recruitment, selection, and onboarding processes for employees) and retaining that talent is paramount. In addition, DEI organizations have no-tolerance policies for bias, harassment, or discrimination of any kind.

Inclusion can be defined as the feeling of belonging and acceptance based on one's whole identity or intersecting identities.[90,91] This belonging creates psychological safety that allows individuals to voice their ideas, opinions, frustrations, and much more.[92] Inclusive workplaces are collaborative, supportive, and respectful. Diverse workplaces are not necessarily inclusive workplaces, which is a common misconception. Ensuring diversity is a good first step, but organizations have to take the next step and ensure the workplace is inclusive. Research indicates that organizations must have an inclusive workplace to leverage diversity and translate it into organizational performance.[93] McKinsey and Company found that equality, openness, and belonging were vital components for creating inclusive workplaces, particularly among organizational leaders and managers.[88]

So, what should the prescription be for the health system and its organizations? First, education and training is needed to develop a shared understanding of what DEI is and why it is important. Simply making DEI visible inside and outside the organization helps create a strong organizational culture of DEI to build upon. Creating the role of a Chief Diversity, Equity, and Inclusion Officer, or a similar role, is a step toward ensuring DEI is a visible strategic priority and systematically embedded in and across an organization. Second, organizations need to set data-driven goals and targets to promote accountability and progress. Reviewing and revising talent acquisition practices can reveal opportunities for improvement and be a great place to start when creating DEI goals. Third, it is important to create an organizational culture that is open, especially around the topics of fairness, discrimination, microaggressions, and multivariate forms of diversity. A high-performing and responsive health system reflects its population. Therefore, a workforce that prioritizes DEI will be positioned to better serve its population while simultaneously improving performance.

Employee Wellness

Organizations are increasingly recognizing that employee wellness is tied to organizational performance and wellness. Healthcare organizations, like other organizations, are recognizing the importance of wellness programs that focus on helping employees balance all components of their wellness (i.e., occupational, spiritual, emotional/mental, financial, social, intellectual, and environmental). Common components of workplace wellness programs include stress reduction, weight loss, smoking cessation, health screenings, exercise, nutrition, and vaccination clinics. Benefits of wellness programs include lower healthcare costs, reduced absenteeism, increased productivity, reduced workers' compensation and disability-related costs, reducing injuries, and improved employee morale and loyalty.[94] Workplace wellness committees provide input into workplace wellness programs and should be established by organizations. Chief wellness officers (CWOs) are emerging in many healthcare organizations to lead employee health and wellness efforts. The COVID-19 pandemic catapulted the wellness of healthcare professionals into the international limelight. In response to the pandemic, CWOs are being incorporated into the emergency command structure of healthcare organizations to try and mitigate job stress and burnout among healthcare professionals before, during, and after a crisis.[95] Employee surveys are a great way to have employees assess their health and identify potentially helpful resources. Additionally, the organization can use the information when negotiating health plan coverage.

Job stress and burnout are both high among healthcare professionals and an integral part of an employee wellness program for healthcare professionals. Job stress refers to "the response people have when presented with work demands and pressures that are not matched to their knowledge and abilities and which challenge their ability to cope."[96] Job stress can lead to job-related burnout. Job-related burnout is "a special type of work-related stress – a state of physical or emotional exhaustion that also involves a sense of reduced accomplishment and loss of personal identity."[97] Individuals in helping professions, like health care, experience higher rates of job-related burnout. This can be the result of extreme activities (i.e. constant high-stress or monotonous activities), lack of work–life balance, work environment, unclear job expectations, and a lack of ability to influence work and work decisions. Some common symptoms of job-related burnout include becoming cynical at work; trouble starting and completing job tasks; becoming irritable with coworkers or patients; difficulty concentrating; misusing food, drugs, or alcohol to feel better; changes in sleep habits; and headaches, bowel issues, or other physical complaints. Employee wellness programs continue to emerge and evolve to care for the health and well-being of caregivers.

▶ The Future of the Healthcare Workforce

Policy makers at every level of government, insurers, educators, providers, and consumers have a vested interest in the issues that pertain to the healthcare workforce. The Association of Academic Health Centers clearly defined those issues in a 1994 publication. Remarkably, the issues remain relevant decades later[98]:

■   The adequacy of supply of health professionals, such as nurses, allied health professionals, primary care physicians, and geriatricians

■   The concern about the supply of faculty to train health professionals

■   The geographic distribution of health professionals, especially shortages in rural and underserved urban areas

■   The underrepresentation of minorities in all health professions

■   The potential supply and poor distribution of specialty physicians

■   The questions about the appropriate scope of practice for various health professionals and concern about legal restrictions on scope of practice for nonphysician practitioners

■   The concern about the quality and relevance of the health professions' educational programs; whether educational institutions are producing the health professionals needed for an effective and productive workforce

■   The costs associated with educating health professionals. The competency testing of healthcare professionals

■   The emergence or revision of professional roles such as technology and the delivery system change

The increasing need for higher levels of education and training to reflect the growing complexity and specialization in medicine and healthcare

The United States has never planned comprehensively or strategically for the development and deployment of its healthcare workforce and, as a result, "the preparation of each generation of health workers is just as fragmented and confusing as the healthcare system they will one day join."[99] Federal and state governments, educational institutions, professional organizations, insurers, and provider institutions have had separate and often conflicting interests in health workforce education and training, regulation, financing, entry-level preparation, and scope of practice. The various levels at which policy decisions have been made and the disparate interests that influence those decisions have presented major obstacles to ensuring a coherent, efficient, and rational health workforce in the United States. Complex supply and demand factors influence workforce requirements, and the prediction of future requirements is severely confounded by the lack of uniform data at national and state levels across the professions.[100] Supply factors include variables such as income variations among professions, licensure requirements, and transferability of skills. Demand is affected by factors such as population demographics, consumer expectations, and payment systems. In the upcoming years, the current workforce shortages in professions such as generalist physicians, nurses, and mental health workers; the disproportionate geographic distribution of many types of providers in urban and rural areas; and underrepresentation of minorities in the health professions are major focal points for future legislation. The aging population, the shifting nature of diseases, healthcare delivery and reimbursement reforms, new technology, and economic factors will continue to change consumer demands and provider expectations, all lending more complexity to the challenges of planning for future workforce requirements.

▶ Discussion Questions

- How does the healthcare workforce influence healthcare delivery in the United States?
- What is the definition of a healthcare professional? Give some examples of the direct and indirect patient care roles healthcare professionals play in delivering care in the United States.
- How does interprofessional education and practice influence healthcare delivery in the United States?
- How do evidence-based practice and clinical practice guidelines influence healthcare delivery?
- What are the four primary mechanisms through which health professionals are credentialed and regulated?
- Discuss the evolving role of physicians.
- What is the difference between the allopathic and osteopathic approaches to medicine?
- What are the major distinctions between primary care and specialty care?
- Why is there an imbalance between primary care and specialty care in the United States?
- What are some of the other independent healthcare professions and allied health professions that are part of the healthcare workforce in the United States?
- What factors influence the demand for healthcare professionals in the United States?
- Define diversity, equity, and inclusion (DEI).
- What are the benefits of DEI programs?
- What is intersectionality?
- What are the goals of employee wellness programs?
- What is job stress and job-related burnout?
- What are some of the causes of job-related burnout?
- What are some of the common symptoms associated with job-related burnout?
- What are future challenges and opportunities that face the healthcare workforce?

CASE 5-1 A Collaborative Systems Approach to Health Care

Written by Caren Rossow, DHA, MBA

Amelia is a young Somali refugee woman with juvenile-onset diabetes. From her apartment, she tests her blood sugar level. The reading, which is electronically transmitted to the Federal Qualified Health Clinic (FQHC) where she is a patient, activates a system of health care and learning that has been carefully created around her. She is a member of an alliance, a team of clinicians, university faculty, health professionals-in-training, and members of her community collaborating to keep her healthy.[1]

Recently, the local university and the FQHC were integrated into a major regional health system, creating an interprofessional learning and healthcare delivery partnership along with the Somali Community Development Alliance (SCDA). The SCDA works with the healthcare alliance to obtain culturally competent health care for their community, as well as role models and an education pipeline for a new generation of Somali health professionals. In turn, the university is graduating healthcare professionals who learned their skills in the community and understand the importance of collaboration, while achieving the Triple Aim—enhancing the patient experience and population health while decreasing overall costs.[1]

(continues)

CASE 5-1 A Collaborative Systems Approach to Health Care *(continued)*

Interprofessional education is defined when two or more professions learn about, from, and with each other to enable effective communication and improve health outcomes.[2] In this context, a professional is all-encompassing that includes individuals with the knowledge, skills, and ability to contribute to the physical, mental, and social well-being of a community.[2]

Medical, nursing, pharmacy, and occupational therapy students from the university learn together, rotating in interprofessional teams to complete their training in an integrated healthcare system that incorporates ambulatory clinics, patient-centered medical homes, and acute care and transitional care units within a community setting. This system setting allows the health science students to build healing relationships with their patients and families, work with traditional and nontraditional providers of care (community health workers), immerse themselves into different cultures, receive an opportunity to coordinate care across various healthcare settings, and participate in systems improvements.[1]

Today, Amelia's blood sugar level is elevated. The results were transmitted electronically via cell phone to the FQHC, triggering an alert in the electronic health record as well as a notification to Amelia that someone from the FQHC would call her. At the FQHC, the nurse preceptor scans the alerts for the day, and on noticing Amelia's elevated blood sugar level, she meets with the interprofessional team. From the meeting, the pharmacy student and Somali community health worker call Amelia on her cell phone, communicating with her in her own language that they have been working with her nurse practitioner preceptor to determine the amount of medications she should take today and provide her with the required dose of insulin.

While on the phone, Amelia relays that she is experiencing other symptoms. They gather all the information and begin to develop a plan of care. After review by her family physician, Amelia is called to come into the FQHC for lab work. A few hours later, the pharmacy student and community health worker call Amelia notifying her that she has a urinary tract infection. They clarify the severity of the infection, question her regarding any allergies to medications, and verify the location of her pharmacy. Education is provided on taking an antibiotic as well as plans for follow-up care. Later that day, the interprofessional healthcare team huddles to discuss several events of the day. The pharmacy student briefly shares Amelia's history and her plan of care focusing on medications, diabetes care, Somali culture, and the role of interprofessional healthcare team members. Concentrating on systems issues, the team members discuss the FQHC's diabetes care goals and their roles in collecting and analyzing data on the care processes and outcomes. The next three days, a member of the interprofessional healthcare team call Amelia for follow-up care. Her blood sugar level has returned to a normal range, and she is feeling much better. **FIGURE 5-9** illustrates the community and health system domain interconnected with interprofessional educational and collaborative practice ultimately improving the health outcomes of the entire domain.[1]

The FQHC has surpassed its performance goals with reducing costs by approximately 20%.[1] The entire system as a whole has benefited by a decrease in hospitalizations and emergency department utilization. Most importantly, the Somali community has achieved health, wellness, and survival statistics that are indistinguishable from other wealthy suburbs nearby.

References

1. Earnest M, Brandt B. Aligning practice redesign and interprofessional education to advance the triple aim outcomes. *J Interprof Care*. 2014;28(6):497-500.
2. World Health Organization. Framework for action on Interprofessional Education and Collaborative Practice. http://www.who.int/hrh/resources/framework_action/en/. Geneva, Switzerland. Published 2010:1-62. Accessed January 23, 2018.

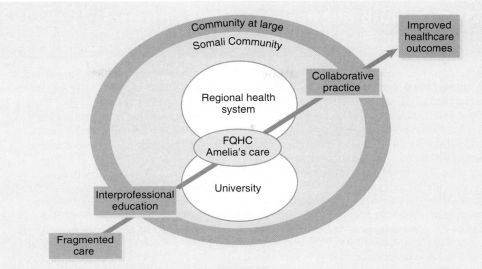

FIGURE 5-9 Community and Health System Domain

Data from Earnest and Brandt. (2014). Aligning Practice Redesign and Interprofessional Education to Advance Triple Aim Outcomes and the World Health Organization. (2010). Framework for Action on Interprofessional Education and Collaborative Practice. Geneva, Switzerland. Retrieved January 23, 2018, from http://www.who.int/hrh/resources/framework_action/en/.

Discussion Questions

1. What are the factors contributing to the community health center's success?
2. How does the community health center impact the health and well-being of individual patients and the broader community?
3. What steps can the clinic take to continue to improve the health and well-being of individual patients and the broader community?

Johnson JA, Anderson DE, Rossow CC. *Health Systems Thinking: A Primer*. Jones & Barlett Learning; 2020.

CASE 5-2 Antibiotic Resistance: It's with Us for the Long Run

It was too good to be true: when penicillin was first introduced in clinical practice during World War II, it had dramatic impacts on a range of infectious diseases, from pneumococcal pneumonia, to gonorrhea, to staphylococcal wound infections. No randomized controlled trials were needed to demonstrate its efficacy or effectiveness compared with previous treatments. In short order, however, higher dosages of penicillin were required, and by the early 1950s, penicillin stopped working altogether for many infections.

In the 1950s, new classes of antibiotics were developed, which headed off a crisis. However, it was already apparent that bacteria had the ability to develop resistance to antibiotics using a range of mechanisms. The more aggressively antibiotics were used, the more common resistance became, especially in hospitals where antibiotics had literally become standard operating procedure.

In addition to the use of antibiotics to treat bacterial infections, it became common clinical practice to try antibiotics as a first-line approach when the cause of the problem was not clear or was most

(continues)

CASE 5-2 Antibiotic Resistance: It's with Us for the Long Run *(continued)*

likely due to a virus. In addition, it was found that antibiotics could modestly increase the growth rate of many animals raised for food. Widespread use of antibiotics in farm animals allowed the development of feedlots and whole industries devoted to raising animals together in close quarters.

By the late 20th century, animal use of antibiotics exceeded human use. These antibiotics often ended up in public water systems, where the runoff from feedlots contaminates streams and groundwater. It has been called a "double hit." We got antibiotics in our food and in our drinking water, both of which promote bacterial resistance.

By the early years of this century, the problem of antibiotic resistance returned with a vengeance. Methicillin-resistant Staphylococcus aureus infections, or MRSA, became widespread not only in hospitals, but in the community as well. Healthy athletes as well as those undergoing outpatient surgeries were now at risk of life-threatening diseases. Community-acquired MRSA skin infections are increasingly common in groups that share close quarters or experience more skin-to-skin contact, such as team athletes, military recruits, and prisoners. However, MRSA infections are being seen in the general community as well, including in individuals without known risk factors.

The problem is broader than staphylococcal infection; in fact, the vast majority of bacteria that causes infections in hospitals are resistant to at least one of the antibiotics previously used for their treatment. Recently, gram-negative infections, which are the most common causes of urinary tract infections and an increasingly frequent cause of pneumonia and postsurgical infections, have often become resistant to multiple antibiotics. The CDC estimates that over 20,000 people per year die in the United States alone from antibiotic-resistant bacterial infections.

Reducing the consequences of the existing antibiotic resistance is critical. Increased hand-washing and use of other sterilizing procedures is underway in healthcare institutions. Parallel precautions might be needed in athletic and fitness facilities. Early nonantibiotic treatments of wounds and other acute conditions is becoming an important intervention.

Previously unrecognized impacts of overuse of antibiotics are increasingly being recognized. These are likely to include increases in childhood asthma and juvenile idiopathic arthritis. There is even suggestive evidence of an increase in childhood obesity associated with early use of antibiotics. These previously unexpected impacts are all being linked to changes in the human microbiome that are due to overuse of antibiotics. The human microbiome consists of billions of bacteria and other microbes that live outside and inside all human beings, most commonly in the gastrointestinal tract.

In recent years, routine feeding of antibiotics to animals has been banned in much of the developed world and is now being curtailed in the United States. New approaches to reducing the development and spread of antibiotic-resistant bacteria are underway, and new classes of antibiotics are under investigation. Before clinical use, they will need FDA approval. Once approved, the FDA will need to decide whether they should be available for all licensed prescribers or restricted to specifically qualified prescribers and/or specific conditions/diseases.

Alternative or complementary approaches, such as greater reliance on vaccinations, may reduce the need for antibiotics. For instance, vaccines to prevent pneumococcal and meningococcal bacterial disease have been highly successful. Use of nonprescription probiotics, or "good bacteria," has been shown to improve the tolerance for, and at times the effectiveness of, existing antibiotics. They are increasingly being used as a routine adjunct to treatment and possibly for prevention.

New approaches to antibiotic resistance may come from the rapidly expanding understanding of the relationship between human health, animal health, and ecosystem health. The issue of antibiotic resistance to treatment is not new, and it is not going away.

Discussion Questions

1. What type of interprofessional team would you propose to address the misuse of antibiotics that are contributing to antibiotic resistance in a primary care clinic or hospital?
2. How can evidence-based practice and clinical practice guidelines be used in providing care to address antibiotic resistance?
3. What recommendations would you share with the interprofessional team related to building a culture of collaboration?

Riegelman R. *Population Health: A Primer*. Jones & Bartlett Learning; 2020.

CASE 5-3 Healthcare Professional Interview Exercise

Written by Kim Davey, PhD, MBA, MA
Samford University, School of Public Health

In this exercise, students are required to conduct an interview with a healthcare professional. Physicians, nurses, health technology professionals, health insurance professionals, public health professionals, social workers, healthcare lawyers, and many other types of professionals would be appropriate to interview. Students will use the interview questions provided below to better understand the variety of healthcare professionals and their role within the United States. Course instructors and students can use the questions as a menu to select the questions that fit the focus of the course and healthcare professional selected. The interview can be conducted via face-to-face meeting, phone, or video conferencing such as Zoom or Skype. The interview should last approximately 40 minutes to 1 hour (no more than 1 hour to respect the time of your interviewee). Students are required to identify a healthcare professional, set up a meeting, and conduct the interview in a timely and professional manner. Students must provide the course instructor with the health professional's contact information to verify the interview was conducted in a professional manner. As a professional courtesy, students should email some of the following questions to their healthcare professional in advance of the scheduled interview. Preparation and planning are key to a conducting a good interview. Researching your interviewee and organization in advance of the interview is helpful. Remember to dress professionally and send the interviewee a thank you following the interview.

Healthcare Professional Interview Questions
Professional Background

Share about your professional background.

- What was your educational path?
- What professional organizations are you a member of and involved with?

Current Professional Position

- Tell me about your current organization (e.g., location(s), size, services, points of pride).
- What is your current title/position? Describe your typical day and key responsibilities.
- What types of healthcare professionals do you regularly work with? How do you work together (e.g., provide patient care, key reporting, projects, operations, budgeting)?

(continues)

CASE 5-3 Healthcare Professional Interview Exercise *(continued)*

- What types of healthcare organizations do you work with? This could be the Joint Commission, insurance commissions or companies, federal/state agencies/departments, etc.
- What is a challenging aspect of your role?
- What is a rewarding aspect of your role?

Healthcare Happenings
- What healthcare trends are you following?
- How do you keep up with what is happening in health care? What do you read? Listen to?

Healthcare Overview
- Will you provide an overview of the U.S. healthcare system from your perspective (e.g., cost, quality, access, private health insurance, public health insurance, primary care, acute care, long-term care, health information technology, etc.)? Select a few topics that are driving your work and share how these elements influence your work.

Healthcare Aims
Think back to Chapter 1 and the Triple Aim for Populations as you select interview questions from this section. Health policies shape financing and ultimately health system outcomes through how care is delivered (or not) to populations. Students can also think about the WHO Health System Framework and Building Blocks from Chapter 1, as shown in Figure 1-2 and Table 1-1.

Costs
- How do changes in healthcare financing and reimbursement influence your healthcare organization, the services, and service providers?
- Can you share more about the shift from fee-for-service to value-based care reimbursement models? Can you share any insights into bundled payments?

Quality and Safety
- How does your organization ensure it delivers the best care, for every patient, every time?
- What programs, surveys, or other efforts are used in your organization to promote quality or used to assess patient experience?
- How are new delivery models changing how your organization approaches quality?

Access
- Are there creative ways your organization is expanding access? New markets? New services? New technology? New care models?
- Can you share insights into how provider shortages are affecting access?
- Can you share insights into what is happening in underserved areas of your community, market, state, etc.?

Population Health
- Can you share any collaborative efforts you have led with other organizations, providers, businesses, or insurers to improve population or community health?
- Can you share insights into how organizations and providers are using health informatics to address the health needs of specific populations (i.e., diabetics, congestive heart failure patients, Medicare beneficiaries, Medicaid recipients, women/infants)?

Health Policies

- Can you provide an example of how health policy influences your organization and work?
- What role has health policy and an evolving healthcare financing/reimbursement landscape played, if any, in focusing on improving quality and safety?
- What role has health policy and an evolving healthcare financing/reimbursement landscape played, if any, in focusing on enhancing value and reducing costs?
- What role has health policy and an evolving healthcare financing/reimbursement landscape played, if any, in focusing on expanding access?
- What role has health policy and an evolving healthcare financing/reimbursement landscape played, if any, in focusing on improving population health?

Future of Healthcare

- How do you think health care will change or advance in the next 5, 10, 15, and 20 years?
- What changes do you anticipate to how health care will be financed or paid for in the future?
- What improvements do you believe these changes or advancements will lead to? What challenges might emerge related to these changes or advancements?

Career and Professional Advice

- What advice do you have for students and/or early career professionals?
- What is your organization looking for (i.e., knowledge, skills, and abilities) in its workforce/employees?
- What professional organizations are you a member of? Why are you a member of the organization(s)? What types of events, professional development, networking, or other opportunities does the organization provide?

Concluding Questions

- Are there any specific questions you would like to ask your interviewee? Here are some additional questions to consider:
  - Does your organization have internship or residency opportunities for students?
  - What is the one thing you wish you could change about our health system?
  - What was the hardest problem you have had to solve in your career? How did you solve it?
  - What innovations do you believe offer the greatest opportunities to positively impact and improve our health system? How? Why?
  - What is a mistake you have made and what did you learn from the mistake?

CHAPTER ACRONYMS

AACN American Association of Colleges of Nursing
AAMC Association of American Medical Colleges
ABMS American Board of Medical Specialties
ACA Affordable Care Act
ACGME Accreditation Council for Graduate Medical Education

ADN Associate Degree in Nursing
APRN Advanced Practice Registered Nurses
CE Continuing Education
CNM Certified nurse-midwife
CRNA Nurse Anesthetists
CWO Chief wellness officers
DDM Doctor of Dental Medicine
DDS Doctor of Dental Surgery

(continues)

CHAPTER ACRONYMS   *(continued)*

DEI Diversity, equity, and inclusion
DMD Doctor of Medical Dentistry
DNP Doctor of Nursing Practice
DO Doctor of Osteopathy
DPM Doctor of Podiatric Medicine
DPT Doctor of Physical Therapy
FQHC Federal Qualified Health Clinic
IMG International medical graduate
LGBTQIA Lesbian, Gay, Bisexual, Transgender, Queer, Intersex, Asexual
LPN Licensed practical nurse
LVN Licensed vocational nurse
MCAT® Medical College Admission Test®
MD Doctor of Medicine

MOC Maintenance of Certification
MRI Magnetic resonance imaging
NCLEX-RN National Council Licensure Examination for RNs
NP Nurse practitioner
NRMP® National Resident Matching Program®
OB-GYN Obstetrics and Gynecology
PA Physician assistant
PA-C Physician assistant-certified
PET Positron Emission Tomography
PharmD Doctor of Pharmacy
PsyD Doctor of Psychology
RN Registered nurse
SCDA Somali Community Development Alliance

References

1. U.S. Department of Labor Bureau of Labor Statistics. Health care and social assistance: NAICS 62. Published June 11, 2021. Accessed June 11, 2021. https://www.bls.gov/iag/tgs/iag62.htm#workforce

2. U.S. Department of Labor Bureau of Labor Statistics. Ambulatory health care services: NAICS 621. Published June 11, 2021. Accessed June 11, 2021. https://www.bls.gov/iag/tgs/iag621.htm

3. U.S. Department of Labor Bureau of Labor Statistics. Hospitals: NAICS 622. Published June 11, 2021. Accessed June 11, 2021. https://www.bls.gov/iag/tgs/iag622.htm

4. U.S. Department of Labor Bureau of Labor Statistics. Nursing and residential care facilities: NAICS 623. Published June 11, 2021. Accessed June 11, 2021. https://www.bls.gov/iag/tgs/iag623.htm

5. U.S. Department of Labor Bureau of Labor Statistics. Social assistance: NAICS 624. Published June 11, 2021. Accessed June 11, 2021. https://www.bls.gov/iag/tgs/iag624.htm

6. U.S. Department of Labor Bureau of Labor Statistics. Healthcare occupations. Published June 11, 2021. Accessed June 11, 2021. https://www.bls.gov/ooh/healthcare/home.htm

7. Niles NJ. *Basics of the U.S. Health Care System.* 4th ed. Jones & Barlett Learning; 2021.

8. Johnson JA, Rossow CC. *Health Organizations: Theory, Behavior, and Development.* 2nd ed. Jones & Bartlett Learning; 2019.

9. Interprofessional Education Collaborative. *Core Competencies for Interprofessional Collaborative Practice: 2011 Original.* Interprofessional Education Collaborative; 2011. Accessed June 11, 2021. https://ipec.memberclicks.net/assets/2011-Original.pdf

10. Interprofessional Education Collaborative. *Team-Based Competencies: Building a Shared Foundation for Education and Clinical Practice.* Interprofessional Education Collaborative; 2011. Accessed June 11, 2021. https://www.gih.org/files/IPE%20conference%20proceedings%20Report_5211.pdf

11. Interprofessional Education Collaborative. *Core Competencies for Interprofessional Collaborative Practice: 2016 Update.* Interprofessional Education Collaborative; 2016. Accessed June 11, 2021. https://ipec.memberclicks.net/assets/2016-Update.pdf

12. World Health Organization. *Framework for Action on Interprofessional Education and Collaborative Practice.* World Health Organization; 2010. Accessed June 11, 2021. http://apps.who.int/iris/bitstream/handle/10665/70185/WHO_HRH_HPN_10.3_eng.pdf;jsessionid=A7D4007128B9DD5F17C691D4E71795DB?sequence=1

13. Wilson B, Austria MJ. What is evidence-based practice? University of Utah Health. Published February 26, 2021. Accessed June 11, 2021. https://accelerate.uofuhealth.utah.edu/explore/what-is-evidence-based-practice

14. National Center for Complementary and Integrative Health. Clinical practice guidelines. Accessed June 11, 2021. https://www.nccih.nih.gov/health/providers/clinicalpractice

15. Romig CL. New Pew Health Professions Commission report released. *AORN J.* 1999;69(1):260-262. doi: 10.1016/s0001-2092(06)62775-0

16. Hansen DA, Mueller JT, Craner RC, Poterack KA. Examining the burden of licensure, certification, and related credentialing costs in young physicians. *Mayo Clin Proc.* 2015;90(12):1795-1736. doi: 10.1016/j.mayocp.2015.09.020

17. Donaho BA. The Pew Commission Report: nursing's challenge to address it. 1997;24(5):507-512.

18. Shi L, Singh DA. *Essentials of the U.S. Health Care System.* 5th ed. Jones & Barlett Learning; 2019.

19. Nelson J. Laborists, defined. *The Hospitalist.* Published October 2011. Accessed February 13, 2021. https://www.the-hospitalist.org/hospitalist/article/124666/laborists-defined

20. Association of American Medical Colleges. The road to becoming a doctor. Published November 2020. Accessed June 11, 2021. https://www.aamc.org/system/files/2020-11/aamc-road-to-becoming-doctor-2020.pdf

21. American Board of Medical Specialities. Specialty and subspecialty certificates. Published 2020. Accessed June 11, 2021. https://www.abms.org/member-boards/specialty-subspecialty-certificates/

22. Association of American Medical Colleges. Who we are. Accessed June 11, 2021. https://www.aamc.org/who-we-are

23. American Osteopathic Association. Commission on Osteopathic College Accreditation. Published 2021. Accessed June 11, 2021. https://osteopathic.org/accreditation/

24. Kalter L. U.S. medical school enrollment rises 30%. Association of American Medical Colleges. Published 2019 July 25. Accessed October 20, 2021. https://www.aamc.org/news-insights/us-medical-school-enrollment-rises-30

25. Association of American Medical Colleges. Preparing aspiring physicians for medical school. Published 2020. Accessed June 11, 2021. https://students-residents.aamc.org/advisors/help-your-advisees-explore-medical-careers/

26. Association of American Medical Colleges. Number of people per active physician by specialty, 2019. Published 2020. Accessed June 11, 2021. https://www.aamc.org/what-we-do/mission-areas/health-care/workforce-studies/interactive-data/number-people-active-physician-specialty-2019

27. Association of American Medical Colleges. Active physicians by age and specialty, 2019. Published 2020. Accessed June 11, 2021. https://www.aamc.org/data-reports/workforce/interactive-data/active-physicians-age-and-specialty-2019

28. Association of American Medical Colleges. Active physicians by sex and specialty, 2019. Published 2020. Accessed June 11, 2021. https://www.aamc.org/data-reports/workforce/interactive-data/active-physicians-sex-and-specialty-2019

29. Association of American Medical Colleges. *The Complexities of Physician Supply and Demand: Projections from 2018 to 2033.* Association of American Medical Colleges; 2020. Accessed June 11, 2021. https://www.aamc.org/system/files/2020-06/stratcomm-aamc-physician-workforce-projections-june-2020.pdf

30. U.S. Department of Labor Bureau of Labor Statistics. Occupational Outlook Handbook: physicians and surgeons. Published 2015. Accessed June 11, 2021. http://www.bls.gov/ooh/healthcare/physicians-and-surgeons.htm

31. Association of American Medical Colleges. Figure 18. Percentage of all active physicians by race/ethnicity, 2018. In: *Diversity in Medicine: Facts and Figures 2019.* Association of American Medical Colleges; 2019. Accessed June 11, 2021. https://www.aamc.org/data-reports/workforce/interactive-data/figure-18-percentage-all-active-physicians-race/ethnicity-2018#:~:text=Diversity%20in%20Medicine%3A%20Facts%20and%20Figures%202019,-New%20section&text=Figure%2018%20shows%20the%20percentage,as%20Black%20or%20African%20American

32. Association of American Medical Colleges. Figure 6. Percentage of acceptees to U.S. medical schools by race/ethnicity (alone), academic year 2018–2019. In: *Diversity in Medicine: Facts and Figures 2019.* Association of American Medical Colleges; 2020. Accessed June 11, 2021. https://www.aamc.org/data-reports/workforce/interactive-data/figure-6-percentage-acceptees-us-medical-schools-race/ethnicity-alone-academic-year-2018-2019

33. Association of American Medical Colleges. Figure 13. Percentage of U.S. medical school graduates by race/ethnicity (alone), academic year 2018–2019. In: *Diversity in Medicine: Facts and Figures 2019.* Association of American Medical Colleges; 2020. Accessed June 11, 2021. https://www.aamc.org/data-reports/workforce/interactive-data/figure-13-percentage-us-medical-school-graduates-race/ethnicity-alone-academic-year-2018-2019

34. Association of American Medical Colleges. *2014 Physician Specialty Data Book.* Association of American Medical Colleges; 2014. Accessed June 11, 2021. https://www.aamc.org/media/8386/download

35. Association of American Medical Colleges. *2015 State Physician Workforce Data Book.* Association of American Medical Colleges; 2015. Accessed June 11, 2021. https://www.aamc.org/data-reports/workforce/report/state-physician-workforce-data-report

36. Association of American Medical Colleges. Medical students, selected years, 1965-2015. Published 2016. Accessed August 23, 2021. https://www.aamc.org/media/8661/download

37. Boyle P. More women than men are enrolled in medical school. Association of American Medical Colleges. Published December 9, 2019. Accessed June 11, 2021. https://www.aamc.org/news-insights/more-women-men-are-enrolled-medical-school

38. O'Brien P. 'All a woman's life can bring': the domestic roots of nursing in Philadelphia, 1830–1885. *Nurs Res.* 1987;36(1):12-17.

39. Stevens R. *In Sickness and in Wealth: American Hospitals in the Twentieth Century.* Basic Books, Inc.; 1989.

40. U.S. Department of Labor Bureau of Labor Statistics. Licensed Occupational Outlook Handbook: practical and licensed vocational nurses. Accessed June 11, 2021. https://www.bls.gov/ooh/healthcare/licensed-practical-and-licensed-vocational-nurses.htm

41. U.S. Department of Labor Bureau of Labor Statistics. Occupational Outlook Handbook: registered nurses. Accessed June 11, 2021. https://www.bls.gov/ooh/healthcare/registered-nurses.htm

42. American Association of Colleges of Nursing. Employment of new nurse graduates and employer preferences for baccalaureate-prepared nurses. Published December 2020. Accessed June 11, 2021. https://www.aacnnursing.org/News-Information/Research-Data-Center/Employment/2020

43. Nursing Explorer. About nursing diploma programs. Accessed February 26, 2021. https://www.nursingexplorer.com/diploma

44. Poghosyan L, Lucero R, Rauch L, Berkowitz B. Nurse practitioner workforce: a substantial supply of primary care providers. *Nurs Econ.* 2012;30(5):268-274, 294.

45. National Association of Clinical Nurse Specialists. What is a CNS? Published 2016. Accessed June 11, 2021. http://www.nacns.org/html/cns-faqs.php

46. U.S. Department of Labor Bureau of Labor Statistics. Occupational Outlook Handbook: nurse anesthetists, nurse midwives, and nurse practitioners: 2014. Accessed June 11, 2021. http://www.bls.gov/ooh/healthcare/nurse-anesthetists-nurse-midwives-and-nurse-practitioners.htm

47. Bullough B, Bullough VL. *Nursing Issues for the Nineties and Beyond.* Springer Publishing Co.; 1994.

48. Neal-Boylan L. PhD or DNP? That is the question. *J Nurse Pract.* 2020;16(2):PA5-A6. doi: 10.1016/j.nurpra.2019.11.015

49. American Academy of Physician Assistants. History. Accessed August 23, 2021. https://www.aapa.org/about/history/

50. U.S. Department of Labor Bureau of Labor Statistics. Occupational Outlook Handbook: physician assistants. Updated April 9, 2021. Accessed June 11, 2021. https://www.bls.gov/ooh/healthcare/physician-assistants.htm

51. U.S. Department of Labor Bureau of Labor Statistics. Occupational Outlook Handbook: how to become a dentist. Updated June 2, 2021. Accessed June 11, 2021. http://www.bls.gov/ooh/healthcare/dentists.htm#tab-4

52. National Comission on Recognition of Dental Specialties and Certifying Boards. Specialty definitions. Published June 2, 2021. Accessed June 11, 2021. https://www.ada.org/en/ncrdscb/dental-specialties/specialty-definitions

53. U.S. Department of Labor Bureau of Labor Statistics. Occupational Outlook Handbook: dentists. Updated June 2, 2021. Accessed June 11, 2021. https://www.bls.gov/ooh/healthcare/dentists.htm#tab-1

54. Shu-Ayanji F, Ogurchak J. Expanding the roles of pharmacists: specialty and beyond. *Pharmacy Times.* Published July 13, 2020. Accessed June 11, 2021. https://www.pharmacytimes.com/news/expanding-the-roles-of-pharmacists-specialty-and-beyond

55. Baker A. The pharmacy job crisis: blame the pharmacy school bubble. *Pharmacy Times.* Published May 26, 2015. Accessed June 11, 2021. https://www.pharmacytimes.com/contributor/alex-barker-pharmd/2015/05/the-pharmacy-job-crisis-blame-the-pharmacy-school-bubble

56. Board of Pharmacy Specialties. BPS specialties. Accessed June 11, 2021. https://www.bpsweb.org/bps-specialties/

57. U.S. Department of Labor Bureau of Labor Statistics. Occupational Outlook Handbook: pharmacists: summary. Updated June 2, 2021. Accessed June 11, 2021. https://www.bls.gov/ooh/healthcare/pharmacists.htm#tab-1

58. U.S. Department of Labor Bureau of Labor Statistics. Occupational Outlook Handbook: pharmacists: job outlook. Updated June 2, 2021. Accessed June 11, 2021. http://www.bls.gov/ooh/healthcare/pharmacists.htm#tab-6

59. U.S. Department of Labor Bureau of Labor Statistics. Occupational Outlook Handbook: pharmacists: work environment. Updated June 2, 2021. Accessed June 11, 2021. https://www.bls.gov/ooh/healthcare/pharmacists.htm#tab-3

60. U.S. Department of Labor Bureau of Labor Statistics. Occupational Outlook Handbook: podiatrists: how to become a podiatrist. Updated April 9, 2021. Accessed June 11, 2021. http://www.bls.gov/ooh/healthcare/podiatrists.htm#tab-4

61. U.S. Department of Labor Bureau of Labor Statistics. Occupational Outlook Handbook: podiatrists. Updated April 9, 2021. Accessed June 11, 2021. https://www.bls.gov/ooh/healthcare/podiatrists.htm

62. U.S. Department of Labor Bureau of Labor Statistics. Occupational Outlook Handbook: podiatrists: working environment. Updated April 9, 2021. Accessed June 11, 2021. https://www.bls.gov/ooh/healthcare/podiatrists.htm#tab-3

63. U.S. Department of Labor Bureau of Labor Statistics. Occupational Outlook Handbook: chiropractors:

summary. Updated April 9, 2021. Accessed June 11, 2021. https://www.bls.gov/ooh/healthcare/chiropractors.htm#tab-1

64. U.S. Department of Labor Bureau of Labor Statistics. Occupational Outlook Handbook: chiropractors: job outlook. Updated April 9, 2021. Accessed June 11, 2021. http://www.bls.gov/ooh/healthcare/chiropractors.htm#tab-6

65. U.S. Department of Labor Bureau of Labor Statistics. Occupational Outlook Handbook: optometrists: how to become an optometrist. Updated April 9, 2021. Accessed June 11, 2021. http://www.bls.gov/ooh/healthcare/optometrists.htm#tab-4

66. U.S. Department of Labor Bureau of Labor Statistics. Occupational Outlook Handbook: optometrists: summary. Updated April 9, 2021. Accessed June 11, 2021. https://www.bls.gov/ooh/healthcare/optometrists.htm

67. U.S. Department of Labor Bureau of Labor Statistics. Occupational Outlook Handbook: optometrists: job outlook. Updated April 9, 2021. Accessed June 11, 2021. http://www.bls.gov/ooh/healthcare/optometrists.htm#tab-6

68. U.S. Department of Labor Bureau of Labor Statistics. Occupational Outlook Handbook: optometrists: work environment. Updated April 9, 2021. Accessed June 11, 2021. https://www.bls.gov/ooh/healthcare/optometrists.htm#tab-3

69. U.S. Department of Labor Bureau of Labor Statistics. Occupational Outlook Handbook: psychologists: summary. Updated April 9, 2021. Accessed June 11, 2021. https://www.bls.gov/ooh/life-physical-and-social-science/psychologists.htm

70. U.S. Department of Labor Bureau of Labor Statistics. Occupational Outlook Handbook: psychologists: work environment. Updated April 9, 2021. Accessed June 11, 2021. https://www.bls.gov/ooh/life-physical-and-social-science/psychologists.htm#tab-3

71. Association of Schools Advancing Health Professions. What is allied health? Accessed June 11, 2021. https://www.asahp.org/what-is

72. U.S. Department of Labor Bureau of Labor Statistics. Occupational Outlook Handbook: clinical laboratory technologists and technicians. Updated June 2, 2021. Accessed June 11, 2021. https://www.bls.gov/ooh/healthcare/clinical-laboratory-technologists-and-technicians.htm

73. U.S. Department of Labor Bureau of Labor Statistics. Occupational Outlook Handbook: clinical laboratory technologists and technicians: work environment. Updated June 2, 2021. Accessed June 11, 2021. https://www.bls.gov/ooh/healthcare/clinical-laboratory-technologists-and-technicians.htm#tab-3

74. U.S. Department of Labor Bureau of Labor Statistics. Occupational Outlook Handbook: radiologic and MRI technologists: summary. Updated April 9, 2021. Accessed June 11, 2021. https://www.bls.gov/ooh/healthcare/radiologic-technologists.htm#tab-1

75. U.S. Department of Labor Bureau of Labor Statistics. Occupational Outlook Handbook: radiologic and MRI technologists: how to become one. Updated April 9, 2021. Accessed June 11, 2021. https://www.bls.gov/ooh/healthcare/radiologic-technologists.htm#tab-4

76. U.S. Department of Labor Bureau of Labor Statistics. Occupational Outlook Handbook: radiologic and MRI technologists: work environment. Updated April 9, 2021. Accessed June 11, 2021. https://www.bls.gov/ooh/healthcare/radiologic-technologists.htm#tab-3

77. U.S. Department of Labor Bureau of Labor Statistics. Occupational Outlook Handbook: nuclear medicine technologists. Updated April 9, 2021. Accessed June 11, 2021. https://www.bls.gov/ooh/healthcare/nuclear-medicine-technologists.htm

78. U.S. Department of Labor Bureau of Labor Statistics. Occupational Outlook Handbook: physical therapists. Updated June 2, 2021. Accessed June 11, 2021. https://www.bls.gov/ooh/healthcare/physical-therapists.htm

79. U.S. Department of Labor Bureau of Labor Statistics. Occupational Outlook Handbook: physical therapist assistants and aides Updated April 9, 2021. Accessed June 11, 2021. https://www.bls.gov/ooh/healthcare/physical-therapist-assistants-and-aides.htm#tab-3

80. U.S. Department of Labor Bureau of Labor Statistics. Occupational Outlook Handbook: occupational therapists. Updated April 9, 2021. Accessed June 11, 2021. https://www.bls.gov/ooh/healthcare/occupational-therapists.htm Updated April 9, 2021.

81. U.S. Department of Labor Bureau of Labor Statistics. Occupational Outlook Handbook: speech-language pathologists. Updated June 2, 2021. Accessed June 11, 2021. https://www.bls.gov/ooh/healthcare/speech-language-pathologists.htm#tab-4

82. U.S. Department of Labor Bureau of Labor Statistics. Occupational Outlook Handbook: social work. Updated April 9, 2021. Accessed June 11, 2021. https://www.bls.gov/ooh/community-and-social-service/social-workers.htm#tab-1

83. U.S. Department of Labor Bureau of Labor Statistics. Occupational Outlook Handbook: rehabilitation counselors. Updated April 9, 2021. Accessed June 11, 2021. https://www.bls.gov/ooh/community-and-social-service/rehabilitation-counselors.htm

84. U.S. Department of Labor Bureau of Labor Statistics. Occupational Outlook Handbook: medical and health services managers. Updated June 2, 2021. Accessed June 11, 2021. https://www.bls.gov/ooh/management/medical-and-health-services-managers.htm#tab-3

85. U.S. Department of Labor Bureau of Labor Statistics. Occupational Outlook Handbook: medical assistants. Updated April 9, 2021. Accessed June 11, 2021. https://www.bls.gov/ooh/healthcare/medical-assistants.htm

86. U.S. Department of Labor Bureau of Labor Statistics. Employment in health care: a crutch for the ailing economy during the 2007–09 recession. Published April 2011. Accessed June 11, 2021. http://www.bls.gov/opub/mlr/2011/04/art2full.pdf

87. University of Albany Center for Health Workforce Studies. Health care employment projections, 2014–2024: an analysis of Bureau of Labor Statistics projections by setting and by occupation 2016. Published April 2016. Accessed June 11, 2021. http://chws.albany.edu/archive/uploads/2016/04/BLS-Health-Care-Employment-Projections_2016.pdf

88. Dixon-Fyle S, Dolan K, Hunt V, Prince S. Diversity wins: how inclusion matters. McKinsey & Company. Published May 19, 2020. Accessed June 11, 2021. https://www.mckinsey.com/featured-insights/diversity-and-inclusion/diversity-wins-how-inclusion-matters#

89. Graham N. The why behind DEI: how diversity, equity, and inclusion initiatives benefit businesses. Workhuman Blog. Accessed June 11, 2021. https://www.workhuman.com/resources/globoforce-blog/the-why-behind-d-i-how-diversity-and-inclusion-initiatives-benefit-business

90. Coaston J. The intersectionality wars. Vox. Published May 28, 2019. Accessed June 11, 2021. https://www.vox.com/the-highlight/2019/5/20/18542843/intersectionality-conservatism-law-race-gender-discrimination

91. Bashford S. The importance of intersectionality in HR. *HR Magazine*. Published September 23, 2019. Accessed June 11, 2021. https://www.hrmagazine.co.uk/content/features/the-importance-of-intersectionality-in-hr.

92. Delizonna L. High-performing teams need psychological safety. Here's how to create it. *Harvard Business Review*. Published August 24, 2017. Accessed June 11, 2021. https://hbr.org/2017/08/high-performing-teams-need-psychological-safety-heres-how-to-create-it

93. Edmondson AC. The role of psychological safety in diversity and inclusion. *Psychology Today*. Published June 22, 2020. Accessed June 11, 2021. https://www.psychologytoday.com/us/blog/the-fearless-organization/202006/the-role-psychological-safety-in-diversity-and-inclusion

94. Society for Human Resource Management. How to establish and design a wellness program. Accessed June 11, 2021. https://www.shrm.org/resourcesandtools/tools-and-samples/how-to-guides/pages/howtoestablishanddesignawellnessprogram.aspx

95. Brower K, Brazeau C, Kiely S, et al. The evolving role of Chief Wellness Officer in the management of crises by health care systems: lessons from the COVID-19 pandemic. *New England Journal of Medicine Catalyst*. Published May 2021. Accessed June 11, 2021.https://catalyst.nejm.org/doi/full/10.1056/CAT.20.0612

96. World Health Organization. Occupational health: stress at the workplace. Published October 19, 2020. Accessed June 11, 2021. https://www.who.int/news-room/q-a-detail/ccupational-health-stress-at-the-workplace

97. Mayo Clinic. Job burnout: how to spot it and take action. Accessed June 11, 2021. https://www.mayoclinic.org/healthy-lifestyle/adult-health/in-depth/burnout/art-20046642

98. McLaughlin C. Health work force issues and policy-making roles. In: Larson PF, Osterweis M, Rubin ER, eds. *Health Workforce Issues for the 21st Century*. Association of Academic Health Centers; 1994:1-3.

99. Health Resources & Services Administration. Review health workforce research. Updated February 2021. Accessed June 11, 2021. https://bhw.hrsa.gov/data-research/review-health-workforce-research

100. Bipartisan Policy Center. The complexities of national health care workforce planning: a review of current data and methodologies and recommendations for future studies. Published February 5, 2013. Accessed June 11, 2021. https://bipartisanpolicy.org/report/complexities-national-health-care-workforce-planning-review-current-data-and/

CHAPTER 6

Hospitals and Integrated Delivery Systems

LEARNING OBJECTIVES

After reading this chapter you should be able to:

- Discuss the history of hospitals in the United States.
- Name the types of hospitals and their roles in care delivery.
- Describe the divisions in hospitals.
- Explain the growth and decline in hospitals.
- Describe the hazards of hospitalization.

KEY TERMS

Accountable Care
  Organization (ACO)
American College of Graduate
  Medical Education (ACGME)

Centers for Medicare and
  Medicaid Services (CMS)
Conditions of Participation
  (CoP)

Diagnosis-Related Group
  (DRG)
Hill-Burton Act
Population Health

CHAPTER OVERVIEW

Hospitals have remained the centerpiece of healthcare delivery since their inception. In this chapter, we will learn about the foundational elements of hospitals as well as how they are organized. The chapter discusses the types of hospitals, key structures, and recent trends related to growth and decline. We will discuss the ways in which patients interface with hospitals as well as their horizontal flow through care delivery.

This chapter also discusses the significant challenges and opportunities created by reforms and efforts to improve the quality of care, increase patient satisfaction, improve the health of populations, and reduce costs. The chapter will conclude with a discussion on integrated delivery and how it has shaped acute care.

Hospitals in the United States were founded to shelter older adults, the dying, orphans, and vagrants. They formed as a means to protect the community from the mentally ill and contagiously sick. Today they are the core entity in the provision of care delivery.

Patients may interface with hospitals in a number of ways to deal with a range of healthcare issues from the acute to the chronic. Our perspective for this chapter will primarily focus on the entry point of patients into hospitals for acute care with acknowledgement of the role of behavioral health as a factor, as shown in **FIGURE 6-1**.

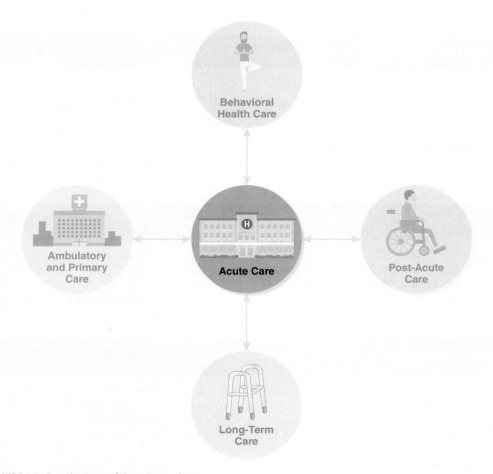

FIGURE 6-1 Continuum of Care Domains

Created by Richard Greenhill.

A hospital is an institution primarily engaged in the provision of a range of services, by or under the supervision of physicians or other service areas.[1] Hospitals fall into two categories: accredited or not accredited. Accreditation is a means to ensure certain operational and quality standards. The Centers for Medicare & Medicaid Services (CMS) is the entity that extends accreditation via approved programs that routinely survey hospitals for compliance on a host of topics related to the health and safety of their patients. Final accreditation of hospitals means that they meet the Conditions of Participation (CoPs). CoPs are important because the "participation" essentially means that they are able to receive government funding from CMS. The government is the largest payer for accredited hospitals in the United States. This is important to mention upfront because many of the internal processes within hospitals are linked to the relationship to funders (e.g., CMS and insurance companies, etc.).

▶ Types of Hospitals

Acute care hospitals are distinguished from long-term care facilities such as nursing homes, rehabilitation centers, and psychiatric hospitals by the fact that the average length of stay for patients is less than 30 days. The following list indicates the types of hospital sponsorships and the number of each type as of January 2021.[2]

1. Nongovernment not-for-profit community hospitals (2,946)
2. Investor-owned (for-profit) community hospitals (1,233)
3. State and local government community hospitals (962)
4. Federal government hospitals or VA hospitals (208)
5. Nonfederal psychiatric hospitals (625)
6. Other (e.g., prison hospitals, college infirmaries) (116)

Hospitals also may be classified as teaching and nonteaching hospitals. Approximately 7% of all 6,090 U.S. hospitals (about 400 hospitals) are teaching facilities affiliated with one or more of the allopathic or osteopathic medical schools in the United States.[2,3] Teaching hospitals provide clinical education for medical students and medical and dental residents. They, and many hospitals not affiliated with medical schools, also provide clinical education for nurses, allied health personnel, and a wide variety of technical specialists. Most teaching hospitals are voluntary, nongovernment, not-for-profit, or government-sponsored public hospitals. The presence of medical school faculty with strong research interests and the availability of medical residents to assist in the collection of clinical data put teaching hospitals at the forefront of clinical research on medical conditions and treatments.

Public hospitals in many localities deliver the fiscally problematic, but essential, community services that other hospitals are reluctant to provide. These high-cost, low-fiscal-return services include sophisticated trauma centers, psychiatric emergency services, alcohol detoxification services, other substance abuse treatments, and burn treatment.

Most for-profit hospitals belong to one of the large hospital management companies that dominate the for-profit hospital network. An increasing number, however, are physician-owned specialty hospitals. Such hospitals usually limit their services to treatments in one of three major specialty categories: orthopedics, surgery, or cardiology.

Although these new specialty hospitals are typically upscale facilities with many patient amenities, they usually operate with greater efficiency and provide excellent care because of the homogeneity of medical foci. Nevertheless, they have raised a series of concerns about their performance and their effect on community hospitals.

Supporters of physician-owned specialty hospitals point out that the physician owners take great pride in the quality of care provided in their hospitals, that they also work in community hospitals, and that their facilities enhance their communities by paying taxes as for-profit companies.[4]

Academic Health Centers, Medical Education, and Specialization

Medical, dental, nursing, pharmacy, and allied health schools and their teaching hospitals are the principal sources of education and training for most healthcare providers. An academic health center is an accredited, degree-granting institution that consists of a medical school, one or more other professional schools, or programs such as dentistry, nursing, pharmacy, public health, and allied health sciences that has an owned or affiliated relationship with a teaching hospital, health system, or other organized care provider.

Much of the basic and clinical research in medicine and other healthcare disciplines is conducted in these health centers and their related hospitals. The teaching hospitals usually provide the most technologically advanced care in their communities and also offer inpatient and ambulatory care for economically disadvantaged populations. Thus, the three objectives of academic health centers—education, research, and service—are fulfilled most adequately by teaching hospitals.

The influence of academic health centers on health care during the last few decades has been extraordinary. The advances that occurred in the medical sciences and technology that resulted in the introduction of life-saving drugs, anesthetics, surgical procedures, and other therapies increased both the use and the costs of hospital services. This increased intervention resulted in increases in both the life expectancy of most Americans and the proportion of the gross national product devoted to health care. These advances also significantly expanded the knowledge base and performance skills required of physicians to practice up-to-date clinical medicine.

Academic health centers responded to advances in medical science and technology by increasing the number of physicians with in-depth expertise in increasingly narrow fields of clinical practice. Specialization and subspecialization grew, subdivided, and grew more. More and more physicians limited their activities to narrower and narrower fields of practice. In doing so, they greatly increased the overall technologic sophistication of hospital practice along with the number of costly consultations that take place among specialist hospital physicians. Specialists and subspecialists also drove increases in the amount of expensive equipment, supplies, and space maintained by hospitals to serve their needs and, in general, the complexity of patient care. The contributions of highly specialized clinical practice to the quality of hospital care have been both extraordinarily beneficial and regrettably negative. Although the superspecialists of U.S. medicine have given the profession its justified reputation for heroic medical and surgical achievements, specialization also has fragmented and depersonalized patient care and produced a plethora of often questionable tests, procedures, and clinical interventions.

The addition of more subspecialists also created a communication problem between the increasing number of physicians and other healthcare professionals involved in the care of individual patients. As anyone with a complicated medical condition who tries to navigate through the system of multiple specialists knows, the easy and reliable transfer of patient records and test results between multiple specialists is often extremely problematic. Ironically, in an age with unprecedented communications and health information technology capabilities, communication of patient information is still a significant challenge for most patients.

While academic health centers have contributed admirably to the advancement of medicine, especially hospital-delivered medical and surgical care, they have not brought their impressive expertise to bear on solving health services delivery problems that have plagued their industry. Rather, the commitments of academic medicine to high-technology research and patient care and its adherence to traditional organizational structures and professional roles have prevented it from taking the lead in correcting healthcare system problems that emanate from fragmented and piecemeal approaches to care delivery. As vast reforms with a population health focus begin to take shape, academic medicine is faced with numerous challenges to prepare for ongoing changes.[5]

▶ Growth and Decline in Numbers of Hospitals

The number of hospitals in the United States increased from 178 in 1873 to 4,300 in 1909. In 1946, when the Hill–Burton Act was passed, there were 6,000 American hospitals, with 3.2 beds available for every 1,000 people. The goal of the Act was to fund expansion of the hospital system to achieve the goal of 4.5 beds per 1,000 people.[6] The system grew thereafter to reach a high of approximately 7,200 acute care hospitals.

During the 1980s, medical advances and cost-containment measures moved many procedures that once required inpatient hospitalization to outpatient settings. Outpatient hospital visits increased by 40% with a resultant decrease in hospital admissions. Fewer admissions and shortened lengths of stay for patients resulted in a significant reduction in the number of hospitals and hospital beds. Healthcare reform efforts and the emergence of managed care as the major form of insurance for U.S. health care resulted in hospital closings and mergers that reduced the number of governmental and community-based hospitals in the United States to approximately 5,700.

▶ Structure and Organizations

In addition to being a caring, people-oriented institution, a hospital also is a multifaceted, high-tech business. It operates just like any other large business, with a hierarchy of personnel, channels of authority and responsibility, constant concern about its bottom line, and a complex organizational structure. The people who work in hospitals exhibit the same range of human characteristics as their counterparts in other businesses. Patients and their families trying to obtain the best possible results from the services of a hospital should base their approach on the same principles they use in dealing with other service organizations. Hospital care consumers need to determine who is in charge, what services to expect from whom and when, with what results, and at what cost.

The following description of hospital structure and organization uses the voluntary not-for-profit community hospital as the example, because this type of institution historically has provided the model for hospital organization. The direction, control, and governance of the hospital are divided among three influential entities: the medical staff, the administration, and the board of directors or trustees. The major operating divisions of a hospital represent areas of the hospital's functions. Although they may use different names, typical divisions are medical, nursing, patient therapy, diagnosis, fiscal, human resources, hotel services, and community relations.

▶ The Patient

In the early development of hospitals, the patient was considered an unavoidable burden to society. In its mercy, society provided the hospital as a refuge. Patients receiving this charity were expected to be grateful for the shelter and nursing care and even for the opportunity to lend their bodies and illnesses for medical students' instruction and practice.

By 1900 more advanced training in nursing, effective anesthetic agents, modern methods of antisepsis and sterilization, and other medical advances had revolutionized hospital practices. Hospitals changed from merely supplying food, shelter, and meager medical care to the unfortunate needy and contagious to providing skilled medical, surgical, and nursing care to everyone. However, the belief persisted that patients in the hospital, removed from their usual social environment, were in a dependent relationship with charitable authorities. Remnants of the idea that these professionals have the knowledge and authority to decide what is best for grateful and uncomplaining patients have persisted to this day, regardless of the expense to the patient or the merit of the services.

Unfortunately, the behavior of many patients and their families has been conditioned to reinforce this philosophy. While hospitalized, otherwise assertive, independent individuals tend to assume a passive and dependent "sick role." Numerous sociologic studies of patients' behavior have concluded that patients who behave in the traditional submissive sick role help to preserve the authoritarian attitude of healthcare providers that most healthcare consumers now consider patronizing and inappropriate.[7]

Medical Division

The medical staff is a formally organized unit within the larger hospital organization. The president or chief of staff is the liaison between the hospital administration and members of the medical staff. Typically, the medical staff consists primarily of medical physicians, but it also may include other doctoral-level professionals, such as dentists and psychologists, and sometimes mid-level providers (e.g., nurse-midwifes, physician assistants, nurse practitioners).

A major role of the medical staff organization is to recommend to the hospital board of directors the appointment of physicians to the medical staff. The board of directors approves and grants various levels of hospital privileges to physicians. Such privileges commonly include the right to admit patients to the hospital, to perform surgery, and to provide consultation to other physicians on the hospital staff. Another medical staff function is to provide oversight and peer review of the quality of medical care in the hospital. It performs this function through a number of medical staff committees, which coordinate their efforts closely with the hospital's administration and committees of the hospital's board of directors.

Members of the medical staff who have completed their training and are in practice are referred to as attending physicians. In addition, the hospital usually has a house staff of physicians who are engaged in residency training programs under the close supervision of attending physicians. These members of the house staff or residents rotate shifts to provide 24-hour coverage for the attending physicians' patients to which they are assigned.

There is no universal rule as to how a hospital's medical departments or divisions should be organized. Most often, the types of practice of the hospital's medical staff determine the specialty components within the medical division. Medicine, surgery, obstetrics and gynecology, and pediatrics usually are major departments. In larger hospitals and in most teaching hospitals, the subspecialty areas of medical practice are represented by departments or divisions of departments. In the internal medicine specialty, subspecialty divisions might include cardiology or cardiac care, nephrology, oncology, gastroenterology, pulmonary medicine, endocrinology, critical care, and a variety of others. In the surgical area, surgical divisions or departments might include orthopedics, thoracic, neurosurgery, cardiac surgery, and plastic and reconstructive surgery. Each department is headed by a physician department head or chairman, and divisions are headed by a chief. These leaders are charged with overseeing the practice and quality of medical services delivered in their department or division. In a teaching hospital, an attending physician is usually appointed as a program director to coordinate the required educational experiences of medical students and residents in their department or division. Program directors are also responsible for maintaining their training program's accreditation, usually with the American College of Graduate Medical Education (ACGME). Training programs have to maintain extensive records documenting all trainees and their educational activities. They also undergo a formalized and periodic reaccreditation evaluation.

Nursing Division

The nursing division usually comprises the single largest component of the hospital's organization. It is subdivided by the type of patient care delivered in the various medical specialties. Nursing units are composed of a number of patient beds grouped within a certain area to allow centralization of the special facilities, supplies, equipment, and personnel pertinent to the needs of patients with particular conditions. For example, the kinds of equipment and skills and the level of patient care needs vary considerably between an orthopedic unit and a medical intensive care unit.

A head nurse, often with the title of "nurse manager," and who is usually a registered nurse, has overall responsibility for all nursing care in their unit. Such care includes carrying out the attending physician's and house staff physician's orders for medications, diet, and various types of therapy. In addition, the nurse manager supervises the unit's staff, which may include nurses' aides and orderlies. The nurse manager also is responsible for coordinating all aspects of patient care, which may include services provided by other hospital units, such as the dietary department, physical therapy department, pharmacy, and laboratories. The nurse manager also has the responsibility of coordinating the services of departments such as social work, discharge planning, and pastoral care for the patients in the unit. Increasingly, nurse managers are often extensively involved in compliance activities of the hospital as well, ensuring that all safety processes are followed and all exceptions to these processes are documented as required.

Because nursing services are required in the hospital at all times, staff is usually employed in three 8-hour shifts or two 12-hour shifts. Normally, the nurse manager of a unit works during the day shift, and two other members of the nursing staff assume what is referred to as "charge duty" on the other two shifts of the day. Charge nurses report to the nurse manager and take the leadership role when the nurse manager is not present on the unit.

A nurse manager may have responsibility for a number of nursing units and report to a member of the hospital's administration, who is usually a vice president for nursing, an assistant administrator, or the chief nursing officer (CNO). It is also common to find an individual with the title of ward clerk or unit secretary on each nursing unit. The ward clerk acts as the nurse manager's administrative assistant and helps to schedule and coordinate the other hospital services related to patient care and administrative issues.

Allied Health Professionals

Not as well-known as the physicians and nurses who are central to the care and treatment of patients in hospitals is the wide array of personnel who provide other hospital services that support the work of the physicians and nurses and others who operate behind the scenes to make the facility run smoothly.

Staff members in an increasingly diverse array of healthcare disciplines are classified as allied health personnel. These professionals support, complement, or supplement the functions of physicians, dentists, nurses, and other professionals in delivering care to patients. They contribute to environmental management, health promotion, and disease prevention.

Allied health occupations encompass as many as 200 types of health careers within 80 different allied health professions. Advancing medical technology is likely to create the need for even more personnel with highly specialized training and relatively unique skills. Those who are responsible for highly specialized or technical services that have a significant impact on health care are prepared for practice through a wide variety of educational programs offered at colleges and universities. The range of allied health professions may be best understood by classifying them by the functions they serve in the delivery of health care. Some disciplines may serve more than one of these functions:

1. Laboratory technologists and technicians
2. Allied health practitioners of the therapeutic sciences
3. Behavioral scientists
4. Specialist support service personnel

Diagnostic Services

Every hospital either maintains or contracts with laboratories to perform a wide array of tests to help physicians diagnose illness or injury and monitor the progress of treatment. One such laboratory is the pathology laboratory, which examines and analyzes specimens of body tissues, fluids, and excretions to aid in diagnosis and treatment. These laboratories are usually supervised by the hospital's pathologist, who is a physician specialist.

Grouped under the rubric "diagnostic imaging services," in addition to basic radiographic images (x-rays), a wide array of more sophisticated imaging equipment that incorporates computer technology is found in these departments, including ultrasonography, computed tomography (CT), magnetic resonance imaging (MRI), and positron emission tomography (PET). Unlike radiograph technology, which is limited to providing images of the body's anatomic structures, these imaging advances have unique abilities to visualize structures in several planes and, with PET, even quantify complex physiologic processes occurring in the human body.

A variety of other diagnostic services also may be available through specific medical specialty or subspecialty departments, such as cardiology and neurology. For example, a noninvasive cardiac laboratory administers cardiac stress testing to assess a patient's heart function during exercise. Obstetricians commonly use an imaging capability called ultrasonography to visualize the unborn fetus.

Rehabilitation Services

Rehabilitation or patient support departments provide specialized care to assist patients in achieving optimal physical, mental, and social functioning after resolution of an illness or injury. One such department is physical medicine, where diagnosis and treatment of patients with physical injuries or disabilities are conducted. This department is headed by a specialist physician called a physiatrist who usually works with a team of physical therapists, occupational therapists, and speech therapists. Other health-related specialists, such as social workers, may provide additional services to support the rehabilitation of patients with complex problems.

Other Patient Support Services

The hospital pharmacy purchases and dispenses all drugs used to treat hospitalized patients. The department is headed by a licensed pharmacist, who also is responsible for pharmacy technicians and others who work under their supervision.

Among other functions, the social services department helps patients about to be discharged to arrange financial support and coordinate needed community-based services. Generally, the social services department assists patients and their families to achieve the best possible social and domestic environment for the patients' care and recovery. Such services are available to all hospital patients and their families.

Discharge planning services (discussed in more detail later in this chapter) may or may not be a part of the social services department. Frequently, staffing includes both nurses and social workers who are responsible for planning posthospital patient care in conjunction with the patients and their families. The discharge planning department becomes involved when the patient requires referral for one or more community services or placement in a special care facility after discharge.

Nutritional Services

The nutritional services department includes food preparation facilities and personnel for the provision of inpatient meals, food storage, and purchasing and catering for hospital events. More than just a kitchen, the nutritional services department must be able to provide numerous special diets ordered for patients as part of their overall care in the hospital. Some examples include diabetic diets, soft diets, liquid diets, and a variety of others. In addition, the department must insure that all patients' meals are prepared taking into account patients' known food allergies. The department also may operate a cafeteria for employees and, in larger hospitals, may sponsor educational programs for student dietitians. An important function of this department's staff is educating patients on dietary needs and restrictions. This department usually is headed by a chief dietitian who has a degree in nutritional science, and it may be staffed by any number of other dietitians and clinical nutrition specialists with specific expertise in dietary assessment and food preparation.

Administrative Departments

Hospitals contain other professional units that provide a wide variety of nonmedical services essential to the management of the hospital's physical plant and business services. Patients are certainly aware of two of them: the admissions department, through which a hospital stay is initiated, and the business office, through which a hospital stay is terminated and patients' bills are generated. These units are two of the many components of the hospital's complex management structure.

The general administrative services of the hospital are headed by a chief executive officer (CEO) or president who has the day-to-day responsibility for managing all hospital business. They are the highest ranking administrative officer and oversee an array of administrative departments concerned with financial operations, public relations, and personnel. Larger hospitals have a chief operating officer (COO), who oversees the operation of specific departments, and a chief financial officer (CFO), who directs the many and varied fiscal activities of the hospital. Those key administrative officers are commonly positioned as corporate vice presidents. The large number of employees and the wide array of individual skills required to staff a hospital competently call for a personnel or human resources department with highly specialized labor expertise. That department usually is headed by a vice president for human resources. Because nursing is such a large component of the hospital's service operations, larger facilities also maintain a CNO at the vice presidential level. Because of the increasing importance of health information technology (HIT) and electronic health records (EHRs) to hospital operations and business functions, chief information officers (CIOs) and chief medical information officers (CMIOs) are becoming more common in hospitals' management structures. CIOs are charged with the management of hospital IT infrastructure. CMIOs, who are usually physicians with a background in clinical informatics, manage the functionality of the hospital's EHR system from the physicians' perspective.

Rights and Responsibilities of Hospitalized Patients

Patients in hospitals have individual rights, many of which are protected by state statutes and regulations. The U.S. Constitution and, in particular, its Bill of Rights, is not suspended when a citizen enters a hospital. In fact, in 1972 and then revised in 1992, the American Hospital Association published a "Patient's Bill of Rights."[8] In 2003, AHA replaced the Patient's Bill of Rights with a brochure titled *The Patient Care Partnership*.[9] The brochure is free to all hospitals, published in eight languages, and made available to hospitals in paper form for a minor cost. The brochure contains six sections and is designed to explain a patient's rights and responsibilities in simple language:

- High-quality hospital care
- A clean and safe environment
- Involvement in your care
- Protection of your privacy
- Help when leaving the hospital
- Help with your billing claims

In addition, hospitals are required by their accrediting body to make this information known to every patient admitted. Even though it was replaced by *The Patient Care Partnership* brochure, many hospitals continue to post and provide all patients with a copy or locally modified version of the AHA Patient's Bill of Rights. The Partnership brochure is an attempt to emphasize that although the ultimate responsibility for everything that happens within the hospital, including the medical care provided, lies with the hospital institution and its board of directors, patients also have an important and active role to play in their care. The Partnership brochure explains that patients are obligated to act responsibly toward physicians and hospitals by cooperating with all reasonable requests for personal and family information. It is to patients' benefit to inform medical or hospital personnel if they do not understand or do not wish to follow instructions. Patients are encouraged to identify to the physician and the hospital a family member or other advocate they wish to be involved in treatment decisions, and to provide contact information.

Patients also need to recognize that hospitals are highly stressful institutional settings and that other patients, as well as the hospital personnel, deserve consideration and respect. In no other institutional setting are individual rights at greater risk of being compromised than in a hospital. However, the risks do not arise from a purposeful disregard for patients by physicians or the hospital staff. The personal integrity of patients may be unintentionally violated as a result of certain institutional circumstances and factors unique to the hospital setting. These institutional circumstances arise from the fact that the hospital, like most complex organizations, has a life of its own, which pulses with an infinite array of daily scheduled events that pervade every aspect of its functioning. There are schedules for changing beds, bathing patients, serving meals, administering medications, obtaining specimens, providing therapy, checking vital signs, performing surgery, housekeeping, admitting, discharging, conducting patient rounds, receiving visitors, performing examinations, and, finally, preparing patients for the night.

The pressure of the daily schedule often makes it difficult for hospital personnel to pay attention to the special needs of individual patients. Even though a patient's particular schedule of tests, procedures, treatments, and examinations is uniquely related to their condition and the physician's orders, it is also influenced by the needs of fellow patients, the schedules of physicians, and numerous others involved directly or indirectly in the patient's care.

A patient's treatment also may be modified by the schedule of institutional events unrelated to their care. Such institutional events may include inspections, safety drills, grand rounds, physician and nurse in-service training, unplanned staffing shortages, and an array of technical problems with any of the hundreds of the pieces of medical equipment required in a modern hospital.

A second reason why patient rights may be in jeopardy in the hospital setting is that physicians are likely to spend only a few minutes a day with each patient. This means that patients depend heavily on the nursing staff and other support personnel for medical and personal care. Ideally, nurses are able to continuously monitor each patient's condition and alert the physician to any change in a patient's status. However, the number of patients for whom a nurse is responsible and the number of tasks the nurse is required to perform during a single work shift make it extremely difficult, or sometimes impossible, to fulfill that obligation. In addition, the increasing number of caregivers involved with each patient provides additional opportunities for failures of communication and subsequent mistakes in the treatment programs for individual patients. Although hospitals continuously strive to develop fail-safe systems to protect patients against the possibility of human error in the delivery of their care, mistakes can and do happen. Medication errors, lost laboratory test results, and failures to implement physician orders are only a few examples.

As noted above, the "Patient Care Partnership" encourages patients to recognize their vulnerability during hospitalization and urges them or their family members to function as active participants in, rather than passive recipients or observers of, hospital care. In addition, state health departments, which license hospitals, ensure the right of patients to make complaints about hospital care and services. Hospitals are required by law to investigate patient complaints and respond to them. In fact, a hospital must provide a written response if a patient so requests.

Informed Consent and Second Opinions

No description of the structure and processes of hospitals is complete without mention of the very important personal decisions regarding medical care that patients are asked to make, often under stressful and intimidating circumstances. A cornerstone of the personal rights of hospitalized patients is the right to know:

- What is being done to them and why
- What the procedure entails
- How the procedure can be expected to benefit them
- What risks or consequences are associated with the procedure
- The probability of risks and consequences

In short, in almost all cases the doctrine of informed consent ensures that patients have ultimate control over their own bodies. This doctrine, first recognized legally in 1914, has been reaffirmed repeatedly over the years. It is now generally recognized to encompass not only the information mentioned above, but also the right to receive information about alternative forms of treatment to the one recommended.[10]

A physician has no legal right to substitute their judgment for the patient's in matters of consent. This principle means that the patient has the absolute right to reject or question a physician's recommendation. For these reasons, it is considered appropriate for patients to obtain second opinions to satisfy concerns about the necessity for various tests and other procedures. Many insurers now require a confirming second opinion before agreeing to pay for certain surgical or other procedures. Medicare and many private health plans cover most of the costs of second opinions.[11,12]

▶ Diagnosis-Related Group Hospital Reimbursement System

Until 1983, a patient stayed in the hospital until the physician decided that they were well enough for discharge. Each hospital monitored its own situation through a utilization review committee composed of physicians and administrators who reviewed the lengths of stay of hospitalized patients to ensure that neither the quality of care nor the efficiency of the hospital was being compromised by physicians' decisions.

During the 1970s and early 1980s, however, the cost of hospital care rose so fast that health insurance companies and corporations that paid huge insurance premiums to cover the hospitalization costs of their workers increased the pressure on federal agencies to find a way to stem the rising tide of hospital expenses. Two factors made change imperative.

First, hospitals were paid a set amount for each day that a patient stayed in the facility. That amount was determined retrospectively by the cost per day per bed to operate the hospital the year before. Under that arrangement, the hospital had no incentive to keep costs down. In fact, if it did, it would receive a smaller daily reimbursement rate the next year than if it spent freely. Furthermore, it became clear to the government and the insurance companies that they were paying not only for uncontrolled costs per hospital day but also for hospital days that were not necessary. On a national scale, hundreds of thousands of hospital days that did not benefit the patients, at a cost of several hundred dollars per day, amounted to a huge and valueless financial burden. Hospital costs were forcing the Medicare program to exceed all financial projections.

Second, payers recognized that not only were unnecessarily long hospital stays expensive, but they also could be dangerous to patients' health. Patients are exposed to infections in hospitals that they would not face at home. In addition, many older patients are at extreme risk of delirium and rapidly losing the ability to perform basic activities of daily living such as dressing, feeding, or toileting themselves during a long stay in a hospital. Patients' risk of falls and deadly hip fractures also is a significant concern. Older patients often emerge from the hospital less able to function than when admitted. Shortened stays in hospitals, especially for older patients, often can be beneficial as well as less expensive.

In 1983, the federal government radically changed the way hospitals would be reimbursed for the costs of treating Medicare patients. The new payment system, referred to as diagnosis-related groups (DRGs), was designed to provide hospitals with a financial incentive to discharge patients as soon as possible. As a prospective payment system, the patient's diagnosis predetermines how much the hospital will be paid, and the hospital knows that amount in advance. The payment is a set amount based on the average cost of treating a particular illness at a certain level of severity. If the patient requires less care or fewer days in the hospital than the DRG average, the hospital is paid the average cost regardless, and the hospital makes money. If the patient requires a longer stay or more care than the DRG average, the hospital loses money.

This carrot-and-stick system was adopted quickly by almost all states and insurance companies and became the standard for insurance reimbursement of hospital costs. It quickly changed hospital behavior. In addition, medical staff became more conservative about ordering tests and procedures of marginal value in diagnosis and treatment. In most cases, the incentive to discharge patients as soon as safely possible did not result in negative consequences for patients.[13]

▶ Discharge Planning

As noted earlier in this chapter, hospitals are responsible for discharge planning functions to help patients arrange for safe and appropriate care after a hospital stay. Using information provided by the patient or the patient's family, a discharge planner must assure that the patient who needs follow-up services obtains them. The planner must then help make the necessary specific arrangements. If the patient requires a transfer to another level of institutional care, such as a nursing home, the discharge planner must arrange that transfer before the patient can be discharged from the hospital.

In implementing the DRG system, Medicare recognized that hospitals' financial incentives to discharge patients as soon as possible should never cause patients to be discharged before they are medically ready and before arrangements have been made to ensure they will receive the necessary posthospital care. Medicare patients who believe that either of these two conditions will not be met by their discharge date have the right to appeal. A hospital's discharge notice must include instructions on how a Medicare-covered patient can have the hospital's decision reviewed by a Medicare Quality Improvement Organization (QIO). A QIO's function under contract with the federal government is to ensure that hospitals and physicians follow Medicare rules. Every geographic area in the United States is covered by a federally designated QIO. A QIO may reverse a decision to discharge and require Medicare to cover the costs of additional hospital days with evidence that the patient is in need of continuing hospital care. Medicare also provides a mechanism to appeal the QIO's decision.[14]

▶ Integrated Delivery

Horizontal Integration

Under the general business definition, horizontally integrated organizations are aggregations that produce the same goods or services. They may be separately or jointly owned and governed, operated as subsidiary corporations of a parent organization, or exist in a variety of other legal or quasi-legal relationships. According to Roger Kropf[15]:

> In the hospital industry, horizontal integration was viewed as potentially advantageous because it could benefit from economies of scale. Large groups of hospitals merged into one organization can purchase supplies and services at a volume discount, hire specialized staff at the corporate level to increase expertise, raise capital less expensively, and market hospital services under a single brand name in a number of communities.

In the 1980s, the horizontal integration strategy spawned large numbers of hospital mergers and acquisitions and significant growth in the number of multihospital systems. Both for-profit and not-for-profit hospitals engaged in horizontal integration in an effort to meet the economic imperatives of the changing industry climate. As the trend in inpatient utilization and lengths of stay continued to decline throughout the 1980s, managed care organizations and other large purchasers of health care increased demands for the availability of comprehensive, continuous care housed within discrete, accountable systems. For this and other reasons, horizontal integration as a primary strategic initiative declined in favor.

The initial wave of hospital consolidations crested in the mid-1990s, and a period of relative calm ensued over the next decade.[16] However, anticipating effects of new healthcare reform measures, the pace of both mergers and acquisitions has quickened rapidly since 2002.[16]

Vertical Integration

Organizations that have vertical integration operate a variety of business entities, each of which is related to the other. In health care, a vertically integrated system includes several service components, each of which addresses some dimension of a population's healthcare needs. The system may be fully comprehensive, with a complete continuum of services ranging from prenatal to end-of-life care. Other systems may contain some, but not all, of the services required by a population. A fully vertically integrated system in its ideal form includes all facilities, personnel, and technologic resources to render the complete continuum of care, which comprises: (1) all outpatient primary care and specialty diagnostic and therapeutic services, (2) inpatient medical and surgical services, (3) short- and long-term rehabilitative services, (4) long-term chronic institutional and in-home care, and (5) terminal care. Such a system also includes all required support services such as social work and health education. In theory, vertically integrated systems offer attractive benefits ("one-stop shopping") to their sponsoring organizations, patients, physicians, and other providers, as well as payers.

Vertically integrated organizations also gain the advantage of an increased market share across a mixture of high-profit, loss-generating, and break-even revenue sources. They benefit from an increased likelihood of retaining patients for many or all their service needs. In addition, they are advantageously positioned to negotiate with managed care organizations by ensuring the availability of comprehensive, continuous care for an insured population at competitive prices. For patients, the most obvious benefit is continuity of care throughout the various system components and improved case management. Physicians and other providers benefit from both greater certainty about the flow of patients to their practices and improved ease of referrals. Managed care organizations and other large purchasers view integrated organizations favorably because of the relative ease of negotiating pricing with one organization instead of several. In addition, quality monitoring, patient case management, and physician and other provider activity can be managed and monitored more efficiently when they are all part of the same organization.

▶ Quality of Hospital Care

Hazards of Hospitalization

Medical errors have been a serious problem in hospitals for decades, but improving patient safety did not become a serious national concern until the late 1990s. Although those in the health professions and knowledgeable members of the public have long been aware of the error-prone nature of hospital care, it was not until the November 1999 release of a report by the prestigious National Academy of Science's Institute of Medicine (IOM) on medical mistakes that the magnitude of hospitalized patient risks gained public knowledge.

By extrapolating the findings of several well-conducted studies of adverse events occurring in hospitals to the 33.5 million hospital admissions in the United States during 1997, the IOM report concluded that at least 44,000 and as many as 98,000 deaths occur annually because of medical errors.[17] The report put the magnitude of the problem in the context of comparable concerns by noting that more people die from medical errors each year than motor vehicle accidents or breast cancer and that medication errors alone kill more people each year than workplace injuries.

Errors are defined as "the failure to complete a planned action as intended or the use of a wrong to achieve an aim."[17] Errors may be attributed to failures in diagnostic, treatment, or surgical procedures; selection or doses of medication; delays in diagnosis or treatment; and a host of other procedural lapses, including communication or equipment failures. There is general agreement that system deficiencies are the most important factor in the problem and not incompetent or negligent healthcare providers. As noted above, miscommunication among overstressed employees is common in busy hospitals. With so many steps and so many people involved in the care of hospital patients, the potential for error grows with every patient day, and small lapses develop into large tragedies.[17]

The 1999 IOM report presented recommendations to improve the quality of care over a 10-year period with a comprehensive strategy for reducing medical errors through a combination of technologic, policy, regulatory, and financial strategies intended to make health care safer. Better use of health information technology that included decision support, avoidance of similar-sounding and look-alike names and packages of medications, and standardization of treatment policies and protocols were suggested to help to avoid confusion and reliance on memory and handwritten communications. The most controversial of the recommendations was the call for a nationwide mandatory reporting system that would require states to report all "adverse events that result in death or serious harm."[17] The impact of the IOM report has been mixed.[18] According to one study, the number of errors may actually be much higher than they were when the IOM report first came out—between 210,000 and 440,000 hospital-based medical errors annually.[19] Another study published in 2015 showed that the number of hospital-acquired conditions dropped 17% over 3 years and drug errors dropped by 19%.[20] There is no doubt that medical error is a topic that will garner continued study and controversy.

The healthcare system and its medical professionals need to make radical changes in cultural attitudes and individual prerogatives before the necessary system changes and reporting requirements can be institutionalized. The 1999 IOM report, which moved awareness of the magnitude of medical errors from the anonymity of hospitals to the nation's media and subsequently to the halls of Congress, produced vociferous debate over issues of mandatory or voluntary reporting. Questions of liability, confidentiality, and avoidance of punishment must be settled before any mandatory reporting legislation can be passed. In the meantime, other recommendations for more focus on patient safety by professional groups, medical societies, healthcare licensing organizations, and hospital administrations could be followed with more immediate benefits.

Historically, it has always been easier to evaluate the quality of the medical care provided in hospitals than that provided in medical offices or other delivery sites because of the availability of comprehensive medical records and other sources of clinical information, systematically collected and stored for later recovery. The definition of quality, however, is extremely complex as it derives from both operational factors and the measures or indicators of quality selected and the value judgments attached to them. For many years, quality was defined as "the degree of conformity with preset standards" and encompassed all the elements, procedures, and consequences of individual patient–provider encounters. Most often, however, the standards against which care was judged were implicit rather than explicit and existed only in the minds of peer evaluators.

The peer review technique commonly used in hospitals until the 1970s had both benefits and failings with the quality assurance process using chart audits. Periodically, an audit committee composed of several physicians appointed by the hospital medical staff would review a small sample of patient records and make judgments about the quality of care provided. Such audits were ineffective for several reasons. First, the evaluators used internalized or implicit standards to make qualitative judgments. Second, there was no rational basis for chart selection that would permit the evaluators to extrapolate the sample findings to the broader patient population. Third, when deficiencies were identified, physician auditors were reluctant to take corrective action because their deficient colleagues might be on the next audit committee reviewing their patient care.

Avedis Donabedian of the University of Michigan made a benchmark contribution to quality-of-care studies by defining the three basic components of medical care—structure, process, and outcome. He defined structural components as the qualifications of the providers, the physical facility, equipment, and other resources, and the characteristics of the organization and its financing.[21] Until the 1960s, the contribution of structure to quality was the primary, if not the only, quality assurance mechanism in health care. Traditionally, the healthcare system primarily relied on credentialing mechanisms, such as licensure, registration, and certification by professional societies and specialty boards, to ensure the quality of clinical care.

The past focus on structural criteria assumed erroneously that enough was known about the relationship of the structural aspects of health care to its processes and outcomes to identify the critical or appropriate structural indicators. Reviews for accreditation by The Joint Commission (TJC), the primary U.S. accrediting body for hospitals, were based almost exclusively on structural criteria. Judgments were made about physical facilities, the equipment, the ratios of professional staff to patients, and the qualifications of various personnel. The underlying assumption of structural quality reviews was that the better the facilities and the qualifications of the providers, the better the quality of the care rendered. It was much later that TJC hospital accreditation included process criteria and outcomes.

The process components identified by Donabedian are what occur during encounters between patients and providers. Process judgments include what was done, how appropriate it was, and how well performed, as well as what was omitted that should have been done. The assumption underlying the use of process criteria is that the quality of the actions taken during patient encounters determines or influences the outcomes. The outcomes of care identified by Donabedian are all the activities that do or do not happen as a result of the medical intervention.

Only recently has hospital quality assurance and TJC criteria focused on the relationships among structure, process, and outcomes. In the past, providers always argued that so many different variables influence the outcomes of medical care that it is inappropriate and unfair to attribute patient outcomes solely to medical interventions. That argument was dismissed, and analytical techniques that collect and analyze data on most or all of potential intervening influences allow the findings to be adjusted for patient differences. Now, quality-of-care data are routinely standardized to account for age, gender, illness severity, accompanying conditions, and other variables that might influence outcomes.

Another quality framework for examining hospitals and the healthcare system is the Triple Aim Initiative developed by the Institute for Healthcare Improvement (IHI).[22] The premise of the Triple Aim is that in order to optimize the healthcare system, three objectives must be addressed simultaneously[22]:

1. Improving the patient experience of care (including quality and satisfaction)
2. Improving the health of populations
3. Reducing the per capita cost of health care

IHI believes that in the current structure of the U.S. healthcare system, no one entity is responsible for all three objectives. IHI contends that without such a structure, real reform is not likely possible. A complete description of the Triple Aim Initiative, its history, and implications is well beyond the scope of this text. Readers are directed to the IHI website (http://www.ihi.org/) on this topic as a starting place for more in-depth research.[22]

Variations in Medical Care

In 1973 two researchers, John Wennberg and Alan Gittlesohn, published the first of a series of papers documenting the variations in the amounts and types of medical care provided to patients with the same diagnoses living in different geographic areas.[23] Those publications emphasized that the utilization and costs of hospital treatment in a community had more to do with the number, physician specialties, and individual preferences of the physicians than the medical conditions of the patients.

With persistent concerns about improving the quality of hospital care and containing soaring costs, various groups formed to survey and report on the quality of hospital care. Chief among them has been the Leapfrog Group, founded in 2000 by the Business Roundtable with support from the Robert Wood Johnson Foundation. Members include more than 160 Fortune 500 corporations and other large private and public sector health benefits purchasers who represent more than 36 million health insurance enrollees.

The Leapfrog Group fields the Leapfrog Hospital Quality and Safety Survey, a voluntary online survey that tracks hospitals' progress toward implementing all 30 of the safety practices endorsed by the National Quality Forum. Leapfrog's website displays each hospital's results and is updated each month with data from additional hospitals; anyone can review the results at no charge. Leapfrog also has compiled the first free online database of programs across the country that offer financial or nonfinancial rewards and incentives for improved performance.[24]

In 2012, the Choosing Wisely campaign was launched "with a goal of advancing a national dialogue on avoiding wasteful or unnecessary medical tests, treatments, and procedures."[25] This campaign was started by the American Board of Internal Medicine (ABIM) Foundation in partnership with Consumer Reports and more than 70 professional medical societies. The campaign tries to "… promote conversations between clinicians and patients by helping patients choose care that is: supported by evidence, not duplicative of other tests or procedures already received, free from harm, and truly necessary."[25] The Choosing Wisely website maintains searchable evidence-based lists of recommendations for both patients and physicians that are shown by the evidence to not be of significant value. Some examples include recommendations to give the flu shot to most all patients, even to those with an allergy to eggs; to NOT get screened for cancer using whole-body CT scanning; and to NOT get screened for cervical cancer with a Pap smear after a hysterectomy in which the cervix was removed.[25]

Overall, it appears that a significant proportion of hospital procedures are performed for inappropriate reasons. The proportion of all procedures judged to be questionable or equivocal also shows wide-ranging variation. "On average, it appears that one-third or more of all procedures performed in the United States are of questionable benefit."[17]

Population Focus

Perhaps the most enveloping changes of health reform for hospitals result from the new focus on outcomes rather than the number of patients served. Historically, medicine and public health have been two separate and distinct entities at most universities,[26] and "population health" was not embraced by hospitals or individual providers as they were both reimbursed on a piecemeal, procedure-by-procedure basis with no accountability for the overall health status of the populations they treated. Health system reforms now require a population focus in which groups composed of many levels of healthcare providers, including hospitals, take responsibility for managing the total health spectrum of a group of patients "to achieve the best possible quality at minimum necessary cost."[26,27] This population focus is understandably foreign to hospitals accustomed to accountability for individual patient outcomes only within their institutions. As Steve Nahm and George Mack noted in the January 21, 2013, edition of *Modern Healthcare*, "Hospitals can no longer live in a four-walls, brick and mortar world. Community-based care will be the future metric against which providers will be measured. That is, their reimbursement will be based on performance of care rendered in multiple provider sites by various types of caregivers, including in-home settings."[28]

An example of how the new population focus manifests in the Affordable Care Act (ACA) is that hospitals now receive significant financial penalties if they incur higher-than-anticipated 30-day Medicare readmission rates. Thirty-day readmissions were targeted because they are associated with high Medicare costs and, usually, poorer patient outcomes. Since this element of the ACA was enacted in 2012, the national 30-day readmission rate has declined from 19% to 18%, representing an approximate national reduction of 150,000 30-day readmissions per year.[29]

Accountable Care Organizations

The ACA provided financial incentives for healthcare providers to form new groups or organizations that leverage the integration and coordination of all aspects of health care to improve quality and reduce costs. These new organizations are called Accountable Care Organizations (ACOs). ACOs are intended to address the well-acknowledged fragmentation of the healthcare system by ensuring care coordination across multiple providers for the entire spectrum of needs so that all patients receive timely and appropriate care, avoiding unnecessary duplication of services, medical emergencies, and hospitalizations.[30] The intent under the ACA was to create a variety of ACO organizations with different incentive models to track and then to identify the models or organizational structures that worked best.

Under the ACA, ACOs are administered through Medicare and can be structured in several different ways[30]:

- *Medicare Shared Savings Program (MSSP)*: A program that helps Medicare fee-for-service program providers join together to become an ACO. Essentially, Medicare provides financial incentives based on documented savings to Medicare.[31]
- *Advance Payment ACO Model*: A supplementary incentive program designed for physician-based and rural providers who have come together voluntarily to provide

coordinated, high-quality care to the Medicare patients they serve. Through the Advance Payment ACO Model, selected participants will receive upfront and monthly payments, which they can use to make important investments in their care coordination infrastructure.[32] This provision was added to the law in response to protests from rural hospitals.[33]

- *Pioneer ACO Model*: A program designed for early adopters of coordinated care in which the member providers share the risk as well as the savings. This model is no longer accepting applications.[34]

Each ACO must be a legally constituted entity within its state and include healthcare providers, suppliers, and Medicare beneficiaries on its governing board. Each one must take responsibility for at least 5,000 Medicare beneficiaries for a period of 3 years.[35] To qualify for support under the ACA, ACOs also must meet Medicare-established quality measures of care appropriateness, coordination, timeliness, and safety.[35] Providers' participation in an ACO is voluntary, and Medicare recipients participating in ACOs are not restricted from using physicians outside of their ACO.[35]

In 2016, a total of 447 ACOs participated in the MSSP, serving more than 8.9 million beneficiaries since the MSSP and Pioneer ACO models began in 2012.[36] MSSP ACOs are evaluated on 33 quality indicators. In a study comparing patients' reports about timely access to care and their primary physicians being informed about specialty care, there were some improvements as reported by ACO Medicare beneficiaries as compared with Medicare patients who were not part of an ACO.[37] CMS reported an estimated $700 million in savings compared to the non-ACO controls over the study period. CMS also estimated a $385 million savings from the Pioneer Programs during the first 2 years of their operation, 2012 and 2013.[38] However, after paying bonuses, the program resulted in a net loss of $2.6 million.[33] Despite the net loss, Health and Human Services Secretary Sylvia Burwell had set a goal of tying 50% of all traditional Medicare payments to quality or value by 2018 through new payment models, including ACOs.[33]

Hospital Value-Based Purchasing Program

CMS began implementing pilot projects for the Hospital Value-Based Purchasing (VBP) Program in 2003. This model has been replicated by private insurers as well, structured to provide incentives to discourage inappropriate, unnecessary, and costly care.[39] Now mandated by the ACA, the VBP Program applies to more than 3,500 U.S. hospitals, enabling them to earn incentive payments based on clinical outcomes and patient satisfaction. "Participating hospitals are paid for inpatient acute care services based on the quality of care, not just quantity of the services they provide."[40] Hospitals with low case volumes and ones that offer only specific specialties such as psychiatry, long-term treatment, rehabilitation, and cancer treatment are exempted.[40] Quality is measured based on a hospital's Total Performance Score (TPS), which is based on how well they meet a number of specific patient care and outcome objectives. These objectives change from year to year as older objectives "top out," or when most hospitals are meeting them. New objectives are cycled in to address known cost or quality problems identified by CMS.

▶ Continuing Change

U.S. hospitals will retain their core roles as the purveyors of the most technologically sophisticated care in the world, the educational practice platforms of physicians and other health professionals, and the sites of clinical research. In the frenetic environment of health system reforms, hospitals now assume yet another role as one component of an integrated system and continuum of community-based care.

Debates and analyses will continue regarding hospitals' roles in the reformed system and healthcare marketplace. Results of government and private entity experiments with the reconfigured roles of hospitals in a new population-focused, value-driven delivery system will yield numerous opportunities for continued refinements that affect both the quality and costs of care. There are reasons for optimism in the prospect of ACOs, with hospitals as major participants, providing excellent patient-centered coordination of care that successfully addresses the negative hallmarks of the healthcare delivery system—fragmentation, duplication, medical errors, and excessive costs. Observers are expressing concern, however, that the newly established ACOs are combining healthcare organizations that otherwise would compete with each other, thus creating networks with dangerous market power.[41]

Critical to the success of hospitals in the new era of reform will be a strong national health information infrastructure. This will require systems that not only will collect and store patients' health information, but also make that information available in many different ways, across traditional institutional and administrative boundaries, to enable the cost savings and quality improvement as part of the reform initiatives.

Recent evidence bears out that there will be great variation in the capability of America's thousands of hospitals to adjust to radical reversals of form and function required by the ACA and other reforms. It is likely that the Darwinian law of nature—survival of the fittest—will determine which hospitals remain to serve the American public in the future.

▶ Discussion Questions

■ How do hospitals interface with the continuum of care delivery?
■ What does hospital type indicate about the patients they serve?
■ How does the Patient's Bill of Rights benefit patients as well as hospital staff? Are there any unintended consequences?
■ What is the difference between vertical and horizontal organizations?
■ Does the focus on accountable care strengthen or weaken hospitals? Why?

CHAPTER ACRONYMS

ABIM American Board of Internal Medicine
ACA Affordable Care Act
ACGME American College of Graduate Medical Education
ACO Accountable Care Organization
AHA American Hospital Association
CEO Chief executive officer
CFO Chief financial officer
CIO Chief information officer
CMIO Chief medical information officer
CMS Centers for Medicare & Medicaid Services

CNO Chief nursing officer
COO Chief operating officer
CoPs Conditions of Participation
CT Computed tomography
DRG Diagnosis-related groups
EHR Electronic health record
HIT Health information technology
IHI Institute for Healthcare Improvement
IOM National Academy of Science's Institute of Medicine
MRI Magnetic resonance imaging

MSSP Medicare Shared Savings Program
PET Positron emission tomography
QIO Quality Improvement Organization
TJC The Joint Commission

TPS Total Performance Score
VBP Value-based purchasing
x-ray Radiographic image

References

1. Stevens R. *In Sickness and in Wealth: American Hospitals in the Twentieth Century*. Basic Books, Inc.; 1989.

2. American Hospital Association. Fast facts on U.S. hospitals, 2021. Accessed February 18, 2021. https://www.aha.org/statistics/fast-facts-us-hospitals

3. American Association of Medical Colleges. Sustaining teaching hospitals. Accessed February 12, 2021. https://www.aamc.org/news-insights/teaching-hospital-sustainability

4. Greenwald L, Cromwell J, Adamache W, et al. Specialty versus community hospitals: referrals, quality, and community benefits. *Health Aff*. 2006;25(1):106-118. doi: 10.1377/hlthaff.25.1.106

5. Shomaker TS. Commentary: preparing for health care reform: ten recommendations for academic health centers. *Acad Med*. 2011;86(5):555-558. doi: 10.1097/ACM.0b013e3182103443

6. Teisberg E, Vayle E. *The Hospital Sector in 1992*. Harvard Business School; 1991.

7. Faulkner M, Aveyard B. Is the hospital sick role a barrier to patient participation? *Nurs Times*. 2002;98(24):35-36.

8. American Hospital Association. AHA Patient's Bill Of Rights. Accessed January 8, 2021. https://www.americanpatient.org/aha-patients-bill-of-rights/

9. American Hospital Association. The Patient Care Partnership. Accessed February 8, 2021. https://www.aha.org/other-resources/patient-care-partnership

10. Dolgin JL. The legal development of the informed consent doctrine: past and present. *Camb Q Healthc Ethics*. 2010;19(1):97-109. doi: 10.1017/S0963180109990284

11. Centers for Medicare & Medicaid Services. Chapter 12: physicians/nonphysician practitioners. In: *Medicare Claims Processing Manual*. Centers for Medicare & Medicaid Services; 2021. Accessed February 9, 2021. https://www.cms.gov/files/document/medicare-claims-processing-manual-chapter-12

12. Patient Advocate Foundation. Second opinions. Accessed February 19, 2021. https://www.patientadvocate.org/download-view/second-opinions/

13. Shortell S, Reinhardt U. *Improving Health Policy and Management: Nine Critical Research Issues for the 1990s*. Health Administration Press; 1992.

14. Kepro. Hospital discharge appeals. Keproqio.com. Accessed February 26, 2021. https://www.keproqio.com/providers/appeals.aspx

15. Kropf R. Planning for health services. In: Kovner AR, ed. *Health Care Delivery in the United States*. Springer Publishing Co.; 1995:353.

16. Zuckerman A. The next wave of mergers and acquisitions. What's your organization's position? *Healthc Financ Manage*. 2009;63(5):60-63.

17. Institute of Medicine Committee on Quality of Health Care in America. Kohn LT, Corrigan JM, Donaldson MS, eds. *To Err Is Human: Building a Safer Health System*. National Academies Press; 2000.

18. The Commonwealth Fund. Five years after "to err is human": what have we learned? Published May 1, 2005. Accessed January 21, 2021. https://www.commonwealthfund.org/publications/journal-article/2005/may/five-years-after-err-human-what-have-we-learned

19. Allen M. How many die from medical mistakes in U.S. hospitals? *ProPublica*. Published September 19, 2013. Accessed January 29, 2021. https://www.propublica.org/article/how-many-die-from-medical-mistakes-in-us-hospitals

20. Cohn J. A picture of progress on hospital errors. Milbank Memorial Fund. Published March 2015. Accessed February 21, 2021. http://www.milbank.org/the-milbank-quarterly/search-archives/article/4022/a-picture-of-progress-on-hospital-errors

21. Donabedian A. Evaluating the quality of medical care. *Milbank Q*. 2005;83(4):691-729. doi: 10.1111/j.1468-0009.2005.00397.x

22. Institute for Healthcare Improvement. The IHI Triple Aim. Accessed February 21, 2021. http://www.ihi.org/engage/initiatives/tripleaim/Pages/default.aspx

23. Wennberg JE, Gittlesohn A. Small area variation in health care delivery. *Science*. 1973;182(4117):1102-1108. doi: 10.1126/science.182.4117.1102

24. The Commonwealth Fund. Leapfrog Group offers first web-based compendium of quality incentive and reward programs. Published June 30, 2004. Accessed February 12, 2021. http://www.commonwealthfund.org/publications/press-releases/2004/jun/leapfrog-group-offers-first-web-based-compendium-of-quality-incentive-and-reward-programs

25. ABIM Foundation. Choosing wisely. Accessed January 8, 2021. http://www.choosingwisely.org/

26. Rao R, Hawkins M, Ulrich T, Gatlin G, Mabry G, Mishra C. The evolving role of public health in medical education. *Front Public Health*. 2020;8:251. doi: 10.3389/fpubh.2020.00251

27. Shah A, Stanford D. The road to population health: key considerations in making the transition. Objective Health webinar. Published November 14, 2012. Accessed February 18, 2021. https://www.beckersasc.com /webinars/PopulationHealthWebinar.pdf

28. Nahm S, Mack G. Goodbye, post-acute care. "Heavy-lifting" will shift to community-based care. *Modern Healthcare*. Published January 19, 2013. Accessed August 9, 2021. https://www.modernhealthcare.com /article/20130119/MAGAZINE/301199993/goodbye -post-acute-care

29. Blumenthal D, Abrams M, Nuzum R. The Affordable Care Act at 5 years. *N Engl J Med*. 2015;372(25): 2451-2458. doi: 10.1056/NEJMhpr1503614

30. Centers for Medicare & Medicaid Services. Accountable Care Organizations (ACOs). Updated March 4, 2021. Accessed August 9, 2021. https:// www.cms.gov/Medicare/Medicare-Fee-for-Service -Payment/ACO

31. Centers for Medicare & Medicaid Services. Shared Savings Program. Updated July 16, 2021. Accessed August 9, 2021. https://www.cms.gov/Medicare/Medicare -Fee-for-Service-Payment/sharedsavingsprogram/index .html?redirect=/sharedsavingsprogram/

32. Centers for Medicare & Medicaid Services. Advance Payment ACO Model. Updated July 19, 2021. Accessed August 9, 2021. https://innovation.cms.gov /initiatives/Advance-Payment-ACO-Model/

33. Gold J. Accountable care organizations, explained. Kaiser Health News. Published September 14, 2015. Accessed February 9, 2021. http://khn.org/news /aco-accountable-care-organization-faq/

34. Centers for Medicare & Medicaid Services. Pioneer ACO Model. Updated May 4, 2021. Accessed August 9, 2021. https://innovation.cms.gov/initiatives/Pioneer -ACO-Model/

35. Centers for Medicare & Medicaid Services. Summary of final rule provisions for Accountable Care Organizations under the Medicare shared savings program. Published October 20, 2011. Accessed February 9, 2021. https://www.cms.gov/newsroom /fact-sheets/summary-final-rule-provisions -accountable-care-organizations-under-medicare -shared-savings-program

36. Centers for Medicare & Medicaid Services. Next Generation ACO model. Updated August 24, 2021. Accessed September 9, 2021. https://innovation.cms .gov/innovation-models/next-generation-aco-model

37. McWilliams JM, Landon BE, Chernew ME, Zaslavsky AM. Changes in patients' experiences in Medicare Accountable Care Organizations. *N Engl J Med*. 2014;371(18):1715-1724. doi: 10.1056/NEJMsa1406552

38. O'Callaghan E, Turner N, Renwick L, et al. First episode psychosis and the trail to secondary care: help-seeking and health-system delays. *Soc Psychiatry Psychiatr Epidemiol*. 2010;45(3):381-391. doi: 10.1007 /s00127-009-0081-x

39. Deloitte Center for Health Solutions. Value-based purchasing: a strategic overview for health care industry stakeholders. Published 2011. Accessed February 5, 2021. http://www.orthodirectusa.com/wp -content/uploads/2013/07/US_CHS_ValueBased Purchasing_031811.pdf

40. Centers for Medicare & Medicaid Services. The Hospital Value-Based Purchasing (VBP) Program. Updated February 18, 2021. Accessed February 22, 2021. https:// www.cms.gov/Medicare/Quality-Initiatives-Patient -Assessment-Instruments/Value-Based-Programs /HVBP/Hospital-Value-Based-Purchasing

41. Caldwell P. Epic fail: Digitizing America's medical records was supposed to help patients and save money. Why hasn't that happened? *Mother Jones*. Published November 2015. Accessed January 22, 2021. http:// www.motherjones.com/politics/2015/10/epic -systems-judith-faulkner-hitech-ehr-interoperability

CHAPTER 7

Ambulatory Care

© STILLFX/iStock/Getty Images Plus/Getty Images

CHAPTER OVERVIEW

This chapter reviews the major elements of ambulatory (or outpatient) care. Ambulatory care encompasses a diverse and growing sector of the healthcare delivery system. Physician services are the chief component; however, hospital outpatient and emergency departments, community health centers, departments of health, and voluntary agencies also contribute important services, particularly for underserved and vulnerable populations. Ambulatory surgery is a continuously expanding component of ambulatory care as new technology allows more procedures to be performed safely and efficiently. Finally, telehealth is discussed as an expanding field affecting the evolving healthcare delivery system.

▶ Overview and Trends

Ambulatory care comprises healthcare services that do not require overnight hospitalization. Once largely consisting of visits to private physicians' offices and hospital outpatient clinics and emergency departments, ambulatory care today encompasses a broad and expanding array of services. The ambulatory care system is an important subsystem and care domain in the United States health system. In health care, patients may access the delivery continuum at different touchpoints or intervals. These touchpoints in the frame of systems thinking are referred to as Care Domains, as shown in **FIGURE 7-1**.

New technological advancements allow medical and diagnostic procedures previously requiring hospitalization to be performed on an outpatient basis. Surgical procedures that previously required a hospital stay are now routinely performed on a same-day, ambulatory basis. In addition to new diagnostic and treatment tools available in the outpatient setting and the advanced technology that made outpatient treatment safe and effective, financial mandates also drove services into the ambulatory arena.

In the late 1980s, prospective hospital reimbursement replaced retrospective payment on a national scale through Medicare's initiation of the diagnosis-related group (DRG) payment system, as discussed in Chapter 4. The new payment system provided financial incentives to decrease the duration of inpatient stays and to increase service delivery efficiency. Hospitals responded to the new payment system by shifting services amenable to outpatient delivery from the more expensive inpatient environment to less expensive and more efficient outpatient or ambulatory delivery settings. Both DRGs and pressures from healthcare insurers and purchasers to control costs contributed to the rapid expansion of managed care. With the goal of providing services in the least expensive, most effective manner possible, managed care organizations exerted a powerful influence that compelled a shift toward the use of ambulatory services to replace more expensive inpatient care.

Ambulatory care capacity has undergone exponential increases in both the hospital-based and non-hospital-based, or "freestanding," settings. Historically, hospitals operated virtually all ambulatory or outpatient clinics within their main facilities or in contiguous facilities on the hospital campuses. Many hospitals still operate ambulatory clinics on-site, and many have retained ambulatory surgical services within their main facilities. For some hospitals, converting underused inpatient units to ambulatory surgical facilities within the hospital provided a cost-effective means to accommodate the shift in site of care.

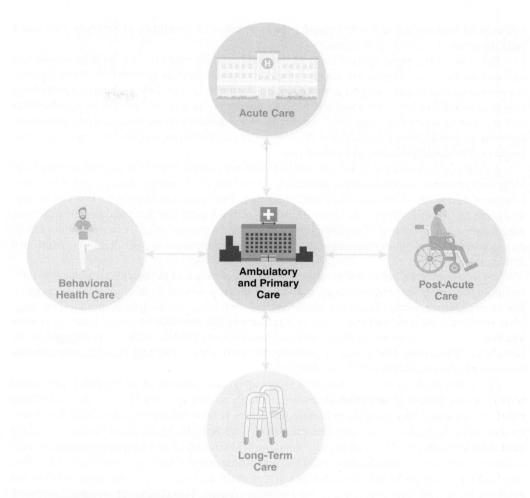

FIGURE 7-1 Ambulatory and Primary Care Domains
Created by Richard Greenhill.

Beginning in the 1980s, hospitals expanded their service networks to include geographically distributed freestanding ambulatory care facilities throughout their service areas, both for routine diagnosis and treatment and for surgical services. Two factors influenced this trend for hospitals. First, the 1980s and 1990s saw increased consumer demand for conveniently located, easily accessible facilities and services. Second, with the growing concerns of inner-city hospitals about competition with other institutions for market share of profitable outpatient services and referrals for inpatient care, hospitals recognized the need to expand their service distribution network by establishing conveniently located facilities. Hospitals also recognized that ambulatory surgical services could be operated more efficiently off-site, removed from complexities such as operating room scheduling that required accommodation to a vast array of physician and inpatient needs. Independent of hospital organizations, for-profit corporations' freestanding facilities providing ambulatory, primary, specialty, and surgical services proliferated. In addition to profitability and cost-control features attractive to insurers, responsiveness to consumer preferences also was a primary driver in these developments.

The 1990s saw a rapid upward trend in the number of ambulatory care facilities owned and operated by hospitals, physicians, and independent chains. Services provided by these facilities are diverse and represent a response to population demographics in their respective service areas as well as reimbursement opportunities. A partial listing of the array of ambulatory care facilities includes cancer treatment, diagnostic imaging of many different types, renal dialysis, pain management, physical therapy, cardiac and other types of rehabilitation, outpatient surgery, occupational health, women's health, and wound care.

A significant corollary to developments in ambulatory care delivery for hospital-operated and independent organizations has been physicians' entry into the business of outpatient diagnostic, treatment, and surgical services previously available to their practices in only the hospital setting. The same factors operative in the larger industry—technological advances making the purchase, maintenance, and operation of required equipment feasible and cost effective in freestanding facilities; consumer demand for convenient, user-friendly environments; and profitability—continued driving this development.

Physician involvement in this arena paralleled that of hospitals in practice areas, such as ophthalmologic surgery for lens replacement and laser therapy, certain types of gynecologic surgery, fiber-optic gastrointestinal diagnosis, chemotherapy, renal dialysis, computed tomography, magnetic resonance imaging, and more. The implications of this trend for hospitals' business volume and revenue were significant as physicians and hospitals emerged as competitors engaged in the same lines of business. These developments significantly altered the long-standing relationships between physicians and their affiliated hospitals.[1]

The ambulatory care delivery system is changing and growing as its various organization models evolve, including new efforts to measure quality relative to costs. The service constellation also is growing and becoming more diverse with many service delivery hybrids. With the implementation of the Patient Protection and Affordable Care Act (ACA), Medicare Access and CHIP Reauthorization Act (MACRA) and accompanying proliferation of new care delivery models such as patient-centered medical homes (PCMHs) and Accountable Care Organizations (ACOs) that emphasize population health, the roles of both primary and specialty ambulatory services are evolving along with their respective reimbursement systems. This chapter provides a framework for understanding the origins, development, and future direction of this important sector of the healthcare delivery system that continues to grow.

▶ Private Medical Office Practice

Private physician office practices constitute the predominant mode of ambulatory care in the United States. In 2016, the most recent year for which data are available, the National Center for Health Statistics (NCHS) estimated that patients made 883.7 million visits to physician offices. Approximately 54.5% of visits were made to primary care physicians (i.e., general and family practice, pediatrics, and internal medicine), 26.5% of visits were made to medical specialists (e.g., dermatology, psychiatry, urology, neurology), and 18.9% were made to surgical specialists (e.g., orthopedic surgery).[2] **FIGURE 7-2** provides a snapshot of the distribution of physician office visits.

The way physicians organize and operate their private practices has evolved from a variety of factors.[3] Physician group practice can be traced to the Mayo Clinic in the late 1800s and generated

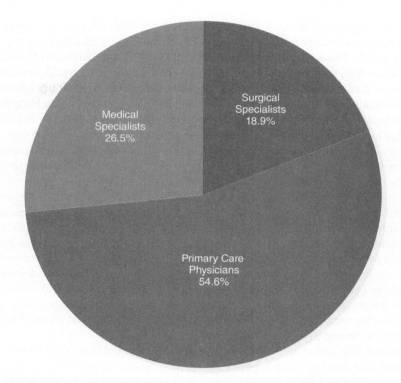

FIGURE 7-2 Percent Distribution of Office Visits by Physician: United States, 2016

Created by Kim Davey. Based on data from Rui P, Okeyode T. National Ambulatory Medical Care Survey: 2016 National Summary Tables. National Center for Health Statistics. Published 2016. Accessed June 11, 2021. https://www.cdc.gov/nchs/data/ahcd/namcs_summary/2016_namcs_web_tables.pdf

considerable controversy among physicians at the time. A 1932 report by a New York private foundation's Committee on the Costs of Medical Care endorsed organized group practices and the use of insurance payments. The American Medical Association (AMA) had long opposed the group practice model and condemned the report, declaring that salaried physicians practicing in groups were unethical. The controversy erupted into a legal battle when the Group Health Association was organized in Washington, D.C., in 1937. The AMA expelled all Group Health Association-salaried physicians. Hospitals received lists of so-called reputable physicians who were not part of group practices. The Medical Society of the District of Columbia and the AMA were subsequently indicted, found guilty, and fined for having conspired to monopolize medical practice.[4] For the next few decades negative confrontations occurred as physicians sought participation in developing group health plans. Participating physicians were socially ostracized and denied hospital privileges. By the 1950s, due to effective legal challenges against organized medicine and a physician shortage, opposition to group practice subsided.

Before 1960, most physicians operated solo practices. Over ensuing years, specialization, changing economics, and the desire for more control over their lifestyles caused physicians to group together, either in single fields, such as primary care, or into multispecialty groups.

The old solo-practice model made the physician responsible for their entire patient caseload 24 hours a day, every day of the year. Before the proliferation of specialties, these physicians provided all medical care for their patients, except for surgery or occasional consultation. The demands on their time and stamina were enormous. Aside from occasional coverage arrangements with a colleague to allow for brief time off, their schedules were relentless and unpredictable.

Beginning in the 1960s, many factors influenced a shift from the solo mode of private practice to group practice. Social movements in the United States yielded heightened awareness of lifestyle adaptations that allowed accommodation for personal growth and balance between professional and personal responsibilities. In the same period, medical specialization burgeoned as the growth in medical knowledge and technologic advances increased exponentially. Rapidly advancing knowledge in every field of medicine and the resulting specialization created new challenges for the solo generalist and the specialist. Most obvious were increasing demands on physicians to maintain a command of an exponentially growing body of diagnostic and therapeutic knowledge in their fields.

The introduction of Medicare reimbursement in 1966 dramatically altered the private medical office and its administrative processes. Before this development, physician reimbursement came from largely two sources—personal patient payments or third-party private insurance. Billing and collection were relatively simple. When Medicare began providing coverage for everyone at the age of 65 years, private physicians' offices found themselves dealing with a vast array of new government regulations and fee schedules. In addition, many Medicare recipients also carried supplemental private insurance contracts. Government regulation, complexity, and volume of billing requirements burgeoned. Solo-practice office administration, once the province of the physicians themselves, possibly with the help of a receptionist and bookkeeper, now required an increased level of sophistication and a great deal more time and attention.

Other factors also influenced the shift to group practice. Inflation fueled office lease and rental expenses. The need for more sophisticated administrative support services increased with advancing technology and more complex billing and record keeping. As technology advanced and diagnostic equipment became available for in-office use, groups could benefit from sharing equipment acquisition costs and ensuring the patient volume necessary to justify ongoing staffing and maintenance. Group practice could provide other economies of scale through shared administrative overhead.[4]

Group practice evolved in two forms. One consisted of groups of physicians in the same discipline, usually primary care, surgery, obstetrics, or pediatrics. The other form was multidisciplinary specialty practices, usually including primary care physicians in collaboration with specialists or subspecialists. There were important features that both generalist and specialist physicians found more attractive in group practice than solo practice. Although typically each physician carried their own caseload of patients, physicians could arrange a routine, preplanned schedule of after-hours and weekend and vacation coverage.

With the continuing growth of medical knowledge required to maintain state-of-the-art competencies and an ever-expanding range of diagnostic and therapeutic alternatives, group practice enabled physicians to access each other's knowledge and experience in an informal consultative environment. This interchange of information provided professional support and introduced an informal system of peer review to each physician's practice, which, in theory, could contribute to the quality of care.

Multispecialty group practices evolved for many of the same reasons as single-specialty groups. For specialists, a major benefit was that group membership reduced reliance on patient referrals from other community physicians because economic incentives made keeping the business inside the group beneficial to all members. Patients also benefited by having diagnosis, treatment, and consultation services available at one location.[5-7] Surgical group practices evolved similarly to those in the general and other specialty medical fields for similar reasons; however, surgeons tend to avoid multispecialty grouping. Instead, most are either general surgeons or specialists in such areas as colorectal, cardiothoracic, vascular, or orthopedic surgery.

In the 1990s, many hospitals acquired physician practices with the goals of capturing new market share, ensuring inpatient admissions, bringing new volume to ancillary departments such as laboratory and radiology, and improving service delivery efficiency to meet the demands of managed care. In succeeding years, hospitals divested from these arrangements due to financial losses resulting from low physician productivity and high overhead expense.[8] However, in the past decade, hospital acquisitions of physician practices accelerated rapidly as hospitals prepared for health reform by creating physician networks that are well positioned to negotiate with health plans, manage coordination of care, monitor quality, and contain costs. There is strong indication that hospital leaders will continue active physician recruitment in the foreseeable future.[4,8] In the past, hospitals targeted primary care physicians for employment but now are also seeking employment from specialists in anticipation of creating "closed integrated healthcare delivery systems."[8] In addition to physicians, staff of hospital-owned physician practices may include nurses, nurse practitioners, physician assistants, medical office assistants, laboratory personnel, clerical staff, information technology personnel, and case management staff.

In 2016, 67.8% of physicians were working in group practices, ranging in size from 2 to over 11 physicians per group. Thus, only around one-third of physicians were in solo practice.[2] The American Hospital Association (AHA) noted that 2018 was the first year that the percentage of employed physicians (47%) exceeded the number of physicians that owned their own practice (46%). In 2016, the number of physicians that owned their own practice was 61%; thus, physician ownership decreased by 15% from 2016 to 2018. A few drivers are cited for this shift in physician ownership and include the need for economies of scale, consumer expectations, a move toward and pressures associated with value-based payment and accepting more financial risk, physician burnout, and student loan debt of medical school graduates and new physicians.[4] From physicians' perspectives, hospital employment has become attractive due to factors such as flat reimbursement rates, complex insurance and health information technology requirements, high malpractice premiums, and the desire for greater work–life balance. For hospitals, employing physicians provides opportunities to gain market share for admissions, the use of diagnostic testing and other outpatient services, and referrals to high-revenue specialty services. Today, an increasing number of physicians are choosing employment by hospitals over private practice and looking to new investor types such as private equity investors, venture capitalists, health plans, and large employers.[3] Given the dynamics of health reform, acquiring physician practices is preparing hospitals to cope with a spectrum of scenarios that range from continuing fee-for-service payment to population health management and financial risk-based reimbursement.[4]

▶ Integrated Ambulatory Care Models

Traditional ambulatory care models reimbursed providers for services on a piecework basis, without requirements for coordinating services between or among providers. This piecework reimbursement promoted using a high volume of interventions, offered providers no compensation for effort to efficiently coordinate services on behalf of patient needs, and lacked methods to aggregate information on patient outcomes.[5] Historically, these models have been service-focused rather than patient-focused and, as a result, highly fragmented and inefficient. The ACA and MACRA system reforms include healthcare delivery and reimbursement principles that make patient health outcomes, rather than delivery of discrete services, the primary focus. In addition, reforms place new emphasis on providers' responsibilities for the overall health outcomes of their total population of patients, not just individuals. This emphasis requires integration and coordination of care across the spectrum of patient needs and among multiple providers in all sectors of the health and human services delivery system. The ACA provides resources to support the development and testing of two service delivery and reimbursement models, PCMHs and ACOs. The overarching goals of these models are to make medical care more effective and efficient, thereby improving the health of populations and reducing costs while increasing both patient and provider satisfaction. The timely, coordinated, and efficient delivery of ambulatory primary care and specialty services is central to both models. To achieve the goals of these programs requires an information system to undergird multiple providers, institutions, payers, and regulators with sufficient sophistication to support all their needs that go well beyond just supporting good patient care.

Patient-Centered Medical Homes

The patient-centered medical home (PCMH) is a "team-based model of care led by a personal physician who provides continuous and coordinated care throughout a patient's lifetime to maximize health outcomes."[6] The PCMH is responsible for providing all of a patient's healthcare needs or appropriately arranging a patient's care with other qualified professionals. This includes the provision of preventive services, treatment of acute and chronic illness, and assistance with end-of-life issues. The model emerged in 1967 and was proposed by the American Academy of Pediatrics.[7] The PCMH applies to all ages of patients with a distinctive orientation toward individual patients' partnership with the provider team in all aspects of their care. The model recognizes that the current reimbursement system fails to meaningfully address multiple patient needs and provider demands for a comprehensive, coordinated, and integrated approach to managing all aspects of an individual's health. **FIGURE 7-3** illustrates the core functions of a PCMH. As such, the PCMH embodies recommendations for major reimbursement reforms that compensate physicians for the time required to provide and arrange for the holistic care necessary to meet the full spectrum of patient needs, not only for in-office, face-to-face encounters.[5] The National Committee for Quality Assurance (NCQA) offers a PCMH recognition program, which was launched in 2008 and was the first program of its kind in the United States.[7] As described by the Agency for Healthcare Research and Quality (AHRQ), the PCMH model embodies a philosophy of advanced primary care (APC) based on the five core principles summarized below, which address the Institute for Healthcare Improvement's "Triple Aim" of improved population health, improved patient experience of care, and reductions in per capita costs[7-10]:

1. Patient-centered: The PCMH supports patients learning to manage and organize their care based upon preferences and ensures that patients, families, and caregivers are included in the development of care plans. It encourages patients to participate in quality-improvement research and health policy efforts.[7,10]

2. Comprehensive: The PCMH offers holistic care from a team of providers that is accountable for the patient's physical and behavioral health needs, including prevention and wellness, acute, and chronic care. The PCMH team establishes practice and population management to identify patients that need follow-up and chronic disease management.[7,10]

3. Coordinated: The PCMH ensures that care is organized across all elements of the broader healthcare system, including specialty care, hospitals, home health care, community services, and long-term care supports. (Elements of the broader healthcare

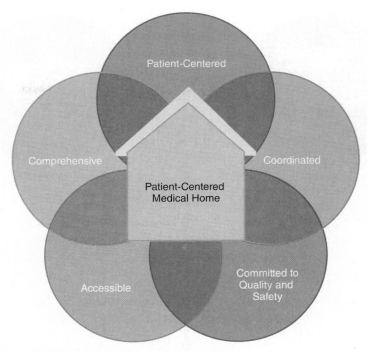

FIGURE 7-3 Patient-Centered Medical Home Core Functions

Created by Kim Davey. Based on information from the Agency for Health Research and Quality. Defining the PCMH. Accessed June 11, 2021. https://pcmh.ahrq.gov/page/defining-pcmh

system are referred to as the "medical neighborhood," and care transitions are coordinated across care settings and services.) This helps minimize costs, confusion, and unnecessary care.[7,10]

4. Accessible: The PCMH delivers accessible service with shorter waiting times, enhanced in-person hours, 24/7 electronic or telephone access, and alternative methods of communication through health information technology.[7,10]

5. Committed to quality and safety: The PCMH demonstrates commitment to quality improvement and the use of data and health information technology and other tools to assist patients and families in making informed decisions about their health.[7,10]

Accountable Care Organizations

The ACO model was a key piece of the ACA and created the Medicare Shared Savings Program, which initially introduced the model to the Medicare-recipient population. An ACO is "a network of doctors and hospitals that shares financial and medical responsibility for providing coordinated care to patients in hopes of limiting unnecessary spending."[11] (See **FIGURE 7-4**.) Primary care is considered the cornerstone of the ACO model, and ideally, PCMHs will be the primary care component of ACOs. Like PCMHs, ACOs are designed to ensure care coordination so that all patients receive timely and appropriate care and avoid unnecessary duplication of services, medical emergencies, and hospitalizations. An ACO may include the following types of provider groups and suppliers of Medicare-covered services[11]:

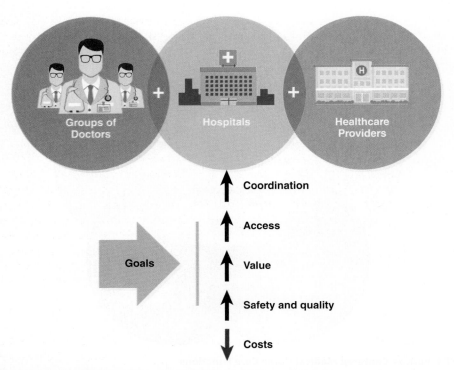

FIGURE 7-4 Accountable Care Organizations: Key Providers and Goals
Created by Kim Davey.

- ACO professionals, including physicians and hospitals in group practice arrangements
- Networks of individual practices of ACO professionals
- Partnerships or joint venture arrangements between hospitals and ACO professionals or hospitals employing ACO professionals
- Other Medicare providers and suppliers as approved by U.S. Department of Health and Human Services

Each ACO must be a legally constituted entity within its state with a governing board that includes service providers, suppliers, and Medicare beneficiaries. Each one must take responsibility for at least 5,000 Medicare beneficiaries for a period of 3 years. To qualify for participation, ACOs must meet Medicare-established quality measures of care appropriateness, coordination, timeliness, and safety. Provider participation in an ACO is voluntary, and Medicare recipients participating in ACOs are not restricted from using physicians outside their ACO.[12]

The ACA provides a payment structure for ACOs that combines fee-for-service payments with shared savings and bonus payments linked with specific quality performance standards for which all providers in an ACO are accountable.[11,12] Like the payment structure for PCMHs, the ACOs shift fee-for-service interventions toward financial rewards for maintaining patients' health. ACO payment model shifts reimbursement toward value-based models that utilize bundled payments for services. These are models that reward providers for quality and outcomes and provide reimbursement based on a bundle of services versus each service (or fee-for-service model). Figure 7-4 illustrates the key goals and providers of ACOs. As of 2020, there were 517 Medicare ACOs caring for 11.2 million beneficiaries.[13] Medicaid ACOs have been created in states across the country to improve patient and population health outcomes while trying to exert downward pressure on healthcare costs. As of 2021, there are several examples of commercial ACOs that are based on the ACO concept but created by private health insurers like Aetna, UnitedHealth, Humana, and Cigna, among others.

▶ Other Ambulatory Care Practitioners

In addition to physicians, several other licensed healthcare professionals conduct practices in ambulatory settings. Among the most common are dentists, podiatrists, social workers, psychologists, physical therapists, and optometrists. Like physicians, they may practice individually or in single-specialty or multispecialty groups. For example, there are general solo-practice dentists and multispecialty dental groups that provide general preventive and curative services, as well as services in specialties such as periodontics and orthodontics. Likewise, psychologists in a group may include both generalists and specialists in forensic, child, and other types of psychological interventions.

▶ Ambulatory Care Services of Hospitals

Acute care, not-for-profit hospitals have operated outpatient clinics since the 1800s. The early ones were located predominantly in urban centers whose indigent populations lacked access to private medical care. At that time, the provision of outpatient services was largely a function of government-sponsored public hospitals. With the proliferation of not-for-profit hospitals beginning in the early 1900s, outpatient clinics provided a means for those hospitals to fulfill part of their charitable mission by serving low-income populations who had little, if any, access to private physicians. Hospital outpatient clinics also provided a teaching setting for university-affiliated hospitals, which trained physicians as part of their community mission. Because hospital outpatient clinics served needy populations, they were a low-status component of the hospital and were characterized as the "stepchild of the institution."[14] Often, medical students and hospital-affiliated physicians of the lowest rank agreed to staff the clinics in return for earning hospital admitting privileges.

Today, hospital outpatient clinics still function as community safety nets for needy populations; however, the status of those clinics is vastly different from their historical predecessors. Far from the "stepchild" image, hospitals now view outpatient clinical services as providing a channel for inpatient admissions and major revenue sources from the use of hospital ancillary services. Today's hospital outpatient clinics are organized along the lines of private physician group practices and are aesthetically pleasant, well equipped, and customer oriented. Trends in treatment in the hospital outpatient setting as contrasted with inpatient care are clear. With respect to the hospitals' financial picture, in 1990 outpatient services revenue constituted 23% of total U.S. voluntary hospital revenues.[15] This figure has continued to rise over succeeding decades, with the outpatient share of total hospital revenue reaching 48% in 2016.[16] Declining hospital admissions and increasing outpatient visits is the current trend.

Because hospital outpatient services were designed to provide teaching and research opportunities, they have been organized along the lines of human organ systems and the diseases affecting them. For example, medical clinics, in addition to general medicine, might include clinics for dermatology (skin), cardiology (heart), gastroenterology (digestive tract), rheumatology (bone and connective tissue), and other specialties. In addition to general surgery, surgical clinics might include specialties such as orthopedics, obstetrics and gynecology, and others. This type of organizational structure allowed focus on patient complaints and illnesses. Beyond this benefit, however, the complex interactions among physicians and patients inherent in this anatomic organization of services have both positive and negative implications for both.

For patients, specialty clinics provide a focused approach to diagnosis and treatment by physicians with special training in their conditions. Also, medical teaching responsibilities in clinics often result in thorough patient examination, diagnostic workups, and case review for the healthcare students' benefit, which might not otherwise occur in a nonteaching setting.

Hospital-based specialty clinics also have drawbacks for patients. Often, specialty clinics treat patients only on certain days each week or month. Patients with multiple conditions may have to visit several specialty clinics, necessitating return visits during which several different physicians examine them. Because communication among physicians in different specialty clinics can be problematic, patients may receive conflicting advice or instruction, may be medicated inappropriately with drugs prescribed by several different specialists, or may "fall through the cracks" when a complaint arises that does not fit the specialty area of one of their providers. Similarly, for the physician, this type of categorical treatment environment requires a high degree of initiative to maintain accurate, current information on patients treated by multiple specialists. Such communication challenges among clinical settings are ripe for the implementation of PCMHs.

Beginning in the early 1980s, several influences began to have an impact on how hospital outpatient clinic services were organized and delivered. One major influence was the adoption of prospective hospital reimbursement, which emphasized decreased lengths of stay and reduced inpatient revenues. Another major factor was the influence of managed care and its emphasis on the role of primary medical care.

Facing declining inpatient revenue, increasing fiscal pressures, and emphasis on primary medicine, hospitals reorganized and expanded outpatient services that focused heavily on primary care. Teaching hospitals planned jointly with their affiliated medical schools, and nonteaching facilities followed suit to expand the array of outpatient services with primary care as the core. Teaching hospitals also created primary care centers under the direction of paid, full-time faculty department heads with administrative, clinical, and teaching responsibilities. Primary care physician employees were organized into group models along the lines of private group practices. This primary care model provided a rational structure for the general medical care of clinic patients and helped ensure appropriate referrals and coordination of patient care within and among outpatient clinic specialty units.

The group model of primary care also supported hospitals' teaching mission by alleviating reliance on voluntary physician staffing of clinic sessions and student supervision responsibilities. Medical students and medical residents were provided a more supportive and consistent learning environment by continuously interacting with members of the practice group instead of interacting with different mentors over the course of their rotations. Patients benefited from improved coordination of their care and the opportunity to develop relationships with attending physicians. Developments in the organization of primary care in hospital-based clinics have made a major contribution to the coordination and appropriate delivery of health care to consumers of hospital-based outpatient clinic services. Trends in the volume of hospital outpatient clinic caseloads and payment sources will be subjects of great interest as hospital markets continue consolidating, quality-of-care improvements are advanced, and delivery costs become the subject of future policy efforts.

▶ Hospital Emergency Services

Recent increases in emergency department (ED) visits are attributed to overall population growth, an increase in illness-related diagnoses, and lack of private health insurance. The uninsured and Medicaid patients demonstrated the greatest increase in rates of ED use as compared with privately insured patients. Of expected sources of payment for ED visits in 2017, private insurance accounted for 31.2%, Medicaid or the Children's Health Insurance Program (CHIP) for 40.3%, and Medicare for 18.5%, Medicare and Medicaid (or dual eligibles) for 3.6%, Uninsured for 8.0%, Worker's compensation for 0.9%, Other for 4.4%, and Unknown for 9.8%, as shown in **FIGURE 7-5**. EDs are the primary portal of entry for hospital admission for uninsured and publicly insured patients.[17]

In the past, like other teaching hospital outpatient clinics, the ED was a place where medical students or medical residents were required to provide coverage as a component of their training. Often, to earn extra income, medical residents would contract to "moonlight" extra hours for their assigned hospital or for other hospital EDs. Nonteaching hospitals also often hired medical residents on a contracted basis to cover the ED or required attending staff to provide rotating coverage. These staffing configurations were less than ideal. Physicians working in EDs often had little training or experience with the illnesses and injuries encountered there, and this haphazard ED staffing was abandoned by the mid-1980s. Expanded knowledge, techniques, and equipment available for the care of critically ill and injured patients and concerns about liability resulted in dramatic changes in how EDs are staffed and organized. Since 1979, emergency medicine has been recognized as a medical specialty with accompanying

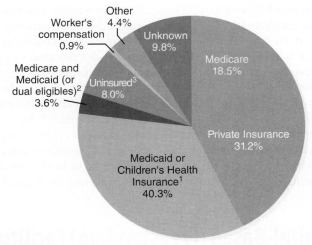

… Category not applicable.
*Estimate does not meet NCHS standards of reliability.
**Total exceeds "All visits" and percentage exceeds 100% because more than one source of payment may be reported per visit.
[1]Children's Health Insurance Program.
[2]Visits are also included in the "Medicaid or CHIP or other state-based program" and "Medicare" categories.
[3]Defined as having only self-pay, no charge, or charity as payment sources.
NOTE: Numbers may not add to totals because of rounding.
SOURCE: NCHS, National Hospital Ambulatory Medical Care Survey, 2017.

FIGURE 7-5 **Source of Payment for Emergency Department Visits: United States, 2017**

Created by Kim Davey. Based on data from Rui P, Kang K. National Hospital Ambulatory Medical Care Survey: 2017 emergency department summary tables. National Center for Health Statistics. Published 2017. Accessed June 6, 2021. https://www.cdc.gov/nchs/data/nhamcs/web_tables/2017_ed_web_tables-508.pdf

requirements for extended specialty training and experience to attain board certification, as in the other medical specialty fields.[18] Now, EDs are staffed by physicians qualified through training and experience in emergency medicine. Many corporations employ groups of board-qualified or board-certified emergency medicine physicians and contract their services to hospitals. Medical schools with accredited training programs in emergency medicine may staff their affiliated hospitals' EDs as a faculty practice group, providing clinical training for emergency department medical residents.

ED staff also includes nurses with advanced education and training in the triage and care of critically ill or injured patients. It also includes an array of other personnel who provide medical and nursing assistance and clerical support. Depending on the needs of the population served by the hospital, ED staff also may include mental health professionals and social workers. On-call arrangements with hospital medical staff of other departments or with contracted professionals assist ED staff to meet patient needs.

Although designed to care for life-threatening illness or injury, the public looks to EDs for medical care that ranges from the critically urgent to the routine, and reasons for ED visits encompass a broad spectrum. Because state and federal regulations require that hospitals turn no one away from an ED without an appropriate medical assessment, patients have learned that EDs are a guaranteed source of care regardless of their ability to pay or the nature of their complaint. EDs are organized to treat episodes of serious illness and injury and are therefore not a good choice for routine care. First, care is much more expensive in an ED than in an appropriate ambulatory setting because it consumes the time of specialist personnel for conditions in which their level of specialty qualification is unnecessary. Second, waiting times are often long because life-threatening cases appropriately have priority. Third, the ED, by its nature, is not organized or staffed to provide follow-up care. To facilitate follow-up care, ED staff often refer patients to ambulatory care services.

Increased ED use coupled with ED closures has resulted in a phenomenon called "ED crowding." Decades-long reports have cited the ongoing need to divert ambulances to alternative EDs because of immediate lack of capacity.[19] Despite the well-documented recognition that inappropriate ED use drives up costs and lacks continuity of care, individuals without resources or who may be unaware of other sources of care find the ED their most accessible choice. Even for individuals with a usual source of primary care, lack of provider availability outside normal business hours contributes to ED use for nonurgent conditions.[20,21] In accordance with the ACA goal of improving access to primary care, recent research evidence suggests that extended-hours access, such as that required in the PCMH model, can help to reduce unnecessary ED use and hospitalizations.[21-23] Such findings are adding strength to the rationale for continued robust support for primary care practices' pivotal role in meeting the population's basic needs.[23]

▶ Non-Hospital-Based (Freestanding) Facilities

Non-hospital-based or freestanding ambulatory care facilities are owned and operated by hospitals, hospital systems or physician groups, independent for-profit or not-for-profit single entities, or corporate chains. Many hospital systems, independent entities, and chains operate multiple ambulatory care facilities that provide a wide array of services, including ambulatory surgery, occupational health services, physical rehabilitation, substance abuse treatment, renal dialysis, cancer treatment, diagnostic imaging, cardiovascular diagnosis, sports medicine, and urgent/emergent care. Technological advances, entrepreneurial business opportunities, cost-reduction initiatives, and consumer preferences for convenient services continue to advance freestanding services as major components of the healthcare delivery system.

The following sections provide an overview of the major types of freestanding facilities that play roles in the rapid expansion of ambulatory care services in the United States.

Urgent Care Centers

The first urgent care centers opened in the 1970s, and as of June 2019 there were 9,279 centers in the United States. There has been more than a 30% increase in the number of centers in the last 5 years.[24] The Urgent Care Association (UCA) defines urgent care services as:

> … (1) a medical examination, diagnosis and treatment for non-life or limb threatening illnesses and injuries that are within the capability of an urgent care center which accepts unscheduled, walk-in patients seeking medical attention during all posted hours of operation and is supported by on-site evaluation services, including radiology and laboratory services; and (2) any further medical examination, procedure and treatment to the extent they are within the capabilities of the staff and facilities available at the urgent care center.[24]

Urgent care centers offer a range of immediate care, screening, and diagnostic services. Immediate care services include treatment for cold and flu, conjunctivitis (or pink eye), rashes, ear infections, fractures, gynecological infections and disorders, sore throats, pneumonia, sprains and strains, upper respiratory infections, urinary tract infections, work-related illness, injuries, and wellness screenings, among others. Several diagnostic tests are offered to help diagnose and treat the conditions mentioned above, including blood counts, diabetic testing, urine pregnancy tests, urinalysis, rapid strep throat cultures, and rapid influenza tests. They also offer occupational health services such as employment screenings (i.e., physicals, urinary drug screening), flu immunizations, and workforce education on injury/illness prevention. Increasingly, urgent care centers are providing telehealth services. These services are provided by family and emergency medicine physicians, physician assistants, nurse practitioners, registered nurses, and radiology technicians, among other healthcare professionals.[24]

A 2019 UCA white paper highlighted the important role urgent care centers play in the health system. The white paper estimated that urgent care centers provided access and care to over 112 million patients in 2018. This accounted for over 23% of all primary care visits in the United States and 12.6% of all outpatient physician visits in 2018.[24] Operating with extended hours including evenings, weekends, and holidays, and accepting patients on a walk-in basis, urgent care centers are filling gaps in the delivery system created by the inflexibility of private physician appointment scheduling and unavailability during nonbusiness hours. This convenience factor is highlighted by the report, which noted that two-thirds of urgent care patients have a regular primary care physician.[24] Urgent care centers provide user-friendly alternatives to the chaotic environment and long waiting times of hospital EDs. Typically located in highly visible facilities such as storefronts in commercial areas, urgent care centers offer convenience and ease of accessibility to their visitors, and their numbers are increasing.[24] Because they are a less-expensive alternative to the hospital ED, health plans usually fully reimburse members' use of urgent care facilities when their physicians are not available. Costs for patients and insurers are also a major factor in urgent care center popularity, with urgent care visits being significantly cheaper than an ED visit. The cost differential is significant as increasing numbers of Americans subscribe to high-deductible health plans in which they pay out-of-pocket charges until an annual spending threshold is met. The expansion of urgent care centers is a clear indication that patients perceive them as a positive alternative to the hospital ED, and for individuals without a primary physician's availability, they meet nonemergency needs in a convenient and consumer-friendly manner.

Retail Clinics

Retail clinics, operated at retail sites such as pharmacies and supermarkets, are a growing form of ambulatory care. The first retail clinics opened in 2000 in the Minneapolis–St. Paul area in grocery stores.[25] Expanding from approximately 300 retail clinic sites in 2007,[26] current projections estimate that the number of retail clinic sites was 1,949 as of January 2019.[27] Total annual patient visits to retail clinics have reached 10.5 million.[28] Retail clinics were operated in 44 states in 2018 and logged more over 40 million patient visits.[29] Clinics are typically located in brand name retailers such as pharmacies, grocery stores, and "big box" stores such as CVS Pharmacies, Walgreens, Amazon, Walmart, and Target. Most retail clinics are owned by pharmacies and big box retailers.[28,30] Known by consumer-friendly names such as "MinuteClinic" and "TakeCare," the clinics represent an entrepreneurial response to patient demand for fast, affordable treatment of easy-to-diagnose conditions. Staffed by nurse practitioners or physician assistants, a physician is not required on-site, although many clinics have physician consultation available by phone. Most clinics accept Medicare, Medicaid, private insurance, and worker's compensation insurance.[28] In 2019, 77% of visits to clinics were covered by insurance.[27]

In the reforming healthcare delivery system, proliferation of these clinics has captured the attention of both health systems and payers. First, the cost of care initiated at retail clinics is significantly lower than that of physician offices, urgent care centers, and EDs. Second, the wide geographic coverage of retail sites and convenient hours of operation have made retail clinics attractive to patients.[31] For health systems, retail clinic locations expand market reach into new areas, expand the primary care network to new populations, and reduce unnecessary ED visits.[28] Payers are integrating retail clinics into their networks to reduce costs (such as those associated with EDs),[32] and patients are also opting for retail services as a way to reduce healthcare costs.[33]

Reactions to retail clinics from the organized medical community vary from acceptance as a patient choice to opposition. Primary care physicians have many concerns about quality and continuity of care and competition. The American Academy of Family Physicians (AAFP) is continuously studying the retail clinic phenomenon. In 2013 it issued a policy affirming its belief that the PCMH is best suited to improving the quality of care. In this policy statement, the AAFP opposed expansion of retail clinic services beyond minor acute illnesses and chronic medical conditions and agreed that retail clinics can be a component of patient-centered care while coordinating with primary care physicians to avoid fragmentation.[34] In a 2015 position paper, the American College of Physicians (ACP) issued recommendations addressing retail clinic expansion, noting that "retail health clinics should serve as an episodic alternative to care from an established primary care practice for relatively healthy patients without complex medical histories."[35] Upon release of the recommendations, the ACP President acknowledged, "Health care delivery models are changing and our patients are embracing and exploring alternatives to the traditional office practice."[35]

As retail clinics continue to proliferate, more research is required to learn about how these entities will fit into the reformed delivery system. This growing ambulatory care enterprise is under close observation by employers, insurers, retailers, investors, and the medical and consumer communities. Retail clinics are established in the mainstream of primary healthcare delivery and will likely continue to be an important component of future primary care delivery systems.

Ambulatory Surgery Centers

The NCHS defines ambulatory surgery as "surgical and nonsurgical procedures performed on an ambulatory (outpatient) basis in a hospital or freestanding center's general operating rooms, dedicated ambulatory surgery rooms, and other specialized rooms such as endoscopy units and cardiac catheterization labs."[36] Federal tracking and reporting on ambulatory surgery through the National Survey of Ambulatory Surgery was first conducted from 1994 to 1996, but discontinued due to lack of resources. After a 10-year hiatus, it was conducted again in 2006, with plans reported in 2015 to include this survey in the National Hospital Ambulatory Medical Care Survey in the future.[37] Therefore, where applicable, ambulatory surgery data is gleaned from other most-recent available sources.

Ambulatory or outpatient surgery accounted for more than 64.5% of all surgeries performed in hospitals in 2012.[38] Since the 1990s, the total number of ambulatory surgery centers (ASCs), including hospital and non-hospital-based, has more than doubled.[39] Now, there are more than 6,000 ASCs operating in the United States, of which over 5,000 are Medicare-certified.[40] Between 2000 and 2007 the number of Medicare-certified ASCs increased at an average annual rate of 7.3%.[41] Since 2007 the growth rate has slowed to an annual average of 2.6%.[41] Ninety-seven percent of ASCs operate as for-profit entities, and 91% are located in urban settings.[41] Approximately 22.3% of ASCs are owned or managed by an ASC management and development company.[41] Physicians have ownership interest in 90% of ASCs, hospitals have ownership interest in 21%, and 3% are owned entirely by hospitals.[42]

In the 1970s, physicians led the development of ASCs because they saw opportunities to establish high-quality and cost-effective alternatives to inpatient surgery. ASCs were physicians' solutions to frustration with hospital bureaucracy, operating room scheduling difficulties, and patient inconvenience. ASCs provided physicians with a high degree of professional autonomy in procedure scheduling and in selecting staff, equipment, and facilities best suited to their specialties and patient needs and preferences.[42]

Advancements in medical technology and changes in reimbursement criteria were the two primary drivers for ambulatory surgical procedures as alternatives to inpatient surgery. One of the most significant factors was advancements in anesthesia that resolved safely and quickly.[42] Advancements in surgical equipment and techniques reduced or eliminated the invasiveness of many procedures and their complications and risks. With these and other technological advances making outpatient surgery safer, mounting financial pressures resulted in Medicare and private insurers requiring that certain procedures be performed in the less costly ambulatory setting unless physicians were able to document the necessity of hospitalization. The initial years of the shift from inpatient to ambulatory surgery provided opportunities for hospitals to convert underused inpatient space into efficient, cost-effective care delivery areas, encouraging the development of separate surgical management systems for ambulatory and complicated cases. At the same time, well-managed ASCs quickly became profitable.

Hospitals responded to the demand for ambulatory surgery as they faced competition from newly formed physician-directed freestanding facilities and insurer demands for lower costs. In 1982, Medicare expanded coverage to include ambulatory surgical procedures, and between 1982 and 1992, outpatient surgeries in community hospitals increased by more than 200%, while inpatient surgical procedures declined by more than 32%.[39,43]

ASCs are among the most highly regulated healthcare entities. Forty-three states and the District of Columbia require licensure of ASCs; the remaining seven states have some form of regulatory requirement. All ASCs qualifying for Medicare reimbursement must undergo a process entailing compliance with federal standards on staff qualifications, safety, equipment, and management. Many ASCs also voluntarily submit to accreditation reviews by The Joint Commission, the Accreditation Association for Ambulatory Health Care, the American Association for Accreditation of Ambulatory Surgery Facilities, or the American Osteopathic Association.[43] In 2015, ASCs serving Medicare beneficiaries began to participate in a new Centers for Medicare & Medicaid Services ASC Quality Reporting Program. ASCs failing to submit required data or to meet established quality criteria may receive a 2% reduction in subsequent years' payment updates. Quality and the patient care experience have benefited significantly from improved technology applied in the ambulatory setting. Patients experience fewer complications, much faster recovery, and less disruption to normal activity than from inpatient surgery. Continuing advances in surgical procedures and anesthetic agents, postoperative management, and other evolving technology provide future opportunities to move even more types of inpatient surgery into the ambulatory setting. Patients view ASC facilities as user friendly and responsive to their needs, with 92% reporting a high degree of satisfaction.[43]

Federally Qualified Health Centers

Federally Qualified Health Centers (FQHCs) originated during Lyndon B. Johnson's presidency in the mid-1960s and represented a facet of that administration's social reform movement, labeled the "war on poverty." Originally authorized by the Office of Economic Opportunity, the Public Health Service assumed coordinating responsibility in the mid-1970s. Funded under Section 330 of the Public Health Service Act, these centers were established in urban and rural communities with common characteristics rooted in federal funding requirements, including focus on the needs of the underserved, comprehensive primary care, professional staffing, community involvement, and partnerships between the public and private sectors. Subsequent amendments to Section 330 established specialized primary care programs for migrant farm workers, the homeless, and residents of public housing.[44,45]

FQHCs may be organized under the aegis of local health departments (LHDs) as part of larger not-for-profit human service organizations or as stand-alone, not-for-profit corporations. All FQHCs must comply with federal requirements to[44,45]:

- Serve a medically underserved population
- Provide appropriate and necessary services with fees adjusted on patients' ability to pay
- Demonstrate sound clinical and financial management
- Be governed by a board, a majority of which includes health center patients

The FQHC model emphasizes coordinated and comprehensive care and reductions in health disparities for low-income individuals, racial and ethnic minorities, rural communities, and other underserved populations. Reflecting these emphases, FQHCs are staffed by multidisciplinary teams that include physicians, nurse practitioners, physician assistants, nurses, dental providers, midwives, behavioral healthcare providers, social workers, health educators, and many others.[45] This team approach assists patients to overcome geographic, cultural, linguistic, and other barriers and to link with other supportive programs and services. FQHCs are required to provide a full range of primary care and preventive services in the fields of family medicine, internal medicine, pediatrics, obstetrics and gynecology, and dentistry, including screenings, laboratory testing, radiology, and, where appropriate, pharmacy services.[45] As population needs dictate, FQHCs also may provide transportation, language translation, and health education services.[46]

FQHC grants are administered by the Health Resources and Services Administration (HRSA) of the U.S. Department of Health and Human Services. Fees for services are based on income, and services are offered without charge for the neediest patients; no patient may be denied services due to inability to pay.[45] The FQHC program has grown substantially over the years, and in 2020 nearly 1,400 centers operated 13,500 delivery sites providing primary and preventive care to nearly 29 million patients in every state, the District of Columbia, Puerto Rico, the U.S. Virgin Islands, and the Pacific Basin (or 1 in 11 people). The number of patients seen increased from 25.9 million in 2016 to 28.6 million in 2020, nearly tripling over the last 20 years.[46] **FIGURES 7-6** and **7-7** depict the important role FQHCs play in the U.S. health system.

Quality improvement has been a recent initiative in FQHCs. Progress has been made with the support of recent federal investments. Most health centers (78%) have been recognized as patient-centered medical homes. This is quite an accomplishment based on the patient population, which tends to be more vulnerable; however, this has not prevented the centers from evidencing strong patient outcomes while controlling costs. FQHCs were able to control disease in 68% of their diabetic patients, exceeding the national average of 59%. They also were able to control blood pressure in 65% of their hypertensive patients, which exceeded the national average of 59%. FQHCs serve as the frontline of the nation's opioid epidemic response through their screening and treatment efforts, with 76% providing substance abuse disorder services. Mental health services are also an important component of care, provided in 96% of FQHCs.[46]

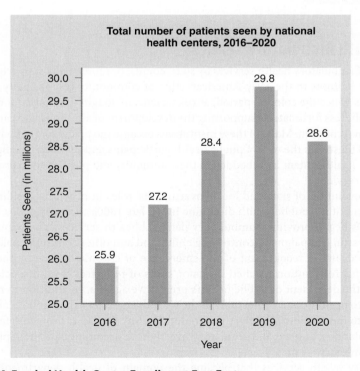

FIGURE 7-6 HRSA-Funded Health Center Enrollment Fast Facts

Created by Kim Davey. Based on data from the Health Resources and Services Administration. Total number of patients seen by National Health Centers, 2016–2020. Updated August 2021. Accessed August 29, 2021. https://data.hrsa.gov/tools/data-reporting/program-data/national

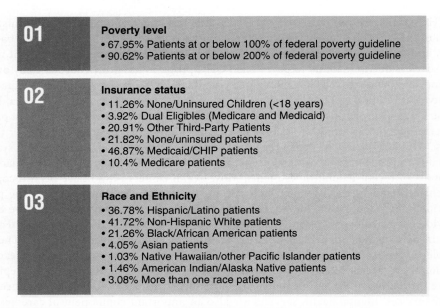

FIGURE 7-7 **HRSA-Funded Health Center Patient Characteristics Summary, 2020**

Created by Kim Davey. Based on data from the Health Resources and Services Administration. Age and race/ethnicity of patients seen by National Health Centers, 2020. Accessed October 28, 2021. https://data.hrsa.gov/tools/data-reporting/program-data/national

Public Health Ambulatory Services

The delivery of ambulatory health services by state, county, or municipally supported governmental entities has its roots in the early American ethic of community responsibility for the care of needy residents. Since the colonial period, altruistic citizens sought the charity of the community to provide for the less fortunate by supporting the development of almshouses to care for the needy and for orphaned children. Many of these institutions became the precursors of community hospitals. **FIGURE 7-8** illustrates the web of public health participants and services. The figure highlights how the public health system is embedded in the community and positioned to provide a number of ambulatory services.

With the evolution of state and local governments' roles in providing welfare services and the development of the public health discipline in the late 1800s and early 1900s, tax-supported state and LHDs began providing ambulatory personal health services. The public health community's successful campaigns in controlling childhood and other communicable diseases were rapidly followed by the recognition of the emergence of chronic disease by the medical care community. This recognition resulted in major shifts of resources toward specialized medical care, albeit to the detriment of public health's preventive agenda. In addition to maintaining its basic mission to promote and protect the public's health and safety, the public health community was expected to mount new initiatives to promote healthy lifestyles, provide safety net services to needy populations, and expand regulatory oversight to accommodate the rapidly expanding medical care industry.[47]

Ambulatory health services that became the domain of health departments included the administration of preventive public health measures such as cancer and chronic disease screening, immunization, high-risk maternal and infant care, family planning, tobacco control, and

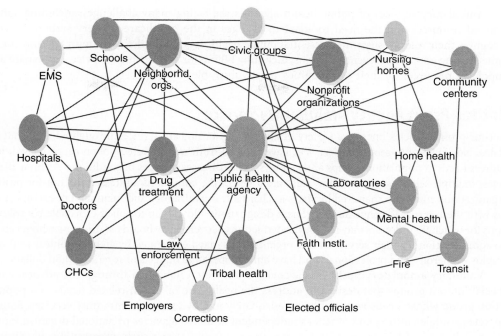

FIGURE 7-8 Public Health Participants

Centers for Disease Control and Prevention (2013). The public health system and the 10 essential public health services. Retrieved from http://www.cdc.gov/nphpsp/essentialservices.html

tuberculosis and sexually transmitted disease screening and treatment. Some LHDs also established FQHCs or other types of community health centers to provide a range of primary care services to needy individuals of all ages.

Today, the scope of ambulatory care services delivered by public health departments ranges across a wide spectrum from prevention-oriented programs, such as immunizations, well-baby care, smoking cessation, and cancer and chronic disease screening and education, to a full suite of personal health services offered through ambulatory care centers. Historically, support for ambulatory public health services has included combinations of city, county, and state funding, plus federal and state disease-specific or block grant funds.

Public health ambulatory services staff may include physicians, nurses, aides, social workers, public health educators, community health workers, and clerical and administrative staff who function under the overall administrative direction of a local health officer. This health officer may or may not be a physician, depending on the population size of the jurisdiction and individual state or municipal requirements. Depending on the geographic area, the governmental aegis may be state, county, or city.

Findings of the National Association of County and City Health Officials (NACCHO) *2019 National Profile of Local Health Departments* reveal the extent to which LHDs are providing ambulatory services.[48] With responses from 2,459 LHDs out of 2,800 surveyed, the report reveals that a significant proportion of local public health agencies continue to directly provide an array of ambulatory services. Some examples of the services most frequently provided are: adult and child immunizations (88%), tuberculosis screening (86%) and treatment (83%), and sexually transmitted disease screening (70%) and treatment (52%). Few LHDs provide direct clinical services to mothers and children, such as prenatal care (30%) and well-child clinics (30%).[48]

Ambulatory services of public health agencies are facing many challenges, including constrained resources and the need to adapt to changes in the healthcare delivery system. LHDs recognize their roles in sustaining essential public health services in their communities and continue seeking additional revenue streams, including billing for some clinical services, to remain as important resources for their communities' most vulnerable citizens.

Not-for-Profit Agency Ambulatory Services

Not-for-profit agencies operate a variety of ambulatory healthcare services throughout the United States. Not-for-profit ambulatory services have evolved from many sources, often cause-related, to address needs of population groups afflicted by specific diseases or types of conditions. Asthma, diabetes, multiple sclerosis, and cerebral palsy are a few of the conditions addressed. As not-for-profit organizations, many are chartered by states as charitable organizations and maintain tax-exempt status with the Internal Revenue Service. These designations allow them to solicit charitable contributions for which their donors may receive tax deductions. Governed by boards of directors who receive no compensation for their services, these organizations may be operated by an all-volunteer staff or employ numerous paid professionals and have annual operating budgets of several million dollars.

Voluntary ambulatory healthcare agencies often were established through the advocacy of special interest groups that desired to address the healthcare or health-related needs of a population group whose needs were not being adequately met by existing community services. Some operate as single entities, and others as independent affiliated agencies of national organizations. Planned Parenthood Federation of America is an example of one such organization. Its clinics provide preventive care, education, gynecologic care, and contraception methods in numerous locations throughout the United States. Another example is the Alzheimer's Association, which provides or assists affected individuals and their caregivers with specialized education and social support and promotes research into the causes of and treatment for the disease. Legislative advocacy related to the organization's interests at the federal, state, and local levels is frequently a major component of not-for-profit organization activity.

Financial support for voluntary ambulatory healthcare agencies is diverse. Sources may include charitable contributions, private payment, third-party insurance reimbursement (including Medicare and Medicaid), and federal, state, or local government grants. In many agencies, a large proportion of clients are uninsured or underinsured and lack personal resources, making financial subsidies crucial to continued viability. Agencies with missions to serve the neediest members of the community continue meeting challenges posed by the ebb and flow of government grant dollars and community economic conditions that affect philanthropic support through efficient business practices and a variety of private fundraising activities.[49] Although voluntary agencies provide only a small fraction of ambulatory care services compared with hospitals and other ambulatory care organizations, they are important as repositories of community values, as symbols of community charity and volunteerism, and as advocates for people with disabilities or special needs.

▸ Telehealth

Though not exclusively in the province of ambulatory care, telehealth (sometimes referred to as telemedicine) is a rapidly expanding field that is increasingly recognized as having a significant impact on the evolving delivery system in general and on ambulatory medicine in particular. There are definite benefits to telehealth from a population health perspective, such as providing care in locations where none exists or is limited (e.g., rural areas), or connecting homebound patients to physicians for consultations. Telehealth allows patients contact with physicians at their offices or institutions or even at a patient's residence. HRSA defines telehealth as "the use of electronic information and telecommunications technologies to support long-distance clinical health care, patient and professional health-related education, public health and health administration."[50] Telehealth is different from telemedicine. Telemedicine "seeks to improve a patient's health by permitting two-way, real time interactive communication between the patient, and the physician or practitioner at the distant site. This electronic communication means the use of interactive telecommunications equipment that includes, at a minimum, audio and video equipment."[51] Telehealth is a broader term that encompasses a range of health activities, including clinical services between a patient and a provider, but also health education and administration activities. Telehealth uses four modalities[52]:

1. Live video (synchronous): Real-time interaction substituting for an in-person encounter using audiovisual telecommunications technology.
2. Store and forward (asynchronous): Transmission of recorded health history that may include digital image results of diagnostic procedures transmitted to a provider (usually a specialist) who uses the information to evaluate a case.
3. Remote patient monitoring (RPM): Personal health and medical data collection from a patient via electronic communication technologies, transmitted to a provider.
4. Mobile health: Mobile communications devices such as cell phones, tablets, and personal digital assistants that send messages ranging from promoting healthy behaviors to alerts about public health threats.

While the benefits of telehealth in terms of cost containment and physician and patient convenience may seem obvious, insurers were slow in initially adopting reimbursement for these services. However, adaptation has significantly accelerated amid the global COVID-19 pandemic. Slow adoption has been attributed principally to the lack of an exact definition of services for billing purposes and accompanying fears that telehealth services will add charges rather than substitute for in-person patient encounters. As of February 2021, billing and reimbursement guidance has been provided. This has allowed services to be expanded across all types of providers. With opportunities for improving access, reducing costs, and responding to patient demands, the utilization of telehealth can be expected to grow.[51]

▶ Future Expansion and Experimentation

The focus of the healthcare delivery system in the United States has shifted from hospitals to expanded use of ambulatory care services. Continuing advances in medical technology, cost-reduction initiatives, and patient demands for convenient, accessible services will drive future ambulatory care growth in all settings. As healthcare reforms continue, the PCMH and ACO models will continue to be subjects of intense study. Analyses will provide fertile opportunities for health services research to inform practitioners and policy makers about these models' effectiveness in achieving the goals of higher quality care, reduced costs, and patient satisfaction.

▶ Discussion Questions

- Define ambulatory care.
- What role do private medical office practices play in the ambulatory care system?
- What are integrated ambulatory care models?
- What are the functions of patient-centered medical homes?
- What are Accountable Care Organizations?
- Discuss the emergence and evolution of ambulatory care services in hospitals.
- Discuss the emergence and evolution of free-standing ambulatory care facilities.
- What role does telehealth play in providing ambulatory care services?

CASE 7-1 Plight After Oversight at Vestavia Medical Services (VMS)

Vestavia Medical Services (VMS) is a physician practice located in a quiet area outside the Baltimore metropolitan area. It is a small practice consisting of two primary care physicians (PCPs), Dr. William Stern, founder of VMS, and Dr. David Stern, Dr. William Stern's son. Paul Parker, a physician assistant (PA), is also employed by the practice. Dr. William Stern's wife has worked as the physician practice manager since the practice's inception. The office staff consists of two nurses, a billing and coding specialist, and a receptionist. The VMS office setting is warm and inviting. Staff members are professional, courteous, and engaging.

Patients are often quoted as saying, "The doctors and staff at this facility treat me like family." The surveys completed after patients' visits resonate with these statements. They indicate the patients are quite pleased with the care they receive at VMS. High ratings are often given in the categories "There was a minimal wait time before seeing a doctor," and "The quality of care I received met my expectations." The doctors are cognizant of the fact that the business is thriving. This is evidenced by the average number of years patients have been seen by each of the providers and is coupled with the increase in patient volume resulting after another local PCP, Dr. Steven Phillip, retired.

One day, after working more than 8 hours at the office, the older Stern told his son, "I love practicing medicine, but a lot has changed since I first began 40 years ago. Back in my day, I believe I saw higher reimbursement rates from private health insurance companies based on the services I provided. As of right now, I feel like I am working harder and getting paid less. I have gotten old, son. I think it's time for me to retire."

It was always understood that Mrs. Stern would relinquish her duties as physician practice manger when her husband retired. The couple plans to spend quality time traveling and enjoying the arts during their golden years. The doctors and Mrs. Stern expect a seamless transition of physician practice manager duties to the new hire. Donna, the daughter of one of William's medical school colleagues, accepted the offer to become practice manager and is starting soon. Donna has a master's degree in Healthcare Management and 10 years of physician practice management experience. In addition to the personal connection, Donna was highly recommended by her previous employer. Mrs. Stern is ready to show Donna "the ropes" to help get her acclimated to VMS and "the way things are done around here." Mrs. Stern plans to discuss a special discount arrangement offered to William's self-paying patients as soon as she meets with Donna.

The younger Dr. Stern knows his father has a soft spot for his uninsured patients and thinks the older Stern's kindness is contributing to his own angst about receiving lower reimbursement for his services. Residents in the area were hit hard by job losses and underemployment after a major employer went out of business. Dr. William Stern is known for offering major discounts, up to 75% off the billed office visit rate, most of which goes uncollected, to his self-paying clients.

David, on the other hand, has a master's degree in Healthcare Management in addition to his Medical Doctor's degree. He is not as generous as his father because he knows the practice is a business. Office procedures involving payment collection for services require attention and process improvement. David is sure he can count on Donna to address procedural shortcomings and to make any changes needed.

Although letters were sent out to the patients informing them of Dr. William Stern's retirement, David began seeing most of his father's former patients immediately after his father retired. He believes the increase in patient volume is due partly to the name association when patients call in requesting an appointment with Dr. Stern. To David's credit, he is a younger version of his father, and patients feel at ease under his care. While David appreciates the compliment when he is told "You are just like your father," he has a much keener sense for delivering quality care while still effectively and efficiently running a business.

Staff members, along with David and the PA, Paul Parker, feel the effects of the practice's growth after accepting new patients, many of whom are former patients of the other local PCP who retired. Dr. David Stern expected he and Paul would begin to see more patients, so the office hours were extended during the week and include Saturday morning appointments. Since Donna is salaried and the practice manager, she is expected to work during office hours. The two nurses, who are hourly staff, rotate on weekends to allow one another to take every other weekend off. The remaining hourly staff are not expected to work overtime, but it is offered to them on a weekly basis. David wants to make sure the physician practice maintains its good reputation in the community. Additionally, he welcomes the opportunity to grow the business.

Donna appears to be a good fit for the practice. She is quite personable and contributes to the familial atmosphere of the office. More importantly, the office appears to be running smoothly under her management. David is impressed with the new practice manager and asks to meet with her 90 days after her initial start date to discuss her performance.

In their meeting, the younger Dr. Stern tells Donna he is pleased with how she manages the office. His father worked hard to establish the business, and he desires to continue his legacy. Most of the former patients are like family to him, and he wants to ensure new patients are made to feel the same. The younger Dr. Stern tells Donna, "We want to continue receiving high marks on our patient survey." Donna is at a loss because she was not informed by Mrs. Stern of any patient surveys; however, she does not let on that she is clearly uninformed about customer satisfaction scores. David requests that he and Donna meet in 1 week to discuss office performance metrics and to review the financial reports.

Donna is elated to hear that David believes she is doing a good job. She is, however, surprised to learn about unfavorable customer satisfaction scores after she accesses patient surveys on the practice's website. To add fuel to the fire, she discovers most of the other retired PCP's former patients are uninsured or have high-deductible health plans (HDHPs). The HDHPs are designed by health insurance companies as a cost-sharing measure to address rising healthcare costs. Since many of the new patients are responsible for reimbursements resulting from these HDHPs, payments were not collected at the time of the patients' visits. There was no determination of the out-of-pocket expenses everyone needed to satisfy before the insurance companies reimbursed the practice. Patients were told no payment was required at the time of service, and they would be billed later.

David has not been informed of the influx of this type of insurance coverage or the high number of uninsured patients by his experienced, newly hired physician practice manager. Industry focus on shared responsibility and the need to compel individuals to manage their health and associated costs are affecting the practice's bottom line unfavorably. There are delays in reimbursement or failed attempts to collect for patient services. Formerly uninsured patients continue to receive discounted

(continues)

CASE 7-1 Plight After Oversight at Vestavia Medical Services (VMS) *(continued)*

rates of 75% off billed charges for office visits. Donna expects to find the new uninsured patients are also receiving the same 75% reduction in fees.

Donna is expected to understand basic bookkeeping as the physician practice manager. She knows patients with HDHPs are on the rise, and the 75% discount offered is standard and aligns with the discounts given by industry providers to the uninsured. Donna did not know that the revenue cycle management was ineffective at VMS. Insurance company reimbursements were not timely, and William allowed patients to pay when they were able, which adds to her chagrin, and more importantly, the amount of uncollected revenue.

She plans to spend the next 7 days focusing on the current state of the office. Mrs. Stern bragged about her husband's successful business and the good relationships he established during his tenure at VMS. Did Mrs. Stern misrepresent the business's viability when she handed the practice management role over to Donna? What is the real reason behind William's decision to retire? Did the good doctor see the "handwriting on the wall"?

In preparation for next week's meeting, Donna decides to start with the patient satisfaction survey. What is really going on? Upon her review of the surveys, Donna sees that both former and new patients are giving low scores in the categories "There was a minimal wait time before seeing a doctor," and "The quality of care I received met my expectations." Prior to her start date, patients gave high marks in these two categories. Based on the patients' comments, Donna now understands that patients believe their wait times are longer and that the providers spend less time in the exam room with them. She should have known better. The timing of the declining score coincides with Dr. Steven Phillip's office closing and the increase in volume at VMS. These findings, along with reimbursement issues, leave Donna a bit unsettled.

Discussion Questions

1. What are the financial implications of this case?
2. Do you believe the quality of services provided by the physicians and staff at VMS is affecting patient reimbursement? Why or why not?
3. What improvements could Donna make to increase future payments from HDHP, private pay, and uninsured patients?
4. As a healthcare management student, Donna asks you to develop talking points related to private health insurance and uninsured trends for next week's meeting. How are these trends impacting practices like VMS? What are some steps practices can take to better manage their patients, revenue cycle, and practice?

CASE 7-2 Accessing Specialty Care for Community Health Center Patients

Written by Lea Nolan

Carol Finn, the executive director of Heartland Community Health, hands Jenny, the health center's referral coordinator and care coordinator, a tissue. Jenny's shedding frustrated tears because this is the third time this week that she's been unable to find a specialty care provider willing to treat one of the health center's uninsured or underinsured patients.

Heartland Community Health Center (CHC) is a federally-qualified health center (FQHC) operating in a medically underserved area (MUA) in a rural section of a midwestern state. FQHCs provide comprehensive primary care services to medically underserved communities regardless of their insurance status or ability to pay. The CHC receives an annual federal Section 330 grant to defray the cost of providing care to its uninsured and underinsured patients. The grant also funds enabling services that support and assist the delivery of primary care and facilitate patients' access to care. Enabling services include case management, eligibility and enrollment services, transportation, interpretation, community health worker programs, and patient education. Uninsured and underinsured patients are charged a sliding fee, based on income, for the primary care services they receive.

Nearly two-thirds of Heartland CHC's 2,700 patients live below the federal poverty line, and 96% have incomes below 200% of poverty (about $20,780 for a family of three). The racial demographics of Heartland CHC's patient population mirrors that of the overall state. More than 85% of patients are White, 9% are Hispanic/Latino, 4% are African-American, and those that remain identify as American Indian or other Native people. As is common among low-income, vulnerable populations, Heartland CHC's patients are more likely to experience a disproportionate share of chronic conditions such as obesity, diabetes, hypertension, high cholesterol, heart disease, cancer, asthma, HIV, mental illness and substance abuse. Nearly a quarter of the center's patients suffer from hypertension. Of those patients with blood pressure < 140/90, more than half (56%) are well controlled with medication, but the remaining 44% are not. More than 14% of the health center's patients have been diagnosed with diabetes and the majority of those (69%) are well controlled. However, 34% of diabetics continue to receive HbA1c results > 9% or have not had a test in more than a year. Only 37% of the health center's asthmatic patients report using appropriate medications.

To meet its patients' needs, the health center provides comprehensive primary and preventive care including sick and well exams, including well gynecological services, immunizations, diagnostic services, screenings, testing for sexually transmitted infections, diagnostic lab and radiology, EKGs, outreach and education, and translation. A behavioral consultant is available to meet with patients and consult with Heartland's providers regarding treatment plans. The health center refers patients who've selected Heartland as their medical home to a dental provider. Similarly, regular patients needing obstetrical/gynecological treatment are referred to an outside partner provider. The center is rapidly growing—its patient population has more than doubled in the last two years. As growth continues, it hopes to provide more services such as dental, obstetrics, pharmacy, and comprehensive outpatient mental health and substance abuse services in-house.

Sadly, many of Heartland CHC's patients need more than primary care. Many require specialty care to treat their chronic conditions. For patients with insurance, especially commercial insurance obtained through an employer, or Medicare, it is relatively easy to see a specialist even in this small community. A nearby not-for-profit general hospital receives no tax support and is entirely self-sufficient. It has 175 beds and specialty clinics that include cardiology, oncology, radiology treatment, nephrology, orthopedics, rheumatology, urology, and pain management among others. Heartland CHC does not have a formal affiliation with the hospital or its specialty clinics, but the providers typically accept appointments for the health center's covered patients. Currently 37% of Heartland CHC's patients have third-party insurance and 19% are enrolled in Medicare. However, obtaining specialty care is more challenging for those with Medicaid, and sometimes downright impossible for those who are either underinsured or uninsured. A fifth of CHC's patient have Medicaid and one quarter remain uninsured.

Since the state has not taken advantage of the Affordable Care Act's (ACA) option to expand Medicaid eligibility for those with incomes up to 138% of the federal poverty level, many low-income residents remain uninsured. In addition, these same individuals do not qualify for subsidies to purchase insurance through the ACA's state marketplace. Other patients—those who purchased low-cost bronze level plans with deductibles of up to $5000 per year per enrollee, along with co-pays and co-insurance—remain underinsured because they cannot afford the out-of-pocket costs of care.

(continues)

CASE 7-2 Accessing Specialty Care for Community Health Center Patients   *(continued)*

These are the patients for whom Jenny, the referral and care coordinator, struggles to find care. She spends the bulk of her time attempting to schedule appointments. Since Medicaid reimbursements are so low, specialists often limit the number of Medicaid patients they will see in a given year. This can lead to wait times of between six and twelve months for an appointment for the health center's Medicaid patients. Finding a provider willing to treat an uninsured patient is even more difficult because specialists generally won't offer sliding fees. Some local specialists are willing to take on one or two uninsured patients each year, but there are limited numbers of providers for each specialty in the community, and Jenny is wary of abusing their kindness lest they refuse to take uninsured patients all together. She often resorts to asking specialists around the state for their help. Even when she finds a willing specialist, they are often located quite a distance away, which poses a challenge for patients who lack reliable transportation and/or can't afford to lose a day out of work to seek care. Faced with no other choice, some patients manage to attend that precious appointment, but some simply forego care, allowing their condition to deteriorate and their suffering to continue until their condition becomes an emergency. Since the CHC's electronic medical record (EMR) system does not interface with the hospital's system, Jenny expends significant effort tracking down reports for patients who do see a specialist or go to the ED. She fears she's falling down on the care coordinator side of her job.

This week, Jenny kept it together as she sought in vain to find a cardiologist willing to treat an underinsured father with an irregular heartbeat, and an orthopedist to help a young uninsured construction worker whose broken arm has not healed properly. But today's failed quest put her over the edge: a young Hispanic girl who is ineligible for either CHIP or Medicaid has severe asthma and needs a pulmonologist. Jenny wipes the tears from her eyes then levels her gaze on her boss Carol. "Isn't there something we can do to help our patients get the specialty care they need?"

Discussion Questions

1. What are the facts in this case?
2. What are three factors contributing to the community health center's problems?
3. What are the consequences of failing to obtain specialty care for the community health center's uninsured and underinsured patients?
4. Are there consequences for the community at large?
5. What are the ethical considerations of charity care? Are specialists in the hospital clinics wrong to limit access to appointments for Medicaid patients or to refuse care to those who are underinsured or uninsured?
6. What strategies could either the executive director or Jenny employ to help increase the community health center's patients' access to specialty care?
7. What health care policy solutions could be implemented to resolve this issue?

Additional Resources

Dickson, V. (September 25, 2014). Underinsured ACA enrollees strain community health centers. *Modern Healthcare*. Retrieved from https://www.modernhealthcare.com/article/20140925/NEWS/309259947/underinsured-aca-enrollees-strain-community-health-centers

Ezeonwu, M. C. (2018). Specialty-care access for community health clinic patients: processes and barriers. *Journal of Multidisciplinary Healthcare, 11*, 109–119. doi: 10.2147/JMDH.S152594 Retrieved from https://www.ncbi.nlm.nih.gov/pmc/articles/PMC5826087/

Health Resources and Services Administration (HRSA). (2017). 2017 Health Center Program Grantee Profiles. Retrieved from https://bphc.hrsa.gov/uds/datacenter.aspx?q=d

National Association of Community Health Centers. (2018, June). *Community Health Center chart book*. Retrieved from http://www.nachc.org/wp-content/uploads/2018/06/Chartbook_FINAL_6.20.18.pdf

Rosenbaum, S., Tolbert, J., Sharac, J., Shin, P., Gunsalus, R., & Zur, J. (2018, March 09). *Community Health Centers: Growing importance in a changing health care system.* Retrieved from https://www.kff.org/report-section/community-health-centers-growing-importance-in-a-changing-health-care-system-issue-brief/

Serafine, M. & Dentler, J. (2015, May 12). Community collaborations: 6 areas of focus for hospital and federally qualified health center partnerships. *Becker's Hospital Review.* Retrieved from https://www.beckershospitalreview.com/hospital-management-administration/community-collaborations-6-areas-of-focus-for-hospital-and-federally-qualified-health-center-partnerships.html

Tu, H. & Postman, C. (2017, September 27) *Strategies by federally-funded health centers to facilitate patient access to specialty care.* Retrieved from https://aspe.hhs.gov/system/files/pdf/259201/SpecialtyAccess.pdf

Buchbinder SB, Shanks NH, Kite BJ. *Introduction to Health Care Management.* 4th ed. Jones & Bartlett Learning; 2021.

CHAPTER ACRONYMS

AAFP American Academy of Family Physicians
ACA Patient Protection and Affordable Care Act of 2010
ACO Accountable Care Organization
ACP American College of Physicians
AHA American Hospital Association
AHRQ Agency for Health Research and Quality
AMA American Medical Association
APC Advanced primary care
ASC Ambulatory surgery center
CHC Community Health Center
CHIP Children's Health Insurance Program
DRG Diagnosis-related group
ED Emergency department
EMR Electronic medical record
FQHC Federally qualified health center

HDHP High-deductible health plan
HRSA Health Resources and Services Administration
LHD Local health department
MACRA Medicare Access and CHIP Reauthorization Act
MUA Medically underserved area
NACCHO National Association of County and City Health Officials
NCHS National Center for Health Statistics
NCQA National Committee for Quality Assurance
PA Physician assistant
PCMH Patient-centered medical home
PCP Primary care physician
RPM Remote patient monitoring
UCA Urgent Care Association
VMS Vestavia Medical Services

References

1. Berenson RA, Ginsburg PB, May JH. Hospital-physician relations: cooperation, competition, or separation? *Health Aff.* 2007;26(1):w31-w43. doi:10.1377/hlthaff.26.1.w31
2. Rui P, Okeyode T. National Ambulatory Medical Care Survey: 2016 National Summary Tables. National Center for Health Statistics. Published 2016. Accessed June 11, 2021. https://www.cdc.gov/nchs/data/ahcd/namcs_summary/2016_namcs_web_tables.pdf
3. American Hospital Association Center for Health Innovation. Evolving physician-practice ownership models. Published 2020. Accessed June 11, 2021. https://www.aha.org/system/files/media/file/2020/02/Market_Insights_MD_Ownership_Models.pdf
4. Kocher R, Sahni NR. Hospitals' race to employ physicians—the logic behind a money-losing proposition. *N Engl J Med.* 2011;364(19):1790-1793. doi:10.1056/NEJMp1101959
5. American College of Physicians. Enhance care coordination through the patient centered medical home (PCMH). Accessed February 21, 2021. https://www.acponline.org/system/files/documents/running_practice/delivery_and_payment_models/pcmh/understanding/pcmh_back.pdf
6. American College of Physicians. Patient-centered medical home. Accessed June 11, 2021. https://www.acponline.org/practice-resources/business-resources/payment/delivery-and-payment-models/patient-centered-medical-home

7. National Committee for Quality Assurance. NCQA PCMH recognition: concepts. Accessed June 11, 2021. https://www.ncqa.org/programs/health-care-providers-practices/patient-centered-medical-home-pcmh/pcmh-concepts/

8. Cotton P. Patient-centered medical home evidence increases with time. *Health Affairs* Blog. Published September 10, 2018. Accessed February 21, 2021. https://www.healthaffairs.org/do/10.1377/hblog20180905.807827/full/

9. Sinaiko AD, Landrum MB, Meyers DJ, et al. Synthesis of research on patient-centered medical homes brings systematic differences into relief. *Health Aff.* 2017;36(3):500-508. doi: 10.1377/hlthaff.2016.1235

10. Institute for Healthcare Improvement. Triple Aim for Populations. Accessed June 11, 2021. http://www.ihi.org/Topics/TripleAim/Pages/default.aspx

11. Gold J. The ABCs of ACOs: Accountable Care Organizations, explained. Kaiser Health News. Published September 14, 2015. Accessed June 11, 2021. https://khn.org/news/aco-accountable-care-organization-faq/

12. Centers for Medicare & Medicaid Services. Summary of Final Rule Provisions for Accountable Care Organizations under the Medicare Shared Savings Program. Published October 20, 2011. Accessed June 11, 2021. https://www.cms.gov/newsroom/fact-sheets/summary-final-rule-provisions-accountable-care-organizations-under-medicare-shared-savings-program

13. Centers for Medicare & Medicaid Services. Shared Saving Program fast facts—as of January 1, 2021. Published January 1, 2021. Accessed June 11, 2021. https://www.cms.gov/files/document/2021-shared-savings-program-fast-facts.pdf

14. Knowles JH. The role of the hospital: the ambulatory clinic. *Bull N Y Acad Med.* 1965;41(1):68-79.

15. Fraser I, Lane L, Linne E, Jones L. Ambulatory care: A decade of change in health care delivery. *J Ambul Care Manage.* 1993;16(4):1-8. doi: 10.1097/00004479-199310000-00003

16. American Hospital Association. Table 4.2: Distribution of inpatient vs. outpatient revenues, 1995–2016. In: *Trendwatch Chartbook 2018.* American Hospital Association; 2018. Accessed February 21, 2021. https://www.aha.org/system/files/2018-05/2018-chartbook-table-4-2.pdf

17. Rui P, Kang K. National Hospital Ambulatory Medical Care Survey: 2017 emergency department summary tables. National Center for Health Statistics. Published 2017. Accessed June 11, 2021. https://www.cdc.gov/nchs/data/nhamcs/web_tables/2017_ed_web_tables-508.pdf

18. American Board of Emergency Medicine. ABEM history. Accessed June 11, 2021. https://www.abem.org/public/about-abem/abem-history

19. Morley C, Unwin M, Peterson GM, Stankovich J, Kinsman L. Emergency department crowding: a systematic review of causes, consequences and solutions. *PLoS One.* 2018;13(8):e0203316. doi: 10.1371/journal.pone.0203316

20. Ugolini C, Leucci AC, Nobilio L, Bertè G. Reorganizing territorial healthcare to avoid inappropriate ED visits: does the spread of community health centres make walk-in-clinics redundant? *BMC Health Serv Res.* 2020;20(1):807. doi: 10.1186/s12913-020-05648-x

21. O'Malley AS. After-hours access to primary care practices linked with lower emergency department use and less unmet medical need. *Health Aff.* 2013;32(1):175-183. doi: 10.1377/hlthaff.2012.0494

22. Pourat N, Davis AC, Chen X, Vrungos S, Kominski GF. In California, primary care continuity was associated with reduced emergency department use and fewer hospitalizations. *Health Aff.* 2015;34(7):1113-1120. doi: 10.1377/hlthaff.2014.1165

23. Bazemore A, Petterson S, Peterson LE, Bruno R, Chung Y, Phillips RL Jr. Higher primary care physician continuity is associated with lower costs and hospitalizations. *Ann Fam Med.* 2018;16(6):492-497. doi: 10.1370/afm.2308

24. Urgent Care Association. Urgent care industry white paper—updated for 2019–2020: industry reports. Published 2020. Accessed June 11, 2021. https://www.ucaoa.org/Resources/Industry-Reports/White-Paper

25. Scott MK. Health care in the express lane: retail clinics go mainstream. California Health Care Foundation. Published September 17, 2007. Accessed June 11, 2021. https://www.chcf.org/publication/health-care-in-the-express-lane-retail-clinics-go-mainstream/

26. Accenture. Number of U.S. retail health clinics will surpass 2,800 by 2017, Accenture forecasts. Published November 12, 2015. Accessed June 11, 2021. https://newsroom.accenture.com/news/number-of-us-retail-health-clinics-will-surpass-2800-by-2017-accenture-forecasts.htm

27. Fein AJ. A tale of two chains: Walgreens exits pharmacy clinics while CVS reinvents in-store care. Drug Channels. Published November 7, 2019. Accessed June 11, 2021. https://www.drugchannels.net/2019/11/a-tale-of-two-chains-walgreens-exits.html

28. Bachrach D, Frohlic J, Garcimonde A, Nevitt K. Building a culture of health: the value proposition of retail clinics. Robert Wood Johnson Foundation. Published April 2015. Accessed June 11, 2021. http://www.rwjf.org/content/dam/farm/reports/issue_briefs/2015/rwjf419415

29. University of Wisconsin Population Health Institute County Health Rankings & Roadmaps. Retail clinics. Updated July 16, 2020. Accessed June 11, 2021. https://www.countyhealthrankings.org/take-action-to-improve-health/what-works-for-health/strategies/retail-clinics

30. Phares J, Dobrzykowski DD, Prohofsky J. How policy is shaping the macro healthcare delivery supply chain: the emergence of a new tier of retail medical clinics. *Bus Horiz*. 2021;64(3):333-345. doi: 10.1016/j.bushor.2021.02.040

31. Mukamel DB, Ladd H, Amin A, Sorkin DH. Patients' preferences over care settings for minor illnesses and injuries. *Health Serv Res*. 2019;54(4):827-838. doi: 10.1111/1475-6773.13154

32. Alexander D, Currie J, Schnell M. Check up before you check out: retail clinics and emergency room use. *J Public Econ*. 2019;178:104050. doi: 10.1016/j.jpubeco.2019.104050

33. Wong CA, Bain A, Polsky D, et al. The use and out-of-pocket cost of urgent care clinics and retail-based clinics by adolescents and young adults compared with children. *J Adolesc Health*. 2017;60(1):107-112. doi: 10.1016/j.jadohealth.2016.09.009

34. American Academy of Family Physicians. Retail clinics. Published 2019. Accessed February 21, 2021. https://www.aafp.org/about/policies/all/retail-clinics.html

35. American College of Physicians. Retail clinics best used as backup to a patient's primary care physician. Published October 13, 2015. Accessed June 11, 2021. https://www.acponline.org/acp-newsroom/retail-clinics-best-used-as-backup-to-a-patients-primary-care-physician

36. Cullen KA, Hall MJ, Golosinskiy A. Ambulatory surgery in the United States, 2006. *Natl Health Stat Report*. 2009;(11):1-25. Accessed June 11, 2021. http://www.cdc.gov/nchs/data/nhsr/nhsr011.pdf

37. Centers for Disease Control and Prevention. National Survey of Ambulatory Surgery. Updated November 6, 2015. Accessed June 11, 2021. http://www.cdc.gov/nchs/nsas.htm

38. National Center for Health Statistics. *Health, United States, 2014: With Special Feature on Adults Aged 55-64*. National Center for Health Statistics; 2015. Accessed June 11, 2021. http://www.cdc.gov/nchs/data/hus/hus14.pdf#091

39. Casalino LP, Devers KJ, Brewster LR. Focused factories? Physician-owned specialty facilities. *Health Aff*. 2003;22(6):56-67. doi: 10.1377/hlthaff.22.6.56

40. Pallardy C, Becker S. 50 things to know about the ambulatory surgery center industry. *Becker's ASC Review*. Updated August 20, 2013. Accessed June 11, 2021. http://www.beckersasc.com/lists/50-things-to-know-about-the-ambulatory-surgery-center-industry.html

41. Koenig L, Doherty J, Dreyfus J, Xanthopoulos J. *An Analysis of Recent Growth of Ambulatory Surgical Centers: Final Report*. KNG Health Consulting, LLC; 2009. Accessed February 26, 2021. https://citeseerx.ist.psu.edu/viewdoc/download?doi=10.1.1.512.4498&rep=rep1&type=pdf

42. Ambulatory Surgery Center Association. Ambulatory surgery centers: a positive trend in health care. Published May 23, 2012. Accessed June 11, 2021. http://www.ascassociation.org/ASCA/Resources/ViewDocument/?DocumentKey=7d8441a1-82dd-47b9-b626-8563dc31930c

43. Ambulatory Surgery Center Association. History: 1980s. Accessed June 11, 2021. http://www.ascassociation.org/aboutus/whatisanasc/history

44. Health Resources and Services Administration Health Center Program. Health Center Program requirements. Accessed June 11, 2021. https://bphc.hrsa.gov/programrequirements

45. Health Resources and Services Administration Health Center Program. What is a health center? Updated August 2021. Accessed August 13, 2021. https://bphc.hrsa.gov/about/what-is-a-health-center/index.html

46. Health Resources and Services Administration Health Center Program. Health Center Program: impact and growth. Updated August 2021. Accessed August 13, 2021. https://bphc.hrsa.gov/about/healthcenterprogram/index.html

47. McGuire M. Collaborative public management: assessing what we know and how we know it. *Public Adm Rev*. 2006;66(Suppl 1):33-43. doi: 10.1111/j.1540-6210.2006.00664.x

48. National Assocation of County and City Health Officals. *2019 National Profile of Local Health Departments*. National Association of County and City Health Officials; 2020. Accessed February 21, 2021. https://www.naccho.org/uploads/downloadable-resources/Programs/Public-Health-Infrastructure/NACCHO_2019_Profile_final.pdf

49. Hostetter M, Klein S. Creating better systems of care for adults with disabilities: lessons for policy and practice. The Commonwealth Fund. Published September 25, 2018. Accessed June 11, 2021. https://www.commonwealthfund.org/publications/case-study/2018/sep/systems-care-adults-disabilities

50. HealthIT.gov. What is telehealth? How is telehealth different from telemedicine? Updated October 17, 2019. Accessed June 11, 2021. https://www.healthit.gov/faq/what-telehealth-how-telehealth-different-telemedicine

51. Medicaid.gov. Telemedicine. Accessed June 11, 2021. https://www.medicaid.gov/medicaid/benefits/telemedicine/index.html

52. Centers for Disease Control and Prevention. Using telehealth modalities. Updated June 10, 2020. Accessed June 11, 2021. https://www.cdc.gov/coronavirus/2019-ncov/hcp/telehealth.html

CHAPTER 8

Long-Term Care and Specialized Services

© STILLFX/iStock/Getty Images Plus/Getty Images

CHAPTER OVERVIEW

Older Americans are not the only segment of the population that have long-term care needs. Many groups may require these types of services. However, older Americans are the fastest-growing proportion of the population and are the major consumers of long-term care services. Advances in medical care have extended the life span for many, with the caveat of accompanying challenges presented by chronic disease and physical limitations. This chapter provides an overview of the major components of the diverse array of long-term care services available in institutional, community-based, and home-based settings for individuals in all age groups who require long-term care. This chapter also reviews the most recent legislation to impact long-term care, the Patient Protection and Affordable Care Act (ACA) of 2010, and recent developments in this area of the healthcare continuum.

▶ Background

Each individual life span, from birth to death, can be viewed as a continuum of events. The unrelenting progression of time is the one constant that expresses the diverse range of life's possibilities. These possibilities include an infant born with a birth defect, a young adult who sustains a traumatic head injury after an automobile accident, or an older adult who suffers a stroke. Unanticipated events such as these have a profound long-term impact on an individual's capacity to develop or to maintain capabilities for self-care and independence. These individuals may require very different kinds and intensities of personal care assistance, health care, and psychosocial and housing services over an extended period. As such, individuals enter the continuum of care at different intervals and points of need. FIGURE 8-1 is a depiction of the continuum of care and a conception of how post-acute and long-term care fit.

The sites of care delivery vary widely for recipients of long-term care based on their age, diagnosis, and self-care capacity. Thus, long-term care requires diversified, yet coordinated, services with system flexibility in response to recipients' changing needs over time.

The ideal healthcare delivery system provides participants with comprehensive personal, social, and medical care services. This ideal system requires mechanisms that continually guide and track individual clients over time through the array of services at all levels and intensities of care that they require.[1] Long-term care has a particular need to use what the American Hospital Association calls a "seamless continuum of care" due to its continuous flow of high costs over an extended period.[2] This promotes the highest quality of life while maintaining vigilance over growing public concerns about cost effectiveness.[3] Services provided to each person should be tailored to meet their individual needs. Service needs vary from assistance with personal care and basic needs to rehabilitation and socialization opportunities. Additionally, the type and extent of physical disability and the intensity of services required determine the environment of long-term care. For example, an older individual with paralysis after a stroke may be able to remain at home with services that supplement family caregivers. Another person with a similar disability may require nursing home placement because that environment best meets their particular requirements and needs.

Optimization of services that promote independence and lifestyle maintenance is complex when considering personal, community, and national resources. The concern about cost effectiveness and the need to include various factors (e.g., reimbursement, personal wishes, family, etc.) indicate the need for a tailored and coordinated menu of services.

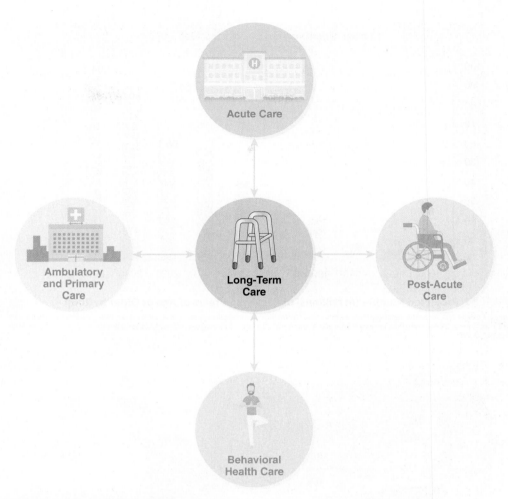

FIGURE 8-1 Continuum of Care Diagram

Created by Richard Greenhill, 2021.

Population demographics including the types and availability of healthcare services in the United States have evolved over the past 70 years. Shifts in the population from extended lifespans, preventive care improvement, and medical advancements have increased the numbers of a segment of the population who will likely require long-term care services. Older adults represent the largest population group requiring long-term care services. Current estimates place the population 65 years of age and older at 56.1 million, or 16.9% of the population, as seen in **FIGURE 8-2**.[4] The number of Americans aged 65 years or older is expected to grow to by 38.6 million by 2060, totaling 94.7 million. The current percentage of the population aged 65 and older is seen in **FIGURE 8-3**.[5] A look at the increase over 10 years from 2009 to 2019 in **FIGURE 8-4** shows just how much the older population has grown and where they are geographically concentrated.[5] The states with the highest percentages of older citizens will need to have clear plan to deal with their long-term care needs.

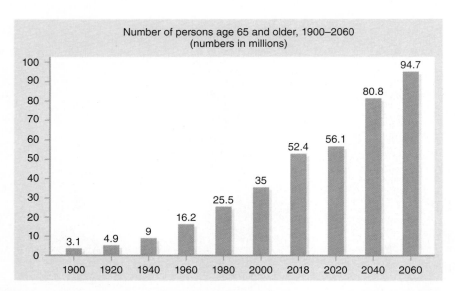

FIGURE 8-2 Projected Number (in Millions) of Persons 65 Years of Age or Older by 2060

Created by R. Greenhill, 2021. Data from U.S. Department of Health and Human Services Administration for Community Living. Number of persons age 65 and older, 1900–2060 (numbers in millions). In: *2020 Profile of Older Americans*. U.S. Department of Health and Human Services; 2021. Accessed August 16, 2021. https://acl.gov/sites/default/files/Aging%20and%20Disability%20in%20America/2020ProfileOlder Americans.Final_.pdf

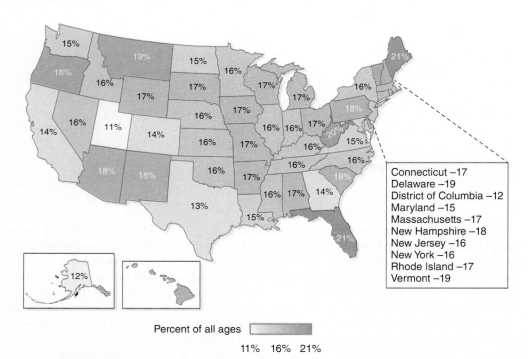

FIGURE 8-3 Persons Age 65 and Older as a Percentage of the Total Population

Created by R. Greenhill, 2021. Data from U.S. Department of Health and Human Services Administration for Community Living. Persons age 65 and older as a percentage of the total population, 2019. In: *2020 Profile of Older Americans*. U.S. Department of Health and Human Services; 2021. Accessed August 16, 2021. https://acl.gov/sites/default/files/Aging%20and%20Disability%20in%20America/2020ProfileOlder Americans.Final_.pdf

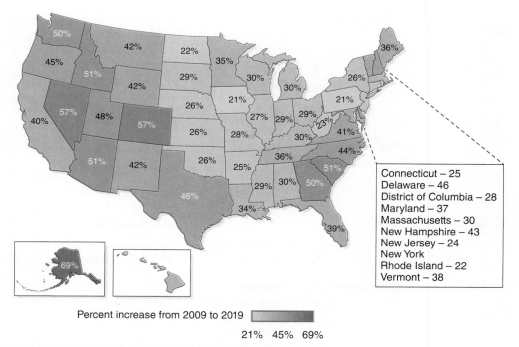

Connecticut – 25
Delaware – 46
District of Columbia – 28
Maryland – 37
Massachusetts – 30
New Hampshire – 43
New Jersey – 24
New York
Rhode Island – 22
Vermont – 38

Percent increase from 2009 to 2019

21%   45%   69%

FIGURE 8-4 Increase in Population Age 65 and Older, 2009 to 2019

Created by R. Greenhill, 2021. Data from U.S. Department of Health and Human Services Administration for Community Living. Increase in population age 65 and older, 2009–2019. In: *2020 Profile of Older Americans.*
U.S. Department of Health and Human Services; 2021. Accessed August 16, 2021. https://acl.gov/sites/default/files/Aging%20and%20Disability%20in%20America/2020ProfileOlderAmericans.Final_.pdf

Many people will grow old alone because of smaller family sizes, single parenting, and divorce. Family members are also now more geographically dispersed, decreasing their availability to care for dependent, older family members. The increasing economic need for family members to delay retirement and work outside the home also reduces the availability of family caregivers to participate in the informal family caregiving system. The COVID-19 pandemic has exacerbated the trend of delayed retirement. One survey indicated that 39% of Americans over 55 years old reported they would now retire between 65 and 69 years old, and 18% indicated 70 to 79 years old as a target.[6]

▶ Development of Long-Term Care Services

The colonists who emigrated from Europe to the New World brought with them many of the social values and institutional models of their native countries. One of these, the almshouse, was a place where the sick, disabled, or older adults who lacked adequate family or financial support could be cared for in a communal setting. Charitable community members purchased private homes and converted them to almshouses that operated as communal residences. Municipal and county governments also created homes and "infirmaries" to care for impoverished older adults. These early models were the basis for "homes for the elderly," which existed until the economic upheavals of the Great Depression and the restructuring of the social welfare system after World War II. **FIGURE 8-5** outlines some of the long-term care milestones in U.S. history.[7]

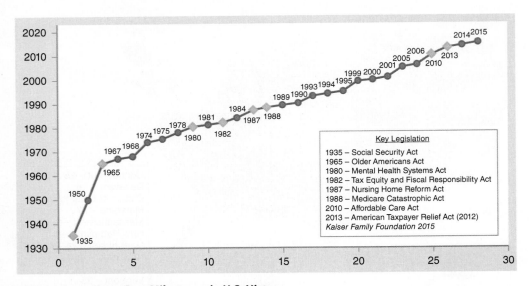

FIGURE 8-5 Long-Term Care Milestones in U.S. History

Created by R. Greenhill, 2021. Data from the Kaiser Family Foundation. Long-term care in the United States: a timeline. Published August 31, 2015. Accessed February 8, 2021. https://www.kff.org/medicaid /timeline/long-term-care-in-the-united-states-a-timeline/

The economic devastation experienced during the Great Depression of the 1930s affected the availability of long-term care services, especially homes for older adults, in several ways. Operating small, private nursing homes became attractive to people in financial danger of losing their homes to mortgage foreclosure because taking in outsiders and providing care generated a new source of income. After the Great Depression, many local charitable agencies could no longer afford to provide care based on the almshouse tradition, and the federal government became more involved in developing, overseeing, and paying for long-term care services as part of the social welfare reforms, such as the 1935 Social Security Act.[8] The Social Security Act provided financial assistance for particular categories of older Americans and people with disabilities. In addition, the Social Security Act established a form of old-age and survivor's insurance that allowed workers and their employers to contribute to a fund that supplemented retirement income. This form of income security reduced the extent of indigence frequently found in the older population and increased the amount of secure income available to older Americans for services and care in later years. Government lending programs available to not-for-profit organizations beginning in the 1950s spurred the development of nursing homes in this sector; major growth in the proprietary (for-profit) sector did not occur until after the passage of Medicare and Medicaid legislation in 1965. The most recent data from Centers for Medicare & Medicaid Services (CMS) reported the ownership basis of nursing homes in the *Nursing Home Data Compendium 2015 Edition*. Now, more than two-thirds operate on a for-profit basis (see **FIGURE 8-6**).[9]

Public and private homes for older adults often varied in the adequacy of care and service provision. Nursing homes often were viewed as places where minimal custodial care required to meet the basic needs of food, clothing, and shelter was provided, sometimes in unhygienic and inhumane environments. Often, nursing homes were places where older and frail adults, some of society's most vulnerable members, were taken to die. They were not seen as options where

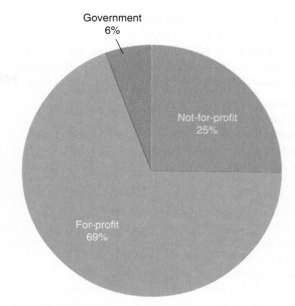

FIGURE 8-6 **Percent Distribution of Nursing Homes by Type of Ownership**

Data from Centers for Medicare & Medicaid Services. *Nursing Home Data Compendium 2015 Edition.* Centers for Medicare & Medicaid Services; 2015. Accessed September 9, 2021. https://www.cms.gov/Medicare
/Provider-Enrollment-and-Certification/CertificationandComplianc/Downloads/nursinghomedatacompendium_508-2015.pdf

residents could receive care to prolong or enhance the quality of their lives. Physical care was often substandard with emotional, spiritual, and social needs ignored. Nursing home residents were often the subject of heavy-handed tactics (use of chemical and physical restraints) due to cognitive disabilities and how they were perceived by staff.

Home nursing care been seen as an alternative to institutional care provided in hospitals and nursing homes. Family members were the traditional home caregivers. An interest in providing formal professional home care services began in the late 1800s as a social response to the unhealthy living conditions of immigrants residing in urban tenements. Such crowded and unsanitary conditions became a public health concern because they were frequently implicated in the spread of contagious diseases, such as tuberculosis, typhoid, and smallpox. Agencies such as the Visiting Nurses Association were established to provide trained nurses to tend to the sick in their homes. Their role quickly expanded to include preventive education regarding hygiene, nutrition, and coordination of social welfare interventions, especially in caring for society's most vulnerable ill, low-income or disabled populations.[10]

The passage of Medicare and Medicaid legislation in 1965 provided more stable sources of reimbursement than were previously available through private pay and charitable funding. It promoted the expansion of the long-term care industry and affected it in several ways. These programs established minimum requirements for standards of care and services for providers to qualify for reimbursement. They also provided funding sources for older Americans, people with disabilities, and those lacking the means to pay for care. This funding simultaneously attracted both the scrupulous and the unscrupulous into the long-term care industry, as it quickly became apparent that being a provider of long-term care could be very profitable.

The long-term care industry came under increasing scrutiny in the early 1970s during congressional hearings on the nursing home industry, which followed the publication of several hundred exposés in newspapers and additional publications such as the Nader Report and Mary Adelaide Mendelson's book, *Tender Loving Greed*. The litany of nursing home corruption cases and abuses that were exposed during that period included the following[11,12]:

- Care that did not recognize the right to human dignity
- A lack of activities for residents
- Untrained and inadequate staff, including untrained administrators
- Unsanitary conditions
- Theft of residents' belongings
- Inadequate safety precautions (especially fire protection)
- Unauthorized and unnecessary use of restraints
- Both overmedication and undermedication of patients
- Failure to act in a timely manner on complaints and reprisals against those who complained
- Discrimination against patients who were members of minority groups
- A lack of dental and psychiatric care
- Negligence leading to injury and death
- Ineffective inspections and nonenforcement of laws that were meant to regulate the nursing home industry
- Reimbursement fraud

Congressional hearings and simultaneous public outcry resulted in stricter enforcement of Medicare and Medicaid guidelines and credentialing as well as increased establishment and enforcement of nursing home and home care licensure. It also resulted in more active accreditation procedures by The Joint Commission, legislation related to reporting of elder abuse, federal guidelines regulating the use of physical restraints, and establishment of ombudsman programs. Each of these measures led to a much more regulated and responsive long-term care industry. Vocal and astute consumers also have provided economic and social mandates for high-quality standards of care, including meaningful, organized quality assurance processes to be maintained in the long-term care industry overall. The Omnibus Budget Reconciliation Act of 1987 legislated new guidelines and restrictions on the use of physical and chemical restraints, established a nursing home resident bill of rights, mandated quality assurance standards, established a standard survey process, and mandated training and educational requirements for nursing home staff.[13]

▶ Modes of Long-Term Care Service Delivery

Long-term care facilities (LTCFs) are institutions such as nursing homes, skilled nursing facilities (SNFs), and assisted living facilities that provide health care to people who are unable to manage independently in the community. This care may represent custodial or chronic care management or short-term rehabilitative services.[14] The site of care delivery categorizes long-term care programs. Institution-based services are those long-term care services provided within an institution such as a nursing home, hospital with inpatient extended care or rehabilitation facility, or inpatient hospice. Community-based services coordinate, manage, and deliver long-term care services such as adult day-care programs, residential group homes, or care in the recipient's home.

Skilled Nursing Care

A skilled nursing facility (SNF) that is Medicare and Medicaid certified is defined as "a facility, or distinct part of one, primarily engaged in providing skilled nursing care and related services for people requiring medical or nursing care, or rehabilitation services."[15] Skilled nursing care is provided by or under the direct supervision of licensed nursing personnel, such as registered nurses and licensed practical nurses, and emphasis is on the provision of 24-hour nursing care and the availability of other types of services. Nursing home residents can be of any age, although most are adults in their later years. The typical nursing home resident is an older woman with cognitive impairment who was living alone on a limited income before nursing home placement. The decreased ability to function independently and a lack of family caregivers are additional factors associated with an increased risk of nursing home admission.

In 2013, CMS reported that 1.4 million Americans resided in 15,643 SNFs.[9] Six out of seven SNF residents, or approximately 86%, are 65 years of age and older.[16] Because SNFs are only one portion of the array of types of long-term care facilities, and an LTCF may provide more than one level of service in the same facility, an exact number of residents in skilled nursing care has been much more difficult to ascertain. The biennial National Study of Long-Term Care Providers (NSLTCP), sponsored by the Centers for Disease Control and Prevention's National Center for Health Statistics (NCHS), is a groundbreaking initiative first implemented in 2012. These recurring studies monitor and detail ongoing trends in the major sectors of the paid, regulated provision of long-term care. The NSLTCP reports include data and overview summaries about nursing homes, home healthcare agencies, hospices, residential care communities, and adult day-services centers. The NSLTCP reports provide reliable and timely statistical information about residents and participants receiving long-term care, agencies that provide those services, and descriptions of services provided.[16]

Annual national expenditures for care in nursing care facilities and continuing care communities continue to rise; in 2014 alone they totaled $155.6 billion. Medicare and Medicaid paid the largest portion (55%), and 45% was funded out-of-pocket, by private insurance, or by third-party or other health insurance. At an average monthly cost of $8,821 for a private room and $7,756 for a semiprivate room, the 2020 national average cost per resident reached $105,852 per year for a private room and $93,072 per year for a semiprivate room.[17] **TABLE 8-1** shows the projections for costs through 2070, as adjusted for an annual inflation rate of 3%.[17]

Despite the burgeoning numbers of older Americans, national nursing home occupancy rates have declined from 84.5% occupancy in 1995 to 80.8% occupancy in 2013.[18] Many factors are cited as contributing to the decline in SNF occupancy rates. Today's older adults are healthier, delaying the need for skilled nursing services. The vastly increased availability of assisted living facilities, defined later in this chapter, and the availability of other community-based assistance through day care and home care also are playing roles in delaying the need for SNF care.

Typical staffing in SNFs includes a physician medical director, a nursing home administrator, a director of nursing, at least one registered nurse on the day and evening shifts, and either a registered nurse or a licensed practical nurse on the night shift. Certified nursing assistants provide direct custodial care under the supervision of licensed nursing personnel and represent the majority of all nursing staff employed by SNFs.[19] SNFs use the services of an array of ancillary professionals who may be employed by the SNFs or contracted. These services include physical therapy, occupational therapy, pharmacy, nutrition, recreational therapy, podiatry, dentistry, laboratory, and hospice.[19] Support staff, including dietary, laundry, housekeeping, and maintenance workers, complete the employee complement. The licensed nursing home administrator, along with the

TABLE 8-1 Projections of Cost by Service Type

Type of Care	2020	2030	2040	2050	2060	2070
In-Home Care						
Homemaker Services	$4,481	$6,022	$8,093	$10,877	$14,617	$19,644
Home Health Aide	$4,576	$6,150	$8,265	$11,107	$14,927	$20,061
Community and Assisted Living						
Adult Day Health Care	$1,603	$2,154	$2,895	$3,891	$5,229	$7,027
Assisted Living Facility	$4,300	$5,779	$7,766	$10,437	$14,027	$18,851
Nursing Home Facility						
Semiprivate Room	$7,756	$10,423	$14,008	$18,826	$25,300	$34,002
Private Room	$8,821	$11,855	$15,932	$21,411	$28,774	$38,670

Created by Richard Greenhill. Data from Centers for Disease Control and Prevention. National Study of Long-Term Care Providers: introduction. Accessed February 4, 2021. http://www.cdc.gov/nchs/data/nsltcp/NSLTCP_FS.pdf

owner/operator, is responsible for carrying out the regulatory mandates regarding the mix and ratio of licensed and unlicensed personnel and the availability of licensed nursing personnel on an around-the-clock basis to provide skilled care and supervision.

Nursing homes are highly regulated by both state licensure and federal certification. The 1987 Omnibus Budget Reconciliation Act increased government involvement in nursing home industry regulation by[13]:

- Mandating regularly scheduled comprehensive assessments of the functional capacity of residents in nursing homes
- Establishing training standards for nursing home aides
- Placing restrictions on the use of physical restraints and psychoactive drugs
- Establishing a nursing home resident bill of rights
- Setting guidelines for the role of the medical director, including continuing education, involvement, and responsibility

States license nursing home administrators. Individual states set criteria for licensure in relationship to minimum age, educational requirements, passing examination scores, and continuing education requirements. The National Association of Boards of Examiners of Long Term Care Administrators "develops and administers the licensing examinations that administrators take to get licensed by their respective states."[20] The examination is required by all states and the District of Columbia.[20] A lack of nursing home compliance with state and federal mandates can lead to penalties such as direct fines, exclusion from Medicare and Medicaid certification, and withdrawal of nursing home licensure. Accreditation through The Joint Commission provides an additional quality check. Although highly desirable, The Joint Commission accreditation remains voluntary.

A 1986 report by the Institute of Medicine, *For-Profit Enterprise in Health Care*, synthesized research on the quality of nursing home care based on for-profit and not-for-profit ownership, noting that for-profit and investor-owned nursing homes tend to provide care of lower quality than their not-for-profit counterparts.[21] These findings have been replicated by other studies over the years.[22] In 2011, the Government Accountability Office reported findings of a first-ever analysis of the 10 largest for-profit nursing home chains, which noted among other findings that these facilities had "the lowest staffing levels; the highest number of deficiencies identified by public regulatory agencies and the highest number of deficiencies causing harm or jeopardy to residents."[22] It is important to note that research findings do not necessarily apply to an individual nursing home, as "some for-profit nursing facilities give excellent care and some not-for-profit nursing facilities give poor care, but the general rule is documented in study after study: not-for-profit nursing facilities generally provide better care to their residents."[22] In response to concerns such as these, the ACA required Medicare and Medicaid-certified SNFs to publicly disclose detailed ownership information, accountability requirements, expenditures, and other information related to quality indicators. It also requires these facilities to publish standardized information reported on the publicly accessible Nursing Home Compare website, which enables Medicare enrollees to compare facilities.[23]

Assisted Living Facilities

Assisted living facilities (ALFs) are appropriate for long-term care for individuals who do not require skilled nursing services and whose needs lie more in the custodial and supportive realm. While a universal interagency definition of assisted living has not yet been achieved, key components include 24-hour oversight, housekeeping services, provision of at least two meals a day, and personal assistance with at least two of the following: bathing, dressing, and use of medications. An underlying philosophy includes accommodation of the individual resident's personal needs to promote independence in a homelike residential setting, coupled with activities and opportunities that promote community and family involvement and maximize the resident's dignity, autonomy, choice, and safety.[24] Assisted living facilities vary significantly in size, ranging from just a few residents to several hundred. They may take the form of small or large homes with just a few residents or large, multiunit apartment complexes with several hundred residents. Many assisted living facilities contract with home health agencies to provide skilled nursing care and with hospice service providers when such services are needed by individual residents. The assisted living population is expected to grow to almost 2 million individuals by 2030.[24]

States carry out oversight and regulation of assisted living facilities at varying levels. These variations in laws and regulations create a diverse operating environment as well as a wide range of terminology and available services for consumers. The quality of facilities, care, and services therefore may be an exclusive function of the policies of the owner organization or a combination of owner and organization policies coupled with state regulatory oversight.

Costs of assisted living are borne largely from private resources, although in certain circumstances supplemental Social Security income, private health insurance, long-term care insurance (LTCI), or special government rent subsidies for low-income older adults may apply. Estimates place the average monthly cost at more than $3,600, but costs can range across a broad continuum depending on the level of amenities desired in a facility and the types of services required. Residents most often fund accommodations from personal resources or from LTCI policies.[17]

Residential institutions such as adult homes, board and care homes, and group homes for people with mental or developmental disabilities also represent assisted living arrangements. Care provided in adult homes has traditionally only been accessible by people who are healthy but limited in their ability to do their own housekeeping, household maintenance, and cooking. Residents must be able, for the most part, to meet their own personal care needs for dressing, eating, bathing, toileting, and ambulation unassisted. Oversight of residents may include services such as supervision of medications to the extent of reminding residents to take their medication or providing some assistance with bathing, grooming, transportation, laundry, and simple housekeeping.

Home Care

Home care is community-based care provided to individuals in their own residences. Home care may be either a long-term provision of supportive care and services to chronically ill clients to avoid institutionalization or short-term intermittent care of clients after an episode of illness or hospitalization. Home care may be provided through the formal system of agency-employed professional home care providers, such as registered nurses, licensed practical nurses, home health aides, physical therapists, occupational therapists, speech-language pathologists, social workers, personal care aides, and homemakers, who make home visits. A considerably smaller number of home care staff may be self-employed individuals who contract privately with clients. An informal system also provides home care through caregivers consisting of family, neighbors, and friends of people in need of healthcare support services. Very often, a combination of both formal and informal systems delivers home care.

Professional home care services originated in social welfare initiatives in the early 1900s in public response to the horrific living conditions of immigrants in U.S. industrialized cities. Public health concerns also gained impetus at that time as the "germ theory" of disease became accepted, and local, state, and national health departments and agencies mandated the control of contagious disease using preventive hygiene and sanitation measures as public health standards.

After Medicare's enactment of reimbursement for home care services in 1965, the number of Medicare-certified home health agencies (HHAs) grew more than threefold to 5,983 between the years 1967 and 1985, with public health agencies dominating the home care industry.[25] In the late 1980s, significant additional growth in the number of agencies ceased due to Medicare reimbursement issues.[25] However, with Medicare reimbursement changes since the 1990s, the number of Medicare-certified, hospital-based, and freestanding for-profit HHAs grew rapidly.[25] The home care industry expanded its scope of services in response to demographic, economic, and legislative changes that include:

- An increase in the number of older people and their expressed desire to remain in their own homes for care whenever possible
- Decreased numbers of informal caregivers that are available to provide in-home care to their relatives
- Increased innovations in high-technology home care that have redefined and expanded the categories of diseases and chronic conditions that can be cared for effectively in the home
- Medicare and Medicaid reimbursement that supported expanded coverage
- The 1999 Olmstead decision of the Supreme Court that upheld the right of citizens to receive care in the community

In 2018, about 3.4 million Medicare beneficiaries received home health services from H
at a Medicare cost of $17.9 billion.[26] Approximately 89% of the freestanding home healthcare agen
cies were classified as proprietary or for-profit.[26]

Eligibility for Medicare reimbursement of home care services originally included four criteria:

1. Home care must include the provision of skilled nursing care or physical, occupational, or speech therapy; or medical social services; or a combination of any of these services as warranted by the patient's condition.
2. The person must be confined to the home.
3. A physician must order that home care services are required.
4. The home care agency must meet the minimum quality standards as outlined by Medicare and must be Medicare certified.

In 2011, under the ACA, Congress added more eligibility criteria for Medicare reimbursement for home care to those listed above. Additional criteria included a requirement for Medicare beneficiaries receiving home care to have a face-to-face office visit encounter or a telehealth visit with a physician or nurse practitioner when home health care is ordered. This change was intended to ensure that beneficiaries receive a complete evaluation when home health care is ordered. Tighter supervision of therapy services provided under the home health benefit was also included. Under the new requirement, patients must be assessed by a qualified therapist at specific therapy intervals.

In 2006 CMS recommended a "post-acute care" (PAC) reform plan that emphasized a patient-centered approach giving more choice and control of post-hospitalization services to patients and caregivers, providing a seamless continuum of care through better service coordination, and ensuring quality services in the most appropriate setting.[27] The reform plan, called Medicaid's "Money Follows the Person" (MFP), set demonstration projects in motion through 2011 by providing grants to states for additional federal matching funds for Medicaid beneficiaries making the transition from an institution back to their homes or to other community settings. The ACA extended the MFP demonstrations through 2016. By mid-2015, 44 states and the District of Columbia had received federal grants under the program, more than 52,140 Medicaid beneficiaries had transitioned through the MFP demonstration, and another 10,265 transitions were in process. MFP continues with some outstanding results.[28]

Other long-term care provisions under the ACA include a "Community First Choice Option" in Medicaid, which provides states with an increased federal Medicaid matching rate to support community-based attendant services for individuals who require an institutional level of care.[29,30] The "Balancing Incentive Program" enhances federal matching funds to states to increase the proportion of Medicaid long-term services and support dollars allocated toward home and community-based services.[30] This program established the Federal Coordinated Health Care Office, charged "to improve the integration of benefits and increase coordination between federal and state governments for individuals receiving both Medicare and Medicaid benefits."[30] This office has launched state demonstration projects to identify and evaluate delivery systems and payment models for individuals eligible for both Medicare and Medicaid that can be rapidly tested and, if successful, replicated in other states.[31]

Research published between 2000 and 2013 in the *New England Journal of Medicine*, the *American Journal of Managed Care, Journal of the American Geriatrics Society, Health Care Financing Review, Cochrane Database of Systematic Reviews*, and other sources notes the significant cost effectiveness of home care when compared with the higher costs of providing institutional care for a variety of conditions, such as the need for intravenous antibiotic therapy, diabetes, chronic

...ionary disease, congestive heart failure, and in the provision of palliative care for
...es.[32]

...ertification of home care agencies requires state licensing.[33] Most states issue a
...ar and require resubmission of an application and an annual state reinspection
...survey team. The state licensing agency has the right to investigate complaints and
to conduct periodic reviews of all licensure requirements. The few agencies that treat only private-pay or private insurance patients may not require a license; however, most home healthcare
agencies want to participate in Medicare and Medicaid, so they maintain certification standards.
Participation in voluntary accreditation indicates that home care agencies have a commitment
to continuous quality improvement. Organizations that are actively engaged in the accreditation
process for home healthcare agencies include the Community Health Accreditation Program, the
Joint Commission, and the Accreditation Commission for Health Care.

Until the proliferation of social programs in the 1960s and 1970s, individuals requiring
long-term health care usually were cared for by family members and/or friends in the family
home. This informal care system provided a valuable social service at little or no public cost. This
arrangement is still the most used system of long-term care, as family members care for more
than 80% of the older adults needing some level of assistance. The informal care system offers
significant savings to the public; however, the potential for caregivers to suffer physical and emotional burnout and the growing inability of family caregivers to fully manage care without outside
assistance have begun to diminish these savings.

Estimates place the market value of long-term care delivered by unpaid family members and
friends at more than $470 billion per year, almost double the annual national healthcare expen-
ditures for nursing home and home care combined.[34] The economic and personal contributions
of the informal caregiving system form the foundation of the nation's chronic care system and
deserve more policy-level attention and support. The federal government took an important
first step to assist family caregivers through the Family and Medical Leave Act (FMLA) of 1993,
providing up to 12 workweeks of unpaid leave per year for the birth of a child or adoption of
a child, or for employees to care for themselves or a sick family member, while ensuring continuation of health benefits and job security.[35] However, the FMLA has serious shortcomings.
It provides only for unpaid leave, a criterion that makes its use financially unfeasible for many
individuals. Also, the FMLA does not cover workers in companies of 50 or fewer employees, or
those employed for less than a year, effectively excluding approximately 40% of U.S. workers;[35]
thus, more needs to be done.

Hospice Care

Hospice is a philosophy supporting a coordinated program of care for the terminally ill. The most
common criterion for admission into a hospice is that the applicant has a diagnosis of a terminal
illness with a limited life expectancy of 6 months or less. Aggressive medical treatment of the
patient's disease may no longer be medically feasible or personally desirable. The disease may have
progressed despite available medical treatments, making continuance of curative treatment futile
or intolerable, or the patient may elect to discontinue such treatment for a variety of personal reasons, such as continued deterioration of quality of life related to treatment side effects.

The term palliative care is often used synonymously with hospice care. Palliative care is care
or treatment given to relieve the symptoms of a disease rather than attempting to cure the disease.
Pain, nausea, malaise, and emotional distress caused by feelings of fear and isolation are only
some of the difficulties that patients encounter during the terminal stages of an illness. Hospice

treatment is directed toward maintaining the comfort of the patient and enhancing the patient's quality of life and sense of independence for as long as possible.

Hospice has its historical roots in medieval Europe. Hospices were originally way stations where travelers on religious pilgrimages received food and rest. Over time, the concept evolved into sanctuaries where impoverished people or those who were sick or dying received care.

English physician Dame Cicely Saunders established St. Christopher's, a hospice located in a London suburb, in 1967, and it became a model for the modern hospice. Here, terminally ill patients received intensive symptom management, modern techniques of pain control, and psychological and emotional support. She brought the founding concepts of the modern hospice to the United States in a lecture tour in the late 1960s, during which she emphasized that dying patients were also on a kind of pilgrimage and needed a more responsive environment than could be provided in high-technology, impersonal, cure-oriented hospitals.

The U.S. hospice movement began as a consumer-based grassroots movement supported by volunteer and professional members of the community. Today, 26.94% of hospice organizations are operating as not-for-profit entities, with 69.65% for-profit and the remaining 3.41% government providers.[36]

U.S. founders shared the belief that the hospice concept was a more humane alternative to the technology-driven, curative emphasis in hospitals. Because the medical system can view choosing to discontinue aggressive medical treatment as a failure, terminally ill patients can feel depersonalized and isolated inside a traditional hospital setting. Ideally, the physician, the patient, and the patient's family jointly recognize the need to refer the patient to a hospice when deciding to stop curative treatment.

The first U.S. hospice was established in New Haven, Connecticut, in 1974. The number of hospices has increased steadily every year, now serving between 1.55 and 1.7 million individuals annually.[36] Growth in the availability of hospice care followed the enactment of 1982 legislation that extended Medicare coverage to hospice services, allowing the movement to escape its prior dependency on grant support and philanthropy.

Consistent with the hospice philosophy, a multidisciplinary team of nurses, social workers, counselors, physicians, and therapists provides services. Hospices also provide drug therapies and medical appliances and supplies. Bereavement services for surviving family members continue for a year or longer after the patient's death. Most hospice organizations also provide bereavement services for the larger community.[36]

A variety of different settings accommodate hospice care, including patient homes, hospitals, SNFs, assisted living facilities, or hospice inpatient facilities. The most important unifying concept about hospice is that no matter where the care is delivered, a specialized multidisciplinary team of healthcare professionals works together to manage the patient's care. Physicians direct multidisciplinary team members with each team member contributing particular skills and expertise to assist in managing pain, alleviating emotional distress, promoting comfort, and maintaining the independence of the hospice patient. Hospice care encompasses the patient's family and routinely includes counseling (including bereavement counseling), spiritual support, and respite care for family members.

The hospice philosophy emphasizes volunteerism, and it is the only healthcare provider category whose Medicare certification requires that at least 5% of total patient care hours are contributed by volunteers. Volunteers typically provide services in three areas[37]:

- ■ Direct support: spending time with patients
- ■ Clinical support: performing clerical services to support care
- ■ General support: fundraising, outreach, and board service

Hospice care has demonstrated its cost savings in care for the terminally ill. The unique blend of care provided by specialized teams, use of volunteers, and frequent use of family members as primary caregivers in the home decreases expenses. The focus on palliative care rather than on cure-oriented care also decreases the cost. A number of research studies have examined the savings from the use of hospice care. Similar to Medicare, annual Medicaid expenditures for hospice care represent only a small fraction of total expenditures.[37]

Managed care organizations and traditional health insurers recognize both the human and economic benefits of hospice care and typically include hospice in their benefit packages. Insurers may have their own team of hospice-type providers within their respective networks or may contract with community hospice organizations to provide hospice care. Medicare-eligible subscribers of Medicare-participating health plans are automatically eligible for hospice care, and services must be provided through a Medicare-certified hospice organization. Patients are not required to obtain a referral from their health plan or to discontinue their managed care contract in order to receive hospice care.

A basic tenet of the hospice philosophy is that hospice care should be available regardless of the ability to pay. When a patient does not have health insurance and does not qualify for Medicare or Medicaid, hospice services still may be available. A hospice may offer a sliding payment scale to patients, with the hospice drawing on internal funds garnered through its fundraising activities to supplement available patient payments.

Ongoing quality assurance to monitor care quality is an inherent concept in hospice care. The three standards used most frequently are licensure, certification, and accreditation. Licensure is based on state-imposed statutes as part of the consumer protection code of a state. Not all states have such licensing statutes. States that have licensing statutes require that hospices within their jurisdiction meet the standards set forth in the law. Certification means that hospices have been examined on the federal level and have been found to at least minimally meet the mandated requirements for Medicare and Medicaid reimbursement. A hospice program that is not certified may still operate legally, but it is ineligible to bill Medicare or Medicaid for its services. As identified above, the same three organizations which accredit home healthcare agencies also accredit hospice agencies.

Respite Care

Family caregivers continue to be a key factor in providing care for many long-term care recipients in their communities, rather than placing them in institutions. Providing care up to 24 hours a day can place enormous physical and emotional stress on family caregivers.

Respite care is temporary surrogate care given to a patient when that patient's primary caregiver(s) must be absent. In the 1970s, formal respite care programs originated to meet the increasing need for assistance after the rapid deinstitutionalization of individuals who had developmental disabilities or mental illness. Since then, the respite care model has expanded to include any family-managed care program that helps to avoid or forestall the placement of a patient in a full-time institutionalized environment by providing planned, intermittent caregiver relief. Respite care offers an organized, reliable system in which both the patient and primary caregiver are beneficiaries.

Respite care may be offered in a variety of settings: the home, a day-care situation, or institutions with overnight care, such as hospitals, nursing homes, or group homes. Respite care providers may include private, public, and voluntary not-for-profit agencies. The length of respite care varies, but it is intended to be short term and intermittent.

Respite care services are highly differentiated. Some are very structured and self-contained; others are highly flexible and exist in a more casual support capacity. A number of services are oriented to treating only patients with a particular ailment, but, for many, the only criterion the patient must meet for admission is that they require supervised medical treatment and nursing care, which usually has been provided by family or friends as primary caregivers. Respite models include:

- Alzheimer's disease care on an inpatient basis with admissions lasting for several weeks
- Community-based, adult day-care centers that offer nursing, therapeutic, and social services
- In-home assistance, where visiting homecare or personal care aides supply services
- Temporary patient furloughs to a hospital or nursing home at regular intervals

Respite care program staffing varies widely, deploying both professionals and nonprofessionals. For example, respite care could be as informal as having a member from the caregiver's church come into the home for a few hours while the caregiver goes out or as professional as a specialized dementia day-care program where nurses, aides, and recreational and physical therapists are specifically educated to care for dementia patients in a structured, caregiving environment. When respite care entails overnight care in an institutional setting, such as a nursing home, hospital, or group home, the staff providing care is the same staff employed by the institution to provide care to their regular patients in the institution.

Formal respite programs in the United States that are financially accessible to all in need have remained sparse. One of the greatest barriers limiting the expanded use of respite care is cost. Family caregivers operating on a limited budget may have difficulty finding funds to compensate a respite provider. Although some respite providers offer care on a sliding scale, almost any fee may exceed the financial means of the family. In these situations, not-for-profit organizations may assist by providing respite assistance at a tolerable cost for patients who meet certain financial or medical parameters.

Historically, there have been few provisions in the Medicare and Medicaid programs to support formal respite care. Medicare contains no allowances for respite, unless services are provided by a Medicare-certified hospice, Medicare-certified hospital, or Medicare-certified nursing home, and copay fees are required. The person receiving respite care may be responsible for 5% of the Medicare-approved amount for respite care. For example, if Medicare pays $100 per day for inpatient respite care, the copay would be $5 per day.[37] Each time a patient receives respite care, Medicare covers up to 5 days. There is no limit to the number of times that a patient can receive respite care. The amount paid for respite care can change each year.[37] Medicaid has stringent requirements regarding the specific type and length of care provided as well as financial eligibility for services and does not pay for respite care directly. Often states use waivers to apply federal funds to offset respite costs for eligible Medicaid recipients. Some states allow family members to receive a wage subsidy for respite services for people over the age of 60 with very low incomes, but eligibility, types of care, and funding vary on a state-by-state basis.[38] Available respite programs offered by voluntary agencies as the result of federal grants often provide services for only specific medical conditions, such as Alzheimer's disease. Both proprietary and not-for-profit organizations are developing specialized dementia and related respite care programs in response to recent federal legislation. Many specialized dementia respite care programs currently are developed and marketed to private-pay customers, but such programs often are beyond the financial capacity of many families.

One of the major barriers to responsive changes in reimbursement for respite care has been that funding mechanisms have viewed respite care as meeting a social need rather than an acute medical care need. In addition, community systems of respite care can be difficult to organize because the level of need is intermittent and unpredictable. Family caregivers, rather than the patients who actually receive the care, are often viewed as the most direct beneficiaries of respite care. With the indisputable conclusion that respite care programs offer society value and cost savings through postponement or avoidance of costly institutionalization, bipartisan federal legislation was developed in 2003 to address respite care issues. Entitled the Lifespan Respite Care Act, more than 200 national, state, and local organizations advocated its passage, culminating in its signing into law in 2006.[39-41] The law authorized $289 million over 5 years for state grants to develop respite programs. According to the National Family Caregivers Association (now renamed Caregiver Action Network, or CAN), the 2006 Act defined respite programs as "coordinated systems of accessible, community-based respite-care services for family caregivers of children and adults with special needs."[39] Passage of this legislation was a landmark because it provided a nationwide acknowledgment of the inherent economic value of the informal family-provided care system. To date, 33 states and the District of Columbia have received Lifespan Respite Care Program grants.[40] The Lifespan Respite Care Reauthorization Act of 2015 requests $75 million, $15 million each year for fiscal years 2016–2020.[40] In addition, as a major thrust of federal initiatives, the Administration on Aging (AoA), part of the U.S. Department of Health and Human Services, has continued to pilot several demonstration programs targeted at determining the cost effectiveness and consumer acceptability of various combinations of community-based services that support older adults' ability to continue living independently.

Adult Day Care

An adult day-care center may provide a supervised program of social activities and custodial care (social model), medical and rehabilitative care through skilled nursing (medical model), or specialized services for patients with Alzheimer's disease or other forms of dementia. An adult day-care center operates during daytime hours in a protective group setting located outside the recipient's home. The primary intent of adult day care is to prevent the premature and inappropriate institutionalization of older adults by providing socialization, health care, or both. Older adults maintain their mental and physical well-being longer and at a higher level when they continue to reside in their homes and their communities. Furthermore, for those who depend on the services of a regular family caregiver, an adult day-care center can provide respite for the caregiver and therapeutic social contacts for the care recipient.[42]

The concept of adult day care grew out of social concern for the quality of life and care of older adults based on the work of Lionel Cousins, who in the 1960s established the first adult day-care center in the United States to "prepare patients for discharge by teaching and promoting independent living skills."[42] Originally, development and growth in such programs were slow because there was no national policy to support the program concept and no permanent funding base because the prototype Medicare and Medicaid programs supported and encouraged institutionalization. However, as the cost of institutionalization, the inhumanity of many nursing homes, and the burden placed on family caregivers were recognized, the focus of long-term care was redirected toward support of community-based care as a preferred alternative to institutionalization.

The services that adult day-care centers offer are similar, but the emphasis varies with the model they follow. Most adult day-care centers offer a variety of medical, psychiatric, and nursing assessments, counseling, physical exercises, social services, crafts, and rehabilitation in activities of daily living skills. Special-purpose adult day-care centers serve particular populations of clients, such as veterans, older adults with mental illnesses, the blind, people with Alzheimer's disease, or people with cerebral palsy, for example.

Staffing patterns of adult day-care programs vary from program to program and are directly related to the type of program and specific services offered; the mix of unskilled and skilled employees depends on the kinds of services being offered. Programs based on the medical model are more likely to employ more registered nurses, occupational therapists, and physical therapists to provide skilled assessment, direct care, and rehabilitative therapies than in a social model, where aides may perform most of the custodial care and a recreational therapist may be employed to plan and deliver recreational and socialization activities. The number of clients enrolled in an adult day-care program varies according to the staffing pattern and facility size. The cost of care may vary widely depending on the range and scope of services provided. Medicare generally does not provide reimbursement for day-care services. Medicaid may provide reimbursement for services in a medical model day-care program, but this practice varies from state to state. Often, services are paid for through private fees or through programs supported by grant funds or by charitable or religious organizations.

Most centers are certified by the particular community agency that is funding the day-care center. Licensure and credentialing ensure that the day-care center meets at least the minimum standards and guidelines set by the overseeing agency that provides grant funding to the community agency and ensure that the overseeing agency has met all criteria for obtaining underlying federal government grants. Adult day-care standards, which include organizational measurement and quality and information systems and outcomes quality, were first published in 1999 by the Commission on Accreditation of Rehabilitation Facilities along with the National Adult Day Services Association. The standards provide quality guidance to adult day-care management, as well as recognition of the value of adult day-care services in the overall continuum of long-term care.[43]

▶ Innovations in Long-Term Care

Innovative long-term care services that meet the diverse medical needs, personal desires, and lifestyle choices of older Americans have made important strides over the years. The continuum of care model recognizes the complex configuration of individual needs and encourages the implementation of programs and services of adequate variety, intensity, and scope to provide the best configuration of care to any individual. Concepts such as aging in place, life care communities, naturally occurring retirement communities, and high-technology home care are some of the changes that offer enriched alternatives to long-term care recipients.

Aging in Place

Moving to a nursing home or dependent care facility is seen by many as a lifestyle change to be steadfastly avoided for as long as possible. Most people prefer to remain actively engaged in their own support and care, in their own residence, and within the context of their own family. Research indicates enhanced quality of life and longevity when older adults are able to remain in their own residences. The term "aging in place" in the context of older and frail people refers to at least partial fulfillment of this desire. An aging-in-place healthcare system allows older adults to maintain their health while living as independently as possible in their own homes, without a costly, and in many cases traumatic, move to an institutional setting. At the federal, state, and local governmental levels, as evidenced by legislation, and at the grassroots level, an increasingly favorable light is shining on the well-documented cost effectiveness of healthcare programs that encourage the aging-in-place concept and the concurrent maintenance of independent living.

Aging-in-place programs bring together a variety of health and other supportive services to enable participants to live independently in their own residences for as long as safely possible. Services that participants receive most frequently include:

- Nursing services provided by registered and licensed nurses
- Home care aide assistance
- Homemaker services to assist with meals and housekeeping
- A 24-hour emergency response system
- Home-delivered groceries
- Transportation to healthcare appointments

In 1972, a model of aging-in-place service delivery, called On Lok Senior Health Services, was established as a demonstration project to provide health services to a selected population of frail older people in San Francisco. The term *On Lok* derives from the Cantonese language, meaning "peaceful and happy abode."[44] Participants in the On Lok program live in their own residences, and an interdisciplinary team of healthcare professionals manages their health care. When institutional care is required (either in a nursing home or hospital) or ancillary diagnostic or specialty physician services are needed, they are provided through contractual arrangements with outside providers. The prototype program was so successful that Congress mandated replication of this model through the establishment of demonstration programs, called the Programs of All-Inclusive Care for the Elderly (PACE), in other parts of the country.[44] The early success of PACE was evidenced by the fact that although clients were certified as eligible for nursing home placement, only 6% were placed in nursing homes; the rest were able to remain in their homes.[45] Also impressive was the low hospitalization rate of participants when compared with typical Medicare beneficiaries of similar health status. Through provisions of the Balanced Budget Act of 1997, PACE earned permanent status as a Medicare-approved benefit.[45]

Continuing Care Retirement and Life Care Communities

Continuing care retirement communities (CCRCs) are available for those Americans who do not wish to stay in their own homes as they get older but are essentially well enough to avoid institutionalization. CCRCs provide residences on a retirement campus, typically in apartment complexes designed for functional older adults. Unlike ordinary retirement communities that offer only specialized housing, CCRCs offer a comprehensive program of social services, meals, and access to contractual medical services in addition to housing. There are three types of CCRCs[46]:

- Life care or extended contract/continuing life care community (CLCC): This is the most expensive option. It offers unlimited assisted living, medical treatment, and skilled nursing care without any additional charges as the resident's needs change over time.
- Modified contract: This contract offers a set of services provided for a specified length of time. When that time is expired, other services can be obtained but will have higher monthly fees.
- Fee-for-service contract: The initial enrollment fee may be lower, but assisted living and skilled nursing are paid for at their market rates.

According to the American Association of Retired Persons (AARP), CCRCs provide the most expensive of all long-term care options and require an entrance fee as well as monthly charges.[46] Fees depend on a variety of factors, including the resident's health status, the type of housing chosen, the size of the facility, and the type of service contract.[46] Cost varies widely, and such programs require upfront entrance fees that can range from $100,000 to $1 million. However, as advocates for this lifestyle point out, many Americans approaching their retirement years have sufficient equity in their homes and investment income to pay the required entrance and monthly maintenance fees.

CLCCs achieve financial viability by using an insurance-based model and, as such, are regulated by state insurance departments as well as other regulatory agencies to which their services may be subject in their respective states. The program administrators establish eligibility criteria for participants using actuarial data from the insurance industry. The future lifetime medical costs of participants are anticipated, and rates and charges are set accordingly. Prospective CLCC residents are provided a contract outlining what the CLCC provides in terms of home accommodations, social activities, services and amenities, and access to on-site levels of health care. Most CLCCs require a one-time entrance fee and a monthly fee, as previously mentioned. There are many variations to the types of contracts offered.[47] In general, services may include the following:

- Meals
- Scheduled transportation
- Housekeeping services
- Housing unit maintenance
- Linen and personal laundry
- Health monitoring
- Wellness programs
- Some utilities
- Social activities
- Home health care
- Skilled nursing care

A life care community offers more comprehensive benefits and support systems for older adults than any other option available today in the United States. Fewer than 1% of older citizens have taken advantage of this option in the past, in great part because of the expense and the requirement of an extended contractual commitment.

Naturally Occurring Retirement Communities

A naturally occurring retirement community (NORC) is a term coined by Professor Michael Hunt of the University of Wisconsin–Madison in the 1980s to describe apartment buildings where most residents were 60 years of age or older. Now, the NORC acronym is widely used to describe apartment complexes, neighborhoods, or sections of communities where residents have opted to remain in their homes as they age.[48] Today, numerous communities throughout the United States formally recognize NORCs.

The AoA recognized NORCs through the development of a competitive grant awards program for demonstration projects designed to test and evaluate methods to assist older Americans in their desire to age in place. Community centers and other not-for-profit organizations competed for grant funding, and demonstration projects were enacted in several states. NORC programs use a combination of services such as case management, nursing, social and recreational activities, health education, transportation, nutrition, and referral linkages to enhance quality of life and safety for older adults who wish to remain in their homes during their aging process.[48] NORCs have appeared to hold much potential as a positive alternative to institutionalization and offer possible cost savings for individuals and governments.[49]

High-Technology Home Care: Hospitals Without Walls

Traditionally, home health care focused on providing supportive care to people with long-term disability and chronic disease. Changes in reimbursement mechanisms to a prospective payment system based on diagnosis-related groups (DRGs) led to the more rapid discharge of all patients from hospitals after episodes of hospitalization for acute illness, exacerbation of chronic disease, progression of disability, or surgery. Patients are frequently discharged to their homes while still requiring advanced intensive therapeutic treatments and relying on complex, high-technology services such as ventilators, kidney dialysis, intravenous antibiotic therapy, parenteral nutrition, or cancer chemotherapy.

The delivery of high-technology home care not only is more cost effective than hospitalization or institutionalization in a nursing home, but it also allows the client to move from the dependent patient role to the more autonomous role as a client in their own residence. Home healthcare agencies have accommodated this trend toward provision of advanced high-technology therapy in the home setting through innovations in the type and organization of the specialty services they provide. Improvements and innovations have taken place in the portability, mobility, reliability, and cost of medical devices such as intravenous therapy pumps, long-term venous access devices, continuous ambulatory peritoneal dialysis equipment, and ventilators. Innovative teams of skilled practitioners in specialized areas such as intravenous therapy and kidney dialysis and the concurrent development of innovative support teams of pharmacists and specialty technicians who prepare and deliver necessary intravenous, parenteral nutrition, and dialysis fluids and medications have made the home setting an appropriate environment for the delivery of high-technology therapies.

▶ Future of Long-Term Care

The United States will need more and diverse long-term care programs in the future to serve increasing needs, especially of older adults. Some of the causes underlying the intensifying need for diverse long-term care service options include:

- Changes in U.S. population demographics
- Social and economic changes in families
- Increasingly sophisticated medical technology
- Greater consumer sophistication and demands

Services such as the provision of transitional health care after hospitalization for medically complex patients through integrated organizations such as patient-centered medical homes and Accountable Care Organizations are components of system reforms to prevent hospital readmissions and improve community-based coordination of care. Demonstrated cost effectiveness and expressed patient preferences for community-based care are reflected in the ACA provisions. As discussed earlier, the ACA promotes increased consumer choice, flexibility, care coordination, and community-based rather than institutional care, holding promise for a more rational, less costly, and more coordinated long-term care system.

In the face of failed federal efforts to address long-term care costs and growing financial challenges among long-term care insurers, it remains clear that political will and continuing advocacy on many fronts will be required to meet the long-term care needs of the burgeoning population of older Americans and others requiring long-term care.

Long-term care employees have traditionally been paid less and given less status than workers in acute care health services. The long-term care industry is enduring an employment crisis with an inadequate number and quality of applicants to fill vacancies in direct caregiver positions across all industry sectors.

Staffing shortages seriously affect the quality of long-term care services. The industry's ability to develop innovative approaches to attracting and retaining staff will have important implications as service demands swell with the aging of the Baby Boomer generation. Given the industry's current unmet needs and rising demands, experimentation, innovation, and advocacy in the long-term healthcare system are sure to continue.

CASE 8-1 Senior Exercise Program

Situation

James Linnon is the Nursing Home Administrator at Retirement Pastures in the southwestern United States. He became alarmed and concerned about complaints he received from several residents at the assisted living center. The complaints were related to the exercise and fitness rehabilitation coaches, Jonny and Tammy, who are interns from a local community college. Jonny and Tammy were new to the center but not new to exercise and fitness. In fact, they were hired as interns due to their vast experience with rehabilitation of geriatric patients. James valued them, as they were part of a grant to establish an exercise routine to meet state rules on activity. The program was a new initiative for the organization, and James had great expectations. The program consisted of a 12-week water aerobics and strength training course designed to give senior residents a sense of purpose and meaning to their lives. The program was an initiative seen as a vital component of the socialization programs offered by the agency in its partnership with senior centers.

James reviewed his notes on the complaints. He was sensitive to the seniors' concerns as he recognized that many of them were adapting to "aging," as he had understood from recent gerontology literature. Seniors complained that Jonny and Tammy yelled at them and embarrassed them for not keeping up. Some noted that Jonny and Tammy came across as condescending to the seniors during the classes. For example, one senior complained that Tammy had a patronizing attitude when she answered their questions and tended to dismiss their concerns, often replying, "Why?" or, "Suck it up." Another senior said that Jonny sometimes acted like they were mentally impaired, overcompensating when he spoke to them and showed them how to perform the exercises. These behaviors were interfering with the seniors' enjoyment and their patience in the learning process. Enthusiasm for the classes was high—there was already a waiting list for the next class session when the current one ended—and James did not want anything to jeopardize it.

Discussion Questions

1. How would you respond to the complaints?
2. Would you replace Jonny and Tammy as instructors for the classes?
3. Explain what intergenerational communication issues may be present. How would you manage them?
4. Describe the challenges of managing and motivating interns who may not make a high salary.

▶ Discussion Questions

- What are the key issues associated with population growth in the United States?
- Compare and contrast the different types of services and how they add value to the care continuum.
- Which issue do you think will be the most pressing for long-term care in the future?
- What is the impact of the FMLA on long-term care? What else needs to be addressed with this type of legislation?
- Describe the value of respite care for the patient and for the caregiver.

CHAPTER ACRONYMS

AARP American Association of Retired Persons
ACA Affordable Care Act
ALF Assisted-living facility
AoA Administration on Aging
CAN Caregiver Action Network
CCRC Continuing care retirement Community
CLCC Continuing life care community
CMS Centers for Medicare & Medicaid Services
DRG Diagnosis-related group
FMLA Family and Medical Leave Act
HHA Home health agency
LTCF Long-term care facility

LTCI Long-term care insurance
MFP Money Follows the Person
NCHS National Center for Health Statistics
NORC Naturally occurring retirement community
NSLTCP National Study of Long-Term Care Providers
PAC Post-acute care
PACE Programs of All-Inclusive Care for the Elderly
SNF Skilled nursing facility

References

1. Evashwick CJ. Strategic management of a continuum of care. *J Long Term Care Adm.* 1993;21(3):13-24.
2. Shortell SM. *Transforming Health Care Delivery: Seamless Continuum of Care.* American Hospital Publishing; 1994:1-7.
3. Jack CM, Paone DL. *Toward Creating a Seamless Continuum of Care: Addressing Chronic Care Needs.* Section for Aging and Long-Term Care Services of the American Hospital Association; 1994:3-5.
4. U.S. Department of Health and Human Services Administration for Community Living. Number of persons age 65 and older, 1900–2060. *In: 2020 Profile of Older Americans.* U.S. Department of Health and Human Services; 2021. Accessed August 16, 2021. https://acl.gov/sites/default/files/Aging%20and%20Disability%20in%20America/2020ProfileOlderAmericans.Final_.pdf
5. U.S. Department of Health and Human Services Administration for Community Living. *2020 Profile of Older Americans.* U.S. Department of Health and Human Services; 2021. Accessed February 17, 2021. https://acl.gov/aging-and-disability-in-america/data-and-research/profile-older-americans
6. Sullivan J. 1 in 8 adults over 55 plan to delay retirement due to COVID. *401K Specialist.* Published December 14, 2020. Accessed December 29, 2020. https://401kspecialistmag.com/1-in-8-adults-over-55-plan-to-delay-retirement-due-to-covid/
7. Kaiser Family Foundation. Long-term care in the United States: a timeline. Published August 31, 2015. Accessed February 8, 2021. https://www.kff.org/medicaid/timeline/long-term-care-in-the-united-states-a-timeline/
8. Shore HH. History of long-term care. In: Goldsmith SB, ed. *Essentials of Long-Term Care Administration.* Aspen; 1994:5-6.
9. Centers for Medicare & Medicaid Services. Nursing homes. Updated August 3, 2021. Accessed

August 16, 2021. https://www.cms.gov/Medicare/Provider-Enrollment-and-Certification/Certification andComplianc/NHs

10. Pavri JM. Overview: one hundred years of public health nursing: visions of a better world. *Imprint*. 1994;41(4):43-48.

11. Glasscote RM, Beigel A, Butterfield A, et al. *Old Folks at Homes: A Field Study of Nursing and Board and Care Homes*. American Psychiatric Association; 1976.

12. Moss FE, Halamandaris VJ. *Too Old, Too Sick, Too Bad*. Aspen; 1977:15-37.

13. Evans JM, Chutka DS, Fleming KC, Tangalos EG, Vittone J, Heathman JH. Medical care of nursing home residents. *Mayo Clin Proc*. 1995;70(7):694. doi: 10.4065/70.7.694

14. Centers for Disease Control and Prevention. Nursing homes and assisted living (long-term care facilities [LTCFs]). Updated June 22, 2020. Accessed January 5, 2021. http://www.cdc.gov/longtermcare/

15. ElderTree Care Management Services. What's the difference between skilled care and long-term care? Accessed February 16, 2021. https://www.eldertreecare.com/blog/whats-the-difference-between-skilled-care-and-long-term-care

16. National Center on Elder Abuse. Abuse of residents of long term care facilities. Accessed December 5, 2020. https://ncea.acl.gov/NCEA/media/docs/Abuse-of-Residents-of-Long-Term-Care-Facilities-(2012)_1.pdf

17. Centers for Disease Control and Prevention. National Study of Long-Term Care Providers: introduction. Accessed February 4, 2021. http://www.cdc.gov/nchs/data/nsltcp/NSLTCP_FS.pdf

18. Genworth. Cost of Care Survey. Accessed February 12, 2021. https://www.genworth.com/aging-and-you/finances/cost-of-care.html

19. National Center for Health Statistics. Table 101. Nursing homes, beds, residents and occupancy rates, by state: United States, selected years 1995–2013. In: *Health, United States, 2014: With Special Feature on Adults Aged 55–64*. National Center for Health Statistics; 2015. Accessed February 5, 2021. http://www.cdc.gov/nchs/data/hus/hus14.pdf

20. Jones AL, Dwyer LL, Bercovitz AR, Strahan GW; National Center for Health Statistics. The National Nursing Home Survey: 2004 overview. *Vital Health Stat*. 2009;13(167):1-155. Accessed February 18, 2021. http://www.cdc.gov/nchs/data/series/sr_13/sr13_167.pdf

21. National Association of Long Term Care Administrator Boards. Programs. Accessed January 5, 2021. http://www.nabweb.org/programs

22. Institute of Medicine. Gray BH, ed. *For-Profit Enterprise in Health Care*. National Academy Press; 1986:510-515.

23. Center for Medicare Advocacy. Non-profit vs. for-profit nursing homes: is there a difference in care? Published March 15, 2012. Accessed February 23, 2021. http://www.medicareadvocacy.org/non-profit-vs-for-profit-nursing-homes-is-there-a-difference-in-care/

24. Center for Medicare Advocacy. Health reform: the nursing home provisions. Published June 17, 2010. Accessed February 15, 2021. http://www.medicareadvocacy.org/health-reform-the-nursing-home-provisions/

25. American Health Care Association National Center for Assisted Living. Facts & figures. Accessed February 6, 2021. https://www.ahcancal.org/Assisted-Living/Facts-and-Figures/Pages/default.aspx

26. National Association for Home Care & Hospice. Basic statistics about home care. Updated 2010. Accessed February 8, 2021. http://www.nahc.org/wp-content/uploads/2017/10/10hc_stats.pdf

27. Medicare Payment Advisory Commission. Chapter 9: home health care services. In: *MEDPAC Report to the Congress: Medicare Payment Policy*. Medicare Payment Advisory Commission; 2020. Accessed January 15, 2021. http://www.medpac.gov/docs/default-source/reports/mar20_medpac_ch9_sec.pdf?sfvrsn=0

28. Centers for Medicare & Medicaid Services. Policy council document: post-acute care reform plan. Published September 28, 2006. Accessed February 21, 2021. http://www.cms.gov/Medicare/Medicare-Fee-for-Service-Payment/SNFPPS/Downloads/pac_reform_plan_2006.pdf

29. Medicaid.gov. Money follows the person. Accessed February 17, 2021. https://www.medicaid.gov/medicaid/long-term-services-supports/money-follows-person/index.html

30. Walker L. Health care reform improves access to Medicaid home and community-based services. American Association of Retired Persons Public Policy Institute. Published June 2010. Accessed January 7, 2021. www.aarp.org/health/health-care-reform/info-06-2010/FS-192.html

31. Reaves EL, Musumeci M. Medicaid and long-term services and supports: a primer. Kaiser Family Foundation. Published December 15, 2015. Accessed February 14, 2021. http://kff.org/medicaid/report/medicaid-and-long-term-services-and-supports-a-primer/

32. Reinhard SC, Kassner E, Houser A. How the Affordable Care Act can help move States toward a high-performing system of long-term services and supports. *Health Aff*. 2011 Mar;30(3):447-453. doi: 10.1377/hlthaff.2011.0099. PMID: 21383363

33. American Association for Homecare. Cost effectiveness of homecare. Accessed February 14,

2021. http://m.nhia.org/Members/memberdocs2005/COST_EFFECTIVENESS_STUDIES_JUNE_8.pdf

34. Centers for Medicare & Medicaid Services. Home health providers. Updated July 15, 2021. Accessed August 17, 2021. https://www.cms.gov/Medicare/Provider-Enrollment-and-Certification/Certification andComplianc/HHAs

35. Reinhard SC, Feinberg LF, Choula R, Houser A. *Valuing the Invaluable: 2015 Update.* AARP Public Policy Institute; 2015. Accessed February 20, 2021. http://www.aarp.org/content/dam/aarp/ppi/2015/valuing-the-invaluable-2015-update-new.pdf

36. Mayer G. The Family and Medical Leave Act (FMLA): an overview. Congressional Research Service. Published September 28, 2012. Accessed February 20, 2021. https://www.fas.org/sgp/crs/misc/R42758.pdf

37. National Hospice and Palliative Care Organization. NHPCO facts and figures: 2020 edition. Published August 20, 2020. Accessed February 28, 2021. https://www.nhpco.org/wp-content/uploads/NHPCO-Facts-Figures-2020-edition.pdf

38. Medicare.gov. Hospice care. Accessed February 28, 2021. https://www.medicare.gov/coverage/hospice-and-respite-care.html

39. Wayne M, White M, Robinson L. Respite care. HelpGuide. Updated November 2020. Accessed February 25, 2021. helpguide.org/articles/caregiving/respite-care.htm

40. U.S. Department of Health and Human Services Administration on Aging. The Lifespan Respite Care program. Accessed February 18, 2021. https://acl.gov/sites/default/files/programs/2018-05/Fact%20Sheet_Lifespan_Respite_Care_2018.pdf

41. Access to Respite Care and Help National Respite Coalition. Seeking congressional cosponsors for Lifespan Respite Care Reauthorization Act of 2015 (HR3913). Accessed March 1, 2021. http://archrespite.org/images/Lifespan_Reauthorization/2015_Reauthorization/Legislative_Alert_2016.pdf

42. Cefalu CA, Heuser M. Adult day care for the demented elderly. *Am Fam Physician.* 1993;47(4):723-724.

43. Lamden RS, Tynan CM, Warnke J, et al. Adult day care. In: Goldsmith SB, ed. *Long-Term Care Administration Handbook.* Jones & Bartlett Learning; 1993:395-396.

44. MacDonnell C. CARF accredits adult day care. *Nurs Homes.* 1999;48:53.

45. Miller JA. *Community-Based Long-Term Care: Innovative Models.* SAGE Publications, Inc.; 1991.

46. Deloitte & Touche, LLP; Deloitte & Touche Consulting Group, LLC. *The Balanced Budget Act of 1997, Public Law 105-33 Medicare and Medicaid Changes.* Deloitte & Touche, LLP; 1997.

47. American Association of Retired Persons. How continuing care retirement communities work. Updated October 24, 2019. Accessed January 5, 2021. https://www.aarp.org/caregiving/basics/info-2017/continuing-care-retirement-communities.html

48. Seniorresource.com. Continuing care retirement communities (CCRCs) and lifecare. Accessed December 28, 2020. http://www.seniorresource.com/hccrc.htm

49. Community-centered solutions for aging at home. *Evidence Matters.* Published 2013. Accessed January 8, 2021. https://studylib.net/doc/14642549/evidence-matters

CHAPTER 9

Behavioral Health Services

CHAPTER OVERVIEW

This chapter provides an overview of behavioral health services in the United States. It examines historical trends and the forces affecting the distribution and types of behavioral health services. Epidemiologic data on the prevalence of psychiatric and substance disorders compared with the nation's behavioral healthcare needs highlight gaps in service adequacy. Special challenges of the

Homeless and incarcerated mentally ill populations are noted. Behavioral health workforce shortages are discussed, as are opportunities for improvement in the financing and delivery of behavioral health services throughout the nation. **FIGURE 9-1** illustrates the behavioral health connection to the various domains of care. It is central to all aspects of health.

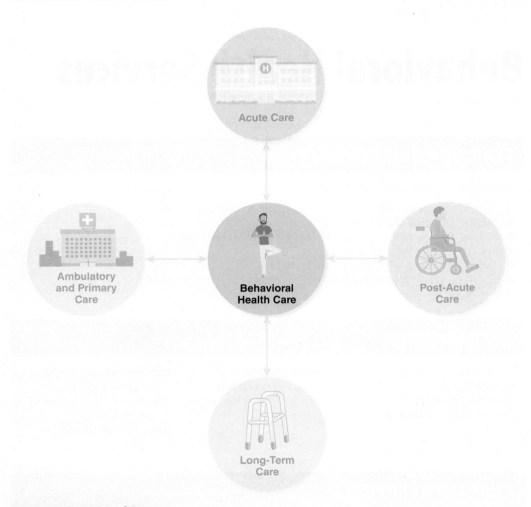

FIGURE 9-1 Domains of Care

Created by Richard Greenhill.

The U.S. Congress, in response to the imperative of addressing issues of cost, quality, and access to healthcare services, passed the Patient Protection and Affordable Care Act (ACA) of 2010. While the nation is still in the implementation phases of the ACA, there have been several attempts at repealing or deconstructing it. When ACA insurance enrollment began in 2013, approximately 44.8 million Americans of all ages were uninsured. By the third quarter of 2018, the law's impact had decreased the number of uninsured to 28.8 million, 12.5% of the total population, with 16 million fewer uninsured than in 2013.[1] Historically, this is the lowest rate of uninsured Americans. However, there is ongoing political polarization regarding whether or not the ACA is necessary, effective, or even harmful, with opinions divided along political party lines.

In the midst of these changes, a new lexicon has emerged, requiring definitions. "Mental health care" is now often referred to as "behavioral health care," with psychiatric care, a medical subspecialty, being but one aspect of an integrated approach to needed services. Usage of terms throughout the country is not uniform. Some jurisdictions, such as states or counties, have departments of mental health, whereas others have departments of behavioral health. The concept of "patient" has been replaced with "consumer" or "person/people." All of these terms will be used in the chapter, depending on the time period and discussion context.

The paradigm for service provision to individuals has shifted from a treatment plan model, which formerly used a diagnosis-anchored, "problem-based" list, to a model that is "strength-based." The "Recovery Movement" has been well underway since 2004 and advocates for the provision of holistic care within the obvious context that a psychiatric illness or behavioral health issue is but one aspect of a person's life. The task of recovery is self-directed, individualized, and person-centered. It is founded on the principles that consumers must have opportunities for choice, self-direction, and empowerment. The model is similar to that used in working with individuals with other disabilities.

The implementation of the ACA, with a significant drop in the number of uninsured throughout the country, has enabled many more people to seek care. This, in turn has resulted in a workforce shortage in the behavioral health field. The workforce shortage is resulting in yet another paradigm shift in service delivery wherein psychiatrists are starting to think more about providing population-based services integrated with primary care providers than restricting services to only those provided directly in psychiatrists' individual, office-based practices. These issues will be discussed more fully later in this chapter.

▶ Background

In the early years of our nation, the mentally ill were confined at home, in jails, or in almshouses, where they received no care and suffered severely. By 1817, a philosophical change occurred in Philadelphia when the Quakers established the first freestanding "asylum" where people with mental illness could receive kind, but firm, treatment while engaged in work, education, and recreation.[2] Effective biological treatments were nonexistent, but psychosocial care was heavily influenced by the European movement for the moral treatment of the mentally ill. Unfortunately, few people nationally could access such care, and most continued to be confined under the most adverse circumstances in overcrowded asylums and hospitals that housed not only the mentally ill, but also criminals and homeless people.

Little changed until the end of World War I, when thousands of soldiers returned, suffering from "war neurosis." This condition, also called "shell shock," was synonymous with current criteria for post-traumatic stress disorder. Finally, in the 1930s and more than a decade after World War I ended, the first effective biological treatments for various types of mental illness emerged in the forms of insulin coma, drug-induced convulsions, electroconvulsive therapy, and psychosurgery. With the end of World War II, the federal government became active in the mental health field, passing the National Mental Health Act in 1946, which resulted in the establishment of the National Institute of Mental Health (NIMH). Federal, state, and county public funds were allocated for mental health training, research, and service. The Department of

Veterans Affairs recognized the need for increased services and established psychiatric hospitals and clinics.

During the 1940s and 1950s, psychiatric care was mainly provided in state-operated psychiatric hospitals.[3] By the mid-1950s, the public psychiatric hospital population peaked at more than half a million people.[4] Fortuitously, this peak corresponded with the development of the first psychoactive medications specifically targeting psychiatric disorders. These agents, chlorpromazine (Thorazine) and reserpine, were used for the treatment of schizophrenia and other psychotic disorders. These pharmaceutical advances profoundly changed patterns of care, reducing the need for convulsive therapies and psychosurgery, and provided patients with effective interventions that allowed them to live outside of a psychiatric hospital. New outpatient services were developed, as were transitional residential facilities, or halfway houses, for the mentally ill. As discussed later in this chapter, in addition to pharmaceutical advances, the implementation of new social programs and the development of community mental health centers for outpatient treatment facilitated a dramatic flow of discharges from psychiatric hospitals over succeeding years. From its peak in the mid-1950s at more than half a million people, by 1994 the number of inpatients in public psychiatric hospitals stood at approximately 72,000.[4]

In 1955, Congress established the Joint Commission on Mental Illness and Health. The Commission attacked the quality of care and inadequate patient access to care in large state and county psychiatric hospitals. The Commission's report stimulated a substantial shift in sites for the provision of mental health services from inpatient state and county psychiatric hospitals to outpatient facilities. This was the first time a federal body had intervened to manage the allocation of resources for the mentally ill. In 1956, Social Security and Disability Insurance became accessible to the mentally ill.

By the early 1960s, the winds of change had been whipped up not only by the Commission, but also by the development of new psychotropic medications and psychosocial treatments that could provide effective intervention outside the hospital. Congress passed the Community Mental Health Act of 1963, resulting in new federal support for community-based services. Subsequently, entitlement programs became accessible to the mentally ill; Medicaid and Medicare in 1965, Supplemental Security Income (SSI) in 1974, and housing subsidies, among others.

Throughout the 1960s and 1970s, the federal government became even more involved in financing mental health care. Community mental health centers developed and expanded, and more health professionals entered the mental health field. By 1980, the number of patient care episodes delivered in organized mental health settings increased nearly fourfold, from 1.7 million to 7 million.[5] Most patients were seen in outpatient settings, and few were severely mentally ill.[6] Insurers became concerned that psychiatric care was an uncontrolled healthcare cost and started limiting coverage for the treatment of mental illness. This was done by placing limits on the amount of service that would be reimbursed, such as lifetime limits, irrespective of the nature of the illness, and by developing discounted fee-for-service contracts with the costs of psychiatric care being reimbursed as a percentage of cost, a system that used different metrics than those used for reimbursement of the cost for nonpsychiatric illnesses. Furthermore, insurers, concerned that psychiatric care would drain their coffers, started issuing contracts that outsourced care and coverage for mental health care, a process referred to as carve-outs. Another method insurers used for cost control was capitation, as discussed in Chapter 4. With capitation, a set amount is paid for care of a defined patient population, irrespective of the amount of service provided. Through these financing initiatives, non-parity of mental illness insurance coverage with insurance coverage for other categories of illness was established. When non-parity occurred, the behavioral health system was defined as "different" from other parts of the healthcare system.

The issue of non-parity in coverage has plagued the financing mechanisms for behavioral health care for decades.

Simultaneously, with the development of new insurance structures and with a shift in focus toward ambulatory care within community mental health centers, many severely mentally ill patients, who formerly had been warehoused in large state or county psychiatric hospitals, were discharged from institutions to community boarding and nursing homes. This deinstitutionalization movement was presented as important to the rehabilitation of those with severe mental illness. Emphasis was placed on the necessity of providing service in community settings. States, through Medicaid, received financial incentives to move patients from inpatient settings to boarding houses. However, community resources remained limited for a variety of reasons, and many severely ill psychiatric patients were not able to access necessary services.

By the late 1970s, healthcare costs had soared, and the federal government became concerned with identifying mechanisms for restraining health-related spending. Limited access to care, including financial barriers, continued to plague those with psychiatric disorders, limiting individual recovery. Consequently, psychosocial rehabilitation programs were expanded under Medicaid. Medicaid payment for outpatient behavioral health care was expanded, and copayment requirements for case management services were reduced. Patients with severe and persistent mental illness became eligible for SSI funding. These changes resulted in a substantial shift in quality of life for this population; however, by the mid-1980s, programs were sharply curtailed again with cutbacks in housing subsidies, social services, and increased exclusion of people with psychiatric and substance abuse disorders from SSI benefits.

By 1990, the locus of mental health care in the United States had shifted from inpatient to outpatient settings. Of the 1.7 million episodes of mental health services delivered in 1955, 77% were in inpatient settings and 23% in outpatient programs. By 1990, 67% of the 8.6 million episodes of mental health services delivered were provided in outpatient programs, 7% in partial hospitalization settings (not 24-hour facilities), and 21% in inpatient services.[7]

Since the 1990s, because of constant and rigorous pressure placed on Congress and legislative bodies by advocacy groups, the focus on severe psychiatric illness returned. The Medicare Prescription Drug, Improvement, and Modernization Act of 2003 expanded drug coverage for older Americans. The Children's Health Insurance Program (CHIP), originally enacted in 1987 and financed jointly by federal and state governments, increased the number of insured children in low-income families. The issue of insurance parity for psychiatric and behavioral health care was finally addressed through the Wellstone–Domenici Parity Act of 2008.[8]

Through insurance coverage for people previously uninsured for financial reasons, or barriers due to preexisting conditions, the ACA improves access to behavioral health services. In these ways, the ACA supports and reinforces the concept of insurance parity.[9]

However, in spite of advancements in therapies, financial assistance, and social supports for the severely mentally ill, negative effects of deinstitutionalization remain pervasive and persistent in the forms of homelessness and criminal incarceration among these individuals. The Substance Abuse and Mental Health Services Administration (SAMHSA) estimated that 26.2% of sheltered homeless people have a severe mental illness and that 34.7% of the same population have chronic substance abuse issues.[10] Another estimate noted that, at minimum, 45% of America's homeless, or 250,000 individuals, were seriously mentally ill at any given point in time.[11] Health policy experts noted that "69 percent of jail inmates have problems related to drugs, alcohol, or both and 64 percent meet the criteria for mental illness at the time of their booking or during the 12 months prior to their arrest."[12] Citing reductions in availability of inpatient mental health services and underfunding of community mental health services, the same authors note that "jails and prisons have become the de facto mental health 'system' for millions of under- or uninsured people with mental health problems and co-occurring mental health and substance abuse conditions."[12] Further, the American Psychiatric Association reported that incarcerated individuals now appear to have more severe types of mental illness than in the past, including psychotic and major mood disorders.[13] For the mentally ill, homelessness and risks of incarceration are highly interrelated. Because homeless people are at a severe disadvantage in accessing, obtaining, and maintaining needed treatment, their untreated conditions can lead to behaviors that subject them to incarceration. This phenomenon is not only profoundly deleterious to mentally ill people, but also to their communities where they overburden already overcrowded hospital emergency departments and strain law enforcement agency resources.[14] With the Medicaid expansion and emphases on care coordination, the ACA offered hope for improving care for both homeless and incarcerated mentally ill people. However, it is clear that given the changes needed in the still very disjointed care delivery system, reaping the benefits of the reforming system for these highly vulnerable populations with complex needs will be extremely challenging for providers and policy makers.[12]

▶ Recipients of Psychiatric and Behavioral Health Services

Psychiatric illness is widespread in the U.S. population. The most recent statistics from the NIMH report that approximately 51.5 million, or 20.6% of American adults, experience a mental illness in a given year.[15] **FIGURES 9-2** and **9-3** depict overall prevalence by gender, age groups, and race.[15]

However, many mental health disorders are temporary and have minimal effects on personal functioning. A subgroup of the population with diagnosed mental illnesses is classified as having a serious mental illness (SMI), resulting in "serious functional impairment which substantially interferes with or limits one or more major life activities."[15] This subgroup, estimated at 13.1 million adults aged 18 years or older, represents approximately 5.2% of all

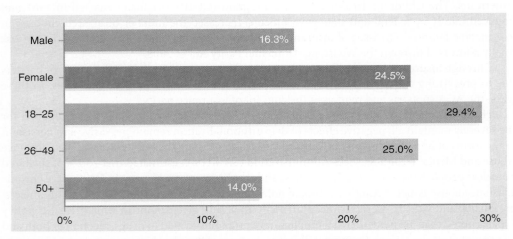

FIGURE 9-2 Prevalence of Any Mental Illness Among U.S. Adults (2019)

Created by Richard Greenhill. Data from National Institute of Mental Health. Prevalence of any mental illness (AMI) among U.S. adults (2019). Accessed February 21, 2021. http://www.nimh.nih.gov/health /statistics/prevalence/any-mental-illness-ami-among-us-adults.shtml

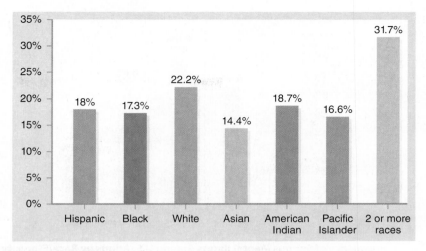

FIGURE 9-3 Prevalence of Any Mental Illness Among U.S. Adults by Race/Ethnicity (2019)

Created by Richard Greenhill. Data from National Institute of Mental Health. Prevalence of any mental illness (AMI) among U.S. adults (2019). Accessed February 21, 2021. http://www.nimh.nih.gov/health/statistics/prevalence/any-mental-illness-ami-among-us-adults.shtml

U.S. adults.[15] This subgroup represents those at greatest risk who have the greatest need for service. **FIGURES 9-4** and **9-5** depict the overall prevalence of SMI and prevalence by gender, age groups, and race.[15]

Neuropsychiatric disorders are the leading cause of disability in the United States, surpassing cardiovascular disease, cancer, and unintentional injuries as measured in units encompassing the

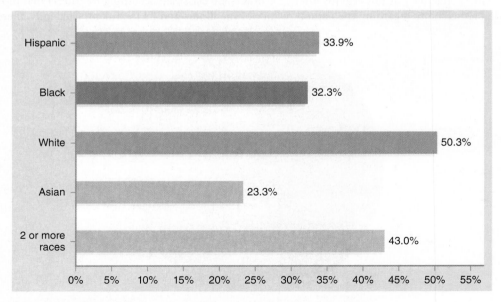

FIGURE 9-4 Prevalence of Serious Mental Illness Among U.S. Adults (2019)

Created by Richard Greenhill. Data from National Institute of Mental Health. Prevalence of any mental illness (AMI) among U.S. adults (2019). Accessed February 21, 2021. http://www.nimh.nih.gov/health/statistics/prevalence/any-mental-illness-ami-among-us-adults.shtml

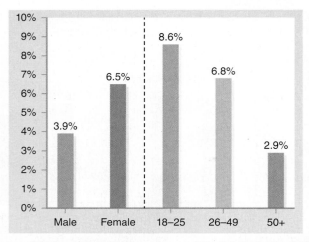

FIGURE 9-5 **Prevalence of Serious Mental Illness Among U.S. Adults by Race/Ethnicity (2019)**

Created by Richard Greenhill. Data from National Institute of Mental Health. Prevalence of any mental illness (AMI) among U.S. adults (2019). Accessed February 21, 2021. http://www.nimh.nih.gov/health/statistics/prevalence/any-mental-illness-ami-among-us-adults.shtml

total burden of disease and defined as disability-adjusted life years (DALYs). DALYs represent the total number of years lost to illness, disability, or premature death within a given population. They are calculated by adding the number of years of life lost to the number of years lived with disability for a certain disease or disorder. **FIGURE 9-6** depicts estimates of mental health services used in 2019 for serious mental illness.[15]

In contrast to widely held assumptions, psychiatric disorders can now be diagnosed and treated as effectively as physical disorders. Disorders are classified according to criteria that provide predictability regarding the natural history of the illness and its treatment. Currently, there

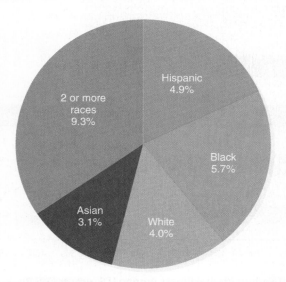

FIGURE 9-6 **Mental Health Services Received Among U.S. Adults with Serious Mental Illness (2019)**

Created by Richard Greenhill. Data from National Institute of Mental Health. Prevalence of any mental illness (AMI) among U.S. adults (2019). Accessed February 21, 2021. http://www.nimh.nih.gov/health/statistics/prevalence/any-mental-illness-ami-among-us-adults.shtml

are 22 diagnostic categories in the 5th edition of the American Psychiatric Association's *Diagnostic and Statistical Manual of Mental Disorders* (DSM-5), and within these categories there are specific diagnostic criteria for more than 300 conditions.[16] Criteria for specific diagnoses in each of these categories have been subjected to extensive field testing for diagnostic reliability and validity.

The coexistence of two diagnoses is called comorbidity. According to NIMH, nearly half of those with any psychiatric disorder meet criteria for two or more disorders, with severity strongly related to comorbidity.[17] Epidemiologic Catchment Area program studies in both clinical and nonclinical settings have determined that the prevalence of substance abuse comorbidity ranges between 23% and 80% depending on the specific psychiatric diagnosis.[18] In addition, clinical studies of people with intellectual disabilities, formerly referred to as mental retardation, have revealed considerable variation in prevalence estimates of comorbid psychiatric disorders, ranging from 30% to 60%.[19] Furthermore, mentally ill individuals have great difficulty in identifying and connecting with medical care services, and even when they do so, they may have overwhelming challenges in complying with treatment plans. These circumstances often result in mentally ill people delaying care and developing medical complications.

▶ Barriers to Care

There are multiple factors associated with lack of access to care. These include:

- Provider geographic distribution
- Financial limitations
- Lack of or inadequate health insurance
- Stigma
- Misunderstandings about the treatability of conditions
- Personal and provider attitudes
- Cultural issues
- A poorly organized care delivery system

Patients with a mental illness and a substance use disorder experience additional barriers secondary to the stigma associated with substance abuse.

Substance abuse, including alcoholism, is a chronic brain disease, like many other psychiatric disorders. However, the general community and, more disturbingly, providers tend not to view substance abuse and addiction as a chronic illness but often instead attribute causality to a lack of will or a moral failure. Furthermore, if there is a relapse, rather than seeing the relapse as a characteristic of the disease, the person who has relapsed is apt to be removed from the treatment program. This is due to providers failing to recognize that by its nature, substance abuse is a chronic illness and is subject to fluctuations that include improvements in function, periods of stabilization, and relapses.[20]

Children and Adolescents

Data on the use of mental health services by children and adolescents diagnosed with mental disorders first became available in 1999 following a NIMH survey of children and adolescents between ages 9 and 17. Only 9% of children and adolescents had been able to access and receive some mental health services in the general medical and specialty mental health delivery sectors. This accounted for fewer than half of those with a diagnosed mental illness. The study found that the largest provider of services to children and youth was the school system.[21] In 2009, results from a larger study indicated that the prevalence of mental health disorders in children aged 4–17 had increased more than 40% between the mid-1990s and 2006, with 7% of this population being diagnosed with at least one psychiatric illness. Increased sensitivity and use of screening tools by primary care physicians appeared to have had a major effect on findings. The rate of mental illness diagnosis among children aged 4–17 seen in primary care offices doubled between 1996 and 2006.[8] However, access to care remains problematic, particularly for children with severe disorders. The American Academy of Child and Adolescent Psychiatry reported in 2018 that there is an ongoing critical shortage of U.S. child and adolescent psychiatrists compounded by severe geographic maldistribution, particularly in low-socioeconomic and rural areas.[22]

Clinical research involving children and adolescents suffering from mental illness has lagged considerably behind that for adults. Inadequate research has been particularly notable regarding pharmaceuticals to treat all types of children's illnesses. In response, Congress passed two laws to increase the study of drugs in children. In 2002, the Best Pharmaceuticals for Children Act (BPCA) was enacted and reauthorized in 2007 to establish and conduct a program for pediatric drug development through the National Institutes of Health (NIH). The BPCA's intent is threefold[23]:

- Identify and prioritize drugs needing study
- Develop study requests in collaboration with NIH, the U.S. Food and Drug Administration, and other organization experts
- Conduct studies on priority drugs after manufacturers decline to do so

The Pediatric Research Equity Act (PREA) of 2003 recognized that some drugs that work for adults may not work for children. The Act also recognizes that a drug's use in children may entail safety concerns or dosage parameters that differ from those in adults. For these reasons, the PREA requires drug companies to study products in children for the same use for which they were approved in adults.[24] These laws have resulted in some gains. Prior to their enactment, more than 80% of the drugs approved for adult use were being used in children, even though their safety and effectiveness had not been established in children. In recent years, the number has been reduced to about 50%. Clearly, there remains much need for improvement.[24]

Although diagnostic techniques have been highly refined through standardized diagnostic interviews and symptom rating scales that facilitate accurate identification of those in need of service, research funding for treatment of mental illness in childhood and adolescence has not kept pace. The effects of a mental disorder on the developmental process of children are only beginning to be appreciated, but they clearly impact development in emotional, social, and cognitive domains. Moreover, few practitioners access research findings regarding treatment efficacy, and there are inadequate numbers of well-trained child and adolescent psychiatrists available for the population at risk. The need for expanding the workforce, developing early interventions, providing treatment and rehabilitation services, and seeking enhanced funding for research is critical.

Older Adults

Although many advances have been made in the treatment of mental disorders, a crisis looms in providing behavioral health services to the older population. Epidemiologic studies have indicated that Baby Boomer cohorts have high prevalence rates for depression, suicide, anxiety, and alcohol and drug abuse.[25] Studies have indicated that one in four older Americans has a significant psychiatric disorder, with depression and anxiety disorders being the most common. The prevalence of psychiatric disorders in the aging population is expected to more than double over the next 25 years, with numbers increasing from 7 to 15 million people.

The implications of these findings on future resource allocation decisions are enormous. Although older adults suffer from many of the same mental disorders as their younger counterparts, diagnosis and treatment are complicated by medical conditions that mimic or mask psychiatric disorders. Older adults also are more likely to be reluctant to report symptoms and tend to emphasize physical complaints, minimizing complaints about their mental status. Stereotypes about aging predispose older adults to believe that adverse mental changes are to be expected, contributing to a tendency to minimize the symptoms associated with a psychiatric disorder. Fears of developing dementia are omnipresent and add to reluctance in symptom disclosure. Such concerns make assessment and accurate diagnosis challenging.[26]

▶ The Organization of Psychiatric and Behavioral Health Services

Psychiatric disorders and behavioral health problems are treated by an array of providers representing multiple disciplines working in both public and private settings. The loose coordination of facilities and services has resulted in the mental health delivery system being referred to as a de facto mental health service system, structured with four highly compartmentalized sectors characterized by poor inter-sector communication and isolated funding streams.[27,28]

The psychiatric and behavioral health sector consists of behavioral health professionals, such as psychiatrists, psychologists, psychiatric nurses, psychiatric social workers, and behavioral health clinicians working in outpatient settings. More recently, providers are hiring peer specialists, people with a psychiatric or substance abuse disorder, who are trained to help others in accessing care and developing a recovery plan. Early reports suggest that peer specialists are particularly helpful in enhancing treatment compliance and community integration.

Most acute care is provided in psychiatric units of general hospitals or beds located throughout hospitals. Intensive treatment for adults and children is provided in private psychiatric hospitals, with residential treatment centers being available for children and adolescents. Public sector facilities include state and county mental hospitals and multiservice facilities that provide or coordinate a wide range of outpatient, intensive case management, partial hospitalization, or inpatient services. Very few long-term care inpatient facilities remain, with most care being provided within the community. Currently, there is a movement away from large community residential facilities for the mentally ill toward an increased focus on independent living accommodations, such as apartments for mentally ill people in need of housing. Case managers work with people to enhance their daily living skills, their use of the public transportation systems, and their ability to access care as well as other resources within the community.

The primary care sector consists of healthcare professionals, such as internists, family practitioners, pediatricians, and nurse practitioners in private office-based practices, clinics, hospitals, and nursing homes. This sector often is the initial point of contact and may be the only source of mental health services for a large proportion of people with psychiatric or behavioral health disorders. The rates of mental health diagnosis in the primary care setting have increased materially in the past decade, doubling for children and increasing by almost 30% for adults.[6]

The human services sector consists of social service agencies, school-based counseling services, residential rehabilitation services, vocational rehabilitation services, criminal justice/prison-based services, and religious professional counselors. With the Great Recession of 2008, the role of this sector shifted as many states faced significant challenges in balancing their budgets.

With increased unemployment and business closures, state revenues were deficient. Consequently, many states decreased services within the human service and mental health sectors. This has resulted in people with mental illness facing even greater financial and resource barriers to accessing care. In addition, many have experienced significant losses in welfare benefits that have resulted in an inability to pay insurance copays for service visits and, more importantly, an inability to pay copays for medication. Decreased personal revenues, including reductions in state-supported general assistance, have resulted in an increase in the homeless population and an increased feeling of desperation among those mentally ill people who have limited financial resources. These economic circumstances and resulting barriers to care have caused exacerbations of symptoms among mentally ill people who previously had been stable and productive. Comorbid substance use and abuse has increased as well as petty crimes. As a consequence, many people with SMI have transitioned from the psychiatric and behavioral health sector into the human service sector, specifically into the criminal justice and prison system. Compounding the tragedy of imprisonment is the limited and variable quality of treatment programs for substance abuse and mental illness within the prison health system. Costs for treating people with a psychiatric disability in prisons far exceed the costs of treating and supporting them within the community. The old adage "a penny wise, a pound foolish" appears to apply to those states where budget cuts have shifted care from programs specifically designed to care for people with mental illness and substance abuse disorders into the criminal justice and prison systems. It remains an abysmal reality that, in fact, the U.S. prisons of today have earned a remarkable resemblance to the early asylums that warehoused individuals prior to scientific understanding of mental illness and treatment. Mentally ill prisoners, like their counterparts from the 1700s and 1800s, without political voice, are among the most vulnerable people in U.S. society.

The volunteer support network sector consists of self-help groups and family advocacy groups. This sector has been invaluable in shifting public attention to people with persistent and severe mental illness. Advocacy groups also have had a major impact on Congress in its appropriations for funding research focused on mental illness and substance abuse disorders through the National Institutes of Health. Numerous national and state public and private advocacy organizations participate in efforts to illuminate the needs of mentally ill and disabled people at the federal state and local levels. Organizations encompass a broad range of activities from lobbying federal and state legislatures on legal and funding issues to promoting behavioral health awareness and reducing mental illness stigma.[29] For organization details, readers are encouraged to consult the reference list and its numerous links.

▶ Paradigm Shifts

Within the last 5 years, there have been two paradigm shifts directed toward turning the de facto mental health system into a more integrated and effective system of care.

Recovery-Oriented Systems of Care

The recovery transformation of the mental health system was first introduced in 2002 by the New Freedom Commission on Mental Health, established by executive order of President George W. Bush.[30] In 2004, there was a National Consensus Conference on Mental Health Recovery and Mental Health Systems Transformation.[31] This invitational conference was sponsored by the U.S. Department of Health and Human Services and the Interagency Committee on

Disability Research in partnership with six other federal agencies. At this conference, recovery was cited as the single most important goal for transforming mental health care in America. The focus on choice, strength-based empowerment of the consumer, and the establishment of hope for a better life culminated in a true paradigm shift for both assessment and treatment planning.

Recovery is the process of pursuing a fulfilling and contributing life, regardless of the difficulties one has faced. Recovery-oriented systems of care (ROSC) provide a holistic and integrated approach to care, seeking to enhance a person's positive self-image and identity. The overarching goals in ROSC are to empower mentally ill people through the provision of choices and a vision of a hopeful future. Evaluations, formerly focused on establishing a diagnosis and a list of problems, are now, through ROSC, person-centered and strength-based. Diagnoses and specific problems remain important but are now viewed as issues that must be managed within the context of life goals that have the potential to enhance the person's quality of life and self-identity. Actively linking a person's strengths with family and community resources are critical steps. Peer specialists facilitate initial contacts between a person and the providers of care and facilitate a person's connections with resources in the community. Resources may be illness related, but they also may be related to the planning of leisure activities, shopping, and other normalizing activities. ROSC shift care from the old episodic care model to one that emphasizes continuity. Choice is provided through the treatment planning process. Both providers and individuals are encouraged to focus beyond symptoms of mental illness and articulate needs and desires for housing, utilization of public transportation systems, employment, leisure activities, or even a weight-reduction strategy. In ROSC, the traditional treatment plan targeting symptom reduction shifts to that of a "hope plan" for the individual's future.[32]

Integration of Primary Care and Behavioral Health Services

More than 60% of people with psychiatric illness are unable to access any kind of psychiatric care, and more than half of those who do access and receive care in primary care settings. In addition, people with psychiatric illness, particularly those with SMI, die 15–20 years earlier than people without psychiatric illness.[33] Moreover, many of the medications used to treat SMI pose an increased risk for the development of metabolic syndrome (high cholesterol, diabetes, and heart disease), whereas others have complex interactions with other medications that the person may be taking for nonpsychiatric conditions. As a result, it is crucial that behavioral health services become increasingly integrated with primary care services. From the perspective of the primary care providers, there is great need for consultation from psychiatrists and behavioral health specialists, particularly given that primary care providers carry much of the burden for early diagnosis of mental illness and substance abuse disorders. Yet, psychiatrists and other behavioral health professionals have traditionally not been involved with the primary care treatment team. Finances have been a major barrier to involvement, particularly the problems posed by insurance nonparity, which has made it difficult, if not impossible, for the behavioral health clinicians to cover costs within a primary care setting.

The ACA provided the mechanisms and funding for massive expansion of insurance coverage through private health insurance exchanges and Medicaid expansion. Under the ACA, the individual mandate for health insurance coverage requires that if the insurance plan provides coverage for psychiatric and behavioral health care, then that coverage must be equivalent to that provided for nonpsychiatric medical disorders. However, an insurer is not required to offer coverage for all behavioral health conditions. This means that insurers, not infrequently, use this loophole as a methodology for trimming costs. Therefore, insurers are able to continue decreasing access to services for behavioral health care. Nonetheless, new models of care are emerging that emphasize the integration of behavioral health services with primary care. Multiple models for facilitating such integration are being studied, with the Collaborative Care Model as the most prominent and evidence-based.[34-36] Within the Collaborative Care Model, the behavioral health provider is not a psychiatrist, but an individual with behavioral health training, such as a psychologist with a master's or doctoral degree, a social worker, or a case worker. Behavioral health providers are usually embedded in a primary care office or clinic and use a variety of screening tools and standardized rating scales to identify patients in need of care. The psychiatrist, as a medical specialist, provides much indirect patient care by reviewing screening interview and standardized rating scales results, conducting caseload-focused registry reviews, and providing follow-up consultation with the behavioral health specialists and the primary care provider. Direct patient care by the psychiatrist is infrequent, but it may be required for complicated cases in which patients are not responding adequately to care provided through the primary care physician and/or the behavioral health specialist.

To date, widespread implementation of integrated care models has been hindered by two major issues: (1) the availability of sustainable funding, and (2) the availability of a sufficient behavioral healthcare workforce. Sustainable financing mechanisms have not been developed adequately or established for any of the integrated care models. Siloed funding streams and the lack of mechanisms for reimbursing providers for indirect patient care through the currently predominant fee-for-service billing systems are a substantial part of the problem. Effective models of integrated care, for the most part, have had grant funding from either the federal or state governments, with some having private foundation funding. As discussed in several other topics of this text, the issue remains as to what mechanisms will be developed that are sufficient for sustainable funding. Bundled payments, case-based rates, and global capitation are under consideration as possible mechanisms for sustaining funding of integrated care programs.

Integrated care also requires access to a considerable behavioral healthcare workforce. Many of the current behavioral health specialists and psychiatrists will require retraining to acquire skills and techniques necessary for working with a population-based care model. Many specialty organizations are working on the development and implementation of new training for practitioners. Many of the retraining programs are being supported by grant funding at this time. What is clear is that the new skills and techniques for service delivery must be subsumed by established training programs if future needs are to be met. Finally, the use of telemedicine for providing care to remote communities and underserved areas will be a critical part of the answer to workforce shortages.[35,37] Nonetheless, even with the challenges of funding programs and workforce development, there is much optimism among both providers and insurers regarding the integration of psychiatric and primary care services. Early reports suggest that the integrative methodology improves health outcomes and, in the long run, will decrease healthcare costs.[38,39]

▶ Financing Psychiatric and Behavioral Health Services

Mental health services are funded in many ways, including private health insurance, Medicaid, Medicare, state and county funding, as well as contracts and grants. As noted in the historic review of mental health services, the history of insurance coverage for behavioral health services has been one of unequal coverage for psychiatric and behavioral health disorders when compared with coverage for nonpsychiatric medical illnesses. As explained previously, "non-parity" has been used to describe insurance inequalities. Insurance inequalities have taken many forms and imposed severe limitations on the amount and kind of care people with chronic and severe mental illness, such as schizophrenia, have been able to access. Recognizing that schizophrenia is a chronic illness not unlike some of the nonpsychiatric chronic illnesses, such as multiple sclerosis, diabetes, stroke, and heart disease, it becomes apparent that the insurers have produced huge inequities biased against people with mental illness.

The Mental Health Parity Act of 1996 was approved by the U.S. Congress with overwhelming bipartisan support. Enacted in 1998, this legislation equated aggregated lifetime limits and annual limits for mental health services with aggregate lifetime and annual limits for medical care; however, the law allowed many cost-shifting loopholes, such as setting limits on psychiatric inpatient days, prescription drugs, outpatient visits, raising coinsurance and deductibles, and modifying the definition of medical necessity.[40] The Act did not require employers to offer mental health coverage, nor did it impose any limits on insurance copayments, deductibles, days, or visits. Furthermore, coverage was not required for people suffering from substance use and abuse disorders, which are psychiatric disorders with substantial public health significance.

In 2008, contained within the Emergency Economic Stabilization Act, Senators Paul Wellstone (D-Minnesota) and Pete Domenici (R-New Mexico) proposed the Mental Health Parity and Addiction Equity Act (MHPAEA) to build upon the Mental Health Parity Act of 1996. Enacted in 2008 with bipartisan support, the law took effect in October 2009. It was intended to end health insurance benefit inequity between mental health and substance abuse benefits and medical/surgical benefits for group health plans with more than 50 employees. Significant features of the legislation include the following:

- Equity coverage applicable to all deductibles, copayments, coinsurance, and out-of-pocket expenses and to all treatment limitations, including frequency of treatment, numbers of visits, days of coverage, or other similar limits
- Parity coverage for annual and lifetime dollar limits with medical coverage
- Broad definition of mental health and substance abuse benefits
- If a plan offers two or more benefit packages, the parity requirements apply to each package
- Mental health/substance abuse benefit coverage is not mandated, but if a plan offers such coverage, it must be provided at parity with other medical/health benefits coverage
- A group health plan or coverage that provides out-of-network coverage for medical/surgical benefits also must provide out-of-network coverage, at parity, for mental health/substance use disorder benefits
- Preserves existing state parity laws and would only preempt a state law that "prevents the application" of the federal Act. Therefore, state parity laws applicable to health insurance coverage continue in effect unless the state laws conflicts with the Act's ban on inequitable financial requirements and treatment limitations[41]

However, as of the end of 2015, it was clear that the intent of the MHPAEA can still be avoided by applying nonquantitative treatment limitations (NQTLs) for almost all of the psychiatric and substance abuse disorders and applying few NQTLs to nonpsychiatric illnesses. NQTLs are defined as treatment limits "which otherwise limit the scope or duration of benefits for treatment and are not expressed numerically."[42] An example of an NQTL is applying a requirement for preauthorization of services.[42] Clearly, regulators need to develop:

- Standards for disclosure of criteria for medical/surgical benefits
- Standards that health plans should use in establishing that the plans have applied NQTLs in a "comparable and no more stringent manner" than for medical/surgical benefits

- Standards for determining what constitutes "recognized clinically appropriate standards of care"
- Standards for delineating parity in scope of service[43]

Before the passage of the MHPAEA of 2008, managed care firms often did not incorporate coverage for mental illness in their basic contracts because of concerns about the costs of chronic care. If coverage was provided, it was "carved out" and outsourced to a subcontractor, known as a managed behavioral healthcare organization (MBHO), which would assume the financial risk as well as the benefits of managing budgets and authorization for access to mental health services. The past practice of limiting mental health benefits to a greater extent than general healthcare benefits is no longer permitted under the federal parity laws, and the U.S. Department of Labor has been charged with monitoring and insuring compliance with parity laws and regulations.

Public sector initiatives have paralleled private sector efforts in using MBHOs to control costs. Recent research indicates that MBHOs, both within the public and private sector, have facilitated access and coordinated care for those in greatest need as more people with SMI are now more likely to receive mental health specialty services than in the past.[44,45]

▶ The Veterans Health Administration

The largest integrated health system in the nation,[46] the Veterans Health Administration (VHA) has made inroads with mental health and behavioral health services. The VHA boasts an integrated model for delivering mental health service support and treatment. Some of the disorders treated and services include: anxiety, bipolar, depression, effects of traumatic brain injury (TBI), military sexual trauma, post-traumatic stress disorder (PTSD), schizophrenia, substance use, suicide prevention, and tobacco, as seen in **TABLE 9-1**.[47] The VHA has robust service offerings for veterans and beneficiaries who need care.

TABLE 9-1 Veterans Health Administration Mental Health Services Provided

Condition or Challenge	Resources & Treatment Options
Anxiety	<ul><li>Cognitive Behavioral Therapy (CBT)</li><li>Medication</li></ul> https://www.mentalhealth.va.gov/anxiety/index.asp
Bipolar	<ul><li>Psychosocial Treatments (Psychoeducation, Cognitive Behavioral Therapy, Illness Management and Recovery, Peer Specialists)</li><li>Medication</li></ul> https://www.mentalhealth.va.gov/bipolar/treatment.asp
Depression	<ul><li>Cognitive Behavioral Therapy for Depression (CBT-D)</li><li>Acceptance & Commitment Therapy for Depression (ACT-D)</li><li>Interpersonal Psychotherapy (IPT)</li></ul> https://www.mentalhealth.va.gov/depression/index.asp

Effects of TBI	■ Mix of Therapies (Cognitive, Physical, Speech, Occupational) ■ Medication ■ Assistive Devices https://www.mentalhealth.va.gov/tbi/index.asp

Post-Traumatic Stress Disorder	■ Cognitive Processing Therapy (CPT)
	■ Prolonged Exposure Therapy (PE)
	■ Eye Movement Desensitization and Reprocessing (EMDR)
	■ Medications
	  • Selective serotonin reuptake inhibitors (SSRIs)
	  • Serotonin-norepinephrine reuptake inhibitors (SNRIs)
	https://www.mentalhealth.va.gov/ptsd/index.asp

Schizophrenia	■ Assertive Community Treatment ■ Supported Employment ■ Cognitive Behavioral Therapy (CBT) ■ Illness Management and Recovery (IMR) ■ Social Skills Training (SST) ■ Medications https://www.mentalhealth.va.gov/schizophrenia/index.asp
Substance Use	■ Cognitive Behavioral Therapy for Substance Use Disorders ■ Motivational Interviewing and Motivational Enhancement Therapy ■ Contingency Management ■ Medications https://www.mentalhealth.va.gov/substance-use/index.asp
Suicide Prevention	■ Lethal Means ■ Support After Suicide Attempt ■ Self-Help options https://www.mentalhealth.va.gov/suicide_prevention/index.asp

Created by Richard Greenhill. Data from U.S. Department of Veterans Affairs. Mental health. Accessed August 22, 2021. https://www.mentalhealth.va.gov/

▶ The Future of Psychiatric and Behavioral Health Services

As previously noted, there have been significant paradigm changes in psychiatric and behavioral healthcare and service organization. Qualitatively, the shift to a recovery model of care provides for a strength-based system, individualized in accord with client-directed life goals and objectives, with the psychiatrist being but one component of an array of providers. First, the hope is that the new paradigm will produce a substantial, sustained shift from the practitioner or provider-driven system focused on diagnosis-anchored problems. Second, it is cautiously anticipated that continued experimentation will produce findings that support the move toward fully integrating psychiatry and behavioral health services with primary care and away from a separate and more isolated model of care. Both of these shifts will be transforming events, which will qualitatively change the face of psychiatric and behavioral health care, if not all health care nationally. However, the real "game changer" is the ACA, which, for vast numbers of Americans, will assure access to affordable health insurance and mandate parity of behavioral health benefits. As these new initiatives and healthcare laws are implemented, it is expected that overall health services will be improved by assuring increased access to needed psychiatric and behavioral health services and by increasing the likelihood that those with SMI will be able to access primary care services. Integration of behavioral health with primary care services will go a long way in reducing untoward effects from drug interactions as well as early interventions for illnesses that are more likely to occur in those with psychiatric illness and on psychotropic medications, such as type II diabetes mellitus and high cholesterol. It is a time of great change and promise in the healthcare delivery system as a whole and for the behavioral health services sector in particular. It is also a time that will require practitioners to be extraordinarily flexible in embracing change with a heightened recognition of the vulnerability of the mentally ill population.

CASE 9-1 Integrating Behavioral Health into Primary Care

Situation

La Buena Ayuda Medical Clinic is a safety net clinic in Ohio. The clinic is funded 95% through grants and the rest from donations. The clinic cares for the Latinx community in a rural, midwestern part of the state. The clinic sees 12,300 annually. Most of the patients are immigrants and low-income residents from all over the state. The clinic has seen a rise in the number of cases of diabetes since the COVID-19 pandemic started; 45% of the patients seen annually. With that, the clinic's medical director, Dr. Lozana, has noticed an increase in patients indicating they feel depressed and anxious—24% of the diabetes cases. The clinic CEO, Donnie Brown, won a 2-year grant to hire a psychologist, five behavioral health specialists, and three licensed clinical social workers (LCSWs) to support the medical team with the increase in new potential patients. The organization has decided to pursue National Committee on Quality Assurance's patient-centered medical home (PCMH) recognition with a Distinction in Behavioral Health Integration (see link below).

Information about PCMH Recognition with Behavioral Health Distinction: https://www.ncqa.org /programs/health-care-providers-practices/patient-centered-medical-home-pcmh/distinction-in-behavioral -health-integration/.

Discussion Questions

1. What considerations do the medical director and psychologist need to take to integrate behavioral health into the clinic's operations?
2. Is La Buena Ayuda ready for PCMH recognition with behavioral health distinction? Why or why not?
3. Do you think the decision to add behavioral health staff is justified? Why or why not?

Reference

1. Florida Department of Elder Affairs. Florida's senior centers. Accessed January 14, 2021. http://elderaffairs.state.fl.us/english/seniorcenter.php

▶ Discussion Questions

- Describe the origins of mental health in the United States. How have things changed and how are they similar to the past?
- With the rise in the number of older adults, what do you think will be the trend for mental health services? Explain your position.
- How does acknowledgement and treatment of behavioral health issues in care enhance care delivery overall?
- Should behavioral health services be integrated throughout the care continuum and not just in primary care? Why or why not?
- What is the impact of poor access to behavioral health on other health conditions?

CHAPTER ACRONYMS

ACA Patient Protection and Affordable Care Act

ACT-D Acceptance & commitment therapy for depression

AMI Any mental illness

BPCA Best Pharmaceuticals for Children Act

CBT Cognitive behavioral therapy

CBT-D Cognitive behavioral therapy for depression

CHIP The Children's Health Insurance Program

CPT Cognitive processing therapy

DALYs Disability-adjusted life years

DSM-5 Diagnostic and Statistical Manual of Mental Disorders

EMDR Eye Movement Desensitization and Reprocessing

IMR Illness Management and Recovery

IPT Interpersonal psychotherapy

LCSW Licensed clinical social worker

MBHO Managed behavioral healthcare organization

MHPAEA Mental Health Parity and Addition Equity Act of 2008

NIH National Institutes of Health

NIMH National Institute of Mental Health

NQTLs Nonquantitative treatment limitations

PCMH Patient-centered medical home

PE Prolonged Exposure Therapy

PREA Pediatric Research Equity Act

PTSD Post-traumatic stress disorder

ROSC Recovery-oriented systems of care

SAMHSA Substance Abuse and Mental Health Services Administration

SMI Serious mental Illness

SNRI Serotonin-norepinephrine reuptake inhibitor

SSI Supplemental Security Income

SSRI Selective serotonin reuptake inhibitor

SST Social Skills Training

TBI Traumatic brain injury

VHA Veterans Health Administration

References

1. Martinez ME, Cohen RA, Zammitti EP. Health insurance coverage: early release of estimates from the national health interview survey, January–March 2018. National Center for Health Statistics. Published August 2018. Accessed January 22, 2021. https://www.cdc.gov/nchs/data/nhis/earlyrelease/Insur201808.pdf

2. Bockoven JS. *Moral Treatment in Community Mental Health*. Springer Publishing Co.; 1972.

3. Fisher WH, Geller JL, Pandiani JA. The changing role of the state psychiatric hospital. *Health Aff.* 2009;28(3);676-684. doi: 10.1377/hlthaff.28.3.676

4. Fuller Torrey E. Deinstitutionalization: a psychiatric "Titanic." In: *Out of the Shadows: Confronting America's Mental Illness Crisis*. John Wiley & Sons; 1997. *PBS Frontline*. Published May 10, 2005. Accessed January 17, 2021. http://www.pbs.org/wgbh/pages/frontline/shows/asylums/special/excerpt.html.

5. Klerman GL. The psychiatric revolution of the past 25 years. In: Gove WR, ed. *Deviance and Mental Illness*. SAGE Publications, Inc.; 1982:180.

6. Mechanic D. Establishing mental health priorities. *Milbank Q.* 1994;72:501-514.

7. Redick RW, Witkin MJ, Atay JE, Manderscheid RW. The evolution and expansion of mental health care in the United States between 1955 and 1990. In: *Mental Health Statistical Note 210*. U.S. Department of Health and Human Services; 1994.

8. Glied SA, Frank RG. Better but not best: recent trends in the well-being of the mentally ill. *Health Aff.* 2009;28(3):637-638. doi: 10.1377/hlthaff.28.3.637

9. 111th U.S. Congress. Public Law 111-148. *The Patient Protection and Affordable Care Act*. U.S. Government Printing Office; 2010.

10. U.S. Department of Health and Human Services Substance Abuse and Mental Health Services Administration. Homelessness programs and resources. Updated March 29, 2019. Accessed February 12, 2021. https://www.samhsa.gov/homelessness-programs -resources

11. Mental Illness Policy Org. 250,000 mentally ill are homeless. 140,000 seriously mentally ill are homeless. Accessed February 14, 2021. https://mentalillness policy.org/consequences/homeless-mentally-ill.html

12. Regenstein M, Rosenbaum S. What the Affordable Care Act means for people with jail stays. *Health Aff.* 2014;33(3):448-454. doi: 10.1377/hlthaff.2013.1119

13. Aufderheide D. Mental illness in America's jails and prisons: toward a public safety/public health model. *Health Affairs* Blog. Published April 1, 2014. Accessed April 12, 2016. http://healthaffairs.org /blog/2014/04/01/mental-illness-in-americas-jails -and-prisons-toward-a-public-safetypublic-health -model/

14. Fuller Torrey E, Fuller DA, Geller J, Jacobs C, Ragosta K. No room at the inn: trends and consequences of closing public psychiatric hospitals: 2005–2010. Treatment Advocacy Center. Published July 19, 2012. Accessed January 22, 2021. https://www .treatmentadvocacycenter.org/storage/documents /no_room_at_the_inn-2012.pdf

15. National Institute of Mental Health. Prevalence of any mental illness (AMI) among U.S. adults (2019). Accessed February 21, 2021. http://www.nimh.nih .gov/health/statistics/prevalence/any-mental-illness -ami-among-us-adults.shtml

16. American Psychiatric Association. *Diagnostic and Statistical Manual of Mental Disorders*. 5th ed. American Psychiatric Press; 2013.

17. National Institute of Mental Health. Questions and answers about the National Comorbidity Survey Replication (NCSR) Study. Accessed February 24, 2021. https://www.nimh.nih.gov/health/topics/ncsr -study/questions-and-answers-about-the-national -comorbidity-survey-replication-ncsr-study

18. Regier DA, Farmer ME, Rae DS, et al. Comorbidity of mental disorders with alcohol and other drug abuse. Results from the Epidemiological Catchment Area (ECA) Study. *JAMA*. 1990;264(19):2511-2518.

19. Kerker BD, Owens PL, Zigler E, Horwitz SM. Mental health disorders among individuals with mental retardation: challenges to accurate prevalence estimates. *Public Health Rep.* 2004;119(4):409-417. doi: 10.1016/j.phr.2004.05.005

20. Substance Abuse and Mental Health Administration. Mental health and substance use disorders. Updated April 30, 2020. Accessed February 25, 2021. https:// www.samhsa.gov/find-help/disorders

21. U.S. Department of Health and Human Services. *Mental Health: A Report of the Surgeon General— Chapter 6*. U.S. Department of Health and Human Services, Substance and Mental Health Services Administration, Center for Mental Health Services, National Institutes of Health, National Institute of Mental Health; 1999:409. Accessed January 24, 2021. https://www.loc.gov/item/2002495357/

22. American Academy of Child and Adolescent Psychiatry. AACAP workforce factsheet. Accessed February 13, 2021. https://www.aacap.org/App_Themes /AACAP/docs/resources_for_primary_care/workforce _issues/workforce_factsheet_updated_2018.pdf

23. National Institutes of Health. Best Pharmaceuticals for Children Act (BPCA). Accessed February 10, 2021. https://bpca.nichd.nih.gov/about/Pages/Index .aspx

24. U.S. Food and Drug Administration. FDA takes steps to encourage pediatric drug studies. Published October 15, 2018. Accessed January 16, 2021. https:// www.fda.gov/news-events/fda-brief/fda-brief-fda -takes-new-steps-encourage-development-novel -treatments-rare-diseases

25. Regier DA, Boyd JH, Burke JD Jr., et al. One-month prevalence of mental disorders in the United States. Based on five Epidemiological Catchment Area sites. *Arch Gen Psychiatry*. 1988;45(11):977-986. doi: 10.1001/archpsyc.1988.01800350011002

26. U.S. Department of Health and Human Services. *Mental Health: A Report of the Surgeon General— Chapter 6*. Rockville, MD: U.S. Department of Health and Human Services, Substance and Mental Health Services Administration, Center for Mental Health Services, National Institutes of Health, National Institute of Mental Health; 1999:340-341. Accessed February 24, 2021. https://profiles.nlm.nih .gov/ps/access/NNBBHS.pdf

27. Regier DA, Narrow WE, Rae DS, Manderscheid RW, Locke BZ, Goodwin FK. The de facto US mental and addictive disorders service system. Epidemiological catchment area prospective 1-year prevalence rates of disorders and services. *Arch Gen Psychiatry*. 1995;50(2):85-94. doi: 10.1001/archpsyc.1993.018201 40007001

28. U.S. Department of Health and Human Services. *Mental Health: A Report of the Surgeon General— Chapter 6*. Rockville, MD: U.S. Department of Health

and Human Services, Substance and Mental Health Services Administration, Center for Mental Health Services, National Institutes of Health, National Institute of Mental Health; 1999:406-407. Accessed February 25, 2021. https://profiles.nlm.nih.gov/ps/access/NNBBHS.pdf

29. American Hospital Association. National mental health organizations. Accessed January 14, 2021. http://www.aha.org/advocacy-issues/mentalhealth/natlorgs.shtml

30. President's New Freedom Commission on Mental Health. *Achieving the Promise: Transforming Mental Health Care in America, Executive Summary, 3-4.* President's New Freedom Commission on Mental Health; 2003. Accessed February 26, 2021. http://govinfo.library.unt.edu/mentalhealthcommission/reports/FinalReport/downloads/downloads.html

31. President's New Freedom Commission on Mental Health. Substance Abuse and Mental Health Services Administration. Interim report of the President's New Freedom Commission on Mental Health. Published October 29, 2002. Accessed January 16, 2021. https://govinfo.library.unt.edu/mentalhealthcommission/reports/Interim_Report.htm

32. U.S. Department of Health and Human Services Substance Abuse and Mental Health Services Administration. *Transforming Mental Health Care in America: The Federal Action Agenda: First Steps.* U.S. Department of Health and Human Services; 2005. Accessed January 10, 2021. http://cretscmhd.psych.ucla.edu/nola/Video/MHR/Governmentreports/TRANSFORMING%20MENTAL%20HEALTH%20CARE%20IN%20AMERICA.pdf

33. Newcomer JW, Hennekens CH. Early death rate for severe mental illness and risk of cardiovascular disease. *JAMA.* 2007;298(15):1794-1796.

34. Katon WJ, Von Korff M, Lin E, et al. Collaborative management to achieve treatment guidelines. Impact on depression in primary care. *JAMA.* 1995;273(13):1026-1031.

35. Katon, WJ, Lin EH, Von Korff M, et al. Collaborative care for patients with depression and chronic illnesses. *N Engl J Med.* 2010;363:2611-2620. doi: 10.1056/NEJMoa1003955

36. Raney LE. Integrating primary care and behavioral health: the role of the psychiatrist in the collaborative care model. *Am J Psychiatry.* 2015;172(8):721-728. doi: 10.1176/appi.ajp.2015.15010017

37. Fortney JC, Pyne JM, Mouden SB, et al. Practice-based versus telemedicine-based collaborative care for depression in rural federally qualified health centers: a pragmatic randomized comparative effectiveness trial. *Am J Psychiatry.* 2013;170(4):414-425. doi: 10.1176/appi.ajp.2012.12050696

38. Collins C, Hewson DL, Munger R, Wade T. *Evolving Models of Behavioral Health Integration in Primary Care.* Millbank Memorial Fund; 2010. Accessed January 19, 2021. http://www.milbank.org/uploads/documents/10430EvolvingCare/10430EvolvingCare.html

39. Butler M, Kane RL, McAlpine D, et al. Integration of mental health/substance abuse and primary care. *Evid Rep Technol Assess.* 2008;(173):1-362.

40. Goodell S. Health policy brief: mental health parity. *Health Affairs.* Published April 3, 2014. Accessed August 18, 2021. http://www.healthaffairs.org/healthpolicybriefs/brief.php?brief_id=112

41. Centers for Medicare & Medicaid Services. Mental Health Parity and Addiction Equity Act (MHPAEA). Accessed January 14, 2021. https://www.cms.gov/CCIIO/Programs-and-Initiatives/Other-Insurance-Protections/MHPAEA

42. Mental Health America. Issue brief: parity. Accessed January 4, 2021. https://www.mhanational.org/issues/issue-brief-parity

43. U.S. Department of Labor. Mental Health Parity and Addiction Equity Act (MHPAEA) FAQs. Accessed January 24, 2021. https://www.dol.gov/agencies/ebsa/about-ebsa/our-activities/resource-center/faqs/mhpaea-1

44. Mechanic D, Bilder S. Treatment of people with mental illness: a decade-long perspective. *Health Aff.* 2004;23(4):84-95. doi: 10.1377/hlthaff.23.4.84

45. Dixon K. Implementing mental health parity: the challenge for health plans. *Health Aff.* 2009;28:663-665. doi: 10.1377/hlthaff.28.3.663

46. U.S. Department of Veterans Affairs. Veterans Health Administration. Updated April 23, 2021. Accessed May 9, 2021. https://www.va.gov/health/aboutvha.asp#:~:text=The%20Veterans%20Health%20Administration%20(VHA,Veterans%20enrolled%20in%20the%20VA

47. U.S. Department of Veterans Affairs. Mental health. Accessed June 1, 2021. https://www.mentalhealth.va.gov/

CHAPTER 10

Public and Population Health

LEARNING OBJECTIVES

After reading this chapter you should be able to:

- Describe public health from a population health perspective.
- Discuss the systems perspective in public health.
- Describe the core functions of public health.
- Identify the essential services of public health.
- Discuss public health management.
- Identify the core competencies of public health professionals.
- Describe Public Health 3.0.
- Discuss the national health objectives from Healthy People 2030.
- Discuss social determinants of health in the context of the national health agenda.
- Describe the multidisciplinary nature of the public health workforce.

KEY TERMS

American Public Health Association (APHA)
Core functions of public health
Council of Education for Public Health

Essential public health services
Healthy People 2030
National Academies of Medicine
Population health
Public Health 3.0

Social determinants of health
Surgeon General
Systems perspective in public health
U.S. Public Health Service

As described by Johnson and Davey in *Essentials of Managing Public Health Organizations*, public health continues to answer the call to promote the health, safety, and well-being of individuals and communities in the United States and around the world.[1] The 21st century is an exciting yet challenging time, a period of both pandemic and promise. Advances in science, technology, policy, and medicine have contributed to progress in all regions of the world.[2] Such advances hold incredible promise for improving health and well-being in the future. This century has also been a perilous time due to radical and disruptive changes in every facet of the physical and social world—including the political, economic, cultural, technological, ecological, and legal. These global and national forces are interacting, producing complex interdependent systems at all levels, from local communities to governments to international organizations. There is now, perhaps more than ever, a need for smart organization and effective management in public health. Coordination of effort though leadership and systems thinking to accomplish goals and meet these challenges necessitate specialized knowledge, skills, and abilities, as well as compassion and care.

▶ Public Health as Population Health

As described in the 4th edition of Shi and Johnson's *Public Health Administration: Principles for Population-Based Management*, "Public health consists of organized efforts to improve the health of populations. The operative components of this definition are that public health efforts are directed to populations rather than to individuals. Public health practice does not rely on a specific body of knowledge and expertise, but rather relies on a dynamic, multidisciplinary approach that often combines the biological, medical, behavioral, and social sciences. By extension, this must also include management as a body of knowledge and practice based on social and behavioral sciences. This definition of public health reflects its central goal, the reduction of disease and the improvement of health in a population."[3] Thus, the fundamental mission of public health, both historically and currently, is to ensure the necessary conditions that promote the health of populations. To further elaborate, Richard Riegelman, founding dean of the School of Public Health and Health Services at George Washington University, states:

> Public health is about what makes us sick, what keeps us healthy, and what we can do TOGETHER about it. When we think about health, what comes to mind first is individual health and wellness. In public health, what should come to mind first is the health

of communities and society as a whole. Thus, in public health the focus shifts from the individual to the population, from me to us.[3]

Shi and Johnson further describe these population-based strategies to improve health, which include, but are not limited to, efforts to control epidemics, ensure safe drinking water and food, reduce vaccine-preventable diseases, improve maternal and child health, and conduct surveillance of health problems. In addition to long-standing efforts to protect populations from infectious disease and environmental health hazards, the public health mission continues to expand to address contemporary health risks such as opioids, tobacco use, obesity, physical inactivity, gun violence, substance abuse, sexually transmitted infections, natural disasters, and bioterrorism. To effectively address both current and emerging health concerns, public health approaches involve multilevel systemic interventions that address the individual, the community, and public policy. The importance of public health and population-based interventions is underscored by achievements in the 20th century, during which the life expectancy for individuals living in developed countries increased from 45 to 75 years. In the 21st century, we have seen this increase to 78 years in the United States and 82 years in Japan.[2] The majority of this gain can be attributed to public health measures such as better nutrition, clean drinking water, and improved air quality, sanitation, and road safety. Both scientific and social factors form the basis for an effective public health intervention. For example, successfully eradicating a vaccine-preventable disease such as measles, or perhaps COVID-19, requires more than the development of an effective vaccine. Acceptance and widespread use of the vaccine in the community depends on a successful public health initiative providing public information and facilitating easy access and safe delivery of the vaccine. Policies in other domains, such as education (schools and universities), to support the initiative further increase the likelihood of success. Unfortunately, many scientific advances are not fully translated into improved health outcomes. For example, in the United States, there is an opioid abuse epidemic.[4] While medical science has developed medications to help mitigate opioid misuse and reverse overdose to prevent death, there are many social, behavioral, and cultural factors that must also be addressed. As described by Haley, Johnson, and Frazier in *Opioids and Population Health: A Primer*, a public health approach must be comprehensive and population based, involving social determinants, epidemiology, harm reduction strategies, community education, and public policy changes when needed.[4] As we see this epidemic continue, it will act increasingly as a syndemic, co-occurring with other public health challenges such as HIV/AIDS and COVID-19. This represents an increase in complexity that necessitates a comprehensive, evidence-informed population health approach that is multisectoral. One instructive way to visualize the scope of population health is provided in **FIGURE 10-1**, which shows the interconnections between care management, quality and safety, health policy, and public health.[5]

▶ Public Health Functions

The Institute of Medicine (IOM) report, *The Future of Public Health*, defined three core functions that public health agencies should be performing.[6] While population health necessarily engages the full spectrum of stakeholders, it is the federal, state, and local public health agencies that are primarily responsible for accomplishing the essential health services. While there is work that may be contracted out to other sectors, both for-profit and not-for-profit, fundamental responsibility remains with the government public health agencies.

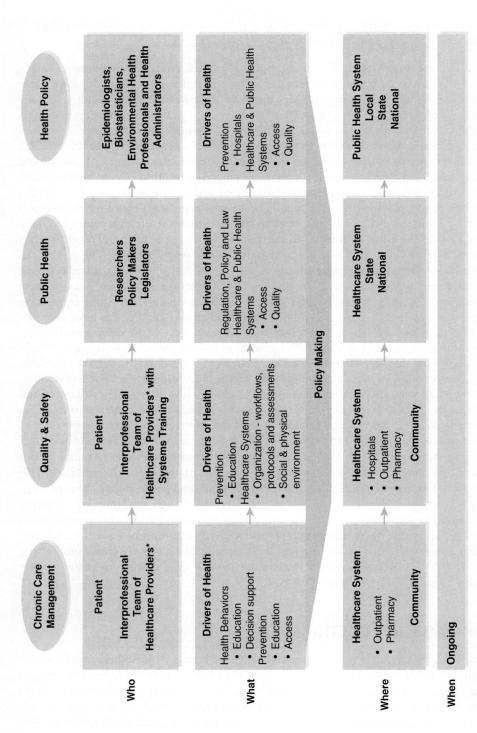

FIGURE 10-1 Pillars of Population Health

Nash DB, Skoufalos A, Fabius RJ, Oglesby WH. *Population Health: Creating a Culture of Wellness*. 2nd ed. Jones & Bartlett Learning; 2016.

* An interprofessional team of healthcare providers includes both clinical (physicians, nurses, pharmacists, allied health professionals, dentists, radiologists) and nonclinical (healthcare administrators, quality, safety, and public health professionals) professionals.

These three core functions are defined as follows[1]:

- Assessment: involves obtaining data to define the health of populations and the nature of health problems
- Assurance: includes the oversight responsibility for ensuring that essential components of an effective health system are in place
- Policy development: includes developing evidence-based recommendations and analysis to guide public policy as it pertains to health

Building on the IOM recommendations, the U.S. Public Health Service (USPHS) and the American Public Health Association (APHA) advocate for a consistent and unified approach to public health. This is reflected in the widely accepted "10 Essential Services" presented in **TABLE 10-1**. A hub-and-spoke chart, shown in **FIGURE 10-2**, can help one better visualize how the core functions and essential services for public health fit together.[1] This framework is used by local, state, and federal agencies throughout the country and has been adapted for other countries as well. On a practical level, it serves as a guide and framework for public health organization design and development, workforce planning and staffing, strategic management, resource allocation, information systems design, and personnel training and development.

TABLE 10-1 Essential Public Health Services
1. **Monitor** health status to identify community health problems.
2. **Diagnose and investigate** health problems and health hazards in the community.
3. **Inform, educate, and empower** people about health issues.
4. **Mobilize** community partnerships to identify and solve health problems.
5. **Develop policies and plans** that support individual and community health efforts.
6. **Enforce** laws and regulations that protect health and ensure safety.
7. **Link** people to the needed personal health services and assure the provision of health care, when otherwise unavailable.
8. **Assure** a competent public health and personal healthcare workforce.
9. **Evaluate** effectiveness, accessibility, and quality of personal and population-based health services.
10. **Research** new insights and innovative solutions to health problems.

Data from Centers for Disease Control and Prevention. 10 essential public health services. Updated March 18, 2021. Accessed September 10, 2021. https://www.cdc.gov/publichealthgateway/publichealthservices/essentialhealthservices.html

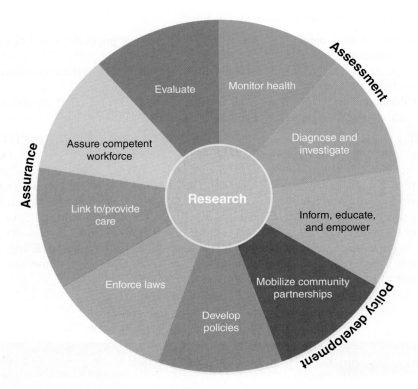

FIGURE 10-2 Core Functions and Essential Public Health Services

Centers for Disease Control and Prevention. 10 essential public health services. Updated March 18, 2021. Accessed September 10, 2021. https://www.cdc.gov/publichealthgateway/publichealthservices
/essentialhealthservices.html

▶ Systems Perspective in Public Health

Today, most would agree that public health and the management of public health services and organizations are best understood from a systems perspective.[1,3,7] As described by health systems scholar James Johnson, "Public health is highly interconnected and interdependent in its relationship to individuals, communities, and the larger society, including the global community. Using the language of systems theory, public health is a complex adaptive system. It is complex in that it is composed of multiple, diverse, interconnected elements, and it is adaptive in that the system is capable of changing and learning from experience and its environment."[7] Shown in **FIGURE 10-3**, the Centers for Disease Control and Prevention (CDC) provides an illustration that demonstrates some of the many interconnections that are commonly linked to a public health agency.[1]

In *Health Systems Thinking: A Primer*, Johnson further explains that the systems approach in public health is more than the relationships that support and facilitate the organization and actions of public health, but also "the mindset of public health professionals" that is salient in public health management, practice, and research.[7] It is also useful to have a systems perspective when looking at the causes of public health problems and challenges. Much of this can be attributed to deficits and poor quality in the social areas of a society. These are referred to as social determinants of health, some of which are shown in **FIGURE 10-4**.[1] While not an

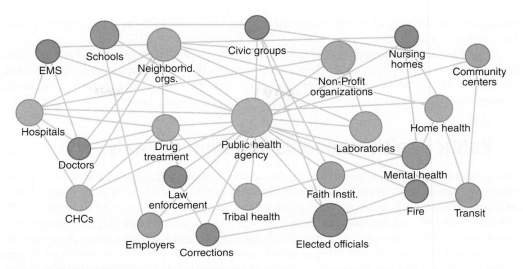

FIGURE 10-3 Public Health Agency Interconnections

Centers for Disease Control and Prevention. The Public Health System and the 10 Essential Public Health Services. Accessed February 5, 2021. https://www.cdc.gov/publichealthgateway/publichealthservices/essentialhealthservices.html

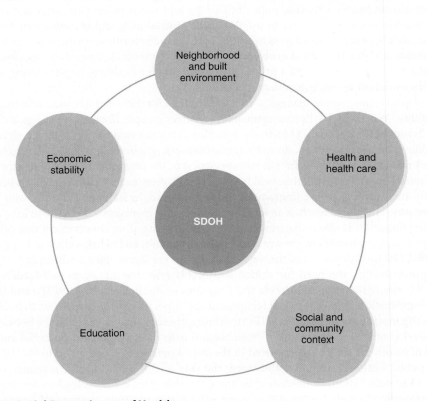

FIGURE 10-4 Social Determinants of Health

DeSalvo KB, Wang YC, Harris A, Auerbach J, Koo D, O'Carroll P. Public health 3.0: a call to action for public health to meet the challenges of the 21st century. *Prev Chronic Dis.* 2017;14:170017. doi: 10.5888/pcd14.170017

exhaustive list, these do show the interconnections that contribute to the larger system of public health in a society.

These social determinants of health can also be used to design programs and address challenges before they happen, making them instrumental in the prevention mandate of public and population health. Social epidemiology is a useful discipline, and applications in community assessment can also be employed to address or preempt many health issues.[1]

▶ Public Health Managers and Professionals

Public health managers and leaders are needed to help their organizations, agencies, and departments navigate complex systems and constantly evolving culture and subcultures to enact change and influence health. Within the public health context, escalating costs, provider shortages, health disparities, obesity and diet-related diseases, the opioid epidemic, climate change, resurgence of infectious diseases, demographic shifts, shrinking budgets, and numerous other challenges are threatening the health and well-being of individuals and communities. These challenges require public health professionals who possess strong management knowledge, skills, and abilities. Public health professionals must be able to manage an evolving and expanding number of public health priorities, programs, professionals, organizations, interorganizational and multisector collaborations, population health activities, policy initiatives, and much more. Countries and communities around the world are looking to public health professionals and organizations for answers and innovative approaches to address health disparities and priorities. Furthermore, public health organizations and practices must evolve to redefine and reinvent themselves in response to environmental forces. Managers have a primary responsibility for enabling, implementing, and overseeing this evolution in public health organizations.

All organizations require managers, who are essential for their maintenance, effectiveness, and sustainability.[8] Whether it be the management of resources (people, finances, buildings, technology), strategy (vision, mission, goals, objectives), behavior dynamics (motivation, conflict, change, decision making), or values (fairness, diversity, responsiveness, accountability, social responsibility), the manager's role and effectiveness in that role are central to the organization's ability to exist and perform its mission and purpose. Public health managers are often leaders within their own professions, and many are leaders in their communities and in the world. In fact, public health, with its public service mission and global reach, is an ideal environment for managers who desire to have a positive and lasting impact. It is also a changing and sometimes demanding environment that offers many challenges and opportunities to grow professionally, personally, and to help others in large and small ways. **TABLE 10-2** identifies some of the ways public health managers make a difference.[1]

In public health, the need for skilled and highly effective managers and leaders is great. The APHA, the Association of Schools and Programs of Public Health (ASPPH), and the World Health Organization (WHO) have all recognized the importance of management in public health systems, organizations, and programs. Furthermore, these groups have called for better management, development, and leadership if public health is to meet its greatest potential and achieve the goal of health for all. This is captured in the WHO perspective, presented in **EXHIBIT 10-1**.

As public health continues to advance, the role of the public health manager will likely expand. One such vision, as described by the CDC, has public health leaders serving as chief health strategists in their communities, partnering across multiple sectors and leveraging data and resources to address social, environmental, and economic conditions that affect health and health equity.[9]

TABLE 10-2 Public Health Practice Profile for Public Health Managers

Public Health Administrators Make a Difference in the Following Ways:

Public Health Purposes
- ✓ Preventing epidemics and the spread of disease
- ✓ Protecting against environmental hazards
- ✓ Preventing injuries
- ✓ Promoting and encouraging healthy behaviors
- ✓ Responding to disasters and assisting communities in recovery
- ✓ Ensuring the quality and accessibility of health services

Essential Public Health Services
- ✓ Monitoring health status to identify community health problems
- ✓ Diagnosing and investigating health problems and health hazards in the community
- ✓ Informing, educating, and empowering people about health issues
- ✓ Mobilizing community partnerships to identify and solve health problems
- ✓ Developing policies and plans that support individual and community health efforts
- ✓ Enforcing laws and regulations that protect health and ensure safety
- ✓ Linking people with needed personal health services and ensuring the provision of health care, when otherwise unavailable
- ✓ Ensuring a competent public health and personal healthcare workforce
- ✓ Evaluating the effectiveness, the accessibility, and the quality of personal and population-based health services
- ✓ Researching new insights and innovative solutions to health problems

Johnson JA, Davey KS. *Essentials of Managing Public Health Organizations*. Jones & Bartlett Learning; 2019.

EXHIBIT 10-1 World Health Organization Perspective on Public Health Management

Effective leadership and management are essential to scaling up the quantity and quality of health services and to Improving population health.

Good leadership and management are about:

- providing direction to, and gaining commitment from, partners and staff;
- facilitating change; and
- achieving better health services through efficient, creative, and responsible deployment of people and other resources.

Strengthening leadership and management requires the fulfillment of four main conditions: adequate numbers of managers deployed, managers with appropriate competencies, functioning management support systems, and a work environment that expects, supports, and rewards good management performance.

While leaders set the strategic vision and mobilize the efforts toward its realization, good managers ensure effective organization and utilization of resources to achieve results and meet the aims.

(continues)

> ## EXHIBIT 10-1 World Health Organization Perspective on Public Health Management *(continued)*
>
> The WHO management framework proposes that good leadership and management at the operational level need to have a balance between four areas:
>
> 1. ensuring an adequate number of managers at all levels of the health system;
> 2. ensuring managers have appropriate competences;
> 3. creating better critical management support systems; and
> 4. creating and enabling the working environment.
>
> The WHO is a strident advocate of systems thinking. These four conditions are closely interrelated. Strengthening one without the others is not likely to work.
>
> Data from DeSalvo KB, Wang YC, Harris A, Auerbach J, Koo D, O'Carroll P. Public health 3.0: a call to action for public health to meet the challenges of the 21st century. *Prev Chronic Dis*. 2017;14:170017. doi: 10.5888/pcd14.170017

Core Competencies for Public Health Managers

The Council on Education for Public Health (CEPH) is the accrediting body for public health. This body oversees the criteria and process for accrediting schools and programs of public health in the United States. The overarching goal of this organization is to prepare students equipped with the requisite knowledge, skills, and abilities to enter the public health workforce at all levels.[10] In 2016, CEPH updated the accreditation criteria for public health schools and programs, revising core competencies to reflect a renewed emphasis on management and leadership as important elements of public health education and practice.[10] We are seeing public health curricula moving toward content and concepts traditionally addressed in healthcare management and administration programs. Likewise, healthcare management and administrative programs are incorporating content and concepts traditionally addressed in public health.[8] Furthermore, to advance professionalism in management and leadership for public health, ASPPH identifies core competencies that can be used in curricular design.[11] These are organized in **TABLES 10-3** and **10-4**.

> ## TABLE 10-3 Management Competencies: Health Policy and Management
>
> ### D. Health Policy and Management*
>
> Health policy and management represent a multidisciplinary field of inquiry and practice concerned with the delivery, quality, and costs of health care for individuals and populations. This definition assumes both a managerial and a policy concern with the structure, process, and outcomes of health services, including the costs, financing, organization, outcomes, and accessibility of care.
>
> *Competencies:* Upon graduation, a student with a Master of Public Health (MPH) should be able to:
>
> D.1 Identify the main components and issues of the organization, financing, and delivery of health services and public health systems in the United States.

D.2 Describe the legal and ethical bases for public health and health services.

D.3 Explain the methods for ensuring community health safety and preparedness.

D.4 Discuss the policy process for improving the health status of populations.

D.5 Apply the principles of program planning, development, budgeting, management, and evaluation in organizational and community initiatives.

D.6 Apply the principles of **strategic planning** and marketing to public health.

D.7 Apply quality and performance improvement concepts to address organizational performance issues.

D.8 Apply "systems thinking" for resolving organizational problems.

D.9 Communicate health policy and management issues using appropriate channels and technologies.

D.10 Demonstrate leadership skills for building partnerships.

*In this series, *health policy* is treated as a separate text and area of inquiry. As such, this text addresses only the health management competencies. Reproduced with permission from Health Policy and Management, MPH Core Competency Model, Association of Schools and Programs of Public Health.

TABLE 10-4 Management Competencies: Leadership

H. Leadership

The ability to create and communicate a shared vision for a changing future, champion the solutions to organizational and community challenges, and energize a commitment to achieve these goals.

Competencies: Upon graduation, it is increasingly important that a student with an MPH be able to:

H.1 Describe the attributes of leadership in public health.

H.2 Describe alternative strategies for collaboration and partnership among organizations, focused on public health goals.

H.3 Articulate an achievable mission, a set of core values, and a vision.

H.4 Engage in dialogue and learn from others to advance public health goals.

H.5 Demonstrate team building, negotiation, and conflict management skills.

H.6 Demonstrate transparency, integrity, and honesty in all actions.

(continues)

TABLE 10-4 Management Competencies: Leadership	*(continued)*
H. Leadership	
H.7 Use collaborative methods for achieving organizational and community health goals.	
H.8 Apply social justice and human rights principles when addressing community needs.	
H.9 Develop strategies for motivating others for collaborative problem solving, decision-making, and evaluation.	

Reproduced with permission from Leadership, MPH Core Competency Model, Association of Schools and Programs of Public Health.

▶ Emerging Scope of Public Health

The National Academy of Medicine and the U.S. Department of Health and Human Services (HHS) promote an initiative called Public Health 3.0.[9] The third-generation model reflects the promise and perils of 21st century public health in the United States.[1] Public Health 3.0, as profiled in **FIGURE 10-5**, is a model and path forward for the field of public health. The model calls on public health to redefine and reinvent itself for the future. The model focuses on the social determinants of health and the need for public health professionals and organizations to engage a broad range of community, industry, education, business, government, and other stakeholders to develop new models to make strategic investments in public health. The overarching goal is to shift the U.S. health system from focusing on sickness and disease to wellness and prevention.[9] The model was developed for the United States; however, it can be adapted and applied to other health systems around the world.[2]

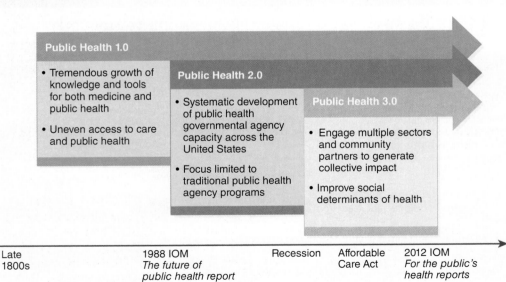

FIGURE 10-5 Public Health 3.0

Hinton et al. (2020, October 29). 10 Things to Know about Medicaid Managed Care. Retrieved from https://www.kff.org/medicaid/issue-brief/10-things-to-know-about-medicaid-managed-care/

Public health has evolved to reinvent and redefine itself with each iteration of the model. The Public Health 1.0 model marked the birth and infancy of public health in the United States. The focus of public health was sanitation, safety, disease surveillance, and the discovery of prevention and treatment methods. As mentioned earlier, the IOM report, *The Future of Public Health,* served as an important inflection point for public health in the United States. The report became a call to action and asked public health to consider what its role was in the face of a number of pressing health challenges.[3] In response, Public Health 2.0 marked the evolution of public health to a mature, refined, focused, and formalized system. Core functions and essential health services emerged from this period and provided considerable clarity to the role of public health.[1,3] Today, public health, especially in the wake of the COVID-19 pandemic, is yet again at another important inflection point.

The vision of Public Health 3.0 is on improving population health by addressing upstream and social factors that influence health, such as working conditions, education, income and economic conditions, neighborhood conditions, and healthcare access. The model stresses local communities and collaboration across sectors to enhance the contexts in which individuals live, learn, work, and play. The model's emphasis is consistent with the population health focus and priorities in HHS's Healthy People 2030 initiative.[12] Both the model and national health priorities emphasize the importance of local health departments in leading and managing initiatives and cross-sector collaboration to address the determinants of health and advance health and well-being. The Public Health 3.0 model recommends[9]:

1. Ensuring a strong public health workforce
2. Strategic, cross-sector partnerships
3. Expanded, flexible, and multisource funding
4. Timely and continuous data, metrics, and analytics to guide public health initiatives at all levels, especially at the sub-county or community level
5. A solid public health infrastructure

The recommendations speak to the essential roles and functions of public health and population health. Though Public Health 4.0 does not currently exist in any formal way, it is only natural for students of public health to wonder, "What's next?" When asked this very question, Jonathan Samet, Dean of the University of Colorado School of Public Health, replied that he sees Public Health 4.0 "resting on 'two pedestals,' the first being the need to gather more and more data from increasingly sophisticated technology and figure out 'the useful signals from that data.' Second, 'We need to have extended interactions with communities in new ways, some of them data-driven. I think we will see that the public health community will recognize that a lot of the things we do are going to require greater engagement with communities.'"[13]

This perspective is consistent with the direction of public health as it continues to evolve in the 21st century while meeting the nation's health objectives in the coming decades.

National Health Objectives: *Healthy People 2020 and Healthy People 2030*

Since 1980, HHS, in collaboration with community partners, has developed 10-year plans that outline key national health and health-related objectives to be accomplished during each decade.

To be more comprehensive by looking at social and health systems as a whole, Healthy People 2020 was differentiated from previous Healthy People initiatives by including multiple new areas in its objective list, such as adolescent health, blood disorders, and blood safety; dementias; genomics; global health; healthcare-associated infections; quality of life and well-being; lesbian, gay, bisexual, and transgender health; older adults; preparedness; sleep health; and social determinants of health. This expansion of foci is demonstrated in **TABLE 10-5.**

TABLE 10-5 *Healthy People 2020* Focus Areas

1.	Access to Health Services	22.	Oral Health
2.	HIV	23.	Environmental Health
3.	Adolescent Health	24.	Physical Activity
4.	Immunization and Infectious Diseases	25.	Family Planning
5.	Arthritis, Osteoporosis, and Chronic Back Conditions	26.	Preparedness
6.	Injury and Violence Prevention	27.	Food Safety
7.	Blood Disorders and Blood Safety	28.	Public Health Infrastructure
8.	Lesbian, Gay, Bisexual, and Transgender Health	29.	Genomics
9.	Cancer	30.	Respiratory Diseases
10.	Maternal, Infant, and Child Health	31.	Global Health
11.	Chronic Kidney Disease	32.	Sexually Transmitted Diseases
12.	Medical Product Safety	33.	Health Communication and Health Information Technology
13.	Dementias, Including Alzheimer's Disease	34.	Sleep Health
14.	Mental Health and Mental Disorders	35.	Health-Related Quality of Life and Well-Being
15.	Diabetes	36.	Social Determinants of Health
16.	Nutrition and Weight Status	37.	Healthcare-Associated Infections
17.	Disability and Health	38.	Substance Abuse
18.	Occupational Safety and Health	39.	Hearing and Other Sensory or Communication Disorders
19.	Early and Middle Childhood	40.	Tobacco Use
20.	Older Adults	41.	Heart Disease and Stroke
21.	Educational and Community-Based Programs	42.	Vision

U.S. Department of Health and Human Services (2016). 2020 Topics and Objectives - Objectives. Available at https://www.healthypeople.gov/2020/topics-objectives

The next 10-year period of national health planning is being addressed in Healthy People 2030 as outlined in it mission and goals presented in **EXHIBIT 10-2**. Although much progress has been made since the Healthy People initiatives began, the United States is still behind other developed nations on key measures of health and well-being, including life expectancy, infant mortality, and obesity. A challenge for Healthy People 2030 is to guide the country in achieving its full potential for health and well-being.

EXHIBIT 10-2 Overview of Healthy People 2030

Vision

A society in which all people can achieve their full potential for health and well-being across the lifespan.

Mission

To promote, strengthen, and evaluate the nation's efforts to improve the health and well-being of all people.

Foundational Principles

Foundational principles explain the thinking that guides decisions about Healthy People 2030.

- Health and well-being of all people and communities are essential to a thriving, equitable society.
- Promoting health and well-being and preventing disease are linked efforts that encompass physical, mental, and social health dimensions.
- Investing to achieve the full potential for health and well-being for all provides valuable benefits to society.
- Achieving health and well-being requires eliminating health disparities, achieving health equity, and attaining health literacy.
- Healthy physical, social, and economic environments strengthen the potential to achieve health and well-being.
- Promoting and achieving the nation's health and well-being is a shared responsibility that is distributed across the national, state, tribal, and community levels, including the public, private, and not-for-profit sectors.
- Working to attain the full potential for health and well-being of the population is a component of decision-making and policy formulation across all sectors.

Overarching Goals

- Attain healthy, thriving lives and well-being, free of preventable disease, disability, injury, and premature death.
- Eliminate health disparities, achieve health equity, and attain health literacy to improve the health and well-being of all.
- Create social, physical, and economic environments that promote attaining the full potential for health and well-being for all.
- Promote healthy development, healthy behaviors, and well-being across all life stages.
- Engage leadership, key constituents, and the public across multiple sectors to take action and design policies that improve the health and well-being of all.

(continues)

EXHIBIT 10-2 Overview of Healthy People 2030 *(continued)*

Plan of Action

- Set national goals and measurable objectives to guide evidence-based policies, programs, and other actions to improve health and well-being.
- Provide data that are accurate, timely, accessible, and can drive targeted actions to address regions and populations with poor health or at high risk for poor health in the future.
- Foster impact through public and private efforts to improve health and well-being for people of all ages and the communities in which they live.
- Provide tools for the public, programs, policymakers, and others to evaluate progress toward improving health and well-being.
- Share and support the implementation of evidence-based programs and policies that are replicable, scalable, and sustainable.
- Report biennially on progress throughout the decade from 2020 to 2030.
- Stimulate research and innovation toward meeting Healthy People 2030 goals and highlight critical research, data, and evaluation needs.
- Facilitate development and availability of affordable means of health promotion, disease prevention, and treatment.

Johnson JA, Davey K. Managing Public Health Organizations. Burlington, MA: Jones and Bartlett. 2020.

As shown in **FIGURE 10-6**, an action model was developed by HHS to assist public health managers and leaders in accomplishing these important national health goals.[1]

From the preliminary work on Healthy People 2030, we can anticipate even further evolution of systems thinking as well as innovation for the development and achievement of the next decade of national health goals and objectives.[1]

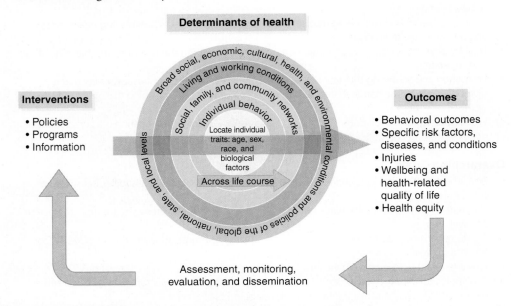

FIGURE 10-6 Action Model to Achieve Overarching National Health Goals

U.S. Department of Health and Human Services.

In order to accomplish these goals and objectives, public health managers and professionals at all levels will be needed for a wide range of roles and occupations. The workforce will necessarily expand and change as new health challenges continue to emerge.

▶ Public Health Organizations

For students studying public health and related fields, there will continue to be many opportunities for employment and career advancement. Some of these will be in managerial and administrative roles while others will be technical or clinical in nature. As stated by Bernard J Turnock in the 3rd edition of *Essentials of Public Health*, "From a functional perspective, it is the individuals involved in carrying out the core functions and essential services of public health who constitute the public health workforce."[14]

Turnock clarifies the multidisciplinary nature of the public health workforce by stating, "There has never been any specific academic degree or unique set of experiences that distinguish public health's workers from those of other fields."[14] As he explains, many public health workers have a primary professional discipline in addition to their role in a public health organization.[15] There are accountants, economists, social workers, biostatisticians, physicians, nurses, lawyers, epidemiologists, urban planners, anthropologists, educators, nutritionists, data analysts, engineers, psychologists, dentists, policy analysts, and many other professionals and support staff carrying out the work of public health. Most of these occupations and professions are identified in **TABLE 10-6**.[1] While this is not an exhaustive list, it does demonstrate range and professional diversity that is perhaps unique to public health.

This work is done in agencies and organizations throughout the country and the world, especially because public health is now in many ways "global health."[2] Furthermore, Turnock sees a challenge and a benefit in this diversification, as he states, "This multidisciplinary workforce, with somewhat divided loyalties to multiple professions, blurs the distinctiveness of public health as a unified profession. At the same time, however, it facilitates the interdisciplinary approaches to community problem identification and problem solving, which are hallmarks of modern public health practice."[14]

The organizations involved in and responsible for public health in the United States are numerous. While not all organizations involved in public health are public agencies, most are. This chapter focuses primarily on the governmental public health infrastructure at the federal, state, territorial, and local levels. However, to illustrate some of the complexity of this infrastructure, a systems and population health perspective are once again helpful. As shown in **FIGURE 10-7**, the public health system is multisectoral with influences, interactions, and partnerships from business, media, education, communities, healthcare delivery, and other public agencies.[1]

There are additional contextual, political, and cultural aspects that should be understood as the backdrop or foundation of the public sector's dominance in public health. Shi and Johnson discuss this as follows.[3] The organization of governmental public health activities in the United States flows directly from the limited federalist system of government based on national, state, and local levels of authority. States occupy pivotal positions within this system because they maintain governmental authority that is not expressly reserved for the federal government. States may choose to exercise this authority directly or delegate it to local agencies and boards in accordance with state constitutional and legislative provisions. In the domain of public health, the federal government is able to exercise authority primarily through its constitutional powers to tax, spend, and regulate. By comparison, state government agencies typically play even larger

TABLE 10-6 Sample of Public Health Occupations and Careers

Career Category with Examples of Titles Used in Public Health Organizations	Bureau of Labor Statistics' Standard Occupational Categories Related to Public Health
Public Health Administration ■ Health Services Manager ■ Public Health Agency Director Health Officer ■ Emergency Preparedness and Response Director	Professional Occupations ■ Emergency Management Directors ■ Medical and Health Services Managers ■ Social and Community Services Managers
Environmental and Occupational Health ■ Environmental Engineer ■ Environmental Health Specialist (entry level) ■ Environmental Health Specialist (midlevel) ■ Environmental Health Specialist (senior level) ■ Occupational Health and Safety Specialist	Professional Occupations ■ Environmental Engineers ■ Environmental Scientists and Specialists (including Health) ■ Health and Safety Engineers (except Mining Safety Engineers and Inspectors) ■ Occupational Health and Safety Specialists Technical Occupations ■ Environmental Engineering ■ Technicians ■ Environmental Science and Protection Technicians (including Health) ■ Occupational Health and Safety Technicians
Public Health Nursing ■ Public Health Nurse (entry level) ■ Public Health Nurse (senior level) ■ Licensed Practical/Vocational Nurse	Professional Occupations ■ Nurse Practitioners ■ Registered Nurses Technical Occupations ■ Home Health Aides ■ Licensed Practical and Licensed Vocational Nurses ■ Nursing Assistants
Epidemiology and Disease Control ■ Disease Investigator ■ Epidemiologist (entry level) ■ Epidemiologist (senior level)	Professional Occupations ■ Epidemiologists ■ Statisticians
Public Health Education and Information ■ Public Health Educator (entry level) ■ Public Health Educator (senior level) ■ Public Information Officer ■ Community Health Workers (and other Outreach Occupations)	Professional Occupations ■ Health Educators ■ **Public Relations** Specialists ■ Technical Occupations ■ Community Health Workers

Other Public Health Professional and Technical Personnel

- Public Health Nutritionist/Dietician
- Public Health Social, Behavioral, and Mental Health Worker
- Public Health Laboratory Worker
- Public Health Physician
- Public Health Veterinarian
- Public Health Pharmacist
- Public Health Oral Health Professional
- Administrative Law Judge/Hearing Officer
- Public Health Program Specialist/Coordinator
- Public Health Policy Analyst
- Public Health Information Specialist

Professional Occupations

- Audiologists
- Administrative Law Judges, Adjudicators, and Hearing Officers
- Dental Hygienists
- Dentists (General Dentist)
- Dieticians and Nutritionists
- Healthcare Social Workers
- Medical and Clinical Laboratory Technologists
 Mental Health Counselors
- Mental Health and Substance Abuse Social Workers
- Microbiologists
- Optometrists
- Pharmacists
- Physician Assistants
- Physicians (Family or General Practitioners)
- Substance Abuse and Behavioral Disorder Counselors
- Veterinarians

Technical Occupations

- Animal Control Workers
- Emergency Medical Technicians and Paramedics
- Medical and Clinical Laboratory Technicians

Turnock BJ. Public Health: What it is and how it Works, MA: Jones & Bartlett Learning; 2016.

FIGURE 10-7 Population Health System

roles in public health regulatory activities while also carrying out substantial responsibilities in public health program administration and resource allocation. States often delegate the primary responsibilities for implementing public health programs within communities to local government agencies. States vary considerably in the range of public health activities that they delegate to local governmental control. Federal agencies play an important role in the public health space because of their ability to formulate and implement a national health policy agenda, as seen with the Healthy People initiatives. Furthermore, they are able to allocate health resources across broad public priorities. Both executive agencies and legislative institutions engage in federal health policy and resource allocation activities. As part of the policy development and administration process, many federal health agencies provide information and technical assistance to state and local agencies as well as nongovernmental organizations. In some cases, federal agencies also engage directly in implementing public health activities within specific communities or populations. Examples of these were previously provided and described in Chapter 3. For example, HHS is the primary public health and social service agency of the United States.[15] The current organizational chart, as shown in **FIGURE 10-8**, demonstrates the incredible range of agencies and programs within HHS.[2]

Many of these agencies comprise the functional units of HHS known as the U.S. Public Health Service (USPHS). A description of this cluster of agencies is provided in **TABLE 10-7**.

One of the most influential positions in USPHS is the Surgeon General. This individual is appointed by the president and serves to help frame and promote the national health agenda. For example, the Surgeon General is currently leading efforts to mitigate the opioid epidemic and the large number of unnecessary deaths due to opioid misuse. A description of the Surgeon General's role is provided in **EXHIBIT 10-3**.

In 2018 HHS initiated its Strategic Plan, which runs through 2022. This plan describes the Department's efforts within the context of five broad Strategic Goals[15]:

- Strategic Goal 1: Reform, Strengthen, and Modernize the Nation's Healthcare System
- Strategic Goal 2: Protect the Health of Americans Where They Live, Learn, Work, and Play
- Strategic Goal 3: Strengthen the Economic and Social Well-Being of Americans Across the Lifespan
- Strategic Goal 4: Foster Sound, Sustained Advances in the Sciences
- Strategic Goal 5: Promote Effective and Efficient Management and Stewardship

One of the most high-profile agencies in HHS is the CDC.[16] Located in Atlanta, Georgia, it was founded there in 1946 as the Communicable Disease Center to combat a malaria epidemic in the southern states. Today, the agency has a global presence, with personnel stationed in 40 different countries. The CDC workforce is composed of nearly 200 different occupations, with over half of these workers having advanced degrees, often in public health and related fields. The official mission of the CDC is as follows[16]:

> CDC works 24/7 to protect America from health, safety and security threats, both foreign and in the U.S. Whether diseases start at home or abroad, are chronic or acute, curable or preventable, human error or deliberate attack, CDC fights disease and supports communities and citizens to do the same.
>
> CDC increases the health security of our nation. As the nation's health protection agency, CDC saves lives and protects people from health threats. To accomplish our mission, CDC conducts critical science and provides health information that protects our nation against expensive and dangerous health threats, and responds when these arise.

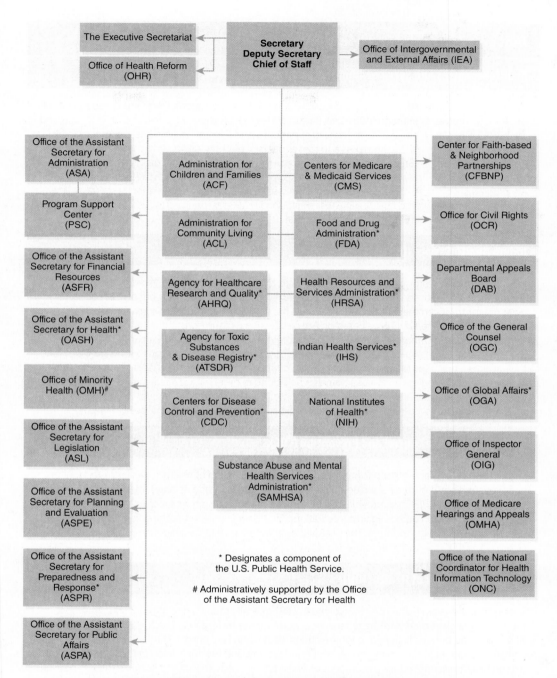

FIGURE 10-8 **U.S. Department of Health and Human Services Organizational Chart**

Courtesy of U.S. Department of Health and Human Services.

TABLE 10-7 U.S. Public Health Service Agencies

Health Resources and Services Administration (HRSA)

HRSA helps provide health resources for medically underserved populations. The main operating units of HRSA are the Bureau of Primary Health Care, Bureau of Health Professions, Maternal and Child Bureau, and the HIV/AIDS Bureau. A nationwide network of community and migrant health centers, augmented by primary care programs for the homeless and the residents of public housing, serve more than 10 million Americans each year. HRSA also works to build the healthcare workforce, and it maintains the National Health Service Corps. The agency provides services to people with AIDS through the Ryan White Care Act programs. It oversees the organ transplantation system and works to decrease infant mortality and improve maternal and child health. HRSA was established in 1982 by bringing together several existing programs. HRSA has nearly 2000 employees, most at its headquarters in Rockville, Maryland.

Indian Health Service (IHS)

IHS is responsible for providing federal health services to American Indians and Alaska Natives. The provision of health services to members of federally recognized tribes grew out of the special government-to-government relationship between the federal government and Indian tribes. This relationship, established in 1787, is based on Article I, Section 8 of the Constitution, and has been given form and substance by numerous treaties, laws, Supreme Court decisions, and Executive Orders. IHS is the principal federal healthcare provider and health advocate for Native Americans, and its goal is to raise their health status to the highest possible level. IHS currently provides health services to approximately 3 million American Indians and Alaska Natives who belong to more than 564 federally recognized tribes in 35 states. IHS was established in 1924; its mission was transferred from the Interior Department in 1955. Agency headquarters are in Rockville, Maryland. IHS has more than 15,000 employees.

Centers for Disease Control and Prevention (CDC)

Working with states and other partners, the CDC provides a system of health surveillance to monitor and prevent disease outbreaks, including bioterrorism events and threats, and it maintains the national health statistics. The CDC also provides for immunization services, supports research on disease and injury prevention, and guards against international disease transmission, with personnel stationed in more than 54 foreign countries. The CDC was established in 1946; its headquarters are in Atlanta, Georgia. The CDC has 11,000 employees.

National Institutes of Health (NIH)

Begun as a one-room Laboratory of Hygiene in 1887, the NIH today is one of the world's foremost medical research centers and the federal focal point for health research. The NIH is the steward of medical and behavioral research for the nation. Its mission is science in pursuit of fundamental knowledge about the nature and behavior of living systems and the application of that knowledge to extend healthy life and reduce the burdens of illness and disability. In realizing its goals, the NIH provides leadership and direction to programs designed to improve the health of the nation by conducting and supporting research in the causes, diagnosis, prevention, and cure of human diseases; in the processes of human growth and development; in the biological effects of environmental contaminants; in the understanding of mental, addictive, and physical disorders; and in the direction of programs for the collection, dissemination, and exchange of information in medicine and health, including the development and support of medical libraries and the training of medical librarians and other health information specialists. Although the majority of NIH resources sponsor external research, there is also a large in-house research program. The NIH includes 27 separate health institutes and centers; its headquarters are in Bethesda, Maryland. The NIH has approximately 19,000 employees.

Food and Drug Administration (FDA)

The FDA ensures that the food we eat is safe and wholesome, that the cosmetics we use will not harm us, and that medicines, medical devices, and radiation-transmitting products, such as microwave ovens, are safe and effective. The FDA also oversees feed and drugs for farm animals and pets. Authorized by Congress to enforce the Federal Food, Drug, and Cosmetic Act and several other public health laws, the agency monitors the manufacture, import, transport, storage, and sale of more than $1 trillion worth of goods annually. The FDA has more than 15,000 employees. Among its staff, the FDA has chemists, microbiologists, and other scientists, as well as investigators and inspectors who visit more than 16,000 facilities a year as part of their oversight of the businesses that FDA regulates. Established in 1906, the FDA has its headquarters in Silver Spring, Maryland.

Substance Abuse and Mental Health Services Administration (SAMHSA)

SAMHSA was established by Congress under Public Law 102-321 on October 1, 1992, to strengthen the nation's healthcare capacity to provide prevention, diagnosis, and treatment services for substance abuse and mental illnesses. SAMHSA works in partnership with states, communities, and private organizations to address the needs of people with substance abuse and mental illnesses, as well as community risk factors that contribute to these illnesses. SAMHSA serves as the umbrella under which substance abuse and mental health service centers are housed, including the Center for Mental Health Services (CMHS), the Center for Substance Abuse Prevention (CSAP), and the Center for Substance Abuse Treatment (CSAT). SAMHSA also houses the Office of the Administrator, the Office of Applied Studies, and the Office of Program Services. SAMHSA's headquarters are in Rockville, Maryland; the agency has about 600 employees.

Agency for Toxic Substances and Disease Registry (ATSDR)

Working with states and other federal agencies, ATSDR seeks to prevent exposure to hazardous substances from waste sites. The agency conducts public health assessments, health studies, surveillance activities, and health education training in communities near waste sites on the U.S. Environmental Protection Agency's National Priorities List. ATSDR also has developed toxicity profiles of hazardous chemicals found at these sites. The agency is closely associated administratively with the CDC; its headquarters are also in Atlanta, Georgia. ATSDR has more than 400 employees.

Agency for Health Care Research and Quality (AHRQ)

AHRQ supports cross-cutting research on healthcare systems, healthcare quality and cost issues, and effectiveness of medical treatments. Formerly known as the Agency for Health Care Policy and Research, AHRQ was established in 1989, assuming broadened responsibilities of its predecessor agency, the National Center for Health Services Research and Health Care Technology Assessment. The agency has about 300 employees; its headquarters are in Rockville, Maryland.

Turnock BJ. Public Health: What it is and how it Works, 6th Ed. MA: Jones & Bartlett Learning; 2016.

EXHIBIT 10-3 Overview of the U.S. Public Health Service

Contributor: Douglas E. Anderson, Col (Ret), USAF, MSC, DHA, MBA, FACHE.

Legacy and Mission

Mission: To protect, promote, and advance the public health and the safety of the nation.

People: 6000+ highly qualified healthcare professionals who are part of the DHHS are led by the U.S. SG.

Services: Largest public health program in the world. The mission is pursued through:

- Rapid and effective response to public health needs and emergencies
- Leadership and excellence in public health practices, advice, and response
- Advancing public health science through research and partnerships

The USPHS SG

- Oversees Public Health Service Commissioned Corps
- Is America's chief health educator on public health topics
- Is responsible for giving the best scientific information on how to improve health and reduce the risk of illness and injury
- Is the leading federal spokesperson on matters of public health
- Reports to the Assistant Secretary for Health, DHHS, and is the principal advisor to the Secretary on public health and scientific issues
- Appointed by the President with the advice and the consent of the U.S. Senate for a 4-year term of office

Health and Healthcare Professions within the USPHS

Physicians	Optometrists
Dentists	Physician assistants
Administrators	Scientists/researchers
Pharmacists	Therapists (including occupational therapy,
Dietitians	physical therapy, speech language pathology,
Engineers	respiratory therapy, and audiology)
Environmental health officers	Veterinarians
Mental health specialists	Other health-related disciplines

USPHS Professionals Work in Most Federal Agencies at Multiple Locations

Disease control and prevention
Biomedical research
Regulation of food and drugs
Mental health care
Substance abuse treatment
Healthcare delivery
International health, and emergency and
humanitarian response

For more information or career opportunities, the USPHS website is https://usphs.gov/

The organizational chart of the agency, presented in **FIGURE 10-9**, demonstrates much of the scope and scale of the CDC's place in public health. Each state and territorial health department has strong relationships with the CDC and helps to form an interdependent system of public health surveillance, monitoring, and education.[17] The CDC readily embraces systems thinking, collaboration, and partnerships to better serve the public.[1,7]

One of the world-class public health agencies that has extraordinary influence in health science, biomedical research, and policy is the National Institutes of Health (NIH), which works with universities and research centers throughout the country to understand the physiological and behavioral causes of disease. The many institutes and centers of NIH are identified in Chapter 12. NIH also houses a Clinical Center to test experimental therapies, and the National Library of Medicine, which serves as a reference library for researchers around the world. It also makes itself accessible by internet to the public.

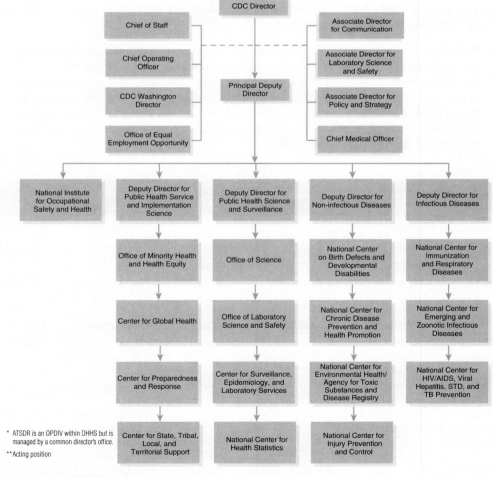

FIGURE 10-9 CDC Organizational Chart

Centers for Disease Control and Prevention, Organizational Chart. Retrieved from https://www.cdc.gov/about/pdf/organization/cdc-org-chart.pdf. Accessed September 12, 2015.

Other Federal Agencies Involved in Public Health

In addition to HHS, there are various federal agencies that work provide their own public health services or have a role in health policy and regulation. These agencies often work in partnership with HHS, but have their own separate missions and responsibilities. These include the Environmental Protection Agency (EPA); the Department of Labor, which houses the Occupational Safety and Health Administration (OSHA); the Department of Agriculture, which does safety inspections and coordinates the Supplemental Nutrition Program for Women, Infants, and Children (WIC); the Department of Homeland Security (DHS); the Department of Veterans Affairs (VA); the Department of Defense (DoD); the Department of Transportation (DOT); and various other agencies and bureaus involved, at least partially, in public health.[1]

In conclusion, given the myriad roles, functions, and benefits of public health and the population health perspective in American society, it may be informative to step back in time and review one of the earliest statements about this very important subject. In 1920, famed American bacteriologist and public health expert Charles-Edward Amory Winslow provided the following seminal definition of public health practice:

> Public health is the science and art of preventing disease, prolonging life, and promoting physical health and efficiency through organized community efforts for the sanitation of the environment, the control of community infections, the education of the individual in principles of personal hygiene, the organization of medical and nursing services for the early diagnosis and preventive treatment of disease, and the development of social machinery which will ensure to every individual in the community a standard of living adequate for the maintenance of health.[6]

INTERVIEW 10-1 Public Health Interview

Scott Harris, MD, MPH, FACP, FIDSA

State Health Officer, Alabama Department of Public Health

Interview conducted by Dr. James A. Johnson

Note: This interview took place November 2019 prior to the first COVID-19 case being diagnosed in the United States.

Dr. Johnson: What are the leading public health challenges in your communities?

Dr. Harris: As younger people leave rural areas for urban ones, the residents of rural areas become relatively older on average, and bear disproportionate burdens of chronic diseases and diseases of aging. Since employment opportunities may be lacking in many rural communities, there are often lower numbers of residents with employer-sponsored health insurance, and it is not surprising that rural residents are less likely overall to have private health insurance than urban residents. This combination of increased disease burden and lower insurance coverage means that local hospitals and providers often provide care that is uncompensated, which in turn can lead to economic stresses on local hospitals and providers (and, not least, the patients themselves!).

Those providers who remain in rural communities are also more likely to be older and in later stages of their careers, and many rural communities find themselves dreading the inevitable retirements of older providers, since it is increasingly difficult for small rural areas to recruit replacements. Younger providers, who are just completing their training and entering the workforce, are increasingly attracted to urban areas with better educational opportunities and more amenities. This is particularly true for medical specialists, who require larger population bases in order to see sufficient numbers of patients. Health care challenges are not the only ones faced by rural communities, of course; it has become difficult for rural communities to recruit potentially high-earning professionals of any kind: attorneys, engineers, high technology workers and others are simply not interested in relocating to rural areas.

Besides the problems of increased disease burden and lack of providers, the residents of rural areas have additional challenges. They are more likely than urban residents to have lower levels of educational attainment, contributing to lower health literacy. Many may lack reliable transportation, making it difficult to travel to relatively distant providers and health care facilities. And all of these issues are compounded by a lack of health insurance!

Dr. Johnson: *Does this differ from what is happening in other states? If so, please provide a few examples.*

Dr. Harris: The demographic shifts that are occurring now in Alabama are similar to those in other states, as young people leave rural communities for opportunities of education and employment. However, Alabama has some special challenges that are not found everywhere. For example, the passage of the Hill-Burton Act in 1946 made federal dollars available to states for the construction of hospitals. Over the next several years, Alabama took advantage of this program to build dozens of new hospitals in rural parts of the state. Since these facilities, which were state of the art at the time of construction, are now several decades old, attempts at renovation may face prohibitive costs, making it difficult for these "Hill-Burton hospitals" to modernize their facilities or add updated technology.

Alabama's Black Belt is a region of about a dozen counties across the midsection of the state that is so named for its black fertile soil that attracted many farmers and planters in our state's early years. The subsequent enslavement of African Americans in Alabama and throughout the Old South has created a legacy of poverty in these rural Black Belt counties, which even today remain impoverished and geographically isolated. The non-medical determinants of health in these low-income, African American communities are associated with significant health disparities and poor health outcomes. Alabama's history of enslavement still occupies a significant place in today's public health landscape.

Dr. Johnson: *In your role as State Health Officer how do you interface with policymakers to address these challenges? Please provide some examples.*

Dr. Harris: Our department has worked diligently to develop personal relationships with members of the Governor's staff, key legislators, and colleagues who serve in other state agencies. For example, one physical aspect of Alabama's Black Belt is the relative impermeability of its soil to water, which creates difficulty in trying to manage residential wastewater. While rural residents in many places use a conventional septic tank to handle sewage and wastewater, these inexpensive systems do not function well in Black Belt soil, which necessitates much more expensive engineered solutions. Sadly, these are often not feasible to many impoverished residents of the Black Belt. ADPH has worked closely with state and local officials from these areas to find federal grants to enable the construction of wastewater systems that can be accessed by residents, and to develop and implement legislation that creates a legal framework for this initiative.

Also, ADPH enlists state legislators to assist us with local issues, whenever possible. For example, our county health departments are funded primarily through the clinical revenue that they earn themselves by the provision of clinical services, but because of the amount of uncompensated care they provide, local health departments also rely on local financial support from city and county governments. ADPH works with state legislators in their districts to help approach local officials

(continues)

with requests for resources. This helps us to build relationships with legislators while improving our credibility with local officials. As the saying goes, all politics is local.

Dr. Johnson: *What are some of the obstacles or barriers you face in this regard?*

Dr. Harris: Because ADPH is a regulatory agency, we sometimes find ourselves in conflict with those we regulate. If a facility receives a poor inspection score, many restaurants, nursing homes, hospitals, tattoo facilities, or other businesses are quick to reach out to local government or state legislators to register their displeasure with ADPH. Legislators generally understand the dilemma we face in our mission to protect the health of the public, but they ultimately answer to the wishes of their constituents, which may create uncomfortable situations on occasion.

Similarly, as the state agency charged with the inspection and regulation of abortion clinics, there is almost no action we can perform that avoids antagonizing at least some of those who are engaged with this polarizing issue. But sometimes, the opposite may be true: public health may be interested in a particular health concern that is of little or no interest to policymakers. A good example is in the area of sexually transmitted infections. While ADPH works hard to explain the public health impact of our state's increasing STI rates, and frequently seeks resources to assist our mission of reducing them, lawmakers are unlikely to hear from constituents who support this, and subsequently we have a difficult time convincing legislators to provide additional support.

A number of issues would seem to be very straightforward from a scientific standpoint, like restrictions on the sale of tobacco or the benefits of syringe service programs in reducing transmission of hepatitis C virus and HIV. However, science does not always triumph, and political calculations are often the deciding factor. This can certainly create frustrating interactions when public health goals conflict with political decisions.

Dr. Johnson: *Please provide a short description of three health improvement or prevention initiatives your Department is currently leading.*

Dr. Harris: The Alabama Department of Public Health (ADPH) is working through our Governor's Children's Cabinet (comprised of other health service agencies and state legislators) to implement a pilot project in three central Alabama counties that have rates of infant mortality above the state average. Our state government partners include the Department of Human Resources, the Department of Mental Health, Medicaid, the Department of Early Childhood Education, and the Governor's Office of Minority Affairs. The pilot is focused on home visitation programs, safe sleep initiatives, utilization of the SBIRT (screening, brief intervention, and referral to treatment) screening tool to identify substance use, depression and domestic violence, breastfeeding, preconception and interconception health care for women who may potentially have high-risk pregnancies, and the use of 17-alpha-hydroxyprogesterone (17P) in women with previous preterm births. Additional ideas include working with insurance payers to make long-acting reversible contraceptives (LARC) available immediately after delivery, and further strengthening of Alabama's perinatal regionalization guidelines.

The Children's Health Insurance Program (CHIP) in Alabama is administered through ADPH and the Centers for Medicare & Medicaid Services (CMS) offers the opportunity to states to draw down federal administrative funds, within the federal administrative cap for states, to be used for demonstration projects that improve the health care of children. ADPH has designed a program to use CHIP coverage that is provided to an "unborn child," effectively providing services to an expecting mother who is determined to be at high-risk for a poor fetal outcome. The project will provide a variety of evidence-based case management / wraparound support services that may include care by nurses, social workers, community health workers or others.

Preventing new cases of HIV infection in our state is a major priority. Given that effective antiretroviral treatment of persons who are living with HIV eliminates the possibility of transmission of the disease to others, the concept of treatment of prevention has added an additional sense of urgency to our goal of ensuring that all infected persons receive appropriate medical therapy. ADPH is currently developing a program to identify persons living with HIV who are not receiving medical care and attempting to re-engage them with the medical community by connecting them to providers. Using laboratory data that identifies HIV-positive persons who do not have evidence of additional follow-up lab studies (e.g. HIV viral loads or T-cell profiles), public health social workers will attempt to contact these persons who are not in care and identify any barriers that may be preventing them from access to providers.

Dr. Johnson: *Please provide any websites developed by your Department that may be helpful to the reader in their understanding of your rural public health efforts.*

Dr. Harris: The Office of Primary Care and Rural Health at the Alabama Department of Public Health maintains a list of important rural health resources and programs, which may be found at our website: http://alabamapublichealth.gov/ruralhealth/index.html

Dr. Johnson: *How has the post-graduate medical training you received in public health, specifically the MPH, been helpful to you in your current leadership role?*

Dr. Harris: My professional background and training are in the realm of clinical medicine, and I began to pursue a Master's in Public Health degree only after changing my career to begin working in public health. I originally saw the degree as the standard credential that I thought I ought to obtain, in order to be on par with my new colleagues. However, my studies in my MPH graduate program opened my eyes to the wider world of public health and has informed everything that I currently do in my role as State Health Officer. Public health is a vast discipline that contains many diverse technical subject matters, from disease control to maternal child health to environmental regulation. My exposure to these areas was tremendously helpful to me as I began to work with public health experts across many different professional fields. My MPH program also introduced me to the theoretical underpinnings of public health, with instruction in areas like public health law, medical economics and medical ethics. I literally developed a new vocabulary, which was necessary for me to understand and communicate in my new profession. Finally, my graduate program helped me to develop many administrative skills that I had never formally studied in my previous career, such as management and finance.

CASE 10-1 A *Giardia* Outbreak?[1]

Situation

"This is the 10th confirmed case of giardiasis we received this week," David said to one of the department's environmental engineers. David works as an environmental health specialist in the Northwest Region office of the Pennsylvania Department of Environmental Protection (DEP), Bureau of Water Standards and Facility Regulation. Several physicians in a local township called his office this week to report positive laboratory tests of *Giardia* cysts in their patients, who were experiencing flulike illnesses with symptoms of persistent diarrhea, nausea, and abdominal cramps. The physicians were growing concerned about a potential outbreak of a waterborne contaminant in the community's water supply, yet they hadn't seen any public announcements from the DEP.

(continues)

CASE 10-1 A *Giardia* Outbreak?[1] *(continued)*

Officials from the local health department had also called earlier in the day to ask if any Boil Water Advisories should be in effect.

One of David's essential duties in his job as an environmental health specialist is to respond to and investigate complaints and violations of Pennsylvania's water supply and wastewater treatment facilities. His department develops surveillance strategies that direct field inspector activities at water supply and wastewater treatment facilities. In addition, he works closely with the Bureau of Watershed Management, which is responsible for planning and managing the water resources in Pennsylvania, including monitoring and regulating water sources to ensure safe drinking water, as required by the Safe Drinking Water Act (SDWA).

The affected local township is a small community in rural Pennsylvania with a population of less than 8,000 located near the Allegheny National Forest. David knows that many rural cities in the mountainous areas of Pennsylvania are particularly susceptible to waterborne contaminants because their water supplies from lakes, ponds, or streams can become contaminated with animal droppings or human sewage discharge. Although water treatment plants have been constructed in many communities, some of the more remote areas still did not have completely effective water systems that were fully risk compliant. David remembers having studied the *Giardia* outbreak that occurred in Bradford, a community not too dissimilar to the local township.

Background

Giardia and *Cryptosporidium* are the most common etiologic agents causing waterborne outbreaks in the United States. *Giardia* and *Cryptosporidium* are protozoan intestinal parasites that cause diarrheal illnesses in people. The parasites are found in every region of the United States and throughout the world. The cysts of the organisms are commonly transmitted from the environment to humans through contaminated water or food. The illnesses associated with the parasites, giardiasis and cryptosporidiosis, are usually acute and can become chronic and last up to 1 or 2 months. From 1965 to 1996, there were 118 outbreaks of giardiasis in the United States with 26,305 reported cases of illness, mainly attributed to the consumption of contaminated drinking water from public and individual water systems, with the majority of cases occurring due to inadequately treated surface water systems.[1]

The State of Pennsylvania was once among the national leaders in the number of recorded waterborne disease outbreaks.[2] The 1979 *Giardia* outbreak in Bradford is an informative reference case. Bradford's water system is supplied from three upland reservoirs. A reservoir is an artificial lake created in a river valley by a dam or built by excavation to store water. Prior to the outbreak, the water from the reservoirs was delivered directly to consumers without any filtration or other barriers. Treatment relied exclusively on chlorination. The water passed out of the reservoirs into the transmission mains. From September to December, 3,500 cases of giardiasis occurred in Bradford. A number of events lead to this outbreak. First, even though chlorination treatment was provided, it was interrupted and deficient at times. Second, heavy rains caused runoff in the watershed, leading to high turbidity. Turbidity is a key test of water quality and represents the cloudiness in water caused by suspended particles. Incidentally, Bradford had applied for and was granted a waiver from the EPA of its obligation to notify the public of the high turbidity measures in the water supply. Although chlorinated, the water was unfiltered before passing through the transmission mains. Third, beavers in the watershed were infected with *Giardia* cysts, contributing to the infection of the water supply. In order to ensure that no future outbreaks of the disease occurred, Bradford constructed a water treatment plant to treat all water delivered to the city. The facility was capable of removing all microorganisms from the water through chemical treatment and filtration.

Next Steps

David's department had been in the process of evaluating local monitoring and sampling equipment in the area, so the field inspection surveys for the local township might have been delayed. If this turned out to be the beginning of an outbreak, his department could be in store for some harsh criticism. The environmental engineers were in the process of coordinating with local inspectors to collect more data, and David thought that this may be the best course of action before alerting the public of a waterborne disease outbreak. David sat down and reflected on the best course of action to take. He considered calling the local health officials to update them on the situation. David thought it might be prudent to ask the local media to alert residents to boil water before consumption. However, his department still needed to determine the cause, and he did not want to risk alarming the public unnecessarily. He knew he should coordinate any external communication activity with his supervisor first, even if it delayed getting the message out to the public. He picked up the phone to call his supervisor and ask for recommendations.

Discussion Questions

1. What course of action should David follow if inspection tests confirm the local township's water supply is contaminated by *Giardia*? (Be sure to read the EPA's *Giardia* fact sheet[2] before answering this question).
2. What parties should David involve in the process of determining an appropriate response by the department?
3. Should David release an official Boil Water Notice to inform the public as a precaution?

References

1. Johnson JA, Musch S. *Multi-Sector Casebook in Health Administration, Leadership, and Management*. Delmar-Cengage; 2013.
2. U.S. Environmental Protection Agency. *Giardia: Drinking Water Fact Sheet*. U.S. Environmental Protection Agency; 2000. Accessed June 10, 2021. https://www.epa.gov/sites/default/files/2015 -10/documents/giardia-factsheet.pdf

Johnson JA, Davey K. Managing Public Health Organizations. Burlington, MA: Jones and Bartlett. 2020.

▶ Discussion Questions

- Compare and contrast public health and population health.
- Discuss who public health benefits from a population health perspective.
- What are some examples of public health initiatives?
- What are the core functions of public health? Describe each one.
- What are the essential services of public health? How do they guide practice?
- Discuss why a systems perspective is so important in public health. Give several examples.
- Why is it important to consider social determinants of health when designing or implementing programs and initiatives?
- What is the role of the public health manager? What competencies should they have?
- What are national health objectives? Discuss them for the current decade.
- Identify various examples of roles and occupations that can be found in public health.

CHAPTER ACRONYMS

ADPH Alabama Department of Public Health
AIDS Acquired Immunodeficiency Syndrome
APHA American Public Health Association
ASPPH Association of Schools and Programs of Public Health
CDC Centers for Disease Control and Prevention
CEPH Council on Education for Public Health
CHIP Children's Health Insurance Program
CMS Centers for Medicare & Medicaid Services
DEP Department of Environmental Protection
DHS Department of Homeland Security
DoD Department of Defense
DOT Department of Transportation
EPA Environmental Protection Agency
HHS U.S. Department of Health and Human Services

HIV Human Immunodeficiency Virus
IOM Institute of Medicine
LARC Long-acting reversible contraceptives
MPH Master's in Public Health
NIH National Institutes of Health
OSHA Occupational Safety and Health Administration
SBIRT Screening, brief intervention, and referral to treatment
SDWA Safe Drinking Water Act
STI Sexually transmitted infection
USPHS United States Public Health Service
VA Department of Veterans Affairs
WHO World Health Organization
WIC Supplemental Nutrition Program for Women, Infants, and Children

▶ Career Exercise

For those who plan to seek management positions or engage in advanced leadership roles in public health agencies and organizations, there is increasingly a preference for additional management education, often beyond the undergraduate level or to augment one's professional or clinical degree. Typically, public health managers have at least an undergraduate degree in fields such as public administration, business administration, behavioral or social sciences, accounting, engineering, life sciences, or a clinical field. However, as managers progress up the organizational ladder into higher level administrative and leadership positions, they will almost always acquire a graduate degree. Most often this will be a Master of Public Health (MPH) or Master of Public Administration (MPA). To a lesser extent, other public health administrators acquire management focused degrees such as Master of Health Administration (MHA), Master of Science (MS) in administration or management, or Master of Business Administration (MBA). However, the largest number of senior administrators in public health agencies have either an MPA or MPH degree. There are also nurses and physicians as well as epidemiologists, engineers, and biostatisticians within the scientific and clinical care units of an organization.

1. If you have an interest in a public health career or want to engage in a leadership role in this domain, how would you position yourself educationally?
2. How could you best utilize your current undergraduate degree?
3. What new competencies would you acquire to help ensure success?
4. What associations might you join and participate in?
5. What experiences, work or voluntary, might you seek outside of the classroom?

References

1. Johnson JA, Davey KS. *Essentials of Managing Public Health Organizations.* Jones & Bartlett Learning; 2019.
2. Johnson JA, Stoskopf C, Shi L. *Comparative Health Systems: A Global Perspective,* 2nd ed. Jones & Bartlett Learning; 2018.
3. Shi L, Johnson JA. *Public Health Administration: Principles for Population-Based Management.* 4th ed. Jones & Bartlett Learning; 2020.
4. Haley SJ, Johnson JA, Frazier LJ. *Opioids and Population Health: A Primer.* Jones & Bartlett Learning; 2022.
5. Nash DB, Skoufalos A, Fabius RJ, Oglesby WH. *Population Health: Creating a Culture of Wellness.* 2nd ed. Jones & Bartlett Learning; 2016.
6. Institute of Medicine. *The Future of Public Health.* National Academies Press; 1988.
7. Johnson JA, Anderson DE, Rossow CC. *Health Systems Thinking: A Primer.* Jones & Bartlett Learning; 2020.
8. Johnson JA, Rossow CC. *Health Organizations: Theory, Behavior, and Development.* 2nd ed. Jones & Bartlett Learning; 2019.
9. DeSalvo KB, Wang YC, Harris A, Auerbach J, Koo D, O'Carroll P. Public health 3.0: a call to action for public health to meet the challenges of the 21st century. *Prev Chronic Dis.* 2017;14:170017. doi: 10.5888/pcd14.170017
10. Council on Education for Public Health. Accessed September 10, 2021. https://ceph.org/
11. Association of Schools and Programs in Public Health. Accessed September 10, 2021. https://www.aspph.org/
12. U.S. Department of Health and Human Services Office of Disease Prevention and Health Promotion. Healthy People 2030 Framework. Updated August 17, 2021. Accessed August 19, 2021. https://www.healthypeople.gov/2020/About-Healthy-People/Development-Healthy-People-2030/Framework
13. Smith T. Looking ahead to Public Health 4.0. University of Colorado Anschutz Medical Campus. Published December 4, 2018. Accessed August 19, 2021. https://www.cuanschutztoday.org/looking-ahead-to-public-health-4-0/
14. Turnock BJ. *Essentials of Public Health.* 3rd ed. Jones & Bartlett Learning; 2016.
15. U.S. Department of Health and Human Services. Accessed September 10, 2021. https://www.hhs.gov
16. Centers for Disease Control and Prevention. Accessed September 10, 2021. https://www.cdc.gov/
17. Schneider MJ. *Introduction to Public Health.* 5th ed. Jones & Bartlett Learning; 2017.

CHAPTER 11

Health Information Technology and Quality

Centralized model of
   health information
   exchange
Clinical decision support
   system (CDSS)
Computerized physician order
   entry (CPOE)
Electronic health record
   (EHR)

Federated model of
   health information
   exchange
Health information
   exchange (HIE)
Health Information
   Technology for Economic
   and Clinical Health
   (HITECH) Act

Information blocking
Meaningful use
Office of the National
   Coordinator for Health
   Information Technology
   (ONCHIT or "the ONC")
Personal health record (PHR)
Regional health information
   organization (RHIO)

CHAPTER OVERVIEW

This chapter outlines major historical developments in the evolution of health information technology and discusses government initiatives to support its implementation. It highlights both benefits and challenges of using this technology and the progress of its implementation to date. The implicit and explicit links to quality of care will be presented throughout.

▶ Background

The concept of using modern health information technology (HIT) to improve the quality and reduce the costs of health care is not new. In fact, the U.S. federal government has facilitated many HIT initiatives for more than 50 years. One of the earliest is traceable back to the Kennedy Administration in the early 1960s. In 2004, the federal government took the most significant step in the history of HIT when President George W. Bush created the Office of the National Coordinator for Health Information Technology (ONCHIT or "the ONC") by Executive Order.[1] It was then legislatively mandated in the American Recovery and Reinvestment Act (ARRA), signed by President Obama on February 17, 2009.[2] Part of the ARRA is the Health Information Technology for Economic and Clinical Health (HITECH) Act, which designated $36.5 billion to promote the development of a nationwide network of electronic health records (EHRs). EHRs are computerized patient records meant to replace paper charts.

Despite a sizable investment and more than a half century of government incentives and technological advancements, the best scientific evidence today indicates that the benefits of HIT on the quality and cost of health care are, at best, mixed.[3] This chapter will explore the history of how HIT has evolved and the imprint HIT has and continues to make on the healthcare system.

▶ Historical Challenges in Implementing Health Information Technology

The use of computers to improve health care in many ways parallels the evolution of the information technology industry. The late 1960s and early 1970s saw several pioneering efforts at a small number of universities to apply HIT to various aspects of healthcare delivery. Early systems were not the ubiquitous, web-based, interactive systems of today but were usually a hybrid of computer and paper integrated into clinical workflows.

One of the earlier noted processes is from the 1970s at Indiana University, where a hybrid approach to HIT was instituted. Their process included a group of data entry clerks who manually entered data on key parts of patients' medical records into a computer. Then, the night before a patient's clinic appointment, a one-page, paper encounter form was printed for the next day's appointment listing the patients' name, record number, medical problem list (i.e., the known diagnoses and medical problems), medication list, medication allergies, and suggestions based on an analysis of the data in the computer system. "Suggestions" were calculated based on the patient information in the computer at the point in time the encounter form was printed (e.g., laboratory results, prescription data, diagnoses, vital signs). The software detected any of 290 agreed-upon patient-care protocols or conditions defined by the biomedical literature and best medical practices. During the clinic visit, the physician would handwrite notes on the paper encounter form and manually annotate the computer-printed problem list, medication list, as well as other items. After the visit, the team of data entry clerks would review the annotated encounter forms and update the computer system to reflect the physician's orders with updates to the patient's condition. The encounter form would then be filed to the patient's paper chart. The Indiana group conducted a study demonstrating a 29% improvement in adherence to agreed-upon treatment protocols in the group of physicians who received the computer "suggestions" for recommended treatments on the encounter forms versus those who did not.[4] Similar systems were designed and built during the same time period at a number of other U.S. universities, including the University of Pittsburgh,[5] the University of Utah,[6,7] Vanderbilt University,[8,9] Duke University,[10] and Harvard University/Massachusetts General Hospital.[11] These pioneering systems were custom designed, built, and maintained by in-house teams of computer programmers and systems engineers. The custom design made these records impractical for widespread use. Despite the limitations, this pioneering work laid the foundation for modern EHR design.

It was not until the 1990s that commercially produced EHR systems became mass marketed and sold to healthcare institutions in high volume. These commercially produced systems allowed hospitals to implement comprehensive EHRs without the prohibitive costs of designing and building custom systems. Instead, hospitals could buy an "off-the-shelf" system that could be configured to meet most of their perceived institutional needs. The "off-the-shelf," commercially produced EHRs of today still require extensive configuration to accommodate a hospital's unique work processes. In addition, some commercial systems are not capable of easily exchanging patients' health information between systems and institutions due to a host of factors. In fact, the configuration differences between institutions are often so significant that even institutions with the same commercial EHR systems cannot electronically exchange patients' records without customized software.

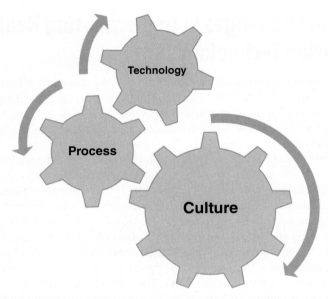

As the installed base of commercial systems expanded, many university researchers who pioneered the early, customized systems began to study the issues with implementation of new HIT in the healthcare setting.[12,13] Researchers learned that there is a great deal more than just selecting the "right system" to ensure successful HIT implementation. **FIGURE 11-1** illustrates the three essential components required for successful HIT implementation.

The first essential component is the technology. However, organizations often devote a lot of energy on this first component with the mistaken belief that merely selecting the "right" technology or the "right EHR" is the most important aspect of HIT implementation.

The second component of successful implementation, workflows (or processes), is a significant consideration due to wide variations in work policies and procedures among clinicians and organizations. An organization's policies and procedures describe and define the processes by which work is carried out. The process component is complex, as it requires a good understanding of all existing work processes. Many processes are not written or formalized, having evolved over the years to accommodate the unique characteristics of a particular organization. Further, actual work processes may significantly differ from those officially documented or assumed to be in place. Many critical work processes are not documented at all. When an HIT system is implemented, it is common for many of the undocumented processes to become apparent for the first time.[14] Undocumented or unknown work processes have been the root cause for many HIT implementation failures.[15]

The third component is the most significant—the institutional and organizational culture.[13] This is the most critical, least studied, and least understood in terms of the HIT implementation components.[16] Ash and Bates summarized the importance of organizational culture with regard to EHR adoption.[12]

There is a significant publication bias in the biomedical literature against revealing HIT implementation failures. The human tendency to avoid admission of mistakes has skewed the body of literature toward successful implementations and studies. This has made it more difficult to study and understand causes associated with HIT implementation failures. The HIT industry would benefit from a shift in culture towards transparent reporting of HIT failures and viewing them as learning opportunities rather than embarrassments.

One notable example of an HIT implementation failure occurred at the Cedars-Sinai Hospital in Los Angeles, California, in 2002. Three months after implementing a new $34 million HIT system, several hundred physicians refused to use it. Cedars-Sinai attempted to implement a new electronic medical record to change the way physicians ordered patient tests and procedures in the hospital. Prior to the new system, physicians documented orders on paper forms in the patients' paper charts. Newly written patient orders were given to nurses or ward clerks for implementation. The new system required physicians to type orders directly into a computer workstation, and the software provided immediate feedback if the order entry was not understood or deemed a mistake. An article in the *Washington Post* reported[17]:

> A veteran physician at the prestigious Cedars-Sinai Medical Center here had been mixing up a certain drug dosage for decades. Every time he wrote the prescription for 10 times the proper amount, a nurse simply corrected it, recalled Paul Hackmeyer. The computers arrived—and when the doctor typed in his medication order, the machine barked at him and he barked back. . . . "What we discovered was that for 20 years he was writing the wrong dose."

This brief story illustrates the three principal HIT implementation components:

- *Technology:* With physicians required to enter orders directly to the computer system, time required to enter orders became dependent on the computer's ordering input format and system response time.
- *Process:* Many undocumented processes in the old system were not carried to the new system. In this example, the nurse's automatic correction of an obvious dosage error was a critical, undocumented process—a nursing check on the orders' accuracy. Although the new system caught the error, the physician user in this case could no longer rely on the nurse's checking and correcting of his orders.
- *Culture:* The new system required physicians to interact with a computer, which took more time than writing orders on paper forms. The new system required physicians to change the way they practiced medicine in the hospital, and, as is common, people dislike change. This was a significant change in physicians' work culture in which nurses had routinely checked and corrected physician orders without communicating the corrections. Physicians also had to deal with a barrage of system alerts when they were imprecise or inaccurate in entering their orders. While potentially enhancing patient safety, responding to the system alerts increased the time (and physician irritation) required for physicians to place orders.

Another historical barrier to broad implementation of HIT is the gap between those who bear the costs of the technology and those who receive its benefits. The purchase and operation of an EHR system represents a major investment for large healthcare organizations and especially for small private physician groups. Not only must physician groups bear the costs of the hardware and software, but they also must support ongoing IT maintenance, staff training, and software upgrade costs. Because small practice groups often have no experience or expertise with IT issues, they also experience anxiety about making decisions necessary to convert from paper to electronic charting. While economies of scale make the marginal costs of adopting EHR technology somewhat lower for large healthcare organizations, these organizations often do not realize the cost savings from their investment. A good example of this is a healthcare system participating in a health information exchange (HIE). HIE systems share patient information across institutions and multiple EHR platforms. This allows patients and physicians access to a patient's comprehensive health record from multiple institutions, regardless of where the patient was seen. HIEs often reduce the number of duplicate laboratory and imaging tests, saving the patient and the payer significant expense.

However, the healthcare system may lose money by not receiving revenue for the duplicate tests not performed and for the expense they bear supporting the HIE. As with large healthcare systems, small practices that invest in EHR technology may not directly benefit from the technology. Patients may receive more age-appropriate screening[18,19] and preventive care,[20] along with reduced duplicate testing, because physicians have access to HIEs and patient records from outside the practice group or health system.[21] However, from a practice's financial perspective, these factors actually may produce a significant disincentive for adopting EHRs.

▶ The Federal Government's Response to Health Information Technology Implementation Challenges

As mentioned previously, the U.S. government has sought ways to incentivize adoption of HIT for more than half a century. **FIGURE 11-2** notes major legislation that continues to influence adoption in health care.

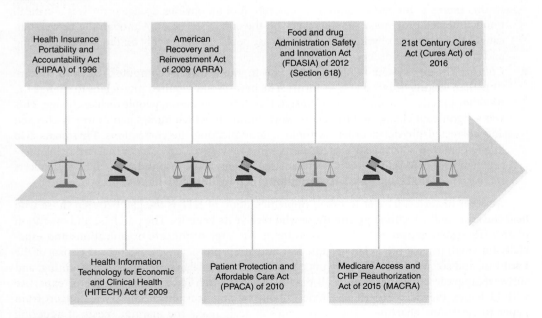

FIGURE 11-2 Key Legislation Impacting HIT

Created by Richard Greenhill.

The largest incentive program to date has been the $36 billion designated in the HITECH Act that created the Medicare and Medicaid Electronic Health Record Incentive Programs.[22] The Center for Medicare & Medicaid Services (CMS) used these funds to incentivize Eligible Professionals (individual physicians in solo or multiphysician practice groups) and Eligible Hospitals as they adopt, implement, upgrade, or demonstrate meaningful use of certified EHR technology to improve patient care. There were three progressive Stages to the "Meaningful Use Program" with deadlines; the largest financial incentives were awarded to Eligible Professionals or Eligible Hospitals who demonstrated the earliest compliance with standards in each Stage.[23] This program was in part an effort to address a portion of the gap between those that bear the costs of HIT implementation (physicians and hospitals) and those who receive most of its benefits (patients, public health agencies, and payers).

Eligible Professionals could receive up to $44,000 through the Medicare EHR Incentive Program and up to $63,750 through the Medicaid EHR Incentive Program. Eligible Professionals were allowed to participate in either the Medicare or Medicaid EHR Incentive Programs, but not both. Eligible Hospitals could participate in both the Medicare and Medicaid incentive programs.[24] Each hospital incentive included a base payment of $2 million plus an additional amount determined by a formula based on the number of discharges per year.[25-27] **TABLE 11-1** compares the Medicare and Medicaid adoption incentive programs for Eligible Professionals and Eligible Hospitals.[22-24,28-34]

TABLE 11-1 Comparison of Medicare and Medicaid Adoption Incentive Programs for Eligible Professionals (Individual Physicians in Solo and Group Practices) and Eligible Hospitals (Including Critical Access Hospitals)		
	Medicare Program	**Medicaid Program**
Eligible Professionals	■ Administered by CMS ■ $44,000 maximum per physician (over 5-year period) ■ 90% or more of practice must be outpatient based ■ Cannot participate in Medicaid Program if enrolled in Medicare Program ■ Must apply for Stage 1 Meaningful Use by 2012 to obtain the maximum incentive ■ Medicare imposes payment penalty on those failing to demonstrate meaningful use beginning 2015	■ Administered by State Medicaid Agency ■ $63,750 maximum per physician Participate (over 5 years) ■ Must have ≤ 30% Medicaid patient volume or ≤ 20% Medicaid patient volume and be a pediatrician or practice predominantly in a Federally Qualified Health Center or Rural Health Clinic and have ≤ 30% patient volume attributable to needy individuals ■ ≤ 90% of practice must be outpatient based ■ Cannot participate in Medicare Program if enrolled in Medicaid Program ■ Can begin to certify for Meaningful Use by 2016 and still receive full incentive ■ Nonparticipants exempt from Medicaid payment reductions

(continues)

TABLE 11-1 Comparison of Medicare and Medicaid Adoption Incentive Programs for Eligible Professionals (Individual Physicians in Solo and Group Practices) and Eligible Hospitals (Including Critical Access Hospitals) *(continued)*		
	Medicare Program	**Medicaid Program**
Hospitals (Including Critical Access Hospitals)	■ Administered by CMS ■ Can begin receiving incentive FY 2011 to FY 2015, but payments will decrease for hospitals that start receiving payments in FY 2014 and later ■ Medicare and Medicaid Program eligible ■ Must apply for Stage 1 Meaningful Use by FY 2013 to receive maximum incentive ■ Hospitals that do not successfully demonstrate meaningful use will be subject to Medicare payment penalties beginning in FY 2015 ■ Incentive payments are based on several factors, beginning with a $2 million base payment	■ Administered by State Medicaid Agency ■ Acute care hospitals (including critical access and cancer hospitals) with at least 10% Medicaid patient volume are eligible ■ Children's hospitals are eligible regardless of their Medicaid volume ■ Can apply for both Medicare and Medicaid Programs ■ Incentive payments are based on a number of factors, beginning with a $2 million base payment

Data from the Centers for Medicare & Medicaid Services and the Office of the National Coordinator for Health Information Technology.

In 2009, the ONC was designated "the principal federal entity charged with coordination of nationwide efforts to implement and use the most advanced health information technology and the electronic exchange of health information."[35] In short, CMS provided the financial incentives for the meaningful use program while the ONC set the requirements. The ONC's mission, noted in its 2016 budget justification to Congress, is to "improve health, health care, and reduce costs through the use of information and technology."[36] **FIGURE 11-3** depicts the ONC's current organizational structure. The ONC had a budget of $60 million in fiscal year 2015.[37] The HITECH Act also created an HIT Policy Committee and the HIT Standards Committee under the auspices of the Federal Advisory Committee Act.[38] Both committees include multiple workgroups with representatives from payers, academia, and the healthcare industry. They address a variety of HIT-related issues including certification/adoption, governance, HIE, meaningful use, privacy and security, quality measures, implementation, and an HIT vocabulary standards committee.[38]

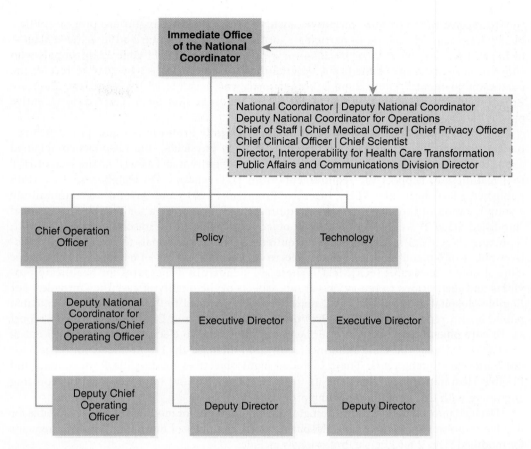

FIGURE 11-3 **Office of the National Coordinator for Health Information Technology Organizational Structure**

Created by Richard Greenhill.

Data from the Office of the National Coordinator of Health Information Technology. About ONC. Updated March 12, 2021. Accessed August 19, 2021. https://www.healthit.gov/topic/about-onc#:~:text=ONC%20is%20the%20principal%20federal,electronic%20exchange%20of%20health%20information

The Health IT Policy Committee makes recommendations to the National Coordinator for Health IT on a policy framework for the development and adoption of a nationwide health information infrastructure, including standards for the exchange of patient medical information. The American Recovery and Reinvestment Act of 2009 (ARRA) requires the Health IT Policy Committee to, at minimum, make recommendations on the eight specific areas in which standards, implementation specifications, and certification criteria are needed.

The Health IT Standards Committee is charged with making recommendations to the National Coordinator for Health IT on standards, implementation specifications, and certification criteria for the electronic exchange and use of health information.

Requirements to demonstrate meaningful use were developed by these committees and the ONC. The evidence for the majority of meaningful use objectives was only at the expert-opinion level. The science of HIT awaits rigorous research studies to validate the choices and designs of the meaningful use criteria.

To receive the maximum incentive payment under the meaningful use program, Eligible Professionals who chose to participate in the Medicare Program had to achieve Stage 1 of Meaningful Use by 2012 or by 2014 for a reduced amount.[31] Eligible Professionals who chose to participate in the Medicaid Program had to achieve Stage 1 by 2016 to receive the maximum payment.[39] Those Eligible Professionals who began to certify under the Medicare Program in 2015 or later or under the Medicaid Program after 2016 received no incentive payments.

By the end of November 2014, only 25.2% of Eligible Professionals and 43.1% of Eligible Hospitals had met Stage 2 requirements.[40,41] Many physicians and hospitals complained about the difficulty and complexity of the reporting requirements as well as the lack of HIT tool readiness to support the requirements from HIT vendors. On October 6, 2015, CMS published a fact sheet titled "EHR Incentive Programs in 2015 and Beyond" to communicate a simplification of the meaningful use requirements.[42] The criteria for Eligible Professional "modified Stage 2" were simplified to 10 objectives, including 1 consolidated public health reporting objective. Previously, Stage 2 required Eligible Professionals to meet 17 core objectives plus 3 of 6 menu objectives and to electronically report 9 out of 64 approved electronic clinical quality measures (eCQMs).[43] (These are standardized measures for healthcare providers and institutions to report on various aspects of the quality of care they provide.) For Eligible Hospitals, modified Stage 2 objectives were reduced to 9, including 1 consolidated public health reporting objective. Previously, Stage 2 required Eligible Hospitals to report on 16 core objectives plus 3 out of 6 menu objectives and to electronically report 16 out of 29 eCQMs.[44] Under the same announcement, CMS finalized the requirements for Stage 3 for 2017 and subsequent years. These included eight objectives for Eligible Professionals and Eligible Hospitals, more requirements for interoperability, and improved quality reporting alignment with CMS quality reporting programs.[42]

Detailed information on the meaningful use requirements for modified Stage 2 is available for Eligible Professionals[45] and Eligible Hospitals.[46] Some examples of meaningful use requirements for modified Stage 2 for Eligible Professionals include:

- Performing a security risk analysis one time per year
- Using clinical decision support to improve performance on high-priority health conditions
- Using computerized physician order entry (CPOE)
- Using an e-prescribing system for at least 50% of prescriptions
- Providing a summary care record when transferring patients from facility to facility
- Providing patient education with HIT
- Performing medication reconciliation at appropriate times
- Providing the capability for patients to view their electronic health information securely online or by downloading or transmitting it directly to a third party
- Using secure electronic messaging (email) to communicate with patients
- Transmitting required public health information electronically to the appropriate agencies

As noted previously, the ONC also has funded several programs to facilitate the adoption of EHRs. Examples include training programs to increase the number of professionals with IT skills required in the healthcare domain. Other programs fund the development of HIE standards across multiple EHR vendor platforms. The ONC also funds annual surveys to track HIT adoption and, more recently, HIT "developer contests" that incentivize innovation in ONC-targeted areas with monetary prizes.

▶ **Healthcare Quality**

Quality in health care is essential to the delivery of appropriate care to patients to reduce suffering and harm. Quality is described by the World Health Organization (WHO) as "the degree to which health services for individuals and populations increase the likelihood of desired health outcomes."[47] Quality is defined differently by people and entities. For example, consider how quality might be defined in the service industry. Restaurant or hotel customers may view quality in terms of cleanliness, presentation, or friendliness of staff. Thus, the term quality is generally in the eye of the beholder. This begs the question of why quality in health care is such an important topic. In 2001, the Institute of Medicine produced a landmark book, *"Crossing the Quality Chasm: A New Health System for the 21st Century,"* that detailed findings of serious issues with healthcare quality in the United States.[48] In health care, there is acknowledgement that health services should meet six domains, plus integration[48]:

- Effective: Care given should be provided to those that need it and based on the best evidence available.
- Safe: Intended care should prevent and avoid causing additional harm.
- Person-centered: Care should be tailored to the extent that it responds to patient needs, values, and preferences.
- Timely: Seekers of care should be able to access it with minimal delay.
- Equitable: A commensurate quality of care should be available for all groups irrespective of race, age, sex, gender, religion, socioeconomic status, political affiliation, or geographic location.
- Integrated: Coordination of care across providers and levels creates continuity and enhances safety.
- Efficient: Care delivery should minimize waste and maximize benefit.

There are generally three main orientations or perspectives in the practice of health care—the patient perspective, the payer perspective, and the health system perspective. Patient satisfaction is not a well-defined concept, but it is an important indicator of quality.[49] Patients often tend to care about bedside manner, cleanliness, and the waiting room as a focal point. This may be because it is difficult for patients to really know the background and record of mistakes linked to their physicians' or nurses' performance. While there are state boards of nursing with data on nurse performance as well as the National Practitioner Data Bank for physicians, that information is not readily available nor easily consumed by the average person seeking care. Therefore, outcomes may be secondary to aesthetics and customer service for patients, as they would not know if their clinicians have provided quality care until after their care is complete (i.e., upon a postsurgical infection, etc.). On the other hand, health systems and insurers are concerned with outcomes (e.g., Did the condition improve? Did the patient return for the same issue within a certain period?). These perspectives are valid; however, this perspective can be tricky as well, as outcomes are dependent on more than just what the hospital or provider does. Quality is of importance to three main groups—health systems, the federal government, and patients. For health systems, quality impacts how they receive funding and reimbursement. Laws such as the Medicare Access and CHIP Reauthorization Act (MACRA) and the Affordable Care Act (ACA) have pushed providers and healthcare facilities to care more about patient outcomes, as many are linked to reimbursement. The other key area of importance to health systems is risk. Risk management is an important function that reduces exposure of the healthcare entity to litigation and other negative outcomes. The federal government cares about quality because of costs and economics. Poor quality negatively impacts patients and consumes resources unnecessarily. Quality is important to patients due to the impact is has on their livelihoods. Patients that are harmed in surgery or through hospital-acquired conditions (HACs) can have reduced quality of life. There are a host of organizations that are involved or have a stake in healthcare quality. **TABLE 11-2** is a basic list of the main entities but, it is not an all-inclusive list.

The U.S. Department of Health and Human Services is an entity run out of the Executive Branch of our government (i.e., the president, the vice president, and the Cabinet). It controls entities such as Centers for Medicare & Medicaid Services (CMS) and the Agency for Healthcare Research and Quality (AHRQ). There are also professional societies that are concerned with quality. The National Association for Healthcare Quality is a member organization that is the certifying body for the Certified Professional in Healthcare Quality (CPHQ) credential. TJC is a key organization that drives quality improvement and patient safety.[50] The DNV-GL is a society based in Norway that is the alternative to TJC for hospital accreditation for CMS reimbursement. All hospitals are not TJC accredited; some are DNV-GL accredited. Then there are many not-for-profit organizations who have their interests directly aligned with healthcare quality. The National Committee for Quality Assurance (NCQA) is the entity that certifies organizations as patient-centered medical homes. The National Quality Forum (NQF) helps to set policy for performance measure reporting. The Institute for Healthcare Improvement (IHI) is the premier organization that provides training and certification for patient safety professionals.

TABLE 11-2 Key Organizations That Have Influence on Quality in the United States	
Organization or Group	**Mission**
The Joint Commission (TJC) https://www.jointcommission.org/	To continuously improve health care for the public, in collaboration with other stakeholders, by evaluating health care organizations and inspiring them to excel in providing safe and effective care of the highest quality and value.[50]
DNV-GL https://www.dnv.com/#dropdown-sector-Healthcare	To safeguard life, property and the environment.[51]
National Association for Healthcare Quality (NAHQ) https://nahq.org/	To prepare a coordinated, competent workforce to lead and advance healthcare quality across the continuum of healthcare.[52]
Commission on the Accreditation of Rehabilitation Facilities (CARF) http://www.carf.org/home/	To promote the quality, value, and optimal outcomes of services through a consultative accreditation process and continuous improvement services that center on enhancing the lives of persons served.[53]

Created by Richard Greenhill.

▶ HIT Opportunities: Improving Healthcare Delivery, Quality, Effectiveness, and Efficiency

With mediocre evidence to date for HIT goals to improve healthcare quality and reduce costs, the question looms: What is the driving force behind the United States' quest to implement HIT? The answer resides in understanding the limitations of the human brain and limited attention span. A healthy human's performance begins to measurably decrease in about 40 minutes while monitoring a continuous process.[54] These limitations explain regulations for work-time breaks for air traffic controllers and anesthesiologists, work-hour limitations for airplane pilots and commercial truck drivers, and, more recently, work-hour limitations for medical students and residents.[55] These regulations recognize that human performance is limited by innate biology and physiology and that fatigue degrades performance. No amount of training or willpower can overcome these biological and physiological limitations. These acknowledgements apply to healthcare delivery, where a physician in a busy outpatient clinic or inpatient ward is much like an air traffic controller monitoring a continuous process. Patients are tightly scheduled with additional patients often "doubled-booked" at the last minute because of acute illness. Every patient must be seen and volumes of data accessed, processed, and synthesized to formulate a diagnosis and a plan of care. At the same time, the physician must document the encounter in detail, complete all required forms and insurance paperwork, respond to electronic pages and phone calls, speak with consultants, manage correspondence, and, in many cases, also supervise advanced practice providers, nurses, and office staff. Stead and Hammond have shown that the amount of data accessed and used by clinicians per medical decision is increasing exponentially despite the fact that physicians' ability to cope with the higher information load remains constant.[56] The driving concept behind the potential of EHRs to improve the quality and reduce the cost of health care is represented in **FIGURE 11-4**.[57]

The ultimate goal is to combine the intuitive strengths of humans with the limitless data retention and recall speed of computers to create a hybrid system that is intuitive with a tireless data processing capability. The physician's medical experience, communication, and intuitive abilities combine with the computer's ability to never tire or forget information. In other words, the computer provides the physician with a computerized clinical decision support system (CDSS). The computer does not supplant the physician's role but enhances it by providing and managing the deluge of patient information to optimize the physician's performance beyond

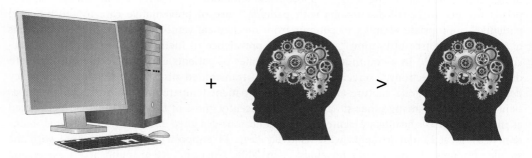

FIGURE 11-4 **Why EHRs Have Potential to Improve Quality and Reduce Costs**

Data from Friedman CP. What informatics is and isn't. *J Am Med Inform Assoc.* 2013;20(2):224-226. doi: 10.1136/amiajnl-2012-001206

the brain's biological capability. However for CDSS to work, "the [computerized] interventions must deliver the right information, to the right person, in the right format, through the right channel, at the right point in workflow."[58] If any of these five requirements are missing, the system will tend to fail. With EHRs, the right place and the right point in the workflow often are when the physician is entering patient orders at a computer workstation—the process termed CPOE. At this place and time, the physician's mind is focused on the patient just seen or the patient they are currently thinking about. This also is the place and time at which it is easiest for the physician to take action, such as writing new orders that result in timely follow-through for a patient's care.

For example, when a physician has completed a patient encounter and enters e-prescriptions in the EHR to be sent to the patient's pharmacy, the computer can present the physician with a pop-up "reminder" that the patient is allergic to the medication being prescribed. It can also indicate that the prescribed medication requires at least annual kidney function monitoring and if the last record of kidney function laboratory work is more than a year old. In this event, the system can present the physician with an option to order the appropriate laboratory work or to ignore the warning with a keystroke or mouse click. Most decision support is designed with these "soft stops" or interventions that allow the physician to heed or ignore the warning as they believe to be most appropriate. CDSS "hard stops" do not allow the physician options to ignore a warning. An example of a "hard stop" could be the use of a very expensive, broad-spectrum antibiotic that by hospital policy can only be ordered by an infectious disease specialist. In this case, the CDSS would not allow the physician to order the medication, but would inform them that an infectious disease consult is required to order the drug and would make ordering that consult a mouse click away. A nonmedical example of a "hard stop" is the automobile design preventing the shift of an automatic transmission out of park and into drive unless the brake petal is depressed. This was implemented after reports of multiple accidental injuries and deaths attributed to unanticipated automobile movements. In this, like the medical example, the decision support system prevents the operator from making an error with a high probability of significant adverse consequences. Because the computer never fatigues, the reminders compensate for physicians' biological limitations, and the human–computer hybrid system outperforms what either could accomplish on its own.

There are hundreds of studies and randomized controlled trials published in the peer-reviewed biomedical literature that have demonstrated how CDSS holds the potential to improve physician performance in myriad healthcare venues. CDSS similarly designed to produce pop-up warnings and recommendations to physicians have been shown to improve ordering of age-appropriate screening tests,[18,19] appropriate antibiotic prescribing for inpatients,[59] appropriate advance directive discussions with patients,[60] use of preventative care for hospitalized patients,[19] appropriate weaning of patients from mechanical ventilators, appropriate reductions of inpatient resource utilization,[61] reduction in prevalence of methicillin-resistant *Staphylococcus aureus* (MRSA) in a community,[62] isolation rates of patients admitted to the hospital with drug-resistant infections,[63] screening for sexually transmitted diseases in hospital emergency departments,[64] accurate capture and recording of patient temperatures by nurses in the inpatient setting,[65] and many other situations. Until recently, most of these studies were performed at major university healthcare centers that had custom-designed EHR software systems maintained by local IT departments with relatively large IT support budgets (compared with the smaller budgets of community hospitals).[16] In 2006, Chaudhry et al. published a systematic review of 257 CDSS studies published up to 2005, concluding that 25% of the studies were from four major academic institutions that all had custom-designed systems and ". . . only 9 studies evaluated multifunctional, commercially developed systems."[16] Therefore, while there are hundreds of studies demonstrating the *potential* for CDSS to improve the quality of care and/or reduce its costs, the appropriate application of this research to typical healthcare settings other than large academic institutions is largely unknown.

The AHRQ commissioned the most systematic, rigorous, and comprehensive review of CDSS studies to date and published the results in 2012.[3] The systematic review analyzed 311 studies in the peer-reviewed biomedical literature and found moderately strong evidence confirming three previously reported factors associated with successful CDSS implementation:

1. Automatic provision of decision support as part of clinician workflow
2. Provision of decision support at time and location of decision making
3. Provision of a recommendation, not just an assessment

The study also identified six additional factors that were correlated with the successful implementation of CDSS:

1. Integration with charting or order entry system to support workflow integration
2. No need for additional clinician data entry
3. Promotion of action rather than inaction
4. Justification of decision support via provision of research evidence
5. Local user involvement in the CDSS development process
6. Provision of decision support results to patients as well as providers

The study found a high strength of evidence for CDSS to improve the ordering and completing of preventive care and ordering and prescribing recommended treatments "across academic, VA, and community inpatient and ambulatory settings that had both locally and commercially developed CDSS systems."[3]

There was a moderate strength of evidence that CDSS improves appropriate ordering of clinical studies, reduces patient morbidity and cost of care, and increases healthcare provider satisfaction. Studies demonstrated a low strength of evidence for CDSS impact on efficiency of the user, length of hospital stay, mortality, health-related quality of life, and "adverse events" or medical errors.

The study also pointed out some significant voids in the current biomedical literature. None of the studies addressed the impact of CDSS on healthcare delivery organization changes, on the number of patients seen per unit of time, on user knowledge, on system cost effectiveness, or on physician workload.

The current cumulative evidence for the benefits of EHRs with CPOE and CDSS is mixed. Even in areas where there is a high strength of evidence, such as improvement in the ordering and completing of preventive care, the effective magnitude of the improvement is small, even though statistically significant.[3]

▶ Health Information Exchanges

Virtually none of the commercially available EHR systems available in today's market or the custom-designed systems at large academic institutions can easily exchange patients' health information with care providers outside of their institutions. Despite more than 50 years of efforts, patients' health information remains "siloed," and "it is not uncommon for a single patient to be cared for by a large number of agencies in a single city, and workers in any one agency usually cannot find out about the activities of others; sometimes they even fail to learn that other agencies are active at all."[66] The barriers to EHR interoperability often become apparent when a patient sees a number of different specialty physicians and attempts to coordinate the flow of information among them. Unlike other industries such as air transportation, the healthcare system has been largely unsuccessful in designing a common platform to allow EHR compatibility among multiple vendor systems. In addition, the Health Insurance Portability and Accountability Act (HIPAA) regulations have had a chilling effect on healthcare institutions' willingness to share data with other institutions due to liability for patient privacy and security of patient data.

Another reason patients' health information is not easily transmitted between various institutions with different EHR systems is that some EHR vendors actively block information transfer. Allegations of information blocking reached a sufficient level that on April 10, 2015, the ONC delivered a "Report to Congress on Health Information Blocking."[67] According to the report, "The full extent of the information blocking problem is difficult to assess, primarily because health IT developers impose contractual restrictions that prohibit customers from reporting or even discussing costs, restrictions, and other relevant details. Still, from the evidence available, it is readily apparent that some providers and developers are engaging in information blocking."[68] The 21st Century Cures Act was an attempt to further reduce information blocking. The ONC issued final guidance noting civil monetary penalties for health IT developers who engage in information blocking.[69]

These and other factors led to development of HIEs with their corresponding administering organizations, regional health information organizations (RHIOs). RHIOs attempt to create systems, agreements, processes, and technology to manage these factors in order to facilitate the appropriate exchange of healthcare information between institutions and across different vendor platforms. While most states and regions of the United States have RHIOs, the actual state of implementation and real data exchange varies widely. For example, some states have active RHIOs that are in the planning stages of establishing relationships with all key stakeholders, creating administration agreements, creating governance structures, securing funding, attempting to develop business models for sustained funding of the organization, etc. Other RHIOs have functioning HIEs where medical data are being exchanged between institutions and across disparate software EHR platforms. The ONC has funded many RHIOS to develop and test their national standards for HIE with the ultimate goal of creating the "Nationwide Health Information Network," which would be a network of regional networks across the whole country. Despite the testing and demonstration projects to date, actively functioning HIEs exist only at regional levels.

Each vendor's building toward one common standard would significantly reduce the technical complexity of data exchange. Unfortunately, vendors' products are still not being built toward one national standard to facilitate electronic HIE. Despite these limitations, there have been significant accomplishments in implementing the data and IT standards necessary to facilitate the exchange of health information among multiple EHR platforms. Today, most institutions participating in HIEs must build or configure "interface engines" that convert an institution's data to the format used by the HIE. This is a major challenge, as no single standard provides sufficient specification of data formats and communication protocols. Rather, a number of standards address various domains of data management. In addition, the voluminous scope of modern health care and continuous advancements in knowledge and technology make managing data in the healthcare domain extremely dynamic and complex.

As an example of this complexity, the Logical Observation Identifiers Names and Codes (LOINC) standard was developed in the 1990s to solve a problem with an older health information communication protocol that specified how clinical data should be identified for transmission between computer systems. LOINC uniquely defines codes for information, such as blood chemistry laboratory tests, and clinical observations, such as patient blood pressure that can be recorded in many different formats. There are currently more than 70,000 LOINC-defined codes for uniquely reporting laboratory tests and clinical observations.[70] For example, there are 419 different codes for reporting blood pressure. With its unique codes for laboratory tests and clinical observations, LOINC enables computer systems receiving the data to generate exact interpretations. This is called semantic interoperability. Semantic interoperability is essential for patient record transmission from one EHR system to another so that the meaning of the critical data contained within the records is not at risk of erroneous interpretation.

Because new laboratory tests are constantly being developed and existing assays are being improved, LOINC creates and disseminates new codes so that semantic interoperability can be maintained. Old codes are not deleted from the system, ensuring that researchers using prior clinical databases can retrieve prior results comparable with new codes. LOINC is supported by the National Library of Medicine (NLM), one of the National Institutes of Health. The LOINC Committee publishes quarterly updates and holds biannual national meetings to discuss proposed new clinical observations and laboratory tests for the assignment of new LOINC codes.

For an HIE to transfer information accurately, each EHR system must map its own internal code for each datum to a standard code to ensure that information passed from one EHR to another in the exchange is interpreted exactly the same by the receiver as by the sender's system. LOINC is one of the many HIT-related standards. The Systematized Nomenclature of Medicine (SNOMED) was originally developed by the College of American Pathologists (CAP) to specify tissue pathologic diagnoses. The same group also developed a standard for clinical observations called SNOMED Clinical Terms (SNOMED CT). LOINC and SNOMED CT domain standards somewhat overlap, but their design characteristics are valuable in different situations; for example, exchanging laboratory results (where LOINC works better) versus coding patient problem lists within EHRs (where SNOMED CT works better). Similar to LOINC, CAP also provides periodic updates to SNOMED CT codes.

To keep track of the many coding standards and the terms within, the NLM built and maintains the Unified Medical Language System (UMLS), which houses a massive "metathesaurus" and a variety of tools for mapping between and discovery of more than 200 biomedically related terminology standards.[71] Because LOINC, SNOMED CT, and the 200 or so other standards are periodically updated, the UMLS also is updated regularly to keep the inter-standard terminology mapping current and accurate.

Using HIEs, designated member groups of healthcare institutions exchange data in a standardized format using a combination of the previously described standards. This cooperation enables access to a comprehensive clinical data set on individual patients across multiple institutions and multiple EHR vendor platforms.

There are three models of HIE architectures: centralized, federated or decentralized, and hybrid.[72] With the centralized architecture design, all member institutions periodically send copies of their clinical data to one central repository where all the data reside together in one format. The advantage of this approach is that a patient's comprehensive data can be maintained in one place and in one format. However, this approach has several disadvantages. First, the frequency with which members contribute and update copies of institutional data can vary, making the comprehensive HIE medical record potentially out of date. Second, aggregating data from multiple institutions creates administrative complexity with regard to HIPAA regulations. HIPAA requires each healthcare institution to maintain security of its patients' data. If an institution's data are "mixed" in the HIE database with data from other institutions, the responsibility of ensuring patient privacy and data

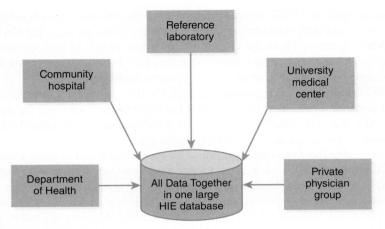

FIGURE 11-5 HIE Centralized Model

security reverts to all HIE member institutions. HIPAA requirements make fulfilling healthcare organization obligations to ensure patient privacy more difficult and complex. Third, when data are aggregated by a third party or HIE, the ability of the source institution to assert control over data contributed to the collective HIE is limited. If, for example, an institution desires to stop participating in an HIE because of concern for patient privacy and data security, it may be technically difficult and time consuming to selectively delete all data from one institution from the HIE database. The centralized model of health information exchange is depicted in **FIGURE 11-5**.

The federated model of health information exchange allows contributing institutions to maintain control over data for which they are responsible under HIPAA. In this model, institutional data resides within each institution's system. The HIE database is small, containing only a master patient index (MPI) housing the identifiers for each patient in the form of each institution's unique patient record numbers along with patient demographic data sufficient to facilitate accurate identification of individual patients with the same or similar names. This information is mapped to all of the institution-specific patient identifiers in the exchange. **FIGURE 11-6** depicts the federated model.

With the federated model, a patient who has medical records at more than one institution in the HIE would have all medical record numbers from the various institutions that store their clinical data linked together in the common MPI, along with basic demographics such as address, date of birth, and Social Security number. This allows for fast and accurate identification of patients named "John Smith," for example, because the MPI maintains sufficient identifying information to ensure selection of the correct patient among all institutions in the exchange.

"John Smith" would be identified from others with the same name by parameters such as date of birth or Social Security number. No clinical data are stored in the MPI. Clinical data usually are maintained in the proprietary format of the particular EHR system used by each institution. Each institution also maintains a copy of the same data in the HIE standardized form. For example, all HIE members could agree to code all laboratory test results using the LOINC standard described earlier. Each institution would create and maintain a database of all patients' laboratory results coded with LOINC. When a user requests a comprehensive record from the HIE, the system would query all of its institutional members in real time to send all the data

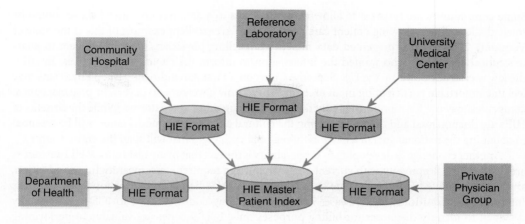

FIGURE 11-6 HIE Federated or Decentralized Model

Institutions maintain copies of their own data at their site in the format used by the HIE. Individual transinstitutional patient records are assembled in real time by searching all institutions' databases only when needed/requested by authorized users. Individual institutions can "opt out" of the HIE at any time by disabling access to their database.

available on a particular patient as identified using the MPI. In this way, when an HIE receives a records request on a particular patient, each institution sends data on the requested patient from the database where all clinical data are in the HIE format. This process ensures that the data are collected securely, assembled into a comprehensive record, and made available to authorized users in real time. This comprehensive record is only accessible on a patient-by-patient basis for immediate patient care purposes; it is not copied to any institution's system. When the user logs out of the HIE, the comprehensive record assembled for that episode of patient care is deleted. The federated model is common, with hybrids being most widely used.

The federated model has several advantages over the centralized model. With the federated model, each institution maintains complete control over its data, simplifying compliance with HIPAA regulations. If, for example, a data breach occurs in the database of an HIE that uses the centralized model, responsibility for the data breach is not always clear. Data breaches in a federated system usually are attributable to a particular institution and not the HIE (unless there is a data breach of the MPI). Another benefit of the federated system is that transinstitutional data can be up-to-the-minute accurate because each time a user requests access, the clinical data from all institutions are assembled in real time. Institutional HIT administrators typically favor the federated model because they have the option of withdrawing from the HIE at any time in order to maintain control of patient privacy and data security under HIPAA guidelines.

While communities with HIEs generally appreciate the benefits of interoperability, the current reality is that most of the operating HIEs are heavily subsidized with federal research grant funding to keep them afloat. The RHIOs that administer the HIEs and seek funding have not developed a business model that can be used in all communities in order to sustain their HIEs independent of federal funding. Some HIEs require each participating institution to pay an annual amount based on their institution's size, the number of physicians, etc. Some have developed services for payers, charging them for access to the comprehensive records available in the HIE. These services allow payers to increase their claims processing efficiency. Other HIEs have developed services to generate comprehensive quality reports to sell to payers desiring to track physician and health plan outcomes or to help them meet the meaningful use requirements for CMS financial eligibility incentives.

Some communities are resistant to allowing payer access to a data resource they believe should be solely dedicated to improving patient care and quality.[73] An excellent example of this is the State of Vermont's 2006 law that prevented data miners from selling physicians' prescribing data to pharmaceutical companies who wanted the information to inform their marketing practices. In 2011, the law was struck down by the U.S. Supreme Court on a First Amendment basis.[74] Physicians may feel uncomfortable participating in an exchange they know government, payers, or pharmaceutical companies may use for monitoring individual practice outcomes and patterns. While the benefits of HIEs are documented and desirable, solving the cultural and business model issues will be essential to obtaining the national goal of a network of regional exchanges that will span the entire country.

Another challenge to developing interoperability is the fact that many institutions' HIT resources are dedicated to keeping up with current quality reporting requirements, meaningful use adoption, and other mandated HIT issues. One example was the CMS-mandated conversion from using the International Classification of Disease, 9th Revision billing codes (ICD-9) to ICD-10. Originally designed to identify diagnoses for billing purposes only, ICD-9 codes are valuable in performing automated chart reviews for quality control and research purposes. However, because of several deficiencies with ICD-9, the new ICD-10 standards were mandated. A full discussion of the key differences between ICD-9 and ICD-10 is well beyond the scope of this book. A focus on just one issue illustrates the magnitude of the change—the impact on the complexity of physician documentation.

There are approximately 13,000 ICD-9 codes and more than 65,000 ICD-10 codes. The greater number of ICD-10 codes is due to the higher specificity of ICD-10. For example, ICD-9 codes did not include laterality (i.e., right and left side of body). ICD-9 has a grand total of two possible codes for a thumb fracture:

815.01	Closed Fracture of the Base of the Thumb (First) Metacarpal
815.11	Open Fracture of Base of Thumb (First) Metacarpal

Some of the codes for the same injury in ICD-10 include:

S62.511B	Displaced fracture of proximal phalanx of right thumb, initial encounter for open fracture
S62.511D	Displaced fracture of proximal phalanx of right thumb, subsequent encounter for fracture with routine healing
S62.511G	Displaced fracture of proximal phalanx of right thumb, subsequent encounter for fracture with delayed healing
S62.511K	Displaced fracture of proximal phalanx of right thumb, subsequent encounter for fracture with nonunion
S62.511P	Displaced fracture of proximal phalanx of right thumb, subsequent encounter for fracture with malunion
S62.511S	Displaced fracture of proximal phalanx of right thumb, sequela

In addition to the six ICD-10 codes listed above, there are 99 additional choices to account for various combinations of displaced/nondisplaced, open/closed, proximal/distal location, right/left, union/nonunion/malunion of fracture, routine/delayed healing, initial/subsequent encounter, and so on. For decades, physicians have been writing their narratives in patient records supporting the billing process for the simpler ICD-9 code set. With ICD-10, the narrative in this example requires sufficient documentation to support the selection of the exact ICD-10 billing code; in other words, the narrative must include mention of displaced/nondisplaced, open/closed, proximal/distal phalanx location, right/left, etc. Failure to do so could result in no reimbursement or even fines from a CMS chart audit. This requirement for added specificity has been the most significant change to the way in which physicians document diagnoses in decades.

▶ The Veterans Health Administration Health Information System

No discussion of HIT, EHRs, and HIEs would be complete without noting the HIT system used by the Veterans Health Administration (VHA). The VHA is a model representing a single-payer healthcare system in the United States. Unlike other components of the healthcare delivery system, the VHA HIT system supports only one payer, one pharmaceutical formulary, one provider group, and one supplier of laboratory testing. All VHA physicians are employees of the same organization, so new policies and practices can be communicated, implemented, and monitored much more easily and efficiently than in the U.S. multipayer, multiformulary, siloed systems. Also, the VHA has one universal EHR system with CPOE and CDSS. The VA EHR is able to code all data in one format that allows veterans who move from state to state to have their entire VHA medical record seamlessly follow them. All these factors have allowed the VHA to offer high-quality care at a relatively reasonable cost. Until the United States creates a single-payer system and uses the same EHR universally, the larger system will suffer from the enormous complexity and costs of developing and maintaining multiple data standards to support the exchange of health information among institutions and across vendor platforms.

▶ Electronic Health Record Adoption Progress in the United States

The National Center for Health Statistics (NCHS) has tracked the use of EHRs in the outpatient setting since 2006.[75] The NCHS specifically defines two levels of adoption as "any" and "basic." This distinction is important because many other surveys report EHR adoption rates but do not define in any detail what "EHR adoption" actually means. This survey uses an exacting definition of "any" and "basic" EHR adoption that produces results that are much more valid than surveys where "adoption" is not well defined. **FIGURE 11-7** illustrates current state of adoption for the outpatient setting.[76] This report indicated that all states with the exception of New York and the District of Columbia have some level of EHR adoption.

The ONC has been tracking hospitals' adoption of EHRs since 2008 using standard definitions of "Certified" and "Basic" EHR systems. **FIGURE 11-8** illustrates the hospital EHR adoption rates.[76] This report showed all states except six and the District of Columbia have made progress to adopt a certified EHR.

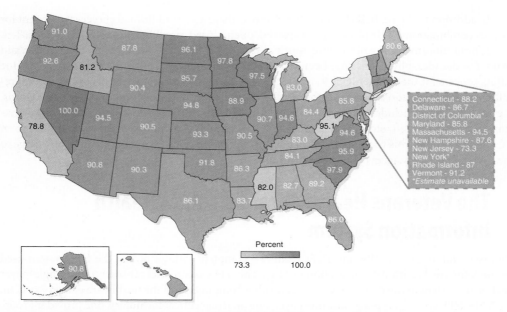

FIGURE 11-7 EHR Adoption Among U.S. Office-Based Physicians, as of 2017[76]

Created by Richard Greenhill.

Data from Myrick KL, Ogburn DF, Ward BW. Table. Percentage of office-based physicians using any electronic health record (EHR)/electronic medical record (EMR) system and physicians that have a certified EHR/EMR system, by U.S. state: National Electronic Health Records Survey, 2017. National Center for Health Statistics. Published January 2019. Updated August 6, 2021. Accessed September 10, 2021. https://www.healthit.gov/data/quickstats/office-based-physician-electronic-health-record-adoption#:~:text=As%20of%202017%2C%20nearly%209,had%20adopted%20a%20certified%20EHR

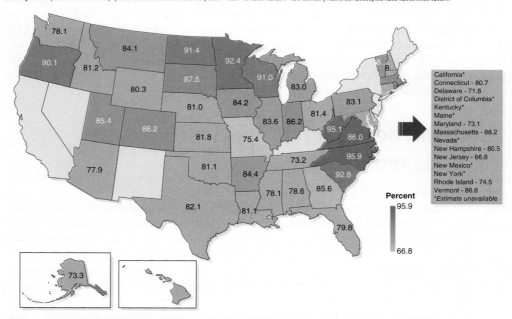

FIGURE 11-8 Certified EHR Adoption Among U.S. Office-Based Physicians, as of 2017[76]

Created by Richard Greenhill.

Data from Myrick KL, Ogburn DF, Ward BW. Table. Percentage of office-based physicians using any electronic health record (EHR)/electronic medical record (EMR) system and physicians that have a certified EHR/EMR system, by U.S. state: National Electronic Health Records Survey, 2017. National Center for Health Statistics. Published January 2019. Updated August 6, 2021. Accessed September 10, 2021. https://www.healthit.gov/data/quickstats/office-based-physician-electronic-health-record-adoption#:~:text=As%20of%202017%2C%20nearly%209,had%20adopted%20a%20certified%20EHR

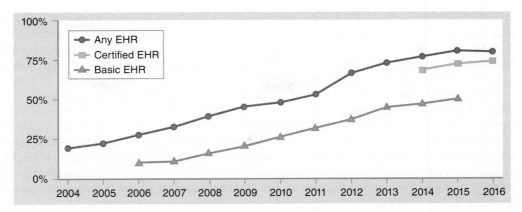

FIGURE 11-9 **Trended EHR Adoption Option Among U.S. Office-Based Physicians, 2004–2016**

Created by Richard Greenhill.

Data from Office of the National Coordinator for Health Information Technology. Office-based physician electronic health record adoption. Updated August 6, 2021. Accessed August 20, 2021. https://www.healthit.gov/data/quickstats/office-based-physician-electronic-health-record-adoption

FIGURE 11-9 illustrates yearly trends and trajectory for adoption in the outpatient setting.[75] This report indicated that as of 2016, nearly 9 in 10 (86%) office-based physicians had adopted any EHR. The types of computerized function for "any" includes patient demographics, problem lists, documented home medication lists, laboratory and radiology results. Nearly 4 in 5 (80%) had adopted a certified EHR, partially or completely electronic, without attached billing systems. Since 2008, office-based physician adoption of any EHRs has more than doubled, from 42% to 86%. ONC and the CDC began tracking adoption of certified EHRs by office-based physicians in 2014.

These trends show a steady increase in adoption of EHRs over the course of time. More will need to be done to assist physician offices with the administrative burden of adopting and maintaining EHR in their practices. Note that EHR adoption rates are typically published every 2 to 3 years by the NCHS and the ONC.

▶ Future Challenges

While there is mounting evidence supporting the value of EHRs with CPOE and CDSS in several well-defined areas such as improving preventive care delivery, extensive meta-analyses report combined average results. There have been several inconclusive and negative studies, and some have actually shown patient harm associated with the installation of CPOE. In one of the most extensively reported analyses, the mortality rate in a neonatal intensive care unit more than doubled after a CPOE system was installed at the University of Pittsburgh.[77] Much has been written about the reasons for this negative result, and despite the finger pointing, there is virtually universal agreement that HIT can be very disruptive to work processes and work cultures, resulting in significant harm to patients.[78] Some have called for more HIT standards and regulation to prevent negative consequences in the same way the U.S. Food and Drug Administration regulates medical devices.[79,80]

Due to the administrative and technical difficulties of achieving the Nationwide Health Information Network, proprietary entities have offered alternate approaches to develop personal health records (PHRs) through which patients create their own records in a standardized format. In these approaches, patients may physically carry records or make them available to caregivers via the Internet. Microsoft, Google, and many other corporate entities have built such systems but with little marketing success. Google Health announced its shutdown on June 24, 2011, after only 3 years of operation. Google joins other lesser-known firms that have decided to close down PHR services.[81] Design of existing PHRs requires patients to have a high level of health literacy and computer savvy. A major reason analysts believed Google Health failed was the newness of the concept and the facts that PHRs are difficult to use and many people find the data entry work necessary to complete their record too laborious.[82] One survey of patients found that only 7% had tried using a PHR and only about 3% continued to use them in 2011.[82] Other barriers to patient adoption include lack of personal health management tools, the difficulty in achieving semantic interoperability such that personal health management tools could be useful, problems vetting the identity of PHR users, patient privacy concerns, and perhaps, most importantly, the lack of a business model to support the long-term operation of PHRs.[81]

In addition to physicians and patients affected by development and implementation of HIT, there are many other healthcare professionals and venues affected by significant complexities and characteristics that make HIT implementation challenging. Many of the same issues previously discussed in this chapter apply to these venues, such as standardized data formats to facilitate data portability, work culture barriers, system costs, training issues, and other matters. For example, some emergency medical services (EMS) providers have begun to use a variety of portable EHRs to collect data at the scenes of patient incidents with systems designed to transmit data to receiving hospitals. The same issues that complicate the ease of universal HIE between healthcare institutions apply to the data exchange between EMS and hospital systems and will not be resolved easily.

To achieve the HIT goals of improving healthcare quality and reducing costs, extensive and rigorous work remains in the research and implementation arenas. After 50 years of efforts, most notably in the past 5 years, government, industry, and academia are only now recognizing the critically important and interdependent roles that standardization, administrative processes, and work cultures play in the achievement of HIT-desired outcomes.

CASE 11-1   Post-EHR Implementation – Delays in the Emergency Department

Situation

Johnathan Robertsen, RN, MSHA is the Senior Director of the Emergency Department at the Care Excellence Medical Center. He is known around the facility for his inclusive leadership and partnership with clinicians (e.g., physicians, ancillary staff, etc.). Since taking over the department 3 years ago, the patient satisfaction scores have increased year over year and are at their highest since it opened. His clinical staff is diverse (in terms of gender and cultures) with an average annual turnover rate of less than 2.5%.

An new electronic health record (EHR) module has been implemented in the Emergency Department (ED). One of the objectives of the implementation will be to capture clinical data that is necessary for quality improvement. Financial data will not be captured in the EHR and is being manually entered on logs that are stored for about 8 years. This storage requirement is for regulatory purposes. The nurses are working hard to input clinical data into the new EHR. However, the average patient hold time has increased by more than 30% due to the nurses having difficulty in entering data into the EHR. Management predicted an increase in ED wait time during the EHR implementation, but was optimistic that the trend would decrease in a few weeks. After 2 months, however, the learning curve continued and the recovery nurses were still having difficulty.

As a result of the EHR input difficulty, delays in routing patients from the ED to nursing units and the intensive care unit (ICU) have been reported. Hospitalists are extremely upset about the delay and maintain cautious concern over patient safety. The average delay time is 30 to 95 minutes. Bed management nurses document the delays in a multifunctional software system that captures data for both clinical and financial purposes. (This system is separate from the newly implemented EHR.) Patients on the day shift tend to make it to units in a timely manner. After day shift, about 40% of patients experience delayed entry upon leaving the ED. Performance indicators have been showing unfavorable results. Declining staff productivity for both the ED and the bed management area is one of the unfavorable performance outcomes. The current staff productivity rate is 75%, but the target percentage is 95%. Productivity is measured by patient volume and the number of worked hours by staff. Despite the declining volume, staffing patterns for both areas have remained unchanged.

Discussion Questions

1. How should the leadership team develop a plan to address the declining performance measures?
2. What data requirements will be needed to make informed decisions?
3. What data requirements do you think are needed to improve staff productivity?
4. Why are performance indicators important and how should they be used to support decision making?
5. How often should performance indicator data be reported and used for management purposes?

Written by Richard Greenhill. Data from Johnson JA, Musch S. *Multi-Sector Casebook in Health Administration, Leadership, and Management.* Cengage Learning; 2013.

▶ Discussion Questions

- The United States has invested a lot of financial resources into HIT efforts. Based on these investments, do you think that HIT has had a positive impact on healthcare delivery? Why or why not?
- What could the federal government do to encourage greater transparency around HIT implementation failures?
- Which legislative action has had the most influence on HIT? Explain your choice.
- There are many laws, rules, and regulations related to HIT. Do you think they are working together or against each other? Discuss your choice.
- Of the three components that drive successful implementation, which can the federal government influence the most?
- Do you think state governments have a role in HIT implementation success? Why or why not?
- Why has CDSS not become more widely used? Which of the components of successful implementation do you believe has slowed its adoption?
- How do you think silos in patient data add risk to care delivery? Which HIE model do you think is the best to reduce silos?
- What can states and the federal government do to support EHR adoption for physician offices?
- Given what you have read, name two challenges that you think are on the horizon for HIT in the United States.

CHAPTER ACRONYMS

ACA Affordable Care Act

AHRQ Agency for Healthcare Research and Quality

ARRA American Recovery and Reinvestment Act

CAP College of American Pathologists

CARF Commission on Accreditation of Rehabilitation Facilities

CDSS computerized decision support system

CMS Centers for Medicare & Medicaid Services

CPHQ Certified Professional in Healthcare Quality

CPOE computerized physician order entry

eCQM electronic clinical quality measures

ED Emergency department

EHR electronic health record

EMR electronic medical record

EMS emergency medical services

HAC Hospital-acquired conditions

HIE health information exchange

HIPAA Health Insurance Portability and Accountability Act

HIT health information technology

HITECH Health Information Technology for Economic and Clinical Health Act

ICD International Classification of Diseases

ICU Intensive care unit

IHI Institute for Healthcare Improvement

IT Information technology

LOINC Logical Observations Identifiers Names and Codes

MACRA Medicare Access and CHIP Reauthorization Act

MPI master patient index

MRSA methicillin-resistant *Staphylococcus aureus*

NAHQ National Association for Healthcare Quality

NCHS National Center for Health Statistics

NCQA National Committee for Quality Assurance

NLM National Library of Medicine

NQF National Quality Forum

ONC Office of the National Coordinator (short for ONCHIT)

ONCHIT Office of the National Coordinator for Health Information Technology

PHR Personal health record

RHIO regional health information organizations

SNOMED CT SNOMED Clinical Terms

SNOMED Systematized Nomenclature of Medicine

TJC The Joint Commission

UMLS Unified Medical Language System

VHA Veterans Health Administration

WHO World Health Organization

References

1. Bush GW. Executive order: incentives for the use of health information technology and establishing the position of the national health information technology coordinator. Published April 27, 2004. Accessed February 14, 2021. http://georgewbush-whitehouse.archives.gov/news/releases/2004/04/20040427-4.html

2. 111th U.S. Congress. *The American Recovery and Reinvestment Act*. Accessed February 14, 2021. https://obamawhitehouse.archives.gov/recovery/about

3. Lobach D, Sanders GD, Bright TJ, et al. Enabling health care decisionmaking through clinical decision support and knowledge management. *Evid Rep Technol Assess (Full Rep)*. 2012;(203):1-784.

4. McDonald CJ. Protocol-based computer reminders, the quality of care and the non-perfectability of man. *N Engl J Med*. 1976;295(24):1351-1355. doi: 10.1056/NEJM197612092952405

5. Yount RJ, Vries JK, Councill CD. The medical archival system: an information retrieval system based on distributed parallel processing. *Inf Process Manage*. 1991;27:379-389. doi: 10.1016/0306-4573(91)90091-Y

6. Gardner RM, Pryor TA, Warner HR. The HELP hospital information system: update 1998. *Int J Med Inform*. 1999;54(3):169-182. doi: 10.1016/s1386-5056(99)00013-1

7. Pryor TA, Gardner RM, Clayton PD, Warner HR. The HELP system. *J Med Syst*. 1983;7(2):87-102. doi: 10.1007/BF00995116

8. Higgins SB, Jiang K, Swindell BB, Bernard GR. A graphical ICU workstation. *Proc Annu Symp Comput Appl Med Care*. 1991:783-787.

9. Giuse DA, Mickish A. Increasing the availability of the computerized patient record. *Proc AMIA Annu Fall Symp.* 1996:633-637.

10. Stead WW, Hammond WE. Computer-based medical records: the centerpiece of TMR. *MD Comput.* 1988;5(5):48-62.

11. Greenes RA, Pappalardo AN, Marble CW, Barnett GO. Design and implementation of a clinical data management system. *Comput Biomed Res.* 1969;2(5): 469-485. doi: 10.1016/0010-4809(69)90012-3

12. Ash JS, Bates DW. Factors and forces affecting EHR system adoption: report of a 2004 ACMI discussion. *J Am Med Inform Assoc.* 2005;12(1):8-12. doi: 10.1197 /jamia.M1684

13. Ash JS, Stavri PZ, Dykstra R, Fournier L. Implementing computerized physician order entry: the importance of special people. *Int J Med Inform.* 2003;69(2-3): 235-250. doi: 10.1016/s1386-5056(02)00107-7

14. Campbell EM, Guappone KP, Sittig DF, Dykstra RH, Ash JS. Computerized provider order entry adoption: implications for clinical workflow. *J Gen Intern Med.* 2009;24(1):21-26. doi: 10.1007/s11606-008-0857-9

15. Bloomrosen M, Starren J, Lorenzi NM, Ash JS, Patel VL, Shortliffe EH. Anticipating and addressing the unintended consequences of health IT and policy: a report from the AMIA 2009 Health Policy Meeting. *J Am Med Inform Assoc.* 2011;18(1):82-90. doi: 10 .1136/jamia.2010.007567

16. Chaudhry B, Wang J, Wu S, et al. Systematic review: impact of health information technology on quality, efficiency, and costs of medical care. *Ann Intern Med.* 2006;144(10):742-752. doi: 10.7326/0003-4819 -144-10-200605160-00125

17. Connolly C. Cedars-Sinai doctors cling to pen and paper. *Washington Post.* Published March 21, 2005. Accessed August 19, 2021. https://www.washing tonpost.com/archive/politics/2005/03/21/cedars-sinai -doctors-cling-to-pen-and-paper/7789c328-61f3 -405c-b2bb-f11e4f7e5baf/

18. Dexter PR, Perkins S, Overhage JM, Maharry K, Kohler RB, McDonald CJ. A computerized reminder system to increase the use of preventive care for hospitalized patients. *N Engl J Med.* 2001;345(13): 965-970. doi: 10.1056/NEJMsa010181

19. Weiner M, Callahan CM, Tierney WM, et al. Using information technology to improve the health care of older adults. *Ann Intern Med.* 2003;139(5 Pt 2):430-436. doi: 10.7326/0003-4819-139-5_part_2-200309021-00010

20. Dexter PR, Perkins SM, Maharry KS, Jones K, McDonald CJ. Inpatient computer-based standing orders vs physician reminders to increase influenza and pneumococcal vaccination rates: a randomized trial. *JAMA.* 2004;292(19):2366-2371. doi: 10.1001 /jama.292.19.2366

21. Overhage JM, Dexter PR, Perkins SM, et al. A randomized, controlled trial of clinical information shared from another institution. *Ann Emerg Med.* 2002;39(1):14-23. doi: 10.1067/mem.2002.120794

22. Centers for Medicare & Medicaid Services. Medicare and Medicaid EHR incentive program basics. Updated April 13, 2021. Accessed August 19, 2021. https://www .cms.gov/Regulations-and-Guidance/Legislation /EHRIncentivePrograms/Basics

23. Office of the National Coordinator for Health Information Technology. Meaningful use. Accessed February 14, 2021. https://www.healthit.gov/topic /meaningful-use-and-macra/meaningful-use

24. Centers for Medicare & Medicaid Services. EHR incentive programs for eligible hospitals & CAHs: what you need to know for 2015 tipsheet. Accessed February 14, 2021. https://www.cms.gov/Regulations -and-Guidance/Legislation/EHRIncentivePrograms /Downloads/2015_NeedtoKnowEP.pdf

25. Centers for Medicare & Medicaid Services. 2016 program requirements. Updated December 12, 2019. Accessed February 14, 2021. https://www.cms.gov /Regulations-and-Guidance/Legislation/EHRIncentive Programs/2016ProgramRequirements

26. Centers for Medicare & Medicaid Services. Medicaid hospital incentive payments calculations. Updated May 2013. Accessed February 14, 2021. https://www .cms.gov/Regulations-and-Guidance/Legislation /EHRIncentivePrograms/Downloads/MLN _TipSheet_MedicaidHospitals.pdf

27. Office of the National Coordinator for Health Information Technology. What is meaningful use? Updated June 1, 2013. Accessed February 14, 2021. https://www.healthit.gov/faq/what-meaningful-use

28. Centers for Medicare & Medicaid Services. EHR Incentive Program for Medicare hospitals: calculating payments. Updated May 2013. Accessed February 14, 2021. https://www.cms.gov/regulations-and-guidance /legislation/ehrincentiveprograms/downloads/mln _tipsheet_medicarehospitals.pdf

29. Centers for Medicare & Medicaid Services. An introduction to: Medicare EHR incentive program for eligible professionals. Accessed February 14, 2021. https://www.cms.gov/regulations-and-guidance /legislation/ehrincentiveprograms/downloads/ehr _medicare_stg1_begguide.pdf

30. Centers for Medicare & Medicaid Services. Eligible hospital and CAH meaningful use table of contents: core and menu set objectives. Updated July 2014. Accessed February 14, 2021. https://www.cms.gov /Regulations-and-Guidance/Legislation/EHRIncen tivePrograms/downloads/Hosp_CAH_MU-TOC .pdf

31. Centers for Medicare & Medicaid Services. Medicare electronic health record incentive payments for eligible professionals. Updated May 2013. Accessed February 14, 2021. https://www.cms.gov/Regulations -and-Guidance/Legislation/EHRIncentivePrograms

/Downloads/MLN_MedicareEHRProgram_TipSheet
_EP.pdf

32. Centers for Medicare & Medicaid Services. Flow chart to help eligible professionals (EP) determine eligibility for the Medicare and Medicaid electronic health record (EHR) Incentive Programs. Published September 2010. Accessed February 15, 2021. https://www.cms.gov/Regulations-and-Guidance /Legislation/EHRIncentivePrograms/downloads /eligibility_flow_chart.pdf

33. Centers for Medicare & Medicaid Services. Eligible hospital information. Updated April 17, 2020. Accessed February 15, 2021. https://www.cms.gov/Regulations -and-Guidance/Legislation/EHRIncentivePrograms /Eligible_Hospital_Information

34. Centers for Medicare & Medicaid Services. Promoting interoperability programs. Updated August 17, 2021. Accessed August 19, 2021. https://www .cms.gov/Regulations-and-Guidance/Legislation /EHRIncentivePrograms

35. Office of the National Coordinator for Health Information Technology. About ONC. Updated March 12, 2021. Accessed August 19, 2021. https://www .healthit.gov/topic/about-onc#:~:text=ONC%20is %20the%20principal%20federal,electronic%20exchange %20of%20health%20information

36. Office of the National Coordinator for Health Information Technology. Justification of estimates for appropriations committees: fiscal year 2016. Accessed February 14, 2021. https://www.healthit.gov /sites/default/files/ONC-FY2016-budget-justification .pdf

37. Office of the National Coordinator for Health Information Technology. Justification of estimates for appropriations committees: fiscal year 2015. Accessed February 15, 2021. https://www.hhs.gov/sites/default /files/budget/fy2015/fy-2015-hhs-congressional -budget-justification.pdf

38. Office of the National Coordinator for Health Information Technology. Health Information Technology Advisory Committee (HITAC). Updated July 14, 2021. Accessed August 19, 2021. https://www .healthit.gov/hitac/committees/health-information -technology-advisory-committee-hitac

39. Centers for Medicare & Medicaid Services. Medicaid electronic health record incentive payments for eligible professionals. Updated May 2013. Accessed February 15, 2021. https://www.cms.gov/Regulations-and-Guidance /Legislation/EHRIncentivePrograms/Downloads /MLN_MedicaidEHRProgram_TipSheet_EP.pdf

40. Healthcare Information and Management Systems Society. Interoperability in healthcare. Accessed August 19, 2021. https://www.himss.org/resources /interoperability-healthcare

41. Office of the National Coordinator for Health Information Technology. National Health IT Policy Committee: recommendations to the National Coordinator for Health IT. Updated February 18, 2021. Accessed August 19, 2021. https://www.healthit .gov/topic/federal-advisory-committees/health -it-policy-committee-recommendations-national -coordinator

42. Centers for Medicare & Medicaid Services. CMS fact sheet: EHR incentive programs in 2015 and beyond. Published October 6, 2015. Accessed February 15, 2021. https://www.cms.gov/newsroom/fact-sheets/cms -fact-sheet-ehr-incentive-programs-2015-and -beyond

43. U.S. Department of Health and Human Services Office of the National Coordinator for Health Information Technology. Eligible professional's guide to Stage 2 of the EHR incentive programs. Published September 2013. Accessed February 15, 2021. https:// www.cms.gov/regulations-and-guidance/legislation /ehrincentiveprograms/downloads/stage2_guide _eps_9_23_13.pdf

44. U.S. Department of Health and Human Services Office of the National Coordinator for Health Information Technology. Stage 2 overview tipsheet. Updated August 2012. Accessed February 15, 2021. https:// www.cms.gov/regulations-and-guidance/legislation /ehrincentiveprograms/downloads/stage2overview _tipsheet.pdf

45. Centers for Medicare & Medicaid Services. Eligible professional EHR incentive program objectives and measures for 2015: table of contents. Accessed February 15, 2021. https://www.cms.gov/Regulations -and-Guidance/Legislation/EHRIncentivePrograms /RequirementsforPreviousYears

46. Centers for Medicare & Medicaid Services. Eligible hospital and critical access hospital EHR incentive program objectives and measures for 2015: table of contents. Accessed February 15, 2021. https://www.cms.gov/Regulations-and-Guidance /Legislation/EHRIncentivePrograms/Requirements forPreviousYears

47. Institute of Medicine Committee on Quality of Health Care in America. *Crossing the Quality Chasm: A New Health System for the 21st Century.* National Academies Press; 2001.

48. World Health Organization. Quality of care. Accessed June 2, 2021. https://www.who.int/health-topics/quality -of-care#tab=tab_1

49. Al-Abri R, Al-Balushi A. Patient satisfaction survey as a tool towards quality improvement. *Oman Med J.* 2014;29(1):3-7. doi: 10.5001/omj.2014.02

50. The Joint Commission. About The Joint Commission. Accessed June 2, 2021. https://www.jointcommission .org/about-us/

51. Det Norske Veritas. About DNV. Accessed June 2, 2021. https://www.dnv.com/about/index.html#drop down-sector-Healthcare

52. National Association for Healthcare Quality. About NAHQ. Accessed June 1, 2021. https://nahq.org/about/about-national-association-healthcare-quality/

53. Commission on the Accreditation of Rehabilitation Facilities. Accessed June 5, 2021. http://www.carf.org/home/

54. Dukette D, Cornish D. *The Essential 20: Twenty Components of an Excellent Health Care Team.* RoseDog Books; 2009:72-74.

55. Parthasarathy S. Sleep and the medical profession. *Curr Opin Pulm Med.* 2005;11(6):507-512. doi: 10.1097/01.mcp.0000183060.60547.40

56. Institute of Medicine. *2007 IOM Annual Meeting Summary: Evidence-Based Medicine and the Changing Nature of Health Care.* National Academies Press; 2008:18-19.

57. Friedman CP. What informatics is and isn't. *J Am Med Inform Assoc.* 2013;20(2):224-226. doi: 10.1136/amiajnl-2012-001206

58. Sirajuddin AM, Osheroff JA, Sittig DF, Chuo J, Velasco F, Collins DA. Implementation pearls from a new guidebook on improving medication use and outcomes with clinical decision support. Effective CDS is essential for addressing healthcare performance improvement imperatives. *J Healthc Inf Manag.* 2009;23(4):38-45.

59. Evans RS, Pestotnik SL, Classen DC, et al. A computer-assisted management program for antibiotics and other antiinfective agents. *N Engl J Med.* 1998;338(4):232-238. doi: 10.1056/NEJM199801223380406

60. Tierney WM, Dexter PR, Gramelspacher GP, Perkins AJ, Zhou XH, Wolinsky FD. The effect of discussions about advance directives on patients' satisfaction with primary care. *J Gen Intern Med.* 2001;16(1):32-40. doi: 10.1111/j.1525-1497.2001.00215.x

61. Tierney WM, Miller ME, Overhage JM, McDonald CJ. Physician inpatient order writing on microcomputer workstations. Effects on resource utilization. *JAMA.* 1993;269(3):379-383.

62. Kho AN, Dexter P, Lemmon L, et al. Connecting the dots: creation of an electronic regional infection control network. *Stud Health Technol Inform.* 2007;129(Pt 1):213-217.

63. Kho A, Dexter P, Warvel J, Commiskey M, Wilson S, McDonald CJ. Computerized reminders to improve isolation rates of patients with drug-resistant infections: design and preliminary results. *AMIA Annu Symp Proc.* 2005:390-394.

64. Rosenman M, Wang J, Dexter P, Overhage JM. Computerized reminders for syphilis screening in an urban emergency department. *AMIA Annu Symp Proc.* 2003:987.

65. Kroth PJ, Dexter PR, Overhage JM, et al. A computerized decision support system improves the accuracy of temperature capture from nursing personnel at the bedside. *AMIA Annu Symp Proc.* 2006:444-448.

66. The Life Sciences Panel of the President's Science Advisory Committee. *Some New Technologies and Their Promise for the Life Sciences.* The White House; 1963. https://www.jfklibrary.org/asset-viewer/archives/JFKPOF/087/JFKPOF-087-003

67. Office of the National Coordinator for Health Information Technology. Report to Congress: report on health information blocking. Published April 2015. Accessed February 15, 2021. https://www.healthit.gov/sites/default/files/reports/info_blocking_040915.pdf

68. DeSalvo KB, Daniel JG. Blocking of health information undermines health system interoperability and delivery reform. Office of the National Coordinator for Health Information Technology. Published April 10, 2015. Accessed February 15, 2021. https://www.healthit.gov/buzz-blog/from-the-onc-desk/health-information-blocking-undermines-interoperability-delivery-reform

69. Office of the National Coordinator for Health Information Technology. *21st Century Cures Act: Interoperability, Information Blocking, and the ONC Health IT Certification Program.* U.S. Department of Health and Human Services; 2020.

70. Lin MC, Vreeman DJ, McDonald CJ, Huff SM. Auditing consistency and usefulness of LOINC use among three large institutions—using version spaces for grouping LOINC codes. *J Biomed Inform.* 2012;45(4):658-666. doi: 10.1016/j.jbi.2012.01.008

71. National Library of Medicine. UMLS quick start guide. Updated July 29, 2016. Accessed August 20, 2021. https://www.nlm.nih.gov/research/umls/quickstart.html

72. Wilcox A, Kuperman G, Dorr DA, et al. Architectural strategies and issues with health information exchange. *AMIA Annu Symp Proc.* 2006;2006:814-818.

73. Sorrell WH. Supreme Court strikes down Vermont prescription privacy law. *VTDigger.* Published June 23, 2011. Accessed February 15, 2021. https://vtdigger.org/2011/06/23/supreme-court-strikes-down-vermont-prescription-drug-privacy-law/

74. The Supreme Court of the United States. *Sorrell, Attorney General of Vermont, et al. v. IMS Health inc. et al.* Published 2011. Accessed February 15, 2021. https://www.supremecourt.gov/opinions/10pdf/10-779.pdf

75. Office of the National Coordinator for Health Information Technology. Office-based physician electronic health record adoption. Updated August 6, 2021. Accessed August 20, 2021. https://www.healthit.gov/data/quickstats/office-based-physician-electronic-health-record-adoption

76. Myrick KL, Ogburn DF, Ward BW. Table. Percentage of office-based physicians using any electronic health record (EHR)/electronic medical record (EMR) system and physicians that have a certified EHR/EMR system, by U.S. state: National Electronic Health

Records Survey, 2017. National Center for Health Statistics. Published January 2019. Updated August 6, 2021. Accessed September 9, 2021. https://www.healthit.gov/data/quickstats/office-based-physician-electronic-health-record-adoption#:~:text=As%20of%202017%2C%20nearly%209,had%20adopted%20a%20certified%20EHR

77. Han YY, Carcillo JA, Venkataraman ST, et al. Unexpected increased mortality after implementation of a commercially sold computerized physician order entry system. *Pediatrics.* 2005;116(6):1506-1512. doi: 10.1542/peds.2005-1287

78. Sittig DF, Ash JS, Zhang J, Osheroff JA, Shabot MM. Lessons from "unexpected increased mortality after implementation of a commercially sold computerized physician order entry system." *Pediatrics.* 2006;118(2): 797-801. doi: 10.1542/peds.2005-3132

79. Miller RA, Gardner RM. Summary recommendations for responsible monitoring and regulation of clinical software systems. American Medical Informatics Association, the Computer-based Patient Record Institute, the Medical Library Association, the Association of Academic Health Science Libraries, the American Health Information Management Association, and the American Nurses Association. *Ann Intern Med.* 1997;127(9):842-845. doi: 10.7326/0003-4819-127-9-199711010-00014

80. Miller RA, Gardner RM. Recommendations for responsible monitoring and regulation of clinical software systems. American Medical Informatics Association, Computer-based Patient Record Institute, Medical Library Association, Association of Academic Health Science Libraries, American Health Information Management Association, American Nurses Association. *J Am Med Inform Assoc.* 1997;4(6):442-457. doi: 10.1136/jamia.1997.0040442

81. Rishel W, Booz RH. Google Health shutdown underscores uncertain future of PHRs. Gartner. Published July 1, 2011. Accessed February 15, 2021. http://www.gartner.com/resources/214600/214682/google_health_shutdown_under_214682.pdf

82. Lohr S. Google is closing its health records service. *New York Times.* Published June 24, 2011. Accessed August 20, 2021. https://www.nytimes.com/2011/06/25/technology/25health.html

CHAPTER 12

Health Services and Systems Research

© STILLFX/iStock/Getty Images Plus/Getty Images

problems of disease or disability, is described along with the rapidly emerging field of health systems research. The goals and initiatives of a major funding source for health services research, the federal Agency for Healthcare Research and Quality, are discussed. Finally, research into the quality of medical care, the problems being addressed, and associated research perspectives and methods are discussed.

The last half of the 1900s and the early 2000s have seen remarkable growth of scientifically rigorous research in medicine, dentistry, nursing, and other health professions. The change from dependence on the clinical impressions of individual physicians, tradition, and other healthcare practitioners to reliance on more accurate scientific findings from carefully controlled studies is one of the most important advances in medicine. Readers of peer-reviewed professional journals can now monitor the progress of basic science and clinical and technologic discoveries, more confident that the published findings were based on research studies designed and conducted to yield statistically significant results.[1]

In contrast, volumes of reports of medical developments that appear in the popular media and on the internet are often premature and, depending on the source, may be cause for skepticism. The imprudent publication of inadequately proved or unproved therapies, the sensationalizing of minor scientific advances, and the promotion of fraudulent devices and treatments create unrealistic patient expectations that often result in disappointment, mistreatment, and costly deceptions. While the internet can be a valuable tool for patients to learn about healthcare issues, it also often provides bad information, which can lead to confusion, anxiety, and false hopes about fraudulent cures.[1]

Despite the advanced state of the internet and modern communications technologies, from both professional and public perspectives, the continuing emergence of new technologies and clinical advances creates ongoing challenges of evaluation, interpretation, and potential applications.

▶ Focus of Different Types of Research

FIGURE 12-1 below illustrates the focus of different types of healthcare research. There are clear distinctions among researchers in terms of methods and the nature of their subsequent findings. Although the kinds of information derived from each type of research may be different, each knowledge gain is an essential step in the never-ending quest to create a more efficient and effective healthcare system.[1]

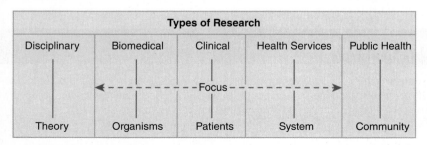

FIGURE 12-1 **Variation in Research Focus**

Reproduced from Young KM, Kroth PJ. *Health Care USA: Understanding its Organization and Delivery.* 9th ed. Jones & Bartlett Learning; 2019.

Clinical research	——————▸	individual level
Biomedical research	——————▸	subindividual level
Health services research	——————▸	individual/population level
Epidemiological research	——————▸	population level
Public health systems research	——————▸	population/systems level
Environmental health research	——————▸	environmental level

FIGURE 12-2 Types of Health-Related Research and Level of Focus

Shi and Johnson also provide a schematic of types of health-related research organized by level of focus.[2] Note that a category titled "Public Health Systems Research" is included, which will be discussed further in this chapter. Another conceptualization of health research can be seen in **FIGURE 12-2**.

Types of Research

Research studies conducted by those in professional disciplines fall into several categories.

Basic Science Research

Basic science research is the work of biochemists, physiologists, biologists, pharmacologists, and others concerned with sciences that are fundamental to understanding the growth, development, structure, and function of the human body. Much of basic science research takes place at the cellular level and is conducted in highly sophisticated laboratories. Other basic research may involve animal or human studies. Whatever its nature, basic science research is an essential antecedent to advances in clinical medicine. Examples of basic research that have led to important advances in medicine are the discovery of DNA (leading to cancer treatments) and neurotransmitters (leading to the development of antidepressants and antiseizure medications).

Clinical Research

Clinical research focuses primarily on the various steps in the process of medical care: the early detection, diagnosis, and treatment of disease or injury; the maintenance of optimal physical, mental, and social functioning; the limitation and rehabilitation of disability; and the palliative care of those who are irreversibly ill. Individuals in all the clinical specialties of medicine, nursing, allied health, and related health professions conduct clinical research, often in collaboration with those in the basic sciences. Much of clinical research is experimental, involving carefully controlled clinical trials of diagnostic or therapeutic procedures, new drugs, or technological developments. Some basics of clinical research are provided in **BOX 12-1**.

Epidemiological Research

Epidemiology is concerned with the distribution and determinants of health, diseases, and injuries in human populations. This type of research often utilizes observational study by collecting observed or reported information about natural phenomena, the characteristics and behaviors of people, aspects of their location or environment, and their exposure to certain circumstances or events.

BOX 12-1   Some Basics of Clinical Research

Clinical trials test a new treatment or drug against a prevailing standard of care. If no standard drug exists or if it is too easily identified, a control group receives a placebo or mock drug to minimize subject bias. To reduce bias further, random selection is used to decide which volunteer patients are in the experimental and control groups. In a well-designed study, none of the personnel associated with the study (e.g., patients, physicians, outcomes assessors) know who is receiving the test drug or treatment until the study is completed and the identifying code revealed.

Research studies have a number of safeguards to protect the safety and rights of human and animal subjects. Studies funded by governmental agencies or foundations are subject to scrutiny by peer review committees or "study sections" that judge the scientific merit of the research design and the potential value of the findings. Next, a hospital- or academically based institutional review board (IRB) ensures the safeguarding of human subjects and appraises the use of animals for research.

Human subjects must provide an informed consent agreement to participate in research to ensure they appreciate both the risks and potential benefits of their participation. Studies with a very low potential for human harm often require only verbal consent, whereas studies that collect blood or tissue from a subject usually require a more formal written consent agreement. The agreement spells out in plain language the risks, benefits, and possible side effects of participation. Some studies may be potentially harmful just based on the mental anguish the subjects may experience by being contacted by investigators or when the subject of the research may be embarrassing or stigmatizing. Subjects must weigh any potential risks against any potential benefits. Often, there are risks but no direct benefits to the subjects other than the knowledge they are helping to advance science.

Data from Koo D, Miner K. Outcome-based workforce development and education in public health. *Annu Rev Public Health*. 2010;31:253-269.

Observational studies may be descriptive or analytical. Descriptive studies use patient records, interview surveys, various databases of existing medical data, and other information sources to identify those factors and conditions that determine the distribution of health and disease among specific populations. They provide the details or characteristics of diseases or biologic phenomena and the prevalence or magnitude of their occurrences. Descriptive studies are relatively fast and inexpensive and often raise questions or suggest hypotheses to be tested. They are often followed by analytic studies, which test hypotheses and try to explain biologic phenomena by seeking statistical associations between factors that may contribute to a subsequent occurrence and the initial occurrence itself.

Some analytic studies attempt, under naturally occurring circumstances, to observe the differences between two or more populations with different characteristics or behaviors. For example, data about smokers and nonsmokers may be collected to determine the relative risk of a related outcome such as lung cancer, or a cohort study may follow a population over time, as in the case of a Framingham, Massachusetts, study.[3] For years, epidemiologists have been studying a cooperating Framingham population to determine associations between variables such as diet, weight, exercise, other behaviors, and characteristics related to heart disease and other outcomes. These observational studies are valuable in explaining patterns of disease or disease processes and providing information about the association of specific activities or agents with health or disease effects.

Experimental Epidemiology   Observational studies are usually followed by experimental studies. In experimental studies, the investigator actively intervenes by manipulating one variable (often called the independent variable) to see what happens to the other (often called the dependent variable, or the one that changes when the independent variable is changed). Although they are the best test of cause and effect, such studies are technically difficult to carry out and often raise ethical issues. For example, it would not be ethical to conduct a clinical trial where one group was going to be exposed to a potential toxin to determine if the toxin caused cancer.

Control populations are used to ensure that other nonexperimental and usually unknown variables are not affecting the outcome. Like clinical trials, such studies may raise ethical issues when experiments involve the use of a clinical procedure that may expose the subjects to significant or unknown risk. Ethical questions also are raised when experimental studies require the withholding of some potentially beneficial drug or procedure from individuals in the control group to decisively prove the effectiveness of the drug or procedure. For example, it would not be ethical to test a new antihypertensive medication using a control group of patients with hypertension who would not receive any treatment, because the risks of untreated hypertension are known to be harmful. In such a case, the control group may receive their usual care with their current antihypertensive medication, and the intervention group would receive a new drug hypothesized to better treat hypertension.

Other Applications of Epidemiologic Methods   Because the population perspective of epidemiology usually requires the study and analysis of data obtained from or about large-scale population samples, the discipline has developed principles and methods that can be applied to the study of a wide range of problems in several fields. Thus, the concepts and quantitative methods of epidemiology have been used not only to add to the understanding of the etiology of health and disease but also to plan, administer, and evaluate health services. Furthermore, the rising interest in studying social determinants of health has advanced the field of social epidemiology. The concepts and methods also are used to forecast the health needs of population groups, to assess the adequacy of the supply of health personnel, and to determine the outcomes of specific treatment modalities in a variety of clinical settings.

Advances in statistical theory and the epidemiology of medical care make it possible to analyze and interpret performance data obtained from the large Medicare and other insurance databases. Many of the research findings of seemingly inexplicable geographic variations in the amount and cost of hospital treatments and in the use of a variety of healthcare services have resulted from the analysis of Medicare claims data and other large health insurance databases.

Health Services Research

Until the 1980s, most medical research was basic science research or research into the biological processes of the human body. However, in the 1980s, the concept of health services research was born.[1,4] Investigators focused on using established scientific methods in basic medical research to study the healthcare system itself. The goal was to find new and more effective means of diagnosis and treatment and, in effect, to improve the quality and length of life.

During the 2 decades following World War II, supply-side subsidy programs dominated federal healthcare policy. Like other subsidy programs, Medicare and Medicaid were politically crafted solutions rather than research-based strategies. Nevertheless, these major healthcare subsidy programs were the driving forces behind the rise of health services research.[1] The continuous collection of cost and utilization data from these programs revealed serious deficiencies in the capability of the healthcare system to efficiently and effectively deliver the knowledge and skills already at hand. In addition, evidence was growing that the large variations in the kinds and amounts of care delivered for the same health conditions represented unacceptable volumes of inappropriate or questionable care and too much indecision or confusion among clinicians about the best courses of treatment. Health services research was borne of the need to improve the efficiency and effectiveness of the healthcare system and to determine which of the healthcare treatment options for each health condition produces the best outcomes.[1,2]

Health Systems Research

Health systems research provides evidence that, when applied, can make health care affordable, safe, effective, equitable, accessible, and patient-centered. The primary purpose of this type of research is to generate new evidence to help healthcare systems and healthcare professionals improve the lives of the patients they serve. For example, findings from health systems research enable frontline clinicians and patients to make better decisions; support healthcare delivery systems; organize care processes to improve safety, effectiveness, and efficacy; and can be used to design healthcare benefits and inform policy.[5] Health policy and systems research (HPSR) is an emerging field that seeks to understand and improve how societies organize themselves in achieving collective health goals and how different actors interact in the policy and implementation processes to contribute to policy outcomes. This type of research can also be global in scope. For example, in the book *Comparative Health Systems: A Global Perspective,* authors Johnson, Stoskopf, and Shi compared health systems of 21 countries across the dimensions of cost, quality, access, and innovation.[6] Given its increasing value in the improvement of health, the World Health Organization publishes an annual report on this type of research. The Alliance for Health Policy and Systems Research describes the field as follows: "It is inter-disciplinary, a blend of economics, sociology, anthropology, political science, public health and epidemiology that together draw a comprehensive picture of how health systems respond and adapt to health policies, and how health policies can shape – and be shaped by – health systems."[7]

At the core of health systems research is systems thinking. Systems thinking takes into consideration that action or changes in one aspect of a health system is likely to affect what results in another. Systems thinking is necessary to navigate the complexity of health systems and to better understand the system-wide effects, both positive and negative, and the planned and unintended consequences of different interventions, policies, and behaviors.[8] Furthermore, it allows for a more adaptive implementation of health system policies and programs.[8] Many examples of these applications and various systems tools are described in Johnson, Anderson, and Rossow's book, *Health Systems Thinking: A Primer,*[9] and a case example that at patient safety from a systems research perspective is provided at the end of this chapter.

▶ Agency for Healthcare Research and Quality

Beginning with John Wennberg's documentation of large differences in the use of medical and surgical procedures among physicians in small geographic areas in the late 1980s, a number of similar studies have brought the value of increasingly more costly health care into serious question.[1,10] Wennberg noted that the rate of surgeries correlated with the numbers of surgeons in a geographic area and that the number of available hospital beds rather than differences among patients correlated with the rate of a population's hospitalization.[11]

He found that per capita expenditures for hospitalization in Boston, Massachusetts, were consistently double those in nearby New Haven, Connecticut.[2,4,5] Widely varying physician practice patterns provided little direction as to the most appropriate use of even the most common clinical procedures. In addition, adequate outcome measures for specific intervention modalities were generally lacking.

The problem did not escape the attention of the 101st U.S. Congress. The development of new knowledge through research has long been held as an appropriate and essential role of the federal government, as evidenced by the establishment and proactive role of the National Institutes of Health (NIH).[12] When it became clear that indecision about the most appropriate and effective ways to diagnose and treat specific medical, dental, and other conditions was contributing to unacceptably large variations in the cost, quality, and outcomes of health care, federal legislation was passed to support the development of clinical guidelines. The Agency for Health Care Policy and Research (AHCPR) was established in 1989.[13] Its priority activities included funding two types of research projects: patient outcome research teams and literature synthesis projects, or meta-analyses. Both the patient outcome research teams and the smaller literature synthesis projects identified and analyzed patient outcomes associated with alternative practice patterns and recommended changes where appropriate. During its decade-long existence, the AHCPR supported studies that resulted in a prodigious array of publications focused on patient care and clinical decision making, technology assessment, the quality and costs of care, and treatment outcomes. Although no longer directly involved in producing clinical practice guidelines, the agency currently assists private sector groups by supplying them with the scientific evidence they need to develop their own guidelines.

Significant changes occurred in the mandate of AHCPR since its 1989 inception. As described by authors Young and Kroth in the 9th edition of *Health Care USA: Understanding its Organization and Delivery,* the agency narrowly escaped the loss of funding and faced possible elimination in 1996 after incurring the wrath of national organizations of surgeons. In keeping with its original mission, AHCPR had issued clinical guidelines.[1] One such guideline discouraged surgery as a treatment for back pain on the grounds that it provided no better outcomes than more conservative treatments.[1] Angry surgeons led a lobbying effort that convinced key members of Congress that the agency was exceeding its authority by establishing clinical practice standards without considering the expertise and opinions of the medical specialists involved.[1,14]

The Healthcare Research and Quality Act of 1999 renamed the AHCPR to the Agency for Healthcare Research and Quality (AHRQ).[5] The mission of AHRQ is to: (1) improve the outcomes and quality of healthcare services, (2) reduce their costs, (3) address patient safety, and (4) broaden effective services through the establishment of a broad base of scientific research that promotes improvements in clinical and health systems practices, including prevention of disease.[8]

While clinical practice guidelines subsequently would be generated by medical specialty and other healthcare organizations, AHRQ's role would be to evaluate recommendations made in the clinical practice guidelines to ensure they were based on a systematic review of the literature (evidence-based) and were revised for currency on a regular basis.

More than 2,000 active, evidence-based clinical practice guidelines that have met the AHRQ evaluation criteria have been collected in a database, organized by searchable topics, and made available online at AHRQ's National Guideline Clearinghouse (http://www.guideline.gov/). AHRQ also maintains a searchable database of nearly 5,000 archived guidelines.

A top priority of AHRQ is transmitting its sponsored research results and new health information to consumers. In addition to a number of consumer-oriented publications, the agency provides information to the public via the internet. Its website (http://www.ahrq.gov) offers a robust array of healthcare information. AHRQ is now a major collaborating organization of the Patient-Centered Outcomes Research Institute (PCORI), which was established by the Affordable

Care Act (ACA). A few examples of AHRQ's research activities that make health care safer and improve quality of care and outcomes is provided in **EXHIBIT 12-1**. Many more examples of AHRQ's health systems and health services research collaborations can be found on their searchable website (https://www.ahrq.gov/programs/index.html).

EXHIBIT 12-1 Sample of AHRQ Research Initiatives

Healthcare Associated Infections

AHRQs work significantly helps in the national effort to reduce healthcare-associated infections (HAIs), which are among the leading threats to patient safety, affecting 1 out of every 31 hospital patients at any one time. More than 1 million HAIs occur across the U.S. healthcare system every year, leading to tens of thousands of deaths and costing billions of dollars.

These AHRQ research projects focus on the applied end of the research continuum and generate evidence for developing and demonstrating effective interventions to reduce HAIs. Clinicians in the field use these research results to combat HAIs.

Comparative Health System Performance Initiative

The agency studies how healthcare delivery systems promote evidence-based practices in delivering care. Three Centers of Excellence to Study High-Performing Health Care Systems are examining different aspects of the health system to understand factors that affect the use of evidence-based medicine.

Treatment of Opioid Abuse in Rural Care Settings

Doctors and nurses in primary care practices—where most rural Americans receive care—need information and tools to provide effective, evidence-based care for patients with opioid addictions. Medication-assisted treatment (MAT) is evidence-based therapy for assisting people with opioid addiction in primary care offices. MAT involves using both medications and behavioral support to empower people to manage their addiction. AHRQ is providing grants to discover how to best support primary care practices and rural communities in delivering MAT.

Practices involved in the initiative will provide access to MAT to individuals struggling with opioid addiction using innovative technology, including patient-controlled smartphone apps, and remote training and expert consultation using Project ECHO—a telehealth program started with AHRQ support that links specialists at an academic hub to primary care providers working on the frontlines in rural communities.

For more on this topic, see Haley, Johnson, and Frazier's book, *Opioids and Population Health: A Primer*.[15]

Patient-Centered Outcomes Research

The agency is charged with disseminating findings from patient-centered outcomes research (PCOR), building capacity to conduct clinical comparative effectiveness research through training, developing a public resource to provide access to PCOR findings, and supporting the incorporation of findings into health information technologies associated with clinical decision support.

Evidence-Based Reports

Through its Evidence-based Practice Centers (EPCs), the agency sponsors the development of reports to assist public and private organizations in their efforts to improve the quality of health care. These EPCs provide timely, comprehensive, science-based information on common, costly medical conditions and new health care technologies and strategies.

Data from Agency for Healthcare Research and Quality. Programs. Accessed June 10, 2021. https://www.ahrq.gov/programs/index.html

▶ Health Services Research and Health Policy

Health services research combines the perspectives and methods of epidemiology, medical social science, sociology, economics, and clinical medicine by applying the basic concepts of epidemiology, biostatistics, process, and outcome measures that reflect the behavioral and economic variables associated with questions of therapeutic effectiveness and cost–benefit. The ability of health services research to address issues of therapeutic effectiveness and cost–benefit during the nation's quest for fiscal exigency has contributed to the field's substantial growth and current value.[1]

The contributions of health services research to health policy are impressive.[2] Major examples identified in Young and Kroth's text[1] include studies of small area variation in medical utilization, the prospective payment system based on diagnosis-related groups, research on inappropriate medical procedures, resource-based relative value scale research, and the background research that supported the concepts of health maintenance organizations and managed care.[1]

The RAND Health Insurance Experiment,[16,17] one of the largest and longest-running health services research projects ever undertaken, began in 1971 and contributed vast amounts of information on the effects of cost sharing on the provision and outcomes of health services. Participating families were assigned to one of four different fee-for-service plans or to a prepaid group practice. Individuals in the various plans differed significantly in their rate of healthcare use, with little measurable effect on health outcomes. The Health Insurance Experiment was followed by two large research studies: the Health Services Utilization Study and the Medical Outcomes Study. The findings of both gave impetus to the federal support of outcomes research.[1] Determining the outcomes and effectiveness of different healthcare interventions aids clinical decision making, reduces costs, and benefits patients.

Quality Improvement

Until the 1990s, health care's impressive accomplishments had made it difficult for healthcare researchers, policy makers, and organizational leaders to publicly acknowledge that poor-quality health care is a major problem within the dynamic and productive biomedical enterprise in the United States. In 1990, after 2 years of study, hearings, and site visits, the Institute of Medicine (IOM) issued a report that cited widespread overuse of expensive invasive technology, underuse of inexpensive "caring" services, and implementation of error-prone procedures that harmed patients and wasted money.[17]

As Young and Kroth so well state, "Although these conclusions from this prestigious body were devastating to healthcare reformers, they were hardly news to health service researchers. For decades, practitioners assumed that quality, like beauty, was in the eye of the beholder, and, therefore, was immeasurable except in cases of obvious violation of generally accepted standards. The medical and other healthcare professions had promoted the image of health care as a blend of almost impenetrable, science-based disciplines, leaving the providers of care as the only ones capable of understanding the processes taking place. Thus, only physicians could judge the work of other physicians."[1]

Health services researchers had known for decades that healthcare quality was measurable and that excellent, as well as poor, care could be identified and quantified. As early as 1966, Avedis Donabedian at the University of Michigan characterized the concept of health care as divided into the components of structure, process, and outcomes and the research paradigm of their assumed linkages, all of which continue to guide quality-of-care investigators to this day.[18]

STRUCTURE → PROCESS → OUTCOMES

Donabedian suggested that the number, kinds, and skills of the providers, as well as the adequacy of their physical resources and the manner in which they perform appropriate procedures should, in the aggregate, influence the quality of subsequent outcomes.[19] Although today the construct may seem like a statement of the obvious, at the time, attention to structural criteria was the major, if not the only, quality assurance activity in favor. It was generally assumed that properly trained professionals, given adequate resources in properly equipped facilities, performed at acceptable standards of quality. For example, for many years, the Joint Commission on Accreditation of Hospitals (now The Joint Commission) made judgments about the quality of hospitals on the basis of structural standards, such as physical facilities and equipment, ratios of professional staff to patients, and the qualifications of various personnel. Later, it added process components to its structural standards and, most recently, has shifted its evaluation process to focus on care outcomes.[1]

Another method for assessing the quality of healthcare practices is based on empirical quality standards. Derived from distributions, averages, ranges, and other measures of data variability, information collected from a number of similar health service providers is compared to identify practices that deviate from the norms. A current popular use of empirical standards is in the patient severity-adjusted hospital performance data collected by health departments and community-based employer and insurer groups to measure and compare both process activities and outcomes. These performance "report cards" are becoming increasingly valuable to the purchasers of care who rely on an objective method to guide their choices among managed care organizations, healthcare systems, and group practices.

▶ Medical Errors

In 1999, the IOM again issued a report on the quality of medical care.[19] Focused on medical errors, the report described mistakes occurring during the course of hospital care as one of the nation's leading causes of death and disability. Citing two major studies estimating that medical errors killed 44,000–98,000 people in U.S. hospitals each year, the report was a stunning indictment of the systems of hospital care at that time. The report contained a series of recommendations for improving patient safety in the admittedly high-risk environments of modern hospitals. One result was establishing a center for patient safety within AHRQ.

▶ Evidence-Based Medicine

According to Sackett et al., "Evidence-based medicine is the conscientious, explicit, and judicious use of current best evidence in making decisions about the care of individual patients. The practice of evidence-based medicine means integrating individual clinical expertise with the best available external clinical evidence from systematic research. Individual clinical expertise refers to the proficiency and judgment that individual clinicians acquire through clinical experience and clinical practice."[20] Although this statement may appear to be a description of the way physicians and other healthcare providers have practiced since the inception of scientific medicine, it reflects a concern that the opposite is true.[1] The wide range of variability in clinical practice, the complexity of diagnostic testing and medical decision making, and the difficulty that physicians have in keeping up with the overwhelming volumes of scientific literature suggest that a significant percentage of clinical management decisions are not supported by reliable evidence of effectiveness.

What constitutes "the best evidence" refers to the highest form of evidence available for the particular medical issue or question in the hierarchy of evidence derived from research. The following, as developed by Young and Kroth,[1] is an abridged summary of the hierarchy of evidence:

1. Systematic review: A meta-analysis of several high-quality randomized, controlled clinical trials. An analysis of multiple analyses has more value, as its conclusions are based on the larger, combined populations studied in all the individual clinical trials. This usually is considered the highest level of evidence but is also the most expensive and difficult to carry out.

2. Randomized controlled clinical trial: A study where patients are randomly assigned to two or more experimental groups where each group is identical to the others with the exception of the treatment they are assigned. Often one of the "treatments" is a placebo or no treatment. Selection of patients is carefully controlled to reduce the potential for any confounder or bias between the experimental groups. Often the study patients, their physicians, and the outcomes assessors are "blinded" to which treatment each patient was randomly assigned, again to minimize potential bias of the results. After systematic reviews, this is generally considered the highest form of evidence.

3. Observational study: An analysis of real-world data. Studies can be either prospective, where one or more groups of patients is followed for a period of time, or retrospective, where existing data representing past clinical events is analyzed.

4. Case series: A published summary of a small number of individual cases in the biomedical literature. These usually occur for extremely rare conditions or for new illnesses or syndromes and often when the diagnosis is unknown. Rigorous analyses usually are not performed. The goal is to attempt identification of the similarities between the cases presented and posit a unifying cause or effective treatment. Case series are generally developed by experts and undergo peer review before they are published.

5. Expert opinion: Usually expresses the opinion of a medical specialist in an area of interest to a particular patient. This is the lowest or least rigorous form of evidence but also the most commonly practiced. It can occur formally, with a referral to a specialist by a patient's primary care physician, or informally, when one physician discusses a case or medical issue with a colleague in person, over the phone, or via email.

The goal of the evidence-based process is to inform the practice of medicine by providing the practitioner with the ability to determine the highest level of evidence for their clinical questions and then use their clinical judgment along with the patients' preferences and values for its application.

Many, if not most, medical decisions are made using the lower levels of evidence (i.e., only expert opinion, case series, or observational evidence). This, of course, would rely on the evidence used being the highest level of evidence that exists at the time of the medical decision. There are many reasons why randomized controlled clinical trials cannot be conducted. They are expensive in terms of time and effort, and they often can raise ethical questions. For example, who would volunteer for a randomized trial of radiation exposure by receiving either harmful doses of radiation or placebo? It would be highly unethical to conduct such a study, so the best science can do is perform observational studies on "natural experiments" where people were accidentally exposed to harmful radiation, such as in the Chernobyl disaster in Ukraine or the Fukushima Daiichi disaster in Japan. Similar examples are populations exposed to toxic chemicals in their water, land, or air. In such cases, observational studies compare the groups exposed to the toxic agents with similar populations from other similar areas that were not exposed. A confounder is a variable that explains the difference in outcome between groups that is not known or compensated for in the observational analysis; in effect, association between variables does not prove causation. While it is difficult to adjust the findings for all possible confounders between the two groups, the evidence produced by such analyses likely will be the highest level that researchers will be able to obtain for toxic exposures.

Another reason observational studies are performed is because the data are readily available and the analyses are often relatively inexpensive. With the ever-increasing amount of data as artifact to our daily lives, many observational studies that were only dreamed of a few years ago can now be performed simply due to the depth and breadth of available data.

One of the major problems with observational studies is the existence of unknown confounders between groups or cohorts. With observational studies, all the confounders must be known and adjusted for in the analysis to ensure accurate results. This is often extremely difficult to do, because there are myriad potential confounders in the real world.

A famous example that illustrates the limitations of observational studies and the value of randomized controlled clinical trials is the research on postmenopausal estrogen supplementation. For a time, the highest level of evidence on the benefits of the use of estrogen supplementation in postmenopausal women used only several observational studies. These observational studies grouped women of similar age, race, and demographics into two groups—those taking estrogen supplementation those and not taking it. The two groups were followed and the rates of heart attack, stroke, bone loss, and other outcomes were documented. Because these studies showed a small but significant benefit for women who took estrogen supplementation in terms of reduced rates of heart attack, stroke, bone loss, and high cholesterol, the studies had enormous influence on the prescribing of supplemental estrogen to postmenopausal women. Eventually, a large, well-designed randomized controlled trial was conducted and, surprisingly, demonstrated that taking estrogen supplementation not only did *not* reduce the rates of heart attack or stroke but actually slightly increased them and increased the rates of invasive breast cancer and pulmonary embolus.[1] What was wrong with all the prior observational studies? It was the fact that women who took supplemental estrogen proactively also were more likely to generally be more health conscious. Further analysis showed that the women in the observational studies who took estrogen also were more likely to see their doctors for preventive checkups, eat more healthfully, and follow preventive instructions from their physicians, such as taking estrogen. It was not that the estrogen reduced the rates of heart attack and stroke in the observational studies, it was that the women who would take estrogen were just healthier than the women who did not take estrogen. The unknown confounder in all the observational studies was the participants' overall health practices, behaviors, and lifestyle choices. Published results of the randomized, controlled, clinical trial resulted in discontinuation of supplemental estrogen prescriptions almost overnight. But, as stated earlier, for many questions in medicine, observational studies will likely be the only ones ever carried out and are therefore the best available evidence. This is why evidence-based practice includes the use of clinical judgment and patient preference and values, as all the available evidence is far from perfect and, in some cases, just incorrect.[1]

▶ Outcomes Research

Insurance companies, state and federal governments, employers, and consumers all look to outcomes research for information to help them make better decisions about what kinds of health care should be reimbursed, for whom, and when.

Because outcomes research evaluates results of healthcare processes in the real world of physicians' offices, hospitals, clinics, and homes, it contrasts with traditional randomized controlled studies that test the effects of treatments in controlled environments. In addition, the research in usual service settings, or "effectiveness research," differs from controlled clinical trials, or "efficacy research," in the nature of the outcomes measured. Traditionally, studies measured health status, or outcomes, with physiologic measurements—laboratory tests, complication rates, recovery, or survival. To capture health status more adequately, outcomes research also should measure a patient's functional status and well-being. Satisfaction with care also must complement traditional measures.

Functional status includes three components that assess patients' abilities to function in their own environment:

1. Physical functioning
2. Role functioning—the extent to which health interferes with usual daily activities, such as work or school
3. Social functioning—whether health affects normal social activities, such as visiting friends or participating in group activities

Personal well-being measures describe patients' sense of physical and mental well-being— their mental health or general mood, their personal view of their general health, and their general sense about the quality of their lives. Patient satisfaction measures the patients' views about the services received, including access, convenience, communication, financial coverage, and technical quality.

Outcomes research also uses meta-analyses, a technique to summarize comparable findings from multiple studies. More importantly, however, outcomes research goes beyond determining what works in ideal circumstances to assessing which treatments for specific clinical problems work best in different circumstances. Appropriateness studies are conducted to determine the circumstances in which a procedure should and should not be performed. Even though a procedure is proved to be effective, it is not appropriate for every patient in all circumstances. The frequency of inappropriate clinical interventions is one of the major quality-of-care problems in the system, and research is underway to develop the tools to identify patient preferences when treatment options are available. Although most discussions about appropriateness stress potential cost savings that could be achieved by reducing unnecessary care and overuse of services, outcomes research may be just as likely to uncover underuse of appropriate services.

It is important to recognize that the ultimate value of outcomes research can be measured only by its ability to incorporate the results of its efforts into the healthcare process. To be effective, the findings of outcomes research must first reach and then change the behaviors of providers,

BOX 12-2 The Patient-Centered Outcomes Research Institute

Empowering the Federal Coordinating Council for Comparative Effectiveness Research, the ACA created the Patient-Centered Outcomes Research Institute (PCORI), a not-for-profit, independent agency dedicated to conducting comparative effectiveness research.[23] PCORI is governed by a board of directors appointed by the U.S. Government Accountability Office and is funded through the Patient-Centered Outcomes Research Trust Fund. Support is derived from the general U.S. Treasury fund, and fees are assessed to Medicare, private health insurance, and self-insured plans. PCORI maintains a strong patient and stakeholder orientation with patient satisfaction recognized as an essential component of quality of care. Although the subjective ratings of health care rendered by patients may be based on markedly different criteria from those considered important by healthcare providers, they capture aspects of care and personal preferences that contribute significantly to perceived quality. PCORI recognizes that it has become increasingly important that the providers' characteristics, organization, and system attributes that are important to patients be identified and monitored. In addition to healthcare providers' technical and interpersonal skills, patient concerns such as waiting times for appointments, emergency responses, helpfulness and communication of staff, and facilities' appearances contribute to patient evaluations of health services delivery programs and subsequent satisfaction with the quality of care received.[24]

PCORI has funded nearly 800 research projects. The top five areas funded included cancer, mental/behavioral health, cardiovascular health, respiratory diseases, and trauma/injury.[23] They also funded the National Patient-Centered Clinical Research Network (PCORNET), thus far composed of 13 clinical data research networks and 20 patient-powered research networks to increase the efficiency of various comparative effectiveness research projects. In the few years that PCORI has been in existence, there are already dozens of papers published on the emerging research findings.

Data from Patient-Centered Outcomes Research Institute. Accessed June 1, 2021. https://www.pcori.org/
Patient-Centered Clinical Research Network. Accessed June 1, 2021. https://pcornet.org/

patients, healthcare institutions, and payers. This is elaborated upon further in the description of patient-centered outcomes research shown in **BOX 12-2** above.

▶ Comparative Effectiveness Research

The American Recovery and Reinvestment Act (ARRA) of 2009 included $1.1 billion over a period of 2 years to expand comparative effectiveness research by AHRQ and NIH. The goal of comparative effectiveness research is to enhance healthcare treatment decisions by providing information to consumers, providers, and payers to improve health outcomes by developing and disseminating evidence "on the effectiveness, benefits, and harms of different treatment options. The evidence is generated from research studies that compare drugs, medical devices, tests, surgeries, or ways to deliver health care."[21] Historically, clinical research examined the effectiveness of one method, product, or service at a time. Comparative effectiveness research compares two or more different methods for preventing, diagnosing, and treating health conditions, using methods such as practical clinical trials, analyses of insurance claim records, computer modeling, and systematic reviews of literature. Disseminating research findings about the effectiveness of treatments relative to other options in a form that is quickly useable by clinicians, patients, policy makers, health plans, and other payers is key to comparative research effectiveness goals. The Kaiser Family Foundation adds another perspective on this kind of research, "identifying the most effective and efficient interventions has the potential to reduce unnecessary treatments, which may help lower costs."[22]

▶ National Institutes of Health

Since the 1950s, the federal government has invested heavily in biomedical research. The ensuing public–private partnership in health has produced some of the finest medical research in the world. The growth of medical knowledge is unparalleled, and the United States can take well-deserved pride in its research accomplishments. Leading the way in biomedical research is NIH, which is made up of 27 different components called Institutes and Centers.[11] Each has its own specific research agenda, often focusing on particular diseases or body systems. NIH's mission is to seek fundamental knowledge about the nature and behavior of living systems and the application of that knowledge to enhance health, lengthen life, and reduce illness and disability. An overview of the agency is provided in **BOX 12-3**.

BOX 12-3 NIH Institutes, Centers, and Offices

- Office of the Director
- National Cancer Institute
- National Eye Institute
- National Heart, Lung, and Blood Institute
- National Human Genome Research Institute
- National Institute of Allergy and Infectious Disease
- National Institute on Aging
- National Institute on Alcohol Abuse and Alcoholism
- National Institute of Arthritis and Musculoskeletal and Skin Diseases
- National Institute of Biomedical Imaging and Bioengineering
- Eunice Kennedy Shriver National Institute of Child Health and Human Development
- National Institute on Deafness and Other Communication Disorders
- National Institute of Dental and Craniofacial Research
- National Institute of Diabetes and Digestive and Kidney Diseases
- National Institute on Drug Abuse
- National Institute of Environmental Health Sciences
- National Institute of General Medical Sciences
- National Institute of Mental Health
- National Institute on Minority Health and Health Disparities
- National Institute of Neurological Disorders and Stroke
- National Institute of Nursing Research
- National Library of Medicine
- Center for Information Technology
- Center for Scientific Review
- Fogarty International Center
- National Center for Complementary and Alternative Medicine
- National Center for Advancing Translational Sciences
- NIH Clinical Center

National Institutes of Health.

NIH's goals are[25]:

- "to foster fundamental creative discoveries, innovative research strategies, and their applications as a basis for ultimately protecting and improving health;
- to develop, maintain, and renew scientific human and physical resources that will ensure the Nation's capability to prevent disease;
- to expand the knowledge base in medical and associated sciences in order to enhance the Nation's economic well-being and ensure a continued high return on the public investment in research; and
- to exemplify and promote the highest level of scientific integrity, public accountability, and social responsibility in the conduct of science.

In realizing these goals, the NIH provides leadership and direction to programs designed to improve the health of the Nation by conducting and supporting research:

- in the causes, diagnosis, prevention, and cure of human diseases;
- in the processes of human growth and development;
- in the biological effects of environmental contaminants;
- in the understanding of mental, addictive and physical disorders; and
- in directing programs for the collection, dissemination, and exchange of information in medicine and health, including the development and support of medical libraries and the training of medical librarians and other health information specialists."

NIH invests about $42 billion annually in medical research for the American people. More than 80% of NIH's funding is awarded for extramural research, largely through almost 50,000 competitive grants to more than 300,000 researchers at more than 2,500 universities, medical schools, and other research institutions in every state. About 10% of NIH's budget supports projects conducted by nearly 6,000 scientists in its own laboratories, most of which are on its campus in Bethesda, Maryland.[12]

It is important to note that NIH goes much beyond biomedical research to inform clinical practice by including health policy and health services research within its scope. One NIH statement on this is as follows: "Health policy and systems research has changed considerably over the last 20 years, but its main purpose remains to inform and influence health policies and systems. Whereas goals that underpin health systems have endured - such as a focus on health equity - contexts and priorities change, research methods progress, and health organizations continue to learn and adapt, in part by using health systems research."[26]

Furthermore, health researchers need to rethink how health systems are conceptualized, to keep up with rapid changes in how we diagnose and manage disease and use information, and to consider factors affecting people's health that go well beyond healthcare systems.[27]

One way this may be done over the next decade is by responding to the health research objectives of the Healthy People 2030 initiative as promulgated by the Department of Health and Human Services. Healthy People provides science-based, 10-year national objectives for improving the health of people nationwide. This national health plan includes three types of objectives—core, developmental, and research—developed by workgroups made up of subject matter experts in specific topics. The research objectives represent public health issues with a high health or economic burden or significant disparities between population groups.

These objectives can help investigators identify research needs, focus on key priority populations, and develop evidence-based interventions that improve health and well-being across the lifespan. **BOX 12-4** identifies the primary research focus areas.

BOX 12-4 Healthy People 2030 Key Research Foci

Access to health services
Adolescent health
Cancer
Disability and health
Early and middle childhood
Health communication and health information technology
Mental health and mental disorders
Physical activity
Public health infrastructure
Social determinants of health
Substance use
Tobacco use
Vision

Data from U.S. Department of Health and Human Services Office of Disease Prevention and Health Promotion. About the objectives. Accessed August 26, 2021. https://health.gov/healthypeople/objectives-and-data/about-objectives

▶ Conclusion

Many, if not most, of the sophisticated new technologies have addressed the need to ameliorate the problems of patients who already have a condition or disease. Both the priorities and the profits intrinsic to the U.S. healthcare system have focused on remedial rather than preventive strategies. Only in the cases of frightening epidemics, such as that of polio in the mid-1900s and AIDS in the 1990s, and now COVID-19 have the requisite moral imperatives prevailed in order to adequately fund research efforts that address the nation's health problems and impending challenges.

The change in emphasis from basic science research toward health services research and population health research will likely continue as the federal government updates its Medicare payment model. This model will require more health services research and health systems research on not only how to improve the health of populations, but also what changes to the existing healthcare infrastructure will be required for the evolving healthcare system. Research must continue to better understand which organizational structures and policies work best for new accountable care organizations. Research also will be needed on what changes to the existing health information technology infrastructure are necessary to better support population health, centralized electronic reporting to various government agencies, and information sharing between multiple healthcare institutions.

The advent of ubiquitous advanced genetic testing will require research on how to analyze, summarize, and present unprecedentedly large volumes of genetic sequencing data into meaningful information that can be used efficiently. Medical education will require updating curricula to include new skills needed by clinicians in areas of population health, systems-based care, health information technology, and basic outcomes research. Continued pressure to improve the quality and drive down the cost of medical care will fuel more comparative effectiveness research to ensure the best and most cost-effective treatments are utilized. Research on what new curricula are needed in this era will be essential as well. In 2020, the American Medical Association's Accelerating Change in Medical Education Consortium published the 2nd edition of the book *Health*

Systems Science, which advocated for medical schools to incorporate systems thinking and systems science research into their curricula.[26] The same trend has generally become evident in schools of public health, nursing, health administration, and health professions.[10]

▶ Discussion Questions

- What are the different types of health-related research? Give an example of each.
- What do each of the different types of research from Question 1 focus on?
- What is meant by outcomes research? Why is it important to focus on outcomes and not simply processes?
- Choose any two research initiatives of AHRQ and describe them. It might be helpful to search the agency's website for more information.
- Discuss why systems thinking has become increasingly relevant to health research.
- Discuss the scope and scale of the National Institutes of Health.
- Have medical schools and health professions schools embraced systems science? If so, how might this help educate more effective graduates who are ready for the real-world challenges they will face?

CASE 12-1   Systems Thinking for Patient Safety

Contributing Author: Stephen M. Powell

According to Johnson and Anderson, systems thinking "focuses on non-linear assumptions about human behavior and feedback loops to determine a systems behavior over time to find leverage points to create the most reliable and innovative health systems that are sustainable with a goal of better health for all."[28] Systems thinking is perfectly suited to address intransient, complex, and seemingly unsolvable problems such as patient safety.

Some estimates suggest that preventable adverse events have become the third leading cause of death in the United States, placing medical errors behind only heart disease and cancer.[29] In the Institute of Medicine (IOM) report *To Err Is Human,* initial estimates of deaths in the United States due to medical errors were reported to be between 44,000 and 98,000 lives each year. The current estimated loss of lives is 400,000 annually—a nearly 10-fold increase over the initial IOM estimates in 2000.[29] Of course, some of the differences may be attributed to mortality surveillance and reporting.[29]

Following the IOM report, healthcare organizations across the United States have launched patient safety programs and interventions to reduce preventable adverse events; however, the pace of improvement is painstakingly slow and often unsustainable over time.[30] The IOM report suggested that medicine and related professions take a "systems approach" to improving patient safety similar to other high-risk industries such as aviation and the nuclear power industry.[31] Health professionals have turned to safety principles attributed to High Reliability Organizations (HROs) that can achieve extremely low incidence in risky situations.[32] Many cross-disciplinary practitioners, researchers, and policymakers began adopting these practices and programs in higher risk healthcare settings, such as operating rooms, intensive care units, emergency departments, and obstetrical care settings. Most programs have focused primarily on training with weaker attempts to change behavior over time, which is necessary in systems thinking. This circumstance begs the question: Is it time to reframe the patient safety problem as a systems problem, requiring systems thinking and a systems approach?

Methods:
CQI on info,
hardware, plant, policy

Recipients of care	Systems for therapeutic action
	Designed to preempt/ rescue from failure
Preparation on:	
• Illness understanding	**Workers:**
• Accessing care systems	Teams trained to preempt/ rescue from/ manage failure
• Advocacy	

Methods:
CQI on competence,
communication, teamwork

FIGURE 12-3 Patient Safety Systems Model

Patient Safety as a System

Emanuel and colleagues submitted a working model or framework to begin viewing patient safety as a system rather than isolated or silo episodes of disjointed care delivery.[33] **FIGURE 12-3** illustrates the model showing its embrace of systems thinking design, human factors, and other systems engineering disciplines along with feedback loops to monitor continuously and improve systems performance. The model shows four interactive elements within patient safety: patients (the recipients of care), healthcare workers (the professionals who deliver care), healthcare systems (the therapeutic care enablers), and the methods of monitoring and improving care (continuous quality improvement). Unfortunately, human failures at the point of care have resulted in a culture of blame and shame among healthcare professionals ("bad" people versus poorly functioning systems).

The dotted lines in the model represent the complex interaction or "permeability" between patient safety systems and stakeholders.[33] Patients and their families are more integrally linked in the practice of safe care than passengers on an airliner or customers of a nuclear power plant due to social determinants of health such as access to prescribed medications and follow-up care after discharge. Patients and families, when possible, must take an active role in the patients' care team advocating for safe and efficient care.[28] Systems of therapeutic care include leadership, management, safety culture, processes, technology, information systems, and equipment. High-functioning teams are critical to the safe delivery of health care requiring nontechnical competency, such as communication, as well as clinical competency or clinical decision-making skills.[32]

Multi-team Patient Safety Systems in Health Care

In 2006, the U.S. Agency for Healthcare Research and Quality with the U.S. Department of Defense Military Health System released the TeamSTEPPS®—Strategies and Tools to Enhance Performance and Patient Safety programming adapting evidence-based research from other HRO sectors such

(continues)

CASE 12-1 Systems Thinking for Patient Safety *(continued)*

as aviation, nuclear power, submarines, and the military special forces.[34] The program includes a comprehensive set of tools, strategies, and implementation methods for developing high-performing teams in the healthcare delivery setting through the building of knowledge, skills, and attitudes including team leadership, situation monitoring, mutual support, and communication. The Joint Commission estimates that as many as 70% of adverse events are the result of ineffective communication.[35] Over the last decade, TeamSTEPPS has become the most widely used teamwork improvement system in health care with specialty programming for acute care, post-acute care, and primary care teams. A key outcome of TeamSTEPPS is a multi-team system (MTS) of care (**FIGURE 12-4**). The MTS uses systems thinking when modeling patient care systems. For instance, a labor and delivery team is the "core" team providing direct patient care to the mother, family, and unborn child. The patient includes the mother and child as well as family. The coordinating team may include a charge (supervisor) nurse and triage nurse at the time of hospital admission. Ancillary and support services can include the laboratory, pharmacy, and blood bank. Administration includes the admitting clerk, department leadership, and clinical education support staff. Contingency teams would include anesthesia should an epidural be ordered to manage pain or a rapid response team should mother or baby suffer a precipitous increase in blood pressure or decrease in oxygen levels.

This example highlights the interdependence of teams and the integrated systems of teams to ensure a safe outcome. If the baby suffers difficulty in breathing after delivery, additional teams such as the neonatal intensive care unit and respiratory therapy would need to be included in the MTS. The MTS ensures that the teams understand their roles and responsibilities as well as the roles and responsibilities of the other teams. This creates a shared mental model—one of the key outcomes of TeamSTEPPS. A shared mental model means that all teams and team members are "on the same page." Numerous TeamSTEPPS studies have shown positive systems improvements in patient safety including a decreased number of adverse events, a decrease in medication and transfusion errors, a decrease in worker safety, including needle stick injury and exposures, and a decrease in communication-related incidents.[36]

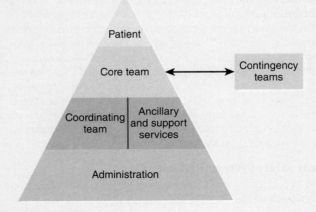

FIGURE 12-4 Multi-team System

Microsystems Thinking

As high-performing clinical and service delivery teams have been strengthened using TeamSTEPPS, other systems-based improvement programming such as clinical microsystems thinking uses a grassroots building block approach to optimize the quality, safety, and costs of our healthcare delivery systems.[37] Health professionals are at the frontline of healthcare delivery—optimally positioning them to design and redesign higher-quality patient care. Clinical microsystem improvement programming uses systems thinking at the smallest systems level known as the microsystem (**FIGURE 12-5**). Surgical patients move through pre-op, operating room, intensive care unit or post-anesthesia care unit, and then to a surgical ward until they are discharged. The mesosystem must provide a coordinated connection between systems using MTS methods. Electronic health records and clinical decision support technology can help bridge clinical knowledge gaps between systems, while the macrosystem provides the hard structure environment, policies, equipment, personnel, and organizational culture. Clinical microsystem improvement teams must first map their current clinical practices and processes. The process mapping informs system variability, waste, and opportunities for improvement. Evidence-based research provides practical improvement options such as a checklist for central line insertion or a proven protocol for the systematic removal of Foley catheters before a patient experiences a catheter-associated urinary tract infection. Teams collect, analyze, and track performance indicators over time to ensure that new interventions are effective, enabling them to make data-driven clinical decisions with their patients.[38]

Engineering Patient Safety Systems

The University of Wisconsin introduced the Systems Engineering Initiative for Patient Safety (SEIPS) model to address the sociotechnical system (work system), processes of care, and the resultant systems outcomes (**FIGURE 12-6**).[39] Systems feedback loops are integral to system learning, adaptation, and continuous improvement. The SEIPS model builds on a successful human factor engineering framework that focuses on systems orientation (with persons central to the work system but not the single failure point) and person-centered design for patients, families, and healthcare professionals to promote higher reliability.[39]

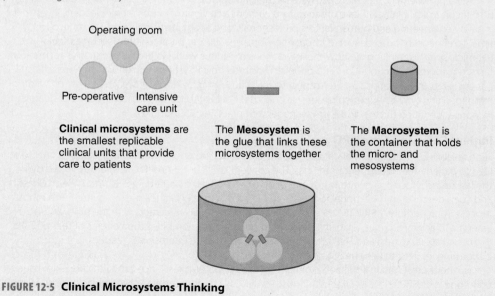

Operating room

Pre-operative   Intensive care unit

Clinical microsystems are the smallest replicable clinical units that provide care to patients

The **Mesosystem** is the glue that links these microsystems together

The **Macrosystem** is the container that holds the micro- and mesosystems

FIGURE 12-5 **Clinical Microsystems Thinking**

(continues)

CASE 12-1 Systems Thinking for Patient Safety *(continued)*

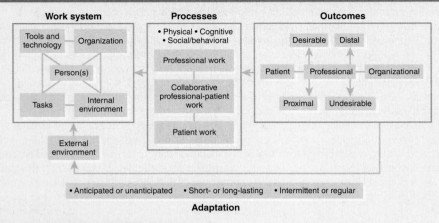

FIGURE 12-6 SEIPS Model for Patient Safety

The SEIPS model has been applied broadly to improve the reliability of patient service delivery pathways such as surgery, intensive care, and medication safety. The SEIPS model attempts to redesign healthcare systems to be more user-friendly, ergonomically efficient, and person-centered. The SEIPS model provides a framework for continuous improvement by providing the feedback loops essential to systems thinking, leading to understanding why a specific outcome (desired or undesired) occurred. The model is sensitive to unintended consequences, behavior drift or normalized deviance, and the external environment from regulators such as the Joint Commission of State Health Departments.[39]

SEIPS provides a comprehensive, systems thinking approach to patient safety, yet the model may be difficult to scale in healthcare organizations without a commitment from senior leaders, investment in safety engineering and human factors professionals, and adequate frontline resources (especially time) to engage in the endeavor of improving work. The SEIPS approach highly leverages socio-technical systems thinking to show the interactions of various work system factors such as technology, tasks, environment, organization, and people.[40] Socio-technical systems thinking is often used in patient safety investigations and retrospective root cause analysis.[40] This approach focuses on what happened and why it happened rather than who did it, allowing learning to occur based on team crisis response, identified threats, and harm management practices (**FIGURE 12-7**).

Patient Safety and the HRO

High reliability in the context of patient safety means reducing preventable serious safety events which lead to patient deaths and serious injuries. The concept of HROs for health care has developed over the last decade, focusing on attributes and principles practiced by other high-risk industries.[32] Chassin and Loeb describe an HRO model for health care built on three pillars: leadership, culture, and robust process improvement.[41] **FIGURE 12-8** demonstrates how each pillar interacts with the other and is essential to achieve higher reliability. This patient safety model combines the benefits of TeamSTEPPS (higher reliability teams) and SEIPS (higher reliability processes/systems) with leadership (higher performing leaders) to achieve high reliability outcomes.

Furthermore, Chassin and Loeb highlight the lack of systems resilience in health care—an essential component of HROs.[41] Other high-risk industries (HROs) are more sensitive to complacency, unwilling

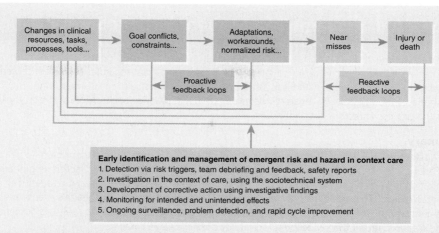

FIGURE 12-7 Socio-technical Approach to Patient Safety Performance and Learning Systems for Threat and Error Management

to accept unnecessary risks, and use errors as a learning opportunity. The HRO model for health care places an increased emphasis on organizational culture—the beliefs, values, and norms about patient safety as well as the impact a pathological culture may have on patient safety. The challenge to adopting the HRO model is the commitment to a significant change in behaviors from the boardroom

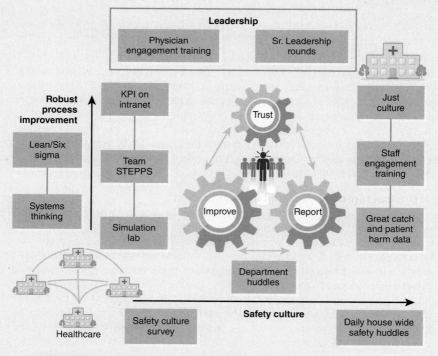

FIGURE 12-8 HRO Methods and Practices in Healthcare Organizations

(continues)

CASE 12-1 Systems Thinking for Patient Safety *(continued)*

to the bedside, meaning that leaders must "walk the talk" while frontline high reliability teams must promote peer-to-peer accountability to safe practice and mutual trust regardless of rank or professional hierarchy. The HRO systems thinking is focused on a journey toward safer care—measuring organizations through maturity levels of implementation and practice while embracing safety science across the process improvement continuum.

Summary

Patient safety requires systems thinking to reduce the impact of preventable patient harm in health care. Patient safety has borrowed heavily from other high-risk industries, human factors, engineering, organizational development, and psychology to develop safer care systems designed to reduce preventable patient harm. Unfortunately, few industry drivers exist to compel health systems to adopt, implement, and sustain systems thinking approaches to patient safety, resulting sadly in pockets of safety excellence rather than widespread scalability of safe, reliable care.

CASE 12-2 COVID-19 from a Systems Perspective: COVID-19 and Application of Systems Thinking Tools

Introduction

The 2019–2020 coronavirus (COVID-19) pandemic is ongoing. This pandemic began in Wuhan, China, and it has spread rapidly, with cases now confirmed in almost every country.[42,43] This case study summarizes the importance of applying systems thinking tools and coordination between individuals, communities, and institutions at all levels to defeat a complex, slow-moving, invisible virus. Part 1 describes the nature of emerging environments and application of systems thinking principles and tools. Part 2 summarizes how data and trends provide the foundation for aspirational goals followed by interventions. Finally, Part 3 challenges leaders to work collaboratively across all levels of society and the world to systematically mitigate the virus.

Part 1: Unstructured and Unfamiliar Environment

A complex adaptive system (CAS), as shown in **FIGURE 12-9**, exhibits stable or ambiguous behaviors, such as those seen in the COVID-19 outbreak. Parts of the system do not convey a perfect understanding of the whole system. Instead, they may provide early indicators or signals.

The outbreak was first identified in December 2019. The World Health Organization (WHO) declared the outbreak to be a public health emergency of international concern on January 30, 2020, and officially recognized it as a pandemic on March 11, 2020.[44,45]

Although CASs are used to represent the whole, they are more complex than the sum of their parts. Emerging events (i.e., symptoms, onset, or travel patterns) of outbreak behavior (i.e., speed, frequency, and reach of spread), risks (i.e., prioritization of response assets such as personal protective equipment [PPE] allocation and available vaccines), constraints (i.e., surge capacity, staffing, infrastructure, and fear), and impacts (i.e., front-line health workers, deaths, mental health, and economics) begin to form patterns.

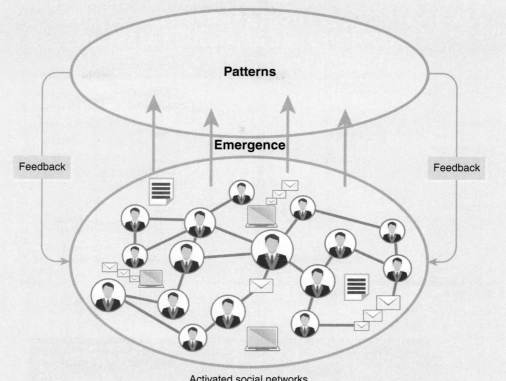

FIGURE 12-9 Complex adaptive systems (CAS)

Anderson DE, from Araz, O.M. Integrating complex system dynamics of pandemic influenza with a multi-criteria decision making model for evaluating public health strategies. *J. Syst. Sci. Syst. Eng.* 22, 319–339 (2013). https://doi.org/10.1007/s11518-013-5220-y

CASs are also adaptive. Based on feedback, they are constantly forming and re-forming. Most CASs never return to their original form.[46,47] In fact, feedback loops are important features of CASs, especially when data begin to drive options for overall protection (i.e., equipment, vaccines), response (i.e., healthcare infra-structure), and recovery (i.e., beds, ventilators) given the surge projections and healthcare capacity.[46]

Emergence of a new reality occurs as a result of interactions, signals, and patterns in the environment. As systems evolve, social networks become activated. As the COVID-19 outbreak activates social networks, their agents and actors forge relation-ships between nodes or social determinants of health (SDH)—public health, health care, social services, transportation, economic systems, public safety, food, schools, and communication systems, etc. These networks will constantly seek equilibrium. Through the interactions of social networks and assessment of patterns, the agents and actors will attain greater situational awareness.[46] They begin to crystallize an unstructured environment.

In **FIGURE 12-10**, connection circles help teams understand the complexity and interdependence of pandemics. For example, teams generate ideas about changing conditions and actions within a system to become more informed through application of analytic tools. As illustrated in Figure 12-10, a causal

(continues)

CASE 12-2 COVID-19 from a Systems Perspective: COVID-19 and Application of Systems Thinking Tools *(continued)*

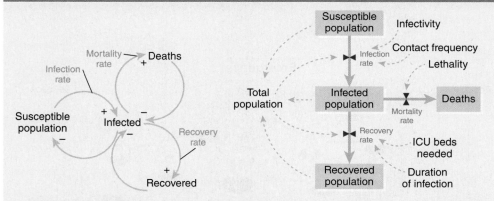

Data from Bala BK, Arshad FM, and Noh KM. (2017). System Dynamics. Springer Texts in Business and Economics. doi:10.1007/978-981-10-2045-2. https://link.springer.com/chapter/10.1007/978-981-10-2045-2_1#

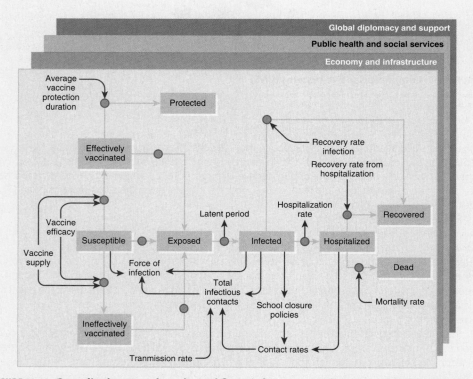

FIGURE 12-10 Causality loops and stocks and flows inform teams about co-evolution of systems

loop diagram (CLD) aids in visualizing how different variables in a system are interrelated—actions, information, and results. The CLD diagram consists of a set of nodes and edges. Nodes represent the variables such as number of test kits, testing stations, and processes to acquire results. Edges are the links representing connections or relationships between variables, such as availability of inventory of masks, gloves, and gowns.[46] Stocks and flows add a higher level of analysis. Unlike CLDs, stock and flow diagrams differentiate between the parts of the system such as patient flow, equipment optimization, and bed availability. They include more details about the elements of the system than do CLDs.[46] This type of analysis must address the root causes or underlying sources of problems and provide a vision for the future.[47]

As systems are modeled, simulated, and analyzed, co-evolution drives new systems and subsystems to interact and influence each other.[46] In the current fight against COVID-19, healthcare, public health, and economic systems and their respective policies and interventions cause the systems to evolve and adapt to each other—often with intended and unintended consequences. Asking "what if" questions using data helps leadership teams develop the best policies and interventions, such as self-isolation, social distancing, economic aid, and travel restrictions.

Part 2: Crystallizing an Unstructured Environment

A behavior over time graph (BOTG) is a simple graphic such as line graph that is used to show patterns of change over time. A BOTG (**FIGURE 12-11**) shows how a parameter increases and decreases as time passes or how it correlates with other variables over time.[46] From the emerging situation, initial ideas, diagramming analysis, and BOTGs, collective insight adds value to the team process. However, insight alone is not enough. Evidence provides an "as-is" foundation but should drive an aspirational "to-be" state.[47]

Next, insights and aspirational goals are translated into measurable policies and interventions (**FIGURE 12-12**). For example, efforts to prevent the virus spreading include travel restrictions, quarantines, curfews, workplace hazard controls, event postponements and cancellations, and facility closures. To be effective, an intervention must be unbiased, self-sustaining, self-correcting when needed, and measurable.

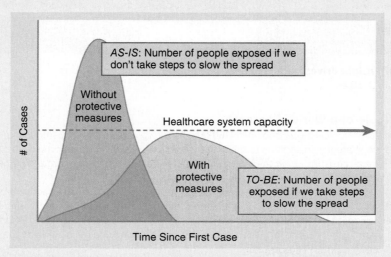

FIGURE 12-11 **Modeling, predicting, and tracking behavior over time followed by an aspiration**
Anderson DE, from Centers for Disease Control and Prevention.

(continues)

CASE 12-2 COVID-19 from a Systems Perspective: COVID-19 and Application of Systems Thinking Tools *(continued)*

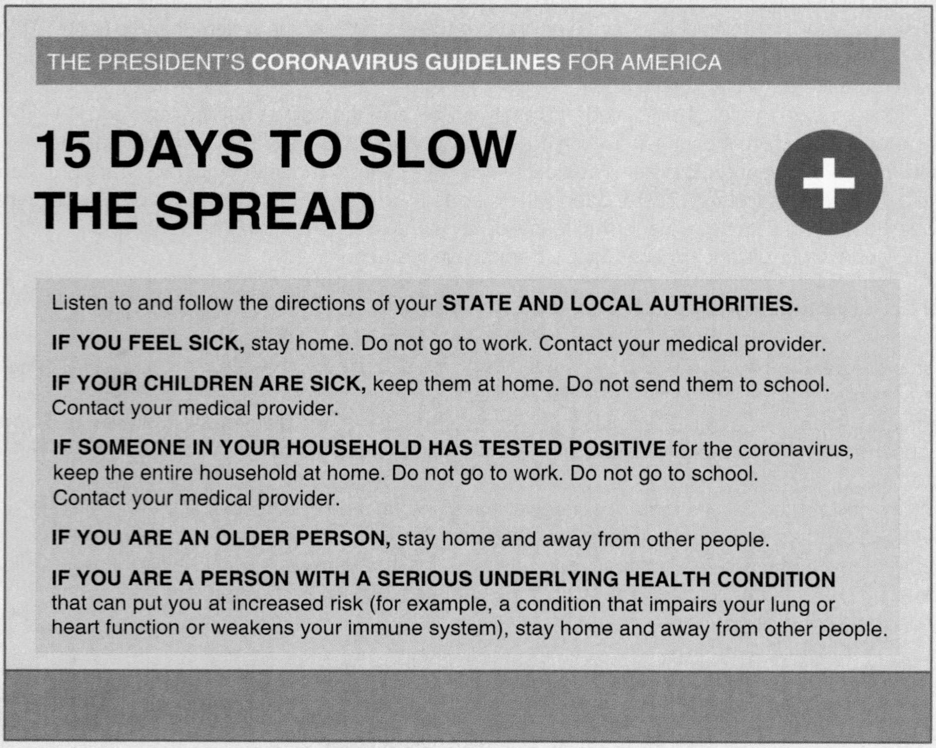

THE PRESIDENT'S **CORONAVIRUS GUIDELINES** FOR AMERICA

15 DAYS TO SLOW THE SPREAD

Listen to and follow the directions of your **STATE AND LOCAL AUTHORITIES.**

IF YOU FEEL SICK, stay home. Do not go to work. Contact your medical provider.

IF YOUR CHILDREN ARE SICK, keep them at home. Do not send them to school. Contact your medical provider.

IF SOMEONE IN YOUR HOUSEHOLD HAS TESTED POSITIVE for the coronavirus, keep the entire household at home. Do not go to work. Do not go to school. Contact your medical provider.

IF YOU ARE AN OLDER PERSON, stay home and away from other people.

IF YOU ARE A PERSON WITH A SERIOUS UNDERLYING HEALTH CONDITION that can put you at increased risk (for example, a condition that impairs your lung or heart function or weakens your immune system), stay home and away from other people.

FIGURE 12-12 Insight drives leaders to generate policies and interventions
U.S. Center for Disease Control and Prevention.

Part 3: "Whole-of-a-World" Approach

Using the social ecological model shown in **FIGURE 12-13**, we can assess factors, barriers, and health communication strategies, in addition to the challenges of prevention, protection, response, and recovery at several levels, including the individual (intrapersonal), interpersonal, organizational, community, and societal levels, as well as the ways in which these levels interact.[47,48]

Figure 12-13 challenges collaborative leaders to engage and mobilize partners across all sectors and levels.[46] Each must leverage the SDHs in accordance with the interventions and policies. The outcomes are evidence-driven results. For example, results of the COVID-19 interventions can be acquired through further data collection and dashboards such as the one maintained by the Johns Hopkins University COVID-19 Resource Center.[49]

Finally, constant intelligent inquiry should follow results, with the aim of assessing progress, making adjustments as necessary, improvising when required, and seeking out opportunities to improve.[46,47]

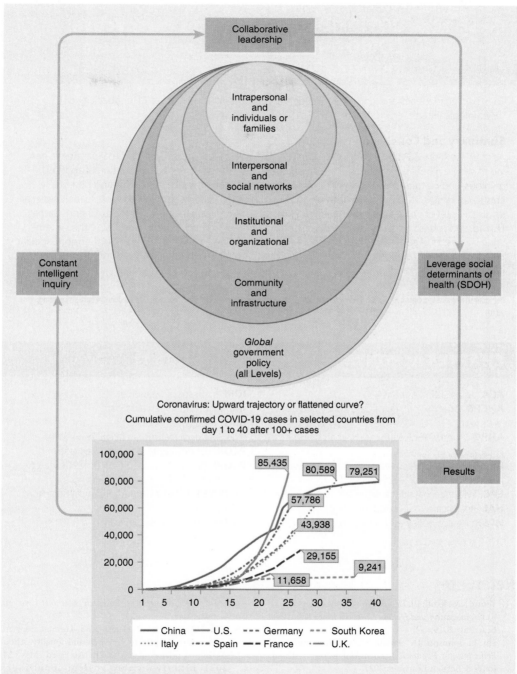

FIGURE 12-13 **"Whole-of-world" approach**

Data from Anderson DE, from McLeroy KR, Steckler A, Bibeau D, eds. The social ecology of health promotion interventions. Health Ed Q 1988;15(4):351–377; and Healthy People 2020 MAP-IT model.

(continues)

CASE 12-2 COVID-19 from a Systems Perspective: COVID-19 and Application of Systems Thinking Tools *(continued)*

To maximize feedback and good ideas, leaders should encourage inquiry and feedback in "psychologically safe" environments.

Summary and Conclusion

As of this writing, COVID-19 has infected millions of people worldwide. The COVID-19 pandemic has led to severe global socioeconomic disruption, such as postponement or cancellation of sporting, religious, and cultural events. It will likely impair healthcare or educational systems and potentially crash economies. Through systems thinking and application of systems thinking tools, leadership at all levels can prevent and slow the spread of COVID-19. This was shown in a study by Lu, Cheng, Qamar, Huang, and Johnson, as reported in the *American Journal of Infection Control*, describing the system-wide successes of several countries such as South Korea, Singapore, and Taiwan.[50] Furthermore, specific antiviral medications approved for COVID-19 can be developed, and the lessons from this experience can be applied in the future.

Reproduced from Shi L, Johnson JA. *Public Health Administration: Principles for Population-Based Management*. 4th ed. Jones & Bartlett Learning; 2020.

CHAPTER ACRONYMS

ACA Affordable Care Act

AHCPR Agency for Health Care Policy and Research

AHRQ Agency for Healthcare Research and Quality

ARRA American Recovery and Reinvestment Act

EPC Evidence-based Practice Center

HAI Healthcare-associated infections

HPSR Health policy and systems research

IOM Institute of Medicine

IRB Institutional review board

MAT Medication-assisted treatment

NIH National Institutes of Health

PCOR Patient-centered outcomes research

PCORI Patient-Centered Outcomes Research Institute

PCORNET Patient-Centered Clinical Research Network

PSNet Patient safety network

References

1. Young KM, Kroth PJ. *Health Care USA: Understanding its Organization and Delivery*. 9th ed. Jones & Bartlett Learning; 2019.
2. Shi L, Johnson JA. *Public Health Administration: Principles for Population-Based Management*. 4th ed. Jones & Bartlett Learning; 2021.
3. National Heart, Lung, and Blood Institute. Framingham Heart Study (FHS). Accessed September 26, 2021. https://www.nhlbi.nih.gov/science/framingham-heart-study-fhs
4. Shi L. *Health Services Research Methods*. 3rd ed. Cengage Learning; 2020.
5. U.S. Department of Health and Human Services Agency for Healthcare Research and Quality. About AHRQ. Updated April 2021. Accessed May 24, 2021. http://www.ahrq.gov/cpi/about/index.html
6. Johnson JA, Stoskopf C, Shi L. *Comparative Health Systems: A Global Perspective*. Jones & Bartlett Learning; 2018.

7. Alliance for Health Policy and Systems Research. What is health policy and systems research (HPSR)? Accessed September 26, 2021. https://ahpsr.who.int/

8. Alliance for Health Policy and Systems Research. *Systems Thinking for Health Systems Strengthening.* World Health Organization; 2009. Accessed September 26, 2021. https://www.who.int/alliance-hpsr/systemsthinking/en/

9. Johnson JA, Anderson DE, Rossow CC. *Health Systems Thinking: A Primer.* Jones & Bartlett Learning; 2020.

10. Wennberg J. Which rate is right? *N Engl J Med.* 1986;314(5):310-311. doi: 10.1056/NEJM198601303140509

11. Wennberg JE, Freeman JL, Shelton RM, Bubolz TA. Hospital use and mortality among Medicare beneficiaries in Boston and New Haven. *N Engl J Med.* 1989;321(17):1168-1173. doi: 10.1056/NEJM198910263211706

12. National Institutes of Health. Accessed June 10, 2021. https://www.nih.gov/

13. Agency for Healthcare Research and Quality. Accessed June 10, 2021. https://www.ahrq.gov/

14. Johnson JA, Jones W. *The AMA and Organized Medicine.* Garland Publishing; 1993.

15. Haley SJ, Johnson JA, Frazier LJ. *Opioids and Population Health: A Primer.* Jones & Bartlett Learning; 2022.

16. Newhouse JP, Manning WG, Duan N, et al. The findings of the RAND health insurance experiment—a response to Welch et al. *Med Care.* 1987;25(2):157-179. doi: 10.1097/00005650-198702000-00009

17. Institute of Medicine Committee to Design a Strategy for Quality Review and Assurance in Medicare. Lohr KN, ed. *Medicare: A Strategy for Quality Assurance. Volume 1.* National Academies Press; 1990.

18. Donabedian A. Evaluating the quality of medical care. 1966. *Milbank Q.* 2005;83(4):691-729. doi: 10.1111/j.1468-0009.2005.00397.x

19. Institute of Medicine Committee on Quality of Health Care in America. Kohn LT, Corrigan JM, Donaldson MS, eds. *To Err Is Human: Building a Safer Health System.* National Academies Press; 2000.

20. Sackett DL, Rosenberg WM, Gray JA, Haynes RB, Richardson WS. Evidence based medicine: what it is and what it isn't. *BMJ.* 1996;312(7023):71-72. doi: 10.1136/bmj.312.7023.71

21. Sox HC. Defining comparative effective research: the importance of getting it right. *Med Care.* 2010; 48(6 Suppl):S7-8. doi: 10.1097/MLR.0b013e3181da3709

22. Kaiser Family Foundation. Explaining health care reform: what is comparative effectiveness research? Published September 29, 2009. Accessed May 20, 2019. http://kff.org/health-costs/issue-brief/explaining-health-care-reform-what-is-comparative/

23. Patient Centered Outcomes Research Institute. Research & results; explore our portfolio. Accessed June 2, 2020. http://www.pcori.org/research-results

24. National Patient-Centered Clinical Research Network. Accessed June 5, 2021. https://pcornet.org/

25. National Institutes of Health. Mission and goals. Updated July 27, 2017. Accessed September 26, 2021. https://www.nih.gov/about-nih/what-we-do/mission-goals

26. Skochelak E. *Health Systems Science.* 2nd ed. Elsevier; 2020.

27. Peters DH. Health policy and systems research: the future of the field. *Health Res Policy Syst.* 2018;16(1):84. doi: 10.1186/s12961-018-0359-0

28. Powell S, Stone R. *The patient survival handbook: avoid being the next victim of medical error.* BookLogix Publishing Services; 2015.

29. Makary MA, Daniel M. Medical error—the third leading cause of death in the US. *BMJ.* 2016;353:i2139.

30. James JT. A new, evidence-based estimate of patient harms associated with hospital care. *J Patient Saf.* 2013;9(3):122-128.

31. Kohn LT, Corrigan JM, Donaldson MS, eds. Institute of Medicine. *To err is human: Building a Safer Health System.* Institute of Medicine; 2000.

32. Powell SM. Creating a systems approach to patient safety through better teamwork. *Biomed Instrum Technol.* 2006;40(3):205-207.

33. Emanuel L, Berwick D, Conway J, et al. What exactly is patient safety? *J Med Regul.* 2009;95(1):13-24.

34. King HB, Battles J, Baker DP, et al. TeamSTEPPS™: team strategies and tools to enhance performance and patient safety. Rockville, MD: *Agency for HealthCare Quality and Research.* 2008.

35. Wu AW, Lipshutz AK, Pronovost PJ. Effectiveness and efficiency of root cause analysis in medicine. *JAMA.* 2008;299(6):685-687.

36. Weaver SJ, Dy SM, Rosen MA. Team-training in healthcare: a narrative synthesis of the literature. *BMJ Qual Saf.* 2014:23(5):359-372.

37. Likosky DS. Clinical microsystems: a critical framework for crossing the quality chasm. *J Extra Corpor Technol.* 2014;46(1):33-37.

38. Nelson EC, Batalden PB, Homa K, et al. Microsystems in health care: Part 2. Creating a rich information environment. *Jt Comm J Qual Saf.* 2003;29(1):5-15.

39. Holden RJ, Carayon P, Gurses AP, et al. SEIPS 2.0: a human factors framework for studying and improving the work of healthcare professionals and patients. *Ergonomics.* 2013;56(11):1669-1686.

40. Burger C, Eaton P, Hess K, et al. System-based approach to managing patient safety in ambulatory care (and beyond). *Patient Safety and Quality Healthcare.* Accessed March 3, 2018. https://www.psqh.com/analysis/system-based-approach-managing-patient-safety-ambulatory-care-beyond/. Nov/Dec 2017

41. Chassin MR, Loeb JM. High-reliability health care: getting there from here. *Milbank Q.* 2013;91(3):459-490.

42. Holshue ML, DeBolt C, Lindquist S, et al. First case of 2019 novel coronavirus in the United States. *N Engl J Med.* 2020;382:929-936.

43. World Health Organization. Coronavirus disease (COVID-19) pandemic. https://www.who.int/emergencies/diseases/novel-coronavirus-2019 Published 2019.

44. Statement on the second meeting of the International Health Regulations (2005) Emergency Committee regarding the outbreak of novel coronavirus (2019-nCoV) [press release]. Geneva, Switzerland: World Health Organization; 2020.

45. Director-General's opening remarks at the media briefing on COVID-19 of 11 March 2020 [press release]. Geneva, Switzerland: World Health Organization; 2020.

46. Johnson JA, Anderson DE, Rossow CC. *Health systems thinking: a primer.* Burlington, MA: Jones & Bartlett Learning; 2020.

47. Johnson JA, Anderson DE. *Systems thinking for health organizations, leadership, and policy: think globally, act locally.* Sentia Publishing; 2017.

48. McLeroy KR, Steckler A, Bibeau D, eds. The social ecology of health promotion interventions. *Health Ed Q.* 1988;15(4):351-377.

49. Johns Hopkins Resource Center: Coronavirus COVID-19 global cases. Coronavirus Resource Center. Accessed March 30, 2020. https://coronavirus.jhu.edu/map.html

50. Lu N, Cheng K-W, Qamar N, Huang K-C, Johnson JA. Weathering COVID-19 storm: successful control measures of five Asian countries. *Am J Infect Control.* 2020;48:851-852.

CHAPTER 13

Preparedness and Emergency Management

LEARNING OBJECTIVES

After reading this chapter you should be able to:

- Define foundational terms associated with emergency preparedness.
- List the four phases of disaster.
- Describe the agencies in the U.S. government associated with disaster preparedness.
- Explain the role of the National Incident Management System.
- Name the roles associated with the Incident Command System.
- Discuss the role of the emergency operations center.
- Describe the role of international and national entities in health preparedness.
- Explain the purpose of the Assistant Secretary for Preparedness and Response.

KEY TERMS

Centers for Disease Control
    and Prevention (CDC)
Disaster
Disaster preparedness

Emergency
Hazards
Incidents
Mitigation

One Health
Response

CHAPTER OVERVIEW

Disasters are a fact of our human existence. Nowhere is disaster preparedness and planning more important than in healthcare delivery. Our healthcare delivery system is sensitive to societal events, especially disasters. This chapter is broken down into three broad areas. First, it gives a general orientation to the emergency management apparatus in the United States. Next, the chapter discusses emergency preparedness and management in healthcare delivery across all levels: international, national regional, and local. Finally, the chapter provides an overview of the linkages between the public and personal healthcare systems in terms of disease outbreaks and describes the Centers for Disease Control and Prevention's (CDC) One Health approach.

Throughout its history, the United States has experienced an array of catastrophic events. The nation has experienced loss of life and resources due to hurricanes, fires, earthquakes, floods, epidemics, and pandemics. In *Comparative Health Systems: A Global Perspective,* authors Johnson, Stoskopf, and Shi noted the potential for health system disruption due to a host of events, including threats, disasters, environmental events, terrorism, and epidemics.[1] These types of events can have profound impacts and disrupt normal operations for healthcare delivery. As an example, **FIGURE 13-1** illustrates key national emergency events that have occurred over the past 100 years.[2,3]

Emergency preparedness activities for the healthcare industry require attention to public health, personal health, and the civil structures of society. First, it is prudent to understand some of the basic vocabulary. Shi and Johnson defined several foundational terms[4]:

- **Emergencies** are typically any occurrence that requires an immediate response. These events can be the result of nature (e.g., hurricanes, tornadoes, and earthquakes), they can be caused by technological or man-made error (e.g., nuclear accidents, bombing, and bioterrorism), or they can be the result of emerging diseases (e.g., Ebola virus in Texas and New York City).
- **Hazards** present the probability of the occurrence of a disaster caused by a natural phenomenon (e.g., earthquake, tropical cyclone), by failure of man-made sources of energy (e.g., nuclear reactor or industrial explosion), or by uncontrolled human activity (e.g., conflicts, overgrazing).

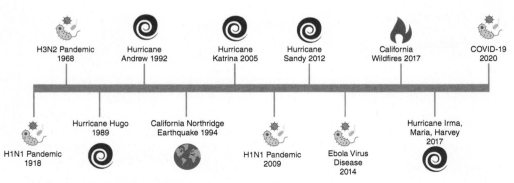

FIGURE 13-1 **Major Emergency Events in the United States, 1918–2020**

FIGURE 13-2 The Four Phases of Disaster

- **Incidents** are "an occurrence or event, natural or man-made, that requires a response to protect life or property. Incidents can, for example, include major disasters, emergencies, terrorist attacks, terrorist threats, civil unrest, wildland and urban fires, floods, hazardous material spills, nuclear accidents, aircraft accidents, earthquakes, hurricanes, tornadoes, tropical storms, tsunamis, war-related disasters, public health and medical emergencies, and other occurrences requiring an emergency response."

Each of these terms describe different areas that healthcare leaders and their organizations must be attentive to. Healthcare facilities depend on their environment for medical supplies, utilities, food, and basic infrastructure support. Thus, a massive hurricane that disrupts the power grid will impact the community in which hospitals exist. A recent example of this is the power failure in Texas due to a winter storm, which halted power to more than 4 million Texans.[5] With Texas being a medical center for the country and the world, this event was nearly catastrophic. Hospitals struggled to provide heat and water for operations and patient care as well as deal with the unintended consequences of desperation from citizen behavior. This is an example of a weather incident in which subarctic temperatures impacted an unprepared state government and utility apparatus with negative implications to all citizens.[6] Disasters tend to follow phases that can be anticipated by planners. **FIGURE 13-2** shows the four phases of disaster and the cycle it tends to take.

Ideally, planning should address each of these phases. Johnson and Rossow described each phase and the level of attention required[1]:

> Mitigation is the cornerstone of disaster management and includes activities to decrease the potential loss of life and property by lessening the impact of disasters. Mitigation should start early, long before a disaster occurs, involving all key stakeholders. The focus of preparedness is to enhance the capacity to respond to an incident. Taking steps to ensure who, what, where, when, and how people and resources are available before an event occurs. Preparedness involves development of training programs for the community, public awareness, logistical support, and communications, early warning, with ongoing monitoring. Response is the implementation of the time-critical plan in order to take action to save lives and to prevent further damage. The recovery phase incorporates actions necessary to maintain and/or return the community to normal after the disaster. Recovery may include repairing buildings, streets, railways, and other infrastructure damaged during the disaster.

▶ Federal Government and Emergency Events

The U.S. federal government is the principal coordinating entity for national emergencies via the Department of Homeland Security (DHS) and its subordinate agencies. The Federal Emergency Management Agency (FEMA) is the key subordinate agency that most often takes the lead for disaster response and intra-agency communication within the first 48 hours following an event. FEMA's mission is "helping people before, during and after disasters."[7] FEMA employs more than 20,000 people and has 10 regional coordinating offices located around the United States. **TABLE 13-1** lists the regions and their states.[8]

FEMA has put forth a shared vision for the future around building a culture of preparedness, readiness for catastrophic disaster, and reduction in complexity.[9] The agency has gained prominence over the years, and **FIGURE 13-3** is a timeline of its evolution.[10]

FEMA works with other national, state, local organizations to plan and respond to disasters. The agency offers a host of tools, education, and even grants to help communities and organizations properly plan for disasters. The Emergency Management Institute (EMI) offers a range of courses on all things related to emergency management. These courses offer an array of insights to introduce individuals, organizations, and the community to emergency management training.

TABLE 13-1 FEMA Regional Coordinating Offices	
FEMA Regional Coordinating Offices	
Region 1	Connecticut, Massachusetts, Maine, New Hampshire, Rhode Island, Vermont
Region 2	New Jersey, New York, Puerto Rico, Virgin Islands
Region 3	District of Columbia, Delaware, Maryland, Pennsylvania, Virginia, West Virginia
Region 4	Alabama, Florida, Georgia, Kentucky, Mississippi, North Carolina, South Carolina, Tennessee
Region 5	Illinois, Indiana, Michigan, Minnesota, Ohio, Wisconsin
Region 6	Arkansas, Louisiana, New Mexico, Oklahoma, Texas
Region 7	Iowa, Kansas, Missouri, Nebraska
Region 8	Guam, American Samoa, Commonwealth of Northern Mariana Islands, Federated States of Micronesia, Colorado, Montana, North Dakota, South Dakota, Utah, Wyoming
Region 9	Arizona, California, Hawaii, Nevada, Pacific Territories
Region 10	Alaska, Idaho, Oregon, Washington

Data from Federal Emergency Management Agency. About us. Accessed February 20, 2021. https://www.fema.gov/about

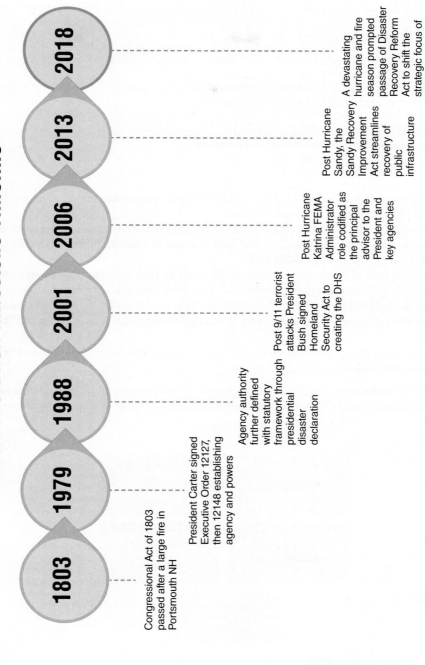

FEMA Evolution Milestone Timeline

1803 — Congressional Act of 1803 passed after a large fire in Portsmouth NH

1979 — President Carter signed Executive Order 12127, then 12148 establishing agency and powers

1988 — Agency authority further defined with statutory framework through presidential disaster declaration

2001 — Post 9/11 terrorist attacks President Bush signed Homeland Security Act to creating the DHS

2006 — Post Hurricane Katrina FEMA Administrator role codified as the principal advisor to the President and key agencies

2013 — Post Hurricane Sandy, the Sandy Recovery Improvement Act streamlines recovery of public infrastructure

2018 — A devastating hurricane and fire season prompted passage of Disaster Recovery Reform Act to shift the strategic focus of FMEA

FIGURE 13-3 Evolution of FEMA

Data from Federal Emergency Management Agency. History of FEMA. Updated January 4, 2021. Accessed February 20, 2021. https://www.fema.gov/about/history

BOX 13-1 FEMA Independent Study Courses

Activities are executed during emergencies via a framework called the National Incident Management System (NIMS). NIMS was established by FEMA as a comprehensive national approach for management of incidents across entities and is intended to[7]:

- Apply across the spectrum of all potential incidents, hazards, and other impacts irrespective of their size, location, or complexity;
- Facilitate public and private cooperation and coordination during incident management activities;
- Serve as a standard approach for incident management

Created by Richard Greenhill. Data from Federal Emergency Management Agency Emergency Management Institute. *Independent Study Program Course Brochure*. Accessed February 20, 2021. https://training.fema.gov/is/crslist.aspx

Many of the courses are free of charge and offer deep knowledge on activities for success. **BOX 13-1** lists FEMA Independent Study Courses.[11]

NIMS is important as it sets a standard for intra-agency coordination at all levels of government (national, state, local, and tribal) to deal with disasters in a sustainable way. The key components of NIMS are illustrated in **FIGURE 13-4**.[7]

The components of NIMS are cascaded to all levels in society. Governments and organizations participate in NIMS through adoption of their own Incident Command Systems (ICSs) modeled off the national framework. These ICSs can be activated at any time (whether a national or local emergency) and are a structured way to manage emergencies. The ICS diagram is shown in **FIGURE 13-5**.[12]

The diagram in Figure 13-5 represents the basic roles and functions required in an ICS. The functions and responsibilities include[12]:

- Incident Commander: The incident commander is the primary individual in charge at the scene of an emergency. They maintain command at the disaster site until relieved or until a

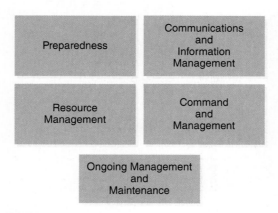

FIGURE 13-4 Components of NIMS

Data from Federal Emergency Management Agency. NIMS: frequently asked questions. Accessed February 20, 2021. https://www.fema.gov/pdf/emergency/nims/nimsfaqs.pdf

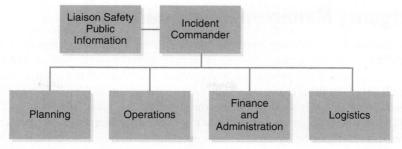

FIGURE 13-5 Incident Command System Diagram

higher echelon arrives (state or federal entities). All media relations, crisis communication, and coordination activities are finalized by the person holding this role.

- Safety: The safety function serves to identify and assess situations for hazards to prevent accidents. In addition, the individual holding this role prepares a safety plan, halts unsafe acts, and corrects any situations or conditions deemed unsafe.
- Liaison: The individual in the liaison role is the point of contact for all entities outside the organization. They also monitor operational progress and work to identify issues among organizations.
- Public Relations/Information: Public relations is the primary face to the media. They prepare briefings and clear content with the incident commander prior to release.
- Operations: This individual gets things done at the operational level. They manage all action plans and operations during an incident and are an important "right hand" to the incident commander.
- Planning: Planners are responsible for meetings as well as supervision of the Incident Action Plan. They are key in determining any specialized resources (human or otherwise) to support the event.
- Logistics: The individual supporting logistics ensures resource availability (except for human resources). They function to estimate and procure resources for all phases and operational periods related to the incident.
- Finance and Administration: This role manages all financial aspects of the incident, including costs analyses, risk management, and expenditures.

Organizations with active disaster planning and preparedness using the ICS model often have a designated place to meet when an incident is called. The location could be anything from a room to a command center and sometimes has a specific name. In terms of incident management, this place is known as an Emergency Operations Center (EOC).[12] Best practices include having two locations designated; a primary and secondary. This follows the notion that the ICS is a standard framework and that staff should know where to go and their function when activated. EOCs should be stocked and equipped with the appropriate materials for an emergency. Equipment might include computers, monitors, televisions, water, food, facilitation materials (flip charts, pens, markers, etc.), phones, two-way radios, printers, and printouts of documents related to emergency management. The EOC is an important part of incident management. It supports the standardization of location for activation of the ICS. It sets the stage for the mindset to address the issue at hand through briefings, action planning, resources, and ultimately incident management. In summary, these foundations set the stage for review of the healthcare delivery system.

▶ Emergency Management in Health Care

By its nature, the healthcare industry is primed to deal with emergency situations. On a daily basis, healthcare facilities deal with patients flowing in from all facets of society with sickness and accidents as chief complaints. Thus, emergency management in health care is a natural phenomenon. In terms of planning, healthcare organizations have more reason to plan for emergencies. Not only is the healthcare industry subject to the same damage from disasters as society, but it must also deal with post disaster consequences. For example, health systems may lose power and have supply chains disrupted during a hurricane, as would any other business; then also need to care for patients and first responders who are impacted. Hurricane Katrina caused catastrophic flooding and loss of life in New Orleans, but also raised the risk of pathogenic bacteria in the drinking water.[13] Thus, anyone exposed to that hazard would potentially seek care at the hospital. Disasters display a clear link between the public health and acute care systems. As such, healthcare organizations must remain vigilant about planning to care for impacted individuals.

▶ Epidemics and Pandemic Preparedness

The healthcare industry is at the tip of the spear for treating diseases. At the time this chapter is being written, the world is in the throes of a "100-year pandemic" caused by a strain of coronavirus (called COVID-19). This type of event is difficult to plan for given the length of time between major events. Also, the efficacy of disease reporting between the acute care system and public health systems (e.g. between local health departments and the CDC) suffers due to poor infrastructure. Therefore, by the time a pathogen is recognized, it may have been in circulation for some time. The complexities in outbreak and epidemic emergency management rest within the political contexts of global, national, state, and local entities. At the global level, the World Health Organization (WHO) acts as the coordinator for disease reporting and surveillance.[13] WHO is the lead international agency charged with planning, prevention, and management of outbreaks deemed public health emergencies of international concern (PHEICs).[14] While this is a noble effort, WHO has been criticized for its handling of outbreaks and other issues. In *State Capacity Influences on Pandemic Preparedness for the Sub-Saharan African Region*, Greenhill et al. found[14]:

> The WHO is the lead UN agency tasked with strategic planning and coordination for disease outbreaks for members in the World Health Assembly (WHA). The WHA comprises a collective group of nation-states, that provide funding for collaboration on issues related to health. The WHA and Director General of the WHO have successfully facilitated the creation of frameworks related to disease coordination and management. While the WHO has experienced remarkable success, it has come under withering criticism from recent challenges related to policy execution. It currently faces a host of issues related to operations and capacity (e.g., competition for funding, lack of accountability mechanisms). These issues directly impact the agency's ability to be effective.

The COVID-19 pandemic has again raised questions about WHO's efficacy as an emergency preparedness coordination entity. Former President Trump was adamant that WHO had not been as transparent as needed when reviewing COVID-19's potential origins in China.[15] Pandemic planning at the global level is as much a political exercise as it is a public health operation.[16] This consideration is key when acknowledging the need for coordination at the international level.

WHO follows the standard of incident management in its practices for disease response. WHO maintains an EOC called the Strategic Health Operations Centre (SHOC) to monitor pandemic and epidemic outbreaks around the world.[17] SHOC is primarily manned when there is a PHEIC declared. Understanding the political dynamics is central to the processes of planning and management.

On the national front, the CDC is the organization responsible for assisting healthcare facilities with collating data and recommendations for standards of treatment during outbreaks.[18] The CDC collects surveillance data from hospitals as well as local public health departments for review of trends. It sends and receives relevant information to and from WHO. This constant exchange is an effort between local, national, and international health agencies to monitor and assist with preparedness. The CDC maintains an EOC in their Atlanta, Georgia, headquarters. The CDC's EOC is monitored 24/7, but it comes to life when there is a public health emergency or threat facing the nation.[19] **FIGURE 13-6** is an illustration of the CDC's EOC activation over the years for public health and other disaster events.[20]

The COVID-19 pandemic has once again highlighted the need to strengthen activities in acute care, public health, and disaster preparedness. Even with all of the information exchange between hospitals and local, national, and international organizations, gaps still exist. Some of the gaps are linked to politics while others are due to infrastructure. Healthcare leaders must remain keenly aware of these factors when planning for preparedness activities.

▶ One Health Preparedness

COVID-19 is believed to have originated as a mutation from bats, which then jumped to humans and ignited the pandemic.[21] While confirmation is ongoing, this hypothesis has reinvigorated attention and discussion on the CDC's One Health approach. Greenhill et. al describe One Health below[14]:

> The One Health initiative resulted from the collective thought of researchers that enhanced collaboration was needed to address vulnerabilities related to the human-environment interface; related to zoonoses potentially impacting humans. The concern for animal-human transmission of disease is not a new concern. Several diseases have resulted from the human-animal relationship, e.g. Lyme disease, HIV, bovine spongiform encephalopathy [BSE] and others.

The key to effective preparedness and management rests with the adoption of systems thinking. Shifts in climate are believed to contribute to more severe weather events. Those events result in disasters that impact ecosystems for animals and humans alike. Subsequently, the healthcare system responds to care for those impacted. Emergency preparedness, like health care, is a team sport.

▶ Healthcare Emergency Preparedness

The federal government has many resources for healthcare entities to aid in planning and preparedness. A key agency focused on health emergency preparedness is the U.S. Department of Health and Human Services (HHS) Office of the Assistant Secretary for Preparedness and

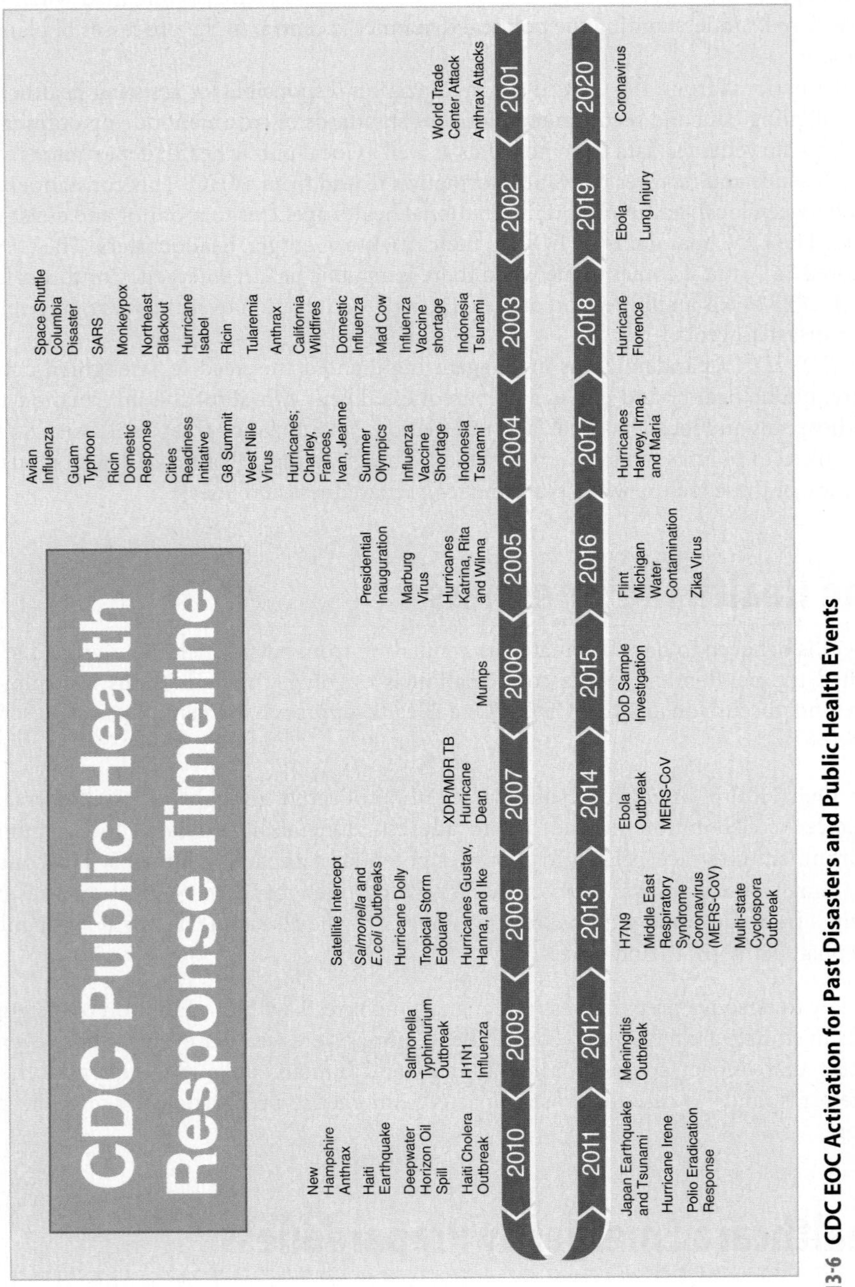

FIGURE 13-6 CDC EOC Activation for Past Disasters and Public Health Events

Response (ASPR). The primary mission of ASPR is to "save lives and protect Americans from 21st century health security threats."[22] They accomplish this through collaboration with hospitals, the community, all levels of government, and biotech companies. ASPR manages 11 programs and initiatives focused on national health security[23]:

- Biomedical Advanced Research and Development Authority (BARDA) Medical Counter-measure Programs
  - Established to deal with chemical, biological, radiological, and nuclear (CBRN) threats
- National Biodefense Strategy
  - Initiative to focus on biothreats to the nation
- Regional Disaster Health Response System
  - Response system to integrate with daily care delivery
- Hospital Preparedness Program
  - Established a foundation for national healthcare preparedness
- Strategic National Stockpile
  - Supplements state and local medical supplies during emergencies
- Critical Infrastructure Protection
  - Coordination and risk management collaborative for preparedness
- Public Health Emergency Medical Countermeasures Enterprise
  - Coordinates CBRN countermeasures; emerging infectious disease preparedness
- Medical Reserve Corps
  - National network of more than 190,000 response volunteers
- Centers for Innovation in Advanced Development and Manufacturing
  - Entity used to streamline manufacture of vaccines and therapeutics
- National Disaster Medical System
  - Aids health system response capabilities during an emergency

Among the many offerings from ASPR, the Technical Resources, Assistance Center, and Information Exchange (TRACIE) is one the most impactful for healthcare delivery. This program offers an array of resources to help healthcare systems plan and prepare for emergencies.

▶ U.S. National Health Security Strategy

ASPR updates the plan called the National Health Security Strategy (NHSS) every 4 years.[24] The 2019–2022 NHSS is a three-part active strategic approach to planning for health security preparedness in the country[24]:

- *Prepare, mobilize, and coordinate a whole-of-government approach*: This objective is concerned with strong collaboration between all levels of government and other key stakeholders (e.g., public partners, private partners, academia, communities, etc.). The belief is that this approach will expand capacity and flexibility for quick mobilization towards prevention of incidents.
- *Protecting the nation from health effects associated with emerging and pandemic infectious diseases and chemical, biological, radiological, and nuclear (CBRN) threats*: This approach expands interoperability and aids in creating a network of actors that can boost health security capacity. It is poised to help with development of new countermeasures to address modern threats and dissemination of appropriate medical countermeasures.

■ *Leverage capabilities in the private sector*: This approach fosters the type of partnerships that can leverage the full weight of private ingenuity. The goal is to incentivize behaviors that encourage preparedness in areas like supply chains to build and maintain efficiency.

The nation faces a host of threats to population health related to all types of disaster events. None is more real than the effects of climate change on health. The 2019–2022 NHSS report indicated that threats related to extreme weather and infectious diseases are continually underfunded and lack coherent response capabilities.[25] Thus, more attention is required to prepare for and mitigate the impact of these types of threats. While there is much political debate on the whole notion of climate change, a report from the U.S. Global Change Research Program highlighted some examples of how climate impacts human health, as shown in **FIGURE 13-7**.[26]

	Climate Driver	Exposure	Health Outcome
Extreme Heat	Frequent, severe, prolonged heat events	Higher temps	Heat-related illness and death
Outdoor Air Quality	Increasing temps and changing precipitation patterns	Worse air quality (e.g, ozone, particulate matter & pollen)	Premature death, acute and chronic cardiovascular and respiratory illness
Floods	Rising sea levels, more intense precipitation, hurricanes and storm surge events	Contaminated water, debris, and essential infrastructure disruptions	Drowning, injuries, mental health consequences, gastrointestinal and other illnesses
Vector-Borne Illness	Changes in temperature extremes and seasonal weather patterns	Earlier and geographically expanded tick activity	Lyme disease
Water-Related Illness	Rising sea surface temperature, changes in precipitation and run off impacting coastal salinity	Recreational water or shellfish contamination with Vibrio species	Vibrio species related diarrhea, intestinal illness, wound and blood stream infections and death
Food-Related Illness	Increases in temperature, humidity, and season length	Increased growth of pathogens with seasonal shifts in diseases such as Salmonella species	Infection with Salmonella species and outbreaks
Mental Health and Well-Being	Climate change impacts, extreme weather	Level of exposure to traumatic events – e.g. disasters	Distress, grief, behavioral health disorders, social impacts

FIGURE 13-7 **Examples of Climate Impact on Health from the U.S Global Change Research Program's** *The Impacts of Climate Change on Human Health in the United States: A Scientific Assessment*

Created by Richard Greenhill. Data from Crimmins A, Balbus J, Gamble J, et al. *The Impacts of Climate Change on Human Health in the United States: A Scientific Assessment*. U.S. Global Change Research Program; 2016. Accessed June 4, 2021. https://s3.amazonaws.com/climatehealth2016/high/ClimateHealth2016_FullReport.pdf

This report listed several key findings that align with scientific research. **TABLE 13-2** lists each area and the findings.[26]

TABLE 13-2 Key Findings in *The Impacts of Climate Change on Human Health in the United States: A Scientific Assessment*	
Area of Concern	**Key Finding Categories**
Temperature-Related Death and Illness	▪ Future increases in temperature-related deaths ▪ Even small differences in seasonal temperatures result in illness and death ▪ Changing tolerances to extreme heat ▪ Some populations at greater risks
Air Quality Impacts	▪ Exacerbation in ozone health impacts ▪ Increased health impacts from wildfires ▪ Worsened allergy and asthma conditions
Impacts on Extreme Events on Human Health	▪ Increased exposure to extreme events ▪ Disruption of essential infrastructure ▪ Vulnerability to coastal flooding
Vector-Borne Diseases	▪ Changes in distributions of vectors and vector-borne diseases ▪ Earlier tick activity and northward range expansion ▪ Changing mosquito-borne disease dynamics ▪ Emergence of new vector-borne pathogens
Water-Related Illness	▪ Seasonal and geographic changes in the risk of waterborne illnesses ▪ Water infrastructure failure ▪ Runoff from extreme precipitation increases exposure risk
Food Safety, Nutrition, and Distribution	▪ Increased risk of food-borne illness ▪ Rising carbon dioxide lowers nutritional value of food ▪ Chemical contaminants in the food chain ▪ Extreme weather limits access to safe foods
Mental Health and Well-Being	▪ Exposure to disasters results in mental health consequences ▪ Specific groups are at higher risk ▪ Climate change threats result in social impacts ▪ Extreme heat increases risk for people with mental illness
Populations of Concern	▪ Vulnerability varies over time and is location-specific ▪ Health impacts vary with age and life stage ▪ Mapping tools and vulnerability indices identify climate health risks ▪ Social determinants of health interact with climate factors to affect health risks

Created by Richard Greenhill. Data from Crimmins A, Balbus J, Gamble J, et al. *The Impacts of Climate Change on Human Health in the United States: A Scientific Assessment*. U.S. Global Change Research Program; 2016. Accessed June 4, 2021. https://s3.amazonaws.com/climatehealth2016/high/ClimateHealth2016_FullReport.pdf

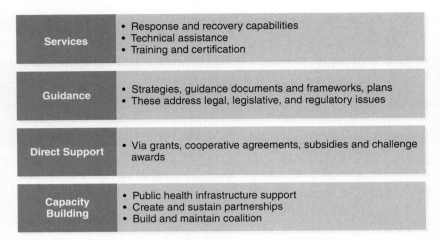

FIGURE 13-8 **Broad Areas for Government Success in Health Security**

Created by Richard Greenhill. Data from U.S. Department of Health and Human Services Office of the Assistant Secretary for Preparedness and Response; Office of Strategy, Policy, Planning, and Requirements. *National Health Security Strategy Implementation Plan 2019–2022.* U.S. Department of Health and Human Services; 2019. Accessed June 9, 2021. https://www.phe.gov/Preparedness/planning/authority/nhss /Documents/2019-2022-nhss-ip-v508.pdf

The federal government devised the *National Health Security Strategy Implementation Plan 2019–2022* as a roadmap to realize its goals.[27] The creators of the policy cite four broad areas for the government that are key to successful health security and implementation of the 2019–2022 plan, as seen in **FIGURE 13-8**.

▶ Hospital Preparedness Program

Under an ASPR Healthcare Readiness cooperative agreement, a program called the Hospital Preparedness Program (HPP) was created.[28] The program was designed to create a foundation for national healthcare preparedness. It is the primary source of federal funding for health system preparedness and focuses on improvement of patient outcomes during emergencies with rapid recovery. The HPP boasts recipients in all 50 U.S. states and eight territories, with 6.8 billion dollars invested as of April 2021.[29] The HPP is the convener for regional collaborations that encourage sustainable healthcare coalitions (HCCs) for healthcare preparedness and response during emergencies.[30] The HCCs are assisted with meeting the core tenets of ASPR's *2017–2022 Health Care Preparedness and Response Capabilities*. This document outlines the high-level objectives that healthcare entities are pushed to meet in order to prepare for, respond to, and recover from emergencies.[31] ASPR lays out expectations and priorities in meeting the goals of the four core Health Care Preparedness and Response Capabilities, as shown in **BOX 13-2**.[31] Rural communities face unique circumstances related to preparedness. **BOX 13-3** lays out perspectives for rural preparedness.

In summary, our healthcare delivery system has opportunities to build upon the work of the national FEMA apparatus for preparedness. Both nationally and internationally, there are a plethora of resources to aid healthcare leaders with planning for disasters, from natural to pandemic.

BOX 13-2 Four Health Care Preparedness Response Capabilities

Capability 1: Foundation for Healthcare and Medical Readiness

Goal   Healthcare organizations and stakeholders create and maintain strong relationships; with hazard identification and risk management. They should address gaps through planning, training, simulation, and resource management.

Capability 2: Health Care and Medical Response Coordination

Goal   Healthcare organizations the HCC, their jurisdiction and the ESF-8 lead agency – plan, share, and analyze information with coordination of medical care to all populations during emergencies.

Capability 3: Continuity of Health Care Service Delivery

Goal   Healthcare organizations, with support from the HCCs and their ESF-8 lead agency, provide uninterrupted and optimal care when health infrastructure is damaged or disabled.

Capability 4: Medical Surge

Goal   Health care organizations (including hospitals, emergency medical services, and other providers) have the ability to provide timely and efficient care – even when demand outpaces supply.

Created by Richard Greenhill. Data from U.S. Department of Health and Human Services Office of the Assistant Secretary for Preparedness and Response. *2017–2022 Health Care Preparedness and Response Capabilities.* U.S. Department of Health and Human Services; 2016. Accessed June 2, 2021. https://www.phe.gov/Preparedness/planning/hpp/reports/Documents/2017-2022-healthcare-pr-capablities.pdf

BOX 13-3 Tips from the Field: Health Professional Expert Advice

What happens when the nearest doctor who takes your insurance is an hour away? Or when you don't have regular access to a car or bus? It is frustrating and can be hazardous to your health when the right care is out there, but you can't get to it. Patients often experience this scenario, which is why patients frequently do not keep appointments or delay receiving care.

In some situations, patients who live in rural communities without transportation access may wait for a medical emergency just to be able to access care by ambulance. Even with public transportation, some patients may find it difficult to utilize, so they have been waiting until they are short of breath, passing out, or in a very frail condition and then calling an ambulance because there are simply no other options.

(continues)

BOX 13-3 Tips from the Field: Health Professional Expert Advice *(continued)*

For healthcare providers, missed appointments mean that we can't address our patients' questions and concerns, or update any changes to the patient's health history or life circumstances, a situation that can be particularly worrisome for patients with diabetes, cancer, and other chronic diseases that require ongoing active care.

Some providers, clinics, and hospitals in both rural and urban areas are using community health workers (CHWs), people who help patients navigate the healthcare system, to assist in coordinating transportation for at-risk patients. CHWs, who generally are not licensed healthcare professionals, will coordinate transportation for patients to and from appointments, motivate them to take their medications, and help them implement positive lifestyle habits. Some hospitals and physicians also use care coordinators: people who, unlike CHWs, are trained in a health-related field, most often social workers or nurses. These coordinators support groups of low-income or chronically ill patients, helping them to understand their care plans and schedule primary-care visits instead of making trips to the Emergency Room.

Although a significant number of patients, especially those with few resources, struggle to find consistent and reliable transportation, there are some options for those in certain areas. Each state has a benefit for people with Medicaid for non-emergency-related visits, covering a certain number of rides per month, and some Medicare Advantage plans also cover a limited number of trips each year. Some states contract with local companies and transportation network companies to provide rides; others enlist volunteers or hire taxis. Some private insurers take similar steps to make transportation more accessible for their clients, although this may involve copays or preapprovals to prove their need for the benefit. In many cases, nonemergency rides must also be requested several days in advance.

For healthcare providers, access to care is a major concern when it comes to delivering timely and needed care to patients living in rural communities. This access to care determines health outcomes for patients and quality of care. **FIGURE 13-9** shows the flow model for the relationship between transportation and health outcomes for Americans living in rural communities.

Recent events, including Hurricane Katrina, California wildfires, and the September 11, 2001, attacks have proven that disasters can occur anywhere at any time. Disaster managers face different challenges and opportunities when handling **emergency preparedness** in rural regions versus urban and suburban regions.

Various research has been conducted showing the susceptibility of urban communities but far less data exist on how rural populations respond to disasters and emergencies.[1] In general, rural communities have a smaller pool of financial resources to support disaster response and clean-up/rebuilding efforts. Besides having limited fiscal resources and manpower, rural communities also face scarce communication systems, which pose challenges when disseminating important messages regarding evacuation and execution of plans.[2]

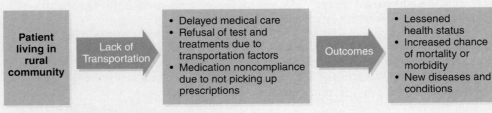

FIGURE 13-9 **Emergency Preparedness**

The four phases of a disaster are: prevention or mitigation, preparedness, response, and recovery.[3] A prevention or mitigation plan decreases the severity of the disaster, whether natural or manmade. By focusing on preparedness efforts, communities and responders can build capacity and identify resources to be utilized during a response. Preparedness plans should include actions that will protect citizens, responders, and facilities during the event and recovery. A prepared community routinely exercises, debriefs, and alters the plan according to changing needs. Routine and direct communication is important when responding to the disaster and during the recovery phase. Communication should include multiple modalities, the ability to reach the appropriate government officials, responders and providers and the scope to communicate the important information to the public to ensure that they are prepared, know what to expect, and know how to act, especially at-risk populations such as the elderly and disabled.[4]

Almost always, rural communities are geographically distant from major urban areas and resources. Geographic challenges for rural areas may include broad deserts, mountain ranges, rivers, and marshy areas, which make travel and communication difficult.[1] Rural communities often find it difficult to attract qualified personnel and as a result, shortages in healthcare personnel and responders create challenges. Subsequently, professional and volunteer staff in rural communities may also have limited experience with major disasters, emergency preparedness, surveillance, or outbreak monitoring. Time and distance also impact the ability of urban professionals and responders to get to the rural communities in the time of emergency and disaster.

Public health and healthcare infrastructure also present limitations to rural communities. In rural communities, emergency first responders are often volunteer-based; therefore, they have less training on emergency preparedness equipment and protocols such as the ability to decontaminate, isolate, and quarantine in the time of a disaster. Decontamination abilities are severely inadequate in rural hospitals and clinics and there is virtually no local experience with decontaminating procedures, except for rural communities located near nuclear plants.

Communications also present a special challenge to rural communities given the lack of reliable communication systems. While many rural communities were among the first to use telecommunications technologies in health care and communication, some forms of communication are not available or simply do not work. Some rural areas still lack Internet capacity, which could support notification in the event of a health alert or bioterrorism emergency. Other rural areas find that telephone connectivity is interrupted.[4]

In general, fiscal resources for rural hospitals and health departments are far more limited than those in major urban areas. Despite the numerous federal and state-level emergency preparedness compliance standards, rural communities have fewer financial monies. The lack of money makes it difficult for rural communities to comply. Rural communities have smaller public health departments and law enforcement agencies, which also present limited resources. There are likely to be fewer healthcare providers overall and, specifically, few specialists who are most needed, like trauma care, infectious disease specialists, and mental health experts. Rural hospitals are less likely to have both the space and equipment to handle the sheer demands of the community. In these situations, the rural hospital emergency departments often must stabilize and transfer the most critical patients to larger facilities. The challenges faced by rural communities can impact their ability to both prepare and react to emergencies and disasters. In summary, rural communities face significant challenges.

Both operational size and geographic location determine when and how well a medical center can respond to disasters. Rural medical centers, often smaller in size, tend to have fewer resources and personnel compared with centers located in urban populations. Due to these constrictions, rural medical centers should activate the emergency preparedness plans earlier than those communities with larger resources.

(continues)

BOX 13-3 Tips from the Field: Health Professional Expert Advice *(continued)*

In times of disaster and emergency, health professionals should modify preparedness plans to fit scope, resources, and surroundings. Rural health professionals should take regular inventory of supplies and the skill sets of their staff to determine what they are lacking and how they would access these resources in the event of an emergency or disaster. Telehealth capabilities are one available resource that is highly valuable in assisting rural communities in tapping into resources and staff during times of need and crisis. Additionally, health professionals working in rural medical centers should maintain their ability to function as ancillaries as they do during normal times of operation.

In addition to identifying resources, it is essential that health professionals also need to be able to identify a strong incident command system. A good incident command system includes strategies for patient evacuations; where to relocate patients; and what equipment, care, and medications need to go with the patient or to be received by the patient at the new center where they are relocated.

An essential part of disaster preparedness is conducting routine drills in preparation for big disasters. The Joint Commission currently necessitates accredited hospitals to conduct several disasters drills annually. Accredited hospitals are then assessed by how well they performed at the drill and where areas of opportunity exist. By conducting routine drills, the health center, health professionals, and community members are prepared for a variety of disasters and emergencies, and all involved parties are actively and successfully communicating and working together.[3] Due to our role as health professionals in emergency preparedness, it is important to pursue disaster training through Federal Emergency Management Agency (FEMA). It is imperative that rural health professionals understand the role they play in emergency preparedness within their communities (See **FIGURE 13-10**).

When patients living in rural communities are diagnosed with illnesses and medical conditions that require care from specialists, they are faced with the reality that they must spend additional time and resources on traveling to healthcare systems that have the needed resources and staff. This could include treatment, tests, consultations, and routine medical appointments. Rural hospitals now have quite a number of options when it comes to providing telemedicine to their patients and all are helpful in allowing patients to receive the care they need without being displaced from their communities and expending mass amounts of time traveling to access that care.

With telehealth, more can be done than just monitoring conditions and health status. Telehealth is an excellent option to educate and engage with patients. Checking in and educating patients at home on a daily basis, in bite size pieces, is transformative. Telehealth providers have the means to intervene immediately when patients have a serious or potentially serious concern, such as a routine blood pressure check.

Providers can expect to see a rise in the number of rural patients receiving treatment right from the comfort of their home or being a part of a medical home, which houses many patients with similar symptoms and diseases for better treatment as a result of telehealth technologies. Additionally, patients can start to use telehealth apps that can be customized to their individual case but also offer the flexibility to specify what sort of information should be displayed.

Telehealth serves as means to connect rural patients to needed care without travel and costs. Telehealth also serves to connect rural providers to urban and metropolitan providers in order to ensure better education, consultations, and community of care.

- Access to specialists without need for travel
- Reduced costs in travel fees and medical care
- Early detection of diseases and conditions
- Reduction of morbidity and mortality

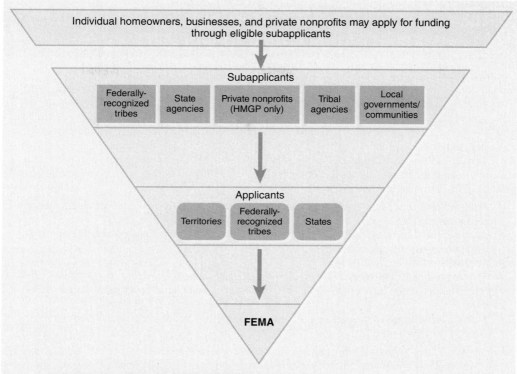

FIGURE 13-10 Flow Chart for Emergency Preparedness

Courtesy of Federal Emergency Management Agency. https://www.fema.gov/sites/default/files/images/pdm_application_flow_chart.jpg

References

1. Brennan, M. A., & Flint, C.G. (2007). Uncovering the hidden dimensions of rural disaster mitigation: Capacity building through community emergency response teams. *Journal of Rural Social Sciences, 22*(2), 111-126.
2. Janssen, D. (2006). Disaster planning in rural America. *Public Manager,* 35(3), 40-43.
3. Federal Emergency Management Agency. (2019). Retrieved from www.fema.org
4. Savoia, E., Lin, L., & Viswanath, K. (2013). Communications in public health emergency preparedness: A systematic review of the literature. *Biosecurity and Bioterrorism: Biodefense Strategy, Practice, and Science, 11*(3), 170-184.

Additional Reading

American Red Cross: http://www.redcross.org.
Centers for Disease Control and Prevention. (2016). Gateway to Health Communication. Retrieved from http:// www.cdc.gov
       /healthcommunication/Campaigns /index.html
CERT programs by state: https://community.fema.gov /PreparednessCommunity/s/cert-find-a-program
The Commonwealth Fund: https://scorecard.common wealthfund.org/
FEMA: http://training.fema.gov
Federal Office on Rural Health Policy: https://www.hrsa .gov/rural-health/index.html
Kaiser Family Foundation. The Affordable Care Act and Insurance Coverage in Rural Areas. https://www.kff.org/uninsured/issue-brief
       /the-affordable-care-act -and-insurance-coverage-in-rural-areas/
Rural Health Information Hub: https://www.ruralhealth info.org/
United States Census Bureau (2018). Quick Facts Maine. Retrieved from: https://www.census.gov/quickfacts /fact/table/ME/PST045218

CASE 13-1 COVID-19: The Importance of Public Health and Global Preparedness

At the close of 2019, the World Health Organization (WHO) China Country Office was notified of pneumonia cases of unknown etiology arising in the city of Wuhan, in China's Hubei province.[32] Those initial cases have since grown into a global pandemic as nations all over the world struggle to contain the spread of COVID-19, a novel coronavirus.[33] To halt its spread, the WHO and countries have stepped up their efforts to limit human-to-human transmission. Their responses highlight the importance of public health and preparedness in mounting an effective defense and containment strategy.

The WHO plays a critical role in global health. As the United Nations' public health arm, it leads the global health response and guides the international community in assessing and containing disease outbreaks. Since it was first notified of cases at the end of 2019, the WHO has:

- Released a national capacity review tool for countries to assess and prepare their ability to mount a response to COVID-19,
- Launched free online educational resources for learning more about COVID-19 and other emerging respiratory viruses,
- Spearheaded research efforts regarding COVID-19,
- Shipped testing kits and personal protection supplies all around the world,
- Issued guidelines on businesses, workplaces, schools, mass gatherings, social distancing, and more, and,
- Maintained an active social media presence to support the wide dissemination of information in a fast and timely manner.[32]

The WHO's ability to direct efforts against COVID-19 comes as a result of its thorough preparation. It has long developed frameworks for the anticipation and implementation of disease outbreak response interventions. These frameworks emphasize the importance of ensuring that health systems and healthcare providers are properly trained and supplied to handle disease outbreaks safely and swiftly. Its commitment to a One Health collaborative approach also allows for early detection by recognizing the close relationship between humans, animals, and their shared environment.[34]

Experts including the WHO have repeatedly emphasized the importance of such preparations and the use of public health measures to combat the spread of disease. Early intervention, including widespread testing, case tracking, and isolation, are critical to keeping cases low.[35,36] If cases continue to grow in number, supplemental measures must be enforced to restrict movement, limit social interaction, and prohibit mass gatherings.[37] Public communication and transparency to ensure that individuals are aware of hallmark symptoms, self-protective behaviors, and new developments that arise are also critical.[36] Such sweeping measures require thorough preparation on behalf of the government or leadership team if they are to act promptly. Health protection infrastructure, skills, and workforce are not easily built up; they must be in place before an outbreak occurs.[38]

The efforts of various countries around the world exemplify the importance of public health and preparedness in combating COVID-19. Among the most significant of these comes from China, the origin of the outbreak. Since its first cases were reported at the end of 2019, China has suppressed its domestic outbreak in just a few months. Much of its success is attributable to speedy, comprehensive action that was taken to find cases, isolate them, and track close contacts.[39] Because of its delayed response in the early stages of the outbreak, China also rolled out broad prevention and control measures that included placing Wuhan on forced lockdown at the height of *chunyun*, the massive increase in travel and movement that occurs around Chinese New Year. The country's public health response has been aligned at all levels of government and is tailored to each region based on local context and epidemic severity.[40] The efficacy of this all-of-government and all-of-society approach has demonstrated the significance of public health and preparedness in mounting a swift and adaptable response.

South Korea's COVID-19 response further highlights the value of taking such measures. Its approach has relied heavily on aggressive testing and contact-tracing; to date, over 360,000 tests have been completed and the country death toll hovers around 140.[41] South Korea's ability to flatten the curve is due to its early employment of a large-scale testing regime and an extensive, detailed tracking system that monitors those who test positive. Although such far-reaching measures have raised privacy concerns, experts and the WHO credit such actions as having reduced the spread of disease.[42] Since daily new cases peaked at 909 at the end of February, South Korea reported just 64 new cases on March 23.[43] Its example illustrates the importance of public health and preparedness in containing the spread of disease.

Other places that have been able to keep COVID-19 cases relatively low include Singapore, Hong Kong, and Taiwan. Although close in proximity to Mainland China, these places, like South Korea, have employed early intervention tactics, strict isolation measures, and painstaking contact-tracing to locate cases before they continue to spread. They also rely on quick, coordinated leadership, strong surveillance monitoring, and rapid public communication and transparency.[44,45]

The downsides of being ill prepared to enact a strong public health response against COVID-19 are apparent in the United States. The United States' lack of preparation traces back to the disbandment of its pandemic response team in 2018.[46] By dissolving the team and calling for budget cuts to public health agencies, the government promoted a shift in priority to other issues, leaving public health and disease outbreak preparation by the wayside. Now, without a centralized team to coordinate across the vast federal system, the U.S. response has been behind the curve. Vice President Mike Pence was put in charge of the U.S. coronavirus response over a month after the first cases appeared.[47] Faulty testing kits initially rolled out by the CDC also led to delays and shortages that prevented local labs and clinics from testing people who needed to be tested.[48] Legislation mandating free COVID-19 testing came almost two months after the virus first appeared on U.S. soil.[49] Contact-tracing has also been spotty at best, partially due to the lack of manpower in overwhelmed health departments.[50]

The high volume of cases the United States is now facing, coupled with shortages of medical equipment and supplies, demonstrate the chilling consequences of neglecting public health and preparedness in fighting against pandemics such as COVID-19. The United States' lack of preparation and lackadaisical attitude towards the outbreak led to an inability to take action early on. It is now the country with the most COVID-19 cases in the world, despite having weeks and even months to prepare. The public health approaches taken by China, South Korea, and other countries that have been able to flatten the curve must be looked to as lessons for how the United States should prepare in the future.

In the twenty-first century, diseases spread faster than ever—human-to-human contact, international travel, and close proximity with other organisms in a shared ecosystem allow pathogens to spread far and wide at unprecedented rates. The actions taken by the WHO and various countries around the world demonstrate the importance of public health and preparedness in tackling and controlling disease out-breaks. Future efforts must focus on putting the hard-learned lessons from COVID-19 to use in preventing, anticipating, and managing future outbreaks.

▶ Discussion Questions

- Describe how FEMA interacts with your state and local emergency agencies.
- What are the advantages and disadvantages of NIMS and ICS?
- Which FEMA courses do you think are most relevant for healthcare professionals?
- What functions would you add to the ICS?
- Name two things you think healthcare systems can do to better prepare for disease outbreaks.

CHAPTER ACRONYMS

ASPR Assistant Secretary for Preparedness and Response

BARDA Biomedical Advanced Research and Development Authority

BSE Bovine spongiform encephalopathy

CBRN chemical, biological, radiological, and nuclear

CDC Centers for Disease Control and Prevention

DHS Department of Homeland Security

EMI Emergency Management Institute

EOC Emergency Operations Center

FEMA Federal Emergency Management Agency

HCC Healthcare Coalition

HHS Department of Health and Human Services

HPP Hospital Preparedness Program

ICS Incident Command System

NHSS National Health Security Strategy

NIMS National Incident Management System

PHEIC Public health emergency of international concern

SHOC Strategic Health Operations Centre

TRACIE Technical Resources, Assistance Center, and Information Exchange

WHA World Health Assembly

WHO World Health Organization

CHWs Community health workers

FEMA Federal Emergency Management Agency

References

1. Johnson JA, Stoskopf C, Shi L. *Comparative Health Systems: A Global Perspective.* 2nd ed. Jones & Bartlett Learning; 2018.

2. Centers for Disease Control and Prevention. Influenza (flu): past pandemics. Updated August 10, 2018. Accessed February 19, 2021. https://www.cdc.gov/flu/pandemic-resources/basics/past-pandemics.html

3. Federal Emergency Management Agency. Historic disasters. Updated July 6, 2021. Accessed August 27, 2021. https://www.fema.gov/disasters/historic

4. Shi L, Johnson JA. *Public Health Administration: Principles for Population-Based Management.* 4th ed. Jones & Bartlett Learning; 2020.

5. Englund W. The Texas grid got crushed because its operators didn't see the need to prepare for cold weather. *Washington Post.* Published February 26, 2021. Accessed August 27, 2021. https://www.washingtonpost.com/business/2021/02/16/ercot-texas-electric-grid-failure/

6. Montgomery D, Romero S. 'Such dire straits': chaos unfolds in Texas hospitals. *New York Times.* Published February 18, 2021. Accessed February 19, 2021. https://www.nytimes.com/2021/02/18/us/texas-hospitals-power-water.html

7. Federal Emergency Management Agency. NIMS: frequently asked questions. Accessed February 20, 2021. https://www.fema.gov/pdf/emergency/nims/nimsfaqs.pdf

8. Federal Emergency Management Agency. About us. Accessed February 20, 2021. https://www.fema.gov/about

9. Federal Emergency Management Agency. Mission & strategic plan. Updated January 4, 2021. Accessed February 20, 2021. https://www.fema.gov/about/mission

10. Federal Emergency Management Agency. History of FEMA. Updated January 4, 2021. Accessed February 20, 2021. https://www.fema.gov/about/history

11. Federal Emergency Management Agency Emergency Management Institute. *Independent Study Program Course Brochure*. Accessed February 20, 2021. https://training.fema.gov/is/crslist.aspx

12. Ready.gov. Incident management. Updated May 26, 2021. Accessed August 27, 2021. https://www.ready.gov/business/implementation/incident

13. Manuel J. In Katrina's wake [published correction appears in *Environ Health Perspect*. 2006;114(2):A90]. *Environ Health Perspect*. 2006;114(1):A32-A39. doi:10.1289/ehp.114-a32

14. Greenhill R, Johnson J, Malone P, Westrum A. *State Capacity Influences on Pandemic Preparedness for the Sub-Saharan African Region*. Dissertation. Central Michigan University; 2019.

15. Hernández JC. Trump slammed the W.H.O. over Coronavirus. He's not alone. *New York Times*. Published April 8, 2020. Updated May 29, 2020. Accessed August 27, 2021. https://www.nytimes.com/2020/04/08/world/asia/trump-who-coronavirus-china.html

16. Greenhill R, Johnson J, Malone P, Westrum A. Customizing health security preparedness activities in Sub-Saharan Africa: leveraging political context to enhance IHR implementation. *Int J Public Adm* 2021:1-12. doi:10.1080/01900692.2020.1867575

17. World Health Organization. Strategic Health Operations Centre (SHOC). Published 2021. Accessed February 20, 2021. https://www.who.int/emergencies/operations

18. Centers for Disease Control and Prevention. Center for Preparedness and Response. Updated August 26, 2021. Accessed August 27, 2021. https://www.cdc.gov/cpr/index.htm

19. Centers for Disease Control and Prevention. CDC's EOC. Updated June 30, 2021. Accessed August 27, 2021. https://www.cdc.gov/cpr/eoc/eoc.htm?CDC_AA_refVal=https%3A%2F%2Fwww.cdc.gov%2Fcpr%2Feoc.htm

20. Centers for Disease Control and Prevention. CDC Public Health Response Timeline. Updated June 30, 2021. Accessed August 27, 2021. https://www.cdc.gov/cpr/eoc/responses.htm

21. Shereen MA, Khan S, Kazmi A, Bashir N, Siddique R. COVID-19 infection: origin, transmission, and characteristics of human coronaviruses. *J Adv Res*. 2020;24:91-98. doi:10.1016/j.jare.2020.03.005

22. U.S. Department of Health and Human Services Office of the Assistant Secretary for Preparedness and Response. Saving lives and protecting Americans from 21st century health security threats. Updated June 28, 2021. Accessed August 27, 2021. https://www.phe.gov/about/aspr/Pages/default.aspx

23. U.S. Department of Health and Human Services Office of the Assistant Secretary for Preparedness and Response. ASPR highlights. Updated March 2, 2021. Accessed August 27, 2021. https://www.phe.gov/about/Pages/highlights.aspx

24. U.S. Department of Health and Human Services Office of the Assistant Secretary for Preparedness and Response. National Health Security Strategy (NHSS). Updated April 30, 2021. Accessed June 1, 2021. https://www.phe.gov/Preparedness/planning/authority/nhss/Pages/overview.aspx

25. U.S. Department of Health and Human Services Office of the Assistant Secretary for Preparedness and Response. *National Health Security Strategy 2019-2022*. U.S. Department of Health and Human Services; 2019. Accessed June 8, 2021. https://www.phe.gov/Preparedness/planning/authority/nhss/Documents/NHSS-Strategy-508.pdf

26. Crimmins A, Balbus J, Gamble J, et al. *The Impacts of Climate Change on Human Health in the United States: A Scientific Assessment*. U.S. Global Change Research Program; 2016. Accessed June 4, 2021. https://s3.amazonaws.com/climatehealth2016/high/ClimateHealth2016_FullReport.pdf

27. U.S. Department of Health and Human Services Office of the Assistant Secretary for Preparedness and Response; Office of Strategy, Policy, Planning, and Requirements. *National Health Security Strategy Implementation Plan 2019-2022*. U.S. Department of Health and Human Services; 2019. Accessed June 9, 2021. https://www.phe.gov/Preparedness/planning/authority/nhss/Documents/2019-2022-nhss-ip-v508.pdf

28. U.S. Department of Health and Human Services Office of the Assistant Secretary for Preparedness and Response. Hospital Preparedness Program (HPP). Updated August 16, 2021. Accessed August 27, 2021. https://www.phe.gov/Preparedness/planning/hpp/Pages/default.aspx

29. U.S. Department of Health and Human Services Office of the Assistant Secretary for Preparedness and Response. Fact sheet: Hospital Preparedness Program (HPP) overview. Accessed June 7, 2021. https://www.phe.gov/Preparedness/planning/hpp/Documents/HPP-FactSheet-April2021-508.pdf

30. U.S. Department of Health and Human Services Office of the Assistant Secretary for Preparedness and Response. About the Hospital Preparedness Program. Updated May 3, 2021. Accessed June 7, 2021. https://www.phe.gov/Preparedness/planning/hpp/Pages/about-hpp.aspx

31. U.S. Department of Health and Human Services Office of the Assistant Secretary for Preparedness and Response. *2017-2022 Health Care Preparedness and Response Capabilities*. U.S. Department of Health and Human Services; 2016. Accessed June 2, 2021. https://www.phe.gov/Preparedness/planning/hpp/reports/Documents/2017-2022-healthcare-pr-capablities.pdf

32. World Health Organization (WHO). (2020, March 25). Rolling updates on coronavirus disease (COVID-19).

https://www.who.int/emergencies/diseases/novel
-coronavirus-2019/events-as-they-happen

33. Zhu N, Zhang D, Wang W, et al.. A novel coronavirus from patients with pneumonia in China, 2019. *N Engl J Med.* 2020;382:727-733. doi: 10.1056/NEJMoa 2001017

34. World Health Organization (WHO). 2018. Managing epidemics: key facts about major deadly diseases. https://www.who.int/emergencies/diseases/managing -epidemics-interactive.pdf

35. Fisher D, Wilder-Smith A. The global community needs to swiftly ramp up the response to contain COVID-19. *Lancet.* 2020;395(10230):1109-1110. doi: https://doi.org/10.1016/S0140-6736(20)30679-6

36. World Health Organization (WHO). 2020. Virtual press conference on COVID-19—11 March 2020. https://www.who.int/docs/default-source/corona viruse/transcripts/who-audio-emergencies-corona virus-press-conference-full-and-final-11mar2020 .pdf?sfvrsn=cb432bb3_2

37. Heymann DL, Shindo N. COVID-19: what is next for public health? *Lancet.* 2020;395(10224):542-545. doi: https://doi.org/10.1016/S0140-6736(20)30374-3

38. Lee A. Wuhan novel coronavirus (COVID-19): Why global control is challenging? *Public Health.* 2020; 179:A1-A2. https://doi.org/10.1016/j.puhe.2020.02.001

39. Belluz J. 2020. China's cases of COVID-19 are finally declining. A WHO expert explains why. *Vox.* https:// www.vox.com/2020/3/2/21161067/coronavirus -covid19-china

40. WHO–China Joint Mission. 2020. Report of the WHO–China joint mission on coronavirus disease 2019 (COVID-19). World Health Organization. https://www.who.int/docs/default-source /coronaviruse/who-china-joint-mission-on-covid -19-final-report.pdf

41. Korea Centers for Disease Control and Prevention (KCDC). 2020. The updates on COVID-19 in Korea as of 27 March. https://www.cdc.go.kr/board/board .es?mid=a30402000000&bid=0030

42. Zastrow M. South Korea is reporting intimate details of COVID-19 cases: Has it helped? *Nature.*

2020. https://www.nature.com/articles/d41586-020 -00740-y doi: 10.1038/d41586-020-00740-y PMID: 32203363

43. Fisher M, Choe SH. March 23, 2020. How South Korea flattened the curve. *The New York Times.* https://www .nytimes.com/2020/03/23/world/asia/coronavirus -south-korea-flatten-curve.html

44. Beech H. March 17, 2020. Tracking the coronavirus: How crowded Asian cities tackled an epidemic. *The New York Times.* https://www.nytimes.com/2020/03 /17/world/asia/coronavirus-singapore-hong-kong -taiwan.html

45. Lai KK, Collins K. March 19, 2020. Which country has flattened the curve for the coronavirus? *The New York Times.* https://www.nytimes.com/interactive /2020/04/03/world/coronavirus-flatten-the-curve -countries.html

46. Lopez G. March 25, 2020. The Trump administration's botched coronavirus response, explained. *Vox.* https://www.vox.com/policy-and-politics /2020/3/14/21177509/coronavirus-trump-covid-19 -pandemic-response

47. Shear MD, Weiland N, Rogers K. February 26, 2020. Trump names Mike Pence to lead coronavirus response. *The New York Times.* https://www.nytimes .com/2020/02/26/us/politics/trump-coronavirus-cdc .html

48. Rabin RC, Sheikh K, Thomas K. March 2, 2020. As coronavirus numbers rise, CDC testing comes under fire. *The New York Times.* https://www.nytimes .com/2020/03/02/health/coronavirus-testing -cdc.html

49. Keith K. Senate passes COVID-19 package #3: The coverage provisions. *Health Affairs.* 2020. https://www .healthaffairs.org/do/10.1377/hblog20200326 .765600/full/

50. Maxmen A. Scientists exposed to coronavirus wonder: Why weren't we notified? *Nature.* 2020; 579(7800). https://www.nature.com/articles/d41586 -020-00823-w

CHAPTER 14

Rural Health Care

CHAPTER OVERVIEW

This chapter provides an overview of rural healthcare, population health, and health delivery in the United States. It examines historical trends and the forces affecting the proper delivery of health care given the geographic distribution challenges of people and services. Healthcare delivery in the United States encompasses the full continuum of care, from outpatient to inpatient, and from postacute care to long-term care. Rural health sometimes overlaps with care in urban centers and at other times is an isolated process; it depends on the geographic circumstances.

© STILLFX/iStock/Getty Images Plus/Getty Images

▶ The Basics of Rural Health

The discussion on rural health has to begin with a basic definition of the term "rural." This term can have different meanings depending on the individual or entity using it. This can make finding viable solutions to the many challenges faced in these communities somewhat difficult. There are three major government entities that have put forth definitions that are most often referenced[1]:

- The U.S. Census Bureau
- The Office of Management and Budget (OMB)
- U.S. Department of Agriculture Economic Research Service (USDA ERS)

The U.S. Census Bureau created a definition by deduction. "Rural" is noted by subtracting from the areas considered urban. Thus, the definition follows a classification of urban versus rural based on a delineation of geographic areas.[2,3] At the time this chapter was written, the 2020 Census Urban and Rural Classification was still under review in the Federal Register. Thus, the authors resorted to use of the last census from 2010. The U.S. Census Bureau determined that urban areas are those that include densely developed areas, including residential and commercial land as well as other nonresidential areas. Urban areas are redefined each in decennial census after application of criteria captured in the process. It defines "rural" as the areas that are left after applying the definition "urban," or those not in an urban area. Urban areas are then further broken down into[4]:

- Urbanized Areas (UAs): composed of 50,000 or more individuals
- Urban Clusters (UC): composed of more than 2,500 and less than 50,000 individuals

TABLE 14-1 further breaks down UAs and UCs from the 2000 and 2010 Censuses and shows the 10-year changes.[4]

TABLE 14-1 Urban, Urbanized, Urban Cluster, and Rural Population, 2010 and 2000: United States

Area	Number of Urban Areas (2010)	Population (2010)	Population (2000)	% of Total Population (2010)	% of Total Population (2000)
Entire U.S.	3,573	308,745,538	281,421,906	-	-
Urban	-	249,253,271	222,360,539	80.7%	79.0%
UA	486	219,922,123	192,323,824	71.2%	68.3%
UC	3,087	29,331,148	30,036,715	9.5%	10.7%
Rural	-	59,492,267	59,061,367	19.3%	21.0%

Created by Richard Greenhill. Data from U.S. Census Bureau. 2010 Census urban and rural classification and urban area criteria. Updated December 2, 2019. Accessed June 9, 2021. https://www.census.gov/programs-surveys/geography/guidance/geo-areas/urban-rural/2010-urban-rural.html

The OMB uses the term rural in the context of "metropolitan statistical areas," or metro areas and nonmetropolitan areas (or nonmetro). Metro areas are central counties with one or more urban areas. Outlying counties are tied to the core counties by commuting patterns where 25% of the workforce commutes to central counties. Nonmetro counties are those outside of the boundaries of a metro area and are further divided into[1]:

- Micropolitan statistical areas: a nonmetro county with an urban cluster of a minimum of 10,000 people
- Noncore counties

The Centers for Disease Control and Prevention uses a further delineated version of this scheme to research comparisons of health and urbanization. The USDA and the Federal Office of Rural Health Policy worked to create the Rural–Urban Commuting Area (RUCA) system.[1] The RUCA system includes RUCA codes, which are a means to characterize rural and urban status relationships in the U.S. Census. **TABLE 14-2** showcases various agency definitions for UAs, UCs, and rural areas.[4]

Variations in the definition of "rural" in the United States resulted from different federal organizations and agencies creating their own definitions to meet their specific organizational needs and purposes. Thus, there are different ways to classify rural versus urban. When considering how this impacts healthcare delivery, the ramifications are tremendous. The ambiguity of these definitions and changes makes crafting coherent health policy complicated.

TABLE 14-2 Comparison of Rural Definitions

Agency and Definition	Geographic Unit Used	Rural Inclusion Criteria	U.S. Rural Population
U.S. Census Bureau: Urbanized Areas (UAs) are geographic areas of 50,000 or more people. Urban Clusters (UCs) are geographic areas of 2,500 to 50,000 people.	Block groups or census blocks	Rural areas encompass all population, housing, and territory not included within an urban area (excluding Puerto Rico)	59,492,267 % of Total Population: 19.3
Office of Management and Budget: Metropolitan areas contain a core urban area population of 50,000 or more. Nonmetropolitan areas contain a population of less than 50,000. This includes both micropolitan areas, with UC populations of 10,000 to 50,000, and all counties that lack an urban core, which are referred to as noncore counties.	County	All nonmetropolitan areas (counties), including micropolitan and noncore counties	46,293,406 % of Total Population: 14.99

(continues)

TABLE 14-2 Comparison of Rural Definitions			*(continued)*
Agency and Definition	**Geographic Unit Used**	**Rural Inclusion Criteria**	**U.S. Rural Population**
USDA: Utilizes the U.S. Census Bureau's UA and UC definitions with information on work commuting. Classification delineates metropolitan, micropolitan, small town, and rural commuting areas with whole numbers 1–10 and further subdivides into 21 secondary codes based on commuting flows—local or to another census tract.	Zip code estimation, census tract	Primary RUCA codes 4 and above (micropolitan area core, population up to 49,999)	51,112,552 % of Total Population: 16.55

Created by Richard Greenhill. Data from U.S. Census Bureau. 2010 Census urban and rural classification and urban area criteria. Updated December 2, 2019. Accessed June 9, 2021. https://www.census.gov/programs-surveys/geography/guidance/geo-areas/urban-rural/2010-urban-rural.html

▶ Rural Health Care

Health care as an industry has struggled with achieving the Institute for Healthcare Improvement's Triple Aim for health care: cost, experience, and quality. A simple look at the complexity in definitions of the term "rural" alone seem to indicate the complexity of delivering care outside of urban areas, which tend to have more resources (e.g., tax revenue, population density, etc.). Rural citizens in the United States face a host of issues that complicate adequate and accessible healthcare delivery. Those issues or disparities include[5]:

- Disproportionate burden of chronic disease relative to the general public
- Restricted access to quality health care
- Poor or lack of health insurance coverage
- Geographic isolation
- Absence of or inadequate public transportation
- Poor infrastructure
- Poor educational attainment
- Poor health literacy
- Higher poverty and unemployment
- Reduced healthcare workforce and lack of access to specialty care
- Limited availability of bilingual providers and interpreter services
- Cultural or social differences and stigma

One could surmise that everything conveyed in this book up to this point is complicated due to the items listed above. These issues make delivery of care that much more complex. In terms of healthcare challenges, the American Hospital Association (AHA) laid out several areas in their annual report on rural issues and classified them as emergent (E), recent (R), and persistent (P)[6]:

- The pervasive opioid epidemic (E)
- Community violence (E)
- Shifting trends in care delivery (R)
- Behavioral health issues (R)
- Demographic as well as economic shifts (R)
- High prescription drug costs (R)
- Low patient volume (P)
- Payer and patient mix (P)
- Medical surge capacity (E)
- Cyber threats and lack of staff to support prevention (E)
- Regulation burden (R)
- Insurance coverage (R)
- Medicaid expansion (R)
- Health plan design (R)
- Workforce shortages (P)
- Limited access (P)

The AHA has taken the mantle as an advocacy entity working to advance meaningful change in these categories related to rural health. Chapter 6 laid out the structures and numbers of hospitals in use. The COVID-19 pandemic placed tremendous financial burden on hospitals, and rural hospitals hit a record during the same period with 20 closing.[7] Twenty might not seem like a lot, but there have been 113 closures since 2010, marking a sharp increase in 2020.[8] **FIGURE 14-1** shows rural hospital closures between 2013 and February 2020.

A breakdown of closures by region can be seen in **FIGURE 14-2**, **FIGURE 14-3**, **FIGURE 14-4**, and **FIGURE 14-5**.

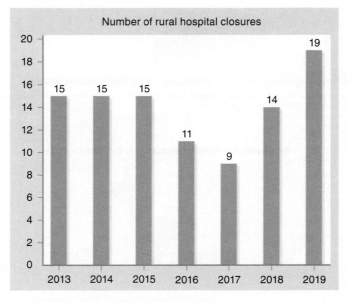

FIGURE 14-1 Rural Hospital Closures, 2013–February 2019

Created by Richard Greenhill. Data from U.S. Government Accountability Office. *Rural Hospital Closures: Affected Residents Had Reduced Access to Health Care Services.*
U.S. Government Accountability Office; 2020. Accessed August 31, 2021. https://www.gao.gov/assets/gao-21-93.pdf

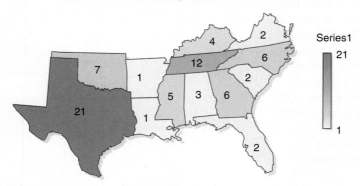

FIGURE 14-2 Rural Hospital Closures, 2013–February 2020: Southern States

Created by Richard Greenhill. Data from U.S. Government Accountability Office. *Rural Hospital Closures: Affected Residents Had Reduced Access to Health Care Services*. U.S. Government Accountability Office; 2020. Accessed August 31, 2021. https://www.gao.gov/assets/gao-21-93.pdf

FIGURE 14-3 Rural Hospital Closures, 2013–February 2020: Midwestern States

Created by Richard Greenhill. Data from U.S. Government Accountability Office. *Rural Hospital Closures: Affected Residents Had Reduced Access to Health Care Services*. U.S. Government Accountability Office; 2020. Accessed August 31, 2021. https://www.gao.gov/assets/gao-21-93.pdf

FIGURE 14-4 Rural Hospital Closures, 2013–February 2020: Northeastern States

Created by Richard Greenhill. Data from U.S. Government Accountability Office. *Rural Hospital Closures: Affected Residents Had Reduced Access to Health Care Services*. U.S. Government Accountability Office; 2020. Accessed August 31, 2021. https://www.gao.gov/assets/gao-21-93.pdf

Southwest rural hospital closures 2013 – 2020

FIGURE 14-5 Rural Hospital Closures, 2013–February 2020: Southwest States

Created by Richard Greenhill. Data from U.S. Government Accountability Office. *Rural Hospital Closures: Affected Residents Had Reduced Access to Health Care Services.* U.S. Government Accountability Office; 2020. Accessed August 31, 2021. https://www.gao.gov/assets/gao-21-93.pdf

The South region (Figure 14-2) of the United States saw 72 closures, broken down as follows: Alabama – 3; Arkansas – 1; Florida – 2; Georgia – 6; Kentucky – 4; Louisiana – 1; Mississippi – 5; North Carolina – 6; Oklahoma – 7; South Carolina – 2; Tennessee – 12; Texas – 21; and Virginia – 2. Texas had 21 closures, the most of any southern state.

The Midwest region (Figure 14-3) of the United States saw 15 closures, broken down as follows: Illinois – 1; Indiana – 1; Kansas – 4; Minnesota – 1; Missouri – 6; Nebraska – 1; and Ohio – 1. Missouri had 6 closures, the most of any Midwest state.

The Northeast region (Figure 14-4) of the United States saw 8 closures, broken down as follows: Maine – 3; Massachusetts – 1; New York – 2; and Pennsylvania – 2.

The Southwest region (Figure 14-5) of the United States saw 6 closures, broken down as follows: Alaska – 1; Arizona – 1; California – 3; and Nevada – 1.

These closures have all compounded the issues mentioned earlier related to social and health-care delivery. The COVID-19 pandemic brought to bear many issues already known in society; rural healthcare delivery issues and disparities were included in that grouping. The light at the end of a dark tunnel for rural health has been the use of innovation and technologies such as telehealth and telemedicine.

▶ Telehealth

Telehealth has and continues to have a hopeful impact in health care, particularly for patients in rural areas who are unable to easily access it. Prior to the COVID-19 pandemic, rural communities experienced great difficulty with recruitment and retention of providers. This placed many providers at further risk of closing, leaving residents without opportunities for adequate care. Telehealth service use exploded during the pandemic and showed just how much technological innovation can reduce this risk. This service enabled residents to receive quality care from providers around the nation. Telehealth also benefits providers, primarily those paid under fee-for-service agreements. Telehealth expands the number of visits and has the potential to reduce no-shows with its added convenience—providing care in the patient's home. While telehealth is a great solution for improving health care in rural communities, the full reach of its implementation and potential issues with quality of service have not been fully realized. Telehealth can also have drawbacks and create a negative experience for patients. Many patients may feel the need to be touched by their provider to determine the status of their condition. While telehealth is convenient, it is impersonal. In addition, many residents who live in rural areas may not have reliable access to internet and cell phone service due to socioeconomic or geographic factors.

▶ Conclusion

Rural healthcare delivery is an important part of the national healthcare delivery system. It is complicated in that many rural patients experience additional barriers to receiving the care they need. One cannot think of rural health without considering the impacts of the social determinants of health and population health. Systems thinking concepts, discussed in earlier chapters, are vital to find sustainable solutions for this important and vulnerable sector of the U.S. healthcare delivery system. As articulated by the National Rural Health Association (NRHA):

> The obstacles faced by health care providers and patients in rural areas are vastly different than those in urban areas. Economic factors, cultural and social differences, educational shortcomings, lack of recognition by legislators and the sheer isolation of living in remote areas all conspire to create health care disparities and impede rural Americans in their struggle to lead normal, healthy lives.[9,10]

Despite the challenges and, in some situations, actual barriers, there is a renewed vigor across states and communities to address these disparities along with federal initiatives and partnerships to improve physical and technological infrastructure for health.

CASE 14-1 Perspectives from the Field
Contributed by Carrie Shaver, University of Indiana

The Hoosier state is popularly imagined as flat and homogenous, populated by more corn and soybean fields than folks, yet the rolling fields, sharp hills, and valleys of southern Indiana were once more densely wooded than any other area east of the Rocky Mountains. Yes, there are corn and soybeans, but the region is also home to leading advanced manufacturing and logistics companies, the flagship campus of the Indiana University system and regional campuses, and one of the world's best cities for modern architecture.

In order to improve health equity within this mixed rural region, significant health disparities necessitate a robust public health response, including commitment to a separate field of practice, study of, and investment in its communities. The confluence of geographic, demographic, cultural, and economic factors greatly influence wellness and life expectancy. While there is substantial variation among counties, rural residents of southern Indiana are more likely than their urban peers to live in poverty, lack a higher education, practice self-destructive health behaviors, have poor healthcare access, and experience adverse health outcomes. Given the evidence of disparities, it is clear that a social justice agenda must include rural southern Indiana.

Dispersed, Dwindling, Aging, and Diversifying Population

Geographic challenges of the region include poor access to transportation and high-speed Internet. There are many miles between home, the grocery store, school, town governmental offices, primary and acute care centers, nonprofit social support agencies, and work. The rural setting can and often does restrict economic and social opportunities. For elderly and poor rural Hoosiers, the challenges posed by distance may not be surmountable without significant public support.

Following the Baby Boom generation, comparatively low birth rates and rising life expectancy have created a dwindling and aging population. In Indiana's rural counties, accelerating outmigration of the working-age population for education and employment opportunities in Indianapolis has generated a labor supply shortage. For example, an internationally renowned mountain biking destination with flowing trails, hilly and densely wooded scenic vistas, and challenging terrain, Brown County, has a replacement rate percentage of 58% and a median age of 46.7 years.[11]

Since 2000, the population's insufficient replacement rates and net domestic migration losses have been offset by positive net international migration.[12] In Johnson County, 60 Central and South American countries are represented by newcomers. A significant demographic shift is happening and the existing white, non-Hispanic residents are largely unaccustomed to immigration and unprepared for their arrival.

Rural Skepticism of Higher Education

Secondary students in southern Indiana's rural communities graduate from high schools at rates comparable to the state and the nation; however, higher educational attainment rates are remarkably low. While 38% of Indiana residents have earned associate degrees, in Switzerland and Crawford counties, only 17% of adults have. Nearly 60% of Orange County's workforce is in low-skilled occupations without formal training.[13]

At the beginning of my career in higher education, I served as a liaison for Indiana University, a state-wide tuition scholarship program, and southcentral Indiana's low-to-moderate income middle school students and families. Tuition-free, post-secondary education was often not significant enough to overcome additional financial barriers, including institutional fees (parking, technology, printing, and textbooks), transportation, food, and housing. In addition, limited local employment prospects lower the perceived value of postsecondary credentialing, especially when federal students loans are needed to supplement scholarships. Young adults who receive bachelor's degrees often do not return to their home communities, further exacerbating community skepticism of the value of higher education.

Limited Economic Prospects

Increasing levels of poverty in southern Indiana are detrimental to the overall wellness and viability of rural life in the region. Rural and rural mixed counties have higher levels of unemployment than urban counties. County to county, there are striking inequalities. For instance, on the southeastern Ohio border, Switzerland County has a 22.2% poverty rate while their neighbor to the north, Ohio County, has an 8.3% rate. Children account for one-third of the poor in rural southern Indiana and concentrated areas of poverty, like those in Switzerland County, have the potential to influence the educational outcomes for all children.[14] Being poor and rural has outsized consequences as access to social services designed to assist is restricted by the very nature of rural living.

Self-Destructive Health Behaviors

Researchers of premature death in rural America have begun calling mortality due to self-destructive health behaviors "despair deaths," positing the likelihood of their occurrence is due to underlying social and economic factors.[15] Rural southern Indiana mirrors the national trends among middle-aged, white, non-Hispanic Americans with shorter lifespans than their parents and grandparents. In Bartholomew

(continues)

County, the prevalence of mortality due to cancer, diabetes, heart disease and stroke, kidney disease, respiratory disease, and substance abuse disorder account for the bulk of age-adjusted death rates. In Jefferson County, the suicide rate grew from 11.2 per 100,000 in 2013 to 41.8 in 2016, more than 3.2 times higher than the national rate.[16]

Substance Abuse

While alcohol and tobacco continue to be the most widely used substances, Hoosiers are more likely to die from an overdose than a car accident.[17] In the community health needs assessment of Bartholomew County, substance abuse was the most cited, by 83.2% of respondents, as a major health issue. Of those informants, heroin or other opioids were identified as the most problematic substance abused in the community, followed by methamphetamine/other amphetamines, alcohol, and prescription medications. In addition, respondents who rated substance abuse as a major problem most identified substance abuse treatment, behavioral health care, and primary care as the most difficult to access in the community.[18]

While 79 of the 92 counties in Indiana have a county-wide response to the opioid epidemic, none provide comprehensive prevention, treatment, and recovery support services. Of southern Indiana counties, five have overdose response projects, four have nonsyringe harm reduction programs, and three have syringe exchange programs.[19]

In 2015, Scott County received national attention when a public health emergency was declared due to an HIV epidemic. From November 18, 2014, to November 1, 2015, 181 residents were diagnosed with HIV and 92.3% were coinfected with the hepatitis C virus.[20] Young adults who were dependent on prescription opiates had switched to injectable opioids or heroin, sharing syringes with one another. Recent computer simulation research found that earlier action in 2010 would have limited the number of infections to 10 of the 215 actual.[21] While a syringe exchange program was finally established, state law is still conflicted. Exchanges reduce needle sharing and HIV incidence and yet needle possession remains illegal in Indiana.

Farm Family Domestic Violence

The remoteness of the home and lack of community resources for survivors of domestic violence in southern Indiana compound the effects of intimate partner violence. Although prevalence rates are roughly the same in rural, mixed, and urban counties, there are distinct barriers. Isolation in rural communities is literal. Neighbors and others who in other settings would be able to identify and report signs of abuse are not physically proximate. Survivors may not have access to a phone or Internet connection, a sole vehicle may be accessed only by the abuser, and work outside of the home may be prohibited.

Even when domestic abuse is recognized and reported, other community members, including law enforcement, may not acknowledge the violence as serious or criminal. Cultural norms of the community may conceptualize the abuse as a private family matter, allowing abusers to continue their behavior and marginalizing the survivors' experience. Economic and familial concerns may also prevent survivors from prioritizing their own health concerns.

There are only 29 domestic violence shelters in Indiana, of which six are located in rural southern counties. Community challenges for rural residents (housing, employment opportunities, education, health care) are especially difficult for this vulnerable population. Healthcare providers, police, educators, and social service professionals must work together to create and sustain appropriate prevention and treatment programs for rural domestic violence survivors.

Health Professions Shortage

The aging population of southern Indiana is creating a rising demand for elder goods and services, including health care. The outmigration of working-age adults not only impacts local employers trying to fill open positions but its rural residents also face healthcare access problems because communities do not have a sufficient number of healthcare professionals. In addition to registered nurse, primary care provider, and specialist shortages, there is limited access to mental health professionals. Critical and hard-to-fill positions also include certification-only employees such as certified medical assistants (CMA), medical lab technicians, certified nursing assistants (CNA), and licensed practical nurses (LPN).

State-wide healthcare workforce development initiatives seek to provide rural residents with education through the community college and employers for stackable credentials leading to higher educational attainment (for instance, CNA to LPN to ASN). In addition, the Indiana Health Care Professional Recruitment and Retention Fund Program (IHCPRRF) provides healthcare professionals a loan repayment to incentivize psychiatric and mental health counselor practice in a specific, federally designated Indiana region experiencing high numbers of opioid deaths.

Discussion Questions

1. From the list, which do you think is the most important to healthcare delivery in the rural setting? Justify your answer.
2. How will health profession shortages impact rural healthcare delivery in your state or area?
3. What can universities do to reduce skepticism in higher education associated with rural areas?

CASE 14-2 Systems Thinking for the Native American Health Initiative

Written by Nitumigaabow Ryan Champagne

In my experience, I have the unique opportunity to lead problem-solving teams. As consultants, our customers often contract with our firm, Grand River Community Development, to help solve a problem or overcome a barrier. While their lists usually are tangible and concrete "problems," we look at the organizational systems and culture before attempting to problem solve. Often, this includes an organizational assessment. Such assessment allows our teams and the customer to see the "bigger picture" and focus on systemic or organizational issues versus program- and department-specific matters. While we employ American Indian consultants nationwide, we do not utilize consultants who are not versed in systemic solutions. These systems are often complex adaptive systems that need a problem solver who understands how relationships, systems, and practices impact organizational culture and productivity. The barrier we often face is getting the customers to understand or embrace the larger need. While I believe they understand and agree, many choose not to explore those types of solutions for fear of staff resistance, personal resistance, and/or lack of capacity to make such changes.

When thinking about systems thinking, one case example comes to mind; it was a rural northern Wisconsin tribe that had a population of about 4000 citizens. They declared a state of emergency due to the high rates of drug usage, dealing, and deaths associated with illegal drugs. The leadership was at a loss on how to combat this crisis. The crisis at hand included the following:

- Twelve deaths related to the sale, consumption, or trafficking of illegal drugs in less than 4 months
- The reported fear of leaving their house after dark due to the illegal drug trafficking and crime associated with such by elders and community members

(continues)

CASE 14-2 Systems Thinking for the Native American Health Initiative *(continued)*

Written by Nitumigaabow Ryan Champagne

- The report by HeadStart that 40% of the children were showing signs of developmental delay due to being born chemically addicted or exposed
- The seemingly ineffectiveness of addressing the crisis by current government programming

The first stage was to identify what the crisis entailed. This process included an analysis of the systems. The common themes that emerged included suicide, drugs, unmet behavioral health needs, and crime. The crisis factors allowed for the tribal council to come together to have a unified leadership and shared vision that the status quo was no longer acceptable. The tribal council decided to contract with our firm to gain an outside perspective and lens on the crisis state. The idea was that their staff and citizens were too close to the situation and could not maintain a systemic view required to assist in developing real solutions to combat the crisis.

Grand River conducted a Community Readiness Assessment to understand the community's current readiness and learn which community achieved a score of 2, which placed them in the domain of denial/resistance. This is normal as most individuals, whether in a social/environmental crisis state or organizational crisis state, have become desensitized to the crisis because the crisis is the status quo or "norm." Post-intervention the tool was used again to measure progress and the community achieved a score of 6.75, which raised them to a level between the initiation and stabilization domains (**FIGURE 14-6**).

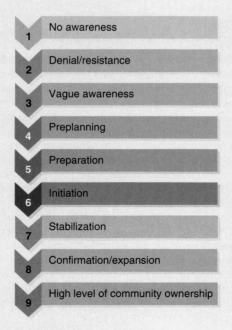

1. No awareness
2. Denial/resistance
3. Vague awareness
4. Preplanning
5. Preparation
6. Initiation
7. Stabilization
8. Confirmation/expansion
9. High level of community ownership

FIGURE 14-6 Stages of Community Readiness

Plested BA, Jumper-Thurman P, and Edwards RW. (2016). Community readiness manual. The National Center for Community Readiness. Colorado State University, Fort Collins, Colorado.

The next step in the process was to have leadership accountability. This step entailed 100% Tribal Council support of a drug-free community by submitting selected individuals to a urinalysis and hair screen, enforced "Zero Tolerance Policy" of drug usage or trafficking in government housing, and enforcement of a drug-free workplace. At first glance, this may not seem like a huge accomplishment but in a socialistic form of government where business, government, and citizenship are interconnected, this was a feat. The next step entailed a comprehensive organizational assessment, which included a systemic review of all their systems in health and human services. The review extended to collaborative agencies that impacted such systems that included the following: law enforcement; judicial, housing, education, and workforce development; and economic development. The systems assessment established baseline data, identified needs and barriers, and recommended strategies that required improvement. The assessment served as a detailed roadmap to follow to allow for systemic change.

Preparing for change requires people to change the way they view problems and solutions from a systems thinking perspective. Grand River conducted a Leadership Policy Academy that provided intensive policy training for tribal council. It allowed the leadership to start thinking of their roles as policymakers and systems change, and it led to dialogue of strategic planning and visioning. The legislators found value in this new way of thinking that they wanted something for their executive management; the Leadership Academy for Tribal Managers was created to meet this need. The tribal managers learned tools for addressing systemic change by engaging the community, implementing change initiatives, leading in a state of crisis, and bridging silos and strategic planning. This was the framework in which they prepared for systemic change and the human factor.

Grand River, along with the traditional tribal community leaders, started the next stage of community engagement. This stage consisted of conducting a series of listening sessions; focus groups with elders, cultural advisors, key stakeholders, and consumers; and a community input survey. This stage allowed us to learn about community perceptions and barriers and problem-solve practical solutions. This stage set the framework of visioning for the community, and their vision is what drove systemic change and community development. Understanding the interconnectedness of these systems and how the community members comprise the most vital part in solutions was critical in this process, as they are the experts of their community.

Policy development and advocacy stage allowed for: creation of policy and legislation; advocacy with federal, state, and local governments; and development of partnerships with local coalitions, state departments, and federal agencies. This stage called on system partners on the local, regional, and macro-levels to share in the solution process. This process allowed a truly encompassing systemic approach to addressing a crisis in a relatively small community. This set the context for the building alliances stage in which Grand River facilitated the process for a formal tribal state partnership and federal partnership. The tribal state partnership addressed social and health disparities, provided funding and technical assistance, and prioritized needs and development of an action plan. Under the tribal law and order act, the tribal federal partnership authorized funding, training, and technical assistance development of tribal action plan—priority funding for federal agencies.

All of the previous steps were needed to be in place to allow for the final steps of strategic planning, reorganization, and implementation. The strategic planning sessions led key stakeholders and the community to recognize the need for reorganizing the Health and Human Services. The first step entailed merging 14 independent siloed programs into three main programs, the creation of Human Services Department, and the recruitment of a national expert to lead the department. The next phase was to create a Health and Human Services Division, which entailed merging the three departments into one division and centralizing the core functions and the administration, which increased efficiencies, bridged silos, and reduced costs. Post-reorganization, a formal strategic plan was adopted that allowed for the initiatives to occur, as shown in **TABLE 14-3**.

(continues)

TABLE 14-3 The System Spectrum and Key Stakeholders

Public Safety	Judicial (Zaagibaa Healing to Wellness Court)	Health Care (Clinic/Public Health)	Health Care (Community-Based Elder Disability)	Health Care (Residential)	Human Services (Crisis/Residential)	Human Services (Funding/Case Management)	Workforce Development	Corrections	Cultural
Surveillance Monitoring System	Adult (Alternative to Corrections)	Prescription Drug Monitoring System	Tribal Operated Waivers	Residential Treatment Center	Emergency Shelter	Title IV-E Pass-through Agreement – Child Welfare	Youth Build	Higher Education in the County Jail	Traditional Healing and Doctoring
Operation Pandora (Interagency Drug Enforcement Approach)	Youth (Early Intervention)	Public Health Awareness Community Campaign	Residential Care Apartment Complex	Permanent Supportive Housing	Peer Supportive Living Homes	Targeted Case Management	Small Business Development in Auxiliary Health and Human Services Vendors	Clinical Services in the County Jail	Ceremonial Roundhouse
Exclusion and Removal (Banishment)		Patient-Centered Medical Home Model				Tribal Wraparound			Family Circles – Grassroots Cultural Intervention
						Comprehensive Community-Based Services			

As the chart demonstrates, these were the major change initiatives that occurred due to a systems thinking perspective, which entailed the following ten-step Tribal Transformation Process: (1) Identifying the Crisis; (2) Unified Leadership; (3) Community Readiness; (4) Accountability of Leadership; (5) Organizational Assessment; (6) Policy Institute; (7) Community Engagement; (8) Policy Development and Advocacy; (9) Building Alliances; and (10) Strategic Planning, Reorganization, and Implementation. Within 3 years, the Grand River Community Development was able to assist the tribe with 21 major self-sustaining initiatives totaling over $15 million brought into the community to start up such initiatives. The annual profit/cost savings from the initiatives totaled more than $5 million.

Discussion Questions

1. How are Tribal Nations and Rural Areas in the United States similar? How are they different? Justify your answer.
2. Considering the Stages of Community Readiness in Figure X, briefly describe how rural healthcare delivery might benefit from this type of mental model.
3. Compare and contrast how Tribal Nations and Rural Areas might benefit from a systems approach to policy.
4. What initiatives are applicable from Table X for Rural Health?

▶ Discussion Questions

- Discuss rurality and how it impacts service delivery and use of resources.
- What are the advantages and disadvantages for providers in rural areas?
- How do you think migration/movement between rural and urban areas impacts rural healthcare delivery?
- What technology do you see as being most important to enhance rural healthcare delivery?
- Read the summary statement from the NRHA and then search their website. Identify and describe three pressing challenges and emerging solutions seen in rural health care.

CHAPTER ACRONYMS

AHA American Hospital Association
E Emergent
NRHA National Rural Health Association
OMB Office of Management and Budget
P Persistent
R Recent
RUCA Rural–Urban Commuting Area
UA Urbanized Area

UC Urban Cluster
USDA U.S. Department of Agriculture
USDA ERS U.S. Department of Agriculture Economic Research Service
IHCPRRF Indiana Health Care Professional Recruitment and Retention Fund Program
CMA certified medical assistants
CNA certified nursing assistants
LPN licensed practical nurses

References

1. Rural Health Information Hub. What is rural? Updated April 8, 2019. Accessed June 13, 2021. https://www.ruralhealthinfo.org/topics/what-is-rural
2. Talbot JA, Burgess AR, Thayer D, Parenteau L, Paluso N, Coburn AF. Patterns of telehealth use among rural Medicaid beneficiaries. *J Rural Health*. 2019;35(3):298-307. doi: 10.1111/jrh.12324
3. U.S. Census Bureau. Urban and rural. Updated June 16, 2021. Accessed August 30, 2021. https://www.census.gov/programs-surveys/geography/guidance/geo-areas/urban-rural.html
4. U.S. Census Bureau. 2010 Census urban and rural classification and urban area criteria. Updated December 2, 2019. Accessed June 9, 2021. https://www.census.gov/programs-surveys/geography/guidance/geo-areas/urban-rural/2010-urban-rural.html
5. Rural Health Information Hub. Overviews of specific issues in a rural context. Updated September 14, 2017. Accessed June 14, 2021. https://www.ruralhealthinfo.org/toolkits/rural-toolkit/1/rural-issues
6. American Hospital Association. Rural Report Executive Summary: challenges facing rural communities

and the roadmap to ensure local access to high-quality, affordable care. Published 2019. Accessed June 14, 2021. https://www.aha.org/system/files /2019-02/rural-report-executive-summary-2019.pdf

7. Ellison A. Why rural hospital closures hit a record high in 2020. *Becker's Hospital Review.* Published March 16, 2021. Accessed June 6, 2021. https://www .beckershospitalreview.com/finance/why-rural -hospital-closures-hit-a-record-high-in-2020.html

8. Ramesh T, Gee E. Rural hospital closures reduce access to emergency care. Center for American Progress. Published September 9, 2019. Accessed June 5, 2021. https://www.americanprogress.org /issues/healthcare/reports/2019/09/09/474001/rural -hospital-closures-reduce-access-emergency-care/

9. Johnson JA, Anderson DE, Rossow CC. *Health Systems Thinking: A Primer.* Jones & Barlett Learning; 2020.

10. National Rural Health Association. About rural health care. Accessed June 14, 2021. https://www .ruralhealthweb.org/about-nrha/about-rural -health-care

11. Waldorf B, McKendree, M. 2013. The aging of rural Indiana's population. *Purdue Extension Center for Rural Development.* Accessed September 22, 2013. https://www.extension.purdue.edu/extmedia/EC /EC-769-W.pdf

12. Waldorf B, Ayres J, McKendree M. 2013. Population trends in rural Indiana. *Purdue Extension Center for Rural Development.* Accessed March 14, 2014. https:// www.extension.purdue.edu/extmedia/EC/EC-767-W .pdf

13. Indiana Business Research Center at the Kelley School of Business, Indiana University & Strategic Development Group, Inc. 2011. *Orange County benchmarking and target industry analysis: Spotlight on a changing region.* Accessed February 14, 2012. https://www.ibrc.indiana.edu/studies/OrangeCounty BenchmarkStudy2011.pdf

14. Waldorf B, Carriere D. 2013. Poverty in rural Indiana. *Purdue Extension Center for Rural Development.* Accessed January 5, 2014. https://www.extension.purdue .edu/extmedia/EC/EC-771-W.pdf

15. Stein EM, Gennuso KP, Ugboaja DC, & Remington PL. The epidemic of despair among White Americans: trends in the leading causes of premature death, 1999-2015. *Am J Public Health.* 2017;107(10):1541-1547

16. King's Daughters' Health. 2018. *Healthy communities of Jefferson County.* Accessed July 31, 2018. https:// www.kdhmadison.org/media/1916/community -meeting-april-2018.pdf

17. Indiana University School of Medicine. 2019. *Opioids abuse crisis.* Accessed March 9, 2020. https://medicine .iu.edu/expertise/indiana-health/opioid-crisis/

18. Professional Research Consultants, Inc. 2018. *Community health needs assessment report: Columbus regional health service area.* Retrieved from https:// www.crh.org/docs/default-source/pdf/2018-prc-chna -report-crh-service-area.pdf

19. Indiana State Department of Health. 2020. *Indiana drug overdose dashboard: County response.* Retrieved from https://www.in.gov/isdh/27393.htm

20. Peters PJ, Pontones P, Hoover KW, et al. HIV infection linked to injection use of oxymorphone in Indiana, 2014–2015. *N Engl J Med.* 2016;375(3):229-239.

21. Gonsalves G, Crawford FW. Dynamics of the HIV outbreak and response in Scott County, IN, USA, 2011–15: a modelling study. *Lancet HIV.* 2018;5(10):e569-e577. doi: 10.1016/S2352-3018(18) 30176-0

CHAPTER 15

Health Care and Future Opportunities

CHAPTER OVERVIEW

This chapter recaps and summarizes selected topics in a future-oriented context. It discusses many ongoing changes and tentatively forecasts future developments in U.S. healthcare system.

▶ Forging the Future

Health care is one of the nation's largest and most important sectors. The healthcare workforce is composed of over 200 different types of professionals (or human factors) that play an important role in influencing healthcare delivery in the United States. The healthcare workforce directly and indirectly influences important health system outcomes like cost, quality, access, patient experience, and overall population health. The U.S. Bureau of Labor Statistics reports that close to 20 million Americans were employed in the healthcare and social assistance industry at the beginning of 2021.[1] A recent healthcare workforce analysis estimates that the United States will need to hire an additional 2.3 million healthcare workers by 2025 to ensure essential health services can be delivered.[2] The U.S. population is cited as the key factor driving the need for more healthcare professionals. Failure to keep a stable workforce will result in shortages, limited access to certain health professionals and services, increased costs, lower quality and patient satisfaction, and many other challenges, undermining population health and well-being. The future of the health system is in the hands of healthcare leaders who will navigate an exciting but uncertain future. **BOX 15-1** provides characteristics future health system leaders will need to possess to steward their people (or workforce) and organizations toward tomorrow.

▶ Technology and the Human Factors of Health Care

The coupling of technology and the human factors of health care (or healthcare professionals) holds exciting promise for the future. Technology is driving disruptive and revolutionary changes in health care every day. The healthcare workforce are the human factors and agents of change positioned to spur technological advancement and adoption across the health system. Medical advances are being made in the methods of diagnosis and treatment, including new or improved equipment, new procedures, and new or improved drugs, among other advances. A promise of technology is reducing practice variation and ensuring healthcare providers are providing a consistent standard of care based on the best scientific evidence for the patients and populations they serve. Further, the hope of technology is that it, along with the healthcare workforce, can achieve higher levels of system integration, cohesion, coordination, and output. As Chapter 1 discussed, health care is a complex adaptive system (CAS), and coupling technology with a strong healthcare workforce provides many exciting opportunities for patients, communities, payers, providers, and overall population health. Future healthcare leaders will need to think about the best ways in which to combine technology and human factors to advance the systems of care under their influence. Systems thinking, as discussed in Chapter 1, will continue to be embraced as healthcare leaders and clinicians seek to address fragmentation, lack of coordination, and other system

BOX 15-1 Key Characteristics of Health Systems Leaders[1] of the Future

1. Acute awareness of the current system, knowing workflow process and best practice standards in the healthcare organization
2. Appreciation of the patterns and structures behind events
3. Willingness to challenge the current systems boundaries
4. Ability to speak to players at all levels of the hierarchy
5. Understanding of how relationships play out before making a decision
6. Conceptualization of the attributes of an improved and successful system
7. Processing of courage and energy to challenge the status quo and seek improvement

[1]Johnson, JA Anderson, DE Rossow C. *Health Systems Thinking: A Primer.*
Republished with permission of Assn for the Advancement of Med Instrumentation, from Five ways to incorporate systems thinking into healthcare organizations. Biomedical instrumentation & technology, Trbovich, P. , 48(s2), 31-36.2014; permission conveyed through Copyright Clearance Center, Inc.

functions in the United States. Further, technology will create additional interactions and inter-dependencies that must be considered and navigated. Talent acquisition, human resources management, and governmental policies must evolve to reflect and keep up with workforce trends to leverage opportunities and mitigate potential perils that will arise as human and technological factors increasingly interact.

▶ Artificial Intelligence (AI) in Health Care

Artificial intelligence (AI) is defined as a type of technology that uses probability and other techniques to perform tasks that apply some type of intelligence or learning.[3] It originated in the 1950s and has become useful in various aspects of medicine (e.g., diagnostics and disease distribution prediction). AI in health care has shown potential to further efforts to improve healthcare quality for patients, but it must be managed effectively to reduce any unintended consequences. The unintended consequences of growth in the use of AI in health care come with concerns about bias, patient privacy, scalability, and costs of implementation.[4]

The actual term "artificial intelligence" was coined by John McCarthy, a computer scientist and professor, in 1956.[5] However, the father of artificial intelligence was none other than British mathematician Alan Turing, who developed the "Turing Test" in 1950. The Turing Test is designed to evaluate a computer's ability to produce a human level of cognitive performance. Turing was known for being the "master code breaker who led the team which succeeded in reading the German highest-level secret codes" during World War II.[6]

AI in medicine can be generally separated into two of categories: virtual and physical Virtual AI includes the type that is used in applications, such as electronic health record (EHR) systems, as well as black box methods (e.g., neural network-based guided treatment decisions). Physical AI is associated with the type used in robots for things like surgery and prosthetics for geriatric care. The application depends on the area in health care and how developed the algorithms are in said area. There is "no one size fits all" application for AI in health care due to a host of complexities.

The Da Vinci Robotic Surgical System

This system "mimics a surgeon's hand movements with better precision and has a 3D view and magnification options which allow the surgeon to perform minute incisions."[7] There are risks and challenges involved in using AI in health care, including how AI systems can learn biased behaviors from the data that they are given and the need to protect patient privacy. Despite these potential issues, AI has a lot of promise and potential to transform healthcare delivery and safety for patients.[7] This is discussed further in the editorial provided by a subject matter expert in **EXHIBIT 15-1** at the end of this chapter.

EXHIBIT 15-1 Perspective on AI and Big Data in Health Care

In this editorial, author Richard Greenhill discusses both the promises and perils of emerging technologies (e.g., AI and Big Data) in terms of healthcare delivery and quality:

"These algorithms have the capability to explore and analyze complex, large data sets and glean insights that would be otherwise impossible. These large complex data fall into the definition of 'big data'. Big data is described in terms of its orientation to the four Vs: volume, veracity, variety, and velocity.

- Volume is the amount of data. In today's world, the internet of things (IoT) and sensor data constantly produce an exhaust of data not seen before.
- The veracity of data relates to the lack of quality and accuracy of data being produced.
- Variety describes the various ways, methods, and types of data being produced.
- The velocity of data describes the speed as well as the constant collection of data.

Thus, big data represents a big opportunity under the right conditions. AI applications that leverage combinations of big data from unconventional sources (e.g. IoT and other sensor data) offer new perspectives. While AI does not represent a new innovation, the accessibility of big data, its analyses, and application broadly in healthcare is. Many clinicians are leveraging AI applications to advance patient care and operations effectiveness. For practitioners, there are a range of opportunities to apply machine learning and deep learning methods to patient safety, project management, and performance improvement. Quality improvement practitioners often collect data to evaluate the snapshot of a process. This snapshot may lack context to other processes in the organization, thereby creating a 'whack-a-mole' paradigm of improvement whereby one problem is solved but other unrecognized ones then emerge. The collection of complete data sets or streaming data offers an opportunity to view organizational quality from a more holistic perspective.

One such application of AI might be around human factors and patient safety. Consider a complete de-identified surgical data set collected for a time period on high-risk surgeries. The data sets may include: the hospital surgery repository, human resources data on days off (e.g. sick time or vacation), and scheduling of operating room staff. AI offers an opportunity to look across these data sets for patterns that point to fatigue or other human factors considerations. While these data might not seem congruent, machine learning tools may uncover important dimensions of interest for improvement. Big data has been successfully used in health care in this fashion for population health management and other areas.

While the potential is exciting, there are challenges related to the workforce and competencies among health-care leaders toward enterprise adoption. The challenges with application of AI methods in health-care quality stem from the vastness of tools and complexities of data mining. This may be less of an issue for quality practitioners as there are natural synergies between the statistical foundations in quality improvement and AI methodologies. For quality improvement practitioners that use advanced statistical methods such as Six Sigma (e.g. Green Belt and Black Belt levels), the methodologies may overlap. However, with any new technological introduction, there are many, key considerations for use of AI methods in health care. They are improperly trained AI models and their ability to perpetuate biases in care delivery, ethics and privacy considerations from the use of sensor data, and AI decision-associated liabilities for mistakes. Quality practitioners as the guardians of safe, accountable, and transparent care must ensure that generalizable improvement is reliable and reduces harm. Emerging technologies offer a new perspective on quality improvement and patient safety as they can help us see beyond the current paradigms."

Reproduced from Greenhill RG. Healthcare quality improvement and emerging technologies: the potential and the pitfalls. *IJQHC Communications.* 2021;1(1). doi: 10.1093/ijcoms/lyab001

▶ Virtual Reality and Simulation

Virtual reality (VR) and simulation are two emerging examples of persuasive (or interactive) technology in use in healthcare delivery. "Captology" is the term used to define persuasive technology, which is an "interactive information technology" designed to assist in purposely changing a person's behavior and/or attitudes using computing technology.[8] The primary purpose of these technologies is to mimic reality in a safe, controlled, and realistic environment. It gives patients the ability to test and change behaviors and attitudes for feedback to improve in a certain area. Simulation also provides a mechanism for improvement of patient safety, quality, and integrity of care professionals. VR and simulation can also enhance the overall effectiveness of education and competency.

▶ Health Professions Supply and Demand

A well-educated and stable healthcare workforce is paramount to a high-functioning health system. A recent healthcare workforce analysis estimates that the United States will need to hire an additional 2.3 million healthcare workers by 2025 to ensure essential health services can be delivered.[9,10] By 2025, the United States is projected to experience a shortage of 446,300 home health aides, 95,000 nursing assistants, 98,700 medical and lab technologists and technicians, and 29,400 nurse practitioners, just to name a few.[9,10] The shortage trend is seen globally; the World Health Organization (WHO) projects a shortage of 4.5 million healthcare professionals worldwide.[11] The healthcare labor market is dire in many parts of the United States and around the world. Turnover rates are increasing among many types of healthcare professionals. Chronic shortages of critical healthcare professionals are combining with changing care delivery and financial models. These factors, along with many others, are colliding and increasing the demands on the healthcare workforce. Job stress and burnout are both high among healthcare professionals, and the COVID-19 pandemic has further exacerbated an already dire situation. Critical shortages are also putting upward pressure on healthcare wages, contributing to higher healthcare costs and potentially jeopardizing health care for millions due to the inability to afford care.

Educational institutions that train healthcare professionals are experiencing shortages. Nursing, respiratory therapy, medical specialties like primary care and psychiatry, and other disciplines are struggling to find faculty to train the next generation of healthcare professionals. Education expectations for the healthcare workforce are at an all-time high and will only increase in response to more technology and complexity. Healthcare professionals will be required to be lifelong learners and remember that education extends well beyond the academic setting. In response, health systems are moving to establish their own educational and training programs to ensure an adequate supply of healthcare providers. For example, Kaiser Permanente, a leading not-for-profit health system, established its own medical school to train primary care physicians. HCA Healthcare, a for-profit health system, purchased a majority stake in a multistate nursing school, Galen College of Nursing, based in Nashville, Tennessee.[12] In the future, the workforce shortages in professions such as generalist physicians, nurses, and mental health workers, the disproportionate geographic distribution of many types of providers in urban and rural areas, and underrepresentation of minorities in the health professions are major focal points for future legislation. Additionally, future legislation is needed to recognize the informal caregiver system in the United States, which is virtually ignored and could be addressed through wage and labor policies. Long-term care facilities are often dangerously understaffed, resulting in a significant amount of informal and uncompensated caregiving by family and community members. Creative and nontraditional staffing, caregiving, and compensation are needed to help alleviate demands on the healthcare workforce where possible in the future.

▶ Workforce Planning and Preparation

There is an urgent need for health policies that prioritize workforce planning to ensure a stable healthcare workforce. Complex supply and demand factors influence workforce requirements, and the prediction of future requirements is severely confounded by the lack of uniform data at national and state levels across the professions. The United States has never planned comprehensively or strategically for the development and deployment of its healthcare workforce and, as a result, the preparation of each generation of health workers is just as fragmented and confusing as the healthcare system they will one day join. Federal and state governments, educational institutions, professional organizations, insurers, and provider institutions have had separate and often conflicting interests in health workforce education and training, regulation, financing, entry-level preparation, and scope of practice. The various levels at which policy decisions have been made and the disparate interests that influence those decisions have presented major obstacles to ensuring a coherent, efficient, and rational health workforce in the United States.

There is great demand for healthcare providers to be able to practice at the highest level of preparation or training. This is also referred to as a health professional's scope of practice, which is simply what a provider is competent in and permitted to perform based on their education and training. States can and often do govern the scope of practice, or how healthcare providers practice in their state. This leads to variation and inefficiency in many practices, communities, and healthcare organizations. Healthcare providers will often move to states that allow them to practice to the full extent of their education and training, or scope of practice, because the work is more rewarding and pays higher salaries. Some providers even live in a state with more a restrictive practice environment and drive across state lines to practice in a state with a less restrictive practice environment. Healthcare administrators are advocating for expanded scopes of practice as the labor market is squeezed by emerging models of care and other environmental factors. Achieving patient outcomes are increasingly a prerequisite for reimbursement and financial viability. Healthcare administrators argue that having a nurse practitioner perform the tasks of a registered nurse is a form of waste and inefficiency that healthcare organizations can no longer tolerate based on the accountable care and value-based models that will continue to dominate health care and health policy. Tensions are high around this topic, as physicians feel their autonomy and prowess is eroding. In fact, the system is trying to free physicians to pioneer new frontiers in medicine and make discoveries to alleviate human suffering and improve health thanks to advances in science and technology. The aging population, the shifting nature of diseases, healthcare delivery and reimbursement reforms, new technology, and economic factors will continue to change consumer demands and provider expectations, all lending more complexity to the challenges of planning for future workforce requirements.

▶ Shift in Sites of Care

The health system is undergoing a seismic shift in terms of the settings in which care is provided, as discussed in previous chapters. Care is shifting from acute care (i.e., inpatient care) to ambulatory care (i.e., outpatient care) settings. This is disrupting and reordering the traditional healthcare delivery models in the United States and challenging traditional healthcare professional roles as well. Technological advances and financial pressures are continuing the push to transfer more modes of treatment to outpatient settings. Recent health policy reforms have created incentives that have shifted delivery from acute care facilities to community-based facilities because they are generally cheaper and easier for patients to access. Freestanding specialty centers that perform some of the same services provided by hospital departments are proliferating. Corporate restructuring is occurring as provider organizations merge or affiliate and form even larger health systems. Although hospitals are still a major employer, recent employment growth has shifted to community-based settings like ambulatory clinics, outpatient surgery centers, home health providers, long-term care facilities, behavioral health clinics, and many other community-based settings. Health policies and reforms will continue to respond to health trends and shift the sites of care to ambulatory care settings. In turn, the healthcare workforce will need the requisite knowledge and skills to work in community-based settings. **BOX 15-2** provides five ways systems thinking can be used by healthcare professionals and organizations to respond to shifts in the sites of care.

BOX 15-2 Five Ways to Incorporate Systems Thinking in Healthcare Organizations

1. Apply a holistic approach to solving problems: Seek a collective view (stakeholder involvement), identify the elements of the system, task dependencies, sequential sequencing order, coordination, and synchronization.
2. Define approaches for evaluating and understanding systems-wide effects.
3. Identify and nurture great systems thinkers.
4. Apply a proactive approach to identify leverage points.
5. Create a culture of systems thinking

BOX 15-3 The 10 Rules to Redesign Health Care[1]

1. Care is based on continuous healing relationships.
2. Care is customized according to the patient's needs and values.
3. The patient is the source of control.
4. Knowledge is shared and information flows freely.
5. Decision-making is evidence based.
6. Safety is a system property.
7. Transparency is necessary.
8. Needs are anticipated.
9. Waste is continuously decreased.
10. Cooperation among clinicians is a priority.

[1]Burlington, MA: Jones & Barlett Learning; 2020.
Reproduced from Institute of Medicine Committee on Quality of Health Care in America. *Crossing the Quality Chasm: A New Health System for the 21st Century*. National Academies Press; 2001.

▶ Interprofessional Teams and Education

The pervasive system changes required to move from an episodic and disjointed care model to one that encompasses a holistic approach to population health needs will require interprofessional teams and education. The increasing specialization and complexity of health care requires that all disciplines work collaboratively to provide safe, effective, quality care at a decreased cost. Collaboration provides an understanding and appreciation for the roles and contributions of each discipline in the care of the patient and the unique community and population a patient belongs to. Interdisciplinary education is a more recent movement and approach to educating and preparing diverse sets of healthcare professionals to work together in practice. This approach to education will continue to enhance interprofessional interactions and in turn improve system function and patient, population, and system outcomes. Health care of the future will depend on health professionals who are able to work within and across their professions to enhance collaboration, communication, and decision making. This will enable a more synergistic influence of grouped knowledge and skills to improve patient safety, outcomes, and satisfaction through evidence-based practice.[13] The future of health care will demand that interprofessional teams use the best evidence-based practices when delivering care. Healthcare organizations of the future will prioritize and emphasize interprofessional teams, evidence-based practice, and clinical practice guidelines. Technology will help ensure the latest evidence is being used in practice through decision support tools. These tools will also be able to track if or when providers deviate from standard practice and match that with patient outcomes. Patient quality and safety data, as discussed in an earlier chapter, will drive healthcare decision making and how delivery will be redesigned in the future. **BOX 15-3** outlines 10 rules for redesigning health care. Interprofessional teams can play a significant role in redesign efforts.

▶ Consumerism and Patient Engagement

The trend is for health care to move from hospitals and clinics to the community and even patients' homes. Technological innovation will impact the healthcare workforce and create higher levels of consumerism among healthcare consumers. Automation will increase as AI, robotic process automation, cognitive computing, and virtual reality/augmented reality change the tasks healthcare professionals perform.[8] New technology is raising consumer expectations about what may be possible. Patients' expectations have considerable influence on their healthcare-seeking behavior, leading to greater demand for and utilization of the latest and best that technology can offer. Technology will be utilized in the future to engage patients in their own health, from prevention to management and even treatment. Companies have turned homes into convenient sites of care through the proliferation of telehealth and at-home diagnostic testing kits. Medical devices are allowing remote monitoring to manage chronic health conditions. The workforce of the future will need to adapt to the rise of consumerism and help patients understand how to engage in their health.

▶ Diversity, Equity, and Inclusion

A high-performing and responsive health system reflects its population. The healthcare needs of the older adult population will also be influenced by its changing racial and ethnic diversity. Minority groups will represent larger proportions of the elderly population. These changes have important implications for the healthcare system and healthcare workforce. There are significant differences in mortality rates, chronic conditions, service preferences, and use, as well as attitudes toward medical care, across racial/ethnic groups. For example, Hispanics have lower rates of diseases such as hypertension and arthritis and higher rates of conditions such as diabetes than Caucasians. African Americans are more likely to require treatment for hypertension, cerebrovascular disease, diabetes, and obesity, and they have persistently higher mortality rates. Therefore, a workforce that prioritizes diversity, equity, and inclusion (DEI) will be positioned to better understand and serve its population while simultaneously improving organizational performance. As discussed in Chapter 5, diversity compounds, and this compounding can lead to higher and higher levels of performance.[9] There are numerous additional benefits associated with DEI, including higher employee engagement, higher productivity, reduced interpersonal conflict, higher levels of learning, reduced stress and overall higher levels of health, increased resilience and trust, and increased organizational commitment.[2]

▶ Employee Wellness

Organizations are increasingly recognizing that employee wellness is tied to organizational performance and wellness. Job stress and burnout are both high among healthcare professionals and are an integral part of a healthcare employee wellness programs. Healthcare organizations, like other organizations, are recognizing the importance of wellness programs that focus on helping employees balance all components of their wellness (i.e., occupational, spiritual, emotional/mental, financial, social, intellectual, environmental). Common components of workplace wellness programs include stress reduction, weight loss, smoking cessation, health screenings, exercise, nutrition, and vaccination clinics. Benefits of wellness programs include lower healthcare costs, reduced absenteeism, increased productivity, reduced workers' compensation and disability-related costs, reduced rates of injury, and improved employee morale and loyalty. Workplace violence is on the rise and is five times higher in health care than in the general population. Healthcare professionals are four times more likely to have to take time off work due to violence-related injuries. The CEO of the Cleveland Clinic, Tom Mihaljevic, noted that their system had collected 30,000 weapons from patients and visitors in 2018 alone.[10] Future polices must focus on employee wellness, from reducing job-related stress and workplace violence to a host of other pressing issues for healthcare professionals.

▶ **Ethical Dimensions and Future Considerations**

Healthcare professionals practicing in today's healthcare system confront a two-faced ethical challenge in assuring their patients receive the best possible care. The first "face" of the challenge is insurers' requirements that providers conform to specific treatment, review, evaluation, reporting, service authorization, and financial criteria for reimbursement. Providers and healthcare organizations typically deal with multiple insurers, which often have differing requirements, creating enormous bureaucratic burdens that subtract substantial time from patient care. As the delivery system moves from volume-driven to value-driven models, it is expected that these burdens will increase. Providers and healthcare organizations already admit the need to sometimes exaggerate the severity of a patient's condition to circumvent insurers' criteria to assure that patients receive necessary care. Another dimension to this ethical challenge recognizes the lure of traditional fee-for-service reimbursement that fuels overuse and wasteful and inappropriate services. The core ethical dilemma resides in how to balance legitimate cost and quality concerns with patients' best interests as the primary consideration. Providers and healthcare organizations will remain "caught in the middle" for the foreseeable future. Future health policy must consider this ethical dimension and actively work to ensure policies promote and incentivize the best evidence-based practices.

The second "face" of ethical challenges results from a "success" problem. Medicine's remarkable technologic advancement in the past 4 decades now enables life prolongation for a range of patients, from very premature infants to the terminally ill, and even to brain-dead individuals with no potential for future functional capacity. In the absence of transparent professional consensus on ethical guidelines to deal with decisions about continuing care in such cases, if a patient's family does not agree with a healthcare professional's recommendations, providers are left without the support of professionally developed guidance or guidance from the healthcare organization.

In addition, among the most critical of future ethical issues are those related to advances in the field of molecular biology, gene manipulation, and gene therapy. The advent of inexpensive technology that will allow scientists to sequence an individual's entire DNA genome in hours is being realized. Health policy continues to allocate millions to continue scaling up the National Institutes of Health's Precision Medicine Initiative, which is focused on developing treatments, diagnostics, and prevention strategies tailored to the individual genetic characteristics of each patient. As genome sequencing becomes more common, a host of unintended consequences and ethical issues will arise. The professional medical community is only beginning dialogue on the future obligations for the holders of individuals' genome data. Traditionally, laboratory tests are analyzed, reported, acted upon, and then archived. Genomic data is different because as more discoveries are made, periodic reanalysis of patients' genomic data could provide extremely valuable information for predicting future disease states and healthcare decision making. American society has not even begun to approach questions regarding by whom, under what circumstances, and even whether such periodic reanalysis will be performed. These loom as significant future questions. In addition, training physicians and other healthcare professionals about implications of the use of human genomic data in their practices will be an enormous future challenge. Enveloping all these challenges are concerns about the potential unethical applications of genome technology. In the future, the need for ethical discernment and transparent consensus on professional guidelines for medical practice will be paramount.

Finally, as discussed in Chapter 12, there are many research-related ethical concerns about conflicts of interest and appropriate public disclosure, some of which have invoked legal actions. Two of these concerns include shifting research funded by pharmaceutical and medical device companies from academic institutions to commercial research firms with obvious vested interests and the shift of the U.S. Food and Drug Administration's funding from the federal government to the same pharmaceutical companies it is intended to monitor. The "Sunshine Act," a provision of the Affordable Care Act, requires disclosures to the Centers for Medicare and Medicaid Services (CMS) about any payments or other transfers of value made to physicians or teaching hospitals and may help to bring these ethical breaches under control. Another continuing ethical issue is the violation of professional ethics found in the growing body of evidence that physicians and health researchers at some of the most prestigious U.S. medical schools have been attaching their names and reputations to scientific publications ghostwritten by employees of pharmaceutical, medical device, and other emerging research and development companies to boost sales of certain products and services. Future policy is needed to keep up with the proliferation of scientific and medical advances to ensure ethical conduct.

The healthcare workforce continues to change in size and composition in response to population and overall health trends as well as political, economic, social/demographic, technological, environmental, and legal/regulatory factors. The future holds many exciting opportunities and challenges for healthcare professionals. Overall, the workforce and health organizations of the future must be adaptable and able to respond to the complex needs of a diverse range of patients and populations.

When we look to the coming decades and the changing healthcare landscape and infrastructure improvements, we may be informed by the perspective presented in **BOX 15-4**.

BOX 15-4 Health System Designs for the 21st Century

Dr. Glenn A. Croxton

A series of papers related to the design of hospitals for the 21st century was presented by the Center for Health Design and Health Care Without Harm at a conference sponsored by the Robert Wood Johnson Foundation, September 2006. The Center for Health Design is a nonprofit research and advocacy organization. Its mission is to transform healthcare settings into healing environments. The healing environment is seen as a vital part of therapeutic treatment and where design of healthcare setting contributes to health rather than adding to the burden of stress.

Health Care Without Harm is an international coalition of 440 groups in 55 countries working to transform the healthcare industry so that it is ecologically sustainable and no longer of harm to people and the environment.

First, Do No Harm

Gary Cohen discussed how healthcare institutions that support the Hippocratic Oath have a special responsibility to ensure that their operations are not major sources of chemical exposure and environmental harm. Until recently, healthcare professionals and hospital administrators were unaware

(continues)

BOX 15-4 Health System Designs for the 21st Century *(continued)*

of their contributions to chemical contaminants and broader societal disease burdens according to Cohen.

Chronic diseases and disabilities now affect more than 90 million men, women, and children in the United States alone. In spite of much advancement in medical practice, the best available data show an increase in the incidence of asthma, autism, birth defects, childhood brain cancer, acute lymphocytic leukemia, endometriosis, Parkinson's disease, and infertility. The economic costs of these diseases by 2020 will exceed US $1 trillion yearly in healthcare cost and lost productivity.

The field of environmental health is attempting to link each of these diseases and disorders to exposure to toxic chemicals. The old way of looking at chemical risk and safety would have missed these links, as they are not as simple as single cause and single effect. Through the new lens of science, we have learned that exposure to toxic chemicals, at levels thought to have been safe, is increasing the chronic disease burden of millions of Americans.

Green Hospitals

The second paper, "Values-Driven Design and Construction: Enriching Community Benefits through Green Hospitals," was presented by Robin Guenther, Gail Vittori, and Cynthia Atwood. They discussed how many hospitals are successfully reaching beyond measures that have economic payback and are achieving community benefits beyond their four walls. Healthcare leaders recognize the high costs of inaction on matters of the environment—such as climate change and chemical contamination on the health of our families, neighbors, and communities at hand and globally. By embedding sustainable design in a broader vision of leadership and mission, these projects and organizations are succeeding in delivering the first generations of sustainable healthcare projects.

Ted Schettler, MD, MPH, identified three tiers of operational environmental performance evolving in hospitals.

- Tier 1: minimum local, state, and national environmental performance
- Tier 2: beyond compliance to measures that save money
- Tier 3: informed by inextricable link between environment and human health and moving beyond both compliance and monetary savings with a long-term plan to reduce environmental footprints

He contended that applying *triple bottom line* approaches to pollution-prevention initiatives—that is, measuring economic, social, and environment benefits—would deliver significant benefits for healthcare organizations and the communities they serve. Early tier 3 hospitals supported this notion. Named one of the state's top four recyclers, the University of Michigan Health System described its program's social benefit as an institution-wide initiative that engages everyone.

As building initiatives accelerate, it is clear that we can apply the same system-tiered performance to organizations engaged in sustainable building. Tier 1 organizations will not undertake green building until they are mandated to do so through legislative policy initiatives. They will not make the link or the organizational leap between the health of their facilities and the patients they serve.

Creating Safe and Healthy Spaces: Selecting Materials that Support Healing

Mark Rossi, PhD, and Tom Lent outlined the relationship of the materials and products used in healthcare facilities to the chemicals to which our communities are exposed. Rossi and Lent further described the opportunities available to healthcare organizations to help society break from its dependence on toxic materials and define the path to healthier, sustainable materials that benefit patients, communities, nature, and the organizational bottom line.

Kaiser Permanente, for example, framed its environmental goals for building design in terms of community health in March 2002 in the "Kaiser Permanente Position Statement on Green Buildings."

Kaiser Permanente's mission is to improve the health of the communities served. In recognition of the critical linkages between environmental health and public health, it is Kaiser's desire to limit adverse impacts upon the environment resulting from the siting, design, construction, and operation of our health facilities. We will address the life cycle impacts of facilities through design and construction standards, selection of material and equipment, and maintenance practices. Additionally, KP will require architects, engineers, and contractors to specify commercially available, cost-competitive materials, products, technologies, and processes—where appropriate—that have positive impact or that limit negative impact on environmental quality and human health.

Preventive Medicine for the Environment: Developing and Implementing Environmental Programs that Work

Laura Brannen suggested moving from the theoretical aspects of why healthcare facilities should adopt green principles to how to do it. According to Brannen, healthcare facilities alone generate a tremendous variety and quantity of waste—at least 2 million tons of waste per year—that may represent real occupational and environmental health threats. Healthcare facilities are the fourth largest consumer of energy, spending US $6.5 billion on energy cost alone and accounting for 11% of all commercial energy use. Water consumption and discharge to public sewer systems are excessive. Wastewater contains toxic laboratory and cleaning chemicals and pharmaceutical compounds, many of which are not broken down in sewage treatment plants and are disposed of in landfills, resulting in sewage sludge applied to farmland and released in rivers and streams.

Finally, Brannen sees healthcare facilities of the future that are high-performance buildings that use less energy and less water, require fewer chemicals to maintain, and are designed for maximum operational waste management systems: where materials are purchased with health and environmental considerations, where materials are used efficiently and staff take responsibility for and participate in waste minimization programs, where end-of-life considerations are maximized, and where reuse and recycling are effective.

Redefining Healthy Food: An Ecological Health Approach to Food Production, Distribution, and Procurement

The fifth paper in this series was presented by Jamie Harvie, who discussed the ecological health approach to food production. According to Harvie, food production, distribution, and procurement intersect with a wide variety of issues. Economics, immigration policy, spirituality, agriculture and trade, culture, environment, and nutrition are but several of the myriad concerns associated with the food we grow and eat. There is perhaps no issue that has such a wide depth of actively involved interest. The complexity of interest requires a system, or ecological, approach. Such an approach is challenging because it is not linear and requires observation of the whole context while seeking to understand the connections between the parts.

Hospital food is big business. In 2004 alone, the top healthcare group purchasing organizations purchased approximately US $2.75 billion worth of food. Although patient food receives considerable attention in the media, it is cafeteria and catered food that make up the largest percentage of the food budget, accounting for approximately 55% to 70% of hospital volume.

Hospital and health systems are not only changing procurement practices to support healthy food systems, they are explicitly identifying the link between healthy food systems and healthy patients, communities, and the planet in their policies and programs. These systems are pioneers in an ecological approach to preventive medicine.

(continues)

Toward an Ecological View of Health: An Imperative for the 21st Century

The final paper presented at the conference was by Ted Schettler, MD, MPH. Schettler began by discussing the relationship between human and environmental health. In 2005, the United Nations released the largest assessment ever undertaken of the health of the earth's ecosystems. More than 1,000 experts from 95 countries prepared the report, which was then reviewed by a large independent board of editors and commented on by hundreds of experts and governments before being released.

The Green Building Council of Australia's environmental rating system, Green Star, has now developed tools to assess buildings in the education, retail, and healthcare sectors. The Green Star—Healthcare rating tool, in particular, aims to address the unique qualities, constraints, and opportunities within hospitals and other medical facilities.

However, it remains much harder to measure the true value of a green hospital because the productivity and operation have different measures and often different management. The majority of hospitals will look at patient recovery time, bed turnover, and staff retention to estimate their attributes and performance. The truly green hospital can look at benefits in all of these areas and more, but the situation requires true, holistic investment in people's health.

Finally, Changi General Hospital is Singapore's first purpose-built, multidisciplinary regional hospital, providing healthcare services to approximately 750,000 people in the eastern and northeastern parts of Singapore. Changi General Hospital instilled several green practices within these grounds. Some of these were waste composting from water conservation (the first hospital to use NewWater), increased energy efficiency of their hospital building and installations, waste-minimization methods to control the generation of unnecessary waste in both the administration and day-to-day running of the hospital, and participation in community grassroots education and staff enrichment programs.

▶ Learning Exercise

Using the Centers for Disease Control and Prevention (CDC) Model presented below, choose any new health technology like AI, VR, or perhaps drones, and explain or speculate on their interface with these domains. You may also consider an evidence-based health system innovation instead of a health technology.

In your chosen example, explain how the domains might interact. You may discuss all five or any subset of them. Share your thoughts with other students in a small group, then with the class.

▶ Description of the Science Impact Framework

The framework illustrates the "Historical Tracing Method" with five domains of CDC scientific influence that define degrees of impact that may not be chronological (the degree of impact is not necessarily a progression; therefore, events captured may not be reflected at every domain). In addition, there may be loop-back at any point. Health outcomes are the ultimate goal; they are driven by the five domains of influence.

CASE 15-1 provides a learning opportunity for students as we look to the future.

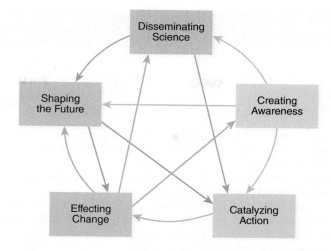

CASE 15-1 Where Else Might We Go?

It can be useful to consider the roads not taken—the measures that have evolved in other, similarly developed countries. This case study briefly reviews the health systems of six roughly comparable countries: Canada, the United Kingdom, Australia, Germany, the Netherlands, and Japan. The approaches are varied, yet all seem to be producing similar results (except costs). Satisfaction surveys for the four English-speaking countries show similar ratings of consumer satisfaction and quality of medical and hospital care; however, self-reported access and expenditures differ widely.

Different Cultures, Different Systems

Canada

Canada's health system initially paralleled the U.S system, but the country switched to a single-payer system incrementally, beginning with initiatives in two provinces. Federal legislation passed in 1957 offered to pay 50% of costs if provinces provided universal hospital coverage; by 1961, all ten provinces were participating. The 1966 Medical Care Act extended this cost-share inducement to universal coverage programs, and universal coverage was fully implemented nationwide in 1971. The federal government's share exceeded 76%, before being lowered.

Key aspects of the Canadian system are:

- Universal coverage under provincial health plans is financed through payroll and income taxes. Many Canadians have private insurance to cover costs the government does not pay and to provide rapid access to scarce services.
- Physicians are typically in private practices, and are paid per visit according to a government fee schedule. Most hospitals are independent public entities that operate within budgets established by the provincial government. Government regulations also affect the prices of prescription drugs.
- Hospitals finance new technology or facilities through the provincial budgeting system, not capital markets. Adoption of new technology such as imaging equipment and surgical capacity is slower than in the United States.
- Rationing occurs through delays in elective services, rather than ability to pay. Lengths of hospital stays have not dropped as rapidly as in U.S. hospitals. Physician visits per person are similar to U.S.

(continues)

CASE 15-1 Where Else Might We Go?   *(continued)*

rates, but percentage of GDP devoted to health care has grown much more slowly. Canada has a similar number of physicians per 1000 population as the United States (2.7 vs. 2.6).

- Concerns exist about access to specialists and primary care after hours. Canadians' levels of satisfaction with their health care are similar to those of U.S. respondents, but they complain a little more about the shortness of physician visits.
- Although it slowed sharply after 1971, growth in per capita spending has picked up since, despite long waits for scanning procedures and "elective" surgery such as hip replacements, cataract removal, and cardiovascular surgery.
- The system has become increasingly fragmented as the provinces have modified their individual systems over the years. Lewis[14] argued that it is "a system in name only."
- Per capita healthcare spending is somewhat lower than in the United States and health outcomes slightly better. No one is sure how much leakage of services and expenditures takes place across the border between the two countries, with U.S. citizens purchasing pharmaceuticals in Canada and Canadians purchasing scarce physician and hospital services in the United States.

England

The British National Health Service (NHS) became a socialized system in 1948 after a gradual movement through voluntary and then mandatory health insurance. Until quite recently, NHS was a government program housed in the Department of Health. Ten strategic health authorities (SHAs) implemented national policies at the regional level. Each general practitioner (GP) operated through a local primary care trust (PCT). PCTs served about 100,000 people each and were responsible for disbursing tax revenues dedicated to health within their service areas. In addition to paying GPs through a system of capitation, allowances, and incentives, PCTs contracted with local consultants (specialists) and the government-owned hospitals. A very small private insurance market was allowed. It has grown in recent years and some physicians practice outside of the NHS. In London, so-called Harley Street physicians cater to the wealthy.

The Health and Social Care Act of 2012 significantly reorganized the NHS. Ostensibly, the reforms were designed to make the system more patient-centric, empower medical providers, increase the focus on clinical outcomes, and provide more local autonomy.

There are really four different health systems: England, Scotland, Wales, and Northern Ireland, with the latter three functioning through block grants from the national government. So, the systems have gradually diverged.

- At the center of the reformed NHS is NHS England with 80% of the population, which was established as the Commissioning Board in October 2012. This independent quasi-governmental agency pushes public funds out to local Clinical Commissioning Groups (CCGs), which replaced PCTs on April 1, 2013. It also promotes quality of care and improvements in health outcomes. The role of the national government has been limited to general oversight of the system and combined strategic leadership for the health and social services systems. SHAs were abolished along with the PCTs.
- CCGs are primarily composed of GPs, but nurses and other providers are represented. The CCGs can commission any health services that meet government standards, including NHS hospitals, consultants (who are typically hospital-based), mental health services, urgent and emergency care, rehabilitation, and community health services.
- The Health and Social Care bill made several other changes to improve coordination, increase democratic input, improve quality and address community public health. For example, leaders of public health, adult social services, children's social services, a consumer representative, and

an elected community representative comprise health and wellbeing boards, which promote coordination across sectors and advise CCGs. An organization called Monitor has authority to license providers beginning April 2014 and is responsible for overseeing the transition of NHS hospitals from government entities to foundations. Public health has become a local responsibility, but a new government agency, Public Health England, performs a national role similar in ways to the role the Centers for Disease Control and Prevention plays in U.S. public health.

- The number of physicians per thousand patients is slightly higher in the United Kingdom than in the United States (2.8 vs. 2.6). British nurses do many things physicians would handle in the United States, including delivering babies.
- Rationing has been based in part on waiting times for treatments for nonacute conditions. These have included cataract removal, hip replacement, and coronary artery bypass surgery, for which patients may wait as much as a year.
- In 2004, the NHS adopted a pay-for-performance system for family physicians that involved 146 quality performance measures. According to Doran et al.,[15] primary care practices met targets for 83% of patients and achieved 97% of the possible points, much more than the 75% anticipated in the budget, resulting in an average of more than $40,000 in additional payments per physician. The result was a substantial budget overrun. Because a major baseline study was not performed, how much of the improvement was due to changed medical care and how much was due to improved documentation is not knowable.
- Long queues were a major political issue in the 1997 elections that brought back the Labour government. That government increased NHS funding, and waiting times dropped. Some management decision-making was also decentralized from the regional SHAs to the local hospitals, whose accountability for quality and cost was increased. At the same time, the government established the National Institute for Health and Care Excellence (NICE) to evaluate procedures, treatments, and technologies and to speed their adoption if the evidence is adequate and favorable. This was in response to reliable evidence of differences in treatments and outcome differences among various geographic areas, regional health authorities, and fund- holder groups.

Australia

Australia has a hybrid public–private healthcare system. A national healthcare system called "Medicare" is financed out of taxation. When established in 1984, Medicare supported government hospitals, medical care, and prescription drugs for the indigent. It also provided grants to state and territorial governments to operate hospitals. The 1999 addition of a Medicare levy—1.5%–2.5% depending on income level—extended these benefits to the general population. Government incentives encourage private insurance, which pays "cost sharing" fees and provides access to private hospitals, specialists, and physicians. About 50% of Australians have private insurance, which pays 11% of healthcare costs.

- Australia has a federal system with the states and territories actually managing the public hospitals and a number of other services, but most primary care and pharmaceutical coverage is paid by the central government.
- Australians seem to have less access problems overall than Canadian and U.S. patients, but they report problems accessing care on nights and weekends and difficulties paying for prescription drugs.
- Australians with insurance entering local public hospitals decide whether to do so as public or private patients. Public patients receive free hospital and physician care. Private patients can choose their doctors. They pay minor charges, but most charges are covered by a combination of Medicare and private insurance.
- Subsidies are limited to pharmaceuticals approved for cost-effectiveness by the independent Pharmaceutical Benefits Advisory Committee.

(continues)

CASE 15-1 Where Else Might We Go? *(continued)*

- Under a program called Lifetime Health Cover, those who join a private health plan before the age of 31 pay a lower premium over their lifetime. Two percent is added to the premium for each year of delay. This is to prevent "hit-and-run" enrollment when people anticipate major expenses and to maintain a larger, healthier risk pool.
- Community rating is mandatory for private health insurance. A "reinsurance" system redistributes the costs of claims among insurers to avoid winners and losers.
- To reduce reliance on public funding, the government provides a 30% rebate on private health insurance costs.
- A government subsidy for the long-term care of older persons includes institutional, community-based, and in-home support. In return, the government controls the supply of long-term beds.
- Australia has 3.5 physicians per 1000 population compared with 2.6 in the United States.

Germany

Chancellor Otto von Bismarck is credited with starting the first national health insurance program in the 1880s. Today, it is built around hundreds of not-for-profit sickness funds that negotiate with labor unions, employers, and providers. The various parties interact quite formally.

- All individuals must have health insurance. A federal unemployment insurance fund pays premiums for the unemployed. A worker's pension fund pays premiums for retired workers. Workers have choices among funds, but funds tend to be linked to an industry or locale.
- Management of the system is split between the states, the Federal government and a number of independent organizations representing employers, providers and insurers. Yet the system is considered very efficient. However, consumer satisfaction tends to be low as well.
- Funds assess premiums on a graduated scale based on income. Co-payments have increased in recent years to cover revenue shortfalls.
- Physician associations receive a fixed amount per person per year, as do hospitals. Hospitals pay hospital-based physicians salaries from their capitation income. Hospitals are reimbursed under a DRG system similar to the U.S. system except that it includes physician services and aftercare for 30 days post discharge. Ambulatory-care physicians are paid either a fee for service or the physician associations pay them a salary from capitated revenues. They generally cannot follow patients into the hospital. Germany has recently started to develop specialized ambulatory care centers for specific diseases with highly integrated services.
- Doctor visits are shorter and more frequent than in the United States, and hospital stays are longer; however, the hospital staffing ratios are much lower. The average cost of a hospital stay in the United States is much greater than that of Germany despite a much longer average length of stay.
- Germany has 4.1 physicians per 1000 population compared with 2.6 in the United States.
- Among developed countries, Germany has the fourth-highest percentage of GDP devoted to health care after the United States, France, and Denmark. Because of cost increases, high unemployment, and an aging population, a 2006 political compromise increased premiums to an average of 15.5% of salaries beginning in 2009. Premiums are pooled, and each insurer receives the same premium per enrollee in an attempt motivate efficiency improvements.

Netherlands

The Netherlands is considered one of the best developed-country health systems.

It has universal coverage, but its delivery system is private with many not-for-profit insurers and independent primary care providers. On top of that there is a mandatory government insurance system for long-term care. Despite premium and co-pay requirements, out-of-pocket costs are low.

- Primary care providers are the gatekeepers in this system. Access to specialists is virtually available only through referral from a GP, including mental health issues. A special program brings mental health services to youth through their schools.
- The Dutch health system is not cheap despite low drug prices and low hospitalization rates.
- This system has focused a great deal on integrated (health and mental) care and coordination of services. Recent legislation (2014 & 2015) has focused on long- term care in the community, on a special program for integrated care for the frail elderly, and psychosocial youth care. These reforms required more involvement by municipalities which had to scramble to build capacity.
- Attempts to allow insurers to limit their networks failed in Parliament in 2014.
- Netherlands institutions while independent are under pressure from the government to follow evidence-based practices.
- The Netherlands has an unusually small number of pharmacists. In 2014 it had 4.27 physicians per 1000 compared to 3.35 for the U.S. International comparisons for nurses are difficult because their roles vary so much. In the United States many nurses have roles outside direct delivery due to the complexity of our insurance systems.
- The Dutch public reports more satisfaction with their health system than do their neighbors.

Japan

Employment-based health insurance is the core of Japan's health system, and it continues to produce the best health outcomes of any of the systems mentioned here; however, some ascribe much of the differential outcomes to demographic and lifestyle issues, especially diet.[1] There is also a national health insurance program financed with national and local taxes. Premiums are scaled to family income. Households not covered by employment-based insurance must belong to community insurance programs under the national plan. Retirees are covered by their former employers or their community plans. There is a high-risk pool available to literally thousands of insurance schemes. The co-pay for most services is 30%.

- The government sets fee schedules for physicians at a level much below U.S. rates. Fees are identical for all plans; however, patients often add 3% or 4% "gifts" to their payments. Fee levels are modified based on utilization. If too many of a procedure are done, the fee is lowered.
- There are both nonprofit and for-profit hospitals, and hospitals may be owned by doctors.
- Most physicians work out of large clinics, some of which are associated with hospitals, and are reluctant to send patients into the hospital because they cannot follow them once they are admitted. Japan has 2.4 physicians per 1000 population compared to the United States with 2.6.
- Specialists are hospital employees and earn less than primary care physicians.
- Clinics usually dispense their own drugs.
- Japanese patients have many more, briefer visits and many more prescriptions than their U.S. counterparts. They also have many fewer admissions, although lengths of stay tend to be much longer.
- There are fewer doctors per capita in Japan than in the United States, and waiting lines tend to be managed on a first-come, first-served basis.
- Japanese hospitals are considered by many to have somewhat outdated equipment and shabby facilities. Physicians do not seem to be customer oriented or highly motivated to meet patients' affective needs.

The government is aware of the collision course the health system is on with a decreasing and aging population.

(continues)

CASE 15-1 Where Else Might We Go? *(continued)*

Other OECD Countries

Most other Organization for Economic Cooperation and Development (OECD) countries have more physicians and nurses per thousand population than the United States. The Netherlands has one of the highest ratios of nurses and recently increased the roles of nurses in primary care. France, Sweden, and Spain had high ratios of physicians per 1000 population (3.3, 4.2, and 3.92, respectively). All physician per 1000 population statistics cited herein come from the OECD data base.

Some Repeating Themes

A number of themes recur in the systems of these various countries. Some represent ideas that have been tried in the United States (under the ACA, in some instances), but all might warrant further consideration as the U.S. system changes over the next 10–20 years.

Universal Coverage

Health care is provided to all. Often it is through a patchwork of public and private funds, but every effort is made to have everyone in the system. General tax revenues (income, payroll, and value added taxes) are used extensively to fund health care, but in most cases, there is a mixture of additional revenue sources, including patient co-payment, employment-based insurance, retirement funds, local government revenues, and private insurance. This patchwork of payment mechanisms does not leave large gaps of uninsured or underinsured citizens. Private insurance and private care are available to those who choose to pay more. Where co-pays are required, a careful effort is made to make sure that ability to pay does not control access to basic care. In the United States, there have been numerous attempts to expand coverage over the last several decades, with ACA being the most ambitious attempt to approach universal coverage.

The Public-Private Pendulum

Anell[16] used the "public-private pendulum" analogy with respect to Sweden. But similar issues have been playing out in England, France, The Netherlands and especially in Australia which has seen at least five changes in the way health care is financed since 1976.[17] For example, while France has universal coverage, 96% of its population also carries complementary health insurance. Vouchers to purchase the private complementary insurance are available to the poor.[18]

Centralized Versus Decentralized Delivery System Controls

Country after country that started out with a centralized healthcare system has decentralized operational control to district or regional authorities. Sometimes their boards are elected separately from the local administrative body. The objectives here are multiple. Sometimes it is privatization, sometimes it is seeking more patient-centered care, and often it is aimed at adding regional and local revenue sources to the mix.

Hospitals Are Budget Constrained

Since the introduction of prospective payment based on diagnostic-related group classifications, hospitals in the United States have operated more as cost centers than revenue centers. A number of countries have established global hospital budgets or capitation budgets for hospitals, often administered through local authorities or trusts. Capital investment is constrained to avoid a hospital arms race.

Specialists Are Salaried and PCPs Incentivized

Income of the universal coverage system is used to pay the salaries of specialists, whereas fee-for-service payments reimburse the primary care providers. They serve as gatekeepers for referrals to specialists and hospitals and do not follow patients into the hospital. They are motivated, therefore, to avoid unnecessary hospitalizations. The British experiment with pay-for-performance was sufficiently successful that. Epstein[19] argued that its time has come for the United States. One might also see it as a way to boost the incomes of primary care physicians in the United States sufficiently to attract new practitioners and bolster the currently dwindling supply.[20]

Large Premium and Risk Pools Are Maintained

Individuals are compelled to belong to one health plan or another. Young and healthy individuals cannot opt out, or where they can, incentives are provided to try to keep them in. Trusts serve very large employers, but the needs of small businesses and individuals are met through required community rating, local community health plans, and tax subsidies. Large premium and risk pools are built in to level the playing field and hold down administrative and marketing costs.

Systems Integration

The integration of the system is provided at the governmental rather than the institutional level. Circuit breakers in the system, especially between hospitals, specialists, and primary care practices, keep individuals and institutions from maximizing utilization. Incentives focus on motivating primary care physicians to control costs and improve quality.

Rationalization and Standardization

A trend toward decentralization of healthcare services is offset in part by setting up staff units that analyze and report on current medical technology, evidence about best practices, and evaluation of the cost-effectiveness of common interventions. These recommendations will probably be worked increasingly into pay-for-performance systems. For example, the Netherlands started with a personal healthcare budget for those in long-term care, but has had to rein in expenses after an expenditure growth rate of 23%.[21]

Labor Substitution

Many countries with lower costs seem to have not only lower professional incomes, but also substitute nurses and pharmacists for physicians, and physician generalists for specialists in their delivery systems.

Pharmaceutical Costs

Most developed countries except New Zealand and the United States constrain or ban direct-to-consumer advertising for prescription drugs (a cost that reached $4.5 billion annually in the United States in 2009), and rely on recommendations by physicians for decision-making. The profit margins of pharmaceutical companies are constrained through a number of mechanisms, depending on what alternatives exist for payment in the national system. In a few cases, physicians may supplement their revenue by dispensing in their practices.

CHAPTER ACRONYMS

AI Artificial intelligence
CAS Complex adaptive system
CDC Centers for Disease Control and Prevention
CMS Centers for Medicare and Medicaid Services
NHS National Health Service
SHAs strategic health authorities
GP general practitioner
PCT primary care trust
CCGs Clinical Commissioning Groups

NICE National Institute for Health and Care Excellence
OECD Organization for Economic Cooperation and DevelopmentDNA deoxyribonucleic acid
DEI Diversity, equity, and inclusion
HER Electronic health record
IoT Internet of Things
VR Virtual reality
WHO World Health Organization

References

1. U.S. Department of Labor Bureau of Labor Statistics Health Care and Social Assistance: NAICS 62. Updated August 26, 2021. Accessed August 31, 2021. https://www.bls.gov/iag/tgs/iag62.htm#workforce

2. Healthcare workforce analysis: Demand for healthcare workers will outpace supply by 2025. Mercer. Accessed June 6, 2021. https://www.mercer.us/our-thinking/career/demand-for-healthcare-workers-will-outpace-supply-by-2025.html

3. Bærøe K, Miyata-Sturm A, Henden E. How to achieve trustworthy artificial intelligence for health. *Bull World Health Organ.* 2020;98(4):257-262. doi: 10.2471/BLT.19.237289

4. Desai AN. Artificial intelligence: promise, pitfalls, and perspective. *JAMA.* 2020;323(24):2448-2449. doi: 10.1001/jama.2020.8737

5. Amisha F, Malik P, Pathania M, Rathaur VK. Overview of artificial intelligence in medicine. *J Family Med Prim Care.* 2019;8(7):2328-2331. doi: 10.4103/jfmpc.jfmpc_440_19

6. Gregory RL. The genius of Alan Turing (1912–1954). *Perception.* 1983;12(6):647–649. doi: 10.1068/p120647

7. Esposito J. How the promise of artificial intelligence will disrupt healthcare. *Health Manag Technol.* 2018;39(1):15.

8. Chow YW, Susilo W, Phillips J, Baek JS, Vlahu-Gjorgievska E. Video games and virtual reality as persuasive technologies for health care: an overview. *J Wirel Mob Netw Ubiquitous Comput Dependable Appl.* 2017;8(3):18-35. doi: 10.22667/JOWUA.2017.09.30.018

9. McConnell, CR, Human Resource Management in Health Care. Burlington, MA: Jones and Bartlett Learning. 2021.

10. Anderson C. Nearly 30,000 weapons seized at Northeast Ohio's Cleveland Clinic facilities in 2018. *19 News.* Updated February 28, 2019. Accessed September 26, 2021. https://www.cleveland19.com/2019/02/28/nearly-weapons-seized-cleveland-clinic-facilities-ceo-calls-violence-against-health-professionals-an-epidemic/

11. Britnell M. *Human: Solving the Global Workforce Crisis in Healthcare.* Oxford University Press; 2019.

12. Paavola A. HCA buys majority stake in multistate nursing school. *Becker's Hospital Review.* Published January 7, 2020. Accessed June 11, 2021. https://www.beckershospitalreview.com/hospital-transactions-and-valuation/hca-buys-majority-stake-in-multistate-nursing-school.html

13. Hahn A SJ. Foundations and health care reform: policy brief: improving workforce efficiency. Accessed May 14, 2020. http://sillermancenter.brandeis.edu/PDFs/Workforce Policy Brief in conf template v2.pdf

14. Lewis S. A system in name only—access, variation, and reform in Canada's provinces. N Engl J Med. 2015;372(6):497-500.

15. Doran T, Fullwood C, Gravelle H, et al. Pay-for-performance programs in family practices in the United Kingdom. *N Engl J Med.* 2006;355(4):375-384.

16. Anell A. The -public-private pendulum—patient choice and equity in Sweden. *N Engl J Med.* 2015;372(1), 1-4.

17. Hall J. Australian health care—the challenge of reform in a fragmented system. *N Engl J Med.* 2015;373(6):493-497.

18. Steffen M. Universalism, responsiveness, sustainability—regulating the French health care system. *N Engl J Med.* 2016;374(5):401-405.

19. Epstein AM. Paying for performance in the United States and abroad. *N Engl J Med.* 2006;355(4):406-408.

20. Basch P. 2006. Pay-for-performance: too much of a good thing—or too worried about the wrong things? Health Affairs Letters. Accessed January 6, 2007. http://content.healthaffairs.org/cgi/eletters/25/5/w412

21. van Ginneken E. Perennial health care reform—the long Dutch quest for cost control and quality improvement. N Engl J M. 2015;373(10), 885-889.

Further Reading

1. Interprofessional Education Collaborative. Core Competencies for Interprofessional Collaborative Practice: 2016 Update. Published 2016. Accessed February 13, 2021. https://nebula.wsimg.com/2f68a39520b03336b41038c370497473?AccessKeyId=DC06780E69ED19E2B3A5&disposition=0&alloworigin=1

2. Interprofessional Education Collaborative. Team-based competencies, buisling a shared foundation for education and clinical practice. Published 2011. Accessed February 13, 2021. https://nebula.wsimg.com/191adb6df3208c643f339a83d47a3f28?AccessKeyId=DC06780E69ED19E2B3A5&disposition=0&alloworigin=1

3. Deloitte Center for Health Solutions. The future of work: how can health systems and health plans prepare and transform their workforce? Published 2019. Accessed June 11, 2021. https://www2.deloitte.com/content/dam/insights/us/articles/4816_fow_health-systems/DI_FoW_health-systems.pdf

4. Dixon-Fyle S, Dolan K, Hunt V, Prince S. Diversity wins: how inclusion matters. Published May 19, 2020. Accessed June 10, 2021. https://www.mckinsey.com/featured-insights/diversity-and-inclusion/diversity-wins-how-inclusion-matters#

5. Graham N. The why behind DEI: how diversity, equity, and inclusion initiatives benefit businesses. Workhuman Blog. Accessed June 10, 2021. https://www.workhuman.com/resources/globoforce-blog/the-why-behind-d-i-how-diversity-and-inclusion-initiatives-benefit-business

6. Johnson JA, Rossow CC. *Health Organizations: Theory, Behavior, and Development*. 2nd ed. Jones & Bartlett Learning; 2019.

7. American Hospital Association. *TrendWatch: Hospital and Health System Workforce Strategic Planning*. American Hospital Association; 2020. Accessed June 6, 2021. https://www.aha.org/system/files/media/file/2020/01/aha-trendwatch-hospital-and-health-system-workforce-strategic-planning2_0.pdf

Appendix: Canadian Health System

Health System Focus on Canada

Contributed by Oluwatosin Omolade Dotun-Olujinmi, DHA, and Felix Asekomhe, MD, CCFP

▶ A Brief History of the Canadian Health System

Health systems consist of all the organizations, institutions, and resources dedicated to producing health actions that reduce inequalities, improves, and protects health.[1] As such, the importance of health systems to the healthy development of individuals, families, and societies can not be overemphasized. However, it is important to note that historical and sociocultural factors contribute significantly to the evolution of any nation's health system,[2,3] and the Canadian health system is not excluded.

The Canadian health system evolved from an independent physician–patient perspective to include some government involvement in the 19th century, and with extensive religious support, the first hospital in Quebec was opened in 1639.[2,4] However, the government's involvement progressively intensified in the financing and delivery of clinical health services through the provincial governments.[2] But it was not until the 1930s that the government became actively involved in health delivery, which was marked by the endorsement of the public health insurance program by the Saskatchewan Medical Association in 1933.[2,5] About a decade afterward, a bill for a national health insurance program was written in Ottawa but failed due to a lack of consensus. As such, the healthcare amendment remained at the provincial level.[2] It was not until 1957, that the federal government enacted the National Hospital and Diagnostic Services Act,[2] which was adopted in all the 10 provinces.

The National Hospital and Diagnostic Services Act enabled an equal hospital-cost sharing between the provincial and federal government for Canadian residents, and constitutionally established the role of the federal government in health care.[2,6,7] Five years later, this act was improved upon through policy deliberation in Saskatchewan, resulting in the Medical Care Insurance Act. This act allowed universal coverage for services provided by physicians in the province and, also became attractive to other provinces and the federal.[2] Hence, in 1966, the federal government passed the Medical Care Act designed to provide universal coverage for physician services under provincially administered programs through equal cost-sharing with the provinces.[2,8] This relates to cash contributions relating to criteria and conditions in respect of insured health services to assure the health of Canadian residents.[9]

The legislation of the Hospital Insurance and Diagnostic Services Act and the Medical Care Act escalated health care costs, thereby necessitating the enactment of the Federal–Provincial Fiscal Arrangements and the Established Programs Financing Act in 1977 to curb the growing cost of health care.[10] This act allowed the federal government to allocate to the provinces combined funding for health care and postsecondary education in an effort to control cost. This was not in the favor of the provincial governments, as they were confronted with infuriated consumers and health-care workforce unions and associations.[10] In response to the growing conflicts and strong advocacy, the federal government revisited the existing four principles of the Medical Care Act, and the tenet of accessibility was added, resulting in the Canada Health Act in 1984.[10]

Canada's Medicare can be considered as a collection of provincial and territorial health insurance plans that is subject to national standards,[11] as shown in **FIGURE A-1** below, and after its enactment, there was notable reform to the legislation to include the Canada Health and Social Transfer legislation in 1995.[12] The legislation of the federal government to increase funds to support primary health care, pharmaceutical management, and technological innovation in delivering health care followed in 2000.[12] Additional reforms were implemented with the establishment of the 10 Year Plan to Strengthen Health Care in 2004, which addressed pertinent issues such as wait times, management, Indigenous health, primary health care, and more.[12] However, the establishment of the Mental Health Commission of Canada and the Canadian Partnership Against Cancer Corporation signifies the growing burden of noncommunicable diseases and mental health amongst Canadians and the need for intervention in these areas.

Several reforms within the Canadian health system demonstrate the efforts of the federal, provincial, and territorial governments in overcoming fragmented institutional structures and decentralization of power, to create insurance models that eliminate financial barriers to care.[11] However, to ensure a health system that is responsive to Canadian's changing health needs, reforms of delivery models and on the social determinants of health by all stakeholders is needed, to achieve a high-quality system built on evidence-based practice and the Canadian values of equity and solidarity.[11]

▶ Overview of Canada's Current Health System

Since the establishment of universal health care coverage, significant changes have occurred within Canada's health system. These changes are evident in the country's governance and leadership, health financing, physical and human resources, and health service delivery.[2,13]

Governance and Leadership: Governance, organization, and delivery of health services is extremely decentralized, but collectively, the federal, provincial, and territorial governments of Canada continue to fund a single-payer health system through transfer payments.[13]

Federal Level: The federal government continues to ensure that the key elements of the Canada Health Act are met by the provinces and territories while providing funds and services to marginalized groups such as Indigenous Peoples, qualified veterans Canadian Armed Forces members, refugees, and prisoners in federal jails.[12,13]

Furthermore, the role of the federal government evolved following several recalls of consumers' products in the past decade from just health care provision to health protection.[14] This role is fulfilled through Health

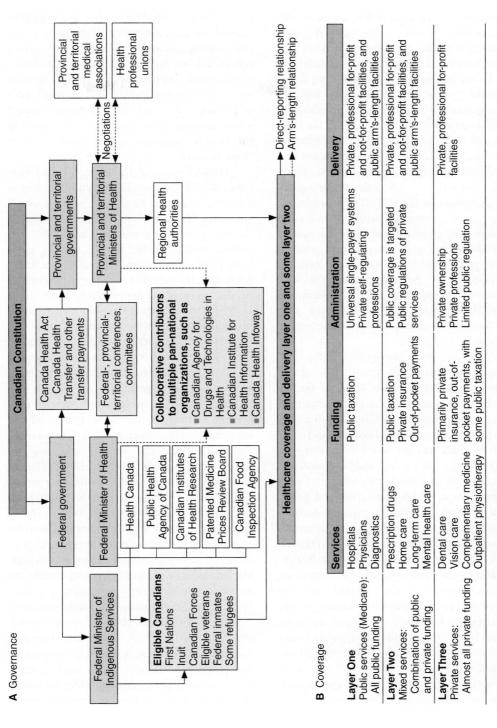

FIGURE A-1 Overview of Canada's Health System

Reproduced from Martin D, Miller AP, Quesnel-Vallée A, Caron NR, Vissandjée B, Marchildon GP. Canada's universal health-care system: achieving its potential. Lancet. 2018;391(10131):1717-1735. doi: 10.1016/S0140-6736(18)30181-8

Canada, the federal agency that consults with the Canadian public, industry, and other stakeholders in the development of laws that protect health and safety and helps to interpret and clarify the legislation surrounding drugs and health products.[13,15] Additionally, with the growing need to improve public health, the federal government operates through the Public Health Agency of Canada in immunization initiatives, infectious diseases prevention and surveillance, emergency preparedness, travel health, and more.[13,16] The role of this agency was paramount in the COVID-19 pandemic, as the agency coordinated with provinces and territories on policies and response strategies.[13] The federal government is also involved in drug price regulation through the Patented Medicine Prices Review Board (PMPRB), in research through the Canadian Institutes of Health Research, and recently in a pan-Canadian system of outpatient pharmaceutical coverage.[13]

Provincial and Territorial Levels: The provinces and territories continue to direct and provide the majority of Canada's health-care services, meeting the national principles in the Canada Health Act.[15] The health coverage is for medically essential hospital and other health facilities services, and it is funded with assistance from federal cash and tax transfers.[15] Moreover, the provinces and territories plan and implement health promotion and public health programs as well as negotiate fee schedules with health professionals.[15] Initially, health planning was conducted through regional health authorities (RHAs) to improve health-care delivery and control cost by decentralizing decision making.[13,15,17] But recently, there has been a trend towards increased administrative centralization by single provincial agencies, as most health professions self-regulate under legal frameworks established by provincial and territorial governments.[17]

Furthermore, the provincial and territorial governments extend benefits not included in the Canada Health Act, such as drugs prescribed outside hospitals, ambulance costs, and hearing, vision, and dental care for certain groups like low-income residents and seniors.[15] Nonetheless, supplementary health services are mostly privately financed through out-of-pocket, individual, or employment-based group insurance plan coverage,[15] necessitating the need for increased health funds to cover these services.

Health Financing: The World Health Organization (WHO) identified health financing as a critical success factor for any health system,[2] and Canada's health system is 70% financed through general tax revenues and 30% from private funds.[18] WHO stated that "a good health financing system raises adequate funds for health, in ways that ensure people can use needed services and are protected from financial risks or hardship at the point of care while providing incentives for providers."[19]

The question of Canada having adequate funds for its health system has been a debate topic for years, especially with the continual growth in health spending since 2017.[13] The increasing cost of healthcare delivery may present a threat to the sustainability of the universal health coverage that has become Canada's pride. The federal spending on health, including the Canada Health Transfer, currently surpasses $43 billion per year,[20] which is more than 15% of total program spending in Ottawa's budget.[19] While provincial and territorial health financing includes over 20% of funds received from transfer payments on a per capita basis, differences in population needs or costs of delivering health care are not a consideration,[13] necessitating private health financing to account for this difference.

Though Canada's share of private health expenditures has been stable over the past 2 decades, nonetheless, it is high in comparison with some other Organisation for Economic Co-operation and Development (OECD) countries due to the narrowness of universal health coverage, which excludes major health goods and services such as prescription medications.[13] For the effectiveness, efficiency, and sustainability of Canada's health system, analysis of the sources of funding channeled to the health system, risk pooling in sharing the burden of health costs through cross-subsidization, and the utilization of different types of payment mechanisms must be reviewed frequently.[19] In addition to the health system's critical success factors discussed above, other factors such as the health workforce and physical resources, including medical technology and health information technology,[2] are worth reviewing within the Canadian health system.

Physical and Human Resources: Over the past 2 decades, most small hospitals in Canada have been closed, and acute care services have been consolidated.[17] Likewise, the number of acute care beds per capita decreased somewhat due to increased day surgeries and shortened discharges and improved noncommunicable management care, which led to reduced hospitalizations.[13] Still, in comparison with other OECD countries, the figures for hospital beds and medical imaging are relatively small.[17] The Canadian Agency for Drugs and Technologies in Health noted in their 2019–2020 report that there are approximately 549 computed tomography (CT) and 378 magnetic resonance imaging (MRI) scanners in Canada.[21] This number is relatively low to serve the entire Canadian population.

Similarly, the integration of information communication technology (ICT) in health care has been rather slow in Canada despite its potential to improve the efficiency and effectiveness of health care, patient safety, and quality of care.[21,22] The quality of health care has been enhanced by ICT by enabling increased adherence to guidelines, enhancing disease surveillance, and decreasing medication errors.[23] The need for increased integration of ICT in clinical care to transform Canada's health system cannot be overemphasized.

According to WHO, the healthcare workforce must be adequate and equally distributed to achieve the best health outcomes.[2] In Canada, there is an established healthcare workforce shortage, especially with physicians and nurses. These groups are not only lacking in number, but they are also unequally distributed across the country in comparison to other OECD countries.[13,24] The immigration of foreign-born health professionals to Canada has been assisting in filling gaps, especially in underserved rural areas.[25] Still, increased investment, accreditation and licensure facilitation, and retention efforts are needed to ensure timely integration of these health professionals into the health system to continue to bridge the shortage gap.[25]

The COVID-19 pandemic has further threatened healthcare workforce supply in Canada, as healthcare workers get disproportionately infected. For example, in Ontario, infected healthcare workers consisted of about 20% of COVID-19 cases by the end of July 2020.[26,27] This percentage is higher than the estimated global rate of healthcare worker infection (14%).[26,28] This calls for concerted efforts amongst all key players within the Canadian health system to develop a more sustainable healthcare workforce for health service delivery.

Health Services Delivery: In *Comparative Health Systems: A Global Perspective*, authors Johnson, Stoskopf, and Shi stated that WHO's critical success factor for a health system is the ability to deliver safe and effective health interventions in a prompt, cost-effective manner, and without financial risk.[2] Importantly, during the COVID-19 pandemic, the federal, provincial, and territorial governments provided services to manage the pandemic. Family physicians remain gatekeepers within the Canadian health system, while most acute care is delivered in hospitals at no cost to patients,[13] and drugs administered are covered under the universal Medicare. This financial protection does not extend to dental, vision, and prescription drugs outside the hospital, nor to nonphysician mental health care,[13] requiring the federal, provincial, and territorial governments to provide coverage for these important healthcare needs to disadvantaged groups.

Furthermore, more Canadians are becoming dissatisfied with health services delivery, as they are confronted with long wait times for specialist services, advanced diagnostics, nonurgent surgery, or while accessing care from urban hospital emergency departments.[13] Likewise, access to primary care is a challenge in remote areas where the shortage of family physicians persists.[13] Nevertheless, the Canadian health system seems to be performing well to some extent, as most health status, access-to-care, and quality-of-care indicators showed Canada to be above the international average.[29]

▶ Major Health System Innovations

The importance of continual innovation within the Canadian health system was emphasized when the federal government launched the Advisory Panel on Healthcare Innovation in 2014.[30] The purpose of the panel is to identify health system innovations that will improve the quality and accessibility of care, while conserving cost, to curb growth in health spending.[30] The critical access of healthcare innovation includes technological transformation via digital health (eHealth).[30]

eHealth: Canadian healthcare systems have undergone immense change due the impacts of new technologies.[31] The provincial government invested in health information and communication technology infrastructures with plans to create electronic health records (EHRs) for all provincial residents.[13] Since the 2000s, information technology has become a standard communication tool in

health care along with other point-of-care data.[32] EHRs have enabled accessibility of health records by authorized healthcare providers, at different care points, while protecting the privacy of patients.[32] This innovation has enabled improved workflow by enhancing accessibility, minimizing errors, and decreasing physical labor, resulting in timely quality care and patient safety.[32]

Furthermore, innovation has enabled better operational performance and financial outcomes at the administrative and organizational levels through the elimination of paper files, the associated handling and storage expenses, and reductions in billing errors.[32,33] Additionally, innovation has enabled data availability and analysis, generating findings that have assisted to inform public health actions, resulting in improved population health. Data from EHRs have assisted in research that has translated to improved societal outcomes.[32,34]

Furthermore, the implementation and utilization of EHRs have contributed to the regeneration of primary health care by enabling the effective coordination and integration of services between care providers.[12] The utilization and application of EHRs are continually optimized to adaptable component-based architectures that can operate perfectly within the workflow of the evolving Canadian healthcare environment.[35]

Integrated Care: Numerous programs such as Health Links in Ontario, Family Medicine Groups in Quebec, Divisions of Family Practice in British Columbia, and the Regulated Health Professions Network in Nova Scotia are established for severely sick patients with complex needs to provide improved integration and coordination of care.[36] Ontario also implemented community-based and multidisciplinary primary care models and bundled payments across different providers, which are designed to improve care coordination for patients as they transition from the hospital to the community.[36]

Universal Drug Coverage: In 2019, the federal government established an Advisory Council on the Implementation of National Pharmacare with an interim report for the possibility of establishing universal drug coverage for prescription drugs prescribed outside of hospitals.[36]

The COVID-19 pandemic seems to have affected the acceleration of this innovation, but the eventual implementation of national drug coverage will denote the biggest expansion of public funding and coverage since the enactment of the Canada Health Act of 1984.[36]

Administrative Centralization: Canada has seen the consolidation of health authorities into centralized decision-making structures to improve efficiency and reduce cost.[12,13,36] For example, in 2017, Saskatchewan consolidated its 12 regional health authorities into a single provincial health authority, Manitoba established a single provincial organization termed "Shared Health" to centralize clinical and administrative services, and Ontario established a single provincial agency in 2019 by consolidating several provincial arm's-length agencies and 14 sub-provincial health authorities.[36] These structural reforms are meant to enhance efficiency.

Primary Care Reform: In the early 2000s, Canadian provinces and territories employed several tools, strategies, and policies to strengthen primary care delivery.[37] These reforms targeted provider reimbursement, organizational infrastructure, quality and safety, and the healthcare workforce in response to the aging population and noncommunicable diseases emerging as a public health priority.[12,37,38]

Reforms focused primarily on primary healthcare delivery, which included the establishment of an increased number of community primary healthcare centers that provide 24-hour healthcare service; development of multidisciplinary, interprofessional primary healthcare teams; greater emphasis on promoting health, preventing illness and injury, and management of noncommunicable diseases; increased coordination and integration of comprehensive health services; and improved work environments for primary healthcare providers.[12,37] These reforms enabled Canada to increase its primary care practitioner-to-population ratio above the average for OECD member countries.[38] Likewise, primary care family medicine became a choice area of specialization for new residents, and primary care providers' recruitment and retention were enhanced through the new model.[38]

The reforms also allowed Canadian provinces to implement a new model of payment (i.e., blended payment arrangements, or fee-for-service systems with capitation or incentive payments) rather than solely a fee-for-service model.[38] Evidence showed that these new models of compensation enhanced evidence-based preventive care and dissemination of information for accessing after-hours care, thereby reducing utilization of emergency care.[38,39] Furthermore, evidence showed that primary physicians' productivity and quality of care had been enhanced because of the reforms.[38]

▶ Emerging Challenges

For decades, the governments have been in pursuit of improved health system performance by addressing persistent issues, such as long wait times for specialist and elective surgical care, fragmented and poorly coordinated care, poor access to non-Medicare services, and disparities in Indigenous health in contrast to other Canadians.[13] However, the COVID-19 pandemic brought emerging challenges to the Canadian health systems, including:

Universal Drug Coverage Challenge: Beginning in 2018, there was an emerging expert and public consensus to include outpatient pharmaceutical therapies in Canada's universal health coverage.[13] However, the COVID-19 pandemic diverted the government and public's attention from Pharmacare to long-term care reform in response to large percentages of cases and deaths in long-term homes and facilities,[13] which somewhat slowed or may threaten the adoption of the proposed universal drug coverage plan.

Uneven Healthcare Spending: Governmental deficits at various levels and public debts because of the massive pandemic expense will inevitably result in health spending restraint after the crisis, thereby affecting other aspects of health.[13] An additional $29 billion in COVID-19-related health system spending was announced in 2020 across the three levels of government for personal protective equipment, screening capacity, compensation of health workers, and vulnerable populations.[40,41] This unanticipated expenditure will result in uneven healthcare spending as unavailability of funds for other public health priorities may persist, such as for noncommunicable diseases and mental health. The COVID-19 pandemic also represents a continued fiscal pressure that will affect both public- and private-sector health care spending in Canada, especially over the short-to-medium term.[41]

Obesity: The rate of obesity is growing rapidly in Canada and negatively impacting overall health status. Additionally, with the COVID-19 pandemic, structural measures such as quarantine restrictions increased rates of sedentary lifestyle, and increased calorie intake has resulted in a higher rate of obesity.[40] This will pose an increased financial burden on the health system due to direct costs in routine management care and indirect costs because of lost workforce productivity.

Other emerging challenges are:

Opioid Crisis: Opioid use disorders have emerged as a major public health crisis in Canada.[13] Opioid overprescribing, a possible result of misleading marketing practices, has played a role in the current opioid crisis.[42] The 2017 Canadian opioid guidelines recommended a multidisciplinary program for patients with chronic noncancer pain using opioids and experiencing serious challenges in tapering.[42] However, accessing these multidisciplinary clinics is a challenge, as there is 1 multidisciplinary pain clinic per 258,000 people.[42] These clinics are mostly located in urban or tertiary care centers, presenting accessibility challenges to individuals in rural areas.[42] Sadly, the services provided at these multidisciplinary clinics are not covered by provincial health plans, and these clinics are not sufficiently equipped to overcome the current opioid crisis.[42]

Vaccine Hesitancy: Vaccine hesitancy is another emerging public health challenge in Canada.[13] 2017 data showed that while most Canadian parents agree that childhood vaccines are safe, there are still apprehensions and knowledge gaps related to vaccines. As such, Canada has not been able to reach its national coverage goals for routine childhood vaccines.[13] Recently, vaccine hesitancy in relation to COVID-19 has been evident, as only approximately 75% of Canadians plan to receive one of the vaccines.[43] Considering WHO's statement that one of the worst threats to global health is vaccine hesitancy, it is critical to gain insights into this emerging challenge.

References

1. World Health Organization. *The World Health Report 2000: Health Systems: Improving Performance.* World Health Organization; 2000. Accessed February 1, 2020. https://www.who.int/whr/2000/en/whr00_en.pdf

2. Johnson JA, Stoskopf C, Shi L. *Comparative Health Systems: A Global Perspective.* 2nd ed. Jones & Barlett Learning; 2018.

3. Starr P. *The Social Transformation of American Medicine: The Rise of a Sovereign Profession and the Making of a Vast Industry.* Basic Books, Inc.; 1982.

4. Roemer MI. *National Health Systems of the World: Volume I: Countries.* Oxford University Press; 1991.

5. Ostry A. The roots of North America's first comprehensive public health insurance system. *Hygiea Internationalis.* 2001;2(1):25-44. doi: 10.3384/hygiea.1403-8668.012125

6. Bernier J. *Disease, Medicine, and Society in Canada: A Historical Overview.* Canadian Historical Association; 2003. Accessed February 1, 2021. https://cha-shc.ca/_uploads/5c38afd70d7cd.pdf

7. Vayda E. The Canadian health care system: an overview. *J Public Health Policy.* 1986;7(2):205-210.

8. Iglehart JL. Revisiting the Canadian health care system. *N Engl J Med.* 2000;342(26):2007-2012. doi: 10.1056/NEJM200006293422624

9. Government of Canada. *Canada Health Act.* R.S.C., 1985, c. C-6. Updated August 25, 2021. Accessed September 2, 2021. https://laws.justice.gc.ca/eng/acts/C-6/FullText.html

10. Canadian Museum of History. Making Medicare: history of health care in Canada, 1914–2007. Accessed February 3, 2021. https://www.historymuseum.ca/cmc/exhibitions/hist/medicare/medic-6h01e.html

11. Martin D, Miller AP, Quesnel-Vallée A, Caron NR, Vissandjée B, Marchildon GP. Canada's universal health-care system: achieving its potential. *Lancet.* 2018;391(10131):1717-1735. doi: 10.1016/S0140-6736(18)30181-8

12. Government of Canada. Canada's health care system. Updated September 17, 2019. Accessed February 3, 2021. https://www.canada.ca/en/health-canada/services/health-care-system/reports-publications/health-care-system/canada.html

13. Marchildon GP, Allin S, Merkur S. Canada: health system review 2020. *Health Syst Transit.* 2020;22(3):i-194. Accessed February 3, 2021. https://apps.who.int/iris/bitstream/handle/10665/336311/HiT-22-3-2020-eng.pdf

14. Bapuji H, Morris K. Consumer product safety in Canada: from enacting to acting. *Policy Options.* Published April 1, 2011. Accessed February 3, 2021. https://policyoptions.irpp.org/magazines/budget-2011/consumer-product-safety-in-canada-from-enacting-to-acting/

15. Government of Canada. Drug and health products. Updated July 22, 2021. Accessed September 2, 2021. https://www.canada.ca/en/health-canada/services/drugs-health-products.html

16. Government of Canada. Public Health Agency of Canada. Updated August 6, 2021. Accessed September 2, 2021. https://www.canada.ca/en/public-health.html

17. Marchildon GP. Health systems in transition: Canada. *Health Syst Transit.* 2013;15(1). Accessed February 5, 2021. https://www.euro.who.int/__data/assets/pdf_file/0011/181955/e96759.pdf

18. Canadian Institute for Health Information. Health spending. Accessed September 26, 2021. https://www.cihi.ca/en/health-spending

19. World Health Organization. Health financing in the Western Pacific. Accessed February 6, 2021. https://www.who.int/westernpacific/health-topics/health-financing

20. Speer S. The Federal Department of Health nears 100: the origins and evolution of the federal role in health care and the case for reform? Macdonald-Laurier Institute. Published August 2018. Accessed February 6, 2021. https://macdonaldlaurier.ca/files/pdf/MLI_BetterHealth%232_FinalWeb.pdf

21. Chao YS, Sinclair A, Morrison A, Hafizi D Pyke L. *CADTH Health Technology Review: The Canadian Medical Imaging Inventory 2019–2020.* Canadian Agency for Drugs and Technologies in Health; 2021. Accessed February 7, 2021. https://cadth.ca/sites/default/files/ou-tr/op0546-cmii3-final-report.pdf

22. Kabashiki IR, Moneke NI. The impact of the use of health information and communication technology on health care delivery in Manitoba, Canada. *J Hosp Adm.* 2014;3(6). doi: 10.5430/jha.v3n6p8

23. Chaudhry B, Wang J, Wu S, et al. Systematic review: impact of health information technology on quality, efficiency, and costs of medical care. *Ann Intern Med.* 2006;144(10):742-752. doi: 10.7326/0003-4819-144-10-200605160-00125

24. Malko AV, Huckfeldt V. Physician shortage in Canada: a review of contributing factors. *Glob J Health Sci.* 2017;9(9). doi: 10.5539/gjhs.v9n9p68

25. Dumont J, Zurn P, Church J, Thi CL. *International Mobility of Health Professionals and Health Workforce Management in Canada: Myths and Realities.* Organisation for Economic Co-operation and Development; World Health Organization; 2008. Accessed February 8, 2021. https://www.who.int/workforcealliance/knowledge/resources/oecd_migration_canada/en/

26. Brophy JT, Keith MM, Hurley M, McArthur JE. Sacrificed: Ontario healthcare workers in the time of COVID-19. *New Solut.* 2021;30(4):267-281. doi: 10.1177/1048291120974358

27. Alam H. Nearly 20 percent of COVID-19 infections in Canada among health-care workers by late July. *Toronto Star.* Published September 19, 2020. Accessed February 8, 2021. https://www.thestar.com/news /canada/2020/09/19/nearly-20-per-cent-of-covid-19 -infections-in-canada-among-health-care-workers -by-late-july.html

28. World Health Organization. Keep health workers safe to keep patients safe: WHO. Published September 17, 2020. Accessed February 8, 2021. https://www.who .int/news/item/17-09-2020-keep-health-workers -safe-to-keep-patients-safe-who

29. Canadian Institute for Health Information. OECD interactive tool: international comparisons—access to care. Accessed February 9, 2021. https://www.cihi.ca /en/oecd-interactive-tool-international-comparisons -access-to-care

30. Government of Canada. *Unleashing Innovation: Excellent Healthcare for Canada: Executive Summary.* Government of Canada; 2015. Accessed February 9, 2021. https:// www.canada.ca/content/dam/canada/health-canada /migration/healthy-canadians/publications/ health-system-systeme-sante/summary-innovation- sommaire/alt/summary-innovation-sommaire-eng .pdf

31. Chauvette A, Paul P. History of nursing informatics in Canada. *Can J Nurs Inform.* 2016;11(4). Accessed February 9, 2021. http://cjni.net/journal/?p=5032

32. Boothe C, Bhullar J, Chahal N, et al. The history of technology in nursing: the implementation of electronic health records in Canadian healthcare settings. *Can J Nurs Inform.* 2020; 15(2). Accessed February 9, 2021. https://cjni.net/journal/?p=7192

33. Menachemi N, Collum TH. Benefits and drawbacks of electronic health record systems. *Risk Manag Healthc Policy.* 2011;4:47-55. doi: 10.2147/RMHP .S12985

34. Samuels J, McGrath T, Fetzer S, Mittal P, Bourgoine D. Using the electronic health record in nursing research: challenges and opportunities. *West J Nurs Res.* 2015;37(10):1284-1294. doi: 10.1177/0193945 915576778

35. Evans RS. Electronic health records: then, now, and in the future. *Yearb Med Inform.* 2016;Suppl 1 (Suppl 1): S48-S61. doi: 10.15265/IYS-2016-s006

36. Tikkanen R, Osborn R, Mossialos E, Djordjevic A, Wharton GA. International Health Care System Profiles: Canada. The Commonwealth Fund. Published June 5, 2020. Accessed February 9, 2021. https://www .commonwealthfund.org/international-health-policy -center/countries/canada

37. Strumpf E, Levesque J, Coyle N, Hutchison B, Barnes M, Wedel RJ. Innovative and diverse strategies toward primary health care reform: lessons learned from the Canadian experience. *J Am Board Fam Med.* 2012;25(Suppl 1):S27-33. doi: 10.3122/jabfm .2012.02.110215

38. Carter R, Riverin B, Levesque JF, et al. The impact of primary care reform on health system performance in Canada: a systematic review. *BMC Health Serv Res.* 2016;16:324. doi: 10.1186/s12913-016-1571-7

39. Hutchison B, Woodward CA, Norman GR, Abelson J, Brown JA. Provision of preventive care to unannounced standardized patients. *Can Med Assoc J.* 1998;158:185-193. Accessed February 10, 2021. https://www.cmaj.ca/content/cmaj/158/2/185.full.pdf

40. Palmer K, Monaco A, Kivipelto M, et al. The potential long-term impact of the COVID-19 outbreak on patients with non-communicable diseases in Europe: consequences for healthy ageing. *Aging Clin Exp Res.* 2020;32(7):1189-1194. doi: 10.1007 /s40520-020-01601-4

41. Canadian Institute for Health Information. *National Health Expenditure Trends: 2020.* Canadian Institute for Health Information; 2021. Accessed February 11, 2021. https://www.cihi.ca/sites/default/files/document /nhex-trends-2020-narrative-report-en.pdf

42. Clarke H, Bao J, Weinrib A, Dubin RE, Kahan M. Canada's hidden opioid crisis: the health care system's inability to manage high-dose opioid patients: fallout from the 2017 Canadian opioid guidelines. *Can Fam Physician.* 2019;65(9):612-614. Accessed February 11, 2021. https://www.cfp.ca/content/cfp/65/9/612.full. pdf

43. Griffith J, Marani H, Monkman H. COVID-19 vaccine hesitancy in Canada: content analysis of Tweets using the Theoretical Domains Framework. *J Med Internet Res.* 2021;24(4):e26874. doi: 10.2196/26874

Epilogue

It is likely you began reading this book with the Foreword, written by Kristina Young, the senior author of the 9th edition. She wrote it this past summer and sought to draw attention to the updates we have presented in the current 10th edition, as well as the context in which we have been writing. The context, as the reader knows is the COVID-19 pandemic that is challenging societies and health systems throughout the world. The United States alone has had nearly 50 million cases and over 700,000 deaths associated with the virus. In addition to morbidity and mortality statistics, the pandemic has disrupted many, if not most, elements of our national economy. The Congressional Budget Office projects $8 trillion in lost output during the next decade. Unfortunately, the pandemic is ongoing and is not likely to resolve until sometime in the future. While public health measures, vaccines, and therapeutics are helping mitigate some of the more dire projections, this is counterbalanced by emerging new strains spreading through the population.

This Epilogue to the 10th edition of *Health Care USA* exists to remind the reader that this book was written during the worst pandemic in 100 years. Much of what has been presented and discussed is shaped by that tragic context. Health systems are still in the process of adapting and evolving, some engaged in envisioning a post-pandemic world, while others are simply doing all they can to function and survive. However, we do know from past pandemics and epidemics that innovations are likely to come about. New investments, especially in preparedness and health technologies, are already underway. Furthermore, federal, state, and local governments are embracing policy that helps individuals, communities, and commerce. Suffice it to say, the post-pandemic landscape of health care will be substantially different than what it is now. Perhaps, having read this book, you will be more empowered with the knowledge of where we have been, where we are today, and a little forethought about where we will be going in the uncertain years ahead.

Finally, you have chosen to study health care at a time when you can have a great impact on the well-being of this country and others. As so often stated in literature and philosophy, in every crisis there is opportunity. This is your time.

—**James A. Johnson**

Glossary

A

Abuse: The Office of the Inspector General defines abuse as "excessive or improper use of a thing, or to use something in a manner contrary to the natural or legal rules for its use. Abuse can occur in financial or non-financial settings." Examples of abuse include billing for unnecessary services, misusing medical codes on claims such as upcoding to increase reimbursement for medical services, or charging excessively for services or supplies.

Academic health center: A university-affiliated complex of professional, academic, and clinical care facilities such as medicine, nursing, pharmacy, dentistry, and allied health professions that are the principal places of education and training for physicians and other healthcare personnel, the sites for most basic medical research, and the settings for clinical trials. Academic health center teaching hospitals are major providers of highly sophisticated patient care required by trauma centers; burn centers; neonatal intensive care centers; and the technologically advanced treatment of cancer, heart disease, and neurologic and other acute and chronic conditions. Academic health center teaching hospitals also provide much of the primary care for the economically disadvantaged populations in their geographical area.

Access: The ability of an individual to obtain healthcare services when needed. In the United States, access is restricted to: (1) those who have health insurance through their employers, (2) those covered under a government healthcare program, (3) those who can afford to buy insurance out of their private funds, and (4) those who are able to pay for services privately.

Accountable Care Organization (ACO): A group of providers and suppliers of health care, health-related services, and others involved in caring for Medicare patients that voluntarily work together to coordinate care for the patients they serve under the original Medicare (not Medicare Advantage managed care) program. The ACA enables ACOs to share in savings to the federal government based on performance in improving quality and reducing healthcare costs.

Accreditation: A process whereby a professional organization or nongovernmental agency grants recognition to a school, educational program, or healthcare institution for demonstrated ability to meet predetermined criteria for established standards. Accreditation contrasts with certification, which is a process through which a state or professional organization attests to an individual's advanced training and performance abilities in a field of healthcare practice.

American College of Graduate Medical Education (ACGME): The independent, not-for-profit professional organization that accredits 3- to 7-year programs of advanced education and clinical practice required by physicians to provide direct patient care in a recognized medical specialty.

Advanced practice registered nurses (APRNs): A type of mid-level provider, or physician extender, are nurses who have education and experience beyond the requirements of an RN. Mid-level providers, or physician extenders, are alternatives to physicians. APRNs generally collaborate with physicians to varying degrees (from close collaborations to independent practice) depending on state laws. APRNs are one category of physician extenders along with physician assistants, physician radiology practitioner assistants, and radiologist assistants. The responsibilities of APRNs exist between those of the RN and physician, which is why they are called mid-level practitioners.

Agency for Healthcare Research and Quality (AHRQ): The federal agency charged with the research, development, and dissemination of evidence-based practice guidelines. AHRQ's National Guideline Clearinghouse maintains an online database organized by searchable topics for more than 2000 evidence-based clinical practice guidelines that have met AHRQ evaluation criteria.

Aging in place: A healthcare system that brings together a variety of health and other supportive services to enable older, frail adults to live independently in their own residences for as long as is safely possible.

Allied health professionals: Represent a varied and complex array of healthcare disciplines that support, complement, or supplement the professional functions of physicians, nurses, dentists, or other health professionals in delivering health care to patients. These professionals can provide both direct and indirect patient care. Additionally, they assist in environmental health control, health promotion, and disease prevention.

Allocation: The federal government (and state governments, to some extent) allocates funds to support various health programs. This is typically done through block grants and categorical grants. All block grants are given to the state governments, which are charged with distributing funds appropriately to specific programs, providers, and organizations. The categorical grants give more control over funds to federal agencies than do block grants, which allow the states greater discretion. Block grants are often given in such categories as child and maternal health, mental health, substance abuse, and migrant health. Categorical grants may be targeted at specific programs such as medical research or health professions education.

Allopathic approach: Views medical treatment as an active intervention to produce a counteracting reaction in an attempt to neutralize the effects of disease.

Alternative medicine: The practice of using non-mainstream treatment approaches in place of conventional medicine.

Alternative Payment Model (APM): A model through which physicians and other healthcare providers accept a measure of financial risk and are reimbursed based upon prudent resource use and the quality of patient outcomes rather than on a piecemeal fee-for-service basis. Examples of APMs include bundled payments for care and accountable care organizations.

Ambulatory care: Services that do not require an overnight hospital stay.

Ambulatory surgery center (ASC): A facility performing surgical and nonsurgical procedures on an ambulatory (outpatient) basis in a hospital or freestanding center's general operating rooms, dedicated ambulatory surgery rooms, and other specialized rooms such as endoscopy units and cardiac catheterization labs.

American Board of Medical Specialties (ABMS): An independent, not-for-profit organization, the ABMS assists its 24 specialty member boards to develop and utilize professional and educational standards that apply to the certification of physician specialists in the United States and internationally.

American Public Health Association (APHA): A Washington, D.C.-based professional organization for public health professionals in the United States.

American Rescue Plan Act: Approved in 2021 to address some of the harsh impacts of the COVID-19 pandemic; President Biden promoted the American Families Plan to further efforts in this regard.

Americans with Disabilities Act (ADA): A civil rights law that prohibits discrimination based on disability.

Analytic studies: Test hypotheses and try to explain biologic phenomena by seeking statistical associations between factors that may contribute to a subsequent occurrence and the initial occurrence itself.

Anti-Kickback Statute: Prohibits paying for patient referrals or providing remuneration (e.g., cash, free rent, expensive meals, medical consultations, medical directorships) for patient referrals.

Artificial intelligence (AI): A type of technology that uses probability and other techniques to perform tasks that apply some type of intelligence or learning.

Assessment (as a core function of public health): Collecting and analyzing data to define population health status and quantify existing or emerging health problems.

Assisted living: A program that provides and/or arranges for daily meals, personal and other supportive services, health care, and 24-hour oversight to people residing in a group residential facility who need assistance with the activities of daily living.

Association of State and Territorial Health Officials (ASTHO): The Association of State and Territorial Health Officials. It represents the public health agencies of all 50 states in the United States, the District of Columbia, the five U.S. territories, and the three freely associated states.

Assurance (as a core function of public health): Governmental public health agency responsibility to ensure that basic components of the healthcare delivery system are in place.

B

Balanced Budget Act of 1997 (BBA): The Act contained significant changes to Medicare and Medicaid. It extended healthcare coverage to uninsured children with a major funding allocation to a new Children's Health Insurance Program (CHIP). The Act also proposed to reduce growth in Medicare and Medicaid spending by $125.2 billion in 5 years. It increased beneficiary premiums for Medicare Part B and required new prospective payment systems for hospital outpatient services, skilled nursing facilities, home health agencies, and rehabilitation hospitals. One of its most significant effects was opening the Medicare program to private insurers through the Medicare+Choice program by allowing financial risk sharing for the Medicare program with the private sector through managed care plans.

Basic science research: Conducted by biochemists, physiologists, biologists, pharmacologists, and others concerned with sciences that are fundamental to understanding the growth, development, structure, and functions of the human body and its responses to external stimuli. Much basic science research is conducted at the cellular level.

Behavioral care: The behavioral care system refers to the individuals, groups, and organizations that provide services that promote mental health, resilience, and well-being, treat mental and substance use disorders, and support individuals that experience and/or are in recovery from these conditions along with their families and communities.

Behavioral scientists: Behavioral scientists include professionals in social work, health education, community mental health, alcoholism and drug abuse services, and other health and human service areas. Bachelor's or master's level degree professionals in these fields counsel and support individuals and families in addressing the personal, economic, and social problems associated with illness, addictions, employment challenges, and disabilities.

Benchmark developments: Major developments that substantially change health care and population health.

Beneficiary: The term used to refer to individuals who are insured by a public health insurance plan because they are receiving a benefit from the government. Insurance pools individual risks and spreads them over a group so that the financial risk is shared by the group through premiums. Members or beneficiaries also engage in cost-sharing, which allows those who are insured to share some of the risk.

Big Data: A field that treats ways to analyze, systematically extract information from, or otherwise deal with data sets that are too large or complex to be dealt with by traditional data-processing application software.

Block grants: Mechanism to shift the federal government's direct support and administration of healthcare programs to state and local governments.

Blue Cross/Blue Shield: Blue Cross Blue Shield Association is a federation of 35 separate United States health insurance companies that provide health insurance in the United States to more than 106 million people.

Bundled Payments for Care Improvement (BPCI) initiative: Developed by the CMS Center for Medicare & Medicaid Innovation (CMMI) that was created by the ACA, the BPCI recognizes that separate Medicare fee-for-service payments for individual services provided during a beneficiary's single illness result in fragmented care with minimal coordination across providers and settings, rewarding service quantity rather than quality. The BPCI is testing whether, as prior research has shown, payments for bundled "episodes of care" can align incentives for hospitals, post-acute care providers, physicians, and other healthcare personnel to collaborate across many settings to achieve improved patient outcomes at lower cost.

C

Capitation: A managed care reimbursement method that prepays providers for services on a per-member per-month basis whether or not services are used. If providers exceed the predetermined capitation amount, they may incur a financial penalty. If providers use fewer resources than predicted, they may retain the excess as profit.

Captology: The term used to define persuasive technology, which is an "interactive information technology" designed to assist in purposely changing a person's behavior and/or attitudes using computing technology.

Case series: A published summary of a small number of individual cases in the biomedical literature that usually occur for extremely rare conditions or for new illnesses or syndromes and often when the diagnosis is unknown, typically without rigorous analyses. Case series generally are developed by experts and undergo peer review before they are published.

Carve-outs: A process through which insurers outsource subscribers' mental illness care oversight to firms specializing in managing service use for mental health diagnoses.

Certificate-of Need (CON): A Certificate of Need (CON) is a legal document that is used to regulate the American healthcare system. In order to be approved, the CON requires that a new healthcare infrastructure be approved by regional governments. Even though most states have CONs in place, they vary in terms and conditions from state to state.

Certification: A regulatory process, much less stringent than licensure, under which a state or professional organization attests to an individual's advanced training and performance abilities in a field of healthcare practice. Specific professions set certification standards for approval by their respective state or professional organizations.

Certified nurse-midwife (CNM): RNs who complete a 1- or 2-year master's degree program in nurse midwifery that has been accredited by the American College of Nurse-Midwives Division of Accreditation. Nurse-midwives are primary care providers for women who are pregnant.

Civilian Health and Medical Program of the Department of Veterans Affairs (CHAMPVA): A comprehensive health program for eligible beneficiaries provided by the Department of Veterans Affairs to individuals that are not eligible for TRICARE. To be eligible for the program, an individual must be the spouse or child of a veteran who is permanently or totally disabled due to service, a veteran who died from a service-related disability, or a veteran who was permanently or totally disabled from a service-related disability at the time of death. Finally, a surviving spouse or child of a veteran who died in the line of duty (not due to misconduct) is eligible for benefits (although most are eligible for TRICARE, not CHAMPVA).

Children's Health Insurance Program (CHIP): Established by the Balanced Budget Act of 1997, CHIP targets uninsured, eligible children for Medicaid enrollment. It has successfully enrolled millions of children in Medicaid and has been re-funded continuously since its inception, including for 2 additional years through the Medicare Access and CHIP Reauthorization Act of 2015 (MACRA).

Chiropractor: Uses a holistic approach to treat their patients. They believe the body can heal itself without medication or surgery and treat the whole body without the use of drugs or surgery. Special care is given to the spine because chiropractors believe that misalignment or irritations of spinal nerves interfere with normal body functions. They manipulate the body using their hands or a machine.

Clinical decision support system (CDSS): An electronic information-based system in which individual patient data is matched with a computerized knowledge base, such as evidence-based clinical practice guidelines, to assist healthcare providers in formulating accurate diagnoses, recommendations, and treatment plans. A CDSS may generate "hard stops" to prevent a disallowed practice or severe errors or "soft stops" that warn of less severe errors and allow physicians to choose to ignore or follow the warning.

Clinical laboratory technologists and technicians: Clinical laboratory personnel who analyze body fluids, tissues, and cells checking for bacteria and other microorganisms; analyze the chemical content of body fluids; test drug levels in blood to monitor the effectiveness of treatment; and match blood for transfusion. Technologists have a bachelor's degree or higher; technicians may hold associate's degrees or certificates.

Clinical nurse specialist: A type of advanced practice nursing role. This specialty role was developed in response to the specific nursing care needs of increasingly complex patients within a hospital setting. Like specialist physicians, clinical nurse specialists are advanced practice specialists with in-depth knowledge and skills that make them valuable adjunct practitioners in specialized clinical settings. The training requirements vary by state but generally include an RN and either a master's or doctoral degree (PhD or DNP) in nursing.

Clinical Observation Unit (COU): Dedicated locations adjacent to hospital EDs or as beds located in other areas of the hospital, COUs use a period of 6-24 hours to triage, diagnose, treat and monitor patient responses while common complaints such as chest pain, abdominal pain, cardiac arrhythmias, and congestive heart failure are assessed.

Clinical practice guidelines: Systematically developed protocols used to assist practitioner and patient decisions about appropriate health care by defining the roles of specific diagnostic and treatment modalities in patient diagnosis and management.

Clinical research: Primarily focuses on steps in the process of medical care such as the early detection, diagnosis, and treatment of disease or injury; the maintenance of optimal, physical, mental, and social functioning; the limitation and rehabilitation of disability; and the palliative care of those who are irreversibly ill. Clinical research is conducted by a variety of professionals in medicine, nursing, and allied health, often in collaboration with basic scientists.

Centers for Disease Control and Prevention (CDC): The the national public health agency of the United States. under the Department of Health and Human Services, and is headquartered in Atlanta, Georgia. Its mission is to protect public health by preventing and controlling disease, injury, and disability. The CDC promotes healthy behaviors and safe, healthy environments. It keeps track of health trends, tries to find the cause of health problems and outbreaks of disease, and responds to new public health threats. The CDC works with state health departments and other organizations throughout the country and the world to help prevent and control disease.

Centers for Medicare and Medicaid Services (CMS): The entity that extends accreditation via approved programs that routinely survey hospitals for compliance on a host of topics related to the health and safety of their patients. Final accreditation of hospitals means that they meet the Conditions of Participation (CoPs).

Coinsurance: A percentage an insured individual pays for healthcare services after the deductible has been paid or met.

Community-rated insurance: Insurance plans in which all individuals in a defined group pay premiums without regard to age, gender, occupation, or health status. Community ratings help ensure nondiscrimination against groups with varying risk characteristics to provide coverage at reasonable rates for the community as a whole.

Complex adaptive systems (CASs): Organizations can be viewed as complex adaptive systems (CASs). These organizations are complex in that they are compose of multiple, diverse, interconnected elements, and equally important. They are also adaptive in that they are capable of changing and learning from experience based on interactions with their dynamic environment. Most organizations, and certainly all health organizations, can be described as CASs that are constantly adjusting to their environment and responding feedback from within and without their environments. Complexity science sees change as inevitable and, thus, the search for a stable state is futile. CASs continuously adjust because they are open to exchanges and interaction with the environment. We see examples of this in healthcare with health policy reforms that try and adjust to health realities across the population. We also see examples of policies that have failed to respond to health realities and thus health challenges persist. CASs have attributes that are consistent with General Systems Theory and the newly emerging complete science.

Comorbidity: When two disorders or illnesses occur in the same person, simultaneously, or one after another.

Comparative effectiveness research: Research designed to inform healthcare decisions by providing evidence on the effectiveness, benefits, and harms of different treatment options. Evidence is generated from research studies that compare drugs, medical devices, tests, surgeries, or ways to deliver health care.

Complementary medicine: Treatment that is not mainstream medicine but is used together with mainstream medicine. An example of complementary medicine would be using acupuncture to treat allergies in addition to obtaining conventional allergy medication prescribed by an allergist.

Computerized physician order entry (CPOE): The process in which a physician enters patient treatment orders into an individual patient's electronic health record.

Conditions of Participation (CoP): These are important because the "participation" essentially means that hospitals are able to receive government funding from CMS. The government is the largest payer for accredited hospitals in the United States. This is important to mention upfront because many of the internal processes within hospitals are linked to the relationship to funders (e.g., CMS and insurance companies, etc.).

Consumer-directed health plans (CDHPs): HDHPs can be combined with either or health savings account or health reimbursement account and are referred to as consumer-directed health plans (CDHPs). The name recognizes that this type of coverage increases the role consumers play in seeking or shopping for services. The deductible is the amount individuals must pay out-of-pocket before insurance coverage begins. While in theory, requiring out-of-pocket spending should promote consumers' prudent choices for care, expert observations and preliminary research are raising some concerns. Only a few of the concerns include: a lack of consumer understanding about how plans actually work, especially about provision of no- or low-cost deductibles for preventive services; evidence that consumers are avoiding necessary and appropriate care due to costs; and evidence that out-of-pocket expenses negatively impact consumers' compliance with medically recommended follow-up care including use of prescription drugs.

Consumerism: An economic and social order that supports the acquisition of goods and services in ever-increasing amounts.

Continuing care retirement community (CCRC): Residences on a retirement campus, typically in apartment complexes designed for functional older adults. Unlike ordinary retirement communities that offer only specialized housing, CCRCs offer a comprehensive program of social services, meals, and access to contractual medical services in addition to housing.

Continuing life care community (CLCC): The most expensive CCRC option. CLCCs offer unlimited assisted living, medical treatment, and skilled nursing care without any additional charges as residents' needs change over time.

Copayment: A fixed payment amount an insured individual pays for healthcare services after the deductible has been paid or met.

Core functions of public health: There are three core functions of public health: assessment, which involves obtaining data to define the health of populations and the nature of health problems; assurance, which includes the oversight responsibility for ensuring that essential components of an effective health system are in place; and policy development, which includes developing evidence-based recommendations and analysis to guide public policy as it pertains to health.

Cost sharing: A strategy to control health service utilization and costs. Health insurance leaves insured individuals unaware of the full cost of the service they are receiving and can lead to overutilization or over consumption of health services. Cost sharing makes individuals more sensitive to the costs associated with medical services, which promotes more responsible behavior and utilization.

Council on Education for Public Health: The accrediting body for public health. This body oversees the criteria and process for accrediting schools and programs of public health in the United States. The overarching goal of this organization is to prepare students equipped with the requisite knowledge, skills, and abilities to enter the public health workforce at all levels.

Credentialing: The certification and licensing of health professionals, typically by state boards and recognized institutions. The process often involves examination.

D

Death with Dignity Acts: Created in response to the growing concern among medical professionals and the public about the extended, painful, and demeaning nature of terminal medical care for patients with certain conditions. An additional consideration was the worry that the extraordinary costs associated with lengthy and futile medical care would exhaust their estates and leave their families with substantial debts.

Deductible: The amount the insured person must first pay before their insurance plan begins to pay.

Deinstitutionalization: The mental health movement beginning in the 1960s through which severely mentally ill patients previously confined to large state or county psychiatric hospitals were discharged to community boarding or nursing homes. The movement marked a major shift of mental health service provision from primarily inpatient settings to community-based facilities.

Dentist: Prevents, diagnoses, and treats tooth, gum, and mouth diseases. They are required to complete 4 years of education at an accredited dental school after completing a bachelor's degree. Dentists are awarded a Doctor of Dental Surgery (DDS), Doctor of Dental Medicine (DDM), or Doctor of Medical Dentistry (DMD) degree. Some states may require a specialty license. To practice in a dental specialty, a dentist must complete a dental residency after dental school in the specialty of choice and then usually must qualify for a special state-based dental license.

Department of Health and Human Services (HHS): The federal government's principal agency concerned with health protection and promotion and provision of health and other human services to vulnerable populations. In addition to administering the Medicare and Medicaid programs, DHHS includes 11 operating divisions.

Department of Veterans Affairs: In addition to medical care, its mission includes education, training, research, and contingency support and emergency management for the Department of Defense medical care system. The VA system provides care to approximately 9 million veterans at 1,293 healthcare facilities that include 171 medical center and 1,112 outpatient sites in 2021. The system is divided into 18 Veterans Integrated Service Networks, or VISNs. These regional networks strive to improve access and care coordination for veterans in a geographic or local area.

Descriptive studies: Identify factors and conditions that determine the distribution of health and disease among specific populations using patient records, interview surveys, various databases, and other information sources to provide the details or characteristics of diseases or biologic phenomena and the prevalence or magnitude of their occurrence. Descriptive studies are relatively fast and inexpensive and often raise questions or suggest hypotheses to be tested by analytic studies.

Determinants of health: The varied factors that affect the health status of populations or groups of people. Health determinants fall into five broad categories that include policymaking, social factors, health services, individual behavior, and biology and genetics. The determinants interact and are interrelated to produce different health outcomes.

Diagnosis-related groups (DRGs): A case payment system that radically changed hospital reimbursement, shifting hospital reimbursement from the retrospective to a prospective basis. The DRG system provided incentives for the hospital to spend only what was needed to achieve optimal patient outcomes. If outcomes could be achieved at a cost lower than the preset payment, the hospital retained an excess payment for those cases. If the hospital spent more to treat cases than allowed, it absorbed the excess costs. This payment system was widely adopted by nongovernmental health insurers.

Disability-adjusted life years (DALYs): The total number of years of life lost to illness, disability, or premature death within a given population.

Disaster: A serious issue occurring over a short or long period of time that causes large-scale human, material, economic, or environmental loss, which exceeds the ability of the affected community or society to cope using its own resources.

Disaster preparedness: The processes and planning necessary for rapid response to disasters.

Disease management programs: MCO programs that attempt to control costs and improve care quality for individuals with chronic and costly conditions through methods such as the use of evidence-based clinical guidelines, patient self-management education, telemedicine, disease registries, risk stratification, proactive patient outreach, and performance feedback to providers. Programs may also use clinical specialists who provide monitoring and support to patients with disease management issues.

Disproportionate share hospital (DSH) payment: Federal law requires these Medicaid payments to states for hospitals serving large numbers of Medicaid and low-income, uninsured individuals. The law establishes an annual DSH allotment for each state. DSH payments provide critical financial supplements to hospitals serving the neediest populations.

Diversity: Refers to understanding, accepting, and valuing individual differences such as experience, skills, knowledge, gender, race, culture, age, sexuality, disability, education, religion, class, and many other dimensions.

Doctor of Medicine (MD): A type of physician. MDs use an allopathic approach, which views medical treatment as an active intervention to produce a counteracting reaction in an attempt to neutralize the effects of disease.

Doctor of Osteopathic Medicine (DO): A type of physician. DOs use an osteopathic approach that takes a more holistic approach to health and stresses preventive medicine in their treatment plans by considering how diet, environment, and other factors influence health and treatment.

Doctorates: There are many doctoral degrees in addition to the MD and DO described above. In health care and health-related professions, these include Doctor of Nursing Practice (DNP), Doctor of Public Health (DrPH), Doctor of Pharmacy (PharmD), Doctor of Physical Therapy (DPT), Doctor of Health Administration (DHA), Doctor of Psychology (PsyD), Doctor of Podiatric Medicine (DPM), Doctor of Optometry (OD), and Doctor of Chiropractic Medicine (DC). There are others, typically associated with medical and health services research fields, such as Doctor of Science (ScD) and Doctor of Philosophy (PhD).

Dual eligible: An individual who qualifies to receive both Medicare and Medicaid benefits.

E

Ecological models: Models that identify causes of public health problems rooted in the physical and/or social environment and behavior related to an individual. Ecological models take into account the vast number of determinants that affect the health status of groups of people and facilitate decisions about the most expeditious path to developing effective interventions.

Electronic health record (EHR): Computerized patient records that essentially replace paper charts.

Emergency: A situation that poses an immediate risk to life, health, property, or environment.

Emergency Medical Treatment and Labor Act (EMTALA): Enacted in the 1995 federal budget because of concerns about inappropriate patient transfers between hospitals prompted by payment considerations. EMTALA requires hospitals to treat everyone who presents in their emergency departments regardless of ability to pay. Stiff financial penalties and risk of Medicare decertification

by hospitals inappropriately transferring patients accompanies the EMTALA legal provisions.

Empirical quality standards: Derived from distributions, averages, ranges, and other measures of data variability, empirical quality standards compare information collected from a number of similar health service providers to identify practices that deviate from norms.

Employer-sponsored health insurance: Generally requires employees to pay a portion of the insurance premium through wage or payroll deductions while Medicare beneficiaries pay some premiums out-of-pocket or have a supplemental health insurance plan to help pay for coverage gaps. Insured individuals, covered through both private and public plans, pay for a portion of healthcare costs out-of-pocket through deductibles and copayments.

Employer mandate: Under the ACA, it requires all businesses with 50 or more full-time equivalent employees to provide health insurance to at least 95% of their full-time employees and dependents up to age 26, or pay a fee by 2018. Employers are subject to a $2,000 fee per full-time employee (in excess of 30 employees). The mandate does not apply to businesses with 49 or fewer employees.

Enrollee: Or member; interchangeable terms that refer to individuals that are insured by a private health insurance plan.

Epidemiological research: Epidemiology is concerned with the distribution and determinants of health, diseases, and injuries in human populations. This type of research often utilizes observational study by collecting observed or reported information about natural phenomena, the characteristics and behaviors of people, aspects of their location or environment, and their exposure to certain circumstances or events.

Equity: Refers to organizational policies that support equal opportunities and fairness for everyone in the organization. The organization is focused on ensuring everyone has opportunities for individual growth, development, and advancement. Equity recognizes that differences exist between employees and that these differences are valuable.

Essential public health services: 1. Monitor health status to identify community health problems. 2. Diagnose and investigate health problems and health hazards in the community. 3. Inform, educate, and empower people about health issues. 4. Mobilize community partnerships to identify and solve health problems. 5. Develop policies and plans that support individual and community health efforts. 6. Enforce laws and regulations that protect health and ensure safety. 7. Link people to the needed personal health services and assure the provision of health care, when otherwise unavailable. 8. Assure a competent public health and personal healthcare workforce. 9. Evaluate effectiveness, accessibility, and quality of personal and population-based health services. 10. Research new insights and innovative solutions to health problems.

Evidence-based clinical practice guidelines: Systematically developed protocols based on extensive research that are considered the most objective and least biased clinical practice guidelines. They serve as a means to assist in preventing the use of unnecessary treatment modalities and in avoiding negligent events, with patient safety and the delivery of consistent high-quality care as foremost priorities.

Evidence-based medicine: The judicious, conscientious, and explicit use of current best evidence in making decisions about the care of individual patients.

Evidence-based practice: Integrates the best available scientific knowledge (i.e., clinical practice guidelines) with clinical skills and experience while considering the unique needs and preferences of a patient.

Exclusion Statute: Prevents providers (individuals and entities) from participating in federal healthcare programs if they have been convicted of Medicare or Medicaid fraud; patient abuse or neglect; felony convictions for health-related fraud, theft, or other financial misconduct; felony convictions for mishandling of controlled substances; defaulting on health education loan or scholarship obligations; receiving kickbacks; submitting false claims; or loss of a practice license.

Experience-rated insurance: Insurance plans that use historically documented patterns of healthcare service utilization for defined populations of subscribers to determine premium charges.

Experimental studies: In experimental studies, the investigator actively intervenes by manipulating one variable to see what happens with the other. Although they are the best test of cause and effect, such studies are technically difficult to carry out and often raise ethical issues. Control populations are used to ensure that other non-experimental variables are not affecting the outcome.

Expert opinion: The lowest or least rigorous form of evidence, but also the most commonly practiced; usually expresses the opinion of a medical specialist in an area of interest to a particular patient; it can occur formally, with a referral to a specialist by a patient's primary care physician, or informally when physicians discuss a case or medical issue with a colleague via phone, email, or face-to-face in an informal setting.

Explicit quality standards: Standards that are professionally developed and agreed on in advance of a quality assessment. Explicit standards minimize the variation and bias that result when judgments are internalized.

F

False Claims Act: States that it is illegal to submit claims to Medicare or Medicaid that are knowingly false or fraudulent. The Act also prohibits subpar goods or services to be sold to the federal government.

Federal Medical Assistance Percentage (FMAP): The federal government matches state Medicaid expenditures based on the FMAP, which is adjusted annually based on a state's average personal income compared with the national average. The formula provides higher matching or reimbursements to states with lower per capita incomes compared with the national average.

Federalism: Prior to ratification of the Constitution by the States, amendments were added to address fundamental principles of human liberty, which are called the Bill of Rights. This founding document also provided the architecture to be used in creating the structure of government. This organization of government involved the separation of powers between three branches: the Executive Branch, composed of the President and Cabinet; the Legislative Branch, made up of two bodies of Congress (the Senate and House of Representatives) to represent the interests of the people and the states through the process of legislation and oversight; and the Judicial Branch, made up of judges and courts, including the United States Supreme Court. Furthermore, the Constitution established two levels of government, the federal and the state. This is often called *federalism* and represents a system of government where two or more levels (i.e., national, state, and local) have certain powers and authority.

Federally Qualified Health Center (FQHC): A community-based primary care center staffed by a multidisciplinary team of healthcare and related support personnel, with fees adjusted based on ability to pay. FQHCs also provide services to link patients with other community resources. Funded by the Health Resources and Services Administration to serve the neediest populations, FQHCs must meet specific operating parameters and may be organized as part of a local health department, a larger human services organization, or a stand-alone, not-for-profit agency.

Federated model of health information exchange: An HIE design in which member institutions maintain their own data at their respective sites in the standardized format used by an HIE. In this model, individual, transinstitutional patient records are assembled in real time by searching all institutions' databases only when requested by authorized users for a particular episode of care.

Focused Practice in Hospital Medicine (FPHM): The American Board of Internal Medicine educational program through which physicians already certified in the internal medicine specialty obtain certification as hospitalists.

Financial risk-sharing: A practice that transfers some measure of financial risk from insurers to providers and beneficiaries. Such transfers of financial risk to beneficiaries commonly take the form of co-payments and deductibles. Co-payments require that beneficiaries pay a set fee each time they receive a covered service, such as a co-payment for each physician office visit. Deductibles require beneficiaries to meet predetermined, out-of-pocket expenditure levels before an insurer assumes payment responsibility. Financial risk-sharing by providers bases their reimbursement levels on insurer-determined parameters related to costs, patient treatment outcomes, and other factors for defined population groups.

Financing: As defined in Shi and Singh's *Essentials of the U.S. Health Care System*, this refers to "any mechanism that gives people the ability to pay for health care services". U.S. healthcare financing continues to evolve and is shaped by a variety of influences or factors, including provider, employer, purchaser, consumer, and political factors. These influences produce major tensions that are reflected in ongoing political debates and policy discussions. Financing issues include the role and responsibility

of the government as a payer, financial responsibilities of employers as purchasers of health insurance, and the impact of payment systems on quality, among other issues. Despite recent health policies, controlling the rising healthcare costs, meeting the needs of aging Americans, reducing health disparities, ensuring health equity, and finding coverage options for uninsured Americans continue to pose fiscal challenges to the United States health system.

Flexner Report: The landmark report resulting from a comprehensive review of the quality of education in U.S. and Canadian medical schools, funded by the Carnegie Foundation. Issued in 1910, the report was a searing indictment of most medical schools of the time. The report gave increased leverage to medical education reformers and stimulated financial support from foundations and wealthy individuals which enabled university-affiliated medical schools to gain significant influence over the direction of medical education.

Fraud: The Office of the Inspector General defines fraud as "wrongful or criminal deception intended to result in financial or personal gain. Fraud includes false representation of fact, making false statements, or by concealment of information." Examples of fraud include billing for unnecessary medical services, misrepresenting diagnoses or procedures to increase reimbursements, paying for referrals, billing for no-show patient appointments, upcoding for medical services or procedures, or billing for services that were not provided or documented in a patient's medical record. Committing fraud can result in criminal, civil and administrative liability and can result in penalties, fines, and even imprisonment. Additionally, providers can lose their practice license while organization can be prohibited from receiving in Federal healthcare program like Medicare or Medicaid.

Food and Drug Administration (FDA): At the beginning of the 20th century, the Pure Food and Drugs Act of 1906 was passed by Congress to provide federal inspection of meat products and prohibit the manufacture, sale, or transportation of adulterated food products and poisonous medicines. As this domain of public policy grew, it was institutionalized in the Executive Branch with the establishment of the Food and Drug Administration (FDA) in 1930. Subsequent legislation and regulations broadened the scope of this policy area to address ever-changing challenges to an increasingly complex and global society. A recent example is the FDA's involvement with other agencies to address the COVID-19 pandemic. This includes facilitating the development of tests, both diagnostic and serologic; supporting the advance of treatments and vaccines for the disease; and working to ensure that healthcare workers and others have the personal protective equipment and other necessary medical products needed to mitigate it.

G

General Systems Theory: Ludwig von Bertalanffy articulated and popularized this theory in his 1968 book entitled *General Systems Theory*. In this book, he sought to unify the field of science. His unique contribution, and that of the General Systems Theory, was trying to understand individual parts of a system as well as how these parts interact through recurring patterns to produce a whole. Prior theories had focused on understanding individual parts in great detail, but they had not considered how the individual parts related to the whole system.

Generalist: Also known as a primary care provider. They are physicians trained in family medicine/general practice, general internal medicine, and general pediatrics in the United States. Primary care providers provide preventive services (e.g., health examinations, immunizations, mammograms, and Pap smears) and treat frequently occurring and less severe problems. Referrals are made to specialists for problems that occur less frequently or require complex diagnostic or therapeutic approaches.

Graduate medical education consortia: Formal associations of medical schools, teaching hospitals, and other organizations involved in the training of medical residents. The consortia provide centralized coordination and direction that encourages the members to function collectively with major aims to improve the structure and governance of residency programs, to increase residents' ambulatory care training experiences, and to address imbalances in physician specialty and location.

Gross domestic product (GDP): The broadest quantitative measure of a nation's total economic activity, representing the monetary value of all goods and services produced within a nation's geographic borders over a specified period.

Group insurance: Refers to when individuals purchase insurance in a group, such as through their employer, which will spread risk among the group members.

H

Hazards: Present the probability of the occurrence of a disaster caused by a natural phenomenon (e.g., earthquake, tropical cyclone), by failure of man-made sources of energy (e.g., nuclear reactor or industrial explosion), or by uncontrolled human activity (e.g., conflicts, overgrazing).

Health: The World Health Organization defines health as "a state of complete physical, mental, and social well-being and not merely the absence of disease or infirmity." This comprehensive concept of health is the one used in this book and serves to inform the discussion of the U.S. health system. This definition also recognizes the influence various health determinants have on individual and population health outcomes.

Healthcare administrators: Also referred to as medical and health service managers, they keep a range of healthcare services and operations running smoothly. Healthcare administrators plan, organize, direct, control, or coordinate medical and health services in hospitals, clinics, nursing care facilities, and group medical practices. Many healthcare administrators are employed in hospital settings, and others work for insurers, clinics, or medical group practices.

Healthcare effectiveness data and information set (HEDIS): A data collection and aggregation system that provides a standardized method for MCOs to collect, calculate, and report information about their performance to allow employers, other purchasers, and consumers to compare different health insurance plans. The HEDIS has evolved through several stages of development and continuously refines its measurements through rigorous reviews and independent audits.

Healthcare professional: Someone who plays a role in delivering health care and includes individuals who provide direct patient care (e.g., physicians, physician assistants, nurses, nurse practitioners, physical therapists, etc.) as well as individuals who indirectly support patients and healthcare delivery (e.g., professionals working in human resources, finance, marketing, environmental services, information technology, etc.).

Health in All Policies (HiAP): An approach to public policies across sectors that systematically considers the health implications of decisions, seeks synergies, and avoids harmful health impacts in order to improve population health and health equity. It improves accountability of policymakers for health impacts at all levels of policymaking. It includes an emphasis on the consequences of public policies on health systems and the determinants of health and well-being.

Health information administrator: Health information administrators are responsible for the activities of the medical records departments of hospitals, skilled nursing facilities, managed care organizations, rehabilitation centers, ambulatory care facilities, and other licensed healthcare entities. They maintain information systems to permit patient data to be received, recorded, stored, and retrieved to assist in diagnosis and treatment and supply research data for tracking disease patterns, evaluating the quality of patient care, verifying insurance claims, and maintaining patient record confidentiality. A bachelor's degree in health information administration is the entry-level credential.

Health information exchange (HIE): Networks that enable exchange among basic levels of interoperability of patient information among electronic health records maintained by individual physicians and healthcare organizations. HIEs are organized and governed by regional health information organizations (RHIOs).

Health Information Technology for Economic and Clinical Health (HITECH) Act: A component of the American Recovery and Reinvestment Act of 2009 dedicated to promoting nationwide adoption and use of electronic health records.

Health insurance marketplace (HIM): The ACA required states to establish health benefit exchanges (now known as health insurance marketplaces, or HIMs) to facilitate individuals' and small employers' choices among health plans. With participation by insurance companies in each state, HIMs created a competitive health insurance market by providing web-based, easily understandable, comparative information for consumers on plan choices and standardized rules regarding health plan offers and pricing.

Health Insurance Portability and Accountability Act (HIPAA): Enacted in 1996 to protect health insurance coverage for workers and their families when they change or lose their jobs. It also established national standards for electronic health care transactions and guidelines for health information privacy and security.

Health policy research: Social, economic, and behavioral research to improve or evaluate health policies

Health services research: A research field combining perspectives and methods of epidemiology, sociology, economics, and clinical medicine. Health services research also uses process and outcome measures reflecting behavioral and economic variables associated with questions of treatment effectiveness and cost–benefit.

Health system: The World Health Organization defines a health system as "the sum total of all the organizations, institutions, and resources whose primary purpose is to improve health." An agreed-upon definition of health is paramount to the discussion of any health system.

Health systems agency (HSA): An organization created by the National Health Planning and Resources Development Act of 1974 that included broad representation of healthcare providers and consumers on governing boards and committees to deliberate and recommend healthcare resource allocations to their respective federal and state governing bodies.

Health system framework: A health system framework consists of all organizations, people, and actions whose primary intent is to promote, restore, or maintain health.

Health systems research: A newer field that addresses the study of the healthcare system itself rather than specific problems of disease or disability.

Healthy People 2030: Since 1980, HHS, in collaboration with community partners, has developed 10-year plans that outline key national health and health-related objectives to be accomplished during each decade. The next 10-year period of national health planning is being addressed in Healthy People 2030. Although much progress has been made since the Healthy People initiatives began, the United States is still behind other developed nations on key measures of health and well-being, including life expectancy, infant mortality, and obesity. A challenge for Healthy People 2030 is to guide the country in achieving its full potential for health and well-being.

High-deductible health plan (HDHP): First dubbed "consumer-driven health plans," the plans are now known as high-deductible health plans (HDHPs). HDHPs' goals are to entice employees with lower premium costs in exchange for agreeing to make out-of-pocket, up-front payments for health services. The HDHP intends to encourage cost-consciousness about the use of healthcare services. Today, HDHPs are the second most common type of plan offered by employers, with 24% of U.S. workers selecting this option.

Hill–Burton Act: The 1946 federal law that provided funding to construct new and expand existing U.S. hospitals.

HMO Act of 1973: Federal legislation enacted by the Nixon administration that provided loans and grants for the planning, development, and implementation of combined insurance and healthcare delivery organizations and required that a comprehensive array of preventive and primary care services be included in the HMO arrangement. By linking the payment for services with the quality of care, the HMO Act paved the way for the proliferation of managed care principles that became the foundation of U.S. health insurance reform in the succeeding 3 decades.

Horizontal integration: Consolidation of two or more hospitals or other entities under one owner through merger or acquisition.

Hospice: A philosophy supporting a coordinated program of care for the terminally ill that focuses on maintaining comfort and quality of life. The most common criterion for admission into hospice is a diagnosis of a terminal illness with a limited life expectancy of 6 months or less.

Hospital Consumer Assessment of Healthcare Providers and Systems Survey (HCAHPS): The first national, standardized, publicly reported survey of patients' perspectives of hospital care created by the Department of Health and Human Services. Results are publicly reported on the CMS "Hospital Compare" website.

Hospitalist: A physician, typically board certified in internal medicine, who specializes in the care of hospital patients. A hospitalist may be an employee of one or more hospitals or an employee of one or more companies that contract with hospitals to provide services.

Human factors: The professionals who play an important role in influencing healthcare delivery in the United States.

I

Implicit quality standards: Standards that rely on the internalized judgments of expert individuals conducting a quality assessment and as such are subject to variation and bias.

Incidents: As defined by authors Shi and Johnson in *Public Health Administration: Principles for Population-Based Management*, "An occurrence or event, natural or manmade, that requires a response to protect life or property. Incidents can, for example, include major disasters, emergencies, terrorist attacks, terrorist threats, civil unrest, wildland and urban fires, floods, hazardous materials spills, nuclear accidents, aircraft accidents, earthquakes, hurricanes, tornadoes, tropical storms, tsunamis, war-related disasters, public health and medical emergencies, and other occurrences requiring an emergency response."

Inclusion: Can be defined as the feeling of belonging and acceptance based on one's whole identity or intersecting identities. This belonging creates psychological safety that allows individuals to voice their ideas, opinions, frustrations, and much more.

Indemnity insurance: A form of insurance in which the insurance company sets allowable charges for services that it will reimburse after services are delivered and allows providers to bill patients for any uncovered excess costs.

Indian Health Service (IHS): Provides health services to Native Americans and Alaska Natives and is an agency within the HHS sponsored by the federal government. The IHS provides comprehensive health services to 574 federally recognized tribes in 37 states, or approximately 2.6 million people.

Information blocking: A practice by some electronic health record providers and developers that actively blocks the transfer of electronic information between institutions with different electronic systems.

Individual mandate: Under the ACA, the requirement that all American citizens (with specific exclusions) obtain health insurance coverage or pay a penalty.

Individual Practice Association (IPA): Physician organizations composed of community-based, independent physicians in solo or group practices that provide services to HMO members.

Informed consent: Legally recognized patient right, formalized in a document for a patient's signature, to ensure patients' understanding of the risks and benefits of a medical intervention.

Institutional Review Board (IRB): Professionally constituted expert groups of individuals who judge the merit of research studies and ensure appropriate and ethical safeguards are provided to protect research subjects' safety. A primary function of an IRB is to ensure fully informed consent and research subjects' understanding of the risks and benefits of participation. A review process to assure integrity and responsibility in the research process. It also serves to protect the interests of research subjects.

Insurance: A mechanism for protecting people and organizations from risk.

Insured: Refers to individuals who have insurance (or are covered by an insurance plan) that provides protection from the risk of significant financial loss.

Integrated delivery system (IDS): May be defined as a network of organizations that provides, or arranges to provide, a coordinated continuum of services to a defined population and is willing to be held clinically and fiscally accountable for the outcomes and health status of that population. For over a decade now, organizational integration to form IDSs has been the hallmark of the U.S. healthcare industry. Integration in the U.S. healthcare delivery system has occurred in response to cost pressures, development of new alternatives for the delivery of health care, the growing power of MCOs, and the need to provide services more efficiently to populations spread over large geographic areas. An IDS represents various forms of ownership and other strategic linkages among major participants, such as hospitals, physicians, and insurers. The objective is to achieve greater integration of healthcare services along the continuum of care.

Interprofessional education: An educational approach in which two or more disciplines collaborate in the learning process with the goal of enhancing interprofessional interactions, thus enhancing the practice of each discipline. The collaboration enhances communication and decision making, enabling a synergistic influence of grouped knowledge and skills to improve patient safety, outcomes, and satisfaction through evidence-based practice.

Interprofessional practice: Defined as using a team-based approach to deliver patient care that promotes the health, safety, and outcomes of patients, clients, families, caregivers, and communities.

International medical graduates (IMGs): Physicians trained in medical schools outside the United States who fill the annual shortfall in U.S. medical school graduates required to staff hospitals. Responsibility for evaluating the credentials of IMGs entering the United States' residency programs lies with the Educational Commission for Foreign Medical Graduates.

Integrative medicine: A treatment approach that brings conventional medicine and complementary medicine together in a coordinated manner.

J

Job stress: As defined by the World Health Organization, job stress is "the response people have when presented with work demands and pressures that are not matched to their knowledge and abilities and which challenge their ability to cope." Job stress can lead to job-related burnout.

Job-related burnout: As defined by the Mayo Clinic, job-related burnout is "a special type of work-related stress – a state of physical or emotional exhaustion that also involves a sense of reduced accomplishment and loss of personal identity." Individuals in helping professions, like health care, experience higher rates of job-related burnout.

L

Laborist: A board-certified physician who provides care to obstetrics and gynecology (OB-GYN) patients in the hospital. The laborist can admit, triage, provide emergency services, manage labor, deliver babies, and generally care for patients who are not assigned to a physician.

Licensed practical nurse (LPN): Or licensed vocational nurse (LVN); works under the direct supervision of a registered nurse (RN) or physician to provide care and administer some medications.

Licensure: The most restrictive form of health professional regulation administered by individual states. It defines a professional's scope of practice and educational and testing requirements to engage legally in the practice of a profession.

Long-term care facility (LTCF): An institution such as a nursing home, skilled nursing facility (SNF), or assisted living facility that provides health care to people who are unable to manage independently in the community. Care may represent custodial or chronic care management or short-term rehabilitative services.

Long-term care system: A variety of individualized, well-coordinated services that promote the maximum possible independence for people with functional limitations and that are provided over an extended period of time in accordance with a holistic approach, while maximizing the person's quality of life. Long-term care needs are not confined only to older Americans, but older Americans are the fastest-growing proportion of the population and are the major consumers of long-term care services. Advances in medical care have made a longer life span possible, with accompanying challenges presented by chronic disease and physical limitations.

M

Maintenance of certification (MOC): An American Board of Medical Specialties (ABMS) requirement of ongoing educational programs and recertification examinations every 10 years in each of the specialties and subspecialties in which a physician is certified. The requirements culminate in an ABMS-sponsored board recertification examination 10 years after first receiving certification and every 10 years thereafter.

Managed behavioral healthcare organization (MBHO): A corporate entity to which a health plan may outsource the management of mental health services for its subscribers. The MBHO assumes the financial risks and benefits of managing treatment budgets and authorization for access to mental health services.

Managed care: A system of healthcare delivery that: 1) seeks to achieve efficiencies by integrating the basic functions of healthcare delivery, (2) employs mechanisms to control (manage) utilization of medical services, and (3) determines the price at which the services are purchased and consequently how much the providers are paid. It is the most dominant healthcare delivery system in the United States today and is available to most Americans. The primary financiers of the managed care system are employers and the government; however, it is not a private–public partnership. Employers purchase insurance for their own employees, but they do so voluntarily. As a result, many small employers do not provide health insurance to their employees. On the other hand, because employer-based health insurance requires cost sharing, many workers choose not to participate even when the employer pays the bulk of the premium costs. Because of variations in the government programs, beneficiaries are either required to obtain healthcare services through a managed care organization (MCO) or through alternative mechanisms.

Managed care plans: The type of program that combines administrative and service costs to achieve better cost control.

Market Justice: In a free market economy, market forces can achieve a fair distribution of healthcare among individuals who are free to purchase the healthcare services they value. In market justice, healthcare is rationed by the willingness and ability of people to pay for healthcare.

Master of Health Administration (MHA): A 2- to 3-year professional degree for healthcare managers and administrators. There are also health administration options in other degree programs, such as public administration (MPA), business administration (MBA), and public health (MPH).

Meaningful use: The criterion defined by the ONC in collaboration with the Centers for Medicare & Medicaid Services that entails meeting a set of time-delineated requirements for eligible professionals and hospitals to qualify for incentive payments under the HITECH Act. In 2015 this criterion was redefined under the Medicare Access and CHIP Reauthorization Act.

Medicaid: Title XIX of the Social Security Act Amendments of 1965, Medicaid is a joint federal/state program providing insurance coverage for a prescribed scope of basic healthcare services to Americans who qualify based on income parameters, established on a state-by-state basis. Medicaid is principally funded from federal general funds with matching dollars to the states and state general funds. Unlike Medicare, which reimburses providers through intermediaries such as Blue Cross, Medicaid directly reimburses providers. Rate-setting formulas, procedures, and policies vary widely among states.

Medical assistant: Checks patients in for appointments, measures and records vital signs, verifies insurance, schedules patient appointments, performs some patient testing, takes patient histories, prepares blood samples for laboratory testing, and provides post-visit instructions and general support. Additionally, medical assistants can give patients injections or medications as directed by a physician and permitted by state law.

Medicare: Title XVIII of the Social Security Act Amendments of 1965, Medicare guarantees a minimum level of health insurance benefits to all Americans beginning at age 65 (and other special needs groups without regard to age). Medicare has four parts: A, B, C, and D, which cover (A) physician and outpatient services, (B) hospital care, (C) participation in managed care plans, and (D) prescription drugs. Most Medicare parts require beneficiary cost sharing. Medicare funds derive largely from payroll taxes levied on all American workers, which are matched by their employers in equal amounts.

Medicare Access and CHIP Reauthorization Act of 2015 (MACRA): Extends funding for Medicaid's Children's Health Insurance Program (CHIP) for 2 years and establishes a physician payment schedule that predictably specifies the inflation rate for Medicare physician reimbursement. MACRA also promotes paying for value and quality of care rather than quantity through programs streamlining physicians' participation in quality reporting and payment incentives using the merit-based incentive payment system (MIPS) and alternative payment models (APMs).

Medicare Advantage: A program through which Medicare beneficiaries may have their benefits administered by managed healthcare organizations (MCOs).

Medicare Prescription Drug, Improvement, and Modernization Act of 2003 (MMA): In addition to adding prescription drug coverage for Medicare beneficiaries, the Act established Medicare Advantage plans with new parameters to replace the Medicare+Choice option created by the Balanced Budget Act of 1997.

Mental Health Parity and Addiction Equity Act: A federal law that generally prevents group health plans and health insurance issuers who provide mental health or substance use disorder (MH/SUD) benefits from imposing less-favorable benefit limitations on those benefits than on medical/surgical benefits.

Merit-based incentive payment system (MIPS): Under the MACRA, combines three previous quality reporting programs into one reporting system, scoring eligible professionals (EPs) on quality, resource use, clinical practice improvement activities, and meaningful use of certified EHR technology. The composite MIPS performance score determines whether EPs will receive an annual upward, downward, or no payment adjustment.

Mid-level practitioner: Health provider who may work at different levels of care.

Mitigation: As discussed in Johnson, Stoskopf, and Shi's *Comparative Health Systems: A Global Perspective*, "Mitigation is the cornerstone of disaster management and includes activities to decrease the potential loss of life and property by lessening the impact of disasters. Mitigation should start early, long before a disaster occurs, involving all key stakeholders. The focus of preparedness is to enhance the capacity to respond to an incident. Taking steps to ensure who, what, where, when, and how people and resources are available before an event occurs. Preparedness involves development of training programs for the community, public awareness, logistical support, and communications, early warning, with ongoing monitoring. Response is the implementation of the time-critical plan in order to take action to save lives and to prevent further damage. The recovery phase incorporates actions necessary to maintain and/or return the community to normal after the disaster. Recovery may include repairing buildings, streets, railways, and other infrastructure damaged during the disaster."

Monolithic model of health information exchange: An HIE design in which all member institutions send clinical data to one central repository where all data reside together in one universal and standardized format. In this model, authorized users may access individual, trans-institutional patient records from the central repository.

Moral hazard: Refers to consumer behavior that leads to higher utilization of healthcare services when the services are covered by insurance.

N

National Academy of Medicine: Formerly called the Institute of Medicine until 2015, is an American nongovernmental, nonprofit organization.

National Association of County and City Health Officials (NACCHO): Provides detailed descriptions of local health department (LHD) characteristics and activities. These health departments support and deliver a variety of health and health-related services and provide direct patient care services in clinics or health centers, referrals for care, and other services particularly focused on underserved populations.

National Center for Complementary and Integrative Health (NCCIH): A center of the National Institutes of Health devoted to defining, through rigorous scientific investigation, the usefulness and safety of complementary and integrative interventions and providing the public with research-based information to guide health care decision making.

National Committee for Quality Assurance (NCQA): The most influential managed care quality assurance organization, formed in 1979. NCQA primary functions are accreditation for MCOs, PPOs, managed behavioral healthcare organizations, new health plans, and disease-management programs; certifying organizations that verify provider credentials and consultation on physician organizations; and utilization management for organizations, patient-centered medical homes, and disease-management organizations and programs.

National Health Care Workforce Commission (NHCWC): Established by the ACA, the NHCWC was mandated to evaluate and make recommendations for the nation's healthcare workforce including education and training support for existing and potential new workers at all levels, efficient workforce deployment, professional compensation, and coordination among different types of providers. Congress has withheld funding, so the NHCWC has never commenced work.

National Healthcare Expenditures (NHEs): Reported annually by the National Center for Health Statistics (NCHS), which is part of the Centers for Disease Control and Prevention (CDC), the U.S. Department of Health and Human Services (HHS), and the Centers for Medicare and Medicaid Services (CMS). Two broad categories of NHEs, historical and projected, are reported.

National Institutes of Health (NIH): Since the 1950s, the federal government has invested heavily in biomedical research. The ensuing public–private partnership in health has produced some of the finest medical research in the world. The growth of medical knowledge is unparalleled, and the United States can take well-deserved pride in its research accomplishments. Leading the way in biomedical research is NIH, which is made up of 27 different components called Institutes and Centers. Each has its own specific research agenda, often focusing on particular diseases or body systems. NIH's mission is to seek fundamental knowledge about the nature and behavior of living systems and the application of that knowledge to enhance health, lengthen life, and reduce illness and disability.

National Prevention, Health Promotion, and Public Health Council: Established by the ACA and chaired by the U.S. Surgeon General, an organization charged with developing and leading a national prevention strategy and making recommendations to the President and Congress for federal policy changes that support public health goals. The Council provides leadership to and coordination of public health activities of 17 federal departments, agencies, and offices and receives input from a 22 nonfederal member, presidentially appointed Prevention Advisory Group.

Natural history of disease: A matrix used by epidemiologists and health services planners that places everything known about a particular disease or condition in the sequence of its origin and progression when untreated. The matrix identifies causes and stages of a particular disease or condition and facilitates matching of causes and stages with appropriate types of interventions intended to prevent the condition's occurrence or to arrest its progress after onset.

Naturally occurring retirement community (NORC): Apartment complexes, neighborhoods, or sections of communities where residents have opted to remain in their homes as they age.

Never events: Egregious medical errors occurring in hospitals, such as wrong-sided surgery, the treatment for which the HHS will not provide reimbursement.

NIH Public Access Policy: Mandated by Congress, it requires authors of all scientific papers on NIH-funded research that are published in the peer-reviewed biomedical journals to deposit their accepted manuscripts in a repository maintained by the National Library of Medicine that is freely searchable on the Internet. Since the NIH policy was implemented, several additional federal agencies adopted the policy including the CDC, Department of Defense, Department of Agriculture, and the AHRQ.

Non-parity: Refers to reimbursement for psychiatric services on bases that are not on par with reimbursement for nonpsychiatric illnesses. Examples include imposition of lifetime limits on eligibility for psychiatric services and selective insurer fee discounts for psychiatric care.

Nonquantitative treatment limitations (NQTLs): Limitations or restrictions of covered insurance benefits which, though not numerically expressed, otherwise limit the scope or duration of benefits for treatment. In assuring parity of mental health with medical/surgical benefits, insurance plans must apply NQTLs in a comparable and no more stringent manner to mental health as compared and medical/surgical benefits.

Not-for-profit ambulatory services: Have evolved from many sources, often cause-related, to address needs of population groups afflicted by specific diseases or types of conditions. Asthma, diabetes, multiple sclerosis, and cerebral palsy are a few of the conditions addressed. As not-for-profit organizations, many are chartered by states as charitable organizations and maintain tax-exempt status with the Internal Revenue Service. These designations allow them to solicit charitable contributions for which their donors may receive tax deductions. Governed by boards of directors who receive no compensation for their services, these organizations may be operated by an all-volunteer staff or employ numerous paid professionals and have annual operating budgets of several million dollars.

Nuclear medicine technologist: Uses diagnostic imaging techniques to detect and map radioactive drugs in the human body. They administer radioactive pharmaceuticals to patients and then monitor the characteristics and functions of tissues or organs in which the radiopharmaceuticals localize.

Nurse anesthetist (CRNA): Provides anesthesia and related care before, during, and after surgical procedures. They provide pain management and some emergency services. CRNAs administer general anesthesia to put patients to sleep so they feel no pain during surgery. They remain with the patient throughout a procedure to monitor vital signs and adjust the anesthesia as necessary.

Nurse practitioner (NP): A registered nurse, typically with a master's degree, who may specialize in a particular area of nursing practice such as primary care, geriatrics, psychiatry, emergency medicine, or other medical fields. Nurse practitioners function under the supervision of physicians and provide diagnostic, preventive, and therapeutic healthcare services and may prescribe medications as allowed by law as delegated by physicians.

O

Observational studies: May be descriptive or analytical; descriptive studies use patient records, interview surveys, existing medical databases, and other information sources to identify factors and conditions that determine the distribution of health and disease among specific populations; descriptive studies are relatively fast and inexpensive and often raise questions or suggest hypotheses to be tested; they are often followed by analytic studies, which test hypotheses that try to explain biologic phenomena by seeking statistical associations between factors that may contribute to a subsequent occurrence and the initial occurrence itself.

Occupational therapist: Assists patients in recovering from accidents, injuries, or diseases to improve their ability to perform tasks in their daily living and work environments.

Office of Management and Budget (OMB): Assists the President in carrying out his budgetary duties. Originally created by the 1921 Budget and Accounting Act as the Bureau of the Budget, it was reconstituted as OMB in 1970. Its primary function is to oversee the development and implementation of the federal budget.

Office of the National Coordinator for Health Information Technology (ONC): The federal agency created to coordinate nationwide efforts to implement health information technology and exchange of health information.

One Health: A collaborative, multisectoral, and transdisciplinary approach—working at the local, regional, national, and global levels—with the goal of achieving optimal health outcomes recognizing the interconnection between people, animals, plants, and their shared environment. CDC's One

Health Office leads the agency's One Health efforts in the United States and abroad.

Optometrist: Examines patients' eyes to diagnose vision problems and eye disease, prescribes drugs for treatment, and prescribes and fits eyeglasses and contact lenses. This professional has a Doctor of Optometry degree and a state license to practice.

Oregon Death with Dignity Act of 1994: Also known as the Oregon Physician-Assisted Suicide Act, it legalized allowing "an adult resident of Oregon, who is terminally ill to voluntarily request a prescription for medication to take his or her life."

Osteopathic approach: A philosophy of medical education with particular focus on the musculoskeletal system. Graduates receive a DO rather than MD degree and are considered as rigorously trained and qualified as their MD degree counterparts.

Outcomes research: Evaluates results of healthcare processes in the real world of physicians' offices, hospitals, clinics, and homes. Insurance companies, state and federal governments, employers, and consumers all look to outcomes research for information to help them make better decisions about what kinds of health care should be reimbursed, for whom, and when.

P

Palliative care: Treatment given to relieve the symptoms of a disease rather than attempting to cure the disease.

Patient-centered medical home (PCMH): A team-based model of care led by a personal physician who provides continuous and coordinated care throughout a patient's lifetime to maximize health outcomes, including appropriately arranging patients' care with other qualified professionals for preventive services, treatment of acute and chronic illness, and assistance with end-of-life issues.

Patient-centered outcomes research: Study of the impact of an intervention from a patient perspective.

Patient-Centered Outcomes Research Institute (PCORI): Created by the ACA as a not-for-profit, independent agency dedicated to conducting comparative effectiveness research, the PCORI is governed by a board of directors appointed by the U.S. Government Accountability Office. The PCORI maintains a strong patient and stakeholder orientation with patient satisfaction recognized as an essential component of quality of care.

Patient engagement: Refers to patients being as informed as possible about their options for treatment, medications, recovery, and all other aspects of the health care system supporting them and providing services.

Patient group: An organized group that represents patients with a specific disease or condition, or collection of diseases or conditions.

Patient Protection and Affordable Care Act (ACA): Enacted in 2010 as an effort to reform the private health insurance market and to provide better coverage for those with preexisting conditions, college-age citizens, and seniors on Medicare. It included provisions for the establishment of a Center for Medicare and Medicaid Innovation and promoted the use of comparative effectiveness research to inform policy and the management of health systems.

Patient Safety Network (PSNET): An AHRQ online access system providing annotated links to the latest patient safety literature and safety news.

Personal health record (PHR): Offered by proprietary companies, a platform on which individual patients create their own records in standardized format to enable them to physically carry records to providers or make them available to providers via the internet.

Pharmacist: Responsible for dispensing prescribed medications. The role of pharmacists is expanding beyond dispensing medication to include advising patients and healthcare providers about the potential side effects of medications, recommending therapeutic alternatives to providers/prescribers, and prescribing medications and monitoring patients after a physician's diagnosis through collaborative practice agreements with physicians.

Physical AI: Associated with the type used in robots for things like surgery and prosthetics for geriatric care.

Physical therapist: Provides services that help restore function, improve mobility, relieve pain, and prevent or limit physical disabilities of patients suffering from injuries or disease. They restore, maintain, and promote overall fitness and health.

Physical therapy assistant or aide: Supervised by physical therapists and assists physical therapists in meeting the needs of an increasing number of patients. Physical therapy assistants observe patients engaged in therapy, help with specific exercises, treat patients via massage and stretching, use devices and equipment like walkers to help patients, and provide patient education based on the treatment plans developed by a physical therapist.

Physician assistant (PA): Provides healthcare services under the supervision of a physician. Most hold master's degrees. PAs are trained to provide diagnostic, preventive, and therapeutic healthcare services as delegated by physicians and prescribe medications as allowed by law. PAs are employed in specialties such as internal medicine, pediatrics, family medicine, orthopedics, emergency medicine, and surgery.

Physician Compare: The CMS website, mandated by the ACA, to provide basic contact, practice characteristics, and clinical quality data on Medicare participating physicians and other healthcare professionals. As of 2016, quality data is available only at the physician group, not individual physician level.

Physician Self-Referral Law: Prohibits physicians from referring patients to facilities with which a physician or a physician's immediate family member has a financial relationship.

Podiatrist: Treats patients with foot diseases and deformities. Podiatric medicine is concerned with the diagnosis and treatment of diseases and injuries of the lower leg and foot. Podiatrists can prescribe drugs; order radiographs, laboratory tests, and physical therapy; set fractures; and perform surgery. They also fit corrective inserts called orthotics, design plaster casts and strappings to correct deformities, and design custom-made shoes. They hold a Doctor of Podiatric Medicine (DPM) degree.

Point-of-service (POS) plan: A POS plan is a hybrid of HMO and PPO plans; called "point-of-service" because beneficiaries can select whether to use a provider in a POS-approved network or seek care outside the POS plan network when a particular medical need arises. Selecting an out-of-network provider without a primary care referral can incur significant out-of-pocket costs.

Policy cycle: The different phases of the policy-making process.

Policy development (as a core function of public health): Generating recommendations from available data to address public health problems, analyzing options for solutions, and mobilizing public and community organizations through implementation plans.

Political determinants of health: There are three fundamental parts to public policy making: problems, stakeholders, and the policy. A fourth dimension, politics, is also present and results in a policy process that is dynamic and changeable. In this regard, Daniel Dawes has written about the "political determinants of health," asserting that when a policy issue aligns with a private sector interest or commercial interest and a government value interest, there is greater likelihood of success in advancing an effective agenda. He provides examples of this with Medicare and Medicaid, the Americans with Disabilities Act, the Mental Health Parity and Addiction Equity Act, and the Affordable Care Act.

Population health: The distribution of health outcomes within a population, the determinants that influence distribution, and the policies and interventions that affect the determinants. Populations can be defined by geography or grouped according to some common element such as employer, ethnicity, medical condition, or some other grouping element. Population health embraces a comprehensive agenda that addresses the healthy and unhealthy, the acutely ill and the chronically ill, the clinical delivery system, and the public sector. While there are many determinants that affect the health of population, the ultimate goal for healthcare providers, public health professionals, employers, payers, and policy makers is the same: health people comprising health population that create productive workforce and thriving communities.

Population health focus: A healthcare system orientation to providing medical care and health-related services that shifts emphasis from individual medical interventions with piecemeal reimbursement to providers' accountability for the outcomes of medical care and overall health status of a defined population group.

Preferred Provider Organization (PPO): Formed by physicians and hospitals to serve the needs of private, third-party payers and self-insured companies, PPOs guarantee a volume of business to hospitals and physicians in return for negotiated fee discounts. PPOs offer attractive features to both physicians and hospitals. Currently, PPOs are the most popular managed care plans.

Premium: Refers to the amount members or beneficiaries generally pay for health insurance every month.

Prescription drug monitoring program (PDMP): A state-operated program using an electronic database which tracks prescribing and dispensing controlled prescription drugs to give pharmacists and prescribers patients' history and identify individuals at high-risk who could benefit from intervention.

Prevention and Public Health Fund: Established by the ACA, the nation's first mandatory funding stream dedicated to improving public health. The Fund is intended to eliminate the prior shortcomings of unpredictable federal budget appropriations for public health and prevention programs. The ACA mandates the Fund's use to improve health and help restrain the rate of growth in private and public sector healthcare costs through programs at the local, state, and federal levels to "curb tobacco use, increase access to primary preventive care services, and help state and local governments respond to public health threats and outbreaks."

Primary prevention: Measures designed to promote health and prevent disease or other adverse health occurrences (e.g., health education to encourage good nutrition, exercise, and genetic counseling) and specific protections (e.g., immunization and the use of seat belts).

Private insurance: Includes four types of coverage: group insurance, individual private insurance, self-insurance, and managed care plans. The insurance companies that provide this coverage can be not-for-profit or for-profit.

Prospective payment system (PPS): PPS is the catch-all term for the case payment system of diagnosis-related groups (DRGs) that Medicare required beginning in 1984. PPS shifted hospital reimbursement from a fee-for-service retrospective mode to a pre-paid prospective mode. The PPS provides incentives for hospitals to spend only what is needed to achieve optimal patient outcomes. If outcomes are achieved at a cost lower than the preset payment, hospitals retain the balance.

Provider-induced demand: A method in which providers purposefully create demand for services and drive up costs of care.

Psychologist: Studies the human mind and human behavior. Research psychologists investigate the physical, cognitive, emotional, or social aspects of human behavior. Psychologists in health services fields provide mental health care in hospitals, clinics, schools, or private settings.

Public Health 3.0: The National Academy of Medicine and the U.S. Department of Health and Human Services (HHS) promote an initiative called Public Health 3.0. The third-generation model reflects the promise and perils of 21st century public health in the United States. Public Health 3.0 is a model and path forward for the field of public health. The model calls on public health to redefine and reinvent itself for the future. The model focuses on the social determinants of health and the need for public health professionals and organizations to engage a broad range of community, industry, education, business, government, and other stakeholders to develop new models to make strategic investments in public health. The overarching goal is to shift the U.S. health system from focusing on sickness and disease to wellness and prevention. The model was developed for the United States; however, it can be adapted and applied to other health systems around the world.

Public health system: According to the Centers for Disease Control and Prevention, the public health system consists of "all public, private, and voluntary entities that contribute to the delivery of essential public health services within a jurisdiction." Public health is unique in its interdisciplinary approach and methods, its emphasis on preventive strategies, its linkage with government and political decision making, and its dynamic adaptation to new problems placed on the agenda. Above all else, it is a collective effort to identify and address the unacceptable realities that result in preventable and avoidable health and quality of life outcomes. It is the composite of efforts and activities that are carried out by people and organizations committed to these ends. The public health system includes public health agencies at the state and local level, healthcare providers, public safety agencies, human service and charity organizations, education and youth development organizations, recreation and arts-related organizations, economic and philanthropic organizations, and environmental agencies and organizations.

Public insurance: This insurance is provided by the state or federal government. Examples include Medicare and Medicaid.

PubMed Central: The National Library of Medicine repository of all scientific papers on NIH-funded research and scientific papers funded by other federal agencies such as the CDC.

Q

Quality Payment Program (QPP): Established by the Medicare and CHIP Reauthorization Act of 2015 (MACRA), the QPP allows physicians to select participation in one of two CMS system options that define the way in which they will be reimbursed for services under Medicare: either the Medicare incentive payment program (MIPS) or the alternative payment model (APM).

R

Radiologic technologist: Works under the supervision of a radiologist, a physician who specializes in the use and interpretation of radiographs and other medical imaging technologies. The radiologic technologist uses radiographs (x-rays), fluoroscopic equipment, and high-tech imaging machines such as ultrasonography, computed tomography, magnetic resonance imaging (MRI), and positron emission tomography (PET). These technologies produce images that allow physicians to study the internal organs, bones, and the metabolic activity of these structures.

Randomized controlled clinical trial: A study where patients are randomly assigned to two or more experimental groups where each group is identical to each other with the exception of the assigned treatment; often one of the "treatments" is a placebo or no treatment. Patient selection is controlled to reduce potential for any confounder or bias between the experimental groups. Study patients, their physicians, and the outcomes assessors are "blinded" to treatment each patient received, randomized to minimize potential bias of results. After systematic reviews, this is generally considered the highest form of evidence.

Readmissions reduction program: Mandated by the ACA, a Medicare program through which payments to hospitals are reduced based on the readmission of patients with specified diagnoses within 30 days of a prior hospitalization. Penalty determinations are based on three prior years' hospital discharge data.

Recovery-oriented systems of care (ROSC): A holistic, integrated, person-centered and strength-based approach to mental health interventions. ROSC views recovery as a process of pursuing a fulfilling life and seeks to enhance a person's positive self-image and identity through linking their strengths with family and community resources. The ROSC shifts care from the old episodic care model to one that emphasizes continuity and provides choice through the treatment planning process.

Regional health information organization (RHIO): Organizations that create systems agreements, processes, and technology to manage and facilitate exchange of health information between institutions and across different vendor platforms within specific geographic areas. RHIOs administer HIEs.

Registered nurse (RN): A nurse who: 1) holds either a nursing diploma, Associate Degree in Nursing, or bachelor's degree in nursing (BSN); 2) has passed the National Council Licensure Examination (NCLEX-RN) administered by the National Council of State Boards of Nursing; and 3) has met all the other licensing requirements mandated by their state's board of nursing. RNs are responsible for recording symptoms of any disease, implementing care plans, coordinating patient care, assisting physicians in the examination and treatment of patients, administering medications and performing medical procedures, supervising other personnel (such as LPNs), and educating patients and families about follow-up care.

Registration: A mechanism of healthcare occupation regulation. Registration began as a mechanism to facilitate contacts and relationships among members of a profession and potential employers or the public. It is the least rigorous of the regulatory processes, ranging from simple listings or registries of people offering a service, such as private duty nurses, to national registration programs of professional or occupational groups that require educational and testing qualifications. Because most registration programs are voluntary, they do not include parameters for competence or disciplinary actions.

Regulation: Public organizations receive their regulatory power either through legislation, as described above, or through executive order from the president, governor, or mayor. This authority often involves a directive to establish administrative procedures and an infrastructure for implementation and enforcement. A recent example would be a governor or mayor, in response to COVID-19, ordering a mandate for everyone in their jurisdiction to wear a mask while in public spaces and to limit the number of people in a restaurant.

Rehabilitation counselor: Provides personalized counseling, emotional support, and rehabilitation therapy to patients limited by physical, mental, developmental, or emotional disabilities to promote independence. Patients may be recovering from illness or injury, have psychiatric problems, or have intellectual deficits. After an injury or illness is stabilized, the rehabilitation counselor tests the patient's motor ability, skill level, interests, and psychological makeup and develops an appropriate training or retraining plan. The goal is to maximize the patient's ability to function in society.

Respite care: Temporary surrogate care given to a patient when that patient's primary caregiver must be absent. It includes any family managed care program that helps to avoid or forestall the placement of a patient in a full-time institutionalized environment by providing planned, intermittent caregiver relief.

Retail clinic: Operated at retail sites such as pharmacies and supermarkets under consumer-friendly names, such as "MinuteClinic" and "TakeCare." Staffed by nurse practitioners or physician assistants, a physician is not required on site. Clinics have physician consultation available by phone.

Registration: Begun as a method to facilitate contacts among professionals and potential employers, registration is the least restrictive form of health professional regulation. Most registration programs are voluntary and range from listings of individuals offering a specific service to professional or occupational groups requiring educational qualifications and testing.

Response: The after-action of disaster that involves human, material, and financial resources needed.

Risk: According to Shi and Singh's *Essentials of the U.S. Health Care System*, this refers "to the possibility of a substantial financial or material loss from some event."

Rural: Geographic locations outside of urban and suburban ares.

Rural health: Rural healthcare delivery is an important part of the national health system. It is complicated in that many rural patients experience additional barriers to receiving the care they need. One cannot think of rural health without considering the impacts of the social determinants of health and population health. Systems thinking concepts are vital to find sustainable solutions for this important and vulnerable sector of the U.S. healthcare delivery system.

Rural health networks: To address challenges of providing a continuum of care with scarce resources, networks join rural healthcare providers in formal, not-for-profit corporations or through informal linkages to achieve a defined set of mutually beneficial purposes. Networks may advocate at local and state levels on rural healthcare issues, cooperate in joint community outreach activities, and seek opportunities to negotiate with insurers to cover services for their communities' populations.

S

Secondary prevention: Early detection and prompt treatment of a disease or condition to achieve an early cure, if possible, or to slow progression, prevent complications, and limit disability. Most preventive health care is currently focused on this level.

Self-funded health insurance: An arrangement through which an employer (or other group, such as a union or trade association) collects and pools premiums into a fund or account used to pay for medical benefit claims instead of using a commercial carrier. Self-funded plans often use the services of an actuarial firm to set premium rates and a third-party administrator to administer benefits, pay claims, and collect data on utilization. Self-funded plans offer advantages to employers, such as avoiding additional administrative and other charges made by commercial carriers, avoiding premium taxes, and enabling interest accrual on cash reserves held in the benefit accounts.

Skilled nursing facility (SNF): A facility, or distinct part of one, primarily engaged in providing skilled nursing care and related services for people requiring medical or nursing care or rehabilitation services. Skilled nursing care is provided by or under the direct supervision of licensed nursing personnel who provide 24-hour nursing care and other types of services.

Social Justice: Justice in terms of the distribution of wealth, opportunities, and privileges within a society.

Social Security Act of 1935: The most significant social initiative ever passed by Congress with the core feature of providing monthly retirement benefits to virtually all working Americans. It was the legislative basis for many major health and welfare programs, including the Medicare and Medicaid programs.

Social worker: Diagnoses and treats clients, patients, and families in relation to an array of mental, behavioral, and emotional issues. They assist in addressing the personal, economic, and social problems associated with everyday life, illness, injury, and disability. Social workers provide social services in hospitals and other health-related settings. Medical and public health social workers provide patients and families with psychosocial support in cases of acute, chronic, or terminal illness. Mental health and substance abuse social workers assess and treat people with mental illness or those who abuse alcohol, tobacco, or other drugs.

Serious mental illness (SMI): Mental illness resulting in profound functional impairment which substantially interferes with or limits one or more major life activities.

Social determinants of health: Public health problems and challenges that can be attributed to deficits and poor quality in the social areas of a society. These are referred to as social determinants of health.

Specialist: A physician who focuses on particular organ systems or diseases in areas such as neurology, nephrology, pulmonology, obstetrics and gynecology, cardiology, dermatology, anesthesiology, ophthalmology, pathology, psychiatry, radiology, surgery, specialized internal medicine, pediatrics, and specialty areas.

Speech-language pathologist: Assesses, diagnoses, and treats patients who have problems with speech, swallowing, and other disorders in hospitals, schools, clinics, and private practice. They help patients improve communication and swallowing disorders due to a variety of causes like stroke, brain injury, hearing loss, developmental delay, Parkinson's disease, autism, and many other conditions.

Staff model: One of the initial types of HMOs. It employed groups of physicians to provide most healthcare needs of its members. HMOs often provided some specialty services within the organization and many contracted for services with community specialists. In the staff model, the HMO operated facilities in which its physicians practiced, providing on-site support services such as radiology, laboratory, and pharmacy. The HMO purchased hospital care and other services for its members through fee-for-service or prepaid contracted arrangements.

Stakeholder: An individual, group, organization, or entity that has an interest in an issue, topic, or outcome. The sometimes shared and often-conflicting concerns, interests, and influences of these constituent groups cause them to shift alliances periodically to oppose or champion specific reform proposals or other changes in the industry.

Stop-loss provision: The maximum out-of-pocket payment an insured individual would be required to pay before their plan pays 100% of costs.

Support services: Are necessary for the highly complex and sophisticated system of health care to function. Service specialists perform administrative, operational, and management duties and often work closely with direct providers of healthcare services.

Supply-side rationing: Focuses on restricting the availability of expensive medical technology and specialty care.

Surgeon General: One of the most influential positions in USPHS is the Surgeon General. This individual is appointed by the president and serves to help frame and promote the national health agenda. For example, the Surgeon General is currently leading efforts to mitigate the opioid epidemic and the large number of unnecessary deaths due to opioid misuse.

Systematic review: A meta-analysis of several high-quality randomized, controlled clinical trials. An analysis of multiple analyses has more value as its conclusions are based on the larger, combined populations studied in all the individual clinical trials. This is usually considered the highest level of evidence but is also the most expensive and difficult to carry out.

Systems perspective in public health: As described by health systems scholar James Johnson, "Public health is highly interconnected and interdependent in its relationship to individuals, communities, and the larger society, including the global community. Using the language of systems theory, public health is a complex adaptive system. It is complex in that it is composed of multiple, diverse, interconnected elements, and it is adaptive in that the system is capable of changing and learning from experience and its environment."

Systems thinking: An approach that reflects the fundamentals of General Systems Theory. Systems thinking allows healthcare professionals to assess the interactions and interdependencies among parts of a system and seek out opportunities to generate sustainable solutions. Systems theory and thinking are helpful in navigating the rapidly changing contexts of healthcare.

T

Teaching hospital: A hospital affiliated with a medical school that provides accredited clinical education programs for medical students, medical and dental residents, and other health professionals.

Telehealth: A collection of means or methods for enhancing health care, public health, and health education delivery and support using telecommunications technologies.

Tertiary prevention: Rehabilitation and maximizing remaining functional capacity when a disease or condition has occurred with residual comprise to physical functionality.

Therapeutic science practitioner: Are essential to the treatment and rehabilitation of patients with diseases and injuries of all kinds. Physical therapists, occupational therapists, speech pathology and audiology therapists, radiation therapists, and respiratory therapists are only some of the allied health disciplines in this category.

Third-party administrator (TPA): A firm contracted by an employer which self-funds employee health insurance to administer benefits, pay claims, and collect data on utilization. Many TPAs also provide case management services for potentially expensive cases to help coordinate care and control employer risk of catastrophic expenses.

Therapeutic science practitioner: Therapeutic sciences practitioners include physical therapists, occupational therapists, speech language pathology and audiology therapists, radiation therapists, and respiratory therapists, representing some of the allied health disciplines in this category. Depending on their field, therapeutic science practitioners' require credentials ranging from bachelor's degrees to doctoral-level educational preparation.

TRICARE: A part of the military medical care system. Dependents of service members, retirees and their dependents, and survivors of deceased members can receive medical care through an insurance program called TRICARE. This program permits the beneficiaries to receive care from military as well as private medical care facilities. Although patients have little choice regarding how services are provided, in general, the military medical care system provides high-quality health care.

Two-midnight rule: A CMS policy that defines hospital stays of less than two-midnights' duration as outpatient visits billable under Medicare Part B, rather than more highly reimbursed inpatient care under Medicare Part A. Exceptions to the rule may be granted only on a case-by-case basis per judgment of the attending physician and supporting documentation. The rule also moved hospital Medicare audits from Recovery Audit Contractors who were paid contingency fees, to independent not-for-profit Quality Improvement Organizations.

U

Uninsured: Refers to an individual without any form of health insurance.

Urban area: The U.S. Census Bureau determined that urban areas are those that include densely developed areas, including residential and commercial land as well as other nonresidential areas.

Urban Cluster (UC): Defined by the U.S. Census Bureau as a community composed of more than 2,500 and less than 50,000 individuals.

Urgent care center: A facility that provides walk-in, extended-hour access for acute illness and injury care that is either beyond the scope or the availability of the typical primary care practice or retail clinic. Urgent care centers also may provide other health services such as occupational medicine, travel medicine, and sports and school physicals.

U.S. Census Bureau: A principal agency of the U.S. Federal Statistical System, responsible for producing data about the American people and the U.S. economy.

U.S. Public Health Service: A collection of agencies of the Department of Health and Human Services concerned with public health, containing eight of the department's eleven operating divisions.

V

Value-based purchasing (VBP): Mandated by the ACA; a Medicare program through which participating hospitals may earn incentive payments based on clinical outcomes and patient satisfaction or incur reductions in Medicare payments based on compliance with Medicare-determined criteria for "clinical processes of care" and "patient experience of care measures."

Vertical integration: A process through which one entity unites related and complementary organizations to create a system that provides a continuum of care. In its most complete form, a vertically integrated system encompasses medical and health-related services required throughout an individual's life span.

Veterans Health Administration (VHA): America's largest integrated healthcare system. The system is divided into 18 Veterans Integrated Service Networks, or VISNs. These regional networks strive to improve access and care coordination for veterans in a geographic or local area.

Virtual AI: Includes the type that is used in applications, such as electronic health record (EHR) systems, as well as black box methods (e.g., neural network-based guided treatment decisions).

Virtual reality: Virtual reality (VR) and simulation are two emerging examples of persuasive (or interactive) technology in use in healthcare delivery. The primary purpose of these technologies is to mimic reality in a safe, controlled, and realistic environment. It gives patients the ability to test and change behaviors and attitudes for feedback to improve in a certain area. VR and simulation can also enhance the overall effectiveness of education and competency.

Voluntary ambulatory healthcare agency: Governed by a volunteer board of directors, a community-based, not-for-profit agency that may provide direct medical care, education, advocacy, or a combination of these services. Many voluntary agencies were established by interest groups to address unmet health or health-related needs of specific population groups. Financial support includes government grants, fees for services, third-party reimbursement, and private contributions.

W

Waste: Defined by the Office of the Inspector General as "the thoughtless or careless expenditure, mismanagement, or abuse of resources to the detriment (or potential detriment) of the United States government. Waste also includes incurring unnecessary costs resulting from inefficient or ineffective practices, systems, or controls."

Withholds: A form of financial risk sharing in which a percentage of the monthly capitated fee is withheld from provider payments to cover potential cost overruns for services such as specialty referrals or hospitalizations. All, part, or none of the withholds may be returned to providers at the end of specified period, depending on financial performance.

World Health Organization (WHO) Health System Framework: WHO promotes the systems thinking approach through its Health System Framework. It identifies six building blocks or core components of health systems that include service delivery, health workforce, health information, medical technology, health financing, and leadership and governance. WHO acknowledged a shift toward systems thinking, and the WHO health system building blocks recognize and utilize systems thinking. These building blocks not only help us to better understand health systems, but they also provide opportunities for system improvement.

Index

Note: Page numbers followed by *f* indicate figures; numbers followed by *t* indicate tables; numbers followed by *e* indicate exhibits; *b* indicate box.